UNITED STATES
Territorial Expansion

W9-BMD-129

CANADA

Lake of the Woods

Lake Superior

Lake Michigan

Lake Huron

Lake Ontario

Lake Erie

St. Lawrence R.

MINNESOTA (1858)

St. Paul ★

WISCONSIN (1848)

Madison ★

Mississippi R.

IOWA (1846)

Des Moines ★

MICHIGAN (1837)

Lansing ★

ORIGINAL UNITED STATES
(By treaty with Britain, 1783)

ILLINOIS (1818)

Springfield ★

INDIANA (1816)

Indianapolis ★

1900

1950

MISSOURI (1821)

Jefferson City ★

opeka ★

2000

OHIO (1803)

Columbus ★

1850

Ohio R.

Frankfort ★

KENTUCKY (1792)

Nashville ★

TENNESSEE (1796)

Tennessee R.

ARKANSAS (1836)

Little Rock ★

Arkansas R.

MISSISSIPPI (1817)

Jackson ★

Red R.

LOUISIANA (1812)

Baton Rouge ★

(Seized from Spain, 1810, 1813)

ALABAMA (1819)

Montgomery ★

Atlanta ★

GEORGIA (1788)

Tallahassee ★

FLORIDA (By treaty with Spain, 1819)

FLORIDA (1845)

Lake Okeechobee

MAINE (1820)

Augusta ★

VT. (1791)

Montpelier ★

N.H. (1788)

Concord ★

Boston

NEW YORK (1788)

Albany ★

MASS. (1788)

Hartford ★

Providence ★

CONN. (1788)

R.I. (1790)

PENN. (1787)

Harrisburg ★

Trenton ★

N.J. (1787)

1800

1790

MD. (1788)

Dover ★

Annapolis

DEL. (1787)

Washington, D.C. ✪

VIRGINIA (1788)

Richmond ★

ORIGINAL THIRTEEN COLONIES

Charleston ★

WEST VIRGINIA (1863)

Chesapeake Bay

Raleigh ★

NORTH CAROLINA (1789)

SOUTH CAROLINA (1788)

Columbia ★

ATLANTIC OCEAN

Gulf of Mexico

MEXICO

CUBA

BAHAMAS

● Geographical center of population per Census year

PUERTO RICO (From Spain, 1898)

ATLANTIC OCEAN

San Juan ★

Charlotte Amalie ★

VIRGIN ISLANDS (From Denmark, 1917)

0   50   100 Miles

0   50   100 Kilometers

0   150   300 Miles

0   150   300 Kilometers

Discover EVEN MORE ABOUT THE PAST ONLINE!

FOR STUDENTS:

The Wadsworth U.S. History Resource Center

Your comprehensive resource for media assets to accompany any U.S. History course!

Explore by Topic, Type of Asset, or Time Period. This rich resource can help you better understand the cultures, conditions, and concepts you will encounter in your study of U.S. History. Assets include Timelines, Images, Primary Sources, Simulations, Web Links, and more!

Timelines

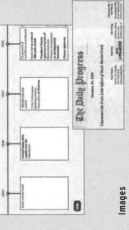

Images

FOR INSTRUCTORS:

Wadsworth HistoryFinder for U.S. History

Create rich and exciting PowerPoint® presentations for your U.S. History course!

With Wadsworth HistoryFinder for U.S. History you can quickly and easily download thousands of assets, including: Photographs, Maps, Art, Primary Sources, and Audio/Video Multimedia Clips.

Photographs

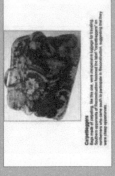

Maps

10P-HI0072

HistoryFinder for U.S. History

Ask your Cengage Learning Representative for more information.

Why Maps?

HISTORICAL EVENTS DO NOT JUST "HAPPEN" —they happen in a specific place. Since events are often dictated by a location's specifics it is important to learn all you can about that place, and a good map can help you do this. Your textbook may include different types of maps:

Demographic or Population Maps show which groups inhabited which regions and how that distribution changed over time.

Geographic-Political Maps show territories occupied by particular nations and empires and the borders between them.

Topographic Maps show natural physical features such as oceans, rivers, elevations,

forests, and deserts and manmade features such as dams and canals.

Expedition Maps show the routes followed by explorers, migrants, invaders, and military forces.

Battle Maps show the encounters and maneuvers of contending armies and navies.

Here are some basic tips to help you to get the most out of a map:

- Always look at the scale, which allows you to determine the distance in miles or kilometers between locations on the map.

- Examine the legend carefully. It explains the colors and/or symbols used on the map.

- Note the locations of mountains, rivers, oceans, and other geographic features, and consider how these would affect such human activities as agriculture, commerce, travel, and warfare.

- Read the map caption thoroughly. It provides important information sometimes not covered in the text itself. The caption may also inform you of additional resources, such as interactive maps, which may be available online.

Liberty Equality Power

AMH 1020

J. Murrin, P. Johnson | J. McPherson | A. Fahs | G. Gerstle | E. Rosenberg | N. Rosenberg

CENGAGE
Learning™

Australia • Brazil • Japan • Korea • Mexico • Singapore • Spain • United Kingdom • United States

CENGAGE
Learning™

Liberty Equality Power: AMH 1020

Liberty Equality Power, Fifth Edition
J. Murrin, P. Johnson | J. McPherson | A. Fahs | G. Gerstle | E. Rosenberg | N. Rosenberg

© 2011 Cengage Learning. All rights reserved.

Executive Editors:
Maureen Staudt
Michael Stranz

Senior Project Development Manager:
Linda deStefano

Marketing Specialist:
Courtney Sheldon

Senior Production/Manufacturing Manager:
Donna M. Brown

PreMedia Manager:
Joel Brennecke

Sr. Rights Acquisition Account Manager:
Todd Osborne

Cover Image:
Getty Images*

*Unless otherwise noted, all cover images used by Custom Solutions, a part of Cengage Learning, have been supplied courtesy of Getty Images with the exception of the Earthview cover image, which has been supplied by the National Aeronautics and Space Administration (NASA).

For product information and technology assistance, contact us at
Cengage Learning Customer & Sales Support, 1-800-354-9706

For permission to use material from this text or product,
submit all requests online at **cengage.com/permissions**
Further permissions questions can be emailed to
permissionrequest@cengage.com

This book contains select works from existing Cengage Learning resources and was produced by Cengage Learning Custom Solutions for collegiate use. As such, those adopting and/or contributing to this work are responsible for editorial content accuracy, continuity and completeness.

Compilation © 2011 Cengage Learning
ISBN-13: 978-1-133-19184-1

ISBN-10: 1-133-19184-3

Cengage Learning
5191 Natorp Boulevard
Mason, Ohio 45040
USA
Cengage Learning is a leading provider of customized learning solutions with office locations around the globe, including Singapore, the United Kingdom, Australia, Mexico, Brazil, and Japan. Locate your local office at:
international.cengage.com/region.

Cengage Learning products are represented in Canada by Nelson Education, Ltd.
For your lifelong learning solutions, visit **www.cengage.com/custom.**
Visit our corporate website at **www.cengage.com.**

Printed in the United States of America

CONTENTS

Omitted for this custom edition

27 THE AGE OF CONTAINMENT, 1946–1953 723

28 AFFLUENCE AND ITS DISCONTENTS, 1953–1963 752

29 AMERICA DURING ITS LONGEST WAR, 1963–1974 786

30 POWER AND POLITICS, 1974–1992 821

Omitted for this custom edition

Omitted for this custom edition

LIST OF MAPS

HISTORY THROUGH FILM

MUSICAL LINKS TO THE PAST

WHY STUDY HISTORY?

Why take a course in American history? This is a question that many college and university students ask. In many respects, students today are like the generations of Americans who have gone before them: optimistic and forward looking, far more eager to imagine where we as a nation might be going than to reflect on where we have been. If anything, this tendency has become more pronounced in recent years, as the Internet revolution has accelerated the pace and excitement of change and made even the recent past seem at best quaint, at worst uninteresting and irrelevant.

But it is precisely in these moments of change that a sense of the past can be indispensable in terms of guiding our actions in the present and future. We can find in other periods of American history moments, like our own, of dizzying technological change and economic growth, rapid alterations in the concentration of wealth and power, and basic changes in patterns of work, residence, and play. How did Americans at those times create, embrace, and resist these changes? In earlier periods of American history, the United States was home, as it is today, to a broad array of ethnic and racial groups. How did earlier generations of Americans respond to the cultural conflicts and misunderstandings that often arise from conditions of diversity? How did immigrants of the early 1900s perceive their new land? How and when did they integrate themselves into American society? To study how ordinary Americans of the past struggled with these issues is to gain perspective on the opportunities and problems that we face today.

History also provides an important guide to affairs of state. What role should America assume in world affairs? Should we participate in international bodies such as the United Nations, or insist on our ability to act autonomously and without the consent of other nations? What is the proper role of government in economic and social life? Should the government regulate the economy? To what extent should the government enforce morality regarding religion, sexual practices, drinking and drugs, movies, TV, and other forms of mass culture? And what are our responsibilities as citizens to each other and to the nation? Americans of past generations have debated these issues with verve and conviction. Exploring these debates, and how they were resolved, will enrich our understanding of the policy possibilities for today and tomorrow.

History, finally, is about stories—stories that we all tell about ourselves; our families; our communities; our ethnicity, race, region, and religion; and our nation. They are stories of triumph and tragedy, of engagement and flight, and of high ideals and high comedy. When telling these stories, "American history" is often the furthest thing from our minds. But, often, an implicit sense of the past informs what we say about grandparents who immigrated many years ago; the suburb in which we live; the church, synagogue, or mosque at which we worship; or the ethnic or racial group to which we belong. How well, we might ask, do we really understand these individuals, institutions, and groups? Do our stories about them capture their history and complexity? Or do our stories wittingly or unwittingly simplify or alter what these individuals and groups experienced? A study of American history helps us first to ask these questions and then to answer them. In the process, we can embark on a journey of intellectual and personal discovery and situate ourselves more firmly than we had thought possible in relation to those who came before us. We can gain a firmer self-knowledge and a greater appreciation for the richness of our nation and, indeed, of all humanity.

Astronomers investigate the universe through telescopes. Biologists study the natural world by collecting plants and animals in the field and then examining them with microscopes. Sociologists and psychologists study human behavior through observation and controlled laboratory experiments.

Historians study the past by examining historical "evidence" or "source" materials—government documents; the records of private institutions ranging from religious and charitable organizations to labor unions, corporations, and lobbying groups; letters, advertisements, paintings, music, literature, movies, and cartoons; buildings, clothing, farm implements, industrial machinery, and landscapes—anything and everything written or created by our ancestors that give clues about their lives and the times in which they lived.

Historians refer to written material as "documents." Excerpts of dozens of documents appear throughout the textbook—within the chapters and in the "Discovery" sections. Each chapter also includes many visual representations of the American past in the form of photographs of buildings, paintings, murals, individuals, cartoons, sculptures, and other historical evidence. As you read each chapter, the more you examine this "evidence," the more you will understand the main ideas of this book and of the course you are taking. The better you become at reading evidence, the better historian you will become.

"Discovery" sections at the end of each chapter assist you in practicing these skills by taking a closer look at specific images, quotes, or maps that will help you to connect the various threads of American history and to excel in your course.

DISCOVERY

In what ways did the ascension of the Jeffersonians to power in 1800 shape the future of America?

GEOGRAPHY AND POLITICS Consider the map of the election of 1800. In what way was the country divided in this vote? How do you think the people in the western territories were likely to vote once the territories became states? What does this map foreshadow about the future of the Federalist Party? By the 1830s, Democratic Republicans called their party by a somewhat different name. Do you know what it was?

In thinking about this question, begin by breaking it down into the components shown below. A discussion of the significance of each component should appear in your answer.

POLITICAL CULTURE Compare the images of Washington and Jefferson on pages 192 and 201. If you didn't know anything about either man, would you say that one of them lived before the other? Which one looks more like a "modern" political leader? Why do you think so?

What does the cartoon on page 202 want you to think about the government Jefferson is seen here "pulling down?" Why is the devil helping Jefferson? Why did Jefferson's attempt to remake (or "pull down") government so upset the Federalists? Consider the map of the election of 1800 in your answer.

GOVERNMENT AND LAW One of the "British crimes" that Madison listed as reasons for declaring war against Great Britain in 1811 was Britain's wielding of "a malicious influence over the Indians of the Northwest Territory." How does the image on page 208 make that point? How is the British soldier depicted? What does the illustration suggest about American views of Native Americans and their actions? What reasons did the British and the Native American have for forming an alliance against white Americans?

Map 7.1 PRESIDENTIAL ELECTION, 1800

	Electoral Vote	
---	Number	%
Jefferson	73	53
Burr	73	53
(Democratic Republican)		
Adams	65	47
Pinckney	64	46
Jay	1	—
(Federalists)		

© Cengage Learning

This concise version of the much admired, *Liberty, Equality, Power* is intended to make the textbook more accessible to a broad range of students and give instructors maximum flexibility in determining how best to use it in their courses. A brief edition, for example, makes it easier for instructors both to reach out to students who might be discouraged by a longer book and to supplement a textbook with readings, web-based exercises, movies, and related materials of their own choosing.

The Concise Fourth Edition won praise for its successful integration of political, cultural, and social history; its thematic unity; its narrative clarity and eloquence; its extraordinary coverage of pre-Columbian America; its attention to war and conquest; its extended treatment of the Civil War; its history of economic growth and change; and its robust map and illustration programs. We have preserved and enhanced all the strengths of the Fourth Edition in this Fifth Edition.

THE *LIBERTY, EQUALITY, POWER* APPROACH

In this book we tell many small stories, and one large one: how America transformed itself, in a relatively brief era of world history, from a land inhabited by hunter-gatherer and agricultural Native American societies into the most powerful industrial nation on earth. This story has been told many times before, and those who have told it in the past have usually emphasized the political experiment in liberty and equality that took root here in the 18th century. We, too, stress the extraordinary and transformative impact that the ideals of liberty and equality exerted on American politics, society, and economics during the American Revolution and after. We show how the creation of a free economic environment, one that nourished entrepreneurship and technological innovation, underpinned American industrial might. We emphasize, too, the successful struggles for freedom that, over the course of the last 230 years, have brought—first to all white men, then to men of color, and finally to women—rights and opportunities that they had not previously known. But we have also identified a third factor in this pantheon of American ideals: power. We examine power in many forms—the accumulation of

economic fortunes that dominated the economy and politics; the dispossession of Native Americans from land that they regarded as theirs; the enslavement of millions of Africans and their African American descendants for a period of almost 250 years; the relegation of women and of racial, ethnic, and religious minorities to subordinate places in American society; and the extension of American control over foreign peoples, such as Latin Americans and Filipinos, who would have preferred to have been free and self-governing. We do not mean to suggest that American power has always been turned to negative purposes. To the contrary: subordinate groups have themselves marshaled power to combat oppression, as in the abolitionist and civil rights crusades, the campaign for woman's suffrage, and the labor movement. In the 20th century, the federal government used its power to moderate poverty and to manage the economy in the interests of general prosperity. While one form of power sustained slavery over many generations, another, greater power abolished the institution in four years. Later, the federal government mobilized the nation's military might to defeat Nazi Germany, World War II Japan, the Cold War Soviet Union, and other enemies of freedom. The invocation of power as a variable in American history forces us to widen the lens through which we look at the past and to complicate the stories we tell. Ours has been a history of freedom and domination, of progress toward democracy and of delays and reverses, of abundance and poverty, of wars to free peoples from tyranny and battles to put foreign markets under American control.

In complicating our master narrative in this way, we think we have rendered American history more exciting and intriguing. Progress has not been automatic, but has been instead the product of ongoing struggles.

In this book we have also tried to capture the diversity of the American past, both in terms of outcomes and in terms of the variety of groups who have participated in America's making. We have not presented Native Americans simply as the victims of European aggression, but as a people diverse in their own ranks, with a variety of systems of social organization and cultural expression. We give equal treatment to the industrial titans of American history—the likes of Andrew Carnegie and John D. Rockefeller—and to those, such as small farmers and skilled workers, who resisted the corporate reorganization of economic life. We dwell on the achievements of 1863, when African Americans were freed from slavery, and of 1868, when they were made full citizens of the United States. But we also note how a majority of African Americans had to wait another 100 years, until the civil rights movement of the 1960s, to gain full access to American freedoms. We tell similarly complex stories about women, Latinos, and groups of ethnic Americans.

Political issues, of course, are only part of America's story. Americans have always pursued individuality and happiness and, in the process, have created the world's most vibrant popular culture. They have embraced technological innovations, especially those promising to make their lives easier and more fun. In light of this history, we have devoted considerable space to a discussion of popular culture, from the founding of the first newspapersin the 18th century to the rise of movies, jazz, and comics in the 20th century, to the cable television and Internet revolutions of recent years. We have pondered, too, how American industry has periodically altered home and personal life by making new products—such as clothing, cars, refrigerators, and computers— available to consumers. In such ways we hope to give our readers a rich portrait of how Americans spent their time, money, and leisure at various points in our history.

NEW TO THIS EDITION

The biggest change to the Fifth Edition was our decision to add a new author, Professor Alice Fahs of the University of California, Irvine. This is the first time in 19 years of work on this textbook that we have reached out to a new historian, and we are delighted that Professor Fahs has decided to join us. Professor Fahs is an accomplished historian of the 19th and early 20th centuries, with special expertise in cultural history and the history of gender. She has already contributed significantly to this edition by substantially reworking chapters 18 and 19, bringing to them her extraordinary knowledge of the period and her accessible and evocative writing style. We invite readers to look closely at those two revised and expanded chapters, and we think they will share our enthusiasm about adding Professor Fahs to our team. We expect her to work on this book for many years, and we are excited by the many contributions she will make.

In preparing for this revision, we solicited feedback from professors and scholars throughout the country, many of whom have used the Concise Fourth Edition of *Liberty, Equality, Power* in their classrooms. Their comments proved most helpful, and many of their suggestions have been incorporated into the Fifth Edition. Thus, in addition to the reworking of chapters 18 and 19

mentioned previously, we have reorganized substantial portions of the content in the antebellum chapters, specifically chapters 7, 8, 11, and 12. We have added an entirely new chapter 32 to give adequate attention to the momentous developments in politics, economics, and culture of the last 20 years. George W. Bush's victories in 2000 and 2004, the destruction of the World Trade Center towers on September 11, 2001, the wars on terrorism and against Iraq, and the 2008 election all receive substantial treatment.

Finally, we have scrutinized each page of the textbook, making sure our prose is clear, the historical issues are well presented, and the scholarship is up to date. This review, guided by the scholarly feedback we received, caused us to make numerous revisions and additions. A list of notable content changes follows.

SPECIFIC REVISIONS TO CONTENT AND COVERAGE

Chapter 18 New title: "A Transformed Nation: The West and the New South, 1865–1900." Includes a new introduction on experiences of homesteader Mary Abell. New material on the industrializing West, as well as a new History Through Film feature on the musical *Oklahoma!*

Chapter 19 New title: "The Emergence of Corporate America, 1865–1900." Includes new material on economic growth, class distinction, and culture.

Chapter 20 Revised to accommodate new material and organization in the preceding chapter. Now includes the History Through Film feature on *The Jazz Singer*, moved from chapter 24.

Chapter 21 Includes the History Through Film feature on *The Great White Hope*, moved from chapter 20.

Chapter 24 New History Through Film feature on *Inherit the Wind*.

Chapter 26 New History Through Film feature on *Casablanca*.

Chapter 30 New title: "Power and Politics, 1974–1992." Material in Fourth Edition Chapters 30 and 31 has been reorganized to provide a better perspective on the recent past and to include addition of new chapter 32. Chapter 30 consists primarily of material from Fourth Edition Chapter 31 (now ending with the first Bush administration). New History Through Film feature on "The First Movie Star President" (Ronald Reagan).

Chapter 31 Chapter 31 now consists primarily of material from Fourth Edition Chapter 30. History Through Film feature on *Star Wars* moved from Fourth Edition Chapter 30.

Chapter 32 Comprised of sections from Fourth Edition Chapter 31 (starting with the Clinton administration) plus considerable new material on George W. Bush's second term, the economy, and the 2008 election.

FEATURES

The popular **History Through Film** essays summarize a film, note interesting historical questions that it raises, and offer commentary on the accuracy or inaccuracy of historical figures and events as seen through the lens of a camera. The Concise Fifth Edition includes one **History Through Film** feature in each chapter.

Visually engaging **Timelines** help students understand the relationships among the events and movements of a particular era. Many chapter sections open with **Focus Questions** to aid students in grasping overarching themes and to organize the knowledge that they are acquiring. These Focus Questions reappear at the end of each chapter in **Chapter Reviews**, which are supplemented by **Critical Thinking Questions** that encourage students to range widely and imaginatively in their thinking about what they have just learned.

Quick Reviews and *Glossary Terms* further contribute to the emphasis we have placed on pedagogy. Quick Reviews appear periodically in the margins to summarize major events, ideas, and movements discussed in the text. Glossary Terms—individuals, ideas, events, legislation, and movements that we have deemed particularly important to an understanding of the historical period in question—appear boldface in the text and then are briefly defined in the margins. We have also assembled all the glossary terms in an alphabetical appendix that appears at the end of the textbook.

SUPPLEMENTS

FOR THE INSTRUCTOR

The Instructor's Companion Website provides instructors access to all of the features of the Student Companion Website, HistoryFinder, the United States History Resource Center, and the eInstructor's Resource Manual. This manual has many features, including instructional objectives, chapter outlines and summaries, lecture suggestions, suggested debate and research topics, cooperative learning activities, and suggested readings and resources. HistoryFinder is a searchable online database that allows instructors to quickly and easily download thousands of assets, including art, photographs, maps, primary sources, and audio/video clips. Each asset downloads directly into a Microsoft® PowerPoint® slide, allowing instructors to easily create exciting PowerPoint presentations for their classrooms.

The PowerLecture with ExamView and Join In, a dual-platform, all-in-one multimedia resource, includes the Instructor's Resource Manual; Test Bank (includes key term identification, multiple-choice, short answer, essay, and map questions); Microsoft® PowerPoint® slides of both lecture outlines and images and maps from the text that can be used as offered, or customized by importing personal lecture slides or other material; and JoinIn® PowerPoint® slides with clicker content. Also included is ExamView, an easy-to-use assessment and tutorial system that allows instructors to create, deliver, and customize tests in minutes. Instructors can build tests with as many as 250 questions using up to 12 question types, and using ExamView's complete word-processing capabilities, they can enter an unlimited number of new questions or edit existing ones.

FOR THE STUDENT

The Student Companion Website allows students to access a wide assortment of resources to help them master the subject matter. The website includes a glossary, flashcards, crossword puzzles, tutorial quizzes, essay questions, critical thinking exercises, web links, and suggested readings. Throughout the text, icons direct students to relevant exercises and self-testing material located on the student companion website.

The Printed Access Card for USHRC, Interactive CL eBook, and Info Trac is an interactive multimedia eBook that links out to rich media assets such as video and MP3 chapter summaries. Through this eBook, students can also access self-test quizzes, chapter outlines, focus questions, chronology and matching exercises, essay and critical thinking questions (for which the answers can be emailed to their instructors), primary source documents with critical thinking questions, and interactive (zoom-able) maps.

The Printed Access Card for Wadsworth American History Resource Center gives students access to a "virtual reader" with hundreds of primary sources including speeches, letters, legal documents and transcripts, poems, maps, simulations, timelines, and additional images that bring history to life, along with interactive assignable exercises. A map feature including Google Earth™ coordinates and exercises will aid in student comprehension of geography and use of maps. Students can compare the traditional textbook map with an aerial view of the location today. It's an ideal resource for study, review, and research. In addition to this map feature, the resource center also provides blank maps for student review and testing.

The **Printed Access Card for WebTutor™ on Blackboard®** and **The Printed Access Card for WebTutor™ on WebCT®** is text-specific, pre-formatted content. With total flexibility, instructors can easily create and manage their own custom course website. WebTutor's course management tool gives instructors the ability to provide virtual office hours, post syllabi, set up threaded discussions, track student progress with the quizzing material, and much more. For students, WebTutor offers real-time access to a full array of study tools, including animations and videos that bring the book's topics to life, plus chapter outlines, summaries, learning objectives, glossary flashcards (with audio), practice quizzes, and weblinks.

The History Handbook, by Carol Berkin of Baruch College, City University of New York and Betty Anderson of Boston University teaches students both basic and history-specific study skills such as how to read primary sources, research historical topics, and correctly cite sources. Substantially less expensive than comparable skill-building texts, *The History Handbook* also offers tips for Internet research and evaluating online sources.

Doing History: Research and Writing in the Digital Age, by Michael J. Galgano, J. Chris Arndt, and Raymond M. Hyser of James Madison University, is a perfect guide whether you are starting down the path as a history major or simply looking for a straightforward, systematic guide to writing a successful paper. This text is an indispensable handbook to historical research. Its "soup-to-nuts" approach to researching and writing about history addresses every step of the process, from locating your sources and gathering information, to writing clearly and making proper use of various citation styles to avoid plagiarism. You'll also learn how to make the most of every tool available to you—especially the technology that helps you conduct the process efficiently and effectively.

The Modern Researcher, Sixth Edition, by Jacques Barzun and Henry F. Graff of Columbia University, a classic introduction to the techniques of research and the art of expression, is used widely in history courses but is also appropriate for writing and research method courses in other departments. Barzun and Graff thoroughly cover every aspect of research, from the selection of a topic through the gathering, analysis, writing, revision, and publication of findings, presenting the process not as a set of rules but through actual cases that put the subtleties of research in a useful context. Part One covers the principles and methods of research; Part Two covers writing, speaking, and getting one's work published.

Rand McNally Atlas of American History, Second Edition, is a comprehensive atlas that features more than 80 maps, with new content covering global perspectives, including events in the Middle East from 1945 to 2005, as well as population trends in the United States and around the world. Additional maps document voyages of discovery; the settling of the colonies; major U.S. military engagements, including the American Revolution and World Wars I and II; and sources of immigrations, ethnic populations and patterns of economic change.

ACKNOWLEDGMENTS

We recognize the contributions of these reviewers, who have provided feedback on *Liberty, Equality, Power: A History of the American People, Concise Fifth Edition:*

David Arnold, Columbia Basin College
Mary Ann Bodayla, Southwest Tennessee Community College
Betty Brandon, University of Southern Alabama
Janet Brantley, Texarkana College
April L. Brown, NorthWest Arkansas Community College
B. R. Burg, Arizona State University
Randy Finley, Georgia Perimeter College
Michael P. Gabriel, Kutztown University
Steven C. Garvey, Muskegon Community College
Wendy Gordon, SUNY Plattsburgh
Sally Hadden, Florida State University
Kevin E. Hall, University of South Florida
Ian Harrison, University of Nevada, Las Vegas
Mary Ann Heiss, Kent State University
Terry Isaacs, South Plains College
Volker Janssen, California State University Fullerton
Catherine Kaplan, Arizona State University
Timothy K. Kinsella, Ursuline College
Greg Kiser, NorthWest Arkansas Community College
C. Douglas Kroll, College of the Desert
David F. Krugler, University of Wisconsin, Platteville
Marianne F. McKnight, Salt Lake Community College
Joel McMahon, Baker College
Salvatore R. Mercogliano, Central Carolina Community College
Caryn E. Neumann, Miami University of Ohio
Margaret E. Newell, Ohio State University
Thomas Ott, University of North Alabama
George S. Pabis, Georgia Perimeter College
Geoffrey Plank, University of Cincinnati
G. David Price, Santa Fe Community College (FL)
Akim D. Reinhardt, Towson University
Jason Ripper, Everett Community College
John Paul Rossi, Penn State Erie
Steven T. Sheehan, University of Wisconsin, Fox Valley
Megan Taylor Shockley, Clemson University
Adam M. Sowards, University of Idaho

Evelyn Sterne, University of Rhode Island

Kristen L. Streater, Collin County Community College, Preston Ridge Campus

Sean Taylor, Minnesota State University, Moorhead

Jerry Tiarsmith, Georgia Perimeter College

Leslie V. Tischauser, Prairie State College

Paul S. Vickery, Oral Roberts University

Stephen Webre, Louisiana Tech University

Bryan Wuthrich, Santa Fe Community College (FL)

We also wish to thank the members of the Wadsworth staff who capably guided the revision and production of this edition: Ann West, Senior Sponsoring Editor; Margaret Manos, Freelance Editor; and Lauren Wheelock and Anne Finley, Content Project Managers. Thanks as well go to Lori Hazzard, our Production Editor at MPS Content Services. Our greatest debt once again is to our longtime developmental editor, Margaret McAndrew Beasley. Margaret's editing skills, organizational expertise, good sense, and belief in this book and its authors keep us going.

John M. Murrin
Paul E. Johnson
James M. McPherson
Alice Fahs
Gary Gerstle
Emily S. Rosenberg
Norman L. Rosenberg

RECONSTRUCTION, 1863–1877

From the beginning of the Civil War, the North fought to "reconstruct" the Union. At first Lincoln's purpose was to restore the Union as it had existed before 1861. But once the abolition of slavery became a Northern war aim, the Union could never be reconstructed on its old foundations. Instead, it must experience a "new birth of freedom," as Lincoln had said at the dedication of the military cemetery at Gettysburg.

But precisely what did "a new birth of freedom" mean? At the very least it meant the end of slavery. The slave states would be reconstructed on a free-labor basis. But what would be the dimensions of liberty for the 4 million freed slaves? Would they become citizens equal to their former masters in the eyes of the law? And on what terms should the Confederate states return to the Union? What would be the powers of the states and of the national government in a reconstructed Union?

IMELINE

| 1863 | 1865 | 1867 | 1869 | 1871 | 1873 | 1875 | 1877 |

■ 1863
Lincoln issues Proclamation of Amnesty and Reconstruction

■ 1865
Andrew Johnson becomes president, announces his reconstruction plan

1865–1869
Andrew Johnson presidency

■ 1866
Congress passes civil rights bill and expands Freedmen's Bureau over Johnson's veto and approves Fourteenth Amendment

■ 1867
Congress passes Reconstruction acts over Johnson's vetoes

■ 1868
Andrew Johnson impeached but not convicted

1869–1877
Ulysses S. Grant presidency

■ 1870
Fifteenth Amendment ratified

1871 ■
Congress passes Ku Klux Klan Act

■ 1872
Liberal Republicans defect from party
• Grant wins reelection

1873 ■
Economic depression begins with the Panic

■ 1874
Democrats win House of Representatives

■ 1876
Disputed presidential election causes constitutional crisis

1877 ■
Compromise of 1877 installs Rutherford B. Hayes as president

WARTIME RECONSTRUCTION

Lincoln pondered these questions long and hard. At first he feared that whites in the South would never extend equal rights to the freed slaves. In 1862 and 1863, Lincoln encouraged freedpeople to emigrate to all-black countries like Haiti. But black leaders, abolitionists, and many Republicans objected to that policy. Black people were Americans: Why should they not have the rights of American citizens instead of being urged to leave the country?

Lincoln eventually was converted to the logic and justice of that view. But in beginning the process of reconstruction, Lincoln first reached out to Southern *whites* whose allegiance to the Confederacy was lukewarm. On December 8, 1863, Lincoln issued his Proclamation of **Amnesty** and Reconstruction, which offered a presidential

amnesty *General pardon granted to a large group of people.*

pardon to Southern whites who took an oath of allegiance to the United States and accepted the abolition of slavery. The plan allowed Southern states to form new governments if the number of adult white males who took the oath equaled 10 percent of the number of voters in 1860.

Because the war was still raging, this policy could be carried out only where Union troops controlled substantial portions of a Confederate state: Louisiana, Arkansas, and Tennessee in early 1864. Lincoln hoped that the process might snowball as Union military victories convinced more and more Confederates that their cause was hopeless. As matters turned out, those military victories were long delayed, and reconstruction in most parts of the South did not begin until 1865. Growing opposition within Lincoln's own party slowed the process as well. Many Republicans believed that white men who had fought *against* the Union should not be rewarded with restoration of their political rights while black men who had fought *for* the Union were denied those rights. The Proclamation of Reconstruction stated that "any provision which may be adopted by [a reconstructed] State government in relation to the freed people of such State, which shall recognize and declare their permanent freedom, provide for their education, and which may yet be consistent, as a temporary arrangement, with their present condition as a laboring, landless, and homeless class, will not be objected to by the national Executive." This seemed to mean that white landowners and former slaveholders could adopt labor regulations and other measures to control former slaves, so long as they recognized their freedom.

RADICAL REPUBLICANS AND RECONSTRUCTION

These were radical advances over slavery, but for many Republicans they were not radical enough. If the freedpeople were landless, they said, provide them with land by confiscating the plantations of leading Confederates as punishment for treason. Radical Republicans also distrusted oaths of allegiance sworn by ex-Confederates. Rather than simply restoring the old ruling class to power, they asked, why not give freed slaves the vote, to provide a genuinely loyal nucleus of supporters in the South?

These radical positions did not command a majority of Congress in 1864. Yet the experience of Louisiana, the first state to reorganize under Lincoln's more moderate policy, convinced even nonradical Republicans to block that policy. Enough white men in the occupied portion of the state took the oath of allegiance to satisfy Lincoln's conditions. They adopted a new state constitution and formed a government that abolished slavery and provided a school system for blacks. But the new government did not grant blacks the right to vote. It also authorized planters to enforce restrictive labor policies on black plantation workers. Louisiana's actions alienated a majority of congressional Republicans, who refused to admit representatives and senators from the "reconstructed" state.

At the same time, though, Congress failed to enact a reconstruction policy of its own. This was not for lack of trying. In fact, both houses passed the Wade-Davis reconstruction bill (named for Senator Benjamin Wade of Ohio and Representative Henry Winter Davis of Maryland) in July 1864. That bill did not enfranchise blacks, but it did impose such stringent loyalty requirements on Southern whites that few of them could take the required oath. Lincoln therefore vetoed it.

Lincoln's action infuriated many Republicans. Wade and Davis published a blistering "manifesto" denouncing the president. This bitter squabble threatened for a time to destroy Lincoln's chances of being reelected. But Union military success in the fall of 1864 reunited the Republicans behind Lincoln. The collapse of Confederate military resistance the following spring set the stage for compromise on a policy for the postwar South. Two days after Appomattox, Lincoln promised that he would soon announce such a policy. But three days later he was assassinated.

ANDREW JOHNSON AND RECONSTRUCTION

FOCUS QUESTION

What were the positions of Presidents Abraham Lincoln and Andrew Johnson and of moderate and radical Republicans in Congress on the issues of restoring the South to the Union and protecting the rights of freed slaves?

In 1864 Republicans had adopted the name "Union Party" to attract the votes of War Democrats and border-state Unionists who could not bring themselves to vote Republican. For the same reason, they also nominated Andrew Johnson of Tennessee as Lincoln's running mate.

Of "poor white" heritage, Johnson had clawed his way up in the rough-and-tumble politics of east Tennessee. This was a region of small farms and few slaves, where there was little love for the planters who controlled the state. Johnson denounced the planters as "stuck-up aristocrats" who had no empathy with the **Southern yeomen** for whom Johnson became a self-appointed spokesman. Johnson was the only senator from a seceding state who refused to support the Confederacy.

Booth's bullet therefore elevated to the presidency a man who still thought of himself as primarily a Democrat and a Southerner. The trouble this might cause in a party that was mostly Republican and Northern was not immediately apparent, however. In fact, Johnson's enmity toward the "stuck-up aristocrats" whom he blamed for leading the South into secession prompted him to utter dire threats against "traitors." "Traitors must be impoverished," he said. "They must not only be punished, but their social power must be destroyed."

Radical Republicans liked the sound of this. It seemed to promise the type of reconstruction they favored—one that would deny political power to ex-Confederates and enfranchise blacks. They envisioned a coalition between these new black voters and the small minority of Southern whites who had never supported the Confederacy. These men could be expected to vote Republican. Republican governments in Southern states would pass laws to provide civil rights and economic opportunity for freed slaves.

JOHNSON'S POLICY

From a combination of pragmatic, partisan, and idealistic motives, therefore, radical Republicans prepared to implement a progressive reconstruction policy. But Johnson unexpectedly refused to cooperate. Instead of calling Congress into session, he moved ahead on his own and issued two proclamations on May 29. The first provided for a blanket amnesty for all but the highest-ranking Confederate officials and military officers and those ex-Confederates with taxable property worth $20,000 or more. The second named a provisional governor for North Carolina and directed him to call an election of delegates to frame a new state constitution. Only white men who had received amnesty and taken an oath of allegiance could vote. Similar proclamations soon followed for other former Confederate states. Johnson's policy was clear: He would exclude both blacks and upper-class whites from the reconstruction process.

Southern yeoman *Farmer who owned relatively little land and few or no slaves.*

Many Republicans supported Johnson's policy at first. But the radicals feared that restricting the vote to whites would open the door to the restoration of the old power structure in the South. They began to sense that Johnson was as dedicated to white supremacy as any Confederate. "White men alone must govern the South," he told a Democratic senator. After a tense confrontation with a group of black men led by Frederick Douglass, Johnson told his private secretary: "I know that damned Douglass; he's just like any nigger, and he would sooner cut a white man's throat than not."

Moderate Republicans believed that black men should participate to some degree in the reconstruction process, but in 1865 they were not yet prepared to break with the president. They regarded his policy as an "experiment" that would be modified as time went on. "Loyal negroes must not be put down, while disloyal white men are put up," wrote a moderate Republican. "But I am quite willing to see what will come of Mr. Johnson's experiment."

SOUTHERN DEFIANCE

As it happened, none of the state conventions enfranchised a single black. Some of them even balked at ratifying the Thirteenth Amendment (which abolished slavery). Reports from Unionists and army officers in the South told of neo-Confederate violence against blacks and their white sympathizers. Johnson seemed to encourage such activities by allowing the organization of white militia units in the South. "What can be hatched from such an egg," asked a Republican newspaper, "but another rebellion?"

Then there was the matter of presidential pardons. After talking fiercely about punishing traitors, and after excluding several classes of them from his amnesty proclamation, Johnson began to issue special pardons to many ex-Confederates, restoring property and political rights. Moreover, under the new state constitutions Southern voters were electing hundreds of ex-Confederates to state offices. Even more alarming to Northerners, who thought they had won the war, was the election to Congress of no fewer than nine ex-Confederate congressmen, seven ex-Confederate state officials, four generals, four colonels, and even the former Confederate vice president, Alexander H. Stephens.

Somehow the aristocrats and traitors Johnson had denounced in April had taken over the reconstruction process. What had happened? Flattery was part of the answer. In applying for pardons, thousands of prominent ex-Confederates or their tearful female relatives had confessed the error of their ways and had appealed for presidential mercy. Reveling in his power, Johnson waxed eloquent on his "love, respect, and confidence" toward Southern whites, for whom he now felt "forbearing and forgiving."

More important, perhaps, was the praise and support Johnson received from leading Northern Democrats. Though the Republicans had placed him on their presidential ticket in 1864, Johnson was after all a Democrat. That party's leaders enticed Johnson with visions of reelection as a Democrat in 1868 if he could manage to reconstruct the South in a manner that would preserve a Democratic majority there.

THE BLACK CODES

That was just what the Republicans feared. Their concern was confirmed in the fall of 1865 when some state governments enacted **Black Codes.**

Black Codes *Laws passed by Southern states that restricted the rights and liberties of former slaves.*

One of the first tasks of the legislatures of the reconstructed states was to define the rights of 4 million former slaves who were now free. The option of treating them exactly like white citizens was scarcely considered. Instead, the states excluded black people from juries and the ballot box, did not permit them to testify against whites in court, banned interracial marriage, and punished them more severely than whites for certain crimes. Some states defined any unemployed black person as a vagrant and hired him out to a planter, forbade blacks to lease land, and apprenticed black youths out to whites.

Northern Republicans saw these Black Codes as a brazen attempt to reinstate a **quasi-slavery.** "We tell the white men of Mississippi," declared the *Chicago Tribune,* "that the men of the North will convert the State of Mississippi into a frog pond before they will allow such laws to disgrace one foot of the soil in which the bones of our soldiers sleep and over which the flag of freedom waves." And, in fact, the Union Army's occupation forces did suspend the implementation of Black Codes that discriminated on racial grounds.

LAND AND LABOR IN THE POSTWAR SOUTH

The Black Codes, though discriminatory, were designed to address a genuine problem. The end of the war had left black–white relations in the South in a state of limbo. The South's economy was in a shambles. Burned-out plantations, fields growing up in weeds, and railroads without tracks, bridges, or **rolling stock** marked the trail of war. Most tangible assets except the land itself had been destroyed. Law and order broke down in many areas. The war had ended early enough in the spring to allow the planting of at least some food crops. But who would plant and cultivate them? One quarter of the South's white farmers had been killed in the war; the slaves were slaves no more. "We have nothing left to begin anew with," lamented a South Carolina planter. "I never did a day's work in my life, and I don't know how to begin."

But despite all, life went on. Slaveless planters and their wives, soldiers' widows and their children, plowed and planted. Confederate veterans drifted home and went to work. Former slave owners asked their former slaves to work the land for wages or shares of the crop, and many did so. But others refused, because for them to leave the old place was an essential part of freedom. "You ain't, none o' you, gwinter feel rale free," said a black preacher to his congregation, "till you shakes de dus' ob de Ole Plantashun offen yore feet" (dialect in original source).

Thus in the summer of 1865 the roads were alive with freedpeople on the move. Many signed on to work at farms just a few miles from their old homes. Others moved into town. Some looked for relatives who had been sold away during slavery or from whom they had been separated during the war. Some wandered aimlessly. Crime increased, and whites organized vigilante groups to discipline blacks and force them to work.

THE FREEDMEN'S BUREAU

Into this vacuum stepped the United States Army and the **Freedmen's Bureau.** Tens of thousands of troops remained in the South until civil government could be restored. The Freedmen's Bureau (its official title was Bureau of Refugees, Freedmen, and Abandoned Lands), created by Congress in March 1865, became the principal agency for overseeing relations between former slaves and owners. Staffed by army officers, the bureau established posts throughout the South to

quasi-slavery *Position that resembled slavery, such as that created by the Black Codes.*

rolling stock *Locomotives, freight cars, and other types of wheeled equipment owned by railroads.*

Freedmen's Bureau Federal agency created in 1865 to supervise newly freed people. It oversaw relations between whites and blacks in the South, issued food rations, and supervised labor contracts.

Photographs and Prints Division, Schomburg/Center for Research in Black Culture, The New York Public Library, Astor, Lenore and Tilden Foundations

SHARECROPPERS WORKING IN THE FIELDS. *This photograph shows two families of sharecroppers picking cotton. Freed slaves resisted landowners' efforts to work them in gangs as they had in slavery, so the owners rented land to black families in return for a share of the crop. These croppers do not appear to be overjoyed with the new system.*

supervise free-labor wage contracts between landowners and freedpeople. The Freedmen's Bureau also issued food rations to 150,000 people daily during 1865, one third of them to whites.

The Freedmen's Bureau was viewed with hostility by Southern whites. But without it, the postwar chaos and devastation in the South would have been much greater. Bureau agents used their influence with black people to encourage them to sign free-labor contracts and return to work.

In negotiating labor contracts, the bureau tried to establish minimum wages. Because there was so little money in the South, however, many contracts called for **share wages**—that is, paying workers with shares of the crop. At first, landowners worked their laborers in large groups called gangs. But many black workers resented this system. Thus, a new system evolved, called **sharecropping,** whereby a black family worked a specific piece of land in return for a share of the crop produced on it. This system represented an uneasy and imperfect compromise between landowners who wanted to control their workers and freedpeople who wanted greater independence.

LAND FOR THE LANDLESS

Freedpeople, of course, would have preferred to farm their own land. "What's de use of being free if you don't own land enough to be buried in?" asked one black sharecropper (dialect in original). Some black farmers did manage to save up enough money to buy small plots of land. Demobilized black soldiers purchased land with their bounty payments, sometimes pooling their money to buy an entire plantation, on which several black families settled. Northern philanthropists helped some freedmen buy land. But for most ex-slaves the purchase of land was impossible. Few of them had money, and even if they did, whites often refused to sell.

share wages *Payment of workers' wages with a share of the crop rather than with cash.*

sharecropping *Working land in return for a share of the crops produced instead of paying cash rent.*

NEW YORK, SATURDAY, MAY 26, 1866.

Library of Congress Prints and Photographs Division [LC-USZ62-111152]

THE BURNING OF A FREEDMEN'S SCHOOL. *Because freedpeople's education symbolized black progress, whites who resented and resisted this progress sometimes attacked and burned freedmen's schools, as in this dramatic illustration of a white mob burning a school during antiblack riots in Memphis in May 1866.*

Several Northern radicals proposed legislation to confiscate ex-Confederate land and redistribute it to freedpeople, but those proposals got nowhere, and the most promising effort to put thousands of slaves on land of their own also failed. In January 1865, after his march through Georgia, General William T. Sherman had issued a military order setting aside thousands of acres of abandoned plantation land in the Georgia and South Carolina Lowcountry for settlement by freed slaves. The army even turned over some of its surplus mules to black farmers. The expectation of **40 acres and a mule** excited freedpeople in 1865. But President Johnson's Amnesty Proclamation and his wholesale issuance of pardons restored most of this property to pardoned ex-Confederates. The same thing happened to white-owned land elsewhere in the South. Placed under the temporary care of the Freedmen's Bureau for subsequent possible distribution to freedpeople, by 1866 nearly all of this land had been restored to its former owners by order of President Johnson.

EDUCATION

Abolitionists were more successful in helping freedpeople get an education. During the war, freedmen's aid societies and missionary societies founded by abolitionists had sent teachers to Union-occupied areas of the South to set up schools for freed slaves. After the war, this effort was expanded with the aid of the Freedmen's Bureau. Two thousand Northern teachers fanned out into every part of the South to train black teachers. After 1870 missionary societies concentrated on making higher education available to African Americans. They founded many of the black colleges in the South. These efforts reduced the southern black illiteracy rate to 70 percent by 1880 and to 48 percent by 1900.

40 acres and a mule *Largely unfulfilled hope of many former slaves that they would receive free land from the confiscated property of ex-Confederates.*

THE ADVENT OF CONGRESSIONAL RECONSTRUCTION

The civil and political rights of freedpeople would be shaped by the terms of reconstruction. By the time Congress met in December 1865, the Republican majority was determined to take control of the process by which former Confederate states would be restored to full representation. Congress refused to admit the representatives and senators elected by the former Confederate states under Johnson's reconstruction policy, and set up a special committee to formulate new terms. The committee held hearings at which southern Unionists, freedpeople, and U.S. Army officers testified to abuse and terrorism in the South. Their testimony convinced Republicans of the need for stronger federal intervention to define and protect the civil rights of freedpeople. However, because racism was still strong in the North, the special committee decided to draft a constitutional amendment that would encourage Southern states to enfranchise blacks but would not require them to do so.

SCHISM BETWEEN PRESIDENT AND CONGRESS

Meanwhile, Congress passed two laws to protect the economic and civil rights of freedpeople. The first extended the life of the Freedmen's Bureau and expanded its powers. The second defined freedpeople as citizens with equal legal rights and gave federal courts appellate jurisdiction to enforce those rights. But to the dismay of moderates who were trying to heal the widening breach between the president and Congress, Johnson vetoed both measures. He followed this action with a speech to Democratic supporters in which he denounced Republican leaders as traitors who did not want to restore the Union except on terms that would degrade white Southerners. Democratic newspapers applauded the president for vetoing bills that would "compound our race with niggers, gypsies, and baboons."

THE FOURTEENTH AMENDMENT

Johnson had thrown down the gauntlet to congressional Republicans. But with better than a two-thirds majority in both houses, they passed the Freedmen's Bureau and Civil Rights bills over the president's vetoes. Then on April 30, the special committee submitted to Congress its proposed Fourteenth Amendment to the Constitution. After lengthy debate, the amendment received the required two-thirds majority in Congress on June 13 and went to the states for ratification. Section 1 defined all native-born or naturalized persons, including blacks, as American citizens and prohibited the states from abridging the "privileges and immunities" of citizens, from depriving "any person of life, liberty, or property without due process of law," and from denying to any person "the equal protection of the laws." Section 2 gave states the option of either enfranchising black males or losing a proportionate number of congressional seats and electoral votes. Section 3 disqualified a significant number of ex-Confederates from holding federal or state office. Section 4 guaranteed the national debt and repudiated the Confederate debt. Section 5 empowered Congress to enforce the Fourteenth Amendment by "appropriate legislation."

The Fourteenth Amendment had far-reaching consequences. Section 1 has become the most important provision in the Constitution for defining and enforcing civil rights. It vastly expanded federal powers to prevent state violations of civil rights. It also greatly enlarged the rights of blacks.

THE 1866 ELECTIONS

During the campaign for the 1866 congressional elections Republicans made clear that any ex-Confederate state that ratified the Fourteenth Amendment would be declared "reconstructed" and that its representatives and senators would be seated in Congress. Tennessee ratified the amendment, but Johnson counseled other Southern legislatures to reject the amendment, and they did so. Johnson then created a "National Union Party" made up of a few conservative Republicans who disagreed with their party, some border-state Unionists who supported the president, and Democrats.

The inclusion of Democrats doomed the effort from the start. Many Northern Democrats still carried the taint of having opposed the war effort, and most Northern voters did not trust them. The National Union Party was further damaged by race riots in Memphis and New Orleans. The riots bolstered Republican arguments that national power was necessary to protect "the fruits of victory" in the South. Perhaps the biggest liability was Johnson himself. In a whistle-stop tour through the North, he traded insults with hecklers and embarrassed his supporters.

Republicans swept the election. Having rejected the reconstruction terms embodied in the Fourteenth Amendment, Southern Democrats now faced far more stringent terms. "They would not cooperate in rebuilding what they destroyed," wrote an exasperated moderate Republican, so "we must remove the rubbish and rebuild from the bottom."

THE RECONSTRUCTION ACTS OF 1867

In March 1867 the new Congress enacted two laws prescribing new procedures for the full restoration of the former Confederate states to the Union. The Reconstruction Acts of 1867 divided the 10 southern states into five military districts, directed army officers to register voters for the election of delegates to new constitutional conventions, and **enfranchised** males aged 21 and older, including blacks, to vote in those elections. When a state had adopted a new constitution that granted equal civil and political rights regardless of race and had ratified the Fourteenth Amendment, it would be declared reconstructed and its newly elected congressmen would be seated.

These measures embodied a true revolution. Just a few years earlier, Southerners had been masters of 4 million slaves and part of an independent Confederate nation. Now they were shorn of political power, with their former slaves not only freed but also politically empowered.

Like most revolutions, the reconstruction process did not go smoothly. Many Southern Democrats breathed defiance and refused to cooperate. The presence of the army minimized antiblack violence. But thousands of white Southerners who were eligible to vote refused to do so, hoping that their nonparticipation would delay the process long enough for Northern voters to come to their senses and elect Democrats to Congress.

Blacks and their white allies organized **Union Leagues** to mobilize the new black voters into the Republican Party. Democrats branded Southern white Republicans as **scalawags** and Northern settlers as **carpetbaggers.** By September 1867,

enfranchise *To grant the right to vote.*

Union Leagues *Organizations that informed African American voters of, and mobilized them to support, the Republican Party.*

scalawags *Term used by Southern Democrats to describe Southern whites who worked with the Republicans.*

carpetbaggers *Northerners who settled in the South during Reconstruction.*

there were 735,000 black voters and only 635,000 white voters registered in the 10 states. At least one third of the registered white voters were Republicans.

President Johnson did everything he could to block Reconstruction. He replaced several Republican generals with Democrats. He had his attorney general issue a ruling that interpreted the Reconstruction acts narrowly, thereby forcing a special session of Congress to pass a supplementary act in July 1867. And he encouraged Southern whites to obstruct the registration of voters and the election of convention delegates.

Johnson's purpose was to slow the process until 1868 in the hope that Northern voters would repudiate Reconstruction in the presidential election of that year, when Johnson planned to run as the Democratic candidate. Indeed, in off-year state elections in the fall of 1867 Republicans suffered setbacks in several Northern states. "I almost pity the radicals," chortled one of President Johnson's aides after the 1867 elections. "After giving ten states to the negroes, to keep the Democrats from getting them, they will have lost the rest."

THE IMPEACHMENT OF ANDREW JOHNSON

Johnson struck even more boldly against Reconstruction after the 1867 elections. In February 1868, he removed from office Secretary of War Edwin M. Stanton, who had administered the War Department in support of the congressional Reconstruction policy. This appeared to violate the Tenure of Office Act, passed the year before over Johnson's veto, which required Senate consent for such removals. By a vote of 126 to 47 along party lines, the House **impeached** Johnson on February 24. The official reason for impeachment was that he had violated the Tenure of Office Act, but the real reason was Johnson's stubborn defiance of Congress on Reconstruction.

Under the U.S. Constitution, impeachment by the House does not remove an official from office. It is more like a grand jury indictment that must be tried by a petit jury—in this case, the Senate, which sat as a court to try Johnson on the impeachment charges brought by the House. If convicted by a two-thirds majority of the Senate, he would be removed from office.

The impeachment trial proved to be long and complicated, which worked in Johnson's favor by allowing passions to cool. The Constitution specifies the grounds on which a president can be impeached and removed: "Treason, Bribery, or other high Crimes and Misdemeanors." The issue was whether Johnson was guilty of any of these acts. His able defense counsel exposed technical ambiguities in the Tenure of Office Act that raised doubts about whether Johnson had actually violated it. Behind the scenes, Johnson strengthened his case by promising to appoint the respected General John M. Schofield as secretary of war and to stop obstructing the Reconstruction acts. In the end, seven Republican senators voted for acquittal on May 16, and the final tally fell one vote short of the necessary two-thirds majority.

THE COMPLETION OF FORMAL RECONSTRUCTION

The end of the impeachment trial cleared the poisonous air in Washington. Constitutional conventions met in the South during the winter and spring of 1867–1868. The constitutions they wrote were among the most progressive in the nation. The

FOCUS QUESTION
Why was Andrew Johnson impeached? Why was he acquitted?

impeach *To charge government officeholders with misconduct in office.*

new state constitutions enacted **universal male suffrage.** Some disfranchised certain classes of ex-Confederates for several years, but by 1872 all such disqualifications had been removed. The constitutions mandated statewide public schools for both races for the first time in the South. Most states permitted segregated schools, but schools of any kind for blacks represented a great step forward. Most of the constitutions increased the state's responsibility for social welfare.

Violence in some parts of the South marred the voting on ratification of these state constitutions. A night-riding white terrorist organization, the **Ku Klux Klan,** made its first appearance during the elections. Nevertheless, voters in seven states ratified their constitutions and elected new legislatures that ratified the Fourteenth Amendment in the spring of 1868. That amendment became part of the U.S. Constitution the following summer, and the newly elected representatives and senators from those seven states, nearly all of them Republicans, took their seats in the House and Senate.

THE FIFTEENTH AMENDMENT

The remaining three Southern states completed the Reconstruction process in 1869 and 1870. Congress required them to ratify the Fifteenth as well as the Fourteenth Amendment. The Fifteenth Amendment prohibited states from denying the right to vote on grounds of race, color, or previous condition of servitude. Its purpose was not only to prevent any future revocation of black suffrage by the reconstructed states but also to extend equal suffrage to the border states and to the North. But the challenge of enforcement lay ahead.

THE ELECTION OF 1868

Just as the presidential election of 1864 was a referendum on Lincoln's war policies, so the election of 1868 was a referendum on the Reconstruction policy of the Republicans. The Republican nominee was General **Ulysses S. Grant.** Though he had no political experience, Grant commanded greater authority and prestige than anyone else in the country. Grant agreed to run for the presidency in order to preserve in peace the victory for Union and liberty he had won in war.

The Democrats turned away from Andrew Johnson and nominated Horatio Seymour, the wartime governor of New York. They adopted a militant platform denouncing the Reconstruction acts as "a flagrant usurpation of power . . . unconstitutional, revolutionary, and void." The platform also demanded "the abolition of the Freedmen's Bureau, and all political instrumentalities designed to secure negro supremacy."

The vice presidential candidate, Frank Blair of Missouri, became the point man for the Democrats. In a public letter he proclaimed, "There is but one way to restore the Government and the Constitution, and that is for the President-elect to declare these [Reconstruction] acts null and void, compel the army to undo its usurpations at the South, disperse the carpet-bag State Governments, [and] allow the white people to reorganize their own governments."

The only way to achieve this bold counterrevolutionary goal was to suppress Republican voters in the South. This the Ku Klux Klan tried its best to do. Federal troops had only limited success in preventing the violence. In Louisiana, Georgia, Arkansas, and Tennessee, the Klan or Klan-like groups committed dozens of murders and intimidated thousands of black voters. The violence helped the Democratic cause in the South but probably hurt it in the North, where many voters perceived the Klan as an organization of neo-Confederate paramilitary guerrillas.

---

universal male suffrage *System that allowed all adult males to vote without regard to property, religious, or race qualifications or limitations.*

Ku Klux Klan *White terrorist organization in the South originally founded as a fraternal society in 1866.*

Ulysses S. Grant *General-in-chief of Union armies who led those armies to victory in the Civil War.*

QUICK REVIEW

GOALS OF RECONSTRUCTION

- To bring ex-Confederate states back into the Union

- To define and protect the rights of ex-slaves

- Johnson's Plan: rapid restoration of states to Union but minimal rights and economic opportunities for freedpeople

- Radical Republicans' plan: equal civil and political rights for freedpeople plus land and education

Library of Congress Prints and Photographs Division [LC-USZ62-119565]

Two Members of the Ku Klux Klan. *Founded in Pulaski, Tennessee in 1866 as a social organization similar to a college fraternity, the Klan evolved into a terrorist group whose purpose was intimidation of southern Republicans. The Klan, in which former Confederate soldiers played a prominent part, was responsible for the beating and murder of hundreds of blacks and whites alike from 1868 to 1871.*

Seymour did well in the South, carrying five former slave states and coming close in others despite the solid Republican vote of the newly enfranchised blacks. But Grant swept the electoral vote 214 to 80. Seymour actually won a slight majority of the white voters nationally, so without black enfranchisement, Grant would have had a minority of the popular vote.

THE GRANT ADMINISTRATION

Grant is usually branded a failure as president. His two administrations (1869–1877) were plagued by scandals. His private secretary allegedly became involved in the infamous **whiskey ring,** a network of distillers and revenue agents that deprived the government of millions of tax dollars; his secretary of war was impeached for selling appointments to army posts and Indian reservations; and his attorney general and secretary of the interior resigned under suspicion of malfeasance in 1875.

Honest himself, Grant was too trusting of subordinates. But not all of the scandals were Grant's fault. This was an era notorious for corruption at all levels of government. The Tammany Hall "Ring" of "Boss" William Marcy Tweed in New York City may have stolen more money from taxpayers than all the federal agencies combined. In Washington, one of the most widely publicized scandals concerned Congress rather than the Grant administration. Several congressmen had accepted

whiskey ring *Network of distillers and revenue agents that cheated the government out of millions of tax dollars.*

stock in the **Credit Mobilier,** a construction company for the Union Pacific Railroad, which received loans and land grants from the government in return for ensuring lax congressional supervision, thereby permitting financial manipulations by the company.

What accounted for this explosion of corruption in the postwar decade? The expansion of government contracts and the bureaucracy during the war had created new opportunities for the unscrupulous. Then came a relaxation of tensions and standards following the intense sacrifices of the war years. Rapid postwar economic growth, led by an extraordinary rush of railroad construction, encouraged greed and get-rich-quick schemes of the kind satirized by Mark Twain and Charles Dudley Warner in their 1873 novel *The Gilded Age,* which gave its name to the era.

CIVIL SERVICE REFORM

But some of the increase in corruption during the Gilded Age was more apparent than real. Reformers focused on the dark corners of corruption hitherto unilluminated because of the nation's preoccupation with war and reconstruction. Thus, the actual extent of corruption may have been exaggerated by the publicity that reformers gave it. In reality, during the Grant administration several government agencies made real progress in eliminating abuses that had flourished in earlier administrations.

One area of progress was civil service reform. Its chief target was the **spoils system.** With the slogan "To the victor belong the spoils," the victorious party in an election rewarded party workers with appointments as postmasters, customs collectors, and the like. The hope of getting appointed to a government post was the glue that kept the faithful together when a party was out of power. The spoils system politicized the bureaucracy and staffed it with unqualified personnel who spent more time working for their party than for the government.

Civil service reformers wanted to separate the bureaucracy from politics by requiring competitive examinations for the appointment of civil servants. This movement gathered steam during the 1870s and finally achieved success in 1883 with the passage of the Pendleton Act, which established the modern structure of the civil service. When Grant took office, he seemed to share the sentiments of civil service reformers. Grant named a civil service commission headed by George William Curtis, a leading reformer and editor of *Harper's Weekly.* But many congressmen, senators, and other politicians resisted civil service reform because **patronage** was the grease of the political machines that kept them in office. They managed to subvert reform, sometimes using Grant as an unwitting ally and thus turning many reformers against the president.

FOREIGN POLICY ISSUES

A foreign policy fiasco added to Grant's woes. The irregular procedures by which his private secretary had negotiated a treaty to annex Santo Domingo (now the Dominican Republic) alienated leading Republican senators, who defeated ratification of the treaty. Grant's political inexperience led him to act like a general who needed only to give orders rather than as a president who must cultivate supporters. The fallout from the Santo Domingo affair widened the fissure in the Republican Party.

But the Grant administration had some solid foreign policy achievements to its credit. Hamilton Fish, the able secretary of state, negotiated the Treaty of Washington

Credit Mobilier *Construction company for the Union Pacific Railroad that gave shares of stock to some congressmen in return for favors.*

spoils system *System by which the victorious political party rewarded its supporters with government jobs.*

patronage *Government jobs given out by political figures to their supporters, regardless of ability.*

in 1871 to settle the vexing "Alabama Claims." These were damage claims against Britain for the destruction of American shipping by the C.S.S. *Alabama* and other Confederate commerce raiders built in British shipyards. The treaty established an international tribunal to arbitrate the U.S. claims, resulting in the award of $15.5 million in damages to U.S. ship owners and a British expression of regret.

The events leading to the Treaty of Washington also resolved another long-festering issue between Britain and the United States: the status of Canada. The seven separate British North American colonies were especially vulnerable to U.S. desires for annexation. In 1867 Parliament passed the British North America Act, which united most of the Canadian colonies into a new and largely self-governing Dominion of Canada.

The successful conclusion of the treaty cooled Canadian–American tensions. It also led to the resolution of disputes over American commercial fishing in Canadian waters. American demands for annexation of Canada faded away. These events gave birth to the modern nation of Canada, whose 3,500-mile border with the United States remains the longest unfortified frontier in the world.

Reconstruction in the South

During Grant's two administrations, the "Southern Question" was the most intractable issue. A phrase in Grant's acceptance of the presidential nomination in 1868 had struck a responsive chord in the North: "Let us have peace." With the ratification of the Fifteenth Amendment, many people breathed a sigh of relief at this apparent resolution of "the last great point that remained to be settled of the issues of the war." It was time to deal with other matters that had been long neglected.

But there was no peace. State governments elected by black and white voters were in place in the South, but Democratic violence protesting Reconstruction and the instability of the Republican coalition that sustained it portended trouble.

Blacks in Office

In the North, the Republican Party represented the most prosperous, educated, and influential elements of the population; but in the South, most of its adherents were poor, illiterate, and propertyless. About 80 percent of Southern Republican voters were black. Although most black leaders were educated and many had been free before the war, the mass of black voters were illiterate ex-slaves. Neither the leaders nor their constituents, however, were as ignorant as stereotypes have portrayed them. Of 14 black representatives and two black senators elected in the South between 1868 and 1876, all but three had attended secondary school and four had attended college. Several of the blacks elected to state offices were among the best-educated men of their day. For example, Jonathan Gibbs, secretary of state in Florida from 1868 to 1872 and state superintendent of education from 1872 to 1874, was a graduate of Dartmouth College and Princeton Theological Seminary. It is true that some lower-level black officeholders, as well as their constituents, could not read or write. But illiteracy did not preclude an understanding of political issues for them any more than it did for Irish American voters in the North, many of whom also were illiterate. Southern blacks thirsted for education. Participation in the Union League and the experience of voting were themselves a form of education. Black churches and fraternal organizations proliferated during Reconstruction and tutored African Americans in their rights and responsibilities.

Linked to the myth of black incompetence was the legend of the "Africaniza-tion" of Southern governments during Reconstruction. The theme of "Negro rule" was a staple of Democratic propaganda. It was enshrined in folk memory and text-books. In fact, blacks held only 15 to 20 percent of public offices, even at the height of Reconstruction in the early 1870s. There were no black governors and only one black state Supreme Court justice. Nowhere except in South Carolina did blacks hold office in numbers anywhere near their proportion of the population.

"CARPETBAGGERS"

Next to "Negro rule," carpetbagger corruption and scalawag rascality have been the prevailing myths of Reconstruction. "Carpetbaggers" did hold a disproportion-ate number of high political offices in Southern state governments during Recon-struction. A few did resemble the proverbial adventurer who came south with nothing but a carpetbag in which to stow the loot plundered from a helpless people. But most were Union Army officers who stayed on after the war as Freedmen's Bureau agents, teachers in black schools, or business investors.

Those who settled in the postwar South hoped to rebuild its society in the image of the free-labor North. Many were college graduates. Most brought not empty carpetbags but considerable capital, which they invested in what they hoped would become a new South. They also invested human capital—themselves—in a drive to modernize the region's social structure and democratize its politics. But they under-estimated the hostility of Southern whites, most of whom regarded them as agents of an alien culture.

"SCALAWAGS"

Most of the native-born whites who joined the Southern Republican Party came from the Upcountry Unionist areas of western North Carolina and Virginia and eastern Tennessee. Others were former Whigs. Republicans, said a North Carolina scalawag, were the "party of progress, of education, of development."

But Democrats were aware that the Southern Republican Party they abhorred was a fragile coalition of blacks and whites, Yankees and Southerners, hill-country yeomen and Lowcountry entrepreneurs, illiterates and college graduates. The party was weakest along the seams where these disparate elements joined, especially the racial seam. Democrats attacked that weakness with every weapon at their com-mand, including violence.

THE KU KLUX KLAN

The generic name for the secret groups that terrorized the Southern countryside was the Ku Klux Klan, but some went by other names (the Knights of the White Camelia in Louisiana, for example). Part of the Klan's purpose was social control of the black population. Sharecroppers who tried to extract better terms from land-owners, or black people who were considered too "uppity," were likely to receive a midnight whipping—or worse—from white-sheeted Klansmen. Scores of black schools, perceived as a particular threat to white supremacy, went up in flames.

But the Klan's main purpose was political: to destroy the Republican Party by terrorizing its voters and, if necessary, murdering its leaders. No one knows the number of politically motivated killings that took place, but it was certainly in

QUICK   REVIEW

ACHIEVEMENTS OF SOUTHERN RECONSTRUCTION

- Election of Republican state governments

- Suppression of Ku Klux Klan

- Creation of black schools, churches, communities

HISTORY THROUGH FILM

BIRTH OF A NATION (1915)

Directed by D. W. Griffith; starring Lillian Gish (Elsie Stoneman), Henry B. Walthall (Ben Cameron), Ralph Lewis (Austin Stoneman), George Siegmann (Silas Lynch)

Few films have had such a pernicious impact on historical understanding and race relations as *Birth of a Nation*. This movie popularized a version of Reconstruction that portrayed predatory carpetbaggers and stupid, brutish blacks plundering a prostrate South and lusting after white women. It perpetuated vicious stereotypes of rapacious black males. It glorified the Ku Klux Klan of the Reconstruction era, inspiring the founding of the "second Klan" in 1915 that became a powerful force in the 1920s (see Chapter 24). The first half of the film offers a conventional Victorian romance of the Civil War. The children of the northerner Austin Stoneman (a malevolent radical Republican who is a thinly disguised Thaddeus Stevens) become friends with the children of the Cameron family, from South Carolina. The Civil War tragically separates the families. The Stoneman and Cameron boys enlist in the Union and Confederate armies and—predictably—face each other on the battlefield. Two Camerons and one Stoneman are killed in the war, and Ben Cameron, badly wounded, is captured, to be nursed back to health by Elsie Stoneman.

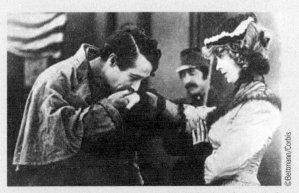

Colonel Ben Cameron (Henry B. Walthall) kissing the hand of Elsie Stoneman (Lillian Gish) in Birth of a Nation.

After the war the younger Camerons and Stonemans renew their friendship. The Stonemans visit South Carolina, and Ben Cameron and Elsie Stoneman, and Phil Stoneman and Flora Cameron, fall in love. If the story had stopped there, *Birth of a Nation* would have been just another Hollywood romance. But Austin Stoneman brings south with him Silas Lynch, an ambitious, leering mulatto demagogue who stirs up the animal passions of the ignorant black majority to demand "Equal Rights, Equal Politics, Equal Marriage." A "renegade Negro," Gus, stalks the youngest Cameron daughter, who saves herself from rape by jumping from a cliff to her death. Silas Lynch tries to force Elsie to marry him. "I will build a Black Empire," he tells the virginal Elsie (Lillian Gish, the Hollywood beauty queen of silent films), "and you as my queen shall rule by my side."

Finally provoked beyond endurance, white South Carolinians led by Ben Cameron organize the Ku Klux Klan to save "the Aryan race." Riding to the rescue of embattled whites in stirring scenes that anticipated the heroic actions of the cavalry against Indians in later Hollywood westerns, the Klan executes Gus, saves Elsie, disperses black soldiers and mobs, and carries the next election for white rule by intimidating black voters. The film ends with a double marriage that unites the Camerons and Stonemans in a symbolic rebirth of a nation, one rightfully based on the supremacy of "the Aryan race."

The son of a Confederate lieutenant colonel, David Wark (D. W.) Griffith was the foremost director of the silent movie era. *Birth of a Nation* was the first real full-length feature film, technically and artistically superior to anything before it. Apart from its place in the history of cinema, though, why should anyone today watch a movie that perpetuates such wrong-headed history and noxious racist stereotypes? Precisely *because* it reflects and amplifies an interpretation of Reconstruction that prevailed from the 1890s to the 1950s, and thereby shaped historical understanding as well as contemporary behavior—as in its inspiration for the Klan of the 1920s.

the hundreds, probably in the thousands. Nearly all the victims were Republicans; most of them were black. In one notorious incident, the "Colfax Massacre" in Louisiana (April 18, 1873), a clash between black militia and armed whites left three whites and nearly 100 blacks dead.

In some places, notably Tennessee and Arkansas, militias formed by Republicans suppressed and disarmed many Klansmen. But in most areas the militias were outgunned and outmaneuvered by ex-Confederate veterans who had joined the Klan. Some Republican governors were reluctant to use black militia against white guerrillas for fear of sparking a racial bloodbath, as happened at Colfax.

The answer seemed to be federal troops. In 1870 and 1871 Congress enacted three laws intended to enforce the Fourteenth and Fifteenth Amendments. Interference with voting rights became a federal offense, and any attempt to deprive another person of civil or political rights became a felony. The third law, passed on April 20, 1871, and popularly called the Ku Klux Klan Act, gave the president power to suspend the writ of **habeas corpus** and send in federal troops to suppress armed resistance to federal law.

Armed with these laws, the Grant administration moved against the Klan. But Grant did so with restraint. He suspended the writ of habeas corpus only in nine South Carolina counties. Nevertheless, there and elsewhere federal marshals backed by troops arrested thousands of suspected Klansmen. Federal grand juries indicted more than 3,000, and several hundred defendants pleaded guilty in return for suspended sentences; the Justice Department dropped charges against nearly 2,000 others. About 600 Klansmen were convicted. Most of them received fines or light jail sentences, but 65 went to a federal penitentiary for terms of up to five years.

THE ELECTION OF 1872

These measures broke the back of the Klan in time for the 1872 presidential election. A group of dissident Republicans had emerged to challenge Grant's reelection. They believed that conciliation of Southern whites rather than continued military intervention was the only way to achieve peace in the South. Calling themselves Liberal Republicans, these dissidents nominated Horace Greeley, the famous editor of the *New York Tribune*. Under the slogan "Anything to beat Grant," the Democratic Party also endorsed Greeley's nomination. On a platform denouncing "bayonet rule" in the South, Greeley urged his fellow Northerners to put the issues of the Civil War behind them.

Most voters in the North were still not prepared to trust Democrats or Southern whites, however. Anti-Greeley cartoons by Thomas Nast showed Greeley shaking the hand of a Klansman dripping with the blood of a murdered black Republican. On Election Day Grant swamped Greeley. Republicans carried every Northern state and 10 of the 16 Southern and border states. But this apparent triumph of Republicanism and Reconstruction would soon unravel.

THE PANIC OF 1873

The U.S. economy had grown at an unprecedented pace since 1867. The first **transcontinental railroad** had been completed on May 10, 1869, when a golden spike was driven at Promontory Summit, Utah Territory, linking the Union Pacific and the Central Pacific. But it was the building of a second transcontinental line, the Northern Pacific, that precipitated a Wall Street panic in 1873 and plunged the economy into a five-year depression.

habeas corpus *Right of an individual to have the legality of his arrest and detention decided by a court.*

transcontinental railroad
Railroad line that connected with other lines to provide continuous rail transportation from coast to coast.

Jay Cooke's banking firm, fresh from its triumphant marketing of Union war bonds, took over the Northern Pacific in 1869. Cooke pyramided every conceivable kind of equity and loan financing to raise the money to begin laying rails west from Duluth, Minnesota. Other investment firms did the same as a fever of speculative financing gripped the country. In September 1873 the pyramid of paper collapsed. Cooke's firm was the first to go bankrupt. Like dominoes, hundreds of banks and businesses also collapsed. Unemployment rose to 14 percent and hard times set in.

THE RETREAT FROM RECONSTRUCTION

Democrats made large gains in the congressional elections of 1874, winning a majority in the House for the first time in 18 years. Public opinion also began to turn against Republican policies in the South. Intra-party battles among Republicans in Southern states enabled Democrats to regain control of several state governments. Well-publicized corruption scandals also discredited Republican leaders. Although corruption was probably no worse in Southern states than in many parts of the North, the postwar poverty of the South made waste and extravagance seem worse. White Democrats scored propaganda points by claiming that corruption proved the incompetence of "Negro-carpetbag" regimes. Northerners grew increasingly weary of what seemed the endless turmoil of Southern politics. Most of them had never had a very strong commitment to racial equality, and they were growing more and more willing to let white supremacy regain sway in the South. "The truth is," confessed a Northern Republican, "our people are tired out with this worn out cry of 'Southern outrages'!!!"

By 1875 only four Southern states remained under Republican control: South Carolina, Florida, Mississippi, and Louisiana. In those states, white Democrats had revived paramilitary organizations under various names: White Leagues (Louisiana); Rifle Clubs (Mississippi); and Red Shirts (South Carolina). Unlike the Klan, these groups operated openly. In Louisiana, they fought pitched battles with Republican militias in which scores were killed. When the Grant administration sent large numbers of federal troops to Louisiana, people in both the North and South cried out against military rule. The protests grew even louder when soldiers marched onto the floor of the Louisiana legislature in January 1875 and expelled several Democratic legislators after a contested election.

FOCUS QUESTION

Why did a majority of the Northern people and their political leaders turn against continued federal involvement in Southern Reconstruction in the 1870s?

THE MISSISSIPPI ELECTION OF 1875

The backlash against the Grant administration affected the Mississippi state election of 1875. Democrats there devised a strategy called the Mississippi Plan. The first step was to "persuade" the 10 to 15 percent of white voters still calling themselves Republicans to switch to the Democrats. Only a handful of carpetbaggers could resist the economic pressures, social ostracism, and threats that made it "too damned hot for [us] to stay out," wrote one white Republican who changed parties.

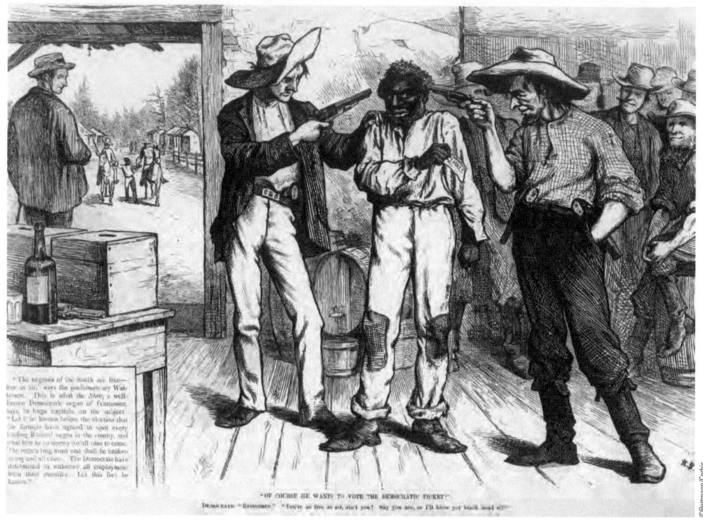

HOW THE MISSISSIPPI PLAN WORKED. *This cartoon shows how black counties could report large Democratic majorities in the Mississippi state election of 1875. The black voter holds a Democratic ticket while one of the men, described in the caption as a "Democratic reformer," holds a revolver to his head and says: "You're as free as air, ain't you? Say you are, or I'll blow your black head off!"*

The second step in the Mississippi Plan was to intimidate black voters, for even with all whites voting Democratic, the party could still be defeated by the 55 percent black majority. Economic coercion against black sharecroppers and workers kept some of them away from the polls. But violence was the most effective method. Democratic "rifle clubs" showed up at Republican rallies, provoked riots, and shot down dozens of blacks in the ensuing melees. Governor Adelbert Ames called for federal troops to control the violence. Grant intended to comply, but Ohio Republicans warned him that if he sent troops to Mississippi, the Democrats would exploit the issue of bayonet rule to carry Ohio in that year's state elections. Grant yielded—in effect giving up Mississippi for Ohio.

Governor Ames did try to organize a loyal state militia. But that proved difficult—and in any case, he was reluctant to use a black militia for fear of provoking a race war. "No matter if they are going to carry the State," said Ames with weary resignation, "let them carry it, and let us be at peace and have no more killing." The Mississippi Plan worked like a charm. What had been a Republican majority of 30,000 in 1874 became a Democratic majority of 30,000 in 1875.

THE SUPREME COURT AND RECONSTRUCTION

Even if Grant had been willing to continue intervening in Southern state elections, Congress and the courts would have constricted such efforts. The new Democratic majority in the House threatened to cut any appropriations intended for use in the South. And in 1876 the Supreme Court handed down two decisions that declared parts of the 1870 and 1871 laws for enforcement of the Fourteenth and Fifteenth Amendments unconstitutional. In *U.S.* v. *Cruikshank* and *U.S.* v. *Reese,* the Court ruled that the Fourteenth and Fifteenth Amendments apply to actions by *states:* "No State shall . . . deprive any person of life, liberty, or property . . . nor deny to any person . . . equal protection of the laws"; the right to vote "shall not be denied . . . by any State." Therefore, the portions of these laws that empowered the federal government to prosecute *individuals* were unconstitutional. The Court did not say what could be done when states were controlled by white-supremacy Democrats who had no intention of enforcing equal rights.

Meanwhile, in the *Civil Rights Cases* (1883), the Court declared unconstitutional a civil rights law passed by Congress in 1875. That law banned racial discrimination in all forms of public transportation and public accommodations. If enforced, it would have effected a sweeping transformation of race relations—in the North as well as in the South. But even some of the congressmen who voted for the bill doubted its constitutionality, and the Justice Department had made little effort to enforce it. Several cases made their way to the Supreme Court, which in 1883 ruled the law unconstitutional, again on grounds that the Fourteenth Amendment applied only to states, not to individuals. Several states, all in the North, passed their own civil rights laws in the 1870s and 1880s, but less than 10 percent of the black population resided in those states. The mass of African Americans lived a segregated existence.

THE ELECTION OF 1876

The mounting revelations of corruption at all levels of government ensured that reform would be the leading issue in the presidential election of 1876. Both major parties gave their presidential nominations to governors who had earned reform reputations in their states: Democrat Samuel J. Tilden of New York and Republican Rutherford B. Hayes of Ohio.

Democrats entered the campaign as favorites for the first time in two decades. It seemed likely that they would be able to put together an electoral majority from a "solid South" plus New York and two or three other Northern states. To ensure a solid South, they looked to the lessons of the Mississippi Plan. In 1876 a new word came into use to describe Democratic techniques of intimidation: **bulldozing.** To bulldoze black voters meant to trample them down or keep them away from the polls. In South Carolina and Louisiana, the Red Shirts and the White Leagues mobilized for an all-out bulldozing effort.

The most notorious incident, the "Hamburg Massacre," occurred in the village of Hamburg, South Carolina, where a battle between a black militia unit and 200 Red Shirts resulted in the capture of several militiamen, five of whom were shot "while attempting to escape." This time Grant did send in federal troops. He pronounced the Hamburg Massacre "cruel, blood-thirsty, wanton, unprovoked . . . a repetition of the course that has been pursued in other Southern States."

bulldozing *Using force to keep African Americans from voting.*

The federal government also put several thousand deputy marshals and election supervisors on duty in the South. Though they kept an uneasy peace at the polls, they could do little to prevent assaults, threats, and economic coercion in backcountry districts, which reduced the potential Republican tally in the former Confederate states by at least 250,000 votes.

DISPUTED RESULTS

When the results were in, Tilden had carried four Northern states, including New York with its 35 electoral votes, and all the former slave states except—apparently—Louisiana, South Carolina, and Florida. From those three states came disputed returns. Since Tilden needed only one of them to win the presidency, while Hayes needed all three, and since Tilden seemed to have carried Louisiana and Florida, it appeared initially that he had won the presidency. But fraud and irregularities reported from several bulldozed districts in the three states clouded the issue. The official returns ultimately sent to Washington gave all three states—and therefore the presidency—to Hayes. But the Democrats refused to recognize the results, and they controlled the House.

The country now faced a serious constitutional crisis. Many people feared another civil war. The Constitution offered no clear guidance on how to deal with the matter. It required the concurrence of both houses of Congress in order to count the electoral votes of the states, but with a Democratic House and a Republican Senate such concurrence was not forthcoming. To break the deadlock, Congress created a special electoral commission consisting of five representatives, five senators, and five Supreme Court justices split evenly between the two parties, with one member, a Supreme Court justice, supposedly an independent—but in fact a Republican.

Tilden had won a national majority of 252,000 popular votes, and the raw returns gave him a majority in the three disputed states. But an estimated 250,000 Southern Republicans had been bulldozed away from the polls. In a genuinely fair and free election, the Republicans might have carried Mississippi and North Carolina as well as the three disputed states. While the commission agonized, Democrats and Republicans in Louisiana and South Carolina each inaugurated their own separate governors and legislatures. Only federal troops in the capitals at New Orleans and Columbia protected the Republican governments in those states.

THE COMPROMISE OF 1877

In February 1877, three months after voters had gone to the polls, the electoral commission issued its ruling. By a partisan vote of 8 to 7—with the "independent" justice voting with the Republicans—it awarded all the disputed states to Hayes. The Democrats cried foul and began a **filibuster** in the House to delay the final electoral count beyond the inauguration date of March 4. But, behind the scenes, a compromise began to take shape. Hayes promised his support as president for federal appropriations to rebuild war-destroyed **levees** on the lower Mississippi and federal aid for a southern transcontinental railroad. Hayes's lieutenants also hinted at the appointment of a Southerner as postmaster general, who would have a considerable amount of patronage at his disposal. Hayes also signaled his intention to end "bayonet rule." He believed that the goodwill and influence of Southern moderates would offer better protection for black rights than federal troops could

filibuster *Congressional delaying tactic involving lengthy speeches that prevent legislation from being enacted.*

levee *Earthen dike or mound, usually along the banks of rivers, used to prevent flooding.*

provide. In return for his commitment to withdraw the troops, Hayes asked for—and received—promises of fair treatment of freedpeople and respect for their constitutional rights.

THE END OF RECONSTRUCTION

Such promises were easier to make than to keep, as future years would reveal. In any case, the Democratic filibuster collapsed and Hayes was inaugurated on March 4. He soon fulfilled his part of the Compromise of 1877: ex-Confederate Democrat David Key of Tennessee became postmaster general; the South received more federal money in 1878 for internal improvements than ever before; and federal troops left the capitals of Louisiana and South Carolina. The last two Republican state governments collapsed. Any remaining voices of protest could scarcely be heard above the sighs of relief that the crisis was over.

QUICK   REVIEW

END OF RECONSTRUCTION

- Growing Northern weariness with the "Southern Question"
- Renewal of Southern white resistance
- Supreme Court limited federal government's enforcement powers
- Federal troops removed from South after disputed election of 1876

C O N C L U S I O N

Before the Civil War, most Americans had viewed a powerful government as a threat to individual liberties. That is why the first 10 amendments to the Constitution (the Bill of Rights) imposed strict limits on the powers of the federal government. But during the Civil War and especially during Reconstruction, it became clear that the national government would have to exert an unprecedented amount of power to free the slaves and guarantee their equal rights as free citizens. That is why the Thirteenth, Fourteenth, and Fifteenth Amendments to the Constitution contained clauses stating that "Congress shall have power" to enforce these provisions for liberty and equal rights.

During the post–Civil War decade, Congress passed civil rights laws and enforcement legislation to accomplish this purpose. Federal marshals and troops patrolled the polls to protect black voters, arrested thousands of Klansmen and other violators of black civil rights, and even occupied state capitals to prevent Democratic paramilitary groups from overthrowing legitimately elected Republican state governments. But by 1875 many Northerners had grown tired of or alarmed by this continued use of military power to intervene in the internal affairs of states. The Supreme Court stripped the federal government of much of its authority to enforce certain provisions of the Fourteenth and Fifteenth Amendments.

The withdrawal of federal troops from the South in 1877 constituted both a symbolic and a substantive end of the 12-year postwar era known as Reconstruction. Reconstruction had achieved the two great objectives inherited from the Civil War: to reincorporate the former Confederate states into the Union, and to accomplish a transition from slavery to freedom in the South. But that transition was marred by the economic inequity of sharecropping and the social injustice of white supremacy. And a third goal of Reconstruction, enforcement of the equal civil and political rights promised in the Fourteenth and Fifteenth Amendments, was betrayed by the Compromise of 1877. In subsequent decades the freed slaves and their descendants suffered repression into segregated second-class citizenship.

QUESTIONS FOR REVIEW AND CRITICAL THINKING

Review

1. What were the positions of Presidents Abraham Lincoln and Andrew Johnson and of moderate and radical Republicans in Congress on the issues of restoring the South to the Union and protecting the rights of freed slaves?
2. Why was Andrew Johnson impeached? Why was he acquitted?
3. What were the achievements of Reconstruction? What were its failures?
4. Why did a majority of the Northern people and their political leaders turn against continued federal involvement in Southern Reconstruction in the 1870s?

Critical Thinking

1. The two main goals of Reconstruction were to bring the former Confederate states back into the Union and to ensure the equal citizenship and rights of the former slaves. Why was the first goal more successfully achieved than the second?
2. Why have "carpetbaggers" and "scalawags" had such a bad historical image? Did they deserve it?

ONLINE RESOURCES

 Visit the companion website to access flashcards, crossword puzzles, exercises, and quizzes related to this chapter: www.cengage.com/history/murrin/libertyequalconc5e.

 See our interactive ebook for map and primary source activities.

ISCOVERY

Evaluate the success with which African Americans were integrated into American society during Reconstruction.

CULTURE AND SOCIETY From your reading in this chapter and your examination of the illustrations shown here, what observations can you make about the role of violence and/or intimidation in suppressing Republican votes across the South in the 1870s? In the cartoon on the Mississippi Plan, how are the two gun-toting Southern whites portrayed? Does this scene appear to represent a spontaneous, isolated incident or a systematic effort to influence votes? What is common between the two images?

In thinking about this question, begin by breaking it down into the components shown below. A discussion of the significance of each component should appear in your answer.

Library of Congress Prints and Photographs Division [LC-USZ62-119565]

TWO MEMBERS OF THE KU KLUX KLAN

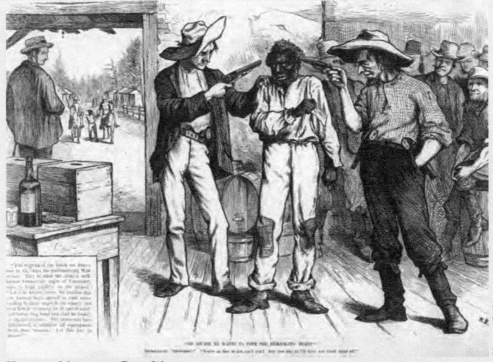

©Bettmann/Corbis

HOW THE MISSISSIPPI PLAN WORKED

Chapter 18 deleted from this edition

THE EMERGENCE OF CORPORATE AMERICA, 1865–1900

A lexis de Tocqueville visited the United States in 1831 and published his famous analysis, *Democracy in America*, in 1835. At that time more than two thirds of all Americans lived on farms and only 10 percent lived in towns or cities with populations larger than 2,500. The overwhelming majority of white males owned property and worked for themselves rather than for wages. What impressed Tocqueville most was the relative absence of both great wealth and great poverty; the modest prosperity of the broad middle class created the impression of equality.

During the next generation the North began to industrialize, cities grew much faster than rural areas, and inequality of wealth and income grew larger. The country's preoccupation with sectional issues prior to the Civil War and the gnawing problems of Reconstruction after the war diverted attention from the economic and social problems associated with industrialism and class inequality. With the depression that followed the Panic of 1873, however, these problems burst spectacularly into public view. For a time, economic growth promised to deflect class conflict. By the 1890s, however, no American could deny that Tocqueville's republic of equality had disappeared.

TIMELINE

| 1869 | 1873 | 1877 | 1878 | 1883 | 1886 | 1887 | 1890 | 1892 | 1893 | 1894 | 1896 |

■ **1869**
Knights of Labor founded

■ **1873**
"Crime of 1873" de-monetizes silver • Financial panic begins economic depression

■ **1877**
Railroad strikes cost 100 lives and millions of dollars in damage

■ **1878**
Bland-Allison Act to remonetize silver passed over Hayes's vetos

■ **1883**
Railroads establish four standard time zones

■ **1886**
Knights of Labor membership crests at 700,000 • Haymarket riot causes antilabor backlash • American Federation of Labor founded

1887 ■
Edward Bellamy publishes *Looking Backward* • Interstate Commerce Act creates the first federal regulatory agency

1890 ■
Congress passes Sherman Antitrust Act • Congress passes Sherman Silver Purchase Act

1892 ■
Homestead strike fails • Populists organize the People's Party

1893 ■
Financial panic begins economic depression • Congress repeals Sherman Silver Purchase Act

1894 ■
"Coxey's army" of the unemployed marches on Washington • Pullman strike paralyzes the railroads and provokes federal intervention

1896 ■
William McKinley defeats William Jennings Bryan for the presidency

AN EXPANSIVE AND VOLATILE ECONOMY

During the 15 years between recovery from one depression in 1878 and the onset of another in 1893, the American economy grew at one of the fastest rates in its history. The **gross national product (GNP)** almost doubled and per capita GNP increased by 35 percent. All sectors of the economy were expanding. The most spectacular growth was in manufacturing, which increased by 180 percent, compared to a 26 percent increase for agriculture.

But this tremendous economic growth was also accompanied by spectacular volatility. The two, in fact, were closely connected. Cycles of overexpansion and overproduction were followed by inevitable cycles of contraction. The Great Railroad Strike of 1877 occurred during an extended depression; 1886, another depression year, saw 1,400 strikes involving half a million workers.

Just as workers struggled to eke out a living, many business owners also periodically faced the threat of failure. The American economy may have grown enormously in this period, but expansion

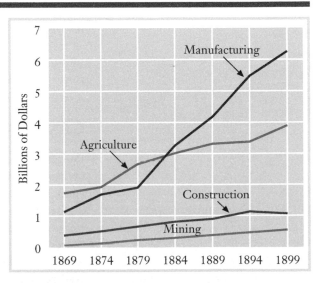

VALUE ADDED BY ECONOMIC SECTOR, 1869–1899 (in 1879 PRICES)

gross national product (GNP)
Total value of all goods and services produced during a specific period.

often meant saturation of markets followed by price-cutting of products, lower profits, and inevitable layoffs.

Still, the enormous growth of the economy in this period meant great opportunity and increased prosperity for many Americans. Titans of industry piled up previously unimaginable fortunes. A flourishing middle class achieved new power, establishing a variety of public institutions such as libraries, symphonies, and museums. The working class, however, shared unequally in this rising prosperity.

ENGINES OF ECONOMIC GROWTH

FOCUS QUESTION
What were the main engines of American economic growth in the last third of the 19th century?

The railroad was the single most important agent of economic growth during these years. Track mileage increased from 30,000 in 1860 to some 200,000 in 1900. Railroad expansion meant a greater need for coal and iron, then steel, to build railroad cars and lay track: Steel production soared from 732,000 tons in 1878 to 10,188,000 tons by 1900. The steel industry itself was a catalyst for a host of other industries, in a pattern repeated across the American industrial landscape.

As a result manufacturing expanded dramatically. Just before the Civil War, there were 140,000 factories and manufacturing shops across the country; this figure had risen to 512,000 in 1899 and included the rise of industrial giants such as Carnegie Steel.

TECHNOLOGICAL INNOVATION AND CELEBRATIONS OF THE MACHINE

Growth in manufacturing spurred invention, and invention in turn spurred increased and more efficient manufacturing. Technological advances during this period included automatic signals, air brakes, and knuckle couplers on the railroads; the Bessemer and then the open-hearth process in steel mills; the telephone, electric light, and typewriter (all in the 1870s); the phonograph and motion pictures (1890s); the electric dynamo (generator), which not only laid the basis for such household items as refrigerators and washing machines but also provided a new source of industrial power that gradually replaced water power and the steam engine; and the internal combustion machine, which made possible the first automobile (1890s) and the first airplane flight by the Wright brothers in 1903.

The antebellum Market Revolution had become a full-fledged Industrial Revolution, and many Americans embraced the new technological order with a sense of pride and wonder.

CHANGES IN BUSINESS ORGANIZATION AND PRACTICE

Railroad companies inaugurated a new era of big business that had profound effects on business practice. Many businesses now organized as corporations rather than single proprietorships: this mode of organization provided a flexible means of raising capital by allowing shares in a company to be sold directly to the public. New, expanded corporations used boards of directors as a management tool, allowing for shared responsibility and promoting a new scale and complexity of enterprise.

Some of the titans of industry made their money by methods that critics considered predatory and were labeled "robber barons." They included William Vanderbilt, Jay Gould, Jim Fisk, and Collis P. Huntington in railroading; **John D. Rockefeller**

John D. Rockefeller *Founder of the Standard Oil Company, whose aggressive practices drove many competitors out of business and made him one of the richest men in America.*

in oil; Andrew Carnegie and Henry Clay Frick in steel; James B. Duke in tobacco; and John Pierpont Morgan in banking. Criticism of the "robber barons" sometimes focused more on the immense power commanded by their wealth than on the wealth itself. Fisk and Gould bribed legislators, manipulated the stock market, exploited workers, and cheated stockholders. Rockefeller either bought out or ruined his competitors, obtained rebates and **drawbacks** on rail shipments of oil, and created a monopoly in his determined efforts to gain control of oil refining. Carnegie and Frick pushed laborers to the limit in 72-hour workweeks, redefined skill levels and changed work rules, and sped up the pace in steel mills in a ceaseless quest for greater efficiency and lower labor costs. Morgan's banking firm built an empire of leveraged financing and interlocking corporate directorates.

Many Americans feared the power wielded by these tycoons. Their monopoly or near-monopoly share of the market in oil, steel, sugar, tobacco, transportation, and other products seemed to violate the ideal of fair competition. To curb that power, an "antitrust" movement emerged in the 1880s. The word **trust** derived from an investment strategy in which the stockholders of several refining companies turned over their shares to Rockefeller's Standard Oil in return for so-called trust certificates. The term came to be applied to all large corporations that controlled a substantial share of any given market. In response to pressures to curb such trusts, several states passed antitrust laws in the 1880s.

But because the larger corporations operated across state lines, reformers turned to Congress. The Sherman Antitrust Act of 1890 was an attempt to declare any form of **"restraint of trade"** illegal, but it was so vague as to be almost useless in the actual prosecution of corporations. In 1895 the Supreme Court dealt the Sherman Act a crippling blow when it ruled in *U.S.* v. *E.C. Knight Company* that manufacturing was not commerce and therefore did not fall under the jurisdiction of the law.

WEALTH AND SOCIETY

Both Rockefeller and Carnegie justified their business practices, as well as their right to wealth, with an emerging belief that racially inherited traits explained variations in the economic, social, and cultural lives of ethnic and racial groups. Many of the nation's intellectuals believed that human society developed according to the "survival of the fittest" principle articulated by the English naturalist Charles Darwin to describe plant and animal evolution. Human history could be understood in terms of an ongoing struggle among races, with the strongest and the fittest invariably triumphing. The wealth and power of the Anglo-Saxon race were ample testimony, in this view, to its superior fitness.

This view, which would become known as **Social Darwinism,** reflected a widely shared belief that human society operated according to principles every bit as scientific as those governing the natural world. The social sciences—economics, political science, anthropology, sociology, psychology—took shape in the late 19th century, each trying to discover the scientific laws governing individual and group behavior. Awed by the accomplishments of natural scientists, social scientists were prone to exaggerate the degree to which social life mimicked natural life; hence the appeal of Social Darwinism.

Social Darwinism was quickly adopted by a broader public, with "survival of the fittest" becoming a popular catchphrase. Such a theory provided a comfortable way of understanding the glaring social inequality of the era: workers were doomed to be permanent wage laborers not because of some fault in the emerging corporate system, but because they themselves were not "fit." The rich, meanwhile, were entitled to every dollar that came their way.

drawbacks *Form of rebate offered to special customers by the railroads.*

trust *Large corporations that control a substantial share of any given market.*

restraint of trade *Activity that prevents competition in the marketplace or free trade.*

Social Darwinism *Set of beliefs that explain human history as an ongoing evolutionary struggle among different groups of people for survival and supremacy. Many used these beliefs to justify inequalities between races, classes, and nations.*

The estimated number of *millionaires* (a word that came into use during this era) was 300 in 1860; by 1892, the number was 4,000. While this was not a large proportion of the population, it was a highly visible group. Many practiced what the economist Thorstein Veblen described in *The Theory of the Leisure Class* (1899) as "conspicuous consumption." They sent agents to Europe to buy paintings and tapestries from impoverished aristocrats. They entertained lavishly in their mansions on Fifth Avenue and their summer homes at Newport. Their extravagant habits gave substance to Mark Twain's labeling of this era as the Gilded Age.

CLASS DISTINCTION AND CULTURAL HIERARCHY

QUICK   REVIEW

ECONOMIC GROWTH

- Marked by rapid technological advances

- Great wealth and economic power of "robber barons" triggered antitrust movement

- Fueled emergence of new middle class

The well-publicized activities of the wealthy sharpened a growing sense of class distinction. Throughout the late 19th century, many Americans worried over the class distinctions they saw emerging around them as part of the corporate reordering of American life. The existence of classes was not new in American society—the middle class itself had emerged in the antebellum era with its own distinctive culture—but now class distinctions seemed sharper, class divides more difficult to cross. Was this acceptable in a republican society that promised equality for all? A source of uneasiness at first, class distinctions became a source of alarm among numerous observers especially in the 1890s, when widespread labor activism challenged the existing social order. But members of different classes would emerge with different proposed solutions to the problems of corporate America. By the 1890s many members of the middle class sought not so much to reduce class distinction as to create additional barriers between classes.

THE CONSOLIDATION OF MIDDLE-CLASS CULTURE

FOCUS QUESTION
How did American middle-class culture change in response to the rise of corporations?

A broad middle class consolidated and extended its social and cultural power during the late 19th century. Race and class went hand in hand: while a thriving African American middle class emerged in African American communities in the post-Civil War era (see Chapter 18), its existence was barely acknowledged by the dominant white middle class. Immersed in a world of goods produced by the new corporate economy, the new white middle class also engaged in distinctive styles of consumption that marked a significant change from antebellum middle-class life.

WHITE-COLLAR WORKERS

The new corporate order produced a need for salaried managers, professionals, office workers, and retail clerks—"white-collar" workers (a reference to detachable, starched white collars for shirts). Agricultural labor dropped from 53 percent of the gainfully employed in 1870, to 35 percent in 1900, and to 21 percent in 1930; clerical work in the same period rose from less than 1 percent to over 8 percent. By 1900 there were 235,000 bank tellers nationwide, 232,000 salesmen and clerks, and 34,000 real estate agents. The profession of engineer, directly related to the expansion of manufacturing, leapt by an astonishing 586 percent between 1870 and 1900. By the 1880s the term "business man" had replaced the antebellum term "merchant."

THE MIDDLE-CLASS HOME

The center of middle-class life was the home and family. But domesticity took on a more consumer-oriented tinge, as the Victorian parlor grew cluttered with doilies, cushions, statuary, clocks, paintings, pianos, and bric-a-brac. Styles of decorating grew more elaborate, reflecting the impact of an expanded world of manufactured consumer goods. By the 1880s, many women of means drew upon an international marketplace of decorating, as well. The 1882 Chicago mansion of Bertha Palmer, for instance, featured a Spanish music room, an English dining room, a Moorish ballroom, a Flemish library, and French and Chinese drawing rooms. By the turn of the century, the profession of interior decorator was well established among a wealthy elite, part of the larger trend of professionalization and the emergence of "experts" in this period.

DEPARTMENT STORES AS MIDDLE-CLASS COMMUNITIES OF TASTE

At the center of the new consuming culture, the new department stores dramatically changed the experience of buying goods in cities. Glittering "palaces of consumption" such as Marshall Field & Co. in Chicago (1865) and R.H. Macy's in New York (1866) changed the experience of shopping. Customers strolled down carpeted aisles—arranged to mimic city streets—and gazed at a dazzling array of goods in glass cases. Ornate interiors with mirrors and lights added to a sensory experience of profusion, color, and excitement. Theodore Dreiser captured the desire that experience created in his novel *Sister Carrie*, as his main character Carrie "passed along the busy aisles, much affected by the remarkable displays of trinkets, dress goods, stationery, and jewelry. Each separate counter was a show place of dazzling interest and attraction." As Carrie left the store, she "longed for dress and beauty with a whole heart."

The stores sought to appeal to middle-class women with a variety of services and amenities, including restaurants, ladies' parlors, check rooms, "retiring rooms," libraries, information bureaus, free wrapping, and free delivery. The new Otis elevator took customers from floor to floor in what were some of the earliest "skyscrapers" of up to ten stories. Store tearooms quickly became popular places for middle-class women to meet in an urban public space—a novelty at the time.

DOMESTICITY VS. WORK

In the late 19th century, an increasing number of women began to explore the world of work—whether out of necessity in the turbulent economy, or because they chose to enter a "wider sphere" of life. By 1900, 21 percent of all women were in the workforce, as opposed to 9.7 percent of women in 1860. After the Civil War women moved into nursing and office work, while continuing to be a mainstay in teaching. By the end of the century middle-class women were also entering the professions of medicine and law in small numbers. College women moved to cities to take up work, living in apartments on their own as "bachelor girls" who were the subject of numerous newspaper articles.

The increased interest in work was reflected in literature of the period. Louisa May Alcott's 1873 *Work*, for instance, imagines an ideal cross-class, cross-race

THE NEW WOMAN. *John Singer Sargent's 1897 portrait of Mr. and Mrs. I. N. Phelps Stokes captures the vibrant, athletic independence of the emerging New Woman. Dressed in a shirtwaist and carrying a straw boater, Edith Minturn Stokes radiates an air of vitality and energy; her husband by contrast is very much in the background.*

world of supportive female workers, while Elizabeth Stuart Phelps spoke for many discontented middle-class women in her 1877 *The Story of Avis*, in which the despairing heroine ultimately gives up being an artist for her marriage. But it was writer and economist Charlotte Perkins Gilman's 1892 biting novella *The Yellow Wallpaper* that spoke most powerfully of a new domestic claustrophobia. In that brief work the unnamed heroine desires to write after the birth of a child but is told by her husband and doctor that she must rest instead and is virtually imprisoned in her home.

Few middle-class observers—men or women—were able to imagine women combining work with family. And yet many women had to do so: the nationally known journalist Jane Croly, for instance, who wrote columns under the name "Jenny June," supported her sick husband and four children as an editor and author during the 1880s before becoming the first female professor of journalism at Rutgers University.

THE WOMEN'S CLUB MOVEMENT AND PUBLIC LIVES

In 1868 the New York Press Club decided to bar women journalists from a celebratory dinner for the great novelist Charles Dickens, who was touring the United States. Jane Croly, insulted and furious, formed the women's club Sorosis (the name was chosen to suggest sisterhood) composed primarily of professional writers. Sorosis met regularly to discuss topics of the day and to exchange professional advice.

Sorosis inaugurated a movement of women's clubs across the nation. Distinct from antebellum moral reform societies, the new women's clubs were secular and had a variety of different purposes, from intellectual discussion to civic reform. Women's clubs also provided a bridge to middle-class women's activism during the Progressive era. By the turn of the century the women's club movement was an important source of support for the revived suffrage movement. What's more, women had used the women's club movement to move into and even take over a variety of civic organizations—a way of practicing politics by other means in an era before women had the vote. Middle-class black women drew on their extensive experiences in church organizations and Republican aid societies to create networks of public civic organizations. African American women also joined the largest women's social organization of the late 19th century, the Woman's Christian Temperance Union. Under the leadership of Frances Willard, the WCTU engaged in a variety of social reform activities nationally and endorsed woman suffrage in 1884.

THE NEW WOMAN

The "New Woman" became a dominant figure of American popular culture in the 1890s. In cartoons, illustrations, paintings, short stories, and essays, the New Woman was athletic, self-confident, young, and independent: she wore the new, less confining fashion of shirtwaists and skirts; rode a bicycle; and even smoked in some images. The painter John Singer Sargent captured this dawning moment of confidence for women in several compelling portraits.

But to some observers the New Woman was a fearsome thing, threatening the sanctity of the home and traditional gender roles. A backlash against middle-class women's new roles was often rooted in new "scientific" expertise. Arguing against women's higher education, for instance, the Harvard Medical School professor Edward H. Clarke asserted in 1873 that intellectual work damaged women's reproductive organs. "A girl could study and learn," he warned, "but she could not do all this and retain uninjured health, and a future secure from neuralgia, uterine disease, hysteria, and other derangements of the nervous system." The Comstock Law (1872) made it illegal to send reproductive literature or devices through the mails on the grounds that they were "obscene." During the bicycle craze of the 1890s, experts warned that it would be unhealthy for women to ride. Women actively resisted these attacks in articles and lectures and through their own actions. Frances Willard of the WCTU took up bicycling at age 53 in part, she said, because she knew her example would "help women to a wider world."

HIGHER EDUCATION AND PROFESSIONAL ORGANIZATIONS

That wider world included education. In the Midwest and the West, universities began to admit women in the 1860s. In the East there were fewer coeducational institutions, but the founding of women's colleges—with Vassar leading the way in 1865—meant that by 1890 women represented approximately 40 percent of all college graduates nationally.

This move into higher education did not translate into greater ease of access to professional education. Women had broken into medical training in 1849 with the admission of Elizabeth Blackwell to Geneva Medical College in upstate New York. But as separate medical colleges gave way to medical schools within universities in the late 19th century, women began to lose ground. Professional organizations often excluded women; at the turn of the century the American Medical Association, a gatekeeper to the profession, was an all-white, all-male organization, as were the American Bar Association, the American Historical Association, and the American Economic Association. Thus, while new professional organizations established much-needed uniform standards and training, they also closed ranks against women and minorities.

MIDDLE-CLASS CULTURAL INSTITUTIONS

Symphonies, opera companies, museums, and public libraries were created in the decades after the Civil War, housed in imposing buildings that transformed the city landscape. The American museum evolved from a warehouse of curiosities to an ornate space for the display of fine art and scientific artifacts. Newly rich art patrons donated collections to establish the Metropolitan and Natural History museums in New York, the Field Museum and the Art Institute in Chicago, and the Fine Arts Museum in Boston.

Museums served as markers of class identity as well as repositories of art. In New York, founders of the Metropolitan Museum of Art made the paternalistic claim in 1880 that they sought to "diffuse knowledge of art in its higher forms of beauty" so as to "educate and refine a practical and laborious people." Yet the museum was ambivalent about those same "laborious people," closing its doors to the public on Sundays—the one day when many workers might have visited—and articulating a fastidious set of rules for behavior within the museum. At one point the museum evicted a patron because he was wearing overalls, which caused a brief newspaper scandal. The museum spent far more energy courting wealthy art collectors with private receptions. For the newly wealthy, the museum offered a form of alchemy: donation could magically transform social status upward.

The attempt to create cultural hierarchy—and physical distance from the working class—was everywhere an aspect of middle-class institution building. In the antebellum period, for instance, performances of Shakespeare had often been rowdy, participatory, cross-class events. By the end of the century, however, the middle class had not only claimed Shakespeare as an icon of high culture, but had succeeded in imposing a new set of standards for audience behavior at the theater. Vocal audience participation gave way to an expectation of total silence during performances as a marker of gentility.

That gentility could also be found in a new art movement: American Impressionism. Influenced by French Impressionism, artists such as William Merritt Chase and Childe Hassam painted light-flecked landscapes or flower-filled urban parks, recording middle-class pleasures in cities devoid of workers. Yet some painters, such as Thomas Eakins or Thomas Anshutz, were already pioneering a style that would develop into the realism of the early 20th century, with its grittier view of city life and less idealized vision of the human form.

Literary magazines sought to create permanent genteel standards. *Century* and *Harper's New Monthly* published serial novels by great authors and a variety of articles and "tasteful" fiction, including an emerging literature of nostalgia for slavery. This white nostalgia for black subordination paralleled growing middle-class alarm over the "insubordination" of the working class in late 19th-century labor strife.

Yet increasingly over the late 19th century mere gentility began to seem arid to a number of middle-class writers. The writer William Dean Howells called for a new "realism" based on close observation of and engagement with life. His novels explored issues that had rarely been touched by American authors, including divorce, the moral bankruptcy of capitalism, and interracial marriage. Discouraged by the widening gulf between the classes, in 1886 Howells even broke with most of his class in his plea for clemency for the defendants in the Haymarket affair (see page 514).

The gulf between the classes also alarmed Edward Bellamy, whose 1888 utopian novel, *Looking Backward*, imagined a world in the year 2000 in which "labor troubles" and social inequities had been eradicated through a form of socialism called Nationalism. Bellamy's powerful fictional indictment of Gilded Age society was one of the most popular novels of the 19th century. More than 160 Nationalist clubs sprang up in which members of the middle class mulled over the possibilities of government ownership of industry. A number of authors and artists in the 1880s and 1890s understood the considerable social costs of the new corporate order.

Yet the drive for class differentiation continued for most in the middle class. As early as 1873, *Scribner's* magazine noted that "the middle class, who cannot live among the rich, and will not live among the poor....go out of the city to find their houses." By the end of the century suburban communities of detached houses, surrounded by lawns, were markers of the middle-class status of businessmen and professionals who worked by day in cities and traveled back and forth by train or streetcar.

RACIAL HIERARCHY AND THE CITY: THE 1893 COLUMBIAN EXHIBITION

A pernicious assumption of racial superiority was threaded throughout white middle-class institutions in the late 19th century. The heart of the 1893 Columbian Exposition in Chicago, a world's fair displaying American achievements to the nation and to the world, was a monumental set of gleaming buildings called the "White City." With its broad, open courts studded with statuary and interspersed with lagoons, canals, fountains, and parks, the White City was a triumph of the City Beautiful movement, whose advocates hoped to impose a new and more refined cultural order on what they saw as a chaotic urban environment.

With paid admissions at 21,480,141 in a nation with a population of 63 million, this was the most successful fair in American history. Its exhibitions celebrated both technological innovations and high cultural achievements. But by far the most popular part of the fair was an amusement strip called the Midway Plaisance, which included "ethnographic" displays of life in "primitive" villages in Africa, Morocco, China, and other locations. It was hard to miss the implication that "civilization" occurred in America and Europe, while "primitivism" belonged to people of color from Africa, the Middle East, and Asia.

The very structure of the fair thus posited the superiority of white, middle-class civilization. Moreover, fair organizers refused African Americans' repeated requests to display black achievements. Outraged, the antilynching crusader Ida B. Wells (see Chapter 18) published a pamphlet titled "The Reason Why the Colored American Is Not in the World's Columbian Exposition." Exploring the intertwined histories of American slavery and racism, it offered a detailed accounting of the refusal by the fair to include African Americans.

THE CITY AND WORKING-CLASS CULTURE

Cities grew rapidly after the Civil War. From 1870 to 1880, for instance, New York grew to over 1 million in population, a 25 percent rate of increase. Chicago's growth was even more startling: from 30,000 residents in 1850 to 500,000 in 1880 to 1,700,000 by 1900. While San Francisco was a much smaller city, it, too, grew at a dramatic rate of 163 percent in the 1870s. In 1860 about one in five Americans lived in cities; by 1900 this number had doubled.

A fast-growing industrial economy created new jobs at an astonishing rate: Between 1870 and 1910 jobs in iron and steel grew by 1,200 percent; in the oil,

The Museum of the City of New York Corbis

New York City in 1885. *This photograph shows the crowded, chaotic nature of lower Manhattan in the 1880s. The scene is Broadway at Cortlandt Street looking south from Maiden Lane. Note the proliferation of utility poles and wires: the telephone and electric lighting had become part of American urban life in the past half-dozen years, radically changing the face of city streets.*

rubber, and chemical industries, by 1,900 percent. Workers came from overseas, with 85 percent of immigrants before 1880 from Germany, Ireland, England, and the Scandinavian countries; after 1880, 80 percent were from eastern and southern Europe. By 1900 more than a third of the U.S. population worked as industrial workers, and most lived in cities.

Working-Class Women and Men

For men, cities often offered a variety of job possibilities—at least in flush times. Cincinnati, for instance, boasted firms that manufactured or processed beer, tobacco, lumber, meat, liquor, clothing, books, carriages, clothes, tools, and baked goods. Women had many fewer opportunities for work; in 1900 only 18.3 percent of the workforce was female. Most working-class families agreed with the middle class that married women's place was in the home. But young single working-class women often worked outside the home before marriage: both young men and women were expected to supplement the family's earnings. In 1900 around a third of all single women living in cities worked for wages in the garment trade and other industries. Young, single workers helped to fuel a lively culture of urban entertainments.

Commercial Amusements

While the poorest workers could not afford commercial amusements, most workers shared in a new culture of leisure that included dance halls, music halls, vaudeville houses, nickelodeons (early storefront movie theaters), and amusement parks. Storefront vaudeville theaters, for instance, began to advertise "cheap amusements" to a broad working public in the 1880s. With roots in such antebellum entertainments as minstrelsy, circuses, and dime museums, vaudeville shows offered a variety of miscellaneous short acts for only a dime: a typical show might include sentimental ballads; acrobats; soft-shoe dances; magicians; mind readers; one-act plays; blackface minstrelsy; sports stars from baseball or boxing; puppeteers; jugglers; and dancing bears.

Amusement parks such as Steeplechase Park at Coney Island, built in 1895, attracted a large working class audience of men and women while soon also appealing to middle-class youth. Older middle-class commentators found the uncatchaperoned mingling of young men and women in an urban public space troubling, even shocking, but it was precisely that loosening of restraint that made Coney Island so pleasurable and exciting.

While vaudeville theaters and amusement parks at first attracted a primarily working-class crowd of pleasure-seekers, they eventually crossed class lines by appealing to large middle-class audiences, as well. Both the working class and the middle class sometimes pushed at the boundaries between them. In the 1880s, for instance, labor unions in New York City petitioned the Metropolitan and Natural History museums to open on workers' free day, Sunday. After a lengthy campaign, in 1892 both museums capitulated.

POPULAR LITERATURE

Urban workers read a variety of dime novels (cheap paperbacks that sold for a dime) and westerns. A flourishing cheap literature reflected the presence of working women in the new industrial order: the popular 1871 story "Bertha the Sewing Machine Girl; or, Death at the Wheel" inspired many imitators and was staged as a play in New York City. Its author, Laura Jane Libbey, published more than 60 novels in the 1880s. For working women, romances featuring wealthy heroines, or working women who discovered that by birth they were actually aristocrats, offered fantasies that—in imagination, at least—closed the gulf between the classes. For working-class men, dime novels told heroic stories in which men overcame numerous obstacles to become owners of factories. Such stories allowed a form of imagined compensation for the loss of independence men actually experienced as permanent wage earners.

EMERGENCE OF A NATIONAL CULTURE

The rise of a corporate society created a gulf between classes in post-Civil War America, but paradoxically it also created a shared national culture. Technological innovations as well as an emerging consumer culture reshaped almost all Americans' lives. Electricity, streetcars, and elevators changed urban dwellers' everyday relationship to physical space. Even people's relationship to time changed. Before 1883 many localities and cities kept their own time, derived from the sun's meridian in each locality. When it was noon in Chicago, for instance, it was 11:50 in St. Louis, 11:38 in St. Paul, and 11:27 in Omaha. This played havoc with railroad timetables. In a sign of corporations' power over American life, in 1883 a consortium of railroads established four standard time zones and put new timetables into effect for these zones. There was some grumbling about the arrogance of railroad presidents changing "God's time." For the most part, however, the public accepted the change, and Congress finally got around to sanctioning standard time zones in 1918.

ADVERTISING

Consumer goods standardized experience as manufacturers produced national brands and advertising became a major American industry. Ad agencies such as J. Walter Thompson (founded in 1878) and N.W. Ayer & Son (founded in 1869), working hand in hand with manufacturers, created national marketing campaigns. Expenditures on advertising increased enormously: from some $50 million in 1867 to $500 million by 1900. But national advertising did not just affect what people chose to buy; it sometimes reflected and spread dominant racial stereotypes. Several national brands—including Aunt Jemima mixes and Cream of Wheat, with its portrayal of the character Rastus—created trademarks images that hearkened back to blackface minstrelsy (a racist entertainment popular in the antebellum period; see Chapter 10) and to mythic images of supposedly happy slaves.

A SHARED VISUAL CULTURE

With their bright, colorful images, advertisements changed daily visual experience and helped to create a shared national visual culture. Technological improvements in lithography and the half-tone process in the 1880s and 1890s lay behind this shared visual culture. Picture postcards and stereographs became popular. The Kodak camera allowed people to take snapshots for the first time, creating a visual record of ordinary life. The most popular magazines and newspapers of the 1890s also created a new shared visual culture. *Ladies' Home Journal*, founded in 1893, argued women's place was in the home and achieved enormous success with its profusion of illustrations, photographs, and advertisements. It reached a circulation of 500,000 within only a few years. Cheap new popular magazines such as *Munsey's* reached hundreds of thousands of national readers with a steady diet of racy stories and photographs of celebrities and chorus girls.

The new sensational or "yellow" newspapers (so called because of the popularity of the *New York World*'s first color comic, "The Yellow Kid") of the late 1880s and early 1890s responded to the demands of an expanded culture of consumption by adding illustrated women's pages, Sunday sections, society pages, and sports pages.

MAIL-ORDER CATALOGUES

For those who lived in rural areas and could not travel to the big city, mail-order companies emerged. Montgomery Ward and Sears, Roebuck published thick catalogues, offering everything from women's underclothing to entire houses. The nation's rapidly expanding rail system sped their goods across the country. The chain store was another retail strategy that spread throughout the country. The Great Atlantic and Pacific Tea Company (A&P) and Woolworth's developed extensive national systems of food and dry goods stores built in small towns and large cities alike.

The department stores, mail-order houses, and chain stores would not have been possible without the standardization of the goods they sold. Standardization had long been central to the American system of manufactures. Already in the 1850s, the American system had allowed for the mass production of many items built with interchangeable parts. Numerous entrepreneurs after the Civil War adapted these basic techniques to the production of additional consumer goods. Fashionable items of clothing and housewares, once obtainable only by the wealthy, could now be made relatively cheaply and quickly. After 1885, the ready-made clothing industry grew two to three times faster than any other industry. By 1915, it was the nation's third largest industry, ranking just behind steel and oil.

A national culture of consumption had grown up in the last decades of the century, but not everyone had equal access to it. Wages that did not keep pace with the booming economy meant less money to spend—not to mention a struggle to put food on the table. "Eight hours for work, eight hours for rest, eight hours for what we will" was a famous slogan of the labor movement in the post–Civil War era. In the demand for "eight hours for what we will," workers voiced their belief that they had a right to leisure time under their own control. As one worker told a Senate committee in 1883, "a workingman wants something besides food and clothes in this country. . . . He wants recreation. Why should not a workingman have it as well as other people?"

What most workers wanted was simple: fair wages and fair conditions in the workplace. They wanted equality in a system in which power had been systematically stripped from them and liberty was legally defined as the right of corporations. Broad-based workers' movements throughout the late 19th century attempted to rectify a situation in which equal opportunities no longer seemed to be available to all.

WORKERS' RESISTANCE TO THE NEW CORPORATE ORDER

Although the average per capita income of all Americans increased by 35 percent from 1878 to 1893, **real wages** advanced only 20 percent. That advance masked sharp inequalities of wages by skill, region, race, and gender. Many unskilled and semiskilled workers made barely enough to support themselves, much less a family; many families, especially recent immigrants (who formed a large part of the blue-collar workforce), needed two or three wage earners to survive.

At the turn of the century, the United States had the unhappy distinction of having the world's highest rate of industrial accidents. Many families were impoverished by workplace accidents that killed or maimed their chief breadwinner. In the factories, managers made decisions about the procedures and pace of operations once made by workers themselves. Many crafts that had once been a source of pride to those who practiced them became just a job that could be performed by anyone. Labor increasingly became a commodity bartered for wages rather than a craft whereby the worker sold the product of his labor rather than the labor itself. For the first time in American history, the census of 1870 reported that a majority of employed persons worked for wages paid by others rather than working for themselves.

For skilled artisans, this was an alarming trend. In 1866, the leaders of several craft unions had formed the National Labor Union. Labor parties sprang up in several states; the Labor Reform candidate for governor of Massachusetts in 1870 won 13 percent of the vote. While the advocacy of an eight-hour day would remain a central demand of the postwar labor movement, the National Labor Union itself withered away in the depression of the 1870s. Workers were virtually powerless to push their agenda. Meanwhile, industrial violence escalated. In the anthracite coalfields of eastern Pennsylvania, the Molly Maguires carried out guerrilla warfare against mine owners. In the later 1870s, the Greenbackers (a group that urged currency expansion to end deflation) and labor reformers formed a coalition that elected several local and state officials plus 14 congressmen in 1878.

THE GREAT RAILROAD STRIKE OF 1877

Railroads were an early focal point of labor strife. Citing declining revenues, several railroads cut wages by as much as 35 percent between 1874 and 1877. When the Baltimore and Ohio Railroad announced its third 10-percent wage cut on July 16, 1877, workers struck.

FOCUS QUESTION
How did post–Civil War economic changes affect working people? How did they respond?

real wages *Relationship between wages and the consumer price index.*

HISTORY THROUGH FILM

THE MOLLY MAGUIRES (1970)

*Directed by Martin Ritt; starring Richard Harris
(James McParlan), Sean Connery (Jack Kehoe),
Samantha Eggar (Mary Raines)*

The gritty realism of *The Molly Maguires* offers a compelling portrait of labor conditions in 19th-century coal mines. Filmed on location in the anthracite region of eastern Pennsylvania, the film takes the viewer deep into the earth, where Irish American miners labored long hours for a pittance at the dangerous, back-breaking, health-destroying job of bringing out the coal that heated American homes and fueled American industry.

These mining communities constituted a microcosm of ethnic and class tensions in American society. Most of the mine owners were Scots-Irish Presbyterians; many foremen, skilled workers, and police were English or Welsh Protestants; most of the unskilled workers were Irish Catholics. This was a volatile mixture, as vividly depicted in the movie. The skilled miners had formed the Workingmen's Benevolent Association, which had won modest gains for its

members by 1873. Many Irish belonged to the Ancient Order of Hibernians, which aided sick miners and supported the widows and orphans of those who died—and there were many such. The inner circle of this order called itself the Molly Maguires, after an antilandlord organization in Ireland that resisted the eviction of tenants. In Pennsylvania, the Mollies retaliated against exploitative owners, unpopular foremen, and the police with acts of sabotage, violence, intimidation, and murder.

The economic depression following the Panic of 1873 exacerbated tensions and violence. The owners hired the Pinkerton detective agency to infiltrate and gather criminal evidence against the Mollies. Detective James McParlan went to work in the mines, gained the confidence of his fellow Irish Americans, and was eventually admitted to the Molly Maguires. For more than two years, he lived a dangerous double existence (foreshortened in the movie) that would have meant instant death if the Mollies had discovered his mole role. In a series of widely publicized trials from 1875 to 1877 in which McParlan was the main witness, dozens of Molly Maguires were convicted and 20 were hanged. Richard Harris and Sean Connery are superb as McParlan and Jack Kehoe, the Mollies' leader. The real Jamie McParlan courted the sister-in-law of one of the Mollies; the film expands this into a poignant romance between McParlan and a retired miner's beautiful daughter. The love interest fits with the film's effective presentation of McParlan's conflicted conscience and the moral ambiguity of his role as the agent of justice (as defined by the ruling class), which requires him to betray the men with whom he had lived, sung, plotted, swapped stories, and carried out raids. What were McParlan's real motives? The film does not successfully answer that question, but neither does history. Most viewers, however, will take from this movie a feeling of empathy with the Mollies, whose protest against terrible conditions drove them to desperate acts of violence.

Sean Connery (Jack Kehoe, right) and Art Lund (a fellow Molly Maguire) prepare to dynamite a coal train in The Molly Maguires.

© Bettmann/Corbis

The Great Railroad Strike was no local, isolated disturbance. It touched a nerve nationally and spread rapidly; within a few days, what had begun as a local protest had traveled to Baltimore, Philadelphia, Pittsburgh, New York, Louisville, Chicago, St. Louis, Kansas City, and San Francisco. Traffic from St. Louis to the East Coast came to a halt. Women as well as men joined angry crowds in the streets; workers from a variety of industries walked out in sympathy; and in some places the strike crossed both gender and racial lines—as in Galveston, Texas, where black laundresses struck for higher wages. Ten states called out their militias. Strikers and militia fired on each other, and workers set fire to rolling stock and roundhouses. By the time federal troops brought things under control in the first week of August, at least 100 strikers, militiamen, and bystanders had been killed, hundreds more had been injured, and uncounted millions of dollars of property had gone up in smoke.

The Great Railroad Strike of 1877, the worst labor violence in U.S. history to that time, underscored the deep discontent of workers nationwide. But this spontaneous, unorganized labor upheaval did not produce solutions to workers' dilemmas. On the contrary, fears of a workers' "insurrection" led to a new cohesion in the middle class, which began to talk of a "war" between capital and labor. Not only did the middle class strongly support military intervention in the wake of 1877, it supported the construction of armories in the nation's largest cities.

THE KNIGHTS OF LABOR

In the wake of 1877, many workers looked to a new labor organization for inspiration. The Knights of Labor had been founded in 1869 in Philadelphia as a secret fraternal organization. Under the leadership of Terence Powderly, a machinist by trade, it became public in 1879 and emerged as a potent national federation of unions, or "assemblies," as they were officially known. The Knights of Labor departed in several respects from the norm of labor organization at that time. Most of its assemblies were organized by industry rather than by craft, giving many unskilled and semiskilled workers union representation for the first time. Some admitted women; some also admitted blacks.

The goal of most members of the Knights was to improve their lot within the existing system through higher wages, shorter hours, and better working conditions. This meant **collective bargaining** with employers; it also meant strikes. But Powderly and the Knights' national leadership discouraged strikes, partly out of practicality: A losing strike often destroyed an assembly, as employers replaced strikes with strikebreakers, called **scabs**.

Another reason for Powderly's antistrike stance was philosophical. Strikes constituted a tacit recognition of the legitimacy of the wage system. In Powderly's view, wages siphoned off to capital a part of the wealth created by labor. The Knights, he said, intended "to secure to the workers the full enjoyment of the wealth they create." This was a goal grounded both in the past independence of skilled workers and in a radical vision of the future—a vision in which workers' cooperatives would own the means of production.

The Knights did sponsor several modest workers' cooperatives. Their success was limited, partly from lack of capital and of management experience and partly because even the most skilled craftsmen found it difficult to compete with machines. Ironically, the Knights gained their greatest triumphs through strikes. In 1884 and 1885, successful strikes against the Union Pacific and Missouri Pacific railroads won prestige and a rush of new members, which by 1886 totaled 700,000. But defeat in a second strike against the Missouri Pacific in spring 1886 was a serious blow. Then came the Haymarket bombing in Chicago.

collective bargaining *Negotiations between representatives of workers and employers on issues such as wages, hours, and working conditions.*

scabs *Strikebreakers who are willing to act as replacements for striking workers, thus undermining the effect of strikes as leverage against company owners.*

URBAN FORTRESSES. *In the 1880s and 1890s, numerous armories were built in cities across the country to protect against a perceived threat from the "dangerous classes"—workers and the poor. This immense, castle-like 1894 armory in Brooklyn, New York, was meant to inspire awe.*

© Bettmann/Corbis

HAYMARKET

Chicago was a center of labor radicalism, including socialist parties and **anarchists**, some of whom were committed to violent destruction of the capitalist system. A national movement centered in that city called for a general strike on May 1, 1886, to achieve the eight-hour workday. Chicago police were notoriously hostile to labor organizers and strikers, so the scene was set for a violent confrontation.

The May 1 showdown coincided with a strike at the McCormick farm machinery plant in Chicago. A fight outside the gates on May 3 brought a police attack on the strikers. Anarchists then organized a protest meeting at Haymarket Square

anarchist *Activist who called for the destruction of the capitalist system so that a new social order could be built.*

on May 4. Toward the end of the meeting, the police suddenly arrived in force. When someone threw a bomb into their midst, the police opened fire. When the melee was over, 50 people lay wounded and 10 dead, 6 of them policemen.

This affair set off a wave of hysteria against labor radicals. Chicago police rounded up hundreds of labor leaders. Eight anarchists went on trial for conspiracy to commit murder, although no evidence turned up to prove that any of them had thrown the bomb. All eight were convicted; four were hanged on November 11, 1887. The case bitterly divided the country. Many workers, civil libertarians, and middle-class citizens branded the verdicts judicial murder, but most Americans applauded them.

The Knights of Labor were caught in this antilabor backlash. Although the Knights had nothing to do with the Haymarket affair, Powderly's opposition to the wage system sounded suspiciously like socialism, perhaps even anarchism. Membership in the Knights plummeted from 700,000 in spring 1886 to fewer than 100,000 by 1890.

As the Knights of Labor waned, a new national labor organization waxed. Founded in 1886, the American Federation of Labor (AFL) was a loosely affiliated association of unions organized by trade or craft: cigar-makers, machinists, carpenters, and so on. Under the leadership of Samuel Gompers, an immigrant cigar-maker, the AFL accepted capitalism and the wage system and worked for better conditions, higher wages, shorter hours, and occupational safety. Most AFL members were skilled workers. AFL membership grew from 140,000 in 1886 to nearly 1 million by 1900.

THE HOMESTEAD STRIKE

During the 1890s strikes occurred with a frequency and a fierceness that made 1877 and 1886 look like mere preludes to the main event. The most dramatic confrontation took place in July 1892 at the Homestead plant, near Pittsburgh, of the Carnegie Steel Company. Carnegie and his plant manager, Henry Clay Frick, were determined to break the power of the country's strongest union, the Amalgamated Association of Iron, Steel, and Tin Workers. Frick used a dispute over wages and work rules as an opportunity to close the plant (a **lockout**), preparatory to reopening it with nonunion workers. When the union called a strike and refused to leave the plant (a **sitdown**), Frick called in 300 Pinkerton guards to oust them. A full-scale gun battle between strikers and Pinkertons erupted, leaving nine strikers and seven Pinkertons dead and scores wounded. Frick persuaded the governor to send in 8,000 militia to protect the strikebreakers, and the plant reopened. Public sympathy, much of it pro-union at first, shifted when an anarchist tried to murder Frick on July 23. The failed Homestead strike crippled the Amalgamated Association.

THE DEPRESSION OF 1893–1897

By the 1890s, the use of state militias to protect strikebreakers had become common. Events after 1893 brought an escalation of conflict. The most serious economic crisis since the 1873–1878 depression was triggered by the Panic of 1893, a collapse of the stock market that plunged the economy into a severe four-year depression. The bankruptcy of the Reading Railroad and the National Cordage Company in early 1893 set off a process that by the end of the year had caused 491 banks and 15,000 other businesses to fail. By mid-1894, the unemployment rate had risen to more than 15 percent.

An Ohio reformer named Jacob Coxey conceived the idea of sending Congress a "living petition" of unemployed workers to press for appropriations to put them

lockout *Act of closing down a business by the owners during a labor dispute.*

sitdown *Act of protest when workers refuse to leave their workplace during a labor dispute to prevent management's use of strikebreakers.*

to work on road building and other public works. "Coxey's army" inspired other groups to hit the road and ride the rails to Washington during 1894. This descent of the unemployed on the capital provoked arrests by federal marshals and troops, and ended when Coxey and others were arrested for trespassing on the Capitol grounds. Coxey's idea for using public works to relieve unemployment turned out to be 40 years ahead of its time.

QUICK   REVIEW

CONFLICT OF CAPITAL AND LABOR IN THE GILDED AGE

- Railroad strikes of 1877

- Knights of Labor emerged as principal labor organization

- Critique by Edward Bellamy

- Depression and strikes in the 1890s

- Haymarket Affair of 1886

THE PULLMAN STRIKE

Even more alarming to middle-class Americans than Coxey's army was the Pullman strike of 1894. George M. Pullman had made a fortune in the manufacture of sleeping cars and other rolling stock for railroads. Workers in his large factory complex lived in the company town of Pullman just south of Chicago, where they enjoyed paved streets, clean parks, and decent houses rented from the company. But Pullman controlled many aspects of their lives, banned liquor from the town, and punished workers whose behavior did not suit his ideas of decorum. When the Panic of 1893 caused a sharp drop in orders for Pullman cars, the company laid off one third of its workforce and cut wages for the rest by 30 percent. But it did not reduce rents in company houses or prices in company stores. Pullman refused to negotiate with a workers' committee, which called a strike and appealed to the American Railway Union (ARU) for help.

The ARU had been founded the year before by Eugene V. Debs. Debs was convinced that the conservative stance of the railroad craft unions was contrary to the best interests of labor. He formed the ARU to include all railroad workers in one union. When George Pullman refused the ARU's offer to arbitrate the strike of Pullman workers, Debs launched a boycott by which ARU members would refuse to run any trains that included Pullman cars. When the railroads attempted to fire the ARU sympathizers, whole train crews went on strike. Rail traffic was paralyzed.

Over the protests of Illinois Governor John P. Altgeld, President Grover Cleveland sent in federal troops. The U.S. attorney general also obtained a federal injunction against Debs under the Sherman Antitrust Act on grounds that the boycott and the strike represented a conspiracy in restraint of trade. This creative use of the Sherman Act was upheld by the Supreme Court in 1895 and became a powerful weapon against labor unions.

For a week in July 1894, the Chicago railroad yards resembled a war zone. Millions of dollars of equipment went up in smoke. Thirty-four people were killed. Finally, 14,000 state militia and federal troops restored order and broke the strike. Debs went to jail for six months. He emerged from prison a socialist.

The Pullman strike was only the most dramatic event of a year in which 750,000 workers went on strike and another 3 million were unemployed. But it was a surge of discontent from farmers that wrenched American politics off its foundations in the 1890s.

FARMERS' MOVEMENTS

FOCUS   QUESTION

What provoked the farmers' protest movements in the last third of the 19th century?

Between 1870 and 1890, America's soaring grain production increased three times as fast as the American population. Only rising exports could sustain such expansion in farm production. But by the 1880s, the improved efficiency of large farms in eastern Europe brought intensifying competition and consequent price declines, especially for wheat. Prices on the world market fell about 60 percent from 1870 to 1895, while the wholesale price index for all commodities declined by 45 percent during the same period.

Victims of a world market largely beyond their control, farmers lashed out at targets nearer home: railroads, banks, commission merchants, and the monetary system. In truth, these institutions did victimize farmers, although not always intentionally.

RESISTANCE TO RAILROADS

The power wielded by the railroad companies inevitably aroused hostility. Companies often charged less for long hauls than for short hauls in areas with little or no competition. The rapid proliferation of tracks produced overcapacity in some areas, which led to rate-cutting wars that benefited some shippers at the expense of others, usually small ones. To avoid "ruinous competition" (as the railroads viewed it), companies formed **pools** by which they divided traffic and fixed their rates. Some of these practices made sound economic sense; others appeared discriminatory and exploitative. Railroads kept rates higher in areas with no competition (most farmers lived in areas served by only one line) than in regions with competition. Grain elevators, many of which were owned by railroad companies, came under attack for cheating farmers.

Farmers responded by organizing **cooperatives** to sell crops and buy supplies. The umbrella organization for many of these cooperatives was the Patrons of Husbandry, known as the Grange, founded in 1867. But because farmers could not build their own railroads, they organized "antimonopoly" parties and elected state legislators who enacted "Granger laws" in several states. These laws established railroad commissions that fixed maximum freight rates and warehouse charges. Railroads challenged the laws in court. Eight challenges made their way to the U.S. Supreme Court, which in *Munn* v. *Illinois* (1877) ruled that states could regulate businesses clothed with a "public interest," including railroads.

The welter of different and sometimes conflicting state laws, plus rulings by the U.S. Supreme Court in the 1880s that states could not regulate interstate railroad traffic, brought a drive for federal regulation. After years of discussion, Congress passed the Interstate Commerce Act in 1887. This act, like most such laws, was a compromise that reflected the varying viewpoints of shippers, railroads, and other pressure groups. It outlawed pools, discriminatory rates, long-haul versus short-haul differentials, and **rebates** to favored shippers. It required that freight and passenger rates must be "reasonable and just." What that meant was not entirely clear, but the law created the Interstate Commerce Commission (ICC) to define it on a case-by-case basis. Because the ICC had minimal enforcement powers, however, federal courts frequently refused to issue the orders it requested. Nevertheless, the ICC had some effect on railroad practices, and freight rates continued to decline during this period as railroad operating efficiency improved.

CREDIT AND MONEY

The long period of price **deflation** from 1865 to 1897, unique in American history, exacerbated the problem of credit. A price decline of 1 or 2 percent per year added that many points cumulatively to the nominal interest rate. If a farmer's main crop was wheat or cotton, whose prices declined even further, his real interest rate was that much greater. Thus it was not surprising that farmers who denounced banks or country-store merchants for gouging them also attacked a monetary system that brought deflation.

pools *Technique used by railroads to divide up traffic and fix rates, thereby avoiding ruinous competition.*

cooperatives *Marketing groups established by such groups as the Farmers Alliance that eliminated "middlemen" and reduced prices to farmers. The idea also was tried by some labor groups and included other types of businesses such as factories.*

rebates *Practice by the railroads of giving certain big businesses reductions in freight rates or refunds.*

deflation *Decline in consumer prices or a rise in the purchasing power of money.*

FOCUS QUESTION
What issues were at stake in the contest between "free silver" and the "gold bugs"?

The federal government's monetary policies worsened deflation problems. After the Civil War, the Treasury moved to bring the **greenback** dollar to par with gold by reducing the amount of greenbacks in circulation. This limitation of the money supply produced deflationary pressures. Western farmers, who suffered from downward pressures on crop prices, were particularly vociferous in their protests against this situation, which introduced a new sectional conflict into politics—not North against South, but East against West. However, parity between greenbacks and gold would not be reached until 1879.

The benefits of parity were sharply debated then and remain controversial today. On the one hand, it strengthened the dollar, placed government credit on a firm footing, and helped create a financial structure for the remarkable economic growth that tripled the GNP during the last quarter of the 19th century. On the other hand, the restraints on money supply hurt the rural economy in the South and West; they hurt debtors who found that deflation enlarged their debts by increasing the value of greenbacks; and they probably worsened the two major depressions of the era by constraining credit.

THE GREENBACK AND SILVER MOVEMENTS

Many farmers in 1876 and 1880 supported the Greenback Party, whose platform called for the issuance of more U.S. Treasury notes (greenbacks). Even more popular was the movement for **free silver**. Until 1873, government mints had coined both silver and gold dollars at a ratio of 16 to 1—that is, 16 ounces of silver were equal in value to one ounce of gold. However, when new discoveries of gold in the West after 1848 placed more gold in circulation relative to silver, that ratio undervalued silver, so that little was being sold for coinage. In 1873 Congress enacted a law, branded as "the Crime of 1873," that ended the coinage of silver dollars.

Soon after the law was passed, the production of new silver mines began to increase dramatically, which soon brought the price of silver below the old ratio of 16 to 1. Silver miners joined with farmers to demand a return to silver dollars. In 1878, Congress responded by passing the Bland-Allison Act requiring the Treasury to purchase and coin not less than $2 million nor more than $4 million of silver monthly. Once again, silver dollars flowed from the mint, but those amounts failed to absorb the increasing production of silver and did little, if anything, to slow deflation. The market price of silver dropped to a ratio of 20 to 1.

Pressure for "free silver"—that is, for government purchase of all silver offered for sale at a price of 16 to 1 and its coinage into silver dollars—continued through the 1880s. The admission of five new Western states in 1889 and 1890 contributed to the passage of the Sherman Silver Purchase Act in 1890. That act increased the amount of silver coinage, but not at the 16-to-1 ratio. Even so, it went too far to suit the **gold bugs**, who wanted to keep the United States on the international gold standard. President Cleveland blamed the Panic of 1893 on the Sherman Silver Purchase Act, which caused a run on the Treasury's gold reserves triggered by uncertainty over the future of the gold standard. Cleveland called a special session of Congress in 1893 and persuaded it to repeal the Sherman Silver Purchase Act, setting the stage for the most bitter political contest in a generation.

GRANGERS AND THE FARMERS' ALLIANCE

Agrarian reformers supported the free silver movement, but many had additional grievances concerning problems of credit, railroad rates, and the exploitation of workers and farmers by the "money power." A new farmers' organization emerged in the 1880s.

greenbacks *Paper money issued by the federal government during the Civil War to help pay war expenses. They were called greenbacks because of their color.*

free silver *Idea that the government would purchase all silver offered for sale and coin it into silver dollars at the preferred ratio between silver and gold of 16 to 1.*

gold bugs *"Sound money" advocates who wanted to keep the United States on the international gold standard and believed the expanded coinage of silver was foolhardy.*

Starting in Texas as the Southern Farmers' Alliance, it expanded into other Southern states and then into the North as well. By 1890 it had evolved into the National Farmers' Alliance and Industrial Union. Reaching out to 2 million farm families, the Alliance set up marketing cooperatives. It served the social needs of farm families by bringing them together, especially in the sparsely settled regions of the West. It also gave farmers a sense of pride and solidarity to counter the image of "hick" and "hayseed."

The Farmers' Alliance developed a comprehensive political agenda. At a national convention in December 1890, it set forth these objectives: a **graduated income tax**; **direct election of U.S. senators**; free and unlimited coinage of silver at a ratio of 16 to 1; effective government control and, if necessary, ownership of railroad, telegraph, and telephone companies; and the establishment of **subtreasuries** (federal warehouses) for the storage of crops, with government loans at 2 percent interest on those crops. The most important of these goals was the setting up of subtreasuries. Government storage would allow farmers to hold their crops until market prices were more favorable. Low-interest government loans on the value of these crops would enable farmers to pay their annual debts and thus escape the ruinous interest rates of the crop lien system in the South and bank mortgages in the West.

These were radical demands for the time. Nevertheless, most of them eventually became law: the income tax and the direct election of senators by constitutional amendments in 1913; government control of transportation and communications by various laws in the 20th century; and the subtreasuries in the form of the Commodity Credit Corporation in the 1930s.

Anticipating that the Republicans and the Democrats would resist these demands, many Alliancemen were eager to form a third party. In Kansas they had already done so, launching the People's Party (whose members were known as Populists) in 1890. But Southerners opposed the idea of a third party. Most of them were Democrats who feared that a third party might open the way for the return of the Republican Party to power.

In 1890, farmers helped elect numerous state legislators and congressmen who pledged to support their cause. But the legislative results were thin. By 1892, many Alliance members were ready to take the third-party plunge.

graduated income tax *Tax based on income with rates that gradually rise as the level of income rises.*

direct election of senators *Constitutional amendment that mandated the election of senators by the people rather than by selection by state legislatures.*

subtreasuries *Plan to help farmers escape the ruinous interest rates of the crop lien system by storing their crops in federal warehouses until market prices were more favorable. Farmers could draw low-interest loans against the value of these crops.*

The Rise and Fall of the People's Party

Enthusiasm for a third party was particularly strong in the plains and mountain states. The most prominent leader of the Farmers' Alliance was Leonidas L. Polk of North Carolina. A Confederate veteran, Polk commanded support in the West as well as in the South. He undoubtedly would have been nominated for president by the newly organized People's Party had not death cut short his career in June 1892.

The first nominating convention of the People's Party met at Omaha a month later. The preamble of their platform expressed the grim mood of delegates. "We meet in the midst of a nation brought to the verge of moral, political, and material ruin," it declared. "The fruits of the toil of millions are boldly stolen to build up colossal fortunes for a few. . . . From the same prolific womb of governmental injustice we breed the two great classes—tramps and millionaires." The platform called for unlimited coinage of silver at 16 to 1; creation of the subtreasury program for crop storage and farm loans; government ownership of railroad, telegraph, and telephone companies; a graduated income tax; direct election of senators; and laws to protect labor unions against prosecution for strikes and boycotts. To ease the lingering tension between Southern and Western farmers, the party nominated Union veteran James B. Weaver of Iowa for president and Confederate veteran James G. Field of Virginia for vice president.

Despite winning 9 percent of the popular vote and 22 electoral votes, Populist leaders were shaken by the outcome. In the South, most of the black farmers who were allowed to vote stayed with the Republicans. Democratic bosses in several Southern states kept white farmers loyal to the party of white supremacy. Only in Alabama and Texas, among Southern states, did the Populists get more than 20 percent of the vote. They did even less well in the older agricultural states of the Midwest, where the largest vote share they gained was 11 percent in Minnesota. Only in distressed wheat states such as Kansas, Nebraska, and the Dakotas and in the silver states of the West did the Populists do well, carrying Kansas, Colorado, Idaho, and Nevada.

The party remained alive, however, and the anguish caused by the Panic of 1893 seemed to boost its prospects. In several Western states, Populists or a Populist–Democratic coalition controlled state governments for a time, and a Populist–Republican coalition won the state elections of 1894 in North Carolina. Women as well as men campaigned for the Populists: Mary Lease, a former homesteader and one of the few women practicing law in Kansas, became famous for her impassioned speeches against corporate power. "We endured hardships, dangers and privations, hours of loneliness, fear and sorrow," she said of the homesteading years. "Yet after all our years of toil and privations, dangers and hardship on the Western frontier, monopoly is taking our homes from us."

President Cleveland's success in getting the Sherman Silver Purchase Act repealed in 1893 drove a wedge into the Democratic Party. Southern and Western Democrats turned against Cleveland. Democratic Senator Benjamin Tillman of South Carolina told his constituents: "When Judas betrayed Christ, his heart was not blacker than this scoundrel, Cleveland, in deceiving the Democracy. He is an old bag of beef and I am going to Washington with a pitchfork and prod him in his fat ribs."

William Jennings Bryan *A two-term Democratic congressman from Nebraska who won the party's presidential nomination in 1896 after electrifying delegates with his "Cross of Gold" speech. Bryan was twice more nominated for president (1900 and 1908); he lost all three times.*

THE SILVER ISSUE

Democratic dissidents stood poised to take over the party in 1896. They adopted free silver as the centerpiece of their program, raising the possibility of fusion with the Populists. Meanwhile, out of the West came a new and charismatic figure, a silver-tongued orator named **William Jennings Bryan**. Only 36 years old, Bryan came to the Democratic convention in 1896 as a delegate. Given the opportunity to make the closing speech in the debate on silver, Bryan brought the house to its feet in a frenzy of cheering with his peroration: "You shall not press down upon the brow of labor this crown of thorns, you shall not crucify mankind upon a cross of gold."

Library of Congress Prints & Photographs Division, LC-US2C4-9712

AN ANTI-BRYAN CARTOON. *This cartoon in* Judge *magazine, entitled "The Sacrilegious Candidate," charged William Jennings Bryan with blasphemy in his "Cross of Gold" speech at the Democratic national convention. Bryan grinds his Bible into the dust with his boot while waving a crown of thorns and holding a cross of gold. In the background a caricature of a bearded anarchist dances amid the ruins of a church and other buildings.*

This speech catapulted Bryan into the presidential nomination. He ran on a platform that not only endorsed free silver but also embraced the idea of an income tax, condemned trusts, and opposed the use of injunctions against labor. Bryan's nomination created turmoil in the People's Party. Although some Populists wanted to continue as a third party, most of them saw fusion with silver Democrats as the road to victory. At the Populist convention, the fusionists got their way and endorsed Bryan's nomination.

THE ELECTION OF 1896

The Republicans nominated **William McKinley**, who would have preferred to campaign on his specialty, the tariff. Bryan made that impossible. Crisscrossing the country, Bryan gave as many as 30 speeches a day, focusing almost exclusively on the free silver issue. Republicans responded by denouncing the Democrats as irresponsible inflationists. Free silver, they said, would demolish the workingman's gains in real wages achieved over the preceding 30 years.

Under the skillful leadership of Ohio businessman Mark Hanna, chairman of the Republican National Committee, McKinley waged a "front-porch campaign" in which various delegations visited his home in Canton, Ohio, to hear carefully crafted speeches that were widely publicized in the mostly Republican press. Hanna sent out an army of speakers and printed pamphlets in more than a dozen languages to reach immigrant voters. His propaganda portrayed Bryan as a wild man from the prairie whose monetary schemes would further wreck an economy that had been plunged into depression during a Democratic administration. McKinley's election, by contrast, would maintain the gold standard, revive business confidence, and end the depression.

William McKinley *A seven-term Republican congressman from Ohio whose signature issue was the protective tariff. He was the last Civil War veteran to be elected president.*

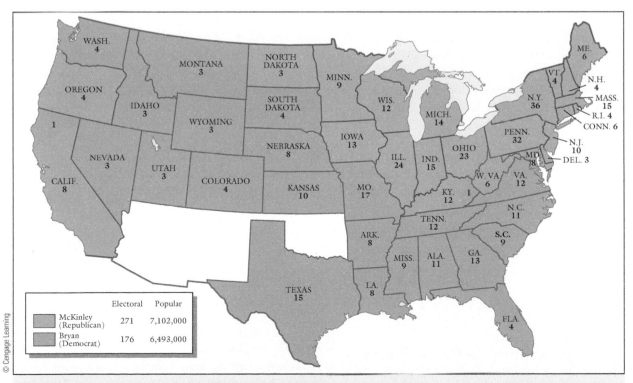

Map 19.1 **PRESIDENTIAL ELECTION, 1896.** *Once again, note the continuity of voting patterns over the two generations from the 1850s to the 1890s by comparing this map with those on pages 374 and 391.*

QUICK   REVIEW

FARMERS' MOVEMENTS AND POPULISM

- Postwar deflation fueled greenback and silver movements

- Farmers' Alliance and People's Party addressed farmers' plight

- Election of 1896 ushered in new era of Republican leadership, economic growth

The 1896 election was the most impassioned and exciting in a generation. Many Americans believed that the fate of the nation hinged on the outcome. The number of voters jumped by 15 percent over 1892. Republicans won a substantial share of the urban, immigrant, and labor vote with the slogan of McKinley as "the advance agent of prosperity." McKinley rode to a convincing victory by carrying every state in the northeast quadrant of the country. Bryan carried most of the rest. Republicans won decisive control of Congress as well as the presidency. They would maintain control for the next 14 years. The election of 1896 marked a crucial turning point in American political history away from the stalemate of the preceding two decades.

Whether by luck or by design, McKinley did prove to be the advance agent of prosperity. The economy pulled out of the depression during his first year in office and entered into a long period of growth—not because of anything the new administration did, but because of the mysterious workings of the business cycle. With the discovery of rich new goldfields in the Yukon, in Alaska, and in South Africa, the silver issue lost potency, and a cascade of gold poured into the world economy. The long deflationary trend since 1865 reversed itself in 1897. Farmers entered a new era of prosperity. Bryan ran against McKinley again in 1900 but lost even more emphatically. The nation seemed embarked on a placid sea of plenty. But below the surface, the currents of protest and reform still ran strong.

C O N C L U S I O N

The 1890s were a watershed in American history. In the past lay a largely rural society and agricultural economy; in the future lay cities and a commercial–industrial economy. Before the 1890s, most immigrants had come from northern and western Europe, and many became farmers. Later immigrants largely came from eastern and southern Europe, and nearly all settled in cities. Before the 1890s, the old sectional issues associated with slavery, the Civil War, and Reconstruction remained important forces in American politics; after 1900, racial issues would not play an important part in national politics for another 60 years. The election of 1896 ended 20 years of even balance between the two major parties and led to more than a generation of Republican dominance.

Most important, the social and political upheavals of the 1890s shocked many people into recognition that the liberty and equality they had taken for granted as part of the American dream was in danger of disappearing before the onslaught of wrenching economic changes. The strikes and violence and third-party protests of the decade were a wake-up call. As the forces of urbanization and industrialism increased during the ensuing two decades, many middle-class Americans supported greater government power to carry out progressive reforms to cure the ills of an industrializing society.

QUESTIONS FOR REVIEW AND CRITICAL THINKING

Review

1. What were the main engines of American economic growth in the last third of the 19th century?
2. How did American middle-class culture change in response to the rise of corporations?
3. How did post–Civil War economic changes affect working people? How did they respond?
4. What provoked the farmer protest movements in the last third of the 19th century?
5. What issues were at stake in the contest between "free silver" and the "gold bugs"?

Critical Thinking

1. Some historians have argued that corporate power went virtually unchecked in the 19th century. Is this true? Why or why not?

2. What are the most significant ways in which the ongoing struggle between capital and labor reshaped American society in the late 19th century?

ONLINE RESOURCES

 Visit the companion website to access flashcards, crossword puzzles, exercises, and quizzes related to this chapter: www.cengage.com/history/murrin/libertyequalconc5e.

 See our interactive ebook for map and primary source activities.

 **DISCOVERY**   *How did post–Civil War economic changes affect American society?*

ECONOMICS AND TECHNOLOGY
Look at the photo of New York City in 1885. How does this picture show the impact of technology on American society? What evidence do you see of emerging changes in transportation? In communication? How do these technologies transform the experience of individuals? How do they transform businesses? Are the resulting changes from these "improvements" all positive for society?

In thinking about this question, begin by breaking it down into the components shown below. A discussion of the significance of each component should appear in your answer.

NEW YORK CITY IN 1885

The Museum of the City of New York Corbis

POLITICS Study the 1896 election map on page 521 and examine in particular the number of electoral votes for individual states and the geographic pattern of voting. What generalizations can you make about the geographic basis of support for each candidate? According to the cartoon on page 520, what institutions and values does William Jennings Bryan threaten?

Chapter 20 deleted from this edition

PROGRESSIVISM

Progressivism took its name from individuals who left the Republican Party in 1912 to join Theodore Roosevelt's new party, the Progressive Party. But the term "progressive" refers to an even larger and more varied group of reformers. Progressives wanted to cleanse politics of corruption and tame the power of the "trusts." They fought against prostitution, gambling, drinking, and vice. They first appeared in municipal politics, organizing to oust crooked mayors and break up local gas or streetcar monopolies. They then carried their fights to the states and finally to the nation. Two presidents, Theodore Roosevelt and Woodrow Wilson, placed themselves at the head of this movement.

Progressivism was popular among several groups with distinct, and often conflicting, aims. On one issue, however, most progressives agreed: the need for an activist government to right political, economic, and social wrongs.

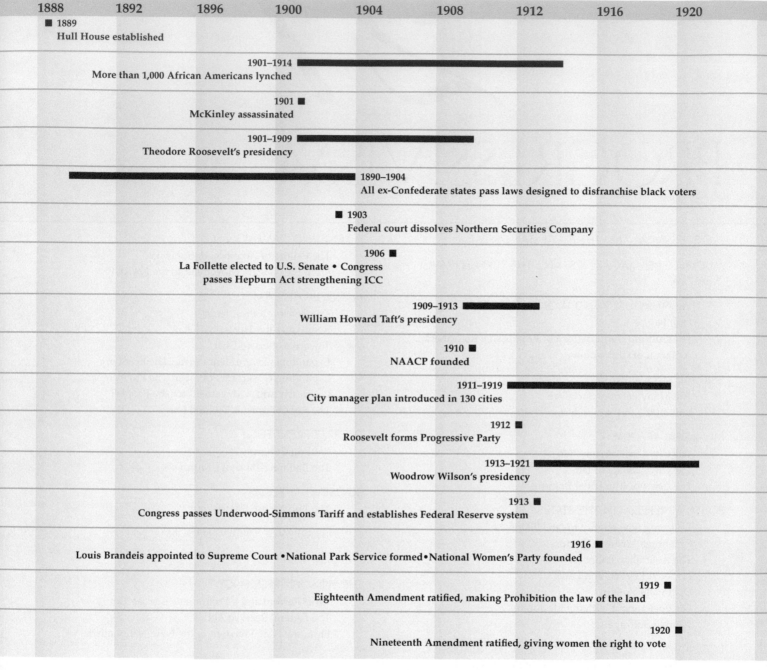

1888	1892	1896	1900	1904	1908	1912	1916	1920

1889
Hull House established

1901–1914
More than 1,000 African Americans lynched

1901
McKinley assassinated

1901–1909
Theodore Roosevelt's presidency

1890–1904
All ex-Confederate states pass laws designed to disfranchise black voters

1903
Federal court dissolves Northern Securities Company

1906
La Follette elected to U.S. Senate • Congress passes Hepburn Act strengthening ICC

1909–1913
William Howard Taft's presidency

1910
NAACP founded

1911–1919
City manager plan introduced in 130 cities

1912
Roosevelt forms Progressive Party

1913–1921
Woodrow Wilson's presidency

1913
Congress passes Underwood-Simmons Tariff and establishes Federal Reserve system

1916
Louis Brandeis appointed to Supreme Court • National Park Service formed • National Women's Party founded

1919
Eighteenth Amendment ratified, making Prohibition the law of the land

1920
Nineteenth Amendment ratified, giving women the right to vote

Some progressives wanted government to become active only long enough to clean up the political process, end drinking, upgrade the electorate, and break up trusts. These problems were so difficult to solve that many other progressives endorsed the notion of a permanently active government—with the power to tax income, regulate industry, protect consumers from fraud, safeguard the environment, and provide social welfare. Many progressives came to see the federal government as the institution best equipped to solve social problems.

Americans had long been suspicious of centralized government, viewing it as the enemy of liberty. The Populists had broken with that view (see Chapter 19), but they had been defeated. So the progressives had to build a new case for strong government as the protector of liberty and equality.

Progressivism and the Protestant Spirit

Progressivism first emerged most strongly among young, mainly Protestant, middle-class Americans who felt alienated from society. Many had been raised in homes where religious conviction was a spur to social action. They were expected to become ministers or missionaries or to infuse religious values into society in some other way. Many did not pursue those callings, but they never lost their zeal for righting moral wrongs and for uplifting the human spirit. They were distressed by the immorality and corruption in American politics and by the gap that separated rich from poor.

Other Protestant reformers preached their faith. This was true of William Jennings Bryan, the former Populist leader who became an ardent progressive and a prominent evangelical. Throughout his political career, Bryan insisted that Christian piety and American democracy were integral. Billy Sunday, a former Major League Baseball player who became the most theatrical preacher of his day, elevated opposition to saloons and the "liquor trust" into a righteous crusade. And Walter Rauschenbusch led a movement known as the Social Gospel, which emphasized the duty of Christians to work for the social good.

Protestants, of course, formed a diverse population, large sections of which showed little interest in reform. Of the many groups of reformers that arose, three were of particular importance, especially in the early years: investigative journalists, who were called muckrakers; the founders and supporters of settlement houses; and socialists.

FOCUS QUESTION
Which groups of Americans spearheaded the progressive movement?

Muckrakers, Magazines, and the Turn Toward "Realism"

The term **muckraker** was coined by Theodore Roosevelt, who had intended it as a criticism of newspaper and magazine reporters who wrote stories about scandalous situations. But it became a badge of honor among journalists who wanted to shock the public into taking action about the troublesome aspects of American life. Ida Tarbell reported on the shady practices by which John D. Rockefeller had transformed his Standard Oil Company into a monopoly. Lincoln Steffens unraveled the webs of bribery and corruption that were strangling local governments in the nation's cities. George Kibbe Turner documented prostitution and family disintegration.

These reporters were part of a tradition of investigative journalism that reached back to the 1870s, when newspaper and magazine writers exposed the corrupt practices of New York City's Boss Tweed and his Tammany Hall machine. The rise of the muckrakers reflected two factors, one economic and the other intellectual, that transformed investigative reporting into something of national importance.

From 1870 to 1909 the number of daily newspapers rose from 574 to 2,600, and their circulation increased from less than 3 million to more than 24 million. During the 1890s magazines also underwent a revolution. Cheap, 10-cent periodicals such as *McClure's Magazine* and *Ladies Home Journal*, with circulations of 400,000 to 1 million, displaced genteel and relatively expensive 35-cent publications such as *Harper's* and *The Atlantic Monthly*. The expanded readership brought journalists money

muckrackers *Investigative journalists who propelled progressivism by exposing corruption, economic monopoly, and moral decay in American society.*

and prestige and attracted many talented and ambitious men and women to the profession. It also made magazine publishers more receptive to stories that would appeal to the masses.

The muckrakers were favored by the turn toward **realism** among the nation's middle class. "Realist" thinking prized detachment, objectivity, and skepticism. Many people, for example, felt that constitutional theory had little to do with the way government in the United States actually worked. What could one learn about bosses, machines, and graft from studying the Constitution? Wasn't the nation's glorification of the "self-made man" and of "individualism" preventing Americans from understanding how corporations, banks, and labor unions—the large-scale organizations—were shaping the nation's economy and society?

In the 1890s, artists and intellectuals set about creating truer representations and more realistic interpretations of American society. Many of them were inspired by the work of investigative journalists; some had been newspapermen themselves. Years of firsthand observation enabled them to describe American society as it "truly was" rather than how it ought to be. They brought shadowy figures to life: the captain of industry who ruthlessly destroyed his competitors; the con artist who tricked young people new to city life; the white slave trader who sold innocent girls into prostitution; and the corrupt policeman under whose protection urban vice flourished.

Middle-class Americans, uneasy about the state of society, read these exposés and became interested in reform. They began pressuring city and state governments to send crooked government officials to jail and to stamp out corruption and vice. Between 1902 and 1916 more than 100 cities launched investigations of the prostitution trade. At the federal level, all three branches of government felt compelled to address the question of "the trusts," the concentration of power in the hands of a few industrialists and financiers. Progressivism crystallized around the abuses that muckrakers exposed.

realism *Form of thinking, writing, and art that prized detachment, objectivity, and skepticism.*

Settlement Houses and Women's Activism

Established by middle-class reformers, settlement houses were intended to help poor immigrant workers cope with the harsh conditions of city living. Much of the inspiration for them came from young, college-trained, Protestant women from affluent backgrounds who rebelled against being relegated solely to the roles of wife and mother. For them, the settlement houses provided a way to assert their independence and apply their talents in socially useful ways.

Hull House

Jane Addams and Ellen Gates Starr established the nation's first settlement house in Chicago in 1889. The two women had been inspired by a visit the year before to London's Toynbee Hall, where a group of middle-class men had been living and working with that city's poor since 1884. Addams and Starr bought a decaying mansion once owned by a prominent Chicagoan, Charles J. Hull, and now surrounded by factories, churches, saloons, and tenements. Addams quickly emerged as the guiding spirit of **Hull House**. She moved into the building and demanded that all workers there do the same. She and Starr enlisted extraordinary women such as Florence Kelley, Alice Hamilton, and Julia Lathrop. They set up a nursery

Hull House *First American settlement house, established in Chicago in 1889 by Jane Addams and Ellen Gates Starr.*

TABLE 21.1

WOMEN ENROLLED IN INSTITUTIONS OF HIGHER EDUCATION, 1870–1930			
Year	Women's Colleges (thousands of students)	Coed Institutions (thousands of students)	Total (thousands of students)	Percentage of All Students Enrolled
1870	6.5	4.6	11.1	21.0%
1880	15.7	23.9	39.6	33.4
1890	16.8	39.5	56.3	35.9
1900	24.4	61.0	85.4	36.8
1910	34.1	106.5	140.6	39.6
1920	52.9	230.0	282.9	47.3
1930	82.1	398.7	480.8	43.7

Source: From Mabel Newcomer, *A Century of Higher Education for American Women* (New York: Harper and Row, 1959), p. 46.

for the children of working mothers, a penny savings bank, and an employment bureau, soon followed by a baby clinic, a neighborhood playground, and social clubs. Determined to minister to cultural as well as economic needs, Hull House sponsored an orchestra, reading groups, and a lecture series. Members of Chicago's widening circle of reform-minded intellectuals, artists, and politicians contributed their energies to the enterprise. In 1893 Illinois Governor John P. Altgeld named Hull House's Florence Kelley as the state's chief factory inspector. Kelley's investigations led to Illinois's first factory law, which prohibited child labor, limited the employment of women to eight hours a day, and authorized the state to hire inspectors to enforce the law.

Meanwhile, Julia Lathrop used her appointment to the State Board of Charities to agitate for improvements in the care of the poor, the handicapped, and the delinquent. With Edith Abbott and Sophonisba Breckinridge, she established the Department of Social Research at the University of Chicago.

The Hull House leaders did not command the instant fame accorded the muckrakers. Nevertheless, their achievements drew increasing public attention. Thousands of women across the country were inspired to build their own settlement houses on the Hull House model. By 1910 Jane Addams had become one of the nation's most famous women.

THE CULTURAL CONSERVATISM OF PROGRESSIVE REFORMERS

In general, settlement house workers were more sympathetic toward the poor, the illiterate, and the downtrodden than the muckrakers were. Jane Addams, though she disapproved of machine politics, saw firsthand the benefits machine politicians delivered to their constituents. She respected the cultural inheritance of the immigrant poor and admired their resourcefulness. Although she wanted them to become Americans, she encouraged them to enrich America with their "immigrant gifts." Her approach was more liberal than that of many other reformers, who wanted to strip immigrants of their "inferior" cultures.

But there were limits to Addams's sympathy for the immigrants. She disapproved of the new working-class entertainments that gave adolescents opportunities for intimate association. She was also troubled by the emergence of the "new woman" and her frank sexuality (see Chapter 20). Addams tended to equate female sexuality with prostitution. She still adhered to Victorian notions of "pure," asexual womanhood.

Underwood & Underwood/Corbis

JANE ADDAMS. *The founder of the settlement house movement, Addams was the most famous woman reformer of the progressive era. This photograph (1930) shows her late in her career, by which time she had dedicated more than 40 years to helping immigrant children and their families.*

In fact, a good many champions of progressive reform were cultural conservatives. In addition to women's sexuality, they frowned on alcohol. Drinking was a serious problem in poor, working-class areas. Settlement house workers were well aware of alcoholism's ill effects and sought to combat it. They called on working people to refrain from drink and worked for legislation to shut down saloons. Progressives joined forces with the Woman's Christian Temperance Union and the Anti-Saloon League. By 1916, their collective efforts had won prohibition of the sale and manufacture of alcoholic beverages in 16 states. In 1919 their crowning achievement was the Eighteenth Amendment to the U.S. Constitution, making Prohibition the law of the land (see Chapter 23).

In depicting alcohol and saloons as evils, however, the prohibition movement ignored the role saloons played in working-class communities. On Chicago's South Side, for example, saloons provided thousands of packinghouse workers with the only decent place to eat lunch. Some saloons catered to particular ethnic groups: They served traditional foods and drinks, provided meeting space for fraternal organizations, and offered camaraderie to men longing to speak in their native tongue. Saloon-keepers sometimes functioned as informal bankers, cashing checks and making small loans. Not surprisingly, many immigrants in Chicago and elsewhere shunned the prohibition movement. Here was a gulf separating the immigrant masses from the Protestant middle class that even compassionate reformers such as Jane Addams could not bridge.

A NATION OF CLUBWOMEN

Settlement house workers constituted only one part of the network of female reformers. Hundreds of thousands of women belonged to local women's clubs. Conceived as self-help organizations in which women would be encouraged to sharpen their minds, refine their domestic skills, and strengthen their moral faculties, these clubs embraced social reform. Clubwomen typically focused their energies on improving schools, building libraries and playgrounds, expanding educational and vocational opportunities for girls, and securing fire and sanitation codes for tenement houses. In so doing, they transformed traditional female concerns about children and families into questions of public policy about education, safety, and hygiene.

QUICK REVIEW

PROGRESSIVISM

- Embraced an activist government to right political, economic, and social wrongs

- Led by middle-class reformers often inspired by Protestant values and fearing more radical critiques of capitalism such as those rooted in socialism

- Intellectual roots in realism

- Conservative undertones most evident in morality crusades over sexuality, temperance, and racial control

SOCIALISM AND PROGRESSIVISM

While issues such as women's sexuality and men's alcoholism drew progressives in a conservative direction, other issues drew them to **socialism**. In the early part of the 20th century, socialism stood for the transfer of industry from private to public control. Socialists believed that such a transfer, usually defined in terms of government

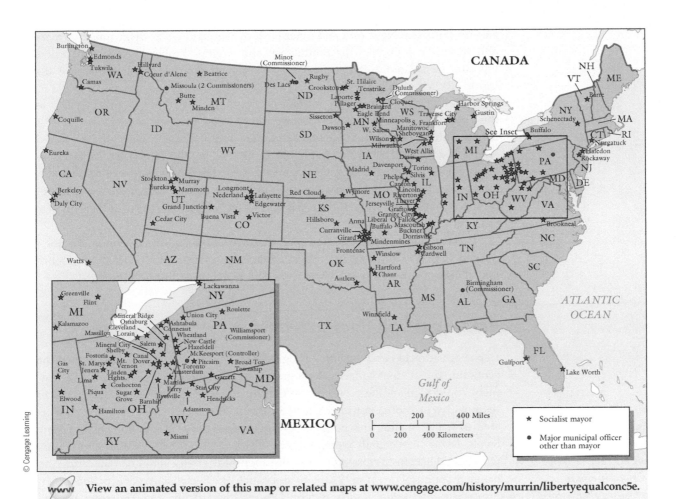

www **View an animated version of this map or related maps at www.cengage.com/history/murrin/libertyequalconc5e.**

Map 21.1 Cities and Towns Electing Socialists as Mayors or as Other Major Municipal Officers, 1911–1920.
This map reveals the strength of socialist electoral support in some unexpected areas: western Pennsylvania; Ohio; Illinois; Minnesota; a cluster of towns where Oklahoma, Missouri, and Kansas meet; Colorado; and Utah.

ownership of private corporations, would allow the laboring masses to control the wealth and power that industrial elites had amassed for themselves.

The Socialist Party of America, founded in 1901, became a political force during the first 16 years of the century, and socialist ideas influenced progressivism. In 1912, at the peak of its influence, the party's presidential candidate, **Eugene Victor Debs,** attracted almost 1 million votes—6 percent of the total votes cast that year. In that same year, 1,200 Socialists held elective office in 340 different municipalities (see Map 21.1). More than 300 newspapers and periodicals spread the socialist gospel. The most important socialist publication was *Appeal to Reason*, published by the Kansan Julius Wayland and sent out each week to 750,000 subscribers. In 1905 Wayland published, in serial form, a novel by an obscure muckraker named Upton Sinclair, which depicted scandalous working conditions in Chicago's meatpacking industry. When it was published as a book in 1906, *The Jungle* created a popular outcry.

The Many Faces of Socialism

Socialists came in several varieties: German working-class immigrants and their descendants in Milwaukee and other Midwest cities; Jewish immigrants from

socialism *Political movement that called for the transfer of industry from private to public control, and the transfer of political power from elites to the laboring masses.*

Eugene V. Debs *Leader of the Socialist Party who received almost a million votes in the election of 1912.*

eastern Europe in New York and other Eastern Seaboard cities; disgruntled farmers and former Populists in the Southwest; and miners, timber cutters, and others laboring in isolated areas in the West who joined the Industrial Workers of the World (IWW) (see Chapter 20).

Socialists differed not only in their occupations and ethnic origins but also in their politics. The IWW was the most radical socialist group, with its incessant calls for revolution. Those who followed Debs were democratic socialists who respected America's political processes and hoped to redeem the American republic by electing Debs president. Evolutionary socialists, led by Victor Berger of Milwaukee, abandoned talk of revolution altogether and chose instead an aggressive brand of reform politics. They were dubbed **gas and water socialists** because of their interest in improving city services.

These differences would, after 1912, fragment the socialist movement. But for a decade or so, these divergent groups managed to coexist due to Debs's eloquence and charisma, which impelled hundreds of thousands to embrace the cause.

SOCIALISTS AND PROGRESSIVES

Debs both attracted and unsettled progressives. On the one hand, he addressed the economic threats that concerned progressives. His confidence that strong government could regulate the economic system mirrored the progressives' own faith in the positive uses of government. Indeed, progressives and socialists often cooperated to win economic and political reforms, especially at the municipal and state levels. Many intellectuals were both socialist and progressive. Walter Lippmann, who would become a close adviser to President Wilson during the First World War, began his political career in 1912 as an assistant to the Socialist mayor of Schenectady. Prominent intellectuals, such as John Dewey, Richard Ely, and Thorstein Veblen, traveled back and forth between the socialist and progressive camps. So did Helen Keller, a leading advocate for the disabled.

gas and water socialists *Term used to describe evolutionary socialists who focused their reform efforts on regulating municipal utilities in the public interest.*

© Hulton Archive/Getty Images

EUGENE V. DEBS. *This photograph captures the energy and charisma of Debs as he addresses a working-class audience in New York during his 1912 presidential campaign.*

On the other hand, Debs's talk of revolution scared progressives, as did his efforts to organize a working-class political movement independent of middle-class control. Although progressives wanted to tame capitalism, they did not want to eliminate it altogether. They wanted to improve conditions for the masses but not cede political control to them. The progressives hoped to offer just enough socialist elements to counter the appeal of Debs's more radical movement. In this, they were successful.

Municipal reform

Progressive reform first arose over control of city transportation networks and utilities. Street railways were typically owned and operated by private corporations, as were electrical and gas systems. These corporations won the right to charge exorbitant rates by bribing city officials who belonged to political machines. They achieved generous reductions in real estate taxes in the same way.

The assault on private utilities and their protectors in city government gained momentum in the 1890s. In St. Louis in 1900, middle-class consumers and small businessmen joined hands with striking workers to challenge the "streetcar trust." In Cleveland, reformer Tom Johnson won election as mayor in 1901, curbed the power of the streetcar interests, and brought honest and efficient government to the city.

Occasionally, a reform politician of Johnson's caliber would rise to power through one of the regular political parties. But this path to power was difficult, especially in cities where the political parties were controlled by machines. Consequently, progressives worked for reforms that could strip the parties of their power. Two of their favorite reforms were the city commission and the city manager forms of government.

THE CITY COMMISSION PLAN

First introduced in Galveston, Texas, in 1900, the city commission shifted municipal power from the mayor and his aldermen to five city commissioners, each responsible for a different department of city government. The impetus for this reform came from civic-minded businessmen determined to rebuild government on the principles of efficient and scientific management that had energized the private sector. The results were often impressive. The Galveston commissioners restored the city's credit, improved its harbor, and built a massive seawall, all on a budget only two-thirds the size of what it had been before. In Houston, Texas; Des Moines, Iowa; Dayton, Ohio; Oakland, California; and elsewhere, commissioners similarly improved urban infrastructures, expanded city services, and strengthened the financial health of the cities.

THE CITY MANAGER PLAN

The city commission system did not always work to perfection. Commissioners rewarded supporters with jobs and contracts and sought undue power and prestige for their respective departments. The city manager plan was meant to overcome such problems. Under this plan, the commissioners continued to set policy, but the implementation of policy now rested with a "chief executive." This official, who was appointed by the commissioners, was to be insulated from the pressures of running for office. The city manager would curtail rivalries between commissioners and ensure that no outside influences interfered with the businesslike management of the city. The job of city manager was explicitly modeled after that of a corporation executive. First introduced in Sumter, South Carolina, in 1911 and then in Dayton, Ohio, in 1913, by 1919 the city manager plan had been adopted in 130 cities.

THE COSTS OF MUNICIPAL REFORM

Although these changes in municipal governance limited corruption and improved services, they were not universally popular. Poor and minority voters, in particular, saw their influence on local affairs diminished by the shift to city commissioners and managers. Previously, candidates for municipal office (other than the mayor) competed in ward elections rather than in citywide elections. Voters in working-class wards commonly elected workingmen to represent them, and voters in immigrant wards made sure that fellow ethnics represented their interests on city councils. Citywide elections diluted the strength of these constituencies. Candidates from poor districts often lacked the money needed to mount a citywide campaign, and they were further hampered by the nonpartisan nature of such elections. Denied the support of a political party or platform, they had to make themselves personally known to voters throughout the city. That was a much easier task for "leading citizens"—manufacturers, merchants, and lawyers—than it was for workingmen.

QUICK REVIEW

MUNICIPAL REFORM

- Shifted local transportation networks and utilities to public control
- Applied principles of business efficiency and scientific management to local government
- Diluted working-class power through nonpartisan and expensive nature of citywide elections

POLITICAL REFORM IN THE STATES

FOCUS QUESTION

How did progressive reformers hope to create a "responsible" or "virtuous" electorate? What were the consequences of their reforms?

Political reform in the cities quickly spread to the states. As at the local level, political parties at the state level were often dominated by corrupt politicians who did the bidding of powerful private lobbies. In New Jersey in 1903, for example, large industrial and financial interests, working through the Republican Party machine, controlled numerous appointments to state government, including the chief justice of the state supreme court, the attorney general, and the commissioner of banking and insurance. Such webs of influence ensured that New Jersey would provide large corporations such as the railroads with favorable legislation.

RESTORING SOVEREIGNTY TO "THE PEOPLE"

Progressives introduced reforms designed to undermine the power of party bosses, restore sovereignty to "the people," and encourage honest, talented individuals to enter politics. One such reform was the direct primary, a mechanism that enabled voters themselves, rather than party bosses, to choose party candidates. By 1916 all but three states had adopted the direct primary. Closely related was a movement to strip state legislatures of their power to choose U.S. senators. State after state enacted legislation that permitted voters to choose Senate candidates in primary elections. In 1912 a reluctant U.S. Senate was obliged to approve the Seventeenth Amendment to the Constitution, mandating the direct election of senators.

A total of 18 states followed the example of Oregon after 1902 by adopting two other reforms, the **initiative** and the **referendum**. The initiative allowed reformers

initiative *Reform that gave voters the right to propose and pass a law independently of their state legislature.*

referendum *Reform that gave voters the right to repeal an unpopular act passed by their state legislature.*

to put before voters in general elections legislation that state legislatures had yet to approve. The referendum gave voters the right in general elections to repeal an act that a state legislature had passed. Less widely adopted was the **recall**, a device that allowed voters to remove from office a public servant who had betrayed the voters' trust. As a further control, numerous states enacted laws that regulated corporate campaign contributions and restricted lobbying activities in state legislatures.

These laws did not eliminate corporate privilege or destroy the power of machine politicians. Nevertheless, they made politics more honest and restored faith in governing institutions.

CREATING A VIRTUOUS ELECTORATE

Progressive reformers sought to create an electorate that recognized the importance of the vote and resisted efforts to manipulate elections. To create this ideal electorate, reformers sought changes in the voting process that would allow "virtuous" citizens to cast their votes free of coercion and intimidation. At the same time, reformers sought to disfranchise citizens who were considered irresponsible and corruptible. In pursuing these goals, progressives substantially altered the composition of the electorate and strengthened government regulation of voting. The results were contradictory. On the one hand, progressives enlarged the electorate by extending the right to vote to women; on the other hand, they supported laws that barred large numbers of minority and poor voters from the polls.

THE AUSTRALIAN BALLOT

Government regulation of voting had begun in the 1890s when virtually every state adopted the **Australian, or secret, ballot**. This reform required voters to vote in private rather than in public. It also required the government, rather than political parties, to print the ballots and supervise the voting. Prior to this time, each political party had printed its own ballot with only its candidates listed. At election time, each party mobilized its loyal supporters. Party workers offered liquor, free meals, and other bribes to get voters to the polls and to "persuade" them to cast the right ballot. Because the ballots were cast in public, few voters who had accepted gifts of liquor and food dared to cross watchful party officials. Critics argued that the system corrupted the electoral process. They also pointed out that it made "ticket-splitting"— dividing one's vote between candidates of two or more parties—difficult.

The Australian ballot solved these problems. Although it predated progressivism, it anticipated the progressives' determination to use government power to encourage citizens to cast their votes responsibly and wisely.

PERSONAL REGISTRATION LAWS

That same determination was apparent in the progressives' support for the personal registration laws that virtually every state passed between 1890 and 1920. These laws required prospective voters to appear at a designated government office with proper identification; only then would they be allowed to register to vote. Frequently, these laws also mandated a certain period of residence in the state prior to registration and a certain interval between registration and actual voting.

Personal registration laws were meant to disfranchise citizens who showed no interest in voting until Election Day when party workers offered them a few dollars

recall *Reform that gave voters the right to remove from office a public servant who had betrayed the voters' trust.*

Australian ballot (secret ballot) *Practice that required citizens to vote in private rather than in public, and required the government (rather than political parties) to supervise the voting process.*

and free rides to the polls. These laws also excluded, however, many poor people who wanted to vote but failed to register, either because their work schedules made it impossible or because they were intimidated. The laws could be particularly frustrating for immigrants who knew little English and who could not get the registration help they needed from city officials.

DISFRANCHISEMENT

Some election laws promoted by the progressives were designed to prevent non-citizen immigrants from voting. In the 1880s, 18 states had passed laws allowing immigrants to vote without first becoming citizens. Progressives reversed this trend. At the same time, the newly formed Bureau of Immigration and Naturalization (1906) made it more difficult to become a citizen. Applicants for citizenship now had to appear before a judge who interrogated them in English on American history and civics.

Progressives defended this new process. The gift of U.S. citizenship, they believed, required responsibility; it was not to be bestowed lightly. This view was understandable, given the electoral abuses progressives had exposed. Nevertheless, the reforms also had the effect of denying the vote to significant numbers of Americans. Nowhere was exclusion more apparent than in the South, where between 1890 and 1904 every ex-Confederate state passed laws designed to strip blacks of their right to vote. Because laws explicitly barring blacks from voting would have violated the Fifteenth Amendment, their exclusion was accomplished indirectly through literacy tests, property qualifications, and poll taxes. Any citizen who failed a reading test, could not sign his name, did not own a minimum amount of property, or could not pay a poll tax lost his right to vote. The citizens who failed these tests most frequently were blacks, who formed the poorest and least educated segment of the Southern population, but a large portion of the region's poor whites also failed the tests.

Many progressives in the North, black and white, criticized Southern **disfranchisement**. But in the South, white progressives rarely challenged it. They had little difficulty using progressive ideology to justify disfranchisement. Progressives everywhere believed that the franchise was a privilege; thus, it could be withheld from those deemed unfit to handle its responsibilities. Progressives in the North excluded immigrants on these grounds. Progressives in the South saw African Americans in the same light.

DISILLUSIONMENT WITH THE ELECTORATE

In the process of ascertaining those "unfit" to hold the franchise, some progressives soured on the electoral process altogether. The more they looked for rational and virtuous voters, the fewer they found. In *Drift and Mastery* (1914), Walter Lippmann developed a theory that ordinary people had been overwhelmed by industrial and social changes. Because these changes seemed beyond their comprehension or control, they "drifted," unable to "master" the circumstances of modern life. Lippmann did not suggest that ordinary people should be barred from voting. But he did argue that political responsibility should be placed in the hands of appointed officials with the training and knowledge necessary to make government effective and just. The growing disillusionment with the electorate, in combination with intensifying restrictions on the franchise, created an environment in which fewer and fewer Americans went to the polls. Voting participation rates fell from 79 percent in 1896 to only 49 percent in 1920.

disfranchisement *Process of barring groups of adult citizens from voting.*

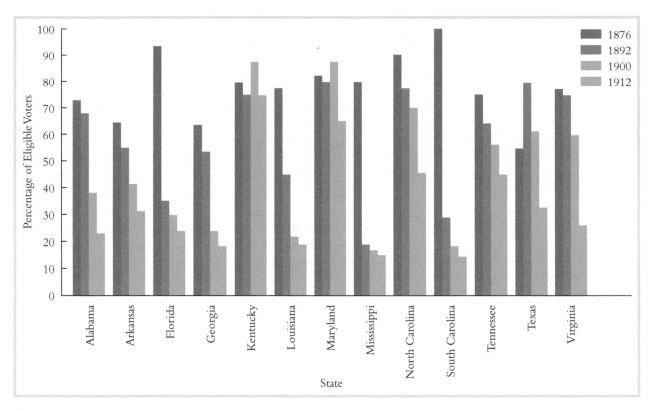

VOTER PARTICIPATION IN 13 SOUTHERN STATES, 1876, 1892, 1900, 1912
Source: Data from *Historical Statistics of the United States, Colonial Times to 1970* (White Plains, NY: Kraus International, 1989).

WOMAN SUFFRAGE

The major exception to this trend was the enfranchisement of women. This momentous reform was embraced by several states during the 1890s and the first two decades of the 20th century. It became federal law with the ratification of the Nineteenth Amendment in 1920. Launched in 1848 at the famous Seneca Falls convention (see Chapter 12), the women's rights movement had floundered in the 1870s and 1880s. In 1890 suffragists came together in a new organization, the **National American Woman Suffrage Association** (NAWSA). Thousands of young, college-educated women campaigned door to door, held impromptu rallies, and pressured state legislators.

Wyoming, which attained statehood in 1890, became the first state to grant women the right to vote, followed in 1893 by Colorado and in 1896 by Idaho and Utah. The main reason for success in these sparsely populated Western states was not egalitarianism but rather the conviction that women's supposedly gentler and more nurturing nature would tame and civilize the rawness of the frontier (see Map 21.2).

This notion reflected a subtle change in the suffrage movement. Earlier generations had insisted that women were fundamentally equal to men, but many of the new suffragists argued that women were different from men. Women, they stressed, possessed a moral sense and a nurturing quality that men lacked. Consequently, they understood the civic obligations implied by the franchise and could be trusted to vote virtuously. Their experience as mothers and household managers, moreover, would enable them to guide local and state governments in efforts to improve education, sanitation, and the condition of women and children in the workforce.

Suffragists were slow to ally themselves with blacks, Asians, and other disfranchised groups. In fact, many suffragists, especially those in the South and West,

National American Woman Suffrage Association *Organization established in 1890 to promote woman suffrage; stressed that women's special virtue made them indispensable to politics.*

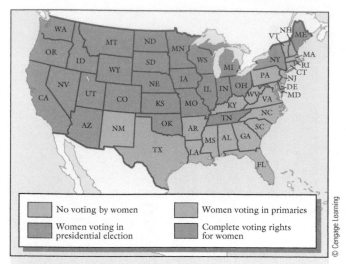

Map 21.2 WOMAN SUFFRAGE BEFORE 1920. *This map illustrates how woman suffrage prior to 1920 had advanced furthest in the West.*

opposed the franchise for Americans of color. They, like their male counterparts, believed that members of these groups lacked reason and morality and thus did not deserve the vote.

Washington, California, Kansas, Oregon, and Arizona followed the lead of the other Western states by enfranchising women in the years from 1910 to 1912. After a series of setbacks in Eastern and Midwestern states, the movement regained momentum under the leadership of Carrie Chapman Catt, who became president of NAWSA in 1915, and the radical Alice Paul, who founded the militant National Women's Party in 1916. Aided by a heightened enthusiasm for democracy generated by America's participation in the First World War (see Chapter 23) and by the decision to shift the movement's focus from individual states to the nation at large, the suffragists achieved their goal of universal woman suffrage in 1920.

Predictions that suffrage for women would radically alter politics turned out to be false. Although the numbers of voters increased after 1920, voter participation rates continued to decline. Still, the extension of the vote to women, 144 years after the founding of the nation, was a great political achievement.

ECONOMIC AND SOCIAL REFORM IN THE STATES

In some states, progressive reform extended well beyond political parties and the electorate. Progressives also wanted to limit the power of corporations, strengthen organized labor, and offer social welfare protection to the weak. State governments were pressured into passing such legislation by progressive alliances of middle-class and working-class reformers and by dynamic state governors.

ROBERT LA FOLLETTE AND WISCONSIN PROGRESSIVISM

Nowhere did the progressives' campaign for social reform flourish as it did in Wisconsin. The movement arose first in the 1890s as citizens began to mobilize against the state's corrupt Republican Party. Then Robert La Follette emerged into prominence.

La Follette was born into a prosperous farming family in 1855. He entered politics as a Republican in the 1880s and embraced reform in the late 1890s. Elected governor in 1900, he secured for Wisconsin both a direct primary and a tax law that stripped the railroad corporations of tax exemptions they had long enjoyed. In 1905 he pushed through a civil service law mandating that every state employee had to meet a certain level of competence. A tireless campaigner and vigorous speaker, "Fighting Bob" won election to the U.S. Senate in 1906. Meanwhile, the growing strength of Wisconsin's labor and socialist movements persuaded progressive reformers to focus their legislative efforts on issues of corporate greed and social welfare. By 1910 reformers had passed state laws that regulated railroad and utility rates, instituted the nation's first state income tax, and provided workers with compensation for injuries, limitations on work hours, restrictions on child labor, and minimum wages for women.

Many of these laws were written by social scientists at the University of Wisconsin, with whom reformers had close ties. In the first decade of the 20th century, John R. Commons, a University of Wisconsin economist, drafted Wisconsin's civil service and public utilities laws. In 1911 Commons designed and won legislative approval for the Wisconsin Industrial Commission, which brought together employers, trade unionists, and professionals and gave them broad powers to investigate and regulate relations between industry and labor in the state. The intention was to treat the rights of labor with the same respect as the rights of industry and to shift policy-making initiative away from political parties and toward administrative agencies run by disinterested professionals.

The "Wisconsin idea" quickly spread to Ohio, Indiana, New York, and Colorado, and in 1913 the federal government established its own Industrial Relations Commission and hired Commons to direct its investigative staff. In other areas, too, reformers began urging state and federal governments to sidestep political parties by establishing government commissions.

PROGRESSIVE REFORM IN NEW YORK

New York was probably second to Wisconsin in the vigor and breadth of its progressive movement. As in Wisconsin, progressives in New York focused first on fighting political corruption. Revelations of close ties between leading Republican politicians and life insurance companies vaulted the reform lawyer Charles Evans Hughes into the governor's mansion in 1907. Hughes immediately established several public service commissions to regulate railroads and utility companies. As in Wisconsin, the growing strength of labor had an effect. Strikes by New York City's garment workers impelled state legislators to examine the condition of workers. With the establishment of the Factory Investigating Committee, New York, like Wisconsin, became a pioneer in labor and social welfare policy.

New York state legislators also were being pressured by middle-class reformers who had worked with the urban poor. This combined pressure from working-class and middle-class constituencies prompted some state Democrats to convert from machine to reform politics. While they opposed prohibition, city commissions, voter registration laws, and other reforms whose intent seemed anti-immigrant and anti-Catholic, they now supported a minimum wage, factory safety, workmen's compensation, the right of workers to join unions, and the regulation of corporations. Their participation in progressivism accelerated the movement's shift away from a preoccupation with political reform and toward questions of economic justice and social welfare.

QUICK REVIEW

ECONOMIC AND SOCIAL REFORM IN THE STATES

- Progressive alliances of middle-class reformers, working-class activists, and dynamic governors pioneered government regulation of the economy

- States regulated railroads and utilities, restricted child labor, and established state income tax, minimum wages, and workmen's compensation

- "Wisconsin idea" brought together employers, trade unionists, and professionals to solve industrial problems

- Modern civil rights movement was born with the founding of the NAACP in 1910

A RENEWED CAMPAIGN FOR CIVIL RIGHTS

As state legislators in New York and elsewhere were refocusing progressivism on economic and social issues, a new generation of African American activists began insisting that the issue of racial equality also be placed on the reform agenda.

THE FAILURE OF ACCOMMODATIONISM

In the 20th century's first decade, black activists increasingly criticized Booker T. Washington's message—that blacks should accept segregation and disfranchisement

FOCUS QUESTION
How did W. E. B. Du Bois's approach to reform for African Americans differ from that of Booker T. Washington?

HISTORY THROUGH FILM

THE GREAT WHITE HOPE (1970)

Directed by Martin Ritt; starring James Earl Jones (Jack Jefferson) and Jane Alexander (Eleanor Backman)

This movie is a fictional retelling of the life of Jack Johnson, the first black world heavyweight boxing champion, and of the furor that his dominance over white boxers, his outspokenness, and his relationships with white women generated in early-20th-century America. The movie opens with white boxing promoters persuading a former white champion (James Bradley) to come out of retirement to battle the black champion, here called Jack Jefferson (rather than Johnson). In a subsequent scene, Jefferson destroys Bradley in the ring and reacts with defiant cheeriness to the boos and racial epithets that rain down upon him from the predominantly white crowd.

James Earl Jones as Jack Jefferson.

© Picture Desk/Kobal Collection/20th Century Fox

Jefferson refuses to accept any of the limitations that white society placed on black men at the time. He is neither submissive nor deferential toward whites, and he openly dates white women. Whites fear and loathe him for defying the era's racial conventions. One evening, federal agents burst in on Jefferson and his white lover, Eleanor Backman (Jane Alexander), and accuse Jefferson of violating the Mann Act, a 1910 law that made it illegal to transport women across state lines for sexual purposes. At Jefferson's trial, prosecutors expected to convince a jury that Backman was coerced into sex, for no white woman, they intended to argue, would have freely chosen to consort with a black man in this way.

Jefferson manages to evade the authorities and flee to Europe, where Backman joins him. The early months abroad are invigorating for both, as Jefferson is celebrated for his fighting prowess and the couple's love for each other flourishes. Soon, however, the opponents dry up, money stops coming in, and a sense of despair grows between the two lovers. Their exile ends disastrously in Mexico, where Backman kills herself after an argument with Jefferson. Jefferson, his spirit finally broken, agrees to throw a fight against the newest Great White Hope, Jess Willard, in return for an opportunity to end his fugitive status and return to the United States.

Made in 1970, the *Great White Hope* was inspired by the brash heavyweight champion of the 1960s, Muhammad Ali. The film is quite faithful to the story of the real Jack Johnson, who dated white women, was arrested for "violating" the Mann Act, fled the country rather than submit to jail, and ultimately lost a heavyweight bout to Jess Willard. The film endows Backman, a fictional character, with more "class" and refinement than the real women who associated with Johnson usually possessed. The film also fictionalizes Johnson's fight against Willard by suggesting that Johnson could have won the fight had he not been required to throw it. Despite these changes, the film successfully recreates the climate of the early years of the 20th century and the white hostility imperiling a black man who dared to assert his pride and independence.

as unavoidable and focus their energies instead on self-help and self-improvement. Washington's accommodationist leadership (see Chapter 18), in their eyes, had brought blacks in the South no reprieve from racism. More than 100 blacks had been lynched in 1900 alone; between 1901 and 1914 at least 1,000 others would be hanged. Increasingly, rumors of black assaults on whites became pretexts for white mobs to rampage through black neighborhoods. In 1908 a mob in Springfield, Illinois, attacked black businesses and individuals; a force of 5,000 state militia was required to restore order. The troops were too late, however, to stop the lynching of two innocent black men.

Washington had long believed that blacks who educated themselves or who succeeded in business would be accepted as equals by whites and welcomed into their society. But, as Washington's critics observed, white rioters in Illinois made no distinction between rich blacks and poor, or between solid citizens and petty criminals. All that had seemed to matter was the color of one's skin.

The Granger Collection, New York

LYNCHING. *This grim photo records the death of five of the approximately 1,000 African Americans who were lynched between 1901 and 1914. The increase in lynching was one measure of the virulence of white racism in the early years of the 20th century.*

FROM THE NIAGARA MOVEMENT TO THE NAACP

Seeing no future in accommodation, **W. E. B. Du Bois** and other young activists, mostly black, came together at Niagara Falls in 1905 to demand full equality. They demanded that African Americans be given the right to vote; that segregation be abolished; and that barriers placed in the path of black advancement be removed. They declared their commitment to freedom of speech, the brotherhood of all peoples, and respect for the workingman.

The 1908 Springfield riot had shaken whites. Some, especially those already involved in social reform, now joined in common cause with the Niagara movement. A conference was planned for Lincoln's birthday in 1909 to revive, in the words of the writer William English Walling, "the spirit of the abolitionists" and to "treat the Negro on a plane of absolute political and social equality." The conference brought together distinguished progressives, black and white, who drew up plans to establish an organization dedicated to fighting racial discrimination and prejudice. In May 1910 the **National Association for the Advancement of Colored People** (NAACP) was officially launched, with Moorfield Storey of Boston as president, Walling as chairman of the executive committee, and Du Bois as the director of publicity and research.

The formation of the NAACP marked the beginning of the modern civil rights movement. The organization launched a magazine, *The Crisis,* edited by Du Bois, to publicize and protest lynchings, riots, and other abuses directed against blacks. Equally important was the Legal Redress Committee, which initiated lawsuits against city and state governments for violating the constitutional rights of African Americans. The committee scored its first major success in 1915, when the U.S. Supreme Court ruled that the so-called grandfather clauses of the Oklahoma and Maryland constitutions violated the Fifteenth Amendment. (These clauses allowed poor, uneducated whites—but not poor, uneducated blacks—to vote, even if they failed to pay their state's poll tax or to pass its literacy test, by exempting from those provisions the descendants of men who had voted prior to 1867.)

By 1914, the NAACP had enrolled thousands of members in scores of branches throughout the United States. The organization's success also stimulated the formation

W. E. B. Du Bois *Leader of the NAACP, the editor of its newspaper,* The Crisis, *and an outspoken critic of Booker T. Washington and his accommodationist approach to race relations.*

National Association for the Advancement of Colored People (NAACP) *Organization launched in 1910 to fight racial discrimination and prejudice and to promote civil rights for blacks.*

of other groups committed to black advancement. Thus, the National Urban League, founded in 1911, pressured urban employers to hire blacks, distributed lists of available jobs and housing in African American urban communities, and developed social programs to ease the adjustment of rural black migrants to city life.

Attacking segregation and discrimination through lawsuits was a slow strategy that would take decades to complete. The NAACP, although growing rapidly, was not large enough to qualify as a mass movement. And its interracial character made the organization seem dangerous to many whites. White NAACP leaders responded to this hostility by limiting the number and power of African American NAACP officials. This policy angered black militants, who argued that a civil rights organization should not be in the business of appeasing white racists. Despite such limitations, the early work of the NAACP was significant. The NAACP gave Du Bois the position he needed to criticize Booker T. Washington's accommodationism. Even before his death in 1915, Washington's influence in black and white communities had begun to recede. The NAACP, more than any other organization, was responsible for resurrecting the issue of racial equality at a time when most white Americans accepted racial segregation and discrimination as normal.

NATIONAL REFORM

FOCUS QUESTION

What were the key similarities and differences in the progressive politics of Theodore Roosevelt and Woodrow Wilson?

The more progressives focused on economic and social matters, the more they sought to increase their influence in national politics. Certain problems demanded national solutions. A patchwork of state regulations, for example, was not enough to curtail the power of the trusts, protect workers, or monitor the quality of consumer goods across America. Moreover, state and federal courts were often hostile toward progressive goals: They repeatedly struck down laws regulating working hours or setting minimum wages, on the grounds that they impinged on the freedom of contract and trade. With a national movement, progressives could force the passage of laws less vulnerable to judicial veto or elect a president who could overhaul the federal judiciary through the appointment of progressive-minded judges.

National leadership was not going to emerge from Congress. The Democratic Party was divided between the reform-Populist wing, led by William Jennings Bryan, and the conservatives who had gathered around Grover Cleveland in the 1890s. The Republican Party was more unified and popular, but it was controlled by a conservative "Old Guard" that was pro-business and devoted to old-style patronage.

National progressive leadership came from the executive rather than the legislative branch, and from two presidents in particular, the Republican Theodore Roosevelt and the Democrat Woodrow Wilson.

THE ROOSEVELT PRESIDENCY

As governor of New York, Roosevelt had shown himself to be a moderate reformer. But even his modest efforts to rid the state's Republican Party of corruption and to institute civil service reform were too much for the state party machine, led by Thomas C. Platt. Consigning Roosevelt to the vice presidency seemed like a safe solution. William McKinley was a young, vigorous politician, in control of his party and his presidency. Then in September 1901, less than a year into his second term, McKinley was shot by an anarchist assassin. The president clung to life for nine days and then died. Upon succeeding McKinley, Theodore Roosevelt, age 42, became the youngest chief executive in the nation's history. Born to an aristocratic New York family, Roosevelt nevertheless developed an uncommon affection for "the people." Asthmatic, sickly, and nearsighted as a boy, he remade himself into a vigorous adult. While Roosevelt indulged his appetite for high-risk adventure, he was also a voracious reader and an accomplished writer. Aggressive and swaggering in his public rhetoric, he was a skilled, patient negotiator in private. A believer in the superiority of his "English-speaking" race, he nevertheless appointed members of "inferior" races to important posts in his administration. Rarely has a president's personality so enthralled the American public.

REGULATING THE TRUSTS

It did not take long for Roosevelt to reveal his flair. In 1902 he ordered the Justice Department to prosecute the Northern Securities Company, a $400 million monopoly that had been set up by financiers and railroad tycoons to control the railroads between Chicago and Washington state. In 1903 a federal court ordered Northern Securities dissolved, and the U.S. Supreme Court upheld the decision the next year. Roosevelt was hailed as the nation's "trust-buster."

But Roosevelt did not want to break up all, or even most, large corporations. Industrial concentration, he believed, brought the United States wealth, productivity, and a rising standard of living. The role of government should be to regulate these industrial giants, to punish those that used their power improperly, and to protect citizens who were at a disadvantage in their dealings with industry. This new role would require the federal government to expand its powers. The *strengthening* of the federal government—not a return to small-scale industry—was the true aim of Roosevelt's antitrust campaign.

TOWARD A "SQUARE DEAL"

Roosevelt displayed his willingness to use government power to protect the economically weak in a bitter 1902 coal miners' strike. Miners in the anthracite fields of eastern Pennsylvania wanted recognition for their union, the United Mine Workers (UMW). They also wanted a 10 to 20 percent increase in wages and an eight-hour day. When their employers, led by George F. Baer of the Reading Railroad, refused to negotiate, they went on strike. In October, the fifth month of the strike, Roosevelt summoned the mine owners and John Mitchell, the UMW president, to the White House. Baer expected Roosevelt to threaten the striking workers with arrest by federal troops if they failed to return to work. Instead, Roosevelt supported Mitchell's request for arbitration and warned the mine owners that if they refused to go along, 10,000 federal troops would seize their property. Stunned, the mine owners agreed to submit the dispute to arbitrators, who awarded the unionists a 10 percent wage increase and a nine-hour day.

The mere fact that the federal government had ordered employers to compromise with their workers carried symbolic weight. Roosevelt enjoyed a surge of support from ordinary Americans convinced that he shared their dislike for ill-gotten wealth and privilege. He also raised the hopes of African Americans when, only a month into his presidency, he dined with Booker T. Washington at the White House.

In his 1904 election campaign, Roosevelt promised that, if reelected, he would offer every American a "square deal." The slogan resonated with voters and helped carry Roosevelt to a victory over the conservative Democrat nominee, Alton B. Parker. To the surprise of many observers, Roosevelt had aligned the Republican Party with the cause of reform.

EXPANDING GOVERNMENT POWER: THE ECONOMY

In 1905 Roosevelt intensified his efforts to extend government regulation of economic affairs. His most important proposal was to give the government power to set railroad shipping rates and thereby to eliminate the industry's discriminatory marketing practices. The government, in theory, already possessed this power through the Interstate Commerce Commission (ICC), a national regulatory body established by Congress in 1887. But the courts had so weakened ICC oversight as to render it virtually powerless. In 1906, Congress passed the Hepburn Act, which significantly increased the ICC's powers of rate review and enforcement. Roosevelt supported the Pure Food and Drug Act, passed by Congress that same year, which protected the public from fraudulently marketed foods and medications. He also campaigned for the Meat Inspection Act (1906), which committed the government to monitoring the quality and safety of meat being sold to American consumers.

EXPANDING GOVERNMENT POWER: THE ENVIRONMENT

Roosevelt also did more than any previous president to extend federal control over the nation's physical environment. Roosevelt viewed the wilderness as a place to live strenuously, to test oneself against nature, and to match wits against strong and clever game. Roosevelt further believed that in the Western landscape Americans could learn something important about their nation's destiny. To preserve this landscape, Roosevelt oversaw the creation of 5 new national parks, 16 national monuments, and 53 wildlife reserves. The work of his administration led directly to the formation of the National Park Service in 1916.

INDEX PEAK, YELLOWSTONE NATIONAL PARK, 1914. *An environmental movement emerged during the progressive era to protect beautiful areas of the American West such as those located in Yellowstone Park, the country's first national park. Thomas Moran painted this image of Index Peak.*

Roosevelt also emerged a supporter of **conservation.** Conservationists cared little for national parks or grand canyons. They wanted to ensure the most efficient use of the nation's resources for economic development. Conservationists believed that the plundering of Western timberlands, grazing areas, water resources, and minerals had reached crisis proportions. Only regulatory controls could conserve the West's economic potential.

To that end, Roosevelt appointed a Public Lands Commission in 1903 to survey public lands, inventory them, and establish permit systems to regulate their use. Soon after, the Departments of Interior and Agriculture decreed that certain Western lands rich in natural resources and waterpower could not be used for agricultural purposes. Government officials also limited waterpower development by requiring companies to acquire permits and then to pay fees for the right to generate electricity on their sites.

When political favoritism within the Departments of the Interior and Agriculture threatened these efforts at regulation, Roosevelt authorized the hiring of university-trained professionals to replace state and local politicians. Scientific expertise, rather than political connections, would now determine the distribution and use of Western lands. Gifford Pinchot, a specialist in forestry management, led the drive for scientific management of natural resources. In 1905 he persuaded Roosevelt to relocate jurisdiction for the national forests from the Department of the Interior to the Department of Agriculture. The newly created National Forest Service quickly instituted a system of competitive bidding for the right to harvest timber on national forest lands. Pinchot and his expanding staff of college-educated foresters also exacted user fees from ranchers who had previously used national forest grazing lands for free. Armed with new legislation and bureaucratic authority, Pinchot and fellow conservationists in the Roosevelt administration declared vast stretches of federal land in the West off-limits to mining and dam construction.

The Old Guard in the Republican Party did not take kindly to these initiatives. When Roosevelt recommended the prosecution of cattlemen and lumbermen who were using federal land illegally, congressional conservatives struck back with legislation (in 1907) that curtailed the president's power to create new government land reserves. Roosevelt responded by seizing another 17 million acres for national forest reserves before the new law went into effect. To his opponents, excluding commercial activity from public land was bad enough. But flouting the will of Congress with a 17-million acre land grab was a violation of constitutional principles governing the separation of powers. Yet Roosevelt's willingness to defy cattle barons, mining tycoons, and other "malefactors of great wealth" added to his popularity.

PROGRESSIVISM: A MOVEMENT FOR THE PEOPLE?

Historians have long debated how much Roosevelt's economic and environmental reforms altered the balance of power between the "interests" and the people. Some have demonstrated that many corporations were eager for federal government regulation—that railroad corporations wanted relief from price wars that were driving them to bankruptcy, for example, and that the larger meatpackers believed that the costs of government food inspections would drive smaller meatpackers out of business. So, too, historians have shown that large agribusinesses, timber companies, and mining corporations in the West believed that government regulation would aid them and hurt smaller competitors. According to this view, government regulation benefited the corporations more than it benefited workers, consumers, and small businessmen.

conservation *Movement that called for managing the environment to ensure the careful and efficient use of nation's natural resources.*

This view has some validity. These early reforms did not go far enough in curtailing corporate power. Corporations fought with some success to turn the final versions of the reform laws to their advantage. But in 1907 the progressive program was still evolving. Popular anger over the power of the corporations and over political corruption remained a driving force. The presence in the Senate of La Follette, Albert Beveridge of Indiana, and other anticorporate Republicans gave that anger a national voice. Before he left office in 1909, Roosevelt would expand his reform program to include income and inheritance taxes, a national workmen's compensation law, abolition of child labor, and the eight-hour work-day. Whether the corporations or the people would benefit most remained unclear.

THE REPUBLICANS: A DIVIDED PARTY

Roosevelt's reforms increased the rift between him and the Old Guard. The financial panic of 1907 widened it further. A failed speculative effort by several New York banks to corner the copper market triggered a run on banks, a severe dip in industrial production, and widespread layoffs. Everywhere, people worried that a devastating depression was in the offing. Indeed, the timely decision of J. P. Morgan and his fellow bankers to pour huge amounts of private cash into the collapsing banks may have saved the day. Prosperity quickly returned, but the jitters caused by the panic lingered. Conservatives blamed Roosevelt's "radical" economic policies for the fiasco. To Roosevelt and his fellow progressives, however, the panic merely pointed up how little impact their reforms had actually made on the reign of "speculation, corruption, and fraud." Roosevelt now committed himself even more strongly to a reform agenda that included an overhaul of the banking system and the stock market. The Republican Old Guard, meanwhile, was more determined than ever to run the "radical" Roosevelt out of the White House. Sensing that he might fail to win his party's nomination, and mindful of a rash promise he had made in 1904 not to run again in 1908, Roosevelt decided not to seek reelection. It was a decision that he would soon regret. Barely 50, he was too young and energetic to end his political career. And much of his reform program had yet to win congressional approval.

THE TAFT PRESIDENCY

Roosevelt thought he had found in **William Howard Taft**, his secretary of war, an ideal successor. Taft had worked closely with Roosevelt on foreign and domestic policies. Roosevelt believed he possessed both the ideas and the skills to complete the reform Republican program.

To reach that conclusion, however, Roosevelt had to ignore some obvious differences between Taft and himself. Taft was not particularly adept at politics. With the exception of a judgeship in an Ohio superior court, he had never held elective office. He was by nature a cautious and conservative man. As Roosevelt's anointed successor, Taft won the election of 1908, defeating the Democrat William Jennings Bryan with 52 percent of the vote. But his conservatism soon revealed itself in his choice of corporation lawyers, rather than reformers, for cabinet positions.

William Howard Taft

Roosevelt's successor as president (1909–1913) who tried but failed to mediate between reformers and conservatives in the Republican Party.

BATTLING CONGRESS

Taft's troubles began when he appeared to side against progressives in a congressional battle over tariff legislation. Progressives had long desired tariff reduction, believing that it would make foreign goods competitive in America and thereby lower prices on consumer goods. Taft himself had raised expectations for tariff reduction when he called Congress into special session to consider a reform bill that called for a modest reduction of tariffs and for an inheritance tax. The bill passed the House but was gutted in the Senate. When congressional progressives pleaded with Taft to use his power to whip conservative senators into line, he pressured the Old Guard into including a 2 percent corporate income tax in their version of the bill, but he did not insist on tariff reductions. As a result, the Payne-Aldrich Tariff he signed into law on August 5, 1909, did nothing to encourage foreign imports. Progressive Republicans, bitterly disappointed, held Taft responsible.

They were further angered when Taft refused to support their efforts to curtail the powers of Speaker of the House Joe Cannon. By 1910 Republican insurgents had entered into an alliance with reform-minded congressional Democrats. Relations between Taft and the progressive Republicans then all but collapsed in a bruising controversy over Taft's conservation policies.

THE BALLINGER-PINCHOT CONTROVERSY

Richard A. Ballinger, secretary of the interior, had aroused progressives' suspicions by reopening for private commercial use 1 million acres of land that the Roosevelt administration had previously brought under federal protection. Then, Gifford Pinchot, still head of the National Forest Service, obtained information implicating Ballinger in the sale of Alaskan coal deposits. Pinchot showed the information, including an allegation that Ballinger had personally profited from the sale, to Taft. Taft defended Ballinger. Pinchot went public with his charges and a congressional investigation ensued. Whatever hope Taft may have had of escaping political damage disappeared when Roosevelt, returning from an African hunting trip by way of Europe in the spring of 1910, staged a public rendezvous with Pinchot in England. In signaling his support for his old friend Pinchot, Roosevelt was expressing displeasure with Taft.

ROOSEVELT'S RETURN

Roosevelt returned to the United States that summer. His craving for the public eye and his conviction that the reform insurgency needed his leadership prompted him to abandon his retirement. In September, Roosevelt embarked on a speaking tour, the high point of which was his elaboration at Osawatomie, Kansas, of his **New Nationalism**, a reform program that called for a strong federal government to stabilize the economy, protect the weak, and restore social harmony.

The 1910 congressional elections confirmed the popularity of Roosevelt's positions. Insurgent Republicans trounced conservative Republicans in primary after primary, and the embrace of reform by the Democrats brought them a majority in the House of Representatives. In 1912, Roosevelt announced that he would challenge Taft for the Republican presidential nomination. In the 13 states sponsoring preferential

New Nationalism *Roosevelt's reform program between 1910 and 1912, which called for establishing a strong federal government to regulate corporations, stabilize the economy, protect the weak, and restore social harmony.*

Library of Congress Prints and Photographs Division [LC-US262-20570]

WOODROW WILSON. *Wilson entered politics after a long career in academia, where he had been a distinguished political scientist, historian, and university president. Here he sits for a full-length portrait soon after his election to the presidency.*

primaries, Roosevelt won nearly 75 percent of the delegates. But the party's national leadership remained in the hands of the Old Guard, and they were determined to deny Roosevelt the Republican nomination. At the Republican convention in Chicago, Taft won renomination on the first ballot.

THE BULL MOOSE CAMPAIGN

Roosevelt had expected this outcome. The night before the convention opened, he had told an assembly of 5,000 supporters that the party leaders would not succeed in derailing their movement. The next day, Roosevelt and his supporters withdrew from the convention and from the Republican Party. The reformers soon reassembled as the new **Progressive Party,** nominated Roosevelt for president and California governor Hiram W. Johnson for vice president, and hammered out this reform platform: sweeping regulation of the corporations, extensive protections for workers, a sharply graduated income tax, and woman suffrage. "I am as strong as a bull moose," Roosevelt roared to his supporters; his proud followers took to calling themselves **Bull Moosers**.

Some of them, however, probably including Roosevelt himself, knew that their mission was futile. They had failed to enroll many of the Republican insurgents who had supported Roosevelt in the primaries but who now refused to abandon the GOP. Consequently, the Republican vote would be split between Roosevelt and Taft, making them both vulnerable to the Democrats' candidate, Woodrow Wilson.

THE RISE OF WOODROW WILSON

Progressive Party *Political party formed by Theodore Roosevelt in 1912 when the Republicans refused to nominate him for president. The party adopted a sweeping reform program.*

Bull Moosers *Followers of Theodore Roosevelt in the 1912 election.*

Few would have predicted in 1908 that the president of Princeton University, Woodrow Wilson, would be the 1912 Democratic nominee for president of the United States. The son of a Presbyterian minister from Virginia, Wilson had practiced law for a short time after graduating from Princeton before settling on an academic career. Earning his doctorate in political science from Johns Hopkins in 1886, he taught history and political science at Bryn Mawr and Wesleyan (Connecticut) before returning to Princeton in 1890. He became president of Princeton in 1902, a post he held until he ran for the governorship of New Jersey in 1910.

Identifying himself with the anti-Bryan wing of the Democratic Party, Wilson attracted the attention of wealthy conservatives. They convinced the bosses of the New Jersey Democratic machine to nominate Wilson for governor in 1910. Wilson accepted the nomination and won the governorship handily. He then shocked his conservative backers by declaring his independence from the state's Democratic machine and moving New Jersey into the forefront of reform. Wilson's Presbyterian upbringing had instilled in him a sense that society should be governed by God's moral law. As a young man, he had come to believe that the social consequences of unregulated industrialization were repugnant to Christian ethical principles. While this belief had receded during his tenure as Princeton University president, it had not disappeared. Its presence in his conscience helped to explain his emergence in 1911 and 1912 as an outspoken progressive.

THE ELECTION OF 1912

At the Democratic convention of 1912, Wilson was something of a dark horse, running a distant second to House Speaker Champ Clark of Missouri. When the New York delegation gave Clark a simple majority of delegates, virtually everyone assumed that he would soon command the two-thirds majority needed to win the nomination. But Wilson's managers held onto Wilson's delegates and began chipping away at Clark's lead. On the fourth day and the 46th ballot, Wilson finally won the nomination. The exhausted Democrats then closed ranks behind their candidate.

Given the split in Republican ranks, Democrats had their best chance in 20 years of regaining the White House. A Wilson victory, moreover, would give the country its first Southern-born president in almost 50 years. Finally, whatever its outcome, the election promised to deliver a hefty vote for reform. Both Roosevelt and Wilson were running on reform platforms, and the Socialist Party candidate, Eugene V. Debs, was attracting large crowds and enthusiasm.

Debate among the candidates focused on the trusts. All three reform candidates agreed that corporations had acquired too much economic power. Debs argued that the only way to ensure popular control of that power was for the federal government to assume ownership of the trusts. Roosevelt called for the establishment of a strong government that would regulate and, if necessary, curb the power of the trusts. This was the essence of his New Nationalism, the program he had been advocating since 1910.

Rather than regulate the trusts, Wilson wanted to break them up. He wanted to reverse the tendency toward economic concentration and thus restore opportunity to the people. This philosophy, which Wilson labeled the **New Freedom,** called for a temporary concentration of governmental power in order to dismantle the trusts. But once that was accomplished, Wilson promised, the government would relinquish its power.

Wilson won the November election with 42 percent of the popular vote to Roosevelt's 27 percent and Taft's 23 percent; Debs garnered 6 percent, the largest in his party's history. The three candidates who had pledged themselves to reform programs—Wilson, Roosevelt, and Debs—together won a remarkable 75 percent of the vote (see Map 21.3).

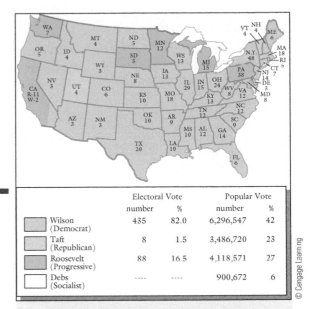

	Electoral Vote		Popular Vote	
	number	%	number	%
Wilson (Democrat)	435	82.0	6,296,547	42
Taft (Republican)	8	1.5	3,486,720	23
Roosevelt (Progressive)	88	16.5	4,118,571	27
Debs (Socialist)	----	----	900,672	6

Map 21.3 **PRESIDENTIAL ELECTION, 1912.** *Taft and Roosevelt split the Republican vote, allowing Wilson to win with a plurality of the popular vote (42 percent) and a big majority (82 percent) of the electoral vote.*

New Freedom *Wilson's reform program of 1912 that called for temporarily concentrating government power so as to dismantle the trusts and return America to 19th-century conditions of competitive capitalism.*

THE WILSON PRESIDENCY

Wilson assembled a cabinet of talented men who could be counted on for wise counsel, loyalty, and influence over key Democratic constituencies. He cultivated a public image of himself as a president firmly in charge of his party and as a faithful tribune of the people.

Federal Reserve Act *Act that brought private banks and public authority together to regulate and strengthen the nation's financial system.*

TARIFF REFORM AND A PROGRESSIVE INCOME TAX

Like his predecessor, Wilson first turned his attention to tariff reform. The House passed a tariff reduction bill within a month, and Wilson used his leadership skills to push the bill through a reluctant Senate. The resulting Underwood-Simmons Tariff of 1913 reduced tariff barriers from approximately 40 to 25 percent. To make up for revenue lost to tariff reduction, Congress then passed the first income tax law. It required the wealthy to pay taxes on a greater *percentage* of their income than the poor.

THE FEDERAL RESERVE ACT

Wilson then asked Congress to overhaul the nation's financial system. Virtually everyone in both parties agreed on the need for greater federal regulation of banks and currency, but there were sharp differences over how to proceed. The banking interests and their congressional supporters wanted the government to give the authority to regulate credit and currency flows either to a single bank or to several regional banks. Progressives opposed the vesting of so much financial power in private hands and insisted that any reformed financial system must be publicly controlled. Wilson worked out a compromise plan that included both private and public controls and marshaled the votes to push it through the House and the Senate. By the end of 1913 Wilson had signed the **Federal Reserve Act**, the most important law passed in his first administration.

The Federal Reserve Act established 12 regional banks, each controlled by the private banks in its region. Every private bank in the country was required to deposit an average of 6 percent of its assets in its regional Federal Reserve bank. The reserve would be used to make loans to member banks and to issue paper currency (Federal Reserve notes) to facilitate financial transactions. The regional banks were also instructed to use their funds to shore up member banks in distress and to respond to sudden changes in credit demands by easing or tightening the flow of credit. A Federal Reserve Board appointed by the president and responsible to the public rather than to private bankers would set policy and oversee activities within the 12 reserve banks.

The Federal Reserve system strengthened the nation's financial structure and was in most respects an impressive political achievement. In its final form, however, it revealed that Wilson was retreating from his New Freedom pledge. The Federal Reserve Board was a less powerful and less centralized federal authority than a national bank would have been, but it nevertheless represented a substantial increase in government control of banking. Moreover, the bill authorizing the system made no attempt to break up private financial institutions that had grown too powerful. Because it sought to work with large banks rather than to break them up, the Federal Reserve system seemed more consonant with the principles of Roosevelt's New Nationalism than with those of Wilson's New Freedom.

FROM THE NEW FREEDOM TO THE NEW NATIONALISM

Wilson's failure to mount a vigorous antitrust campaign confirmed his drift toward a New Nationalism program. For example, in 1914 Wilson supported the Federal Trade Commission Act, which created a government agency by that name to regulate business practices.

GROWTH IN FEDERAL EMPLOYMENT, 1891–1917
Source: Reprinted by permission from *The Federal Government Service*, ed. W. S. Sayre (Englewood Cliffs, NJ: Prentice-Hall, 1965), p. 41

The FTC might have been used to prosecute trusts for "unfair trade practices." But the Senate stripped the FTC Act's companion legislation, the Clayton Antitrust Act, of virtually all provisions that would have allowed vigorous government prosecution of the trusts. Wilson supported this weakening of the Clayton Act, having decided that the breakup of large-scale industry was no longer practical or preferable. The purpose of the FTC, in Wilson's eyes, was to help businesses, large and small, to regulate themselves in ways that contributed to national well-being. In accepting the existing structure of business and in seeking to regulate its behavior, Wilson had become, in effect, a New Nationalist.

At first, his New Nationalism led him to support business interests. But in late 1915 Wilson moved to the left, in part because he feared losing his reelection in 1916. The Bull Moosers of 1912 were retreating back to the Republican Party. To halt the progressives' rapprochement with the GOP, Wilson bid for their support by nominating Louis Brandeis to the Supreme Court. Not only was Brandeis a respected progressive, he was also the first Jew nominated to serve on the country's highest court. Congressional conservatives did everything they could to block his confirmation. But Wilson was better organized, and by June his forces in the Senate had emerged victorious. Wilson followed up this victory by pushing through Congress the first federal workmen's compensation law (the Kern-McGillicuddy Act, which covered federal employees), the first federal law outlawing child labor (the Keating-Owen Act), and the first federal law guaranteeing workers an eight-hour day (the Adamson Act, which covered the nation's 400,000 railway workers). The number of Americans affected by these acts was in fact rather small; nevertheless, Wilson had reoriented the Democratic Party to a New Nationalism that cared as much about the interests of the powerless as the interests of the powerful.

Trade unionists flocked to Wilson, as did most of the prominent progressives who had followed the Bull Moose in 1912. Meanwhile, Wilson had appealed to the supporters of William Jennings Bryan by supporting legislation that made federal credit available to farmers in need. He had put together a reform coalition capable of winning a majority at the polls. From 1916 on, the Democrats, rather than the Republicans, became the chief guardians of America's reform tradition.

By 1916 the ranks of middle-class progressives had swelled. Working-class protest had also accelerated in scope and intensity. In Lawrence, Massachusetts, in 1912, and in Paterson, New Jersey, in 1913, for example, the IWW organized strikes of textile workers that drew national attention, as did the 1914 strike by Colorado mine workers that ended with the infamous Ludlow massacre (see Chapter 20). These protests revealed the growing influence of working-class constituencies—immigrants, women, the unskilled—long considered inconsequential both to American labor and party politics. Assisted by radicals, these groups had begun to fashion a more inclusive and politically demanding labor movement.

QUICK   REVIEW

WILSON'S EFFORTS AT NATIONAL REFORM

- Claimed he would break up corporate trusts ("New Freedom"), but ended up similar to Roosevelt in his efforts to regulate them

- Most important laws overhauled financial system, reduced tariffs, instituted national income tax, and offered some groups of workers protection at workplace

- Appointed Louis Brandeis to Supreme Court

C O N C L U S I O N

By 1916, the progressives had accomplished a great deal. They exposed and curbed some of the worst abuses of the American political system. They enfranchised women and took steps to protect the environment. They broke the hold of laissez-faire economic policies on national politics and replaced it with the idea of a strong federal government committed to economic regulation and social justice. They enlarged the executive branch by establishing new commissions and agencies charged with administering government policies. The progressives, in short, had presided over the emergence of a new national state, one in which power increasingly flowed away from municipalities and states and toward the federal government. There was a compelling logic to this reorientation: A national government stood a better chance of solving the problems of economic inequality, mismanagement of natural resources, and consumer fraud than did local and state governments. The promise of effective remedies, however, brought new dangers. In particular, the new national state gave rise to a bureaucratic elite. The university-educated experts who staffed the new federal agencies, progressives argued, would bring to the political process the very qualities that party politicians allegedly lacked: knowledge, dedication, and honesty. But many of these new public servants were not entirely disinterested. Some had ties to the businesses they were expected to regulate. Some allowed personal prejudices against women, immigrants, and minorities to shape government policy. Some believed that "the people" could not be trusted. For these reasons, the progressive state did not always enhance democracy or secure the people's sovereignty.

QUESTIONS FOR REVIEW AND CRITICAL THINKING

Review

1. Which groups of Americans spearheaded the progressive movement?
2. How did progressive reformers hope to create a "responsible" or "virtuous" electorate? What were the consequences of their reforms?
3. How did W. E. B. Du Bois's approach to reform for African Americans differ from that of Booker T. Washington?
4. What were the key similarities and differences in the progressive politics of Theodore Roosevelt and Woodrow Wilson?

Critical Thinking

1. Progressivism sought to reform all of American society—its politics, its economy, and culture. What were the most important reforms in each of these realms? Were these reforms successful in achieving their aims?
2. When the Progressive reform movement peaked during the first Wilson administration (1913–1917), did it bring Americans greater liberty and equality than they had known in 1900?

ONLINE RESOURCES

 Visit the companion website to access flashcards, crossword puzzles, exercises, and quizzes related to this chapter: www.cengage.com/history/murrin/libertyequalconc5e.

 See our interactive ebook for map and primary source activities.

ISCOVERY

Was progressivism successful in reforming politics and culture in America?

GOVERNMENT AND LAW Examine the graph on voter participation. Compare the percentage of voter participation in 1876 to that of 1912, noting the significant decrease. What factors account for the drop over these elections? Why did the greatest decline in voting occur in the Southern states? Is this decline in voting attributable to changes wrought by the progressive movement, or is it more the result of resistance to progressivism?

In thinking about this question, begin by breaking it down into the components shown below. A discussion of the significance of each component should appear in your answer.

CULTURE AND SOCIETY Study the table on women and higher education on page 555. How did women's activism and education help them achieve electoral power? What role did women like Jane Addams (page 556) play in both the progressive and women's movements? Did women achieve significant, long-lasting reforms? What reforms did they consider the most important? What methods did they use to achieve them? Have women today achieved all that the progressive reformers hoped to achieve?

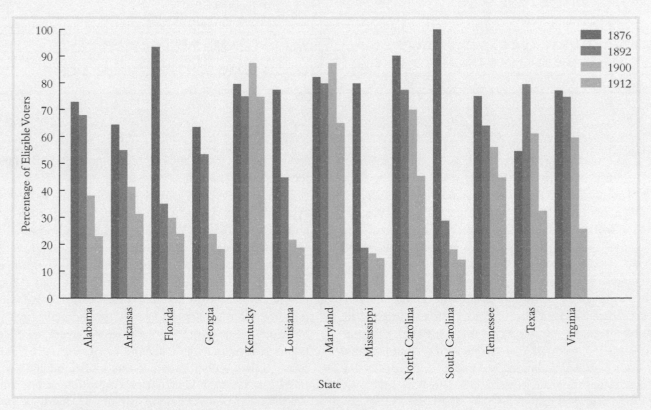

VOTER PARTICIPATION IN 13 SOUTHERN STATES, 1876, 1892, 1900, 1912

22

BECOMING A WORLD POWER, 1898–1917

For much of the 19th century most Americans were preoccupied by continental expansion. Elections rarely turned on international events, and presidents rarely made their reputations as statesmen in the world arena. The diplomatic corps was small and inexperienced. The government projected its limited military power westward and possessed virtually no capacity or desire for involvement overseas.

The nation's rapid industrial growth in the late 19th century forced a turn away from such continentalism. Technological advances, especially the laying of transoceanic cables and the introduction of steamship travel, diminished America's physical isolation. The babel of languages one could hear in American cities testified to how much the Old World had penetrated the New. Then, too, Americans watched anxiously as England, Germany, Russia, Japan, and other industrial powers intensified their competition for overseas markets and colonies. Some believed America too needed to enter this contest.

War with Spain in 1898 gave the United States an opportunity to upgrade its military and acquire colonies and influence in the Western Hemisphere and Asia. But subjugating the peoples of Cuba, Puerto Rico, and the Philippines did not sit well with all Americans. It seemed as though the United States was becoming the kind of nation that many Americans had long despised—one that valued power more than liberty. Exercising imperial power did not trouble Roosevelt, who wanted to create an international system in which a handful of industrial nations pursued their global economic interests, dominated world trade, and kept the world at peace. It did concern Woodrow Wilson, however, who sought to devise a policy toward postrevolutionary Mexico that restrained American might and respected Mexican desires for liberty.

TIMELINE

1892	1896	1900	1904	1908	1912	1916	1920

■ **1893**
Frederick Jackson Turner publishes an essay announcing the end of the frontier

■ **1898**
Spanish-American War (April 14–August 12)
• U.S. takes control of Philippines, Guam, and Puerto Rico and annexes Hawaii

1899–1902
American-Filipino War

■ **1899–1900**
U.S. pursues "Open Door" policy toward China

■ **1900**
U.S. annexes Puerto Rico • Boxer Rebellion

■ **1901**
Cuba adopts constitution favorable to U.S. interests

1904 ■
"Roosevelt corollary" to Monroe Doctrine proclaimed

1904–1914
U.S. builds Panama Canal

■ **1905**
Roosevelt negotiates end to Russo-Japanese War

1906–1917
U.S. intervenes in Cuba, Nicaragua, Haiti,
Dominican Republic, and Mexico

■ **1907**
"Gentlemen's agreement" restricts Japanese immigration to U.S. and
ends discrimination against Japanese schoolchildren in California

1907–1909
Great White Fleet circles the earth

1909–1913
William Howard Taft conducts "dollar diplomacy"

THE UNITED STATES LOOKS ABROAD

By the late 19th century many Americans had become interested in extending their country's influence abroad. The most important groups were Protestant missionaries, businessmen, and imperialists.

PROTESTANT MISSIONARIES

Protestant missionaries were among the most active promoters of American interests abroad. Overseas missionary activity grew quickly between 1870 and 1900, most of it directed toward China. Convinced of the superiority of the Anglo-Saxon race, Protestant missionaries considered it their Christian duty to teach the gospel to the "ignorant" Asian masses and save their souls. Missionaries also believed that their efforts would free those masses from their racial destiny, enabling them to become "civilized."

BUSINESSMEN

For different reasons, industrialists, traders, and investors also began to look overseas, sensing that they could make fortunes in foreign lands. Exports of American manufactured goods rose substantially after 1880. By 1914 American foreign investment equaled 7 percent of the nation's gross national product. Companies such as Kodak Camera, Singer Sewing Machine, Standard Oil, American Tobacco, and International Harvester had become multinational corporations with overseas branch offices.

Some industrialists became intrigued by the prospect of clothing, feeding, and housing China's 400 million people. James B. Duke, who headed American Tobacco, was selling 1 billion cigarettes a year in East Asian markets. Looking for ways to fill empty boxcars heading west from Minnesota to Tacoma, Washington, the railroad tycoon James J. Hill imagined stuffing them with wheat and steel destined for China and Japan. Although export trade with East Asia during this period never fulfilled the expectations of Hill and other industrialists, their talk about the "wealth of the Orient" convinced politicians of its importance to American economic health.

Events of the 1890s only intensified the appeal of foreign markets. First, the 1890 U.S. census announced that the frontier had disappeared; America had completed the task of westward expansion. Then, in 1893 a young historian named Frederick Jackson Turner published an essay, "The Significance of the Frontier in American History," that articulated what many Americans feared: that the frontier had been essential to the growth of the economy and to the cultivation of democracy. It was

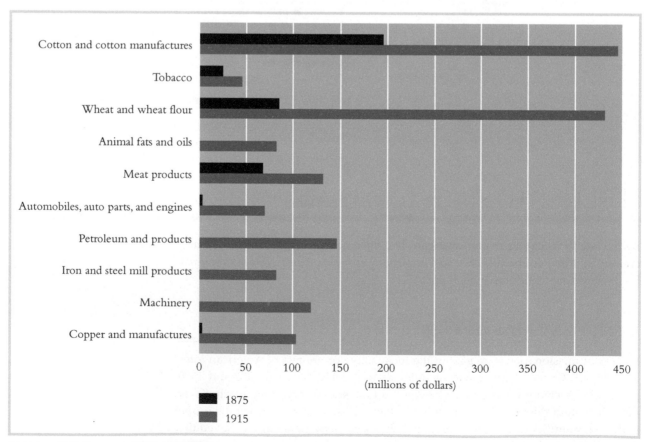

LEADING U.S. EXPORTS, 1875 AND 1915
Source: Data from *Historical Statistics of the United States, Colonial Times to 1970* (White Plains, N.Y.: Kraus International, 1989).

the wilderness, Turner argued, that had transformed the Europeans who settled the New World into Americans. They shed their European clothes, tools, social customs, and political beliefs and acquired distinctively "American" characteristics: rugged individualism, egalitarianism, and a democratic faith. How, Turner wondered, could the nation continue to prosper now that the frontier had gone?

In recent years, historians of the American West have criticized **Turner's "frontier thesis."** They have argued that the very idea of the frontier as uninhabited wilderness overlooked the tens of thousands of Indians who occupied the region and that much else of what Americans believe about the West is based more on myth than on reality.

Even though these points are valid, they would have meant little to Americans living in Turner's time. For them, as for Turner, concern about the disappearing frontier expressed a fear that the increasingly urbanized and industrialized nation had lost its way. Turner's essay appeared just as the country was entering the deepest, longest, and most conflict-ridden depression in its history (see Chapter 19). What could the republic do to regain its economic prosperity and political stability? Where would it find its new frontiers? One answer to these questions focused on overseas markets.

Turner's "frontier thesis *Theory developed by historian Frederick Jackson Turner, who argued that the frontier had been central to the shaping of American character and the success of the U.S. economy and democracy.*

IMPERIALISTS

A group of politicians, intellectuals, and military strategists viewed overseas economic expansion as a key ingredient in the pursuit of world power. They believed that the United States should build a strong navy, solidify a sphere of influence in the Caribbean, and extend markets into Asia. Their desire to control ports and territories beyond the continental borders of their own country made them imperialists. Many of them were also Social Darwinists, who believed that America's destiny required that it prove itself supreme in international affairs.

Perhaps the most influential imperialist was Admiral Alfred Thayer Mahan. In a widely read book, *The Influence of Sea Power upon History, 1660–1783* (1890), Mahan argued that all past empires, beginning with Rome, had relied on their capacity to control the seas. He called for the construction of a U.S. navy with enough ships and firepower to make its presence felt everywhere in the world. To be effective, that global fleet would require a canal across Central America. It would also require

TABLE 22.1

THE U.S. NAVY, 1890–1914: EXPENDITURES AND BATTLESHIP SIZE				
Fiscal Year	Total Federal Expenditures	Naval Expenditures	Naval Expenditures as Percent of Total Federal Expenditures	Size of Battleships (average tons displaced)
1890	$318,040,711	$22,006,206	6.9%	11,000
1900	520,860,847	55,953,078	10.7	12,000
1901	524,616,925	60,506,978	11.5	16,000
1905	657,278,914	117,550,308	20.7	16,000
1909	693,743,885	115,546,011	16.7	27,000 (1910)
1914	735,081,431	139,682,186	19.0	32,000

Sources: (for expenditures) E. B. Potter, *Sea Power: A Naval History* (Annapolis: Naval Institute Press, 1982), p. 187; (for size of ships) Harold Sprout, *Toward a New Order of Sea Power* (New York: Greenwood Press, 1976), p. 52.

a string of far-flung service bases. Mahan recommended that the U.S. government take possession of Hawaii and other strategically located Pacific islands with superior harbor facilities.

Presidents William McKinley and Theodore Roosevelt would eventually make almost the whole of Mahan's vision a reality. But in the early 1890s Mahan doubted that Americans would accept the responsibility and costs of empire. Many Americans still insisted that the United States should not aspire to world power by acquiring overseas bases and colonizing foreign peoples.

Mahan underestimated the government's alarm over the scramble of Europeans to expand their empires. Every administration from the 1880s on committed itself to a "big navy" policy. Already in 1878 the United States had secured rights to Pago Pago, a superb deep-water harbor in Samoa (a collection of islands in the southwest Pacific inhabited by Polynesians), and in 1885 it had leased Pearl Harbor from the Hawaiians. Both harbors were expected to serve as fueling stations for the growing U.S. fleet. These attempts to project U.S. power overseas had already deepened the U.S. government's involvement in the affairs of distant lands. In 1889 the United States established a protectorate over part of Samoa. In the early 1890s President Grover Cleveland's administration was increasingly drawn into Hawaiian affairs, as tensions between American sugar plantation owners and native Hawaiians upset the islands' economic and political stability. In 1891 plantation owners managed to depose the Hawaiian king and put into power Queen Liliuokalani. When Liliuokalani strove to establish her independence, the planters, assisted by U.S. sailors, overthrew her too. Cleveland declared Hawaii a protectorate in 1893, but he resisted the imperialists in Congress who wanted to annex the islands.

By this time, imperialist sentiment in Congress and throughout the nation was being fueled by "jingoism." Jingoists were nationalists who thought that a swaggering foreign policy and a willingness to go to war would enhance their nation's glory. This predatory brand of nationalism emerged not only in the United States but in Britain, France, Germany, and Japan as well. The anti-imperialist editor of *The Nation*, E. L. Godkin, exclaimed in 1894: "The number of men and officials of this country who are now mad to fight somebody is appalling." Spain's behavior in Cuba in the 1890s gave those men and officials the war they sought.

THE SPANISH-AMERICAN WAR

FOCUS   QUESTION

In going to war against Spain in 1898, was the United States impelled more by imperialist or anti-imperialist motives?

Relations between the Cubans and their Spanish rulers had long been deteriorating. A revolt in 1868 had taken the Spanish 10 years to subdue. In 1895 the Cubans staged another revolt. The fighting was brutal. Cuban forces destroyed large areas of the island to render it uninhabitable by the Spanish. The Spanish army, led by General Valeriano Weyler, responded in kind, forcing large numbers of Cubans into concentration camps. Denied adequate food, shelter, and sanitation, an estimated 200,000 Cubans died of starvation and disease.

Such tactics inflamed U.S. public opinion. Many Americans sympathized with the Cubans. Americans were kept well informed about Spanish misdeeds by accounts in the *New York Journal*, owned by William Randolph Hearst, and the *New York World*, owned by Joseph Pulitzer. Hearst and Pulitzer were transforming newspaper publishing in much the same way that other publishers had revolutionized the magazine business (see Chapter 21). To boost circulation they sought out sensational and shocking stories and then described them in lurid detail. They were accused of engaging in **yellow journalism**, embellishing stories with titillating details when the true reports did not seem dramatic enough.

The sensationalism of the yellow press and its frequently jingoistic accounts were not sufficient to bring about American intervention in Cuba, however. In the final days of his administration, President Cleveland resisted mounting pressure to intervene. William McKinley, who succeeded him in 1897, harshly denounced the Spanish, with the aim of forcing Spain into concessions that would satisfy the Cuban rebels and bring an end to the conflict. Initially, this strategy seemed to be working: Spain relieved "Butcher" Weyler of his command, stopped incarcerating Cubans in concentration camps, and granted Cuba limited autonomy. But the Spaniards who lived on the island refused to be ruled by a Cuban government, and the Cuban rebels continued to demand full independence. Late in 1897, when riots broke out in Havana, McKinley ordered the battleship *Maine* into Havana harbor to protect U.S. citizens and their property. Two unexpected events then set off a war. The first was the February 9, 1898, publication in Hearst's *New York Journal* of a letter stolen from Depuy de Lôme, the Spanish minister to Washington, in which he described McKinley as "a cheap politician" and a "bidder for the admiration of the crowd." The de Lôme letter also implied that the Spanish were not serious about resolving the Cuban crisis through negotiation and reform. The news embarrassed Spanish officials and outraged the United States. Then, only six days later, the *Maine* exploded in Havana harbor, killing 260 American sailors. Although subsequent investigations revealed that the most probable cause of the explosion was a malfunctioning boiler, Americans were certain that it had been the work of Spanish agents. "Remember the Maine!" screamed the headlines in the yellow press. On March 8, Congress responded to the clamor for war by authorizing $50 million to mobilize U.S. forces. In the meantime, McKinley notified Spain of his conditions for avoiding war: Spain would pay an indemnity for the *Maine,* abandon its concentration camps, end the fighting with the rebels, and commit itself to Cuban independence. On April 9, Spain accepted all the demands but the last. Nevertheless, on April 11, McKinley asked Congress for authority to go to war. Three days later Congress approved a war resolution, which included a declaration (spelled out in the Teller Amendment) that the United States would not use the war as an opportunity to acquire territory in Cuba. On April 24, Spain responded with a formal declaration of war against the United States.

yellow journalism *Newspaper stories embellished with sensational or titillating details when the true reports did not seem dramatic enough.*

"Remember the *Maine!*" *The explosion of the battleship* Maine *in Havana harbor on February 15, 1898, killed 260 American sailors and helped drive the United States into war with Spain.*

Chicago History Museum

"A SPLENDID LITTLE WAR"

Secretary of State John Hay called the fight with Spain "a splendid little war." Begun in April, it ended in August. More than 1 million men volunteered to fight, and fewer than 500 were killed or wounded in combat. The American victory over Spain was complete, not just in Cuba but in the neighboring island of Puerto Rico and in the Philippines, Spain's strategic possession in the Pacific.

Actually, the war was more complicated than it seemed. The main reason for the easy victory was U.S. naval superiority. In the war's first major battle, a naval engagement in Manila harbor in the Philippines on May 1, a U.S. fleet commanded by Commodore George Dewey destroyed an entire Spanish fleet. On land, the story was different. On the eve of war the U.S. Army consisted of only 26,000 troops. A force of 80,000 Spanish regulars awaited them in Cuba. Congress immediately increased the Army to 62,000 and called for an additional 125,000 volunteers. The response to this call was astounding, but outfitting, training, and transporting the new recruits overwhelmed the Army's capacities. Its standard-issue, blue flannel uniforms proved too heavy for fighting in Cuba. Most of the volunteers had to make do with old Civil War rifles that still used black, rather than smokeless, powder. Moreover, the Army was unprepared for the effects of malaria and other tropical diseases.

That many Cuban revolutionaries were black also came as a shock to the U.S. forces. In their attempts to arouse support for the Cuban cause, U.S. newspapers

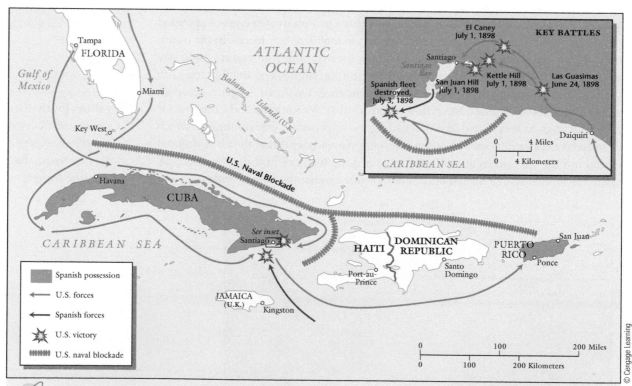

www   View an animated version of this map or related maps at www.cengage.com/history/murrin/libertyequalconc5e.

Map 22.1 **SPANISH-AMERICAN WAR IN CUBA, 1898.** *This map shows the following: the routes taken by U.S. ships transporting troops from Florida to Cuba; the concentration of troop landings and battles around Santiago, Cuba; and a U.S. naval blockade, stretching hundreds of miles from Puerto Rico to Cuba, that attempted to keep the Spanish troops in Cuba and Puerto Rico from being reinforced.*

had portrayed the Cuban rebels as fundamentally similar to white Americans, with an "Anglo-Saxon tenacity of purpose." The Spanish oppressors, by contrast, were depicted as dark complexioned and as possessing the characteristics of their "dark race": barbarism, cruelty, and indolence. The U.S. troops' first encounters with Cuban and Spanish forces dispelled these myths. Their Cuban allies appeared poorly outfitted, rough in their manners, and primarily black skinned. The Spanish soldiers appeared well disciplined, tough in battle, and light complexioned.

The Cuban rebels were actually skilled guerrilla fighters, but racial prejudice prevented most U.S. soldiers and reporters from crediting their military accomplishments. Instead, they judged the Cubans harshly—as primitive, savage, and incapable of self-control or self-government. White U.S. troops preferred not to fight alongside the Cubans; increasingly, they refused to coordinate strategy with them.

At first, the U.S. Army's logistical shortcomings and its racial misconceptions did little to diminish the American soldiers' hunger for a good fight. No one was more eager for battle than Theodore Roosevelt who, along with Colonel Leonard Wood, led a volunteer cavalry unit composed of Ivy League gentlemen, western cowboys, sheriffs, prospectors, Indians, and a small number of Hispanics and ethnic European Americans. Roosevelt's **Rough Riders**, as the unit came to be known, landed with the invasion force and played an active role in the three battles fought in the hills surrounding Santiago (see inset of Map 22.1). Their most famous action was a furious charge up Kettle Hill into the teeth of Spanish defenses. Roosevelt's bravery was stunning, though his judgment was faulty. Nearly 100 men were killed or wounded in the charge. Reports of Roosevelt's bravery overshadowed the equally brave performance of black troops, notably the **9th and 10th U.S. Cavalry**, which played a pivotal role in clearing away Spanish fortifications on Kettle Hill. One Rough Rider commented: "If it had not been for the Negro cavalry, the Rough Riders would have been exterminated." The 24th and 25th Infantry Regiments, also composed of black soldiers, performed equally vital tasks in the U.S. Army's conquest of the adjacent San Juan Hill.

African American soldiers risked their lives despite the segregationist policies that confined them to all-black regiments. At the time, Roosevelt gave them full credit for what they had done, but soon after returning home he began minimizing their contributions, even to the point of calling their behavior cowardly. Like most white American officers and enlisted men of the time, Roosevelt had difficulty believing that blacks could fight well.

The taking of Kettle Hill, San Juan Hill, and other high ground surrounding Santiago gave the U.S. forces a substantial advantage over the Spanish defenders. Nevertheless,

Rough Riders *Much-decorated volunteer cavalry unit organized by Theodore Roosevelt and Leonard Wood to fight in Cuba in 1898.*

9th and 10th U.S. Cavalry *African American army units that played pivotal roles in the Spanish-American war.*

LEADERS OF THE CUBAN STRUGGLE FOR INDEPENDENCE. *By 1898 Cubans had been fighting to free their country from Spain for 30 years. This lithograph, a souvenir of the Grand Cuban-American Fair held in New York in 1896, depicts five key leaders of the Cuban struggle: Máximo Gómez (upper left), Antonio Maceo (upper right), Calixto García (bottom right), and Salvador Cisneros (bottom left). At the center is José Martí, the "Father of the Revolution," killed in battle in 1895.*

Library of Congress Prints and Photographs Division [LC-USZ62-101802]

ROUGH RIDERS AND 10TH CAVALRY. *Roosevelt stands with his Rough Riders (top image) while members of the 10th Cavalry pose in the bottom image. Both groups played pivotal roles in the battles of San Juan and Kettle Hills, but America would celebrate only the Rough Riders, not the black cavalrymen.*

logistical and medical problems nearly did them in. The troops were short of food, ammunition, and medical facilities. Their ranks were devastated by malaria, typhoid, and dysentery; more than 5,000 soldiers died from disease. Fortunately, the Spanish had lost the will to fight. On July 3 Spain's Atlantic fleet tried to retreat from Santiago harbor and was promptly destroyed by a U.S. fleet. The Spanish army in Santiago surrendered on July 16; on July 18 the Spanish government asked for peace. While negotiations for an armistice proceeded, U.S. forces overran Spanish defenses on the neighboring island of Puerto Rico. On August 12 the U.S. and Spanish governments agreed to an armistice. But before the news could reach the Philippines, the United States had captured Manila and had taken prisoner 13,000 Spanish soldiers.

The armistice required Spain to relinquish its claim to Cuba, cede Puerto Rico and the Pacific island of Guam to the United States, and tolerate the American occupation of Manila until a peace conference could be convened in Paris on October 1, 1898. At that conference, American diplomats startled their Spanish counterparts by demanding that Spain also cede the Philippines to the United States. After two months of stalling, the Spanish government agreed to relinquish its coveted Pacific colony for $20 million, and the transaction was sealed by the Treaty of Paris on December 10, 1898.

THE UNITED STATES BECOMES A WORLD POWER

FOCUS QUESTION
What were the different mechanisms of control that the United States used to achieve its aims in Hawaii, Cuba, the Philippines, Puerto Rico, and China?

America's initial war aim, to oust the Spanish from Cuba, was supported by both imperialists and anti-imperialists, but for different reasons. Imperialists hoped to incorporate Cuba into a new American empire; anti-imperialists hoped to see the Cubans gain their independence. But only the imperialists condoned the U.S. acquisition of Puerto Rico, Guam, and the Philippines. President McKinley had cast his lot with the imperialists. First, he annexed Hawaii, giving the United States permanent control of Pearl Harbor. Then, he set his sights on establishing a U.S. naval base at Manila. Never before had the United States sought such a large military presence outside the Western Hemisphere (see Map 22.2).

In a departure of equal importance, McKinley announced his intent to administer much of this newly acquired territory as U.S. colonies. Virtually all the territory previously gained by the United States had been settled by white Americans, who had eventually petitioned for statehood and been admitted to the Union with the same rights as existing states. Of these new territories, however, only Hawaii would be allowed to follow a traditional path toward statehood. There, the powerful American sugar plantation owners prevailed on Congress to pass an act in 1900

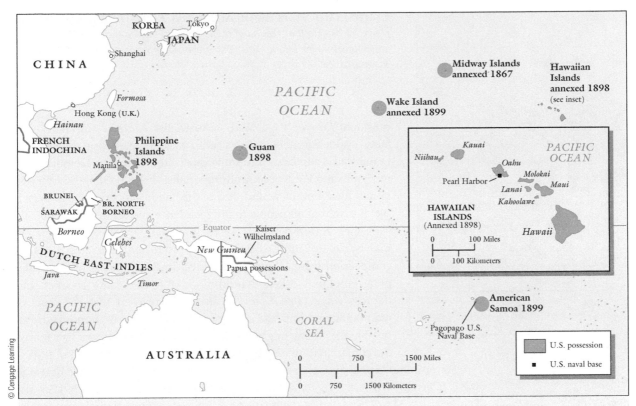

***Map 22.2* AMERICAN SOUTH PACIFIC EMPIRE, 1900.** *By 1900, the American South Pacific empire consisted of a series of strategically located islands with superior harbor facilities, stretching from the Hawaiian Islands and Samoa in the middle of the Pacific to the Philippines on the ocean's western edge.*

extending U.S. citizenship to all Hawaiian citizens and putting Hawaii on the road to statehood. No group of white Americans resided in the Philippines: The decision to make the country a U.S. colony was taken mainly to prevent other powers, such as Japan and Germany, from gaining a foothold somewhere in the 400-island archipelago and launching attacks on the American naval base in Manila.

The McKinley administration might have taken a different course. It might have negotiated a deal with **Emilio Aguinaldo**, a Filipino anticolonial leader, that would have given the Philippines independence in exchange for a U.S. naval base at Manila. An American fleet stationed there would have been able to protect both U.S. interests and the fledgling Philippine nation from predatory assaults by Japan, Germany, or Britain. Alternatively, the United States might have annexed the Philippines outright and offered Filipinos U.S. citizenship as the first step toward statehood. But McKinley believed that self-government was beyond the capacity of the "inferior" Filipino people. The United States would undertake a solemn mission to "civilize" the Filipinos and thereby prepare them for independence. Until that mission was complete, the Philippines would be ruled by American governors appointed by the president.

THE DEBATE OVER THE TREATY OF PARIS

The proposed acquisition of the Philippines aroused opposition both in the United States and in the Philippines. The Anti-Imperialist League enlisted the support of several elder statesmen in McKinley's own party, as well as former Democratic

Emilio Aguinaldo *Anticolonial leader who fought for independence of the Philippines, first from Spain and then from the United States.*

Bettmann/CORBIS

UNITED STATES STOPS EMILIO AGUINALDO. *Political cartoon in* Puck *magazine depicts the great hand of the United States smashing Filipino anticolonial leader Emilio Aguinaldo, who led an uprising against the United States in 1899.*

president Grover Cleveland, industrialist Andrew Carnegie, and labor leader Samuel Gompers. William Jennings Bryan, meanwhile, marshaled a vigorous anti-imperialist protest among Democrats in the South and West. Some anti-imperialists believed that the subjugation of the Filipinos would violate the nation's most precious principle: the right of all people to independence and self-government.

Other anti-imperialists were motivated more by self-interest than by democratic ideals. U.S. sugar producers, for example, feared competition from Filipino producers. Trade unionists worried that poor Filipino workers would flood the U.S. labor market and depress wage rates. Some businessmen warned that the costs of maintaining an imperial outpost would exceed any economic benefits that the colony might produce. Still other anti-imperialists feared the contaminating effects of contact with an "inferior" Asian race.

The anti-imperialists almost dealt McKinley and his fellow imperialists a defeat in the U.S. Senate, where the Treaty of Paris had to be ratified. On February 6, 1899, the Senate voted 57 to 27 in favor of the treaty, only one vote beyond the minimum two-thirds majority required for ratification. Two last-minute developments may have brought victory. First, William Jennings Bryan, in the days just before the vote, abandoned his opposition and announced his support for the treaty. Second, on the eve of the vote, Filipinos rose in revolt against the U.S. army of occupation. With another war looming and the lives of American soldiers imperiled, a few senators who had been reluctant to vote for the treaty may have felt obligated to support the president.

THE AMERICAN-FILIPINO WAR

The acquisition of the Philippines immediately embroiled the United States in a brutal war to subdue the Filipino rebels. In four years of fighting, more than 120,000 American soldiers served in the Philippines, and more than 4,200 died. The war brought Americans face to face with an unpleasant truth: that U.S. actions in the Philippines were virtually indistinguishable from Spain's actions in Cuba. Like Spain, the United States refused to acknowledge a people's aspiration for self-rule. Like "Butcher" Weyler, American generals permitted their soldiers to use savage tactics. Whole communities suspected of harboring guerrillas were driven into concentration camps, while their houses, farms, and livestock were destroyed. American soldiers executed so many Filipino rebels that the ratio of Filipino dead to wounded reached 15 to 1. One New York infantryman wrote home that his unit had killed 1,000 Filipinos in retaliation for the murder of a single American soldier. Estimates of total Filipino deaths from gunfire, starvation, and disease range from 50,000 to 200,000.

The United States finally gained the upper hand after General Arthur MacArthur (father of Douglas) was appointed commander of the islands in 1900. MacArthur did not lessen the war's ferocity, but he understood that it could not be won by guns alone. He offered amnesty to Filipino guerrillas who agreed to surrender, and he

QUICK   REVIEW

AMERICAN-FILIPINO WAR, 1899–1902

- Savage fighting to subdue Filipino rebels who would not accept U.S. control of their nation

- General Arthur MacArthur pacified the Philippines through ruthless attacks on rebels and concessions to those who agreed to live under U.S. rule

- In 1901 William Howard Taft became the first U.S. "governor-general" of the Philippines and sponsored public works programs

- Most fighting ended in 1902, although sporadic skirmishing continued until 1913

MUSICAL LINK TO THE PAST

MUSIC FOR PATRIOTS

Composer: John Philip Sousa
Title: "Stars and Stripes Forever" (c. 1895)

In the five years following the writing of "Stars and Stripes Forever," John Philip Sousa was probably the most famous musician in America. When he and his band arrived in town, a holiday atmosphere ensued: Flags flew, schools closed, and businesses released their workers for the day. International respect for American music grew as Sousa helped dispel the pervasive stereotype that the United States could not produce high-culture musical works and performers. While most famous composers had built their reputations on symphonies, for Sousa, symphonies were pretentious, full of padding, and dawdled before they reached their most crowd-pleasing sections. Sousa favored short, snappy, and often patriotic three-minute pieces such as "Stars and Stripes Forever."

Sousa viewed music as entertainment: he insisted on giving audiences what they wanted, and plenty of it. He did not mandate what audiences should hear, as most classical conductors did; instead, he allowed them to render their choices democratically, with applause. He mixed high-brow and low-brow material, classical themes with march music, and frequently used humor in his arrangements, purposely avoiding what he regarded as the stuffiness of classical concerts. If audiences wished to hear "Stars and Stripes Forever" as an encore over and over (and they consistently did, until he

died in 1932), then Sousa and his men would service them, with no withering of enthusiasm.

Besides his own works, Sousa championed the works of young and struggling American composers, but he demanded to know the stories behind their compositions. Musical inspiration, in Sousa's opinion, needed to be generated from "glorious events"; he avoided material from "atheistic composers" or those "crazily in love" because such works would not produce the appropriate nationalist feelings that he wished to cultivate in his audiences. "This was my mission. The point was to move all of America, while busied in its everyday pursuits, by the power of direct and simple music," he proclaimed in 1910. "I wanted to make a music for the people, a music to be grasped at once."

It was hardly an accident that Sousa's period of greatest popularity coincided with the wave of patriotic feeling that swept over America during the second half of the 1890s. The economy was recovering from the depression, and America was successfully flexing its muscles in a war with Spain. Many Americans wanted to wave the stars and stripes. They found special inspiration in Sousa's music.

1. Does music, even instrumental music such as Sousa's, have the power to generate a patriotic mood?
2. Have recent years in America—from 1896 until 2010—produced music whose influence on Americans has been similar to that of Sousa's in the 1890s?

 Listen to an audio recording of this music on the Musical Links to the Past CD.

cultivated close relations with the islands' wealthy elites. McKinley supported this effort to build a Filipino constituency sympathetic to the U.S. presence. To that end, he sent William Howard Taft to the islands in 1900 to establish a civilian government. In 1901 Taft became the colony's first "governor-general." He transferred many governmental functions to Filipino control and sponsored a program of public works (roads, bridges, schools) that would give the Philippines the infrastructure necessary for economic development and political independence. By 1902 this dual strategy of ruthless war against those who had taken up arms and concessions to those who were willing to live under benevolent American rule had crushed the revolt, though sporadic fighting continued until 1913.

THE "WATER CURE" IN THE PHILIPPINES. *This extraordinary photograph shows U.S. soldiers forcing water into the mouth of a Filipino guerrilla to the point where it would overflow his esophagus and pour into his breathing channels, creating the sensation of drowning. The image reveals U.S. forces using brutal tactics to break down the resistance of their Filipino opponents.*

"A Philippine Album: American Era Photographs" by Jonathan Best (Bookmark, Manila 1998)

CONTROLLING CUBA AND PUERTO RICO

Helping the Cubans achieve independence had been one of the major rationalizations for the war against Spain. But in 1900, when General Leonard Wood, now commander of U.S. forces in Cuba, authorized a constitutional convention to write the laws for a Cuban republic, the McKinley administration made clear it would not easily relinquish control of the island. At McKinley's urging, the U.S. Congress attached to a 1901 army appropriations bill the **Platt Amendment** delineating three conditions for Cuban independence. First, Cuba would not be permitted to make treaties with foreign powers. Second, the United States would have broad authority to intervene in Cuban political and economic affairs. Third, Cuba would sell or lease land to the United States for naval stations. The delegates to Cuba's constitutional convention were so outraged by these conditions that they refused even to vote on them. But the dependence of Cuba's vital sugar industry on the U.S. market and the continuing presence of a U.S. army on Cuban soil rendered resistance futile. In 1901, by a vote of 15 to 11, the delegates reluctantly wrote the Platt conditions into their constitution.

Cuba's status differed little from that of the Philippines. Both were politically subordinate to the United States. In the case of Cuba, economic dependence closely followed political subjugation. Between 1898 and 1914 American trade with Cuba increased more than tenfold, while investments more than quadrupled. The United States intervened in Cuban political affairs a total of five times between 1906 and 1921 to protect its economic and political interests and those of indigenous ruling elites with whom it had become closely allied. The economic, political, and military control that the United States imposed on Cuba would fuel anti-American sentiment there for years to come.

Puerto Rico received somewhat different treatment. The United States did not think independence appropriate. Nor did it follow its Cuban strategy by granting Puerto Rico nominal independence under informal economic and political controls. Instead, it annexed the island outright with the Foraker Act (1900). This act

Platt Amendment *Clause that the U.S. forced Cuba to insert into its constitution, giving the U.S. broad control over Cuba's foreign and domestic policies.*

contained no provision for making the inhabitants citizens of the United States. Puerto Rico was designated an "unincorporated" territory, which meant that Congress would dictate the island's government and specify the rights of its inhabitants. Puerto Ricans were allowed no role in designing their government, nor was their consent requested. With the Foraker Act, Congress had, in effect, invented a new, imperial mechanism for ensuring sovereignty over lands deemed vital to U.S. economic and military security. The U.S. Supreme Court upheld the constitutionality of this mechanism in a series of historic decisions, known as the Insular Cases, in the years from 1901 to 1904.

In some respects Puerto Rico fared better than "independent" Cuba. Puerto Ricans were granted U.S. citizenship in 1917 and won the right to elect their own governor in 1947. Still, Puerto Ricans enjoyed fewer political rights than Americans in the 48 states. Moreover, throughout the 20th century they endured a poverty rate far exceeding that of the mainland.

The subjugation of Cuba and the annexation of Puerto Rico troubled Americans far less than the U.S. takeover in the Philippines. Since the first articulation of the Monroe Doctrine in 1823, the United States had, in effect, claimed the Western Hemisphere as its sphere of influence. Within that sphere, many Americans believed, the United States possessed the right to act unilaterally to protect its interests. Before 1900 most of its actions (with the exception of the Mexican War) had been designed to limit the influence of European powers. After 1900, however, it assumed a more aggressive role, seizing land, overturning governments it did not like, and forcing its economic and political policies on weaker neighbors.

CHINA AND THE "OPEN DOOR"

Except for Hawaii, the Philippines, and Guam, the United States made no effort to take control of Pacific islands or Asian territory. Such a policy might well have triggered war with other world powers already well established in the Pacific. The United States opted for a diplomatic rather than a military strategy to achieve its foreign policy objectives. In China, in 1899 and 1900, it proposed the policy of the "Open Door."

The United States was concerned that the actions of the other world powers in China would block its own efforts to open up China's markets to American goods. Britain, Germany, Japan, Russia, and France each coveted its own chunk of China, where it could monopolize trade, exploit cheap labor, and establish military bases. By the 1890s each of these powers was building a sphere of influence, either by wringing economic and territorial concessions from the weak Chinese government or by seizing outright the land and trading privileges it desired.

To prevent China's breakup and to preserve U.S. economic access to the whole of China, McKinley's secretary of state, John Hay, sent **Open Door notes** to the major world powers. The notes asked each power to open its Chinese sphere of influence to the merchants of other nations and to grant them reasonable harbor fees and railroad rates. Hay also asked each power to respect China's sovereignty by enforcing Chinese tariff duties in the territory it controlled.

None of the world powers was eager to endorse Hay's requests, though Britain and Japan gave provisional assent. France, Germany, Russia, and Italy responded evasively, indicating their support for the Open Door policy in theory but insisting that they could not implement it until all the other powers had done so. Hay then put the best face on their responses by declaring that all the powers had agreed to observe his Open Door principles and that he regarded their assent as "final and

Open Door notes (1899–1900)
Foreign policy tactic in which the United States asked European powers to respect China's independence and to open their spheres of influence to merchants from other nations.

HISTORY THROUGH FILM

TARZAN, THE APE MAN (1932)

*Directed by W. S. Van Dyke; starring Johnny
Weismuller (Tarzan), Maureen O'Sullivan (Jane Parker),
Neil Hamilton (Harry Holt), C. Aubrey Smith
(James Parker), and Cheeta the Chimp*

Tarzan was one of the most popular screen figures of the 1930s, 1940s, and 1950s. Based on the bestselling novels of Edgar Rice Burroughs, this Tarzan movie, like the ones that followed, was meant to puncture the civilized complacency in which Americans and other westernized, imperial peoples had enveloped themselves. The movie opens with an American woman, Jane Parker, arriving in Africa to join her father, James, and his crew as they search for a mythic elephant graveyard said to contain untold riches in ivory tusks. Jane is depicted as bright, energetic, and attractive; she defies conventional expectations

for women. The white male adventurers, however, are portrayed as greedy, haughty, contemptuous of the African environment, and ignorant. The Africans who act as their servants and guides are presented as primitive and superstitious, more like animals than humans. This expedition in search of ivory is destined for disaster. Its members succumb to attacks by the wild animals and "wild humans" who inhabit this "dark continent." During one such attack by hippos and pygmies, Tarzan, played by handsome Olympic swimming champion Johnny Weismuller, comes to the rescue, scaring off the attackers by mobilizing a stampede of elephants with a piercing, high-pitched, and unforgettable jungle cry. He takes Jane, who has become separated from the group, to his tree house. Thus begins one of the more unusual screen romances.

Tarzan's origins are not explained, though one infers that he was abandoned by whites as a baby and raised by apes. He has none of the refining features of civilization—decent clothes, language, manners—but he possesses strength, honesty, and virtue. As Jane falls in love with Tarzan and decides to share a jungle life with him, we, the viewers, are asked to contemplate, with Jane, the benefits of peeling off the stultifying features of civilized life (which seem to drop away from Jane along with many of her clothes) and returning to a simpler, more wholesome, and more natural form of existence.

Although the movie critiques and lampoons the imperial pretensions and smugness of the West, it never asks viewers to see the indigenous African peoples as anything other than savage. Tarzan may be ignorant of civilized customs, but he is white and, as such, equipped with the "native" intelligence and character of his race. The African characters in the movie show no such intelligence or character. They are presented as weak and superstitious or as brutally aggressive and indifferent to human life. Thus *Tarzan, the Ape Man* manages to critique the West without asking Western viewers to challenge the racism that justified the West's domination of non-Western peoples and territories.

© Bettmann/Corbis

Johnny Weismuller and Maureen O'Sullivan as Tarzan and Jane.

definitive." The rival powers may have been impressed by Hay's diplomacy, but whether they intended to uphold the United States' Open Door policy was not at all clear.

The first challenge to Hay's policy came from the Chinese themselves. In May 1900 a nationalist Chinese organization, colloquially known as the **Boxers**, sparked an uprising to rid China of all "foreign devils" and foreign influences. Hundreds of Europeans were killed, as were many Chinese men and women who had converted to Christianity. When the Boxers laid siege to the foreign legations in Beijing and cut off communication between that city and the outside world, the imperial powers raised an expeditionary force to rescue the diplomats and punish the Chinese rebels. The force broke the Beijing siege in August and ended the Boxer Rebellion soon thereafter.

Hay now sent out a second round of Open Door notes, asking each power to respect China's political independence and territorial integrity, in addition to guaranteeing unrestricted access to its markets. Worried that Chinese rebels might strike again, the imperialist rivals responded more favorably. Britain, France, and Germany endorsed Hay's policy outright. With that support, Hay was able to check Russian and Japanese designs on Chinese territory. Significantly, when the imperial powers decided that the Chinese government should pay them reparations for their property and personnel losses during the Boxer Rebellion, Hay convinced them to accept payment in cash rather than in territory. By keeping China intact and open to free trade, the United States had achieved a major foreign policy victory.

Boxers *Chinese nationalist organization that instigated an uprising in 1900 to rid China of all foreign influence.*

THEODORE ROOSEVELT, GEOPOLITICIAN

Roosevelt had been a driving force in the transformation of U.S. foreign policy during the McKinley administration. As assistant secretary of the navy, as a military hero, as a vigorous speaker and writer, and then as vice president, Roosevelt worked tirelessly to remake the country into one of the world's great powers. He fervently believed that the English-speaking character of the nation destined it for supremacy in both economic and political affairs. He did not assume, however, that international supremacy would automatically accrue to the United States. A nation, like an individual, had to strive for greatness. It had to build a military force that could convincingly project power overseas—and it had to be prepared to fight.

Roosevelt's appetite for a good fight caused many people to rue the ascension of this "cowboy" to the White House after McKinley's assassination in 1901. But behind his blustery exterior was a shrewd analyst of international relations. As much as he craved power for himself and the nation, he understood that the United States could not rule every portion of the globe through military or economic means. Consequently, he sought to bring about a balance of power among the great industrial nations through negotiation rather than war. Such a balance would enable each imperial power to safeguard its key interests and contribute to world peace and progress.

Absent from Roosevelt's geopolitical thinking was concern for the interests of less powerful nations. Roosevelt had little patience with the claims to sovereignty of small countries or the human rights of weak peoples. In his eyes, the peoples of

FOCUS QUESTION
What were the similarities and differences in the foreign policies of Theodore Roosevelt, William Howard Taft, and Woodrow Wilson?

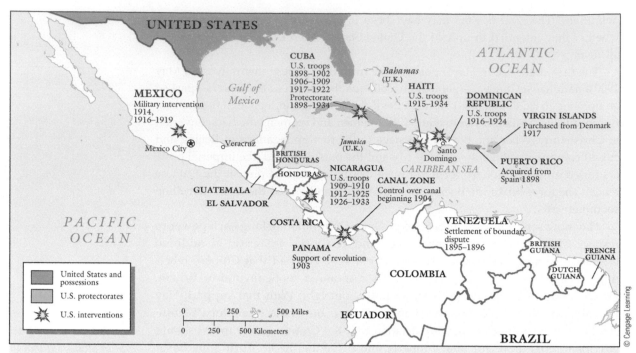

Map 22.3 UNITED STATES PRESENCE IN LATIN AMERICA, 1895–1934. *The United States possessed few colonies in Latin America but intervened (often repeatedly) in Mexico, Cuba, Nicaragua, Panama, Haiti, the Dominican Republic, and Venezuela to secure its economic and political interests.*

Latin America, Asia (with the exception of Japan), and Africa were racially inferior and thus incapable of self-government or industrial progress.

THE ROOSEVELT COROLLARY

Ensuring U.S. dominance in the Western Hemisphere ranked high on Roosevelt's list of foreign policy objectives. In 1904 he issued a "corollary" to the Monroe Doctrine, which had asserted the right of the United States to keep European powers from meddling in hemispheric affairs. In his corollary Roosevelt declared that the United States possessed a further right: the right to intervene in the domestic affairs of hemispheric nations to quell disorder and forestall European intervention. The **Roosevelt corollary** formalized a policy that the United States had already deployed against Cuba and Puerto Rico in 1900 and 1901. Subsequent events in Venezuela and the Dominican Republic had further convinced Roosevelt of the need to expand the scope of U.S. intervention in hemispheric affairs.

The governments of both Venezuela and the Dominican Republic were controlled by corrupt dictators. Both had defaulted on debts owed to European banks. Their delinquency prompted a German-led European naval blockade and bombardment of Venezuela in 1902 and a threatened invasion of the Dominican Republic by Italy and France in 1903. The United States forced the German navy to retreat from the Venezuelan coast in 1903. In the Dominican Republic, after a revolution had chased the dictator from power, the United States assumed control of the nation's customs collections in 1905 and refinanced the Dominican national debt through U.S. bankers.

The corrupt, dictatorial regimes that ruled some Latin America nations had generated conditions conducive to bankruptcy, social turmoil, and foreign intervention.

Roosevelt corollary *1904 corollary to the Monroe Doctrine, stating that the United States had the right to intervene in domestic affairs of hemispheric nations to quell disorder and forestall European intervention.*

The United States now took aggressive actions to correct those conditions, but rarely in Roosevelt's tenure did the United States show a willingness to help the Latin American peoples who had suffered under these regimes to establish democratic institutions or achieve social reform. When Cubans seeking genuine national independence rebelled against their puppet government in 1906, the United States sent in the Marines to silence them.

THE PANAMA CANAL

Roosevelt's interest in Latin America also engendered the building of the **Panama Canal** across Central America. Central America's narrow width, especially in its southern half, made it the logical place to build a canal. In fact, a French company had obtained land rights and had begun construction of a canal across the Colombian province of Panama in the 1880s. But even though a "mere" 40 miles of land separated the two oceans, the French were stymied by technological difficulties and the financial costs of literally moving mountains. Moreover, French doctors found they were unable to check the spread of malaria and yellow fever among their workers. By the time Roosevelt entered the White House in 1901, the French Panama Company had gone bankrupt.

Roosevelt was not deterred by the French failure. He first presided over the signing of the Hay-Pauncefote Treaty with Great Britain in 1901, releasing the United States from an 1850 agreement that prohibited either country from building a Central American canal without the other's participation. He then instructed his advisers to develop plans for a canal across Nicaragua. The Panamanian route chosen by the French was shorter than the proposed Nicaraguan route and the canal begun by the French was 40 percent complete. The company that possessed the rights to the unfinished Panamanian canal, however, wanted $109 million for it—more than the United States was willing to pay. In 1902 the company reduced the price to $40 million, a sum that Congress approved. Secretary of State Hay quickly negotiated an agreement with Tomas Herran, the Colombian chargé d'affaires in Washington. The agreement, formalized in the Hay-Herran Treaty, accorded the United States a six-mile-wide strip across Panama on which to build the canal. Colombia was to receive a one-time $10 million payment and annual rent of $250,000.

The Colombian legislature, however, rejected the proposed fee as insufficient and sent a new ambassador to the United States with instructions to ask for a one-time payment of $20 million and a share of the $40 million being paid to the French company. Actually, the Colombians (not unreasonably) were hoping to stall negotiations until 1904, when they would regain the rights to the canal zone and consequently to the $40 million payment promised to the French company.

Although Colombia was acting within its rights, Roosevelt would not tolerate the delay. Unable to get what he wanted through diplomatic means, he encouraged the Panamanians to revolt against Colombian rule. The Panamanians had staged several rebellions in the previous 25 years, all of which had failed. But the 1903 rebellion succeeded, mainly because a U.S. naval force prevented Colombian troops from landing in Panama. Meanwhile, the U.S.S. *Nashville* put U.S. troops ashore to help the new nation

Panama Canal *An engineering marvel completed in 1914 across the new Central American nation of Panama. Connecting the Atlantic and Pacific Oceans, it shortened ship travel between New York and San Francisco by 8,000 miles.*

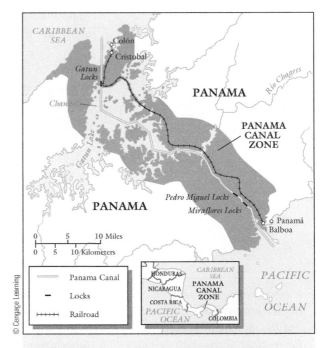

Map 22.4 PANAMA CANAL ZONE, 1914. *This map shows the route of the completed canal through Panama and the 10-mile-wide zone surrounding it that the United States controlled. The inset map locates the Canal Zone in the context of Central and South America.*

secure its independence. The United States formally recognized Panama as a sovereign state only two days after the rebellion against Colombia began.

Philippe Bunau-Varilla, a director of the French company from which the United States had bought the rights to the canal, declared himself the new state's diplomatic representative. As the duly appointed Panamanian delegation embarked for the United States to negotiate a canal deal, Bunau-Varilla rushed to Washington, where he and Secretary of State Hay signed the Hay–Bunau-Varilla Treaty (1903). It granted the United States a 10-mile-wide canal zone in return for $10 million down and $250,000 annually. Thus, the United States secured its canal by dealing not with the legitimate Panamanian government but with Bunau-Varilla's French company. When the Panamanian delegation arrived in Washington, its hands were tied. If it objected to the counterfeit treaty, the United States might withdraw its troops from Panama, leaving the new nation at the mercy of Colombia. Roosevelt's severing of Panama from Colombia prompted angry protests in Congress, but he was not perturbed, later gloating, "I took the Canal Zone and let Congress debate!"

Roosevelt turned the building of the canal into a test of American ingenuity and willpower. Engineers overcame every obstacle; doctors developed drugs to combat malaria and yellow fever; armies of construction workers "made the dirt fly." The canal remains a testament to the labor of some 30,000 workers, imported mainly from the West Indies, who, over a 10-year period, labored 10 hours a day, six days a week, for only 10 cents an hour. Completed in 1914, the canal shortened the voyage from San Francisco to New York by more than 8,000 miles and significantly enhanced the international prestige of the United States (see Map 22.4).

In 1921 the United States paid the Colombian government $25 million as compensation for its loss of Panama. It took Panama more than 70 years, however, to regain control of the 10-mile-wide strip of land that Bunau-Varilla, in connivance with the U.S. government, had bargained away in 1902. President Jimmy Carter signed a treaty in 1977 providing for the reintegration of the Canal Zone into Panama, and the canal itself was transferred to Panama in 2000.

KEEPING THE PEACE IN EAST ASIA

In Asia, Roosevelt's main objective was to preserve the Open Door policy in China and the balance of power in East Asia. The chief threats came from Russia and Japan, both of whom wanted to seize large chunks of China. At first, Russian expansion into Manchuria and Korea prompted Roosevelt to support Japan when in 1904 it launched a devastating attack on the Russian Pacific fleet anchored at Port Arthur, China. But once the ruinous effects of the war on Russia became clear, Roosevelt entered into secret negotiations to arrange a peace. He invited representatives of Japan and Russia to Portsmouth, New Hampshire, and prevailed on them to negotiate a compromise. The settlement, reached in 1905, favored Japan by perpetuating its control over most of the territories it had won during the brief **Russo-Japanese War**. Its chief prize was Korea, which became a protectorate of Japan, but Japan also acquired the southern part of Sakhalin Island, Port Arthur, and the South Manchurian Railroad. Russia avoided having to pay Japan a large indemnity and it retained Siberia, thus preserving its role as an East Asian power. Finally, Roosevelt protected China's territorial integrity by inducing the armies of both Russia and Japan to leave Manchuria. Roosevelt's success in ending the Russo-Japanese War won him the Nobel Prize for Peace in 1906.

Although Roosevelt succeeded in negotiating a peace between these two world powers, he generally was not troubled by challenges to the sovereignty of weaker

Russo-Japanese War *Territorial conflict between imperial Japan and Russia mediated by Theodore Roosevelt at Portsmouth, New Hampshire. The peace agreement gave Korea and other territory to Japan, ensured Russia's continuing control over Siberia, and protected China's territorial integrity.*

Asian nations. Sometimes he even encouraged such challenges. In a secret agreement with Japan (the Taft-Katsura Agreement of 1905), for example, the United States agreed that Japan could dominate Korea in return for a Japanese promise not to attack the Philippines. And in the Root-Takahira Agreement of 1908, the United States recognized Japanese expansion into southern Manchuria.

In Roosevelt's eyes the overriding need to maintain peace with Japan justified ignoring the claims of Korea and, increasingly, of China. Roosevelt admired Japan's industrial and military power and regarded Japanese expansion into East Asia as a natural expression of its imperial ambition. The task of American diplomacy, he believed, was first to allow the Japanese to build a secure sphere of influence in East Asia and second to encourage them to join the United States in pursuing peace rather than war. This was a delicate diplomatic task that required both sensitivity and strength, especially when anti-Japanese agitation broke out in California in 1906.

White Californians had long feared the presence of Asian immigrants (see Chapter 20). They had pressured Congress into passing the Chinese Exclusion Act of 1882, which ended most Chinese immigration to the United States. Then they turned their racism on Japanese immigrants. In 1906 the San Francisco school board ordered the segregation of Asian schoolchildren so that they would not "contaminate" white children. In 1907 the California legislature debated a law to bar further Japanese immigrants from entering the state. Anti-Asian riots erupted in San Francisco and Los Angeles, encouraged in part by hysterical stories in the press about the "yellow peril."

Militarists in Japan began talking of a possible war with the United States. Roosevelt assured the Japanese government that he too was appalled by the white Californians' behavior. In 1907 he reached a **gentlemen's agreement** by which the Tokyo government promised to halt the immigration of Japanese adult male laborers to the United States in return for Roosevelt's pledge to end anti-Japanese discrimination in California. Roosevelt did his part by persuading the San Francisco school board to rescind its segregation ordinance.

At the same time, Roosevelt worried that the Tokyo government would interpret his sensitivity to Japanese honor as weakness. So he ordered the main part of the U.S. fleet to embark on a 45,000-mile world tour, including a splashy stop in

gentlemen's agreement (1907)
Agreement by which the Japanese government promised to halt the immigration of its adult male laborers to the United States in return for President Theodore Roosevelt's pledge to end the discriminatory treatment of Japanese immigrant children in California's public schools.

ANTI-ASIAN HYSTERIA IN SAN FRANCISCO. *In 1906, in the midst of a wave of anti-Asian prejudice in California, the San Francisco school board ordered the segregation of all Asian schoolchildren. Here, a nine-year-old Japanese student submits an application for admission to a public primary school and is refused by the principal, Miss M. E. Dean.*

North Wind Picture Archives

Tokyo Bay. Many Americans deplored the cost of the tour and feared that the appearance of the U.S. Navy in a Japanese port would provoke military retaliation. Roosevelt brushed his critics aside, and, true to his prediction, the Japanese were impressed by the **Great White Fleet's** show of strength. Their response seemed to lend validity to the African proverb Roosevelt often invoked: "Speak softly and carry a big stick." Roosevelt's policies lessened the prospect of a war with Japan while preserving a strong U.S. presence in East Asia.

Great White Fleet *Naval ships sent on a 45,000-mile world tour by President Roosevelt (1907–1909) to showcase American military power.*

WILLIAM HOWARD TAFT, DOLLAR DIPLOMAT

William Howard Taft brought impressive credentials to the job of president. He had gained valuable experience in colonial administration as the first governor-general of the Philippines. As Roosevelt's secretary of war and chief negotiator for the Taft-Katsura agreement of 1905, he had learned a great deal about conducting diplomacy with imperialist rivals. Yet Taft lacked Roosevelt's grasp of balance-of-power politics and capacity for leadership in foreign affairs. Further, Taft's secretary of state, Philander C. Knox, a corporation lawyer from Pittsburgh, had no diplomatic expertise. Knox's conduct of foreign policy seemed to be directed almost entirely toward expanding opportunities for corporate investment overseas, prompting critics to deride his policies as **dollar diplomacy**. Knox, Taft, and their supporters did believe that American overseas investment would, by itself, create prosperity and political stability in the countries that were its recipients. But this approach made it hard for them to grasp the complexity both of international relations and of the internal politics of particular countries.

dollar diplomacy *Diplomatic strategy formulated under President Taft that focused on expanding American investments abroad, especially in Latin America and East Asia.*

Their neglect of these issues caused a diplomatic reversal in East Asia. Knox, prodded by his banker friends, sought to expand American economic activities

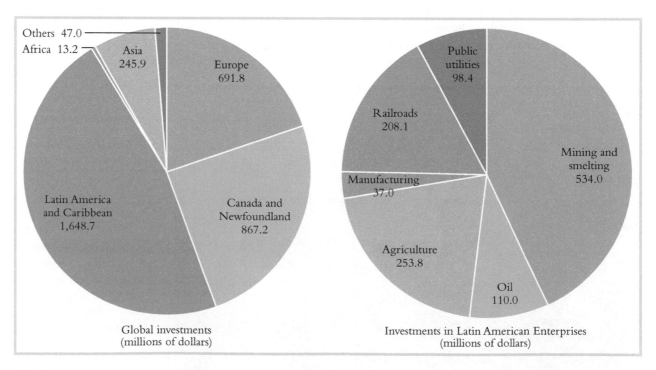

Global investments (millions of dollars)

Others 47.0
Africa 13.2
Asia 245.9
Europe 691.8
Latin America and Caribbean 1,648.7
Canada and Newfoundland 867.2

Investments in Latin American Enterprises (millions of dollars)

Public utilities 98.4
Railroads 208.1
Manufacturing 37.0
Mining and smelting 534.0
Agriculture 253.8
Oil 110.0

U.S. GLOBAL INVESTMENTS AND INVESTMENTS IN LATIN AMERICA, 1914
Source: From Cleona Lewis, *America's Stake in International Investments* (Washington, D.C.: The Brookings Institute, 1938), pp. 576-606.

throughout China—even in Manchuria, where they encroached on the Japanese sphere of influence. In 1911 Knox proposed that a syndicate of European and American bankers buy the South Manchurian Railroad (then under Japanese control) to open up north China to international trade. Japan reacted by signing a friendship treaty with Russia, its former enemy, which signaled their joint determination to exclude American, British, and French goods from Manchurian markets. As a result, Knox's plans for a syndicate fell apart. Similar efforts by Knox to increase American trade with Central and South China triggered further hostile responses from the Japanese and the Russians, contributing to the collapse of the Chinese government and the onset of the Chinese Revolution in 1911.

Dollar diplomacy worked better in the Caribbean. Knox encouraged American investment in the region. Companies such as United Fruit of Boston, which established extensive banana plantations in Costa Rica and Honduras, grew so powerful that they were able to influence both the economies and the governments of Central American countries. When political turmoil threatened their investments, the United States simply sent in its troops. Thus, when Nicaraguan dictator José Santos Zelaya reportedly began negotiating with a European country to build a second trans-Isthmian canal in 1910, a force of U.S. Marines toppled his regime. Marines landed again in 1912 when Zelaya's successor, Adolfo Diaz, angered Nicaraguans with his pro-American policies. This time the Marines were instructed to keep the Diaz regime in power. Except for a brief period in 1925, U.S. troops would remain in Nicaragua continuously from 1912 until 1933.

WOODROW WILSON, STRUGGLING IDEALIST

Woodrow Wilson's foreign policy in Latin America initially appeared to be no different from that of his Republican predecessors. In 1915 the United States sent troops to Haiti to put down a revolution; they remained as an army of occupation for 21 years. In 1916, when the people of the Dominican Republic refused to accept a treaty making them more or less a protectorate of the United States, Wilson forced them to accept the rule of a U.S. military government. When German influence in the Danish West Indies began to expand, Wilson purchased the islands from Denmark, renamed them the Virgin Islands, and added them to the U.S. Caribbean empire (see Map 22.3).

Still, Wilson's relationship with Mexico in the wake of its revolution reveals that he was troubled by a foreign policy that ignored a less powerful nation's right to determine its own future. In his dealings with Mexico, however, he was not motivated solely by his fondness for democracy. He also feared that political unrest there could lead to violence, social disorder, and revolutionary governments hostile to U.S. economic interests. If a democratic government could be put in place in Mexico, property rights would be respected and U.S. investments would remain secure. Wilson's desire both to encourage democracy and to limit the extent of social change made it difficult to devise a consistent foreign policy toward Mexico. The Mexican Revolution broke out in 1910 when dictator Porfirio Diaz was overthrown by democratic forces led by Francisco Madero. Madero's talk of democratic reform frightened many foreign investors. Thus, when Madero himself was overthrown early in 1913 by Victoriano Huerta, a conservative general who promised to protect foreign investments, the dollar diplomatists breathed a sigh of relief. Henry Lane Wilson, the U.S. ambassador to Mexico, had helped to engineer Huerta's coup. Before close relations between the United States and Huerta could be worked out, however, Huerta's men murdered Madero.

Woodrow Wilson, who became president shortly after Madero's assassination in 1913, might have overlooked it and entered into close ties with Huerta on condition that he protect American property. Instead, Wilson refused to recognize Huerta's "government of butchers" and demanded that Mexico hold democratic elections. Wilson favored Venustiano Carranza and Francisco ("Pancho") Villa, two enemies of Huerta who commanded rebel armies and who claimed to be democrats. In April 1914 Wilson seized upon the arrest of several U.S. sailors by Huerta's troops to send a fleet into Mexican waters. He then ordered the U.S. Marines to occupy the Mexican port city of Veracruz and to prevent a German ship there from unloading munitions meant for Huerta's army. In the resulting confrontation between U.S. and Mexican forces, 19 Americans and 126 Mexicans were killed. The battle brought the two countries dangerously close to war. Eventually, however, American control over Veracruz weakened and embarrassed Huerta's regime to the point where Carranza was able to take power.

Carranza, though, did not behave as Wilson had expected. He rejected Wilson's efforts to shape a new Mexican government and announced an extensive land-reform program. If the program went into effect, U.S. petroleum companies would lose control of their Mexican properties, a loss that Wilson deemed unacceptable. So Wilson now threw his support to Pancho Villa, who seemed more willing to protect U.S. oil interests. When Carranza's forces defeated Villa's forces in 1915, Wilson reluctantly withdrew his support of Villa and prepared to recognize the Carranza government.

Furious that Wilson had abandoned him, Villa and his soldiers pulled 18 U.S. citizens from a train in northern Mexico and murdered them, along with another 17 in an attack on Columbus, New Mexico. Wilson obtained permission from Carranza to send a U.S. expeditionary force under General John J. Pershing into Mexico. Pershing's troops pursued Villa's forces for 300 miles but failed to catch them. The U.S. troops did, however, clash twice with Mexican troops under Carranza's command, bringing the countries to the brink of war once again. Because the United States was about to enter the First World War, Wilson could not afford a fight with Mexico. So, in 1917, he quietly ordered Pershing's troops home and grudgingly recognized the Carranza government.

Wilson's policies toward Mexico in the years from 1913 to 1917 seemed to have produced few concrete results, except to reinforce an already deep antagonism among Mexicans toward the United States. His repeated changes in strategy, moreover, seemed to indicate a lack of skill and decisiveness in foreign affairs. Actually, however, Wilson recognized something that Roosevelt and Taft had not: that more and more peoples of the world were determined to control their own destinies. Somehow the United States had to find a way to support their democratic aspirations while also safeguarding its own economic interests.

C O N C L U S I O N

We can assess the dramatic turn in U.S. foreign policy after 1898 either in relation to the foreign policies of rival world powers or against America's own democratic ideals. By the first standard, U.S. foreign policy looks impressive. The United States achieved its major objectives in world affairs: It tightened its control over the Western Hemisphere and projected its military and economic power into Asia. It did so while sacrificing relatively few American lives and while constraining the jingoistic appetite for truly extensive military adventure and conquest. By contrast, in 1900 the British Empire extended over 12 million square miles and embraced one-fourth of the world's population. At times, American rule could be brutal, but on the whole it was no more severe than British rule and significantly less severe than that of the French, German, Belgian, or Japanese imperialists. McKinley, Roosevelt, Taft, and Wilson all placed limits on U.S. expansion and avoided, prior to 1917, extensive foreign entanglements and wars.

If measured against the standard of America's own democratic ideals, however, U.S. foreign policy after 1898 must be judged more harshly. It demeaned the peoples of the Philippines, Puerto Rico, Guam, Cuba, and Colombia as inferior and primitive and denied them the right to govern themselves. In choosing to behave like the imperialist powers of Europe, the United States abandoned its longstanding claim that it was a different kind of nation, one that valued liberty more than power.

Many Americans of the time judged their nation by both standards and thus faced a dilemma. On the one hand, they believed that the size, economic strength, and honor of the United States required it to accept the role of world power and policeman. On the other hand, they continued to believe they had a mission to spread the values of 1776 to the farthest reaches of the earth. The Mexico example demonstrates how hard it was for the United States to reconcile these two very different approaches to world affairs.

QUESTIONS FOR REVIEW AND CRITICAL THINKING

Review

1. In going to war against Spain in 1898, was the United States impelled more by imperialist or anti-imperialist motives?
2. What were the different mechanisms of control that the United States used to achieve its aims in Hawaii, Cuba, the Philippines, Puerto Rico, and China?
3. What were the similarities and differences in the foreign policies of Theodore Roosevelt, William Howard Taft, and Woodrow Wilson?

Critical Thinking

1. What is the appropriate standard for judging the 1898 turn in U.S. foreign policy: the policies of rival world powers or America's own democratic ideals?
2. If you had been president, secretary of state, or a leading senator in the period 1898–1917, with the power to alter U.S. foreign policy, what, if anything would you have changed? What leads you to believe that your change of policy would not only have been desirable but successful?

ONLINE RESOURCES

 Visit the companion website to access flashcards, crossword puzzles, exercises, and quizzes related to this chapter: www.cengage.com/history/murrin/libertyequalconc5e.

 See our interactive ebook for map and primary source activities.

DISCOVERY

Was American foreign policy imperialist or anti-imperialist? Did it spread liberty?

GEOGRAPHY AND FOREIGN POLICY Examine the two maps on pages 586 and 589. What areas did the U.S. seek to influence or come to control during these years? What propelled the United States to exercise its influence abroad? How successful was it in its aims? In which of these areas does the United States still exercise control or influence?

FOREIGN POLICY Examine the political cartoon and think about the reading in this chapter. What do you think the cartoonist is saying about American involvement in the Philippines? What is the significance of the toy rocking horse and its label "Dictatorship?" What is the significance of the burning ship in the background (on the right)? Do you think the cartoonist was in favor of American policies in the Pacific? Why or why not?

In thinking about this question, begin by breaking it down into the components shown below. A discussion of the significance of each component should appear in your answer.

Bettmann/CORBIS

UNITED STATES STOPS EMILIO AGUINALDO

WAR AND SOCIETY, 1914–1920

The First World War broke out in Europe in August 1914. The Triple Alliance of Germany, Austria-Hungary, and the Ottoman Empire squared off against the Triple Entente of Great Britain, France, and Russia. The United States entered the war on the side of the Entente (the Allies, or Allied Powers, as they came to be called) in 1917. Over the next year and a half, the United States converted its immense and sprawling economy into a disciplined war production machine, raised a 5-million-man army, and provided both the war matériel and troops that helped propel the Allies to victory.

But the war also convulsed American society more deeply than any event since the Civil War. This war was the first "total" war, meaning that it required combatants to devote virtually all their resources to the fight. The U.S. government pursued a degree of industrial control and social regimentation unprecedented in American history.

This government buildup was a controversial measure in a society that had long distrusted government power. Moreover, significant numbers of Americans from a variety of constituencies opposed the war. To overcome this opposition, President Woodrow Wilson couched American war aims in disinterested and idealistic terms: The United States, he claimed, wanted a "peace without victory," a "war for democracy," and liberty for the world's oppressed peoples.

Many in the United States and abroad responded enthusiastically to Wilson's ideals. But Wilson could not deliver a "peace without victory" without the support of England and France, and this support never came. At home, disadvantaged groups stirred up trouble by declaring that American society had failed to live up to its democratic and egalitarian ideals. Wilson supported repressive policies to silence these rebels and to enforce unity and conformity on the American people. In the process, he tarnished the ideals for which America had been fighting.

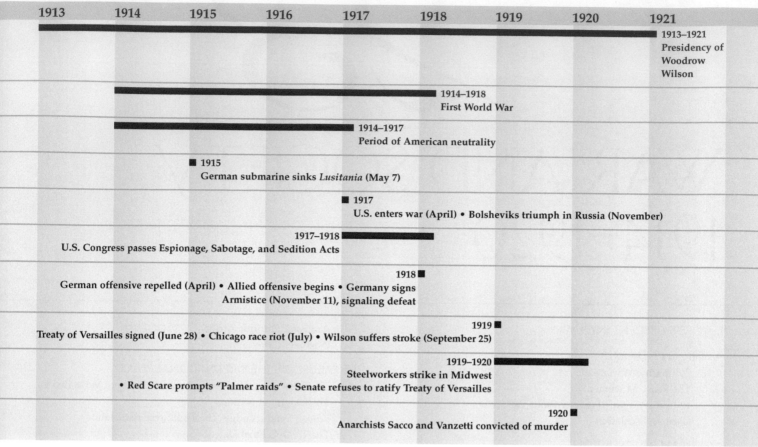

1913	1914	1915	1916	1917	1918	1919	1920	1921

1913–1921
Presidency of Woodrow Wilson

1914–1918
First World War

1914–1917
Period of American neutrality

1915
German submarine sinks *Lusitania* (May 7)

1917
U.S. enters war (April) • Bolsheviks triumph in Russia (November)

1917–1918
U.S. Congress passes Espionage, Sabotage, and Sedition Acts

1918
German offensive repelled (April) • Allied offensive begins • Germany signs Armistice (November 11), signaling defeat

1919
Treaty of Versailles signed (June 28) • Chicago race riot (July) • Wilson suffers stroke (September 25)

1919–1920
Steelworkers strike in Midwest
• Red Scare prompts "Palmer raids" • Senate refuses to ratify Treaty of Versailles

1920
Anarchists Sacco and Vanzetti convicted of murder

$\mathcal{E}$UROPE'S DESCENT INTO WAR

On June 28, 1914, in Sarajevo, Bosnia, a Bosnian nationalist assassinated Archduke Franz Ferdinand, heir to the Austro-Hungarian throne. This act was meant to protest the Austro-Hungarian imperial presence in the Balkans and to encourage the Bosnians, Croatians, and other Balkan peoples to join the Serbs in establishing independent nations. Austria-Hungary responded to this provocation on July 28 by declaring war on Serbia, holding it responsible for the archduke's murder.

The conflict might have remained local if a series of treaties had not divided Europe into two hostile camps. Germany, Austria-Hungary, and Italy, the so-called **Triple Alliance**, had promised to come to each other's aid if attacked. Italy would soon leave this alliance, to be replaced by the Ottoman Empire. Arrayed against the nations of the Triple Alliance were Britain, France, and Russia in the **Triple Entente**. Russia was obligated by another treaty to defend Serbia against Austria-Hungary, and consequently on July 30 it mobilized its armed forces to go to Serbia's aid. That brought Germany into the conflict to protect Austria-Hungary from Russian attack. On August 3 German troops struck not at Russia itself but at France, Russia's western ally. To reach France, German troops had marched through neutral Belgium. On August 4 Britain reacted by declaring war on Germany.

Complicated alliances and defense treaties of the European nations hastened the rush toward war. But equally important was the competition that existed among the major powers to build the strongest economies, the largest armies and

Triple Alliance *One set of combatants in First World War, consisting of Germany, Austria-Hungary, and Italy. When Italy left the alliance, this side became known as the Central Powers.*

Triple Entente *One set of combatants in First World War, consisting of Britain, France, and Russia. As the war went on, this side came to be known as the Allies or Allied Powers.*

THE ROAD TO WAR,
SUMMER 1914

1 June 28
   Assassination at Sarajevo

2 July 28
   Austria-Hungary declares
   war on Serbia

3 July 30
   Russia begins mobilization

4 August 1
   Germany declares war
   on Russia

5 August 3
   Germany declares war
   on France

6 August 4
   Great Britain declares war
   on Germany

7 August 6
   Russia and
   Austria-Hungary at war

8 August 12
   Great Britain declares war
   on Austria-Hungary

Legend:
- Allied powers and possessions, 1916
- Central powers and Ottoman Empire, 1916
- Neutral countries
- British naval blockade
- Trench line, Western front, 1915
- Eastern front, 1915

© Cengage Learning

View an animated version of this map or related maps at
www.cengage.com/history/murrin/libertyequalconc5e.

Map 23.1 EUROPE GOES TO WAR. *In the First World War, Great Britain, France, and Russia squared off against Germany, Austria-Hungary, and the Ottoman Empire. Most of the fighting occurred in Europe along the western front in France (purple line) or the eastern front in Russia (red line). This map also shows Britain's blockade of German ports. British armies based in Egypt (then a British colony) clashed with Ottoman armies in Arabia and other parts of the Ottoman Empire.*

GASSED, **BY JOHN SINGER SARGENT.** *An artist renders the horror of a poison gas attack in the First World War. The Germans were the first to use this new and brutal weapon, which contributed greatly to the terror of war.*

QUICK   REVIEW

CAUSES OF FIRST WORLD WAR

- Competition among European nations to build strongest economies, largest navies, and grandest empires created international friction and instability

- Assassination of Archduke Franz Ferdinand prompted Austria-Hungary to declare war on Serbia

- Intricate series of treaties compelled Russia, England, and France to go to war with Serbia, and Germany to support Austria-Hungary

navies, and the grandest colonial empires. Britain and Germany, in particular, struggled for European and world supremacy. Historians believe that several advisers close to the German emperor, Kaiser Wilhelm II, urged going to war against Russia and France. They expected that a European war would be swift and decisive—in Germany's favor.

But there was to be no quick victory. The two camps were evenly matched. Moreover, the first wartime use of machine guns and barbed wire made it easier to defend against attack than to go on the offensive. On the western front, after the initial German attack narrowly failed to take Paris in 1914, the two opposing armies confronted each other along a battle line stretching from Belgium in the north to the Swiss border in the south (see Map 23.1). Troops dug trenches to protect themselves from artillery bombardment and poison gas attacks. Commanders on both sides mounted suicidal ground assaults on the enemy by sending tens of thousands of infantry, armed only with rifles, bayonets, and grenades, out of the trenches and directly into enemy fire. Barbed wire further retarded forward progress, enabling enemy artillery and machine guns to cut down appalling numbers of men. Many who were not killed in combat succumbed to disease that spread rapidly in the cold, wet, and rat-infested trenches. In eastern Europe the armies of Germany and Austria-Hungary squared off against those of Russia and Serbia. Though the eastern front did not employ trench warfare, the combat was no less lethal. By the time the First World War ended, total casualties, both military and civilian, had reached 37 million.

AMERICAN NEUTRALITY

FOCUS QUESTION

Why did the U.S. policy of neutrality fail, and why did the U.S. get drawn into war?

Soon after the fighting began, Woodrow Wilson told Americans that this was a European war; neither side was threatening a vital U.S. interest. The United States would therefore proclaim its **neutrality** and maintain normal relations with both sides. Normal relations meant that the United States would continue trading with both camps. A few groups opposed Wilson's neutrality policy, but most Americans applauded Wilson's determination to keep the country out of war.

Neutrality was easier to proclaim than achieve, however. Many Americans identified more with Britain than with Germany. They shared with the English a language, ancestry, and a commitment to liberty. Germany's acceptance of monarchical rule, the prominence of militarists in German politics, and the weakness of democratic traditions inclined U.S. officials to judge Germany harshly.

The United States had strong economic ties to Great Britain as well. In 1914 the United States exported more than $800 million in goods to Britain and its allies, compared with $170 million to Germany and Austria-Hungary (which came to be known as the Central Powers). Once war erupted, the British and then the French turned to the United States for food, clothing, munitions, and other war supplies. Bankers began to issue loans to the Allied Powers, further knitting together the U.S. and British economies and giving American investors a direct stake in an Allied victory. Moreover, the British navy had blockaded German ports, which limited U.S. trade with Germany.

The Wilson administration protested the search and occasional seizure of American merchant ships by the British navy. But it never retaliated by suspending loans or exports to Great Britain. To do so might have plunged the U.S. economy into a recession. In failing to protect its right to trade with Germany, the United States compromised its neutrality and allowed itself to be drawn into war.

SUBMARINE WARFARE

To combat British control of the seas, Germany unveiled a terrifying new weapon, the *Unterseeboot*, or U-boat, the first militarily effective submarine. On May 7, 1915, without warning, a German U-boat torpedoed the British passenger liner *Lusitania*, en route from New York to London. The ship sank in 22 minutes, killing 1,198 men, women, and children, 128 of them U.S. citizens. Americans were shocked by the sinking. The Germans claimed that the *Lusitania* was secretly carrying a large store of munitions to Great Britain (a charge later proved true). But this did not stop Wilson from denouncing the sinking of the *Lusitania* and demanding that Germany pledge never to launch another attack on the citizens of neutral nations, even when they were traveling in British or French ships. Germany acquiesced to Wilson's demand.

The resulting lull in submarine warfare was short-lived. In early 1916 the Allies began to arm their merchant vessels with guns and depth charges capable of destroying German U-boats. Considering this a provocation, Germany renewed its campaign of surprise submarine attacks. In March 1916 a German submarine torpedoed the French passenger liner *Sussex*, causing a heavy loss of life and injuring several Americans. Again Wilson demanded that Germany spare civilians from attack. In the so-called *Sussex* pledge, Germany once again relented but warned that it might resume unrestricted submarine warfare if the United States did not prevail upon Great Britain to permit neutral ships to pass through the naval blockade.

The German submarine attacks strengthened the hand of Theodore Roosevelt and others who had been arguing that war with Germany was inevitable and that the United States must prepare to fight. Wilson could no longer ignore these critics. But, to forestall the necessity of American military involvement, he dispatched his closest foreign policy adviser, Colonel Edward M. House, to London in January 1916 to draw up a peace plan with the British foreign secretary, Lord Grey. In the House-Grey memorandum of February 22, 1916, Britain agreed to ask the United States to negotiate a settlement between the Allies and the Central Powers. The British believed that the terms of such a peace settlement would favor the Allies. They were furious when Wilson revealed that he wanted an impartial, honestly negotiated peace in which the

neutrality *U.S. foreign policy from 1914 to 1917 that called for staying out of war but maintaining normal economic relations with both sides.*

Lusitania *British passenger liner sunk by a German U-boat on May 7, 1915, killing more than 1,000 men, women, and children.*

INDIANAPOLIS, IND., AUGUST 5, 1916.

Wisconsin Historical Society

THE HORROR OF WAR. *This cover of the* United Mine Workers Journal *(1916) presents the Great War in the bleakest possible terms: as giving the Grim Reaper license to claim the bodies and souls of Europe's young men. Progressive labor unions were part of the broad coalition in the United States opposed to America's entry into war.*

claims of the Allies and Central Powers would be treated with respect. Britain now rejected U.S. peace overtures, and relations between the two countries grew unexpectedly tense.

THE PEACE MOVEMENT

Underlying Wilson's 1916 peace initiative was a vision of a new world order in which relations between nations would be governed by negotiation rather than war and in which justice would replace power as the fundamental principle of diplomacy. In a major foreign policy address on May 27, 1916, Wilson formally declared his support for an international parliament dedicated to the pursuit of peace, security, and justice for all the world's peoples.

Many Americans supported Wilson's efforts to promote international peace rather than conquest and to keep the United States out of war. In 1915 an international women's peace conference at The Hague (in the Netherlands) had drawn many participants from the United States. A substantial pacifist group emerged among the nation's Protestant clergy, and progressives and socialists urged the United States to steer clear of this European conflict. In April 1916 the new American Union Against Militarism pressured Wilson to continue pursuing the path of peace. The country's sizable Irish and German ethnic populations, determined to block any formal military alliance with Great Britain, also supported Wilson's peace campaign.

WILSON'S VISION: "PEACE WITHOUT VICTORY"

The 1916 presidential election revealed the breadth of peace sentiment. Wilson ran as the "peace president" who had "kept us out of war." Combining the promise of peace with a pledge to push ahead with progressive reform, Wilson won a narrow victory over the pro-war Republican, Charles Evan Hughes. Wilson appeared before the Senate on January 22, 1917, to outline his plans for peace. He reaffirmed his commitment to an international parliament or League of Nations. But for such a league to succeed, Wilson argued, it would have to be handed a sturdy peace settlement. This entailed a **peace without victory.** A settlement that did not crown a victor or humiliate a loser would ensure the equality of the combatants, and "only a peace between equals can last."

Wilson listed the crucial principles of a lasting peace: freedom of the seas; disarmament; and the right of every people to self-determination, democratic self-government, and security against aggression. Wilson was advocating a new world order, one that would allow all the earth's peoples, regardless of their size or strength, to achieve political independence and to participate as equals in world affairs. These views, rare from the leader of a world power, stirred the masses of Europe and elsewhere caught in deadly conflict.

peace without victory *Woodrow Wilson's 1917 pledge to work for a peace settlement that did not favor one side over the other but ensured an equality among combatants.*

GERMAN ESCALATION

But Wilson's oratory came too late to serve the cause of peace. Sensing the imminent collapse of Russian forces on the eastern front, Germany had decided to throw its full military might at France and Britain. At sea it prepared to unleash its submarines to attack all vessels heading for British ports. Germany knew that this last action would compel the United States to enter the war, but it was gambling on being able to strangle the British economy and leave France isolated before significant numbers of American troops could reach European shores.

Wilson continued to hope for a negotiated settlement until February 25, when the British intercepted and passed on to the president a telegram from Germany's foreign secretary, Arthur Zimmermann, to the German minister in Mexico. The infamous **Zimmermann telegram** instructed the minister to ask the Mexican government to attack the United States in the event of war between Germany and the United States. In return, Germany would pay the Mexicans a large fee and regain for them the "lost provinces" of Texas, New Mexico, and Arizona. Wilson, Congress, and the American public were outraged.

In March news arrived that Tsar Nicholas II's autocratic regime in Russia had collapsed and been replaced by a liberal-democratic government. As long as the tsar ruled Russia and stood to benefit from the Central Powers' defeat, Wilson could not honestly claim that America's going to war against Germany would bring democracy to Europe. Russia's fledgling democratic government's need for support gave Wilson the rationale he needed to justify American intervention.

Appearing before a joint session of Congress on April 2, Wilson declared that the United States must enter the war because "the world must be made safe for democracy." Congress broke into thunderous applause. On April 6, Congress voted to declare war by a vote of 373 to 50 in the House and 82 to 6 in the Senate.

The United States thus embarked on a grand experiment to reshape the world. Wilson had given millions of people around the world reason to hope. Although he was taking America to war on the side of the Allies, he stressed that the United States would fight as an "Associated Power," a phrase meant to underscore America's determination to keep its war aims pure and disinterested.

Still, Wilson understood all too well the risks of his undertaking. If the American people went to war, he predicted, "they'll forget there ever was such a thing as tolerance. To fight you must be brutal and ruthless, and the spirit of ruthless brutality will enter into the very fibre of our national life, infecting Congress, the courts, the policeman on the beat, the man in the street."

Zimmerman telegram *Telegram from Germany's foreign secretary instructing the German minister in Mexico to ask that country's government to attack the United States in return for German assistance in regaining Mexico's "lost provinces" (Texas, New Mexico, and Arizona).*

AMERICAN INTERVENTION

The entry of the United States into the war gave the Allies the muscle they needed to defeat the Central Powers, but it almost came too late. The French and British armies had bled themselves white by taking the offensive in 1916 and 1917 and had scarcely budged the trench lines. The Germans had been content simply to hold their trench position in the West, for they were engaged in a huge offensive against the Russians in the East. But a second Russian revolution in November 1917 had brought to power a socialist government under Vladimir Lenin and his Bolshevik Party and it immediately pulled Russia out of the war. Germany threw all its military might into the western front.

QUICK REVIEW

PATH TO U.S. INTERVENTION

- Economic and cultural ties with Great Britain compromised American neutrality

- U-boat attacks on British and French shipping made Germany an easy target for U.S. condemnation

- Wilson quieted antiwar movement by promising "peace without victory"

- Zimmermann telegram in February 1917 outraged U.S. public opinion

- Overthrow of Russian tsar Nicholas II in March 1917 enabled Wilson to declare that America was fighting a "war for democracy"

John J. Pershing *Commander of the American Expeditionary Force that began landing in Europe in 1917 and that entered battle in the spring and summer of 1918.*

Not only did the French and British now have to cope with a much larger German force, but they also had to weather the political storm unleashed by Lenin's decision to publish the texts of secret Allied treaties showing that Britain and France, like Germany, had plotted to enlarge their nations and empires through war. The revelation that the Allies were fighting for land and riches rather than democratic principles outraged people in France and Great Britain, demoralized Allied troops, and threw the French and British governments into disarray. The treaties also embarrassed Wilson, who had brought America into the war to fight for democracy, not territory. Wilson sought to restore the Allies' credibility by unveiling, in January 1918, a concrete program for peace. His Fourteen Points (discussed later in this chapter) rejected territorial aggrandizement as a legitimate war aim.

In March and April 1918, Germany launched its offensive against British and French positions, sending Allied troops reeling. A ferocious assault against French lines on May 27 met little resistance; German troops advanced 10 miles a day until they reached the Marne River, within striking distance of Paris. The French government prepared to evacuate the city. At this perilous moment, a large American army arrived to reinforce what remained of the French lines.

In fact, these American troops, part of the American Expeditionary Force (AEF) commanded by General **John J. Pershing**, had begun landing in France almost a year earlier. But it took months to build up a sizable and disciplined force. The United States had had to create a modern army from scratch. Men had to be drafted, trained, supplied with food and equipment; ships for transporting them to Europe had to be found or built. In France, Pershing put his troops through additional training before committing them to battle. He was determined that the American soldiers—or "doughboys," as they were called—should acquit themselves well on the battlefield. The army he ordered into battle to counter the German spring offensive of 1918 fought well. Many American soldiers fell, but Paris was saved, and Germany's best chance for victory slipped away.

Buttressed by this show of AEF strength, the Allied troops staged a major offensive of their own in late September. Millions of Allied troops advanced across the 200-mile-wide Argonne forest in France, cutting German supply lines. By late October, they had reached the German border. Faced with an invasion of their homeland and with mounting popular dissatisfaction with the war, German leaders asked for an armistice, to be followed by peace negotiations based on Wilson's Fourteen Points. Having forced the Germans to agree to numerous concessions, the Allies ended the war on November 11, 1918.

Mobilizing for "Total" War

FOCUS QUESTION

What problems did the United States encounter in mobilizing for total war, and how successfully were the problems overcome?

Compared to Europe, the United States suffered little from the war. The deaths of 112,000 American soldiers paled in comparison to European losses: 900,000 by Great Britain, 1.2 million by Austria-Hungary, 1.4 million by France, 1.7 million by Russia, and 2 million by Germany. The U.S. civilian population was also spared most of the war's ravages—the destruction of homes and industries, the shortages of food and medicine, the spread of disease—that afflicted millions of Europeans. Only the flu epidemic that swept across the Atlantic from Europe in 1919 to claim approximately 500,000 American lives caused wholesale suffering and death.

Still, the war had a profound effect on American society. Every military engagement the United States had fought since the Civil War had been limited in scope.

The First World War was different. It was a **total war** to which every combatant nation had committed virtually all its resources. The scale of the effort for the United States became apparent early in 1917 when Wilson asked Congress for a conscription law that would permit the federal government to raise a multimillion-man army. The United States would also have to devote much of its agricultural, transportation, industrial, and population resources to the war effort if it wished to end the European stalemate. Who would organize this massive effort? Who would pay for it?

ORGANIZING INDUSTRY

At first Wilson pursued a decentralized approach to mobilization, delegating tasks to local defense councils throughout the country. When that effort failed, Wilson created several centralized federal agencies, each charged with supervising nationwide activity in its assigned economic sector.

The success of these agencies varied. The Food Administration, headed by mining engineer Herbert Hoover, was able to increase production of basic foodstuffs through the use of economic incentives and delivered food to millions of troops and European civilians. At the other extreme, the Aircraft Production Board and Emergency Fleet Corporation did a poor job of supplying the Allies with combat aircraft and merchant vessels. On balance, the U.S. economy performed wonders in supplying troops with uniforms, food, rifles, munitions, and other basic items; it failed badly, however, in producing more sophisticated weapons and machines such as artillery, aircraft, and ships.

Most of the new government war agencies were more powerful on paper than in fact. Consider, for example, the **War Industries Board** (WIB). The WIB floundered for the first nine months of its existence, as it lacked the statutory authority to force manufacturers and the military to adopt its plans. Only the appointment of Wall Street investment banker Bernard Baruch as WIB chairman in March 1918 turned the agency around. Rather than attempting to force manufacturers to do the government's bidding, Baruch permitted industrialists to charge high prices for their products. He won exemptions from antitrust laws for corporations willing to

total war *New kind of war requiring every combatant to devote virtually all its economic and political resources to the fight.*

War Industries Board *U.S. government agency responsible for mobilizing American industry for war production.*

"The migrants arrived in great numbers," Panel 40 from The Migration Series. (1940-41); text and title revised by the artist, 1993). Tempera on gesso on composition board, 12 x 18". Gift of Mrs. David M. Levy. (28.19#2.20) The Museum of Modern Art, New York, NY. © Digital Image © The Museum of Modern Art/Licensed by SCALA/Art Resource, NY

THE MIGRATION OF THE NEGRO, PANEL 40: "THE MIGRANTS ARRIVED IN GREAT NUMBERS," BY JACOB LAWRENCE. In this painting, a noted artist shows African American sharecroppers and tenant farmers crossing the countryside as they leave the rural South for northern centers of industry.

comply with his requests. In general, he made war production too lucrative an activity to resist. However, he did not hesitate to unleash his wrath upon corporations that resisted WIB enticements.

Under Baruch's forceful leadership, production increased substantially, and manufacturers discovered the financial benefits of cooperation between the public and private sectors. But Baruch's favoritism toward large corporations hurt smaller competitors. Moreover, the cozy relationship between government and corporate America violated the progressive pledge to protect the people against the "interests."

SECURING WORKERS, KEEPING LABOR PEACE

The government worried as much about labor's cooperation as about industry's compliance. War increased the demand for industrial labor while cutting the supply. European immigrants had long been the most important source of new labor for American industry, and during the war they stopped coming. Meanwhile, millions of workers already in American were conscripted into the military and thus lost to industry.

Manufacturers responded to the labor shortage by recruiting new sources of labor from the rural South; 500,000 African Americans migrated to Northern cities between 1916 and 1920. Another half-million white Southerners followed the same path during that period. Hundreds of thousands of Mexicans left their homeland for jobs in the Southwest and Midwest. Approximately 40,000 Northern women found work as streetcar conductors, railroad workers, metalworkers, and munitions makers and in other jobs customarily reserved for men. The number of female clerical workers doubled between 1910 and 1920, with many of these women finding work in government war bureaucracies.

These workers alleviated but did not eliminate the nation's labor shortage. Workers were quick to recognize the benefits to be won from the tight labor market. They quit jobs they did not like and took part in strikes and other collective actions in unprecedented numbers. Union membership almost doubled, from 2.6 million in 1915 to 5.1 million in 1920. Workers commonly sought higher wages and shorter hours through strikes and unionization. They also struck in response to managerial attempts to speed up production and tighten discipline. As time passed, increasing numbers of workers began to wonder why the war for democracy in Europe had no counterpart in their factories at home. "Industrial democracy" became the battle cry of an awakened labor movement.

Wilson's willingness to include labor in his 1916 progressive coalition reflected his awareness of labor's potential power. In 1918 he bestowed prestige on the newly formed **National War Labor Board** (NWLB) by appointing former president William Howard Taft as one of its two cochairmen. The NWLB brought together representatives of labor, industry, and the public to resolve labor disputes.

RAISING AN ARMY

National War Labor Board *U.S. government agency that brought together representatives of labor, industry, and the public to resolve labor disputes.*

To raise an army, the Wilson administration committed itself to conscription—the drafting of most men of a certain age, irrespective of their family's wealth, ethnic background, or social standing. The Selective Service Act of May 1917 empowered the administration to do just that. By war's end, local Selective Service boards had registered 24 million young men age 18 and older, and had drafted nearly 3 million of them into the military. Another 2 million volunteered for service.

WOMEN DOING "MEN'S WORK." *Labor shortages during the war allowed thousands of women to take industrial jobs customarily reserved for men. Here women operate pneumatic hammers at the Midvale Steel and Ordnance Company, Nicetown, Pennsylvania, 1918.*

Relatively few men resisted the draft, even among recent immigrants. Foreign-born men constituted 18 percent of the armed forces—a percentage greater than their share of the total male population. Almost 400,000 African Americans served, representing approximately 10 percent of armed forces, the same as the percentage of African Americans in the total population.

The U.S. Army, under the command of Chief of Staff Peyton March and General John J. Pershing, had to fashion these ethnically and racially diverse millions into a professional fighting force. Teaching raw recruits to fight was hard enough, Pershing and March observed; teaching them to put aside their racial and ethnic

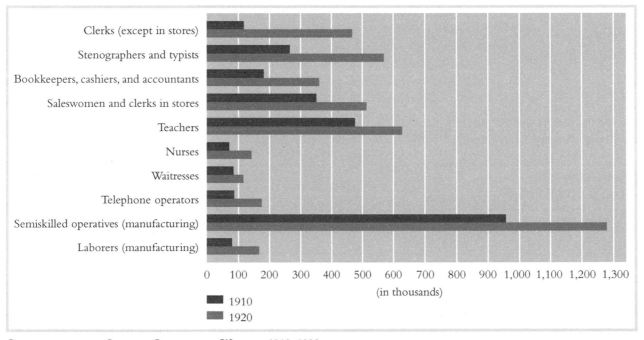

OCCUPATIONS WITH LARGEST INCREASE IN WOMEN, 1910–1920
Source: Joseph A. Hill, *Women in Gainful Occupations, 1870–1920*, U.S. Bureau of the Census, Monograph no. 9 (Washington, D.C.: Government Printing Office, 1929), p. 33.

prejudices was a task they declined to tackle. Rather than integrate the armed forces, they segregated black soldiers from white. Virtually all African Americans were assigned to all-black units that were barred from combat. Being stripped of a combat role was particularly galling to blacks, who, in previous wars, had proven themselves to be among the best American fighters.

For a time, the military justified its intensified discrimination against blacks by referring to the results of rudimentary "IQ" (intelligence quotient) tests administered by psychologists to 2 million AEF soldiers. These tests allegedly "proved" that native-born Americans and immigrants from the British Isles, Germany, and Scandinavia were well endowed with intelligence, while African Americans and immigrants from southern and eastern Europe were poorly endowed. But these tests were scientifically so ill conceived that their findings revealed nothing about the true distribution of intelligence in the population. In 1919 the military discontinued the IQ testing program.

Given the racial and ethnic tensions among American troops and the short time Pershing and his staff had to train recruits, the AEF's performance was impressive. The most decorated soldier in the AEF was Sergeant Alvin C. York of Tennessee, who captured 35 machine guns and 132 prisoners and who killed 17 German soldiers with 17 bullets. York had learned his marksmanship hunting wild turkeys in the Tennessee hills.

One of the most decorated AEF units was **New York's 369th Regiment,** a black unit recruited in Harlem. Bowing to pressure from civil rights groups that some black troops be allowed to fight, Pershing had offered the 369th to the French army. The 369th entered the French front line and scored one major success after another. In gratitude for its service, the French government decorated the entire unit with one of its highest honors—the *Croix de Guerre.*

PAYING THE BILLS

As chief purchaser of supplies for the multimillion-man U.S. military, the government incurred huge debts. To help pay its bills, it sharply increased tax rates. The new taxes hit the wealthiest Americans the hardest: The richest were slapped with a 67 percent income tax and a 25 percent inheritance tax. Corporations were ordered to pay an "excess profits" tax. The revenues brought in by the taxes, however, provided only about one third of the $33 billion the government ultimately spent on the war. The rest came from the sale of **Liberty bonds**. These were 30-year bonds the government sold to individuals with a return of 3.5 percent in annual interest.

The government offered five bond issues between 1917 and 1920, and all were quickly sold out, thanks, in no small measure, to a high-powered sales pitch that equated bond purchases with patriotic duty. The Treasury Department blanketed the country with posters, sent bond salesmen into virtually every American community, enlisted Boy Scouts to go door to door, and staged rallies at which movie stars such as Mary Pickford, Douglas Fairbanks, and Charlie Chaplin stumped for the war.

AROUSING PATRIOTIC ARDOR

The Treasury's bond campaign was only one aspect of an extraordinary government effort to arouse public support for the war. In 1917 Wilson set up a new agency, the **Committee on Public Information** (CPI), to popularize the war. Under the chairmanship of George Creel, a Midwestern progressive and a muckraker, the CPI distributed 75 million copies of pamphlets explaining U.S. war aims in several

New York's 369th Regiment *Black army unit recruited in Harlem that served under French command and was decorated with the* Croix de Guerre *for its valor.*

Liberty bonds *Thirty-year government bonds with an annual interest rate of 3.5 percent sold to fund the war effort.*

Committee on Public Information *U.S. government agency established in 1917 to arouse support for the war and, later, to generate suspicion of war dissenters.*

languages. It trained a force of 75,000 "Four Minute Men" to deliver succinct, uplifting war speeches to groups in their home cities and towns. It papered the walls of countless public institutions (and many private ones) with posters, placed advertisements in mass-circulation magazines, sponsored exhibitions, and peppered newspaper editors with thousands of press releases on the progress of the war.

Faithful to his muckraking past, Creel wanted to give the people "the facts" of the war, believing that well-informed citizens would see the wisdom of Wilson's policies. He also felt his work gave him an opportunity to achieve the progressive goal of uniting all Americans into a single moral community. Americans everywhere learned that the United States had entered the war "to make the world safe for democracy," to help the world's weaker peoples achieve self-determination, and to bring a measure of social justice into the conduct of international affairs. Americans were asked to affirm those ideals by doing everything they could to support the war.

This uplifting message imparted to many a deep love of country and a sense of participation in a grand democratic experiment. It also, however, impelled many Americans to demand that the United States live up to its democratic ideals at home as well as abroad. Workers rallied to the cry of "industrial democracy." Women seized upon the democratic fervor to bring their fight for suffrage to a successful conclusion (see Chapter 21). African Americans began to dream that the war might deliver them from second-class citizenship. European ethnics believed that Wilson's support of their countrymen's rights abroad would improve their own chances for acceptance and advancement in the United States.

Although the CPI had helped to unleash it, this new democratic enthusiasm troubled Creel and others in the Wilson administration. The United States, after all, was still divided along class, ethnic, and racial lines. Workers and industrialists regarded each other with suspicion. Cultural differences compounded this class division, for the working class was overwhelmingly ethnic in composition, while the industrial and political elites consisted mainly of long-settled native-born families. Progressives had fought hard to overcome these divisions. They had tamed the power of capitalists, improved the condition of workers, encouraged the Americanization of immigrants, and articulated a new, more inclusive idea of American nationhood. But their work was not complete when the war broke out, and the war itself widened the remaining social and cultural fissures. The decision to authorize the CPI's unity campaign indicates that the progressives understood how widespread the discord was. Still, they had not anticipated that the promotion of democratic ideals at home would exacerbate, rather than lessen, existing social and cultural conflicts.

WARTIME REPRESSION

By early 1918 the CPI's campaign had developed a more coercive side. Inflammatory advertisements called on patriots to report on neighbors, coworkers, and ethnics whom they suspected of subverting the war effort. Propagandists called on immigrants to repudiate ties to their homeland, native language, and ethnic customs. The CPI spread lurid tales of German atrocities and encouraged the public to see movies like *The Prussian Cur* and *The Beast of Berlin.* The Justice Department arrested thousands of German and Austrian immigrants whom it suspected of subversive activities. Congress passed the Trading with the Enemy Act, which required foreign-language publications to submit all war-related stories to post office censors for approval.

German Americans became the objects of popular hatred. American patriots sought to expunge every trace of German influence from American culture. In Boston, performances of Beethoven's symphonies were banned. Libraries removed

The Art Archive/Eileen Tweedy/Picture Desk

THE CAMPAIGN OF FEAR. *By 1918, the government's appeal to Americans' best aspirations—to spread liberty and democracy—had been replaced by a determination to arouse fear of subversion and conquest. Here the German enemy is depicted as a terrifying brute who violates Lady Liberty and uses his* kultur *club to destroy civilization.*

works of German literature from their shelves, while Theodore Roosevelt and others urged school districts to prohibit the teaching of the German language. Some school boards burned the German books in their districts (see Table 23.1).

German Americans were at risk of being fired from work, losing their businesses, and being assaulted on the street. A St. Louis mob lynched an innocent German immigrant whom they suspected of subversion. After only 25 minutes of deliberation, a St. Louis jury acquitted the mob leaders, who had defended their crime as an act of patriotism. German Americans began hiding their ethnic identity, changing their names, speaking German only in the privacy of their homes, and celebrating their holidays only with trusted friends.

The anti-German campaign escalated into a general anti-immigrant crusade. Congress passed the **Immigration Restriction Act of 1917,** which declared that all adult immigrants who failed a reading test would be denied admission to the United States. The act also banned the immigration of laborers from India, Indochina, Afghanistan, Arabia, the East Indies, and several other countries within an "Asiatic Barred Zone." Congress also passed the Eighteenth Amendment to the Constitution, which prohibited the manufacture and distribution of alcoholic beverages. The crusade for Prohibition was not new, but anti-immigrant feelings gave it added impetus. Prohibitionists pictured the nation's urban ethnic ghettos as scenes of drunkenness, immorality, and disloyalty. The Eighteenth Amendment was quickly ratified by the states, and in 1919 Prohibition became the law of the land.

More and more, the Wilson administration relied on repression to achieve domestic unity. In the **Espionage, Sabotage, and Sedition Acts** passed in 1917 and 1918, Congress gave the administration sweeping powers to silence and even imprison dissenters. These acts went far beyond outlawing behavior such as spying for the enemy, sabotaging war production, and calling for the enemy's victory. By making it illegal to write or utter any statement that could be construed as profaning the flag, the Constitution, or the military, they constituted the most drastic restriction of free speech at the national level since enactment of the Alien and Sedition Acts of 1798 (see Chapter 8).

Government repression fell most heavily on the Industrial Workers of the World (IWW) and the Socialist Party. Both groups had opposed intervention in 1917. Although they subsequently muted their opposition, they continued to insist that the true enemies of American workers were to be found in the ranks of American employers, not in Germany or Austria-Hungary. The government responded by banning many socialist materials from the mails and by disrupting socialist and IWW meetings. By the spring of 1918 government agents had arrested 2,000 IWW members, including the entire executive board. Many of those arrested would be sentenced to long jail terms. Eugene V. Debs, the head of the Socialist Party, received a 10-year jail term for making an antiwar speech in Canton, Ohio, in the summer of 1918. Citizens organized groups to enforce patriotism. The largest of these, the

Immigration Restriction Act of 1917 *Measure that denied any adult immigrant who failed a reading test entry into the United States, and banned immigration from the "Asiatic Barred Zone."*

Espionage, Sabotage, and Sedition Acts *Laws passed in 1917 and 1918 that gave the federal government sweeping powers to silence and even imprison dissenters.*

TABLE 23.1

RENAMED GERMAN AMERICAN WORDS	
Original	**"Patriotic" Name**
hamburger	Salisbury steak, liberty steak, liberty sandwich
sauerkraut	liberty cabbage
Hamburg Avenue, Brooklyn, New York	Wilson Avenue, Brooklyn, New York
Germantown, Nebraska	Garland, Nebraska
East Germantown, Indiana	Pershing, Indiana
Berlin, Iowa	Lincoln, Iowa
pinochle	liberty
German shepherd	Alsatian shepherd
Deutsches Hans of Indianapolis	Athenaeum of Indiana
Germania Maennerchor of Chicago	Lincoln Club
Kaiser Street	Maine Way

Source: From La Vern J. Rippley, *The German Americans* (Boston: Twayne, 1976), p. 186; and Robert H. Ferrell, *Woodrow Wilson and World War I, 1917–1921* (New York: Harper and Row, 1985), pp. 205–206.

American Protective League, routinely spied on fellow workers and neighbors, opened the mail and tapped the phones of those suspected of disloyalty, and harassed young men who were thought to be evading the draft. Attorney General Thomas Gregory publicly endorsed the group and sought federal funds to support its "police" work.

The spirit of coercion even infected institutions that had long prided themselves on tolerance. In July 1917 Columbia University fired two professors for speaking out against U.S. intervention in the war. The National Americanization Committee, which before 1917 had pioneered a humane approach to the problem of integrating immigrants into American life, now supported surveillance, internment, and deportation of aliens suspected of anti-American sentiments.

Wilson did attempt to block some repressive legislation; for example, he vetoed both the Immigration Restriction Act and the Volstead Act (the act passed by Congress to enforce Prohibition), only to be overridden by Congress. But Wilson did little to halt Attorney General Gregory's prosecution of radicals or Postmaster General Burleson's campaign to exclude Socialist Party publications from the mail. He ignored pleas from progressives that he intervene in the Debs case. His acquiescence in these matters cost him dearly among progressives and socialists. Wilson believed, however, that once the Allies won the war and arranged a just peace in accordance with the Fourteen Points, his administration's wartime actions would be forgiven and the progressive coalition would be restored.

Fourteen Points *Plan laid out by Woodrow Wilson in January 1918 to give concrete form to his dream of a "peace without victory" and a new world order.*

THE FAILURE OF THE INTERNATIONAL PEACE

In the month following Germany's surrender on November 11, 1918, Wilson was confident about the prospects of achieving a just peace. Both Germany and the Allies had publicly accepted the **Fourteen Points** as the basis for negotiations. Wilson's international prestige was enormous. To capitalize on his fame, Wilson broke with diplomatic precedent and decided to head the American delegation to the Paris Peace Conference in January 1919 himself. Some

FOCUS QUESTION

What were Woodrow Wilson's peace proposals, and how did they fare?

2 million French citizens lined the parade route in Paris to catch a glimpse of "Wilson, *le juste* [the just]."

In the Fourteen Points, Wilson had translated his principles for a new world order into specific proposals for world peace and justice. The first group of points called for all nations to abide by a code of conduct that embraced free trade, freedom of the seas, open diplomacy, disarmament, and the resolution of disputes through mediation. A second group, based on the principle of self-determination, proposed redrawing the map of Europe to give the subjugated peoples of the Austro-Hungarian, Ottoman, and Russian empires national sovereignty. The last point called for establishing a League of Nations, an assembly in which all nations would be represented and in which all international disputes would be given a fair hearing and an opportunity for peaceful solutions.

THE PARIS PEACE CONFERENCE AND THE TREATY OF VERSAILLES

Although representatives of 27 nations began meeting in Paris on January 12, 1919, to discuss Wilson's Fourteen Points, negotiations were controlled by the "Big Four": Wilson, Prime Minister David Lloyd George of Great Britain, Premier Georges Clemenceau of France, and Prime Minister Vittorio Orlando of Italy. When Orlando quit the conference after a dispute with Wilson, the Big Four became the Big Three. Wilson quickly learned that his negotiating partners' support for the Fourteen Points was much weaker than he had believed. Indeed, Clemenceau and Lloyd George refused to include most of Wilson's points in the peace treaty. The points having to do with freedom of the seas and free trade were omitted, as were the proposals for open diplomacy and Allied disarmament. Wilson won partial endorsement of the principle of self-determination: Belgian sovereignty was restored, Poland's status as a nation was affirmed, and the new nations of Czechoslovakia, Yugoslavia, Finland, Lithuania, Latvia, and Estonia were created. Some lands of the former Ottoman Empire—Armenia, Palestine, Mesopotamia, and Syria—were to be placed under League of Nations' trusteeships with the understanding that they would someday gain their independence. But Wilson failed in his efforts to block a British plan to transfer former German colonies in Asia to Japanese control, an Italian plan to annex territory inhabited by 200,000 Austrians, and a French plan to take from Germany its valuable Saar coal mines (see Map 23.2).

Nor could Wilson blunt the drive to punish Germany for its wartime aggression. In addition to awarding the Saar basin to France, the Allies gave portions of northern Germany to Denmark and portions of eastern Germany to Poland and Czechoslovakia. Germany was stripped of virtually its entire navy and air force, and forbidden to place soldiers or fortifications in western Germany along the Rhine. In addition, Germany was forced to admit its responsibility for the war. In accepting this "war guilt," Germany was, in effect, agreeing to compensate the victors in cash ("reparations") for the pain and suffering it had inflicted on them.

Lloyd George and Clemenceau brushed off the protests of those who viewed this desire to prostrate Germany as a cruel and vengeful act. That the German people, after their nation's 1918 defeat, had overthrown the monarch (Kaiser Wilhelm II) who had taken them to war, and had reconstituted their nation as a democratic republic, won them no leniency. On June 28, 1919, Great Britain, France, the United States, Germany, and other European nations signed the Treaty of Versailles. In 1921, an Allied commission notified the Germans that they were to pay the victors $33 billion, a sum well beyond the resources of a defeated and economically ruined Germany.

Map 23.2 EUROPE AND THE NEAR EAST AFTER THE FIRST WORLD WAR. *The First World War and the Treaty of Versailles changed the geography of Europe and the Near East. Nine nations in Europe, stretching from Yugoslavia in the south to Finland in the north, were created (or re-formed) out of the defeated Austro-Hungarian and Ottoman Empires. In the Near East, meanwhile, Syria, Lebanon, Palestine, Transjordan, and Iraq were carved out of the Ottoman Empire, placed under British or French control, and promised eventual independence.*

THE LEAGUE OF NATIONS

The Allies' single-minded pursuit of self-interest disillusioned many liberals and socialists in the United States, but Wilson seemed undismayed. He had won approval of the most important of his Fourteen Points—the one that called for the creation of the League of Nations. The League, whose structure and responsibilities were set forth in a Covenant attached to the peace treaty, would usher in Wilson's new world order. Drawing its membership from the signatories to the Treaty of Versailles (except, for the time being, Germany), the League would function as an international parliament and judiciary, establishing rules of international behavior and resolving disputes between nations through rational and peaceful means.

The League, Wilson believed, would redeem the failures of the Paris Peace Conference. Under its auspices, free trade and freedom of the seas would be achieved, reparations against Germany would be reduced or eliminated, disarmament of the Allies would proceed, and the principle of self-determination would be extended to peoples outside Europe. Moreover, the League would have the power to punish aggressor nations through economic isolation and military retaliation.

WILSON VERSUS LODGE: THE FIGHT OVER RATIFICATION

For the League to succeed, however, Wilson had to convince the U.S. Senate to ratify the Treaty of Versailles. Wilson knew that this would not be easy. The Republicans had gained a majority in the Senate in 1918, and two groups within their ranks were determined to frustrate Wilson's ambitions. One group was a caucus of 14 Midwesterners and Westerners known as the **irreconcilables**. Most of them were conservative isolationists who had long wanted the United States to preserve its separation from Europe, but a few were prominent progressives who had voted against the declaration of war in 1917. Under no circumstances would they support a plan that would embroil the United States in European affairs.

The second opposition group was led by Senator **Henry Cabot Lodge** of Massachusetts. Its members rejected Wilson's belief that every group of people on earth had a right to form their own nation; that every state, regardless of its size, should have a voice in world affairs; and that disputes between nations could be settled in open, democratic forums. They subscribed instead to Theodore Roosevelt's vision of a world controlled by a few great nations, each militarily strong, secure in its own sphere of influence, and determined to avoid war through a carefully negotiated balance of power. These Republicans preferred to let Europe return to the power politics that had prevailed before the war rather than experiment with a new world order that might constrain and compromise U.S. strength and autonomy.

Lodge and his supporters raised important questions about the power given the League by **Article X of the Covenant** to undertake military actions against aggressor nations. Did Americans want to authorize an international organization to decide when the United States would go to war? Was this not a violation of the Constitution, which vested war-making power solely in Congress? Even if the constitutional problem could be solved, how could the United States ensure that it would not be forced into a military action that might damage its national interest?

It soon became clear, however, that several Republicans, especially Lodge, were more interested in humiliating Wilson than in engaging in debate. They accused Wilson of promoting socialism through his wartime expansion of government power. They were angry that he had failed to include any distinguished Republicans in the Paris peace delegation. And they were bitter about the 1918 congressional elections, when Wilson had argued that a Republican victory would embarrass the nation abroad. As chairman of the Senate Foreign Relations Committee, Lodge did everything possible to obstruct ratification. When his committee finally reported the treaty to the full Senate, it came encumbered with nearly 50 amendments whose adoption Lodge made a precondition of his support. Some of the amendments expressed reasonable concerns—namely, that participation in the League not diminish the role of Congress in determining foreign policy or compromise the sovereignty of the nation. But many were meant only to complicate the task of ratification.

irreconcilables *Group of 14 Midwestern and Western senators who opposed the Treaty of Versailles.*

Henry Cabot Lodge *Republican Senator from Massachusetts who led the campaign to reject the Treaty of Versailles.*

Article X of the Covenant *Addendum to the Treaty of Versailles that empowered the League of Nations to undertake military actions against aggressor nations.*

TABLE 23.2

WOODROW WILSON'S FOURTEEN POINTS, 1918: RECORD OF IMPLEMENTATION	
1. Open covenants of peace openly arrived at	Not fulfilled
2. Absolute freedom of navigation upon the seas in peace and war	Not fulfilled
3. Removal of all economic barriers to the equality of trade among nations	Not fulfilled
4. Reduction of armaments to the level needed only for domestic safety	Not fulfilled
5. Impartial adjustments of colonial claims	Not fulfilled
6. Evacuation of all Russian territory; Russia to be welcomed into the society of free nations	Not fulfilled
7. Evacuation and restoration of Belgium	Fulfilled
8. Evacuation and restoration of all French lands; return of Alsace-Lorraine to France	Fulfilled
9. Readjustment of Italy's frontiers along lines of Italian nationality	Compromised
10. Self-determination for the former subjects of the Austro-Hungarian Empire	Compromised
11. Evacuation of Romania, Serbia, and Montenegro; free access to the sea for Serbia	Compromised
12. Self-determination for the former subjects of the Ottoman Empire; secure sovereignty for Turkish portion	Compromised
13. Establishment of an independent Poland with free and secure access to the sea	Fulfilled
14. Establishment of a League of Nations affording mutual guarantees of independence and territorial integrity	Compromised

Source: From G. M. Gathorne-Hardy, *The Fourteen Points and the Treaty of Versailles*, Oxford Pamphlets on World Affairs, no. 6 (1939), pp. 8–34; and Thomas G. Paterson et al., *American Foreign Policy: A History, 2nd ed.* (Lexington, Mass.: D. C. Heath, 1983), vol. 2, pp. 282–293.

Despite Lodge's obstructionism, the treaty's chances for ratification by the required two-thirds majority of the Senate were still good. Many Republicans were prepared to vote for ratification if Wilson indicated a willingness to accept some of the proposed amendments. But Wilson refused to compromise and announced that he would carry his case to the people. In September 1919 he undertook a whirlwind cross-country tour in which he addressed as many crowds as he could reach, sometimes speaking for an hour at a time, four times a day.

On September 25, after giving a speech at Pueblo, Colorado, Wilson suffered excruciating headaches throughout the night. His physician ordered him back to Washington, where on October 2 he suffered a near-fatal stroke. Wilson hovered near death for two weeks and remained seriously disabled for another six. Wilson's wife, Edith Bolling Wilson, and his doctor isolated him from Congress and the press, withholding news they thought might upset him and preventing the public from learning how much his body and mind had deteriorated.

Many historians believe that the stroke impaired Wilson's political judgment. He refused to consider any of the Republican amendments to the treaty, even after it had become clear that compromise offered the only chance of winning U.S. participation in the League of Nations. When Lodge presented an amended treaty for a ratification vote on November 19, Wilson ordered Senate Democrats to vote against it; 42 (of 47) Democratic senators complied, and with the aid of 13 Republican irreconcilables, the Lodge version was defeated. Only moments later, the unamended version of the treaty—Wilson's version—received only 38 votes.

THE TREATY'S FINAL DEFEAT

As the magnitude of the calamity became apparent, supporters of the League in Congress, the nation, and the world urged the Senate and the president to reconsider. Wilson would not budge. A bipartisan group of senators desperately tried to work out a compromise without consulting him. When that effort failed, the Senate put to a vote, one more time, the Lodge version of the treaty. Because 23 Democrats, most of them Southerners, still refused to break with Wilson, this last-ditch effort at ratification failed.

The judgment of history lies heavily upon these events, for many believe that the flawed treaty and the failure of the League contributed to Adolf Hitler's rise and the outbreak of a second world war more devastating than the first. It is necessary to ask, then, whether American participation in the League would have significantly altered the course of world history.

The mere fact of U.S. membership in the League would not have magically solved Europe's postwar problems. The U.S. government was inexperienced in diplomacy and prone to mistakes. Its freedom to negotiate solutions to international disputes would have been limited by the large number of American voters who remained strongly opposed to U.S. entanglement in European affairs. Even if such opposition could have been overcome, the United States would still have confronted European countries determined to go their own way.

Nevertheless, one thing is clear: No stable international order could have arisen after the First World War without the full involvement of the United States. The League of Nations required American authority and prestige in order to operate effectively as an international parliament. We cannot know whether the League, with American involvement, would have offered the Germans a less humiliating peace, allowing them to rehabilitate their economy and salvage their national pride; nor whether an American-led League would have stopped Hitler's expansionism before it escalated into full-scale war in 1939. Still, it seems fair to suggest that American participation would have strengthened the League and improved its ability to bring a lasting peace to Europe.

THE POSTWAR PERIOD: A SOCIETY IN CONVULSION

FOCUS QUESTION

What issues convulsed American society in the immediate aftermath of war, and how were they resolved?

The end of the war brought no respite from the forces convulsing American society. Workers wanted to regain the purchasing power they had lost to inflation. Employers were determined to halt or reverse the wartime gains labor had made. Radicals saw in this conflict between capital and labor the possibility of a socialist revolution. Conservatives were certain that the revolution had already begun. Returning white servicemen were nervous about regaining their civilian jobs and looked with hostility on the black, Hispanic, and female workers who had been recruited to take their places. Black veterans were in no mood to return to segregation and subordination.

LABOR–CAPITAL CONFLICT

Nowhere was the escalation of conflict more evident than in the workplace. In 1919, 4 million workers—one fifth of the nation's manufacturing workforce—went on strike. In January 1919, a general strike paralyzed the city of Seattle. By August, walkouts had been staged by 400,000 Eastern and Midwestern coal miners, 120,000 New England textile workers, and 50,000 New York City garment workers. Then came two strikes that turned public opinion sharply against labor. In September, Boston policemen walked off their jobs after the police commissioner refused to negotiate with their newly formed union. Rioting and looting soon broke out. Massachusetts governor Calvin Coolidge refused to negotiate with the policemen, called out the National Guard to restore order, and then fired the entire police force.

Hard on the heels of the policemen's strike came a strike by more than 300,000 steelworkers in the Midwest. No union had established a footing in the steel industry since the 1890s, when Andrew Carnegie had ousted the ironworkers' union from his Homestead, Pennsylvania, mills. Most steelworkers labored long hours (the 12-hour shift was still standard) for low wages in dangerous workplaces. The organizers of the **1919 steel strike** had somehow managed to persuade steelworkers with varied skill levels and ethnic backgrounds to put aside their differences and demand an eight-hour day and union recognition. When the employers rejected those demands, the workers walked off their jobs. Employers responded by procuring armed guards to beat up the strikers and by hiring nonunion labor to keep the plants running. In many areas, local and state police prohibited union meetings, ran strikers out of town, and opened fire on those who disobeyed orders. In Gary, Indiana, a confrontation between unionists and armed guards left 18 strikers dead. To gain public support for their antiunion campaign, industry leaders painted strike leaders as violent radicals bent on the destruction of political liberty and economic freedom. They succeeded in arousing public opinion against the steelworkers, and the strike collapsed in January 1920.

RADICALS AND THE RED SCARE

The steel companies succeeded in putting down the strike by fanning the public's fear that revolutionary sentiment was spreading among the workers. Radical sentiment was indeed on the rise. Mine workers and railroad workers had begun calling for the permanent nationalization of coal mines and railroads. Longshoremen in San Francisco and Seattle refused to load ships carrying supplies to the White Russians who had taken up arms against Lenin's Bolshevik government. Socialist trade unionists mounted the most serious challenge to Samuel Gompers's control of the American Federation of Labor (AFL) in 25 years. In 1920, nearly a million Americans voted for the Socialist presidential candidate Debs, who ran his campaign from jail.

This radical surge did not mean, however, that leftists had fashioned themselves into a single movement or political party. On the contrary, the Russian Revolution had split the American Socialist Party. One faction, which would keep the name Socialist and would continue under Debs' leadership, insisted that radicals follow a democratic path to socialism. The other group, which would take the name Communist, wanted to establish a Lenin-style "dictatorship of the proletariat." Small groups of anarchists, some of whom advocated campaigns of terror to speed the revolution, represented yet a third radical tendency.

Few Americans noticed the disarray in the radical camp. Most assumed that radicalism was a single, coordinated movement bent on establishing a communist government on American soil. Beginning in 1919, this perceived **"Red Scare"** prompted government officials and private citizens to embark on yet another campaign of repression.

The postwar repression of radicalism resembled the wartime repression of dissent. Thirty states passed sedition laws to punish people who advocated revolution. Numerous public and private groups intensified Americanization campaigns designed to strip foreigners of their "subversive" ways and remake them into loyal citizens. A newly formed veterans' organization, the American Legion, took on the

1919 steel strike *Walkout by 300,000 steelworkers in the Midwest demanding union recognition and an eight-hour day. It was defeated by employers and local and state police forces, who sometimes resorted to violence.*

Red Scare *Widespread fear in 1919–1920 that radicals had coalesced to establish a communist government on American soil. In response, U.S. government and private citizens undertook a campaign to identify, silence, and, in some cases, imprison radicals.*

HISTORY THROUGH FILM

REDS (1981)

*Directed by Warren Beatty; starring Warren Beatty
(John Reed), Diane Keaton (Louise Bryant), Edward
Herrmann (Max Eastman), Jerzy Kosinski
(Grigory Zinoviev), Jack Nicholson (Eugene O'Neill),
and Maureen Stapleton (Emma Goldman)*

This epic film attempts to integrate the history of the American Left in the early 20th century with a love story about two radicals of that era, John "Jack" Reed and Louise Bryant. Reed was a well-known radical journalist whose dispatches from Russia during its 1917 revolution, published as a book *Ten Days That Shook the World,* brought him fame and notoriety. Bryant was an integral member of the radical circles that gathered in apartments and cafés in New York's Bohemian Greenwich Village before and during the First World War.

At times, the love principals in this movie seem to resemble Warren Beatty and Diane Keaton more than they do the historical figures they are meant to represent. In general, however, the movie successfully conveys an important and historically accurate message about the American Left during this period: namely, that its participants wanted to revolutionize the personal as well as the political. Equality between men and women, women's right to enjoy the same sexual freedom as men, and marriage's impact on personal growth and adventure were debated with the same fervor as building a radical political party and accelerating the transition to socialism. (See the section, The New Sexuality and the New Woman, in Chapter 20.)

Reds is also a serious film about political parties and ideologies. The film follows the arc of John Reed's and Louise Bryant's lives from their prewar days as discontented members of the Portland, Oregon, social elite, through their flight to the freedom and radicalism of Greenwich Village, to the hardening of their radicalism as a result of repression during the First World War at home and the Bolshevik triumph in November 1917. Beatty has recreated detailed and complex stories about internal fights within the Left both in the United States and Russia, through which he seeks to show how hopes for social transformation went awry. To give this film added historical weight, Beatty introduces "witnesses," individuals who actually knew the real Reed and Bryant and who appear on screen periodically to share their memories, both serious and whimsical, about the storied couple and the times in which they lived.

Diane Keaton as Louise Bryant and Warren Beatty as John Reed, together in Russia in the midst of that country's socialist revolution.

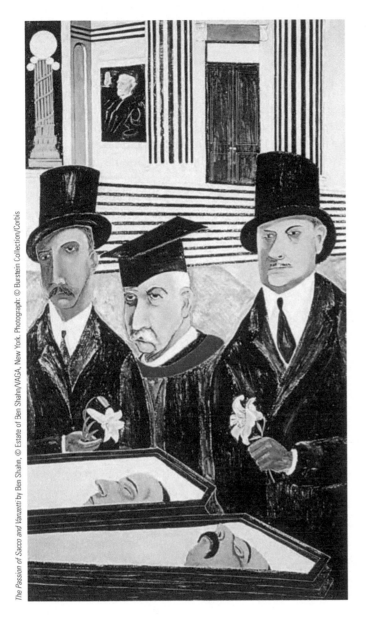

The Passion of Sacco and Vanzetti by Ben Shahn, © Estate of Ben Shahn/VAGA, New York. Photograph: © Burstein Collection/Corbis

THE PASSION OF SACCO AND VANZETTI, BY BEN SHAHN. The 1920 trial and 1927 execution of Nicola Sacco and Bartolomeo Vanzetti became the passion of many immigrants, liberal intellectuals, and artists (such as Ben Shahn), who were convinced that the two anarchists had been unfairly tried and convicted.

American Protective League's role of identifying seditious individuals and organizations and ensuring the public's devotion to "100 percent Americanism."

The Red Scare reached its climax on New Year's Day 1920, when federal agents broke into the homes and meeting places of thousands of suspected revolutionaries in 33 cities. Directed by Attorney General A. Mitchell Palmer, these widely publicized "Palmer raids" were meant to expose the extent of revolutionary activity. Palmer's agents uncovered three pistols, no rifles, and no explosives. Nevertheless, they arrested more than 4,000 people and kept many of them in jail for weeks without formally charging them with a crime. Finally, those who were not citizens (approximately 600) were deported and the rest were released. As the meager results of the Palmer raids became known, many Americans began to wonder whether they had exaggerated the threat of dissent and subversion.

But the political atmosphere remained hostile to radicals, as the **Sacco and Vanzetti case** revealed. In May 1920, two Italian-born anarchists, Nicola Sacco and Bartolomeo Vanzetti, were arrested in Brockton, Massachusetts, and charged with armed robbery and murder. Both men proclaimed their innocence and insisted they were being punished for their political beliefs. Indeed, their foreign accents and

Sacco and Vanzetti case (1920)
Controversial conviction of two Italian-born anarchists accused of armed robbery and murder.

MARCUS GARVEY, BLACK NATIONALIST. *This portrait was taken in 1924, after Garvey's conviction on mail fraud charges.*

Library of Congress Prints and Photographs Division [LC-USZ61-1854]

their espousal of anarchist doctrines in the courtroom inclined many Americans, including the judge who presided at their trial, to view them harshly. Despite the weak case against them, they were convicted of first-degree murder and sentenced to death. Their lawyers attempted numerous appeals, all of which failed. Anger over the verdicts began to build among Italian Americans, radicals, and liberal intellectuals. Protests compelled the governor of Massachusetts to appoint a commission to review the case, but no new trial was ordered. On August 23, 1927, Sacco and Vanzetti were executed, still insisting that they were innocent.

RACIAL CONFLICT AND THE RISE OF BLACK NATIONALISM

The more than 400,000 blacks who served in the armed forces believed that a victory for democracy abroad would help them achieve democracy for themselves at home. At first, the segregation they encountered in the military did not weaken their conviction that they would be treated as full-fledged citizens upon their return. But the discrimination they experienced after the war was difficult to endure. Many blacks who had found jobs in the North were fired to make way for returning white veterans. Returning black servicemen had to scrounge for poorly paid jobs as unskilled laborers. In the South, lynch mobs targeted black veterans who refused to tolerate the usual insults and indignities.

The worst antiblack violence after the war occurred in the North. In Chicago, in July 1919, a black teenager who had been swimming in Lake Michigan was killed by whites after coming too close to a whites-only beach. Rioting soon broke out, with white mobs invading black neighborhoods, torching homes and stores, and attacking innocent residents. Led by war veterans, some of whom were armed, blacks fought back, turning the border areas between white and black neighborhoods into battle zones. Fighting continued for five days, leaving 38 dead (23 black, 15 white) and more than 500 injured. Race rioting in other cities pushed the death total to 120 before summer's end.

The riots made it clear to blacks that the North was not the Promised Land. Confined to unskilled jobs and to segregated neighborhoods with substandard housing and exorbitant rents, black migrants in Chicago, New York, and other Northern cities suffered economic hardship throughout the 1920s. The NAACP carried on its campaign for civil rights and racial equality, but many blacks no longer shared its belief that they would one day be accepted as first-class citizens. They turned instead to an immigrant from Jamaica, **Marcus Garvey**. Garvey called on blacks to give up their hopes for integration and to set about forging a separate black nation. He reminded blacks that they possessed a rich culture stretching back over the centuries that would enable them to achieve greatness as a nation. Garvey wanted to build a black nation in Africa that would bring together all the world's people of African descent. In the short term, he wanted to help American and Caribbean blacks achieve economic and cultural independence.

QUICK   REVIEW

POSTWAR SOCIAL DISORDER

- Labor strikes surged in 1919; most were defeated

- Bolshevik Revolution in Russia (1917) generated fears of communist uprising in the United States (the "Red Scare"), prompting widespread repression

- Black migration north increased racial tensions and triggered urban race riots in 1919

- Disillusionment among African Americans led many to support Marcus Garvey's black nationalist movement

Garvey's call for black separatism and self-sufficiency—black nationalism, as it came to be called—elicited a remarkable response among African Americans. In the early 1920s, the Universal Negro Improvement Association (UNIA), which Garvey had founded, enrolled millions of members. His newspaper, *The Negro World*, reached a circulation of 200,000. Garvey's most visible economic venture was the Black Star Line, a shipping company with three ships flying the UNIA flag from their masts.

This black nationalist movement did not endure for long. Garvey entered into bitter disputes with other black leaders, including W. E. B. Du Bois, who regarded him as a flamboyant, self-serving demagogue. Garvey sometimes showed poor judgment, as when he expressed support for the Ku Klux Klan on the grounds that it shared his pessimism about the possibility of racial integration. Garvey also squandered UNIA money on ill-conceived business ventures. In 1923 he was convicted of mail fraud involving the sale of Black Star Line stock and was sentenced to five years in jail. In 1927 he was deported to Jamaica and the UNIA folded. But Garvey's philosophy of black nationalism endured.

> **Marcus Garvey** *Jamaican-born black nationalist who attracted millions of African Americans in the early 1920s to a movement calling for black separatism and self-sufficiency.*

C O N C L U S I O N

The resurgence of racism in 1919 and the consequent turn to black nationalism among African Americans were signs of how the high hopes of the war years had been dashed. Industrial workers, immigrants, and radicals also found their pursuit of liberty and equality interrupted by the fear, intolerance, and repression unleashed by the war. Of the reform groups, only woman suffragists made enduring gains—especially the right to vote—but for the feminists in their ranks, these steps forward did not compensate for the collapse of the progressive movement and, with it, their program of achieving equal rights for women across the board.

A similar disappointment engulfed those who had embraced and fought for Wilson's dream of creating a new and democratic world order. The world in 1919 appeared as volatile as it had been in 1914. More and more Americans, perhaps even a majority, were coming to believe that U.S. intervention had been a mistake.

In other ways, the United States benefited a great deal from the war. By 1919, the American economy was by far the world's strongest. The nation's economic strength triggered an extraordinary burst of growth in the 1920s, and millions of Americans rushed to take advantage of the prosperity that this "people's capitalism" had put within their grasp. But even affluence failed to dissolve the class, ethnic, and racial tensions that the war had exposed. And the failure of the peace process added to Europe's problems, delayed the emergence of the United States as a leader in world affairs, and created the preconditions for another world war.

QUESTIONS FOR REVIEW AND CRITICAL THINKING

Review

1. Why did the U.S. policy of neutrality fail, and why did the U.S. get drawn into war?
2. What problems did the U.S. encounter in mobilizing for total war, and how successfully were the problems overcome?
3. What were Woodrow Wilson's peace proposals, and how did they fare?
4. What issues convulsed American society in the immediate aftermath of war, and how were they resolved?

Critical Thinking

1. Did the First World War do more to enhance or interrupt the pursuit of liberty and equality on the home front?
2. Do you think that the chances of a second world war breaking out in Europe in the late 1930s would have been substantially lessened had Woodrow Wilson prevailed on the U.S. Senate to ratify the Treaty of Versailles in 1919, thereby bringing the United States into the League of Nations?

ONLINE RESOURCES

 Visit the companion website to access flashcards, crossword puzzles, exercises, and quizzes related to this chapter: www.cengage.com/history/murrin/libertyequalconc5e.

 See our interactive ebook for map and primary source activities.

 ISCOVERY　*What role did nationalism play in the war and on the home front in World War I?*

GEOGRAPHY Study the two maps on pages 607 and 621. Which nations and empires lost the most territory following World War I? What new countries emerged following the war? How many "empires" existed in Europe and the Middle East after World War I? How were League of Nations trusteeships different from colonies? Did the collapse of empires, the emergence of new nations, and the shifting borders of existing nations weaken or intensify expressions of nationalism among Europe's peoples? What were the consequences of this development?

In thinking about this question, begin by breaking it down into the components shown below. A discussion of the significance of each component should appear in your answer.

WAR AND SOCIETY Read through the renamed German American words in the table. In what ways do the new words express an American nationalism? How do you think you would react if you were a German American living at that time? Does this kind of erasure of foreign culture still occur during wartime or international disputes? If so, can you think of a recent example?

TABLE 23.1

RENAMED GERMAN AMERICAN WORDS	
Original	**"Patriotic" Name**
hamburger	Salisbury steak, liberty steak, liberty sandwich
sauerkraut	liberty cabbage
Hamburg Avenue, Brooklyn, New York	Wilson Avenue, Brooklyn, New York
Germantown, Nebraska	Garland, Nebraska
East Germantown, Indiana	Pershing, Indiana
Berlin, Iowa	Lincoln, Iowa
pinochle	liberty
German shepherd	Alsatian shepherd
Deutsches Hans of Indianapolis	Athenaeum of Indiana
Germania Maennerchor of Chicago	Lincoln Club
Kaiser Street	Maine Way

Source: From La Vern J. Rippley, *The German Americans* (Boston: Twayne, 1976), p. 186; and Robert H. Ferrell, *Woodrow Wilson and World War I, 1917–1921* (New York: Harper and Row, 1985), pp. 205–206.

24

THE 1920s

In 1920 Americans elected a president, Warren G. Harding, who could not have been more different from his predecessor, Woodrow Wilson. A Republican, Harding presented himself as a common man with common desires. In his 1920 campaign he called for a "return to normalcy." Although he died in office in 1923, his carefree spirit is thought to characterize the 1920s.

To many Americans, indeed, the decade was one of fun rather than reform, of good times rather than high ideals. It was, in the words of novelist F. Scott Fitzgerald, the "Jazz Age," a time when the quest for personal gratification seemed to replace the quest for public welfare.

Despite Harding's call for a return to a familiar past, America seemed to be rushing headlong into the future. The word "modern" began appearing everywhere: modern times, modern women, modern technology, the modern home, modern marriage. Although the word was rarely defined, it connoted certain beliefs: that science was a better guide to life

than religion; that people should be free to choose their own lifestyles; that sex should be a source of pleasure for women as well as men; that women and minorities should be equal to and enjoy the same rights as white men.

Many Americans, however, reaffirmed their belief that God's word transcended science; that people should obey the moral code set forth in the Bible; that women were not equal to men; and that blacks, Mexicans, and eastern European immigrants were inferior to Anglo-Saxon whites. They made their voices heard in a resurgent Ku Klux Klan and the fundamentalist movement and on issues such as evolution and immigration.

Modernists and traditionalists confronted each other in party politics, in legislatures, in courtrooms, and in the press. Their battles make it impossible to think of the 1920s merely as a time for the pursuit of leisure. Nor were the 1920s free of the economic and social problems that had troubled Americans for decades.

1920	1921	1922	1923	1924	1925	1926	1927	1928	1929	1930

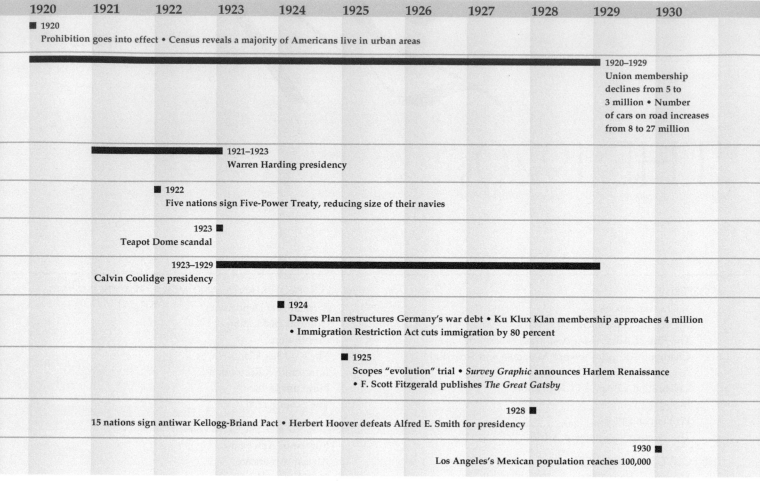

■ 1920
Prohibition goes into effect • Census reveals a majority of Americans live in urban areas

1920–1929
Union membership declines from 5 to 3 million • Number of cars on road increases from 8 to 27 million

1921–1923
Warren Harding presidency

■ 1922
Five nations sign Five-Power Treaty, reducing size of their navies

1923 ■
Teapot Dome scandal

1923–1929
Calvin Coolidge presidency

■ 1924
Dawes Plan restructures Germany's war debt • Ku Klux Klan membership approaches 4 million • Immigration Restriction Act cuts immigration by 80 percent

■ 1925
Scopes "evolution" trial • *Survey Graphic* announces Harlem Renaissance • F. Scott Fitzgerald publishes *The Great Gatsby*

1928 ■
15 nations sign antiwar Kellogg-Briand Pact • Herbert Hoover defeats Alfred E. Smith for presidency

1930 ■
Los Angeles's Mexican population reaches 100,000

$\mathcal{P}$ROSPERITY

FOCUS QUESTION
What were the achievements and limitations of "people's capitalism" in the 1920s?

For a time after the war ended, the country experienced economic turmoil and depression. Workers struck to protest wage reductions or increased work hours. Farmers were hit by a severe depression as overseas demand for American foodstuffs fell from its peak of 1918 and 1919. Disgruntled workers and farmers joined forces to form statewide farmer-labor parties. In 1924 the two groups formed a national Farmer-Labor Party. Robert La Follette, their presidential candidate, received 16 percent of the vote that year.

Then the third-party movement fell apart. Its collapse reflected a rising public awareness of how vigorous and productive the economy had become. Beginning in 1922 the nation embarked on a period of remarkable growth. From 1922 to 1929 gross national product grew at an annual rate of 5.5 percent. The unemployment rate never exceeded 5 percent, and real wages rose about 15 percent.

A CONSUMER SOCIETY

The rate of economic growth was matched by the variety of products being produced. In the 19th century economic growth had rested primarily on the production of capital goods, such as factory machinery and railroad tracks. In the 1920s, however,

Good Times. *This illustration captures the lighthearted and risqué character of the 1920s: a woman with rolled-down stockings puts on her "party face" as a man welcomes her into his car with an illegal bottle of booze.*

growth rested more on consumer goods. Some products, such as cars and telephones, had been available since the early 1900s, but in the 1920s their sales reached new levels. Other consumer goods became available for the first time: tractors, washing machines, refrigerators, electric irons, radios, and vacuum cleaners. The term **consumer durable** was coined to describe such goods, which, unlike food, clothing, and other "perishables," were meant to last. Even "perishables" took on new allure. Scientists had discovered the importance of vitamins in the diet and began urging Americans to consume more fresh fruits and vegetables. Improvements in refrigeration and in packaging, meanwhile, made it possible to transport fresh produce long distances and to extend its shelf life in grocery stores. And more stores were being operated by large grocery chains that could afford the latest refrigeration and packaging technology.

The public responded to these innovations with excitement. American industry had made fresh food and stylish clothes available to the masses. Refrigerators, vacuum cleaners, and washing machines would spare women the drudgery of housework. Radios would expand the public's cultural horizons. Automobiles, asphalt roads, service stations, hot dog stands, "tourist cabins" (the forerunners of motels), and traffic lights seemed to herald a wholly new civilization. By the middle of the decade the country was a network of paved roads. Camping trips and long-distance vacations became routine. Farmers and their families could now hop into their cars and head for the nearest town with its stores, movies, amusement parks, and sporting events. Suburbs proliferated, billed as the perfect mix of urban and rural life. Young men and women everywhere discovered that cars were a place where they could "make out," and even make love, without fear of reproach by prudish parents or prying neighbors.

In the 1920s Americans also discovered the benefits of owning stock. The number of stockholders in AT&T, the nation's largest corporation, rose from 140,000 to 568,000. By 1929 as many as 7 million Americans owned stock, many of them people of ordinary, middle-class means.

A People's Capitalism

Capitalists boasted that they had created a **people's capitalism** in which virtually all Americans could participate. Now everyone could have a share of luxuries and amenities. Poverty, capitalists claimed, had been banished, and the gap between rich and poor had been closed.

Actually, although wages were rising, millions of Americans still did not earn enough income to partake fully of the marketplace. Social scientists Robert and Helen Lynd discovered, in their classic study of Muncie, Indiana, that working-class families who bought a car often lacked money for other goods. One housewife admitted, "We don't have no fancy clothes when we have the car to pay for. . . . The car is the only pleasure we have." But many industrialists were reluctant to increase wages, and workers lacked the organizational strength to force them to pay more. One solution came with the introduction of consumer credit. Car dealers, home

consumer durable *Consumer good that was meant to last, such as a washing machine or a radio.*

people's capitalism *An egalitarian capitalism in which all Americans could participate and enjoy the consumer goods that U.S. industry had made available.*

The Granger Collection, New York

appliance salesmen, and other merchants began to offer installment plans that enabled consumers to make a down payment and promise to pay the rest in installments. By 1930 15 percent of all purchases were made on the installment plan. Even so, few poor Americans benefited from the consumer revolution. Middle-class Americans bought most of the consumer durables, fresh vegetables, and stocks.

THE RISE OF ADVERTISING AND MASS MARKETING

Even middle-class consumers had to be wooed. How could they be persuaded to buy another car only a few years after they had bought their first one? General Motors had the answer. In 1926 it introduced the annual model change. Its cars were given a different look every year; GM engineers changed headlights and chassis colors, streamlined bodies, and added new features. The strategy worked. GM leaped past Ford and became the world's largest car manufacturer.

Henry Ford reluctantly introduced his Model A in 1927 to provide customers with a colorful alternative to the drab Model T. Having spent decades selling a product renowned for its utility and reliability, Ford did not believe that sales could be increased by appealing to the intangible hopes and fears of consumers. He was wrong. The desire to be beautiful, handsome, or sexually attractive; to exercise power and control; to demonstrate competence and success; to escape anonymity, loneliness, and boredom; to experience pleasure—all such desires, once activated, could motivate a consumer to buy a new car even when the old one was still serviceable, or to spend money on goods that might have once seemed frivolous.

Arousing such desires required more than bright colors, sleek lines, and attractive packaging. A product had to be promoted as the answer to the consumer's desires. Ad campaigns by professional advertising firms played upon the emotions and vulnerabilities of their target audiences. One cosmetics ad decreed: "Unless you are one woman in a thousand, you must use powder and rouge. Modern living has robbed women of much of their natural color." A mouthwash ad warned about one unsuspecting gentleman's bad breath—"the truth that his friends had been too delicate to mention"—while a tobacco ad matter-of-factly declared: "Men at the top are apt to be pipe-smokers. . . . It's no coincidence—pipe-smoking is a calm and deliberate habit—restful, stimulating. His pipe helps a man think straight. A pipe is back of most big ideas."

Advertising professionals believed they were helping people to manage their lives in ways that would increase their satisfaction and pleasure. American consumers, especially in the middle class, responded enthusiastically. Many were newcomers to middle-class ranks, searching for ways to affirm—or even create—their new identity. Men new to middle-class jobs in offices and banks needed reassurance, as did their stay-at-home wives. Vacuum cleaners and washing machines would make homemakers more efficient. Cosmetics would aid wives in their "first duty"—to be beautiful to their men.

CHANGING ATTITUDES TOWARD MARRIAGE AND SEXUALITY

That husbands and wives were encouraged to pursue sexual satisfaction together was one sign of how much prescriptions for married life had changed since the 19th century, when women were thought to lack sexual passion and men were tacitly expected to satisfy their drives through extramarital liaisons. Modern husbands

MUSICAL LINK TO THE PAST

WOMEN SINGERS AND THE BIRTH OF MODERN COUNTRY MUSIC

Composer: A. P. Carter
(credited as writer but probably was not)
Title: "Single Girl, Married Girl" (1927)
Performers: The Carter Family

Plaintive and never preachy, "Single Girl, Married Girl" explores women's roles and marriage in ways rarely seen in the country music of the 1920s. As she did throughout her career, Sara Carter, a country music pioneer, sang simply and passionately about the lives of common people, in this case women: "Single girl, single girl, she goes to the store and buys . . . Married girl, married girl, she rocks the cradle and cries . . . Single girl, single girl, she's going where she please . . . Married girl, married girl, baby on her knees." Is Sara sad or angry about the plight of this "married girl" tied down by her baby, or is she just plainly stating how women's lives change when children arrive? In either case, Sara Carter, in this song, offers us a glimpse of how country women of the 1920s, often thought to be conservative in outlook, were themselves struggling to balance traditional female responsibilities (in this case, motherhood) with the freedoms that modern society seemed to be offering young women.

The national commercialization of country and blues music in the 1920s opened up new, but still limited, roles for women in the mass media. The Carter Family was by far the most successful of the initial female country groups, producing hit recordings that sold throughout the United States, England, and South Africa, among other places. The group consisted of Sara, who played autoharp and contributed lead vocals; her sister-in-law Maybelle on guitar; and her husband A. P., who occasionally sang with them, but whose most important job was traveling in search of material for the group, for which he often took unwarranted credit (a common practice at the time). Victor Records's talent scout Ralph Peer discovered them at an open talent audition held in Bristol, Tennessee, on August 2, 1927. This recording, made at those sessions, provides us with a historic glimpse of the birth of modern country music.

The Carter women were relegated to the background in publicity for the group. Posters promised a "morally good" program in which a man (A. P.) appeared onstage, an important promise because women who performed popular music independently were considered morally suspect. Also, despite general agreement that Sara had a major hand in writing and arranging Carter Family material, her name rarely surfaced in the credits, where A.P.'s name typically dominated. Despite such caveats, the Carter Family represented an important example of the trend of women claiming new kinds of identities and expression in the modern mass media. Sara seemed to be an innovator in her personal life as well—her relatives described her as "very liberated" for a Southern woman in the 1920s and 1930s, wearing slacks, shooting big game, writing and arranging music, openly smoking, and divorcing A.P. in 1938.

1. Why do you think women performing music independently were frowned on and viewed by many as morally suspect during this period?

Listen to an audio recording of this music on the Musical Links to the Past CD.

---

and wives were expected to share other leisure activities as well—dining out, playing cards with friends, going to the movies, attending concerts, and discussing the latest selection from the newly formed Book-of-the-Month Club.

The public pursuit of pleasure was also noticeable among young and single middle-class women. The so-called **flappers** of the 1920s donned short dresses, rolled their stockings down, wore red lipstick, and smoked in public. Flappers were signaling their desire for independence and equality, but they did not intend

flappers *Rebellious middle-class young women who signaled their desire for independence and equality through style and personality rather than through politics.*

to achieve those goals through politics, as had their predecessors in the woman suffrage movement. Rather, they aimed to create a new female personality endowed with self-reliance, outspokenness, and a new appreciation for the pleasures of life.

AN AGE OF CELEBRITY

FOCUS QUESTION

What was the age of celebrity, and what caused it to arise?

The pursuit of pleasure became both an individual and a group endeavor. Mass marketers began to understand the money that could be made by staging mega-events that tens of thousands would attend and that radio announcers would broadcast to millions. Newspapers and word of mouth ensured that these events would be discussed for days, even months. This trend became most pronounced in baseball and boxing. When Yankee Stadium opened in 1923, its size dwarfed every other sport amphitheater in the country. To succeed in such a venue, sports required not just stirring athletic competitions but individual athletes who seemed larger than life. No sports figure achieved greater fame than did George Herman "Babe" Ruth, who overcame the hardships of a poor and orphaned youth to become the slugging star, the "Sultan of Swat," of the New York Yankees. In the 1920s Ruth hit more home runs than baseball experts had thought humanly possible, culminating in 1927, when he hit a magical 60, a record that would last for 34 years and that would be surpassed only three times in the 20th century. A close second in popularity to Ruth was heavyweight prizefighter Jack Dempsey, whose combination of ruthlessness and efficiency in the ring and gentleness outside it enthralled millions.

Charles A. Lindbergh *First individual to fly solo across the Atlantic (1927) and the greatest celebrity of the 1920s.*

Americans also found celebrities in the movies, among stars such as comedian Charlie Chaplin and the exotically handsome Rudolph Valentino. Movie stars became so familiar on the silver screen that fans longed for news about their private lives as well, an interest that the movie industry was eager to exploit. Perhaps no single individual achieved more fame and adoration, however, than **Charles A. Lindbergh**, the young pilot who, in 1927, became the first person to cross the Atlantic in a solo flight. Piloting his single-engine monoplane, *The Spirit of St. Louis*, Lindbergh flew nonstop (and without sleep) for 34 hours from the time he took off from Long Island until he landed at Le Bourget Airport in Paris. Thousands of Parisians were waiting for him at the airfield. When he returned to New York, an estimated 4 million fans lined the parade route.

This fame could not have happened without the new machinery of celebrity culture—aggressive journalists, radio commentators, promoters, and others who understood how to turn fame to profit. It mattered, too, that Lindbergh performed his feat in an airplane, one of the era's exciting innovations. But Lindbergh's celebrity involved more than hype and technology: He accomplished what others said could not be done, and he did it on his

Library of Congress Prints and Photographs Division [LC-USZ62-93443]

CHARLES A. LINDBERGH AND THE *SPIRIT OF ST. LOUIS*. *Lindbergh poses before the plane that will carry him from Long Island to Paris in the first solo flight across the Atlantic.*

own. In an industrialized, bureaucratized world, Lindbergh demonstrated that an individual could still make a difference.

CELEBRATING A BUSINESS CIVILIZATION

In the 1920s industrialists, advertisers, and merchandisers began to claim that their work was at the heart of American civilization. In 1924 President Calvin Coolidge declared that "the business of America is business." Even religion became a business. Bruce Barton, in his bestseller *The Man That Nobody Knows* (1925), depicted Jesus as an executive "who picked up twelve men from the bottom ranks of business and forged them into an organization that conquered the world."

Some employers adopted benevolent policies toward their employees. They set up employee cafeterias, staffed on-site medical clinics, and engaged psychologists to counsel troubled workers. They built ball fields and sponsored industry leagues. They published employee newsletters and gave awards to employees who did their jobs well and with good spirit. Some even gave employees a voice in determining working conditions. The purpose of these measures—collectively known as welfare capitalism—was to encourage loyalty to the firm and to convince employees that capitalism could work in their interests.

INDUSTRIAL WORKERS

Many industrial workers benefited from the nation's prosperity, enjoying rising wages and a reasonably steady income. Skilled craftsmen in the older industries of construction, railroad transportation, and printing fared especially well. Semiskilled and unskilled industrial workers, however, had to contend with a labor surplus throughout the decade. As employers replaced workers with machines, the aggregate demand for industrial labor increased at a lower rate than it had in the preceding 20 years. Even so, rural whites, blacks, and Mexicans continued their migration to the cities, stiffening the competition for factory jobs. Employers could hire and fire as they saw fit and were therefore able to keep wage increases lagging behind productivity increases.

This softening demand for labor helps to explain why many working-class families did not benefit much from the decade's prosperity or from its consumer revolution. An estimated 40 percent of workers remained mired in poverty, unable to afford a healthy diet or adequate housing, much less costly consumer goods.

The million or more workers who labored in the nation's two largest industries, coal and textiles, suffered the most during the 1920s. Throughout the decade, both industries experienced severe overcapacity. By 1926 only half of the coal mined each year was being sold. Unemployment in New England textile cities sometimes approached 50 percent. One reason was that many textile industrialists had opened factories in the South, where taxes and wages were lower. But the southern textile industry also suffered from excess capacity, and prices and wages continued to fall. Plant managers put constant pressure on their workers to speed up production. Workers loathed the frequent "speed-ups" of machines and the "stretch-outs" in the number of spinning or weaving machines each worker was expected to tend. By the late 1920s labor strife and calls for unionization were rising in both the South and the North.

Most unions, however, lost ground in the 1920s as business and government remained hostile to labor organization. A conservative Supreme Court whittled away at labor's legal protections. In 1921 it ruled that lower courts could issue

The Man That Nobody Knows
Bruce Barton's bestselling 1925 book depicting Jesus as a business executive.

injunctions against union members, prohibiting them from striking or picketing an employer. State courts also enforced what union members called **yellow dog contracts**, written pledges by employees not to join a union while they were employed. Any employee who violated that pledge was subject to immediate dismissal. These measures crippled efforts to organize trade unions. Membership fell from a high of 5 million in 1920 to fewer than 3 million in 1929—a mere 10 percent of the nation's industrial workforce. Other forces contributed to the decline, too. Many workers, especially those benefiting from welfare capitalist programs, decided they no longer needed trade unions. And the labor movement hurt itself by moving too slowly to open its ranks to semiskilled and unskilled factory workers.

WOMEN AND WORK

Female workers experienced the same hardships as men in the industrial workforce, and fewer of the benefits. They were largely excluded from the ranks of skilled craftsmen and thus missed out on the substantial wage increases that men in those positions enjoyed. Where women held the same jobs as men, they usually earned less. Thus, a female trimmer in a meatpacking plant typically made 37 cents an hour, only two-thirds what a male trimmer earned.

White-collar work established itself, in the 1920s, as a magnet for women. This sector grew rapidly in a decade in which corporations expanded and refined their managerial and accounting practices. Discrimination prevented women from becoming managers, accountants, or supervisors themselves, but they did dominate the ranks of secretaries, typists, filing clerks, bank tellers, and department store clerks. By the 1930s 2 million women, or 20 percent of the female workforce, labored in these and related occupations. Initially, these positions had a glamour that factory work lacked. Work environments were cleaner and brighter, and women had the opportunity—indeed were expected—to dress well and fashionably. Still,

yellow dog contracts *Written pledges by employees promising not to join a union while they were employed.*

AMELIA EARHART, AVIATOR.
In 1932 Earhart became the first female aviator to fly solo across the Atlantic, matching the feat that Charles Lindbergh had accomplished in 1927. In 1935 Earhart became the first individual, male or female, to fly nonstop from Hawaii to California.

© Hulton-Deutsch Collection Corbis

wages were low and managerial authority was absolute. Unions had virtually no presence in white-collar places of employment.

Women with ambitions usually focused on "female" professions, such as teaching, nursing, social work, and librarianship. Opportunities in several of these fields, especially teaching and social work, were growing, and women responded by enrolling in college in large numbers. Indeed, the number of female college students increased by 50 percent during the 1920s. Some of these college graduates used their skills in new fields, such as writing for women's magazines. A few, drawing strength from their feminist forebears during the Progressive Era, managed to crack such male bastions of work as mainstream journalism and university research and teaching. In every field of endeavor, some women demonstrated that the female sex possessed the talent and drive to match or exceed what men had done. Thus, in 1932, Amelia Earhart became the first woman to fly the Atlantic solo, matching Lindbergh's feat and inspiring women everywhere. Even so, Earhart's feat failed to improve opportunities for women who wanted to work as pilots. In the airline industry, as in most lines of work, gender prejudices remained too entrenched. Women who had broken the gender line remained, by and large, solitary figures.

The Women's Movement Adrift

Many supporters of the Nineteenth Amendment to the Constitution, which, in 1920, gave women the right to vote, expected it to transform American politics. Women voters would reverse the decline in voter participation, cleanse politics of corruption, and launch reform initiatives that would improve the quality of life for women and men alike. This female-inspired transformation, however, failed to materialize. Voter participation rates did not increase, nor did American politics become imbued with female-inspired virtue and honesty. The women's movement, instead, seemed to succumb to the same exhaustion and frustration as had the more general progressive movement from which it had emerged 20 years earlier. Younger women searching for independence and equality (such as the flappers) often turned away from reform altogether, preferring a lifestyle that emphasized private achievement and personal freedom to a political career devoted to improving the collective status of America's women. Those who continued to agitate for reform found progress more difficult to achieve once the conservative Republican administrations of Harding and Coolidge came to power.

Nevertheless, some female reformers made significant strides. In 1921 one group succeeded in getting Congress to pass the **Sheppard-Towner Act**, a social welfare program that provided federal funds for prenatal and child health care centers throughout the United States. It remained in effect until 1929. In 1923, Alice Paul and the National Women's Party (see Chapter 21) prevailed on Congress to consider an Equal Rights Amendment (ERA) to the Constitution, phrased as follows: "Men and women shall have equal rights throughout the United States and every place subject to its jurisdiction." The National American Woman Suffrage Association, the major force behind the struggle for suffrage, transformed itself in 1920 into the **League of Women Voters** (LWV). During the next decade, the LWV worked to encourage women to run for elective office, to educate voters about the issues before them, and to improve the condition of those Americans—the poor, female and child laborers, the mentally ill—who needed assistance.

Sometimes the women's movement was stymied not just by external opposition but also by internal division—as it was over the ERA. Supporters insisted that there could be no compromise with the proposition that women were the equals of men, but, the LWV countered, child rearing and mothering duties did render women

Sheppard-Towner Act *Major social welfare program providing federal funds for prenatal and child health care, 1921–1929.*

League of Women Voters *Successor to National American Woman Suffrage Association, it promoted women's role in politics and dedicated itself to educating voters.*

NEW OCCUPATIONS FOR WOMEN. *By the 1920s employers preferred women for the telephone operator jobs that were proliferating. The fancy dresses and high heels worn by the women in this photograph underscore the white-collar status of this job.*

different from men in key respects and thus, in some instances, in need of special treatment by Congress and other lawmaking bodies.

The question of women's difference crystallized around the issue of protective labor legislation for women. Over the years, a series of state and federal laws had given women protections at the workplace—limitations on the hours of labor, prohibitions on overnight work, and other such measures—that men did not have. Many reformers considered these measures vital to protecting the masses of women workers from the worst forms of exploitation and thus enabling them to have enough time and energy to perform their roles as mothers and wives. Fearing that the ERA would render this protective legislation unconstitutional, the LWV and its allies opposed it. But Alice Paul and her supporters argued that female protective laws did not really benefit women; instead, employers used them as an excuse to segregate women in stereotyped jobs that were mostly low status and low paying, and thus to deny women the opportunities for advancement and fulfillment open to men.

This issue of whether women should be treated like men in all respects or be offered protections that no man enjoyed was a genuinely complicated one, and women activists would continue to argue about it with each other for decades. In the 1920s, however, their inability to speak with a single voice on this matter weakened their cause.

THE POLITICS OF BUSINESS

FOCUS QUESTION
What were the similarities and differences in the politics of Harding, Coolidge, and Hoover?

Republican presidents governed the country from 1921 to 1933. In some respects, their administrations resembled those of the Gilded Age, when presidents were mediocre, corruption was rampant, and the government's chief objective was to remove obstacles to capitalist development. But in other respects, the state-building tradition of Theodore Roosevelt lived on, although in somewhat altered form.

HARDING AND THE POLITICS OF PERSONAL GAIN

Warren Gamaliel Harding defeated the Democrat James M. Cox for the presidency in 1920. From modest origins as a newspaper editor in the small town of Marion, Ohio, Harding had risen to the U.S. Senate chiefly because the powerful Ohio Republican machine knew it could count on him to do its bidding. He gained the presidency for the same reason. The Republican Party bosses believed that almost anyone they nominated in 1920 could defeat the Democratic opponent; they chose Harding because they could control him. Harding's good looks and geniality made him a favorite with voters, and he swept into office with 61 percent of the popular vote.

Aware of his own intellectual limitations, Harding included talented men in his cabinet. But he lacked the will to alter his ingrained political habits. He had built his political career on a willingness to please the lobbyists who came to his Senate office asking for favors and deals. He had long followed Ohio boss Harry M. Daugherty's advice and would continue to do so with Daugherty as his attorney general.

It seems that Harding kept himself blind to the widespread use of public office for private gain that characterized his administration. His old friends, the "Ohio gang," got rich selling government appointments, judicial pardons, and police protection to bootleggers. The shadiest deal involved Secretary of the Interior Albert Fall in what became known as the **Teapot Dome scandal**. Fall had secretly leased government oil reserves at Teapot Dome, Wyoming, and Elk Hills, California, to two oil tycoons, who then paid him almost $400,000. Fall spent a year in jail. He was not the only Harding appointee to do so. Charles R. Forbes, head of the Veterans' Bureau, would go to Leavenworth Prison for swindling the government out of $200 million in hospital supplies. Forbes's lawyer committed suicide, as did an associate of Attorney General Daugherty, apparently to avoid being indicted and brought to trial. Daugherty himself managed to escape conviction and incarceration for bribery by burning incriminating documents. Still, Daugherty was forced to leave office in disgrace. Harding grew depressed when he finally realized what had been going on. In summer 1923, in poor spirits, he left Washington for a West Coast tour. He died from a heart attack in San Francisco. The train returning his body to Washington attracted crowds of mourners who little suspected the web of corruption and bribery in which Harding had been caught.

COOLIDGE AND THE POLITICS OF LAISSEZ-FAIRE

Harding's successor, Vice President Calvin Coolidge, quickly put to rest the anxiety aroused by the Harding scandals. He never socialized with the "boys," nor was he tempted by corruption. He believed that the best government was the government that governed least, and that the welfare of the country hinged not on politicians but on the people—their willingness to work hard, to be honest, to live within their means.

Coolidge gained national visibility in September 1919, when as governor of Massachusetts he stood firm against Boston's striking policemen (see Chapter 23). His reputation as a man who battled labor radicals earned him a place on the 1920 national Republican ticket. After succeeding Harding, Coolidge won his party's presidential nomination handily in 1924 and easily defeated his Democratic opponent, John W. Davis.

Coolidge took greatest pride in those measures that reduced the government's control over the economy. The Revenue Act of 1926 slashed the high income and

Teapot Dome scandal *Secretary of Interior Albert Fall allowed oil tycoons access to government oil reserves in exchange for $400,000 in bribes.*

associationalism *Herbert Hoover's approach to managing the economy. Firms and organizations in each economic sector would be asked to cooperate with each other in the pursuit of efficiency, profit, and the public good.*

estate taxes that progressives had pushed through Congress during the First World War. Coolidge trimmed the Federal Trade Commission's power to regulate business affairs and supported Supreme Court decisions invalidating Progressive Era laws that had strengthened organized labor and protected children and women from exploitation.

HOOVER AND THE POLITICS OF "ASSOCIATIONALISM"

Republicans in the 1920s did more than simply lift government restraints and regulations from the economy. Some, led by Secretary of Commerce Herbert Hoover, conceived of government as a dynamic, even progressive, economic force. Hoover did not want government to control industry, but he did want government to persuade private corporations to abandon their wasteful, selfish ways and turn to cooperation and public service. Hoover envisioned an economy built on the principle of association. Industrialists, wholesalers, retailers, operators of railroad and shipping lines, small businessmen, farmers, workers, doctors—each of these groups would form a trade association whose members would share economic information, discuss problems of production and distribution, and seek ways of achieving greater efficiency and profit. Hoover believed that the very act of associating in this way—an approach historian Ellis Hawley has called **associationalism**—would convince participants of the superiority of cooperation over competition, of negotiation over conflict, of public service over narrow self-interest.

Hoover's ambition as secretary of commerce was to make his department the orchestrator of economic cooperation. During his eight years in that post, from 1921 to 1929, he organized more than 250 conferences and brought together government officials, businessmen, policymakers, and others who had a stake in strengthening the economy. Hoover achieved some notable successes: He persuaded farmers to join together in marketing cooperatives, steel executives to abandon the 12-hour day for their employees, and some groups of bankers in the South to organize their institutions into associations with adequate resources and expertise. His dynamic conception of government did not endear him to Coolidge, who declared in 1927: "That man has offered me unsolicited advice for six years, all of it bad."

THE POLITICS OF BUSINESS ABROAD

Republican domestic policy disagreements over whether to pursue laissez-faire or associationalism spilled over into foreign policy as well. As secretary of commerce, Hoover intended to apply associationalism to international relations. He wanted the world's leading nations to meet regularly in conferences, to limit military build-ups, and to foster an international environment in which capitalism could flourish. Aware that the United States must help create such an environment, Hoover hoped to persuade American bankers to adopt investment and loan policies that would aid European recovery. If they refused to do so, he was prepared to urge the government to take an activist, supervisory role in foreign investment.

In 1921 and 1922 Hoover participated in the Washington Conference on the Limitation of Armaments. Although he did not serve as a negotiator at the conference—Secretary of State Charles Evans Hughes reserved that role for himself and his subordinates—he did supply Hughes's team with a wealth of economic information and proposals for disarmament. Those proposals gave U.S. negotiators a decided advantage over their European and Asian counterparts and

QUICK REVIEW

REPUBLICAN PRESIDENCIES, 1921–1933

- Struggle between laissez-faire and associationalism shaped policy debates

- Warren G. Harding (1921–1923) guided by political lobbyists and cronies

- Calvin Coolidge (1923–1929) driven by the ideal that the best government was a government that governed least

- Herbert Hoover (1929–1933) promoted the idea that government should persuade private corporations to abandon their wasteful, selfish ways and embrace cooperation and public service

helped them win a stunning accord, the **Five-Power Treaty**, by which the United States, Britain, Japan, France, and Italy agreed to scrap more than 2 million tons of their warships. Hughes also obtained pledges from all the signatories that they would respect the "Open Door" in China, long a U.S. foreign policy objective (see Chapter 22).

These triumphs redounded to Hughes's credit but not to Hoover's, and Hughes used them to consolidate his control over foreign policy. Hughes's reputation continued to grow when he solved a crisis in Franco-German relations. The victorious Allies had imposed on Germany an obligation to pay $33 billion in war reparations (see Chapter 23). In 1923, when the impoverished German government suspended its payments, France sent troops to occupy the Ruhr valley, whose industry was vital to the German economy. German workers retaliated by going on strike, their actions threatening to undermine the country's economic recovery. Hughes responded by compelling the French to attend a U.S.-sponsored conference in 1924 to restructure Germany's debt obligation.

The conference produced the **Dawes Plan** (after the Chicago banker and chief negotiator, Charles G. Dawes), which reduced German reparations payments from $542 million to $250 million annually and called on U.S. and foreign banks to stimulate the German economy with $200 million in loans. Within a matter of days, banker J. P. Morgan Jr. raised more than $1 billion from American investors. Money poured into German financial markets, and the German economy was apparently stabilized.

The Dawes Plan won applause on both sides of the Atlantic. But the U.S. money flooding into Germany soon created new problems. American investors were so eager to lend to Germany that their investments became speculative and unsound. At this point, a stronger effort by the U.S. government to direct loans to sound investments, a strategy that Hoover would have supported, might have helped. But neither Hughes nor his successor as secretary of state, Frank Kellogg, was interested in such initiatives; nor was Secretary of the Treasury Mellon. Republicans were now content to leave investment decisions in the hands of private bankers.

Republicans did depart from their hands-off approach to foreign affairs in two other areas. The first was in their pursuit of disarmament and world peace. The Five-Power Treaty, negotiated by Hughes in 1921 and 1922, was a major success. Later in the decade, Secretary of State Kellogg drew up a treaty with Aristide Briand, the French foreign minister, outlawing war as a tool of national policy. In 1928, representatives of the United States, France, and 13 other nations met in Paris to sign the Kellogg-Briand Pact. Hailed as a great stride toward world peace, the pact soon attracted the support of 48 other nations. Coolidge viewed the treaty as an opportunity to scale back the military and further reduce the size of the U.S. government. Unfortunately, the pact contained no enforcement mechanism and thus would do little to slow the next decade's descent into militarism and war.

The Republican administrations of the 1920s also took a hands-on approach in Latin America. The U.S. government continued its policy of intervening in the region's internal affairs to protect U.S. interests, and investments there more than doubled from 1917 to 1929. Republican administrations did attempt to curtail American military involvement in the Caribbean, pulling troops out of the Dominican Republic in 1924 and Nicaragua in 1925. But U.S. Marines were sent back to Nicaragua in 1926 to end a war between liberal and conservative Nicaraguans and to protect American property; this time they stayed until 1934. U.S. troops, meanwhile, occupied Haiti continuously between 1919 and 1934, keeping in power governments friendly to U.S. interests.

Five-Power Treaty *1922 treaty in which the United States, Britain, Japan, France, and Italy agreed to scrap more than 2 million tons of their warships.*

Dawes Plan *1924 U.S.-backed agreement to reduce German reparation payments by more than half. The plan also called on banks to invest $200 million in the German economy.*

FARMERS, PROTESTANTS, AND MORAL TRADITIONALISTS

FOCUS QUESTION
What did farmers and Protestants fear about America in the 1920s, and how did they respond?

Although many Americans benefited from the prosperity of the 1920s, others did not. Overproduction was impoverishing substantial numbers of farmers, and many of them also believed that the country was being overrun by racially inferior and morally suspect immigrants.

AGRICULTURAL DEPRESSION

The 1920s brought hard times to the nation's farmers. European agriculture, disrupted by the war, quickly restored itself. Foreign demand for American foodstuffs fell precipitously, as did prices. Tractors increased productivity, leading to further drops in prices. By 1929 the annual per capita income of rural Americans was only $223, one quarter that of the nonfarm population. Millions were forced to sell their farms. Radical groups of farmers, such as the Nonpartisan League of North Dakota and farmer-labor parties in Minnesota and Wisconsin, sprang up to draw attention to the agricultural crisis. By the second half of the decade, however, leadership had passed from farming radicals to farming moderates, and from small farmers in danger of dispossession to larger farmers and agribusinesses seeking to extend their holdings. The more powerful agricultural interests, lobbying through such organizations as the Farm Bureau Federation, pressured Congress to set up economic controls that would protect them from failure. Their proposals, embodied in the McNary-Haugen bill, called on the government to purchase surplus U.S. crops at prices that enabled farmers to cover their production costs. The McNary-Haugen bill passed Congress in 1926 and in 1928, only to be vetoed by President Coolidge both times.

CULTURAL DISLOCATION

A sense of cultural dislocation further demoralized farmers, who had long perceived themselves as the backbone of the nation—hardworking, honest, democratic, liberty loving, and God-fearing. The 1920 census challenged the validity of that view. For the first time, a majority of Americans now lived in urban areas (see Map 24.1). The economic and cultural vitality of the nation seemed to be shifting from the countryside to the city. Industry, the chief engine of prosperity, was an urban phenomenon. Amusement parks, department stores, professional sports, movies, cabarets, and theaters had emerged in cities; so had flashy fashions and open sexuality. Cities also were the home of secular intellectuals who had scrapped their belief in Scripture and in God and had embraced science.

All through the Progressive Era rural white Americans had believed that the cities could be redeemed, that city dwellers could be reformed, that the Protestant values of rural America would triumph. War had undermined that confidence and had replaced it with the fear that urban masses and secular culture would rule and ruin America.

These fears grew even more intense as the consumer culture of the city penetrated the countryside. Even small towns now sported movie theaters and automobile dealerships. Radios carried news of city life into isolated farmhouses. The growth in the circulation of national magazines also broke down the wall separating country from city.

Rural Americans were ambivalent about this cultural invasion. On the one hand, country dwellers were eager to participate in the consumer marketplace. On

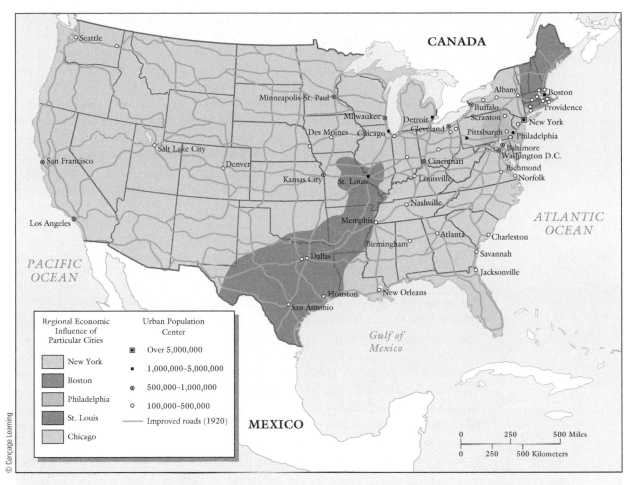

Map 24.1 URBANIZATION, 1920. *By 1920 New York City had surpassed 5 million people, and Boston, Philadelphia, Pittsburgh, Detroit, Chicago, and St. Louis had surpassed 1 million. Another 10 cities, from Los Angeles, California, to Buffalo, New York, had surpassed 500,000. This color-coded map also shows the regions in which the country's five largest cities exercised economic influence.*

the other, they worried that by doing so they would expose the countryside to atheism, immorality, and radicalism. Their determination to protect their imperiled way of life was manifested by their support of Prohibition, the Ku Klux Klan, immigration restriction, and religious fundamentalism.

PROHIBITION

The Eighteenth Amendment to the Constitution, which prohibited the manufacture and sale of alcohol, went into effect in January 1920, supported by a large and varied constituency that included farmers, middle-class city dwellers, feminists, and progressive reformers. It soon became apparent, however, that **Prohibition** was doing more to encourage law breaking than alcohol abstinence. With only 1,500 federal agents to enforce the law, the government could not possibly police the drinking habits of 110 million people. With little fear of punishment, those who wanted to drink did so, either brewing liquor at home or buying it from speakeasies and bootleggers. Because the law prevented legitimate businesses from manufacturing liquor, organized crime simply added alcohol to its business portfolio. Mobsters procured much of their liquor from Canadian manufacturers, smuggled it across the border,

Prohibition *Constitutional ban on the manufacture and sale of alcohol in the United States (1920–1933).*

protected it in warehouses, and distributed it to speakeasies. Al Capone's Chicago-based mob alone employed 1,000 men to protect its liquor trafficking, which was so lucrative that Capone became the richest (and most feared) gangster in America.

These unexpected consequences caused many early advocates of Prohibition, especially in the cities, to withdraw their support. That was not the response of Prohibition's rural, Protestant supporters, however. The violence spawned by illegal liquor trafficking confirmed their view that alcohol was an agent of evil that had to be eradicated. The high-profile participation of Italian, Irish, and Jewish gangsters in the bootleg trade merely reinforced their view that Catholics and Jews were threats to law and morality. Many rural Protestants became more, not less, determined to rid the country of liquor once and for all; many resolved to rid the country of Catholic and Jewish influence as well.

The Ku Klux Klan

The original **Ku Klux Klan**, formed in the South in the late 1860s, had died out with the defeat of Reconstruction and the reestablishment of white supremacy (see Chapter 17). The new Klan was created in 1915 by William Simmons, a white southerner who had been inspired by D. W. Griffith's racist film, *Birth of a Nation*, in which the early Klan was depicted as having saved the nation (and especially its white women) from predatory blacks. By the 1920s control of the Klan had passed to a Texas dentist, Hiram Evans, and its ideological focus had expanded from a loathing of blacks to a hatred of Jews and Catholics as well. Evans's Klan propagated a nativist message that the country should contain—or better yet, eliminate—the influence of Jews and Catholics and restore "Anglo-Saxon" racial purity, Protestant supremacy, and traditional morality to national life. Evans's message swelled Klan ranks and expanded its visibility and influence in the North and South alike. By 1924 as many as 4 million Americans are thought to have belonged to the Klan, including the half-million members of its female auxiliary, Women of the Ku Klux Klan.

In some respects, the Klan functioned just as many other fraternal organizations did. It offered members friendship networks, social services, and conviviality. Its rituals, regalia, and mock-medieval language (the Imperial Wizard, Exalted Cyclops, Grand Dragons, and so on) gave initiates the same sense of superiority, valor, and mystery that many other fraternal societies imparted to their members. But the Klan's determination to stir up hate toward blacks, Catholics, and Jews marked it as a different and dangerous kind of fraternal association.

Immigration Restriction

Although most white Protestants never joined the Klan, many did respond to the Klan's nativist argument that the country and its values would best be served by limiting the entry of outsiders. That was the purpose of the **Immigration Restriction Act of 1924 (Johnson-Reed Act)**.

By the early 1920s most Americans believed that the country could no longer accommodate the million immigrants who had been arriving each year prior to the war and the more than 800,000 who arrived in 1921. Industrialists did not need unskilled European laborers to operate their factories, their places having been taken either by machines or by African American and Mexican workers. Most labor movement leaders were convinced that the influx of workers unfamiliar with English and with trade unions was weakening labor solidarity. Progressive reformers no longer believed that immigrants could be easily Americanized or that harmony between the native-born and the foreign-born could be readily achieved. Congress responded to constituents'

Ku Klux Klan *Fraternal organization reborn in 1915 that achieved popularity in the 1920s through its calls for Anglo-Saxon purity, Protestant supremacy, and the subordination of blacks, Catholics, and Jews.*

Immigration Restriction Act of 1924 (Johnson-Reed Act) *Limited immigration to the United States to 165,000 a year, shrank immigration from southern and eastern Europe to insignificance, and banned immigration from East and South Asia.*

"SPOILING THE BROTH" *This anti-immigrant cartoon, appearing in 1921, shows America's fabled melting pot being forced to take in far more immigrants from Europe and Asia than it could possibly handle. The result were hundreds of thousands, even millions, of immigrants being disgorged from the pot as "unassimilated aliens."*

© The Granger Collection, New York

concerns by passing an immigration restriction act in 1921. Then, in 1924, the more comprehensive Johnson-Reed Act imposed a yearly quota of 165,000 immigrants from countries outside the Western Hemisphere.

The sponsors of the 1924 act believed that certain groups—British, Germans, and Scandinavians, in particular—were racially superior and that, consequently, these groups should be allowed to enter the United States in greater numbers. However, because the Constitution prohibited the enactment of explicitly racist laws, Congress had to achieve this racist aim through subterfuge. Lawmakers established a formula to determine the annual immigrant quota for each foreign country, which was to be computed at 2 percent of the total number of immigrants from that country already resident in the United States in the year 1890. In that year, immigrant ranks had been dominated by the British, Germans, and Scandinavians, so the new quotas would thus allow for a relatively larger influx of immigrants of these nationalities (see Table 24.1). Immigrant groups that were poorly represented in the 1890 population—Italians, Greeks, Poles, Slavs, and Eastern European Jews—were effectively locked out. The Johnson-Reed Act also reaffirmed the longstanding policy of excluding Chinese immigrants, and it added Japanese and other East and South Asians to the list of groups that were altogether barred from entry. The act did not officially limit immigration from nations in the Western Hemisphere, chiefly because agribusiness interests in Texas and California had convinced Congress that cheap Mexican laborers were indispensable to their industry's prosperity. Still, the establishment of a border patrol along the U.S. Mexican border and the imposition of a $10 head tax on all prospective Mexican immigrants made entry into the United States more difficult for Mexicans than it had been.

The Johnson-Reed Act accomplished Congress's underlying goal. Annual immigration from transoceanic nations fell by 80 percent. The large number of available slots for English and German immigrants regularly went unfilled, while the miniscule number of slots reserved for Italians, Poles, Eastern European Jews, and others prevented hundreds of thousands of them from entering the country. A "national origins" system put in place in 1927 reduced the total annual quota further, to 150,000, and reserved more than 120,000 of these slots for immigrants from northwestern Europe.

Remarkably few Americans, outside of the ethnic groups that were being discriminated against, objected to these laws at the time they were passed—an indication of how broadly acceptable racism and nativism had become.

FUNDAMENTALISM

Of all the forces reacting against urban life, Protestant fundamentalism was perhaps the most enduring. **Fundamentalists** regard the Bible as God's word and thus the source of all "fundamental" truth. They believe that every event depicted in the

fundamentalists *Those who regarded the Bible as God's word and thus the source of all fundamental truth. Its followers believed that every event depicted in the Bible happened just as the Bible described it.*

TABLE 24.1

ANNUAL IMMIGRANT QUOTAS UNDER THE JOHNSON-REED ACT, 1925–1927

Northwest Europe and Scandinavia		Eastern and Southern Europe		Other Countries	
COUNTRY	QUOTA	COUNTRY	QUOTA	COUNTRY	QUOTA
Germany	51,227	Poland	5,982	Africa (other than Egypt)	1,100
Great Britain and Northern Ireland	34,007	Italy	3,845	Armenia	124
Irish Free State (Ireland)	28,567	Czechoslovakia	3,073	Australia	121
Sweden	9,561	Russia	2,248	Palestine	100
Norway	6,453	Yugoslavia	671	Syria	100
France	3,954	Romania	603	Turkey	100
Denmark	2,789	Portugal	503	New Zealand and Pacific Islands	100
Switzerland	2,081	Hungary	473	All others	1,900
Netherlands	1,648	Lithuania	344		
Austria	785	Latvia	142		
Belgium	512	Spain	131		
Finland	471	Estonia	124		
Free City of Danzig	228	Albania	100		
Iceland	100	Bulgaria	100		
Luxembourg	100	Greece	100		
Total (number)	142,483	Total (number)	18,439	Total (number)	3,745
Total (%)	86.5%	Total (%)	11.2%	Total (%)	2.3%

Note: Total annual immigrant quota was 164,667.
Source: From *Statistical Abstract of the United States* (Washington, D.C.: Government Printing Office, 1929), p. 100.

Bible, from the creation of the world in six days to the resurrection of Christ, happened exactly as the Bible describes it. For fundamentalists, God is a deity who intervenes directly in the lives of individuals and communities.

The rise of the fundamentalist movement from the 1870s through the 1920s roughly paralleled the rise of urban-industrial society. Fundamentalists recoiled from the "evils" of the city—from what they perceived as its poverty, its moral degeneracy, its irreligion, and its crass materialism. Fundamentalism took shape in reaction against two additional aspects of urban society: the growth of liberal Protestantism and the revelations of science. **Liberal Protestants** believed that religion had to be adapted to the skeptical and scientific temper of the modern age. The Bible was to be mined for its ethical values rather than for its literal truth. Liberal Protestants removed God from his active role in history and refashioned him into a distant and benign deity who watches over the world but does not intervene to punish or to redeem. They turned religion away from the quest for salvation and toward the pursuit of good deeds, social conscience, and love for one's neighbor. Fundamentalism arose in part to counter the "heretical" claims of the liberal Protestants.

Liberal Protestants and fundamentalists both believed that science posed the greatest challenge to Christianity. Scientists argued that rational inquiry was a better guide to the past and to the future than prayer and revelation. Scientists even challenged the ideas that God had created the world and had fashioned mankind in his own image. These were beliefs that many religious peoples, particularly

liberal Protestants *Those who believed that religion had to be adapted to science and that the Bible was to be mined for ethical values rather than for its literal truth.*

fundamentalists, simply could not accept. Conflict was inevitable. It came in 1925, in Dayton, Tennessee.

THE SCOPES TRIAL

No aspect of science aroused more anger among fundamentalists than Charles Darwin's theory of evolution. There was no greater blasphemy than to suggest that man emerged from lower forms of life instead of being created by God almighty. In Tennessee in 1925 fundamentalists succeeded in getting a law passed forbidding the teaching of "any theory that denies the story of the divine creation of man as taught in the Bible."

For Americans who accepted the authority of science, denying the truth of evolution was as ludicrous as insisting that the sun revolved around the earth. They ridiculed the fundamentalists, but worried that passage of the Tennessee law might signal the onset of a campaign to undermine First Amendment guarantees of free speech. The American Civil Liberties Union began searching for a teacher who would be willing to challenge the constitutionality of the Tennessee law. They found their man in John T. Scopes, a 24-year-old biology teacher in Dayton. After confessing that he had taught evolution to his students, Scopes was arrested. The case quickly attracted national attention. William Jennings Bryan announced that he would help to prosecute Scopes, and the famous liberal trial lawyer Clarence Darrow rushed to Dayton to lead Scopes's defense. That Bryan and Darrow had once been allies in the progressive movement only heightened the drama. A small army of journalists, led by H. L. Mencken, descended on Dayton.

The trial dragged on, and most observers expected Scopes to be convicted. (He was.) But it took an unexpected turn when Darrow persuaded the judge to let Bryan testify as an "expert on the Bible." Darrow knew that Bryan's testimony would have no bearing on the question of Scopes's innocence or guilt. His aim was to expose Bryan as a fool for believing that the Bible was a source of literal truth and thus to embarrass the fundamentalists. In a brilliant confrontation, Darrow made Bryan's defense of the Bible look silly, and he then led Bryan to admit that the "truth" of the Bible was not always easy to accept. In that case, Darrow asked, how could fundamentalists be so sure that everything in the Bible was literally true?

In his account of the trial, Mencken portrayed Bryan as a pathetic figure who had been devastated by his humiliating experience on the witness stand, a view popularized in the 1960 movie, *Inherit the Wind*. When Bryan died only a week after the trial ended, Mencken claimed that the trial had broken Bryan's heart.

Bryan deserved a better epitaph than the one Mencken had given him. Diabetes caused his death, not a broken heart. Nor was Bryan the innocent fool that Mencken made him out to be. Bryan remembered when social conservatives had once used Darwin's phrase "survival of the fittest" to prove that the wealthy and politically powerful were racially superior to the poor and powerless (see Chapter 19). His rejection of Darwinism evidenced his democratic faith that all human beings were creatures of God and thus capable of striving for perfection and equality.

The public ridicule attendant on the Scopes trial took its toll on fundamentalists. Many retreated from politics and refocused their attention on purging sin from their own hearts rather than from the hearts of others. In the end, the fundamentalists prevailed on three more states to prohibit the teaching of evolution. But the controversy had even more far-reaching effects. Worried about losing sales, publishers quietly removed references to Darwin from their science textbooks, a policy that would remain in force until the 1960s.

QUICK REVIEW

CULTURAL CONSERVATISM AND MORAL TRADITIONALISM

- Rural Americans feared dominance of cities, industry, immigrants, and mass culture

- Immigrants targeted through Prohibition (1920) and immigration restriction (1921, 1924)

- Ku Klux Klan gained support as racist and nativist protector of Anglo-Saxon purity

- Fundamentalism surged; Scopes Trial (about evolution) became rallying point

HISTORY THROUGH FILM

INHERIT THE WIND (1960)

Directed by Stanley Kramer;
starring Fredric March (Matthew Harrison Brady), Spencer
Tracy (Henry Drummond), Gene Kelly (E. K. Hornbeck), Dick
York (Bertram T. Cates), Claude Akins (Rev. Jeremiah Brown),
and Donna Anderson (Rachel Brown)

Inherit the Wind is a fictionalized drama about the 1925 Scopes Trial in Dayton, Tennessee. It begins with the arrest of Bertram T. Cates (the name given by the moviemakers to the John T. Scopes character) and ends with his conviction on the charge of breaking a state law that prohibits teaching evolution in Tennessee schools. The climactic moment in the movie, as in the real Scopes story, is the courtroom clash between Matthew Harrison Brady (a thinly fictionalized version of William Jennings Bryan) and Henry Drummond (the Clarence Darrow character) over the Bible, truth, and scientific inquiry. *Inherit the Wind* shaped an entire generation's understanding of the Scopes trial. The film's broad influence makes it a particularly fruitful historical document to explore.

Spencer Tracy playing Henry Drummond (the fictional Clarence Darrow) on left and Fredric March playing Matthew Harrison Brady (the fictional William Jennings Bryant) on right.

© John Springer Collection/CORBIS

The film's director, Stanley Kramer, made several movies with political themes. *Home of the Brave* (1949) explored racism in the U.S. army; *On the Beach* (1959) examined the social consequences of nuclear war; *Judgment at Nuremberg* (1961) investigated Nazi criminality. Critics have noted that Kramer often sacrificed historical and personal nuance in order to drive home his political point. In *Inherit the Wind*, for example, Kramer portrays the Scopes camp in the most positive possible light. To help viewers identify with E. K. Hornbeck (meant to represent the irascible Baltimore-based journalist, H. L. Mencken), he casts the amiable Gene Kelly in the role. Drummond (representing Darrow) is celebrated not only for his commitment to defending science and reason but for having more integrity than anyone else in the courtroom. Kramer does try to endow Brady (the Bryan character) with positive qualities and to honor him for his past achievements in politics. Ultimately, however, Kramer depicts Brady as pompous, calculating, and, by the trial's end, dangerously out of control—exaggerations, at best, of William Jennings Bryan.

This caricature of Brady/Bryan derives from the movie's origins as a play of the same name, published in 1955. The playwrights were not especially concerned with making Brady resemble William Jennings Bryan; rather, they wanted him to act as a stand-in for an entirely different figure in American politics: Senator Joseph McCarthy, who led a campaign in the 1950s to oust communists and their supporters from their jobs in the U.S. government. McCarthy's anticommunist operation was terrifying not just to the radicals he sought to expose but also to people who believed that his unscrupulous methods threatened America's core values. In identifying Brady with McCarthy, the playwrights sought to discredit both men. (See Chapter 27 for a discussion of Joseph McCarthy.)

The play and movie also introduce to the 1920s evolution battle an entirely fictitious fire-and-brimstone preacher, Reverend Jeremiah Brown, who, in the manner of a 1950s McCarthyite, viciously and publicly condemns anyone who dares to challenge the authority of those in power—including his own daughter, Rachel. In both play and movie, Brown

and Brady successfully manipulate public opinion, much as McCarthy did.

That Kramer allowed his movie about a trial in the 1920s to be influenced by events he lived through in the 1950s is an interesting subject to discuss. How much of a historian's view of the past is shaped by the times in which he or she lives?

However much *Inherit the Wind* comments on politics in 1950s America, the final courtroom scene, in which Drummond and Brady face off over the meaning of science and religion, offers a glimpse of what was at stake in 1925 when a trial in a small town in Tennessee transfixed the nation.

ETHNIC AND RACIAL COMMUNITIES

The 1920s were a decade of change for ethnic and racial minorities. Some minorities benefited from the prosperity of the decade; others created and sustained vibrant subcultures. All, however, experienced a surge in discrimination that made them uneasy in Jazz Age America.

EUROPEAN AMERICANS

European American immigrants were concentrated in the cities of the Northeast and Midwest. A large number were semiskilled and unskilled industrial laborers and suffered economic insecurity as a result. In addition, they faced cultural discrimination. Catholics generally opposed Prohibition, viewing it as a crude attempt by Protestants to control their behavior. Southern and Eastern Europeans, particularly Jews and Italians, resented immigration restriction and the implication that they were unworthy of citizenship. Their exclusion from universities, professions, and clubs to which they sought access increased during the decade. Many pointed to the double standards that made life more difficult for them than for the native born. Italians, for example, were outraged by the execution of Nicola Sacco and Bartolomeo Vanzetti in 1927 (see Chapter 23). Had the two men been native-born Protestants, Italians argued, their lives would have been spared.

Contrary to the claims of nativists that it could not be done, many southern and Eastern European immigrants reconciled their own culture with American culture. Ethnic associations flourished in the 1920s. Children learned their native languages and customs at home and at church if not at school, and they joined with their parents to celebrate their ethnic heritage.

But these immigrants and their children also flocked to movies and amusement parks, to baseball games and boxing matches. Children usually entered more enthusiastically into the world of American mass culture than did their immigrant parents, but this did not mean that they were leaving their own culture behind. Youngsters who went to the movies did so with friends from within their community. Ethnics who played sandlot baseball often did so in leagues organized around churches or ethnic associations. In these early days of radio, ethnics living in large cities could find programs in their native language and music from their native lands.

Increasingly convinced of their rights as Americans, European American ethnics resolved to develop the political muscle needed to defeat the forces of nativism

FOCUS QUESTION
How were the experiences of ethnic and racial groups in 1920s America similar, and how were they different?

TABLE 24.2

DEMOCRATIC PRESIDENTIAL VOTING IN CHICAGO BY ETHNIC GROUPS, 1924 AND 1928		
	Percent Democratic	
	1924	1928
Czechoslovaks	40%	73%
Poles	35	71
Lithuanians	48	77
Yugoslavs	20	54
Italians	31	63
Germans	14	58
Jews	19	60

Source: From John M. Allswang, *A House for All Peoples: Ethnic Politics in Chicago, 1890–1936* (Lexington: University Press of Kentucky), p. 42.

and to turn government policy in a more favorable direction. One sign of this determination was a sharp rise in the number of immigrants who became U.S. citizens. Armed with the vote, ethnics turned out on Election Day to defeat unsympathetic city councilmen, mayors, state representatives, and even an occasional governor. Their growing national strength first became apparent at the Democratic National Convention of 1924, when urban-ethnic delegates almost won approval of planks calling for the repeal of Prohibition and condemnation of the Klan. Then, after denying the presidential nomination to the presumed favorite, William G. McAdoo, they nearly secured it for their candidate, **Alfred E. Smith**, the Irish American governor of New York. McAdoo represented the rural and southern constituencies of the Democratic Party. His forces ended up battling Smith's urban-ethnic forces for 103 ballots, until the two men gave up and supporters from each camp switched their votes to a compromise candidate, the corporate lawyer John W. Davis.

The nomination fight devastated the Democratic Party in the short term, and the popular Coolidge easily defeated the little-known Davis. However, the convention upheaval of 1924 also marked an important milestone in the bid by European American ethnics for political power. They would achieve a second milestone at the Democratic National Convention of 1928 when, after another bitter struggle, they secured the presidential nomination for Al Smith. Never before had a major political party put forward a Catholic for the presidency. Herbert Hoover crushed Smith in the general election, as nativists stirred up anti-Catholic prejudice yet again, and as large numbers of southern Democrats either stayed home or voted Republican (see Map 24.2). But there were encouraging signs in the campaign, none more so than Smith's beating Hoover in the nation's 12 largest cities. European Americans would yet have their day (see Table 24.2).

AFRICAN AMERICANS

Despite the urban race riots of 1919 (see Chapter 23), African Americans continued to leave their rural homes for the industrial centers of the South and the North. In major areas of settlement, such as New York City and Chicago, complex societies emerged consisting of workers, businessmen, professionals, intellectuals, artists, and entertainers. Social differentiation intensified as various groups—long-resident northerners and newly arrived southerners, religious conservatives and cultural radicals, African Americans and African Caribbeans—found reason to disapprove of one another's

Alfred E. Smith *Irish American, Democratic governor of New York who became in 1928 the first Catholic ever nominated for the presidency by a major party.*

ways. Still, the diversity and complexity of urban black America were thrilling, nowhere more so than in Harlem, the "Negro capital."

Not even the glamour of Harlem could erase the reality of racial discrimination, however. Most African Americans could find work only in New York City's least-desired and lowest-paying jobs. Because they could rent apartments only in areas that real estate agents and banks had designated as "colored," African Americans experienced the highest rate of residential segregation of any minority group. Harlem became a black ghetto, an area set apart from the rest of the city by the skin color of its inhabitants, by its higher population density and poverty rate, by its higher incidence of infectious diseases, and by the lower life expectancy of its people (see Table 24.3). At the same time, substantial numbers of New York City's European ethnics were leaving their lower Manhattan ghettos for the "greener" pastures of Brooklyn and the Bronx.

Blacks did achieve some economic breakthroughs in the 1920s. Henry Ford, for example, hired large numbers of African Americans to work in his Detroit auto factories. Yet even here a racist logic was operating, for Ford believed that black and white workers, divided along racial lines, would not challenge his authority.

Many African Americans grew pessimistic about achieving racial equality. After Marcus Garvey's black nationalist movement collapsed in the mid-1920s (see Chapter 23), no comparable organization arose to take its place. The NAACP continued to fight racial discrimination, and the Urban League carried on quiet negotiations with industrial elites to open up jobs to African Americans--but the victories were small, and white allies were scarce. The political initiatives emerging among European ethnics had few counterparts in the African American community.

In terms of black culture, however, the 1920s were remarkably vigorous and productive. Black musicians coming north to Chicago and New York brought with them their distinctive musical styles, most notably the blues and ragtime. Influenced by the harmonies and techniques of European classical music, these southern styles metamorphosed into jazz. Urban audiences found this new music irresistible. In Chicago, Detroit, New York, New Orleans, and elsewhere, jazz musicians came together in cramped apartments, cabarets, and nightclubs to jam, compete, and entertain. Jazz seemed to express something quintessentially modern. Jazz musicians broke free of

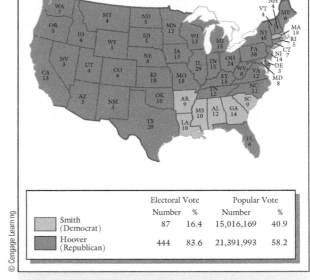

Map 24.2 PRESIDENTIAL ELECTION, 1928. *This map shows Hoover's landslide victory in 1928, as he carried all but eight states and won almost 84 percent of the electoral vote.*

TABLE 24.3

DEATH RATES FROM SELECTED CAUSES FOR NEW YORK CITY RESIDENTS, 1925		
Cause of Death	Total Population	African American Population
General death rate (per 1,000 population)	11.4	16.5
Pneumonia	132.8	282.4
Pulmonary tuberculosis	75.5	258.4
Infant mortality (per 1,000 live births)	64.6	118.4
Maternal mortality (per 1,000 total births)	5.3	10.2
Stillbirths (per 1,000 births)	47.6	82.7
Homicide	5.3	19.5
Suicide	14.8	9.7

Note: Rate is per 100,000 population, unless noted.
Source: Cheryl Lynn Greenberg, *"Or Does It Explode?" Black Harlem in the Great Depression* (New York: Oxford University Press, 1991), p. 32.

Harlem Renaissance *1920s African American literary and artistic awakening that sought to create works rooted in black culture instead of imitating white styles.*

convention, improvised, and produced new sounds that gave rise to new sensations. Both blacks and whites found in jazz an escape from the routine, the predictability, and the conventions of their everyday lives.

THE HARLEM RENAISSANCE

Paralleling the emergence of jazz was a black literary and artistic awakening known as the **Harlem Renaissance**. Black novelists, poets, painters, sculptors, and playwrights created works rooted in their own culture instead of imitating the styles of white Europeans and Americans. The movement had begun during the war, when blacks sensed that they might at last be advancing to full equality. It was symbolized by the image of the "New Negro," who would no longer be deferential to whites but who would display his or her independence through talent and determination. Langston Hughes, a young black poet, said of the Harlem Renaissance: "We younger Negro artists who create now intend to express our individual dark-skinned selves without fear or shame. If white people are pleased, we are glad. If they are not, it doesn't matter. We know we are beautiful. And ugly, too." In 1925, *Survey Graphic*, a white liberal magazine, devoted an entire issue to "Harlem—the Mecca of the New Negro."

These cultural advances did not escape white prejudice. The most popular jazz nightclubs in Harlem, most of which were owned and operated by whites, refused to admit black customers. The only African Americans who were permitted inside were the jazz musicians, singers and dancers, prostitutes, and kitchen help. Moreover, black musicians often had to play what the white patrons wanted to hear. Duke Ellington, for example, featured "jungle music," which for whites revealed the "true" African soul—sensual, innocent, primitive. Artists and writers experienced similar pressures. Many of them depended for their sustenance on the support of wealthy white patrons. Those patrons were generous, but they wanted a return on their investment. Charlotte Mason, the New York City matron who supported Hughes and another black writer, Zora Neale Hurston, for example, expected them to entertain her friends by demonstrating "authentic Negritude."

MEXICAN AMERICANS

After the Johnson-Reed Act of 1924, Mexicans became the country's chief source of immigrant labor. A total of 500,000 Mexicans entered the United States in the 1920s. Most settled in the Southwest. In Texas three of every four construction workers and 8 of every 10 migrant farm workers were Mexicans. In California, Mexican immigrants made up 75 percent of the state's agricultural workforce.

Mexican farm laborers in Texas worked long hours for little money. They were usually barred from becoming machine operators or assuming other skilled positions. Forced to follow the crops, they had little opportunity to develop settled homes and communities. Farm owners rarely required the services of Mexican workers for more than several days or weeks, and few were willing to spend the money required to provide decent homes and schools. Houses typically lacked even wooden floors or indoor plumbing. Mexican laborers found it difficult to protest these conditions. Their knowledge of English and American law was limited. Many were in debt to employers who had advanced them money and who threatened them with jail if they failed to fulfill the terms of their contract. Others feared deportation; they lacked visas, having slipped into the United States illegally rather than pay the immigrant tax or endure harassment from the border patrol.

Increasing numbers of Mexican immigrants, however, found their way to California. Some escaped agricultural labor altogether for construction and manufacturing

"**LOS MADRUGADORES.**" *Led by Pedro J. Gonzalez (seated, on left), this popular Mexican group sang corridos in live performances and on KMPC, a Spanish-language radio station in 1920s Los Angeles.*

Chicano Studies Research Library, University of California, Los Angeles

jobs. Mexican men in Los Angeles worked in the city's large railroad yards, at the city's numerous construction sites, as unskilled workers in local factories, and as agricultural workers in the fruit and vegetable fields of Los Angeles County. Mexican women labored in the city's garment shops, fish canneries, and food processing plants.

The Los Angeles Mexican American community increased in complexity as it grew in size. By the mid-1920s it included a growing professional class, a proud group of *californios* (Spanish speakers who had been resident in California for generations), a large number of musicians and entertainers, a small but energetic band of entrepreneurs and businessmen, conservative clerics and intellectuals who had fled or been expelled from revolutionary Mexico, and Mexican government officials who had been sent to counter the influence of the conservative exiles and strengthen the ties of the immigrants to their homeland. This diverse mix gave rise to much internal conflict, but it also generated cultural vitality. Indeed, Los Angeles became the same kind of magnet for Mexican Americans that Harlem had become for African Americans. Mexican musicians flocked to Los Angeles, as did Mexican playwrights. The city supported a vigorous Spanish-language theater. Mexican musicians performed on street corners, at ethnic festivals and weddings, at cabarets, and on the radio. Especially popular were folk ballads, called *corridos*, that spoke to the experiences of Mexican immigrants.

This flowering of Mexican American culture in Los Angeles could not erase the low wages, high rates of infant mortality, racial discrimination, and other hardships Mexicans faced; nor did it encourage Mexicans to mobilize themselves as a political force. Unlike European immigrants, Mexican immigrants showed little interest in becoming American citizens and acquiring the vote. Yet the cultural vibrancy of the Mexican immigrant community did sustain many individuals who were struggling to survive in a strange, and often hostile, environment.

californios Spanish-speaking people whose families had resided in California for generations.

THE "LOST GENERATION" AND DISILLUSIONED INTELLECTUALS

Many native-born, white artists and intellectuals also felt uneasy in America in the 1920s. Their unease arose not from poverty or discrimination but from alienation. They despaired of American culture and regarded the average American as anti-intellectual, small-minded, materialistic, and puritanical. The novelist Sinclair Lewis ridiculed small-town Americans in *Main Street* (1920), "sophisticated" city dwellers in *Babbitt* (1922), physicians in *Arrowsmith* (1925), and evangelicals in *Elmer Gantry* (1927).

Before the First World War intellectuals and artists had been deeply engaged with "the people." Although they were critical of many aspects of American society, they believed that they could help bring about a new politics and improve social conditions. Some of them joined the war effort before the United States had officially intervened. Ernest Hemingway, John Dos Passos, and e. e. cummings, among

FOCUS QUESTION
To whom did the phrase "Lost Generation" refer, and what caused these individuals to become disillusioned?

others, sailed to Europe and volunteered their services to the Allies, usually as ambulance drivers carrying wounded soldiers from the front.

America's intellectuals were shocked by the war's effect on American society. The wartime push for consensus created intolerance of radicals, immigrants, and blacks. Not only had many Americans embraced conformity for themselves, but they seemed determined to force conformity on others. The young critic Harold Stearns wrote in 1921 that "the most moving and pathetic fact in the social life of America today is emotional and aesthetic starvation." Before these words were published, Stearns had sailed for France. So many alienated young men like Stearns showed up in Paris that Gertrude Stein, an American writer whose Paris apartment became a gathering place for them, took to calling them the **Lost Generation**. These writers and intellectuals managed to convert their disillusionment into a new literary sensibility. The finest works of the decade focused on the psychological toll of living in what the poet T. S. Eliot referred to as *The Waste Land* (1922). F. Scott Fitzgerald's novel *The Great Gatsby* (1925) told of a man destroyed by his desire to be accepted into a world of wealth, fancy cars, and fast women. In the novel *A Farewell to Arms* (1929), Ernest Hemingway wrote of an American soldier overwhelmed by the senselessness and brutality of war who deserts the army for the company of a woman he loves. The playwright Eugene O'Neill created characters haunted by despair, loneliness, and unfulfilled longing.

Writers innovated in style as well as in content. Sherwood Anderson blended fiction and autobiography in his collection of interrelated stories, *Winesburg, Ohio* (1919). John Dos Passos, in *Manhattan Transfer* (1925), mixed journalism with more traditional literary methods. Hemingway wrote in an understated, laconic prose that somehow drew attention to his characters' rage and vulnerability. White southern writers found a tragic sensibility surviving from the South's defeat in the Civil War that spoke to their own loss of hope. One group of southern writers, calling themselves "the Agrarians," argued that the enduring agricultural character of their region offered a more hopeful path to the future than did the mass-production and mass-consumption regime that had overtaken the North. In 1929 William Faulkner published *The Sound and the Fury*, the first in a series of novels set in northern Mississippi's fictional Yoknapatawpha County. With compassion and understanding, Faulkner explored the violence and terror that marked relationships among family members and townspeople.

DEMOCRACY ON THE DEFENSIVE

Disdain for the masses led some intellectuals to question democracy itself. If ordinary people were as stupid, prejudiced, and easily manipulated as they seemed, how could they be entrusted with the fate of the nation? Walter Lippmann, a former radical and progressive, declared that modern society had rendered democracy obsolete. In his view, average citizens, buffeted by propaganda emanating from powerful opinion makers, could no longer make the kind of informed, rational judgments that were needed to make democracy work. Lippmann's solution—and that of many other political commentators—was to shift government power from the people to educated elites. Those elites, who would be appointed rather than elected, would conduct foreign and domestic policy in an informed, intelligent way.

These antidemocratic views did not go uncontested. The philosopher **John Dewey** was the most articulate spokesman for the "pro-democracy" position. He acknowledged that the concentration of power in a few giant organizations had eroded the authority of political institutions. But democracy was not doomed, he insisted. People could reclaim their freedom by making big business subject to

Lost Generation *Term used by Gertrude Stein to describe U.S. writers and artists who fled to Paris in the 1920s after becoming disillusioned with America.*

John Dewey *Philosopher who believed that American technological and industrial power could be made to serve the people and democracy.*

government control. The government could then use its power to democratize corporations and regulate the communications industry to ensure that every citizen had access to the facts needed to make reasonable, informed political decisions.

Dewey's views attracted the support of a wide range of liberal intellectuals and reformers, including Robert and Helen Lynd; Rexford Tugwell, professor of economics at Columbia; and Felix Frankfurter, a rising star at Harvard Law School. Some of these activists had ties to labor leaders and to New York governor Franklin D. Roosevelt. They formed the vanguard of a new liberal movement that was committed to taking up the work the progressives had left unfinished.

But these reformers were without power, except in a few states. The Republican Party had driven reformers from its ranks. The Democratic Party was crippled by a split between its principal constituencies—rural Protestants and urban ethnics—over Prohibition, immigration restriction, and the Ku Klux Klan. The labor movement was moribund. The Socialist Party had never recovered from the trauma of war and Bolshevism. La Follette's Farmer-Labor Party, after a promising debut, had stalled. John Dewey and his friends tried to launch yet another third party, but they failed to raise money or arouse mass support. Reformers took little comfort in the presidential election of 1928. Hoover's smashing victory suggested that the dominance of the Republicans would continue for a long time.

C O N C L U S I O N

Signs abounded in the 1920s that the American economy had become more prosperous, more consumer oriented, even somewhat more egalitarian. Moves to greater equality within marriage, to enhanced liberty for single women, and to greater opportunities for minority writers and artists suggested that economic change was propelling social change as well.

But many working-class and rural Americans benefited little from the decade's prosperity. Changes in social life aroused resistance, especially from farmers and small-town Americans who feared that the rapid growth of cities was rendering their white, Protestant America unrecognizable. Ethnic and racial minorities, as a result, experienced discrimination. As the decade ended, many of the issues that had divided the traditionalists and modernists—whether science should supplant religion; whether the federal government had the authority to enforce morality on individual citizens (as it was doing with Prohibition); and whether Americans who were not white Protestants should be first class citizens—remained unresolved.

QUESTIONS FOR REVIEW AND CRITICAL THINKING

Review

1. What were the achievements and limitations of "people's capitalism" in the 1920s?
2. What was the age of celebrity? What caused it to arise?
3. What were the similarities and differences in the politics of Harding, Coolidge, and Hoover?
4. What did farmers and Protestants fear about America in the 1920s, and how did they respond?
5. How were the experiences of ethnic and racial groups in 1920s America similar, and how were they different?
6. To whom did the phrase "Lost Generation" refer, and what caused these individuals to become disillusioned?

Critical Thinking

1. Can the deep cultural differences that divided America in the 1920s best be explained by where people lived (country vs. city), where they were born (in the United States or abroad), their race (white or not), their wealth or poverty, or something else?
2. A Great Depression was the furthest thing from Americans' minds in the 1920s. Reviewing carefully what you have learned about the economy in those years, can you spot areas of economic trouble that contemporaries may have overlooked?

ONLINE RESOURCES

 Visit the companion website to access flashcards, crossword puzzles, exercises, and quizzes related to this chapter: www.cengage.com/history/murrin/libertyequalconc5e.

 See our interactive ebook for map and primary source activities.

 ISCOVERY   *How did the disillusionment that followed World War I shape social and cultural conflict in the 1920s?*

CULTURE AND SOCIETY The image below illustrates many characteristics of American life in the 1920s, specifically 1925. What does it suggest about the general mood of the country and activities of daily life? How does it convey changes that had taken place in the previous decade for women? How does it show "rebellion" against the previous generation and its values? What values were women challenging at this point? After gaining the right to vote in 1919, what aspects of life did women want to change or control?

In thinking about this question, begin by breaking it down into the components shown below. A discussion of the significance of each component should appear in your answer.

IMMIGRATION AND SOCIETY Examine the table on page 648 and the textual analysis in the section on immigration restriction on pages 646 and 647. The table identifies the countries that were given large annual immigrant quotas by the Immigration Restriction Act of 1924 (also known as the Johnson-Reed Act) and those that were given small annual quotas. Which countries received the largest quotas? Which countries received the smallest quotas? How were these quotas determined? What did Congress hope to accomplish with this legislation? Was the legislation successful?

GOOD TIMES

The Granger Collection, New York

THE GREAT DEPRESSION AND THE NEW DEAL, 1929–1939

The Great Depression began on October 29, 1929—"Black Tuesday"—with a spectacular stock market crash. On that one day, the value of stocks plummeted $14 billion. By the end of that year, stock prices had fallen 50 percent from their September highs. By 1932, the worst year of the depression, they had fallen another 30 percent. Meanwhile the unemployment rate had soared to 25 percent.

Many Americans who lived through the Great Depression were never able to forget the scenes of misery. In cities, the poor meekly awaited their turn at ill-funded soup kitchens. Scavengers poked through garbage cans for food, scoured railroad tracks for coal that had fallen from trains, and sometimes ripped up railroad ties for fuel. Hundreds of thousands of Americans built makeshift shelters out of cardboard, scrap metal, and whatever else they could find in the

Timeline

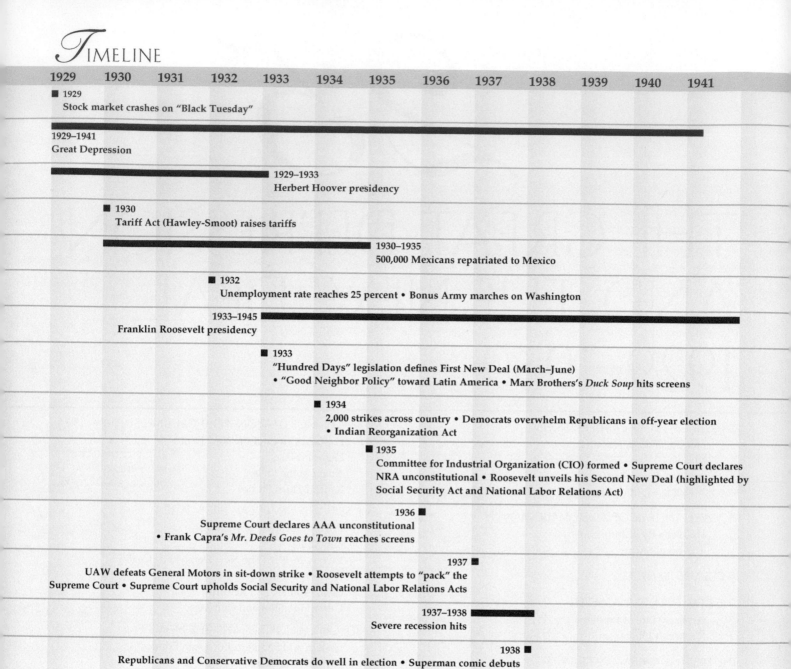

1929	1930	1931	1932	1933	1934	1935	1936	1937	1938	1939	1940	1941

■ 1929
Stock market crashes on "Black Tuesday"

1929–1941
Great Depression

1929–1933
Herbert Hoover presidency

■ 1930
Tariff Act (Hawley-Smoot) raises tariffs

1930–1935
500,000 Mexicans repatriated to Mexico

■ 1932
Unemployment rate reaches 25 percent • Bonus Army marches on Washington

1933–1945
Franklin Roosevelt presidency

■ 1933
"Hundred Days" legislation defines First New Deal (March–June)
• "Good Neighbor Policy" toward Latin America • Marx Brothers's *Duck Soup* hits screens

■ 1934
2,000 strikes across country • Democrats overwhelm Republicans in off-year election
• Indian Reorganization Act

■ 1935
Committee for Industrial Organization (CIO) formed • Supreme Court declares
NRA unconstitutional • Roosevelt unveils his Second New Deal (highlighted by
Social Security Act and National Labor Relations Act)

1936 ■
Supreme Court declares AAA unconstitutional
• Frank Capra's *Mr. Deeds Goes to Town* reaches screens

1937 ■
UAW defeats General Motors in sit-down strike • Roosevelt attempts to "pack" the
Supreme Court • Supreme Court upholds Social Security and National Labor Relations Acts

1937–1938
Severe recession hits

1938 ■
Republicans and Conservative Democrats do well in election • Superman comic debuts

1939 ■
75,000 hear Marian Anderson sing at Lincoln Memorial
• John Steinbeck publishes *The Grapes of Wrath*

---

city dump. They called their towns "Hoovervilles," after the president they despised for his apparent refusal to help them.

The Great Depression brought cultural crisis as well as economic crisis. In the 1920s, many Americans had made business values—economic growth, freedom of enterprise, and acquisitiveness—synonymous with national values. But with the prestige of business in decline, how could Americans regain their hope and recover their confidence in the future?

The gloom broke in early 1933 when Franklin Delano Roosevelt became president and unleashed the power of government to regulate capitalist enterprises, to restore the economy to health, and to guarantee the social welfare of Americans unable to help themselves. Roosevelt called his pro-government program a "new deal for the American people." In the short term, the New Deal did not restore prosperity to America. But the "liberalism" that the New Deal championed was accepted by millions, who agreed with Roosevelt that only a large and powerful government could guarantee Americans their liberty.

CAUSES OF THE GREAT DEPRESSION

There had been other depressions, or "panics," in American history, but none as severe or as enduring as the one that began in 1929. What caused the **Great Depression**?

STOCK MARKET SPECULATION

In 1928 and 1929 the New York Stock Exchange had undergone a remarkable run-up in prices. Money had poured into the market. But many investors were buying on a 10 percent "margin"—putting up only 10 percent of the price of a stock and borrowing the rest from brokers or banks. They expected to be able to resell their shares within a few months at dramatically higher prices, pay back their loans from the proceeds, and still clear a handsome profit. And, for a while, that is exactly what they did. But the possibility of making a fortune with an investment of only a few thousand dollars only intensified investors' greed. Money flowed into risky enterprises. Speculation became rampant. The stock market spiraled upward, out of control. When confidence in future earnings faltered in October 1929, creditors began demanding that investors who had bought stocks on margin repay their loans. Many could not. The market crashed from its dizzying heights.

Still, the crash, by itself, does not explain why the Great Depression lasted as long as it did. Poor decision making by the Federal Reserve Board, an ill-advised tariff that took effect soon after the Depression hit, and a lopsided concentration of wealth in the hands of the rich deepened the economic collapse and made recovery more difficult.

MISTAKES BY THE FEDERAL RESERVE BOARD

In 1930 and 1931, the Federal Reserve curtailed the amount of money in circulation and raised interest rates, thereby making credit more difficult for the public to secure. This tight money policy was a mistake. What the economy needed was the opposite: an expanded money supply, lower interest rates, and easier credit. Such a course would have enabled debtors to pay their creditors. Instead, the Federal Reserve plunged an economy starved for credit deeper into depression.

AN ILL-ADVISED TARIFF

The Tariff Act of 1930, also known as the Hawley-Smoot Tariff, accelerated economic decline abroad and at home. It raised tariffs on not only 75 agricultural goods but also 925 manufactured products. Industrialists had convinced their supporters in the Republican-controlled Congress that such protection would give American industry much-needed assistance. But the legislation was a disaster. Angry foreign governments retaliated by raising their own tariff rates to keep out American goods. International trade, already weakened by the tight credit policies of the Federal Reserve, was dealt another blow.

FOCUS QUESTION
What caused the crash of 1929, and why did the ensuing depression last so long?

Great Depression *Economic downturn triggered by the stock market crash in October 1929 and lasting until 1941.*

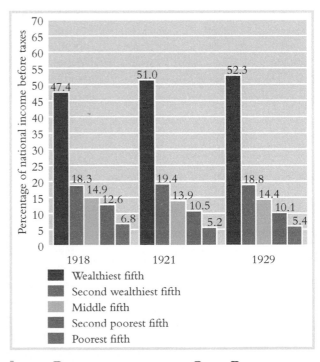

INCOME DISTRIBUTION BEFORE THE GREAT DEPRESSION
Source: From Gabriel Kolko, *Wealth and Power in America: An Analysis of Social Class and Income Distribution* (New York: Praeger, 1962), p. 14.

A MALDISTRIBUTION OF WEALTH

A maldistribution in the nation's wealth that had developed in the 1920s also stymied economic recovery. Between 1918 and 1929 the share of the national income that went to the wealthiest 20 percent of the population rose by more than 10 percent, while the share that went to the poorest 60 percent fell by almost 13 percent. (See chart on p. 661.) The Coolidge administration contributed to this maldistribution by lowering taxes on the wealthy. The deepening inequality of income distribution slowed consumption and held back the growth of consumer-oriented industries. Even when the rich spent lavishly, they still spent a smaller proportion of their total incomes on consumption than wage earners did. Had more of the total increase in national income found its way into the pockets of average Americans during the 1920s, the demand for consumer goods would have been steadier and the newer consumer industries would have been correspondingly stronger. Such an economy might have recovered more quickly from the stock market crash of 1929. But recovery from the Great Depression did not come until 1941, more than a decade later.

HOOVER: THE FALL OF A SELF-MADE MAN

In 1928 Herbert Hoover seemed to represent living proof that the American dream could be realized by anyone who was willing to work for it. A Stanford University geology major, a mining engineer, and a skilled manager, Hoover rose quickly in corporate ranks. His government service began during the First World War, when he won an international reputation for his success in feeding millions of European soldiers and civilians. In the 1920s, he was an active and influential secretary of commerce (see Chapters 23 and 24). As the decade wound down, no American seemed better qualified to become president of the United States, an office that Hoover assumed in March 1929. "We in America today are nearer to the final triumph over poverty than ever before in the history of any land," he had declared in August 1928. A little more than a year later, the Great Depression struck.

HOOVER'S PROGRAM

To cope with the crisis, Hoover first turned to the "associational" principles he had followed as secretary of commerce. He encouraged organizations of farmers, industrialists, and bankers to share information, bolster one another's spirits, and devise policies to aid recovery. Farmers would restrict output, industrialists would hold wages at pre-Depression levels, and bankers would help each other remain solvent.

Hoover pursued a more aggressive set of economic policies once he realized that associationalism was failing. To ease a concurrent European crisis, Hoover secured a one-year moratorium on loan payments that European governments owed American banks. He steered through Congress the Glass-Steagall Act of 1932, intended to help American banks meet the demands of European depositors who wished to convert their dollars to gold. And to ease the crisis at home he created the Reconstruction Finance Corporation (RFC) in 1932 to make $2 billion available in loans to ailing banks and to corporations willing to build low-cost housing, bridges, and other public works. The Home Loan Bank Board, set up that same year, offered funds to financial institutions that lent money for home construction and mortgages.

Despite this new activism, Hoover was uncomfortable with the idea that the government was responsible for restoring the nation's economic welfare. When RFC projects in 1932 gave rise to the largest peacetime deficit in U.S. history, Hoover cut back on RFC expenditures. He also insisted that the RFC issue loans only to healthy institutions that could repay them and that it favor public works, such as toll bridges, that were likely to become self-financing. As a result of these constraints, the RFC spent considerably less than Congress had mandated.

Hoover was especially reluctant to engage the government in providing relief to unemployed and homeless Americans. To give money to the poor, he insisted, would destroy their desire to work, undermine their sense of self-worth, and erode their capacity for citizenship.

THE BONUS ARMY

In the spring of 1932 a group of Army veterans challenged Hoover's policies. In 1924 Congress had authorized a $1,000 bonus for First World War veterans in the form of compensation certificates that would mature in 1945. Now the veterans were demanding that the government pay the bonus immediately. Calling themselves the Bonus Expeditionary Force, a group from Portland, Oregon, hopped onto empty boxcars of freight trains heading east, determined to march on Washington. As the impoverished "army" moved eastward, their ranks multiplied so that by the time they reached the capital their number had swelled to 20,000. The so-called **Bonus Army** set up camp near the Capitol and petitioned Congress for early payment of the bonus. The House of Representatives agreed, but the Senate turned them down. Hoover refused to meet with them. In July, federal troops led by Army Chief of Staff Douglas MacArthur and 3rd Cavalry Commander George Patton

Bonus Army *Army veterans who marched on Washington, D.C., in 1932 to lobby for economic relief but who were rebuffed by Hoover.*

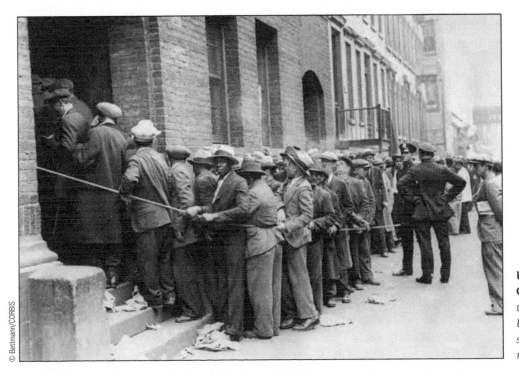

UNEMPLOYED MEN IN NEW YORK CITY, 1931. *The thousands of men waiting to register at the Emergency Unemployment Relief office became so frustrated that they rioted. Police reserves arrived to restore order.*

© Bettmann/CORBIS

attacked the veterans' encampment, set the tents and shacks ablaze, and dispersed the protesters. In the process, more than 100 veterans were wounded and one infant was killed.

News that veterans and their families had been attacked in the nation's capital hardened anti-Hoover opinion. In the 1932 elections, Hoover received only 39.6 percent of the popular vote and just 59 (of 531) electoral votes. Hoover left the presidency a bewildered man, reviled by many Americans for what they took to be his indifference to suffering and his ineptitude in dealing with the economy's collapse.

A CULTURE IN CRISIS

The economic crisis of the early 1930s expressed itself not just in politics but also in culture, especially literature and cinema. Edmund Wilson traveled the country in 1930 and 1931 writing essays about how Americans had lost their way and knew not where to turn. A sense of aimlessness and hopelessness characterized the Studs Lonigan trilogy (1932–1935) by James T. Farrell. In another decade, Farrell might have cast his scrappy Irish American protagonist, Studs, as an American hero who, through pluck, guile, and force of character, rises from poverty to wealth, success, and influence. But Studs lacks focus and is too easily overcome by the harshness of his environment. He dies poor and alone, not yet 30. Meanwhile, Nathaniel West was publishing *Miss Lonelyhearts* (1933) and *A Cool Million* (1934), novels similarly built around central characters succumbing to failure, drift, even insanity.

Parallel themes of despair are evident in such popular movies as *Fugitive from a Chain Gang* (1932), in which an industrious and honorable man, James Allen, returns from Europe a war hero, only to sink into vagabondage. Caught by the police when he becomes an innocent accessory to a crime, Allen is sentenced to 10 years on a Georgia chain gang. Unable to tolerate the hardship and injustice of his punishment, Allen escapes from jail. But he is condemned to being a man always on the run, unable to prove his innocence, earn a decent living, or build enduring relationships. This powerful, utterly bleak film won an Academy Award for Best Picture.

Less bleak but still sobering were gangster movies, especially *Little Caesar* (1930) and *The Public Enemy* (1931), which told stories of hard-nosed, crooked, violent men who became wealthy and influential by living outside the law and bending their environment to their will. Moviegoers were gripped by the intensity, suspense, and violence of gangster–police confrontations in these films, but they were drawn, too, to the gangsters themselves, modern-day outlaws who demonstrated how tough it was to succeed in America and how it might be necessary to break the rules.

Lawlessness also surfaced in the wild comedy of Groucho, Chico, Harpo, and Zeppo Marx, vaudevillians who, in the 1920s and 1930s, made the transition to the silver screen. The Marx Brothers ridiculed authority figures, broke every rule of etiquette, smacked around their antagonists (and each other), and mangled the English language. Anarchy ruled their world. The Marx Brothers offered moviegoers a 90-minute escape from the harsh realities of their daily lives.

Some Marx Brothers movies carried a more serious message. *Duck Soup* (1933) is a withering political satire set in the fictional nation of Fredonia. Fredonia's dictatorial leaders are pompous and small-minded, its legal system is a fraud, and its clueless citizens are easily misled. At the movie's end, Fredonians are called to arms through spectacularly ludicrous song-and-dance scenes, and then led off to fight a meaningless but deadly war. While hilarious to watch, *Duck Soup* also delivers the dispiriting message that people cannot hope to better themselves through politics, for politics has been emptied of all meaning and honesty. This cinematic sentiment echoed the conviction of many Americans in 1932 and early 1933 that their own politicians, especially Hoover and the Republicans, had failed them in a time of need.

THE DEMOCRATIC ROOSEVELT

Between 1933 and 1935, the country's mood shifted sharply, and politics would, once again, generate hope rather than despair. This change was largely attributable to the personality and politics of Hoover's successor, **Franklin D. Roosevelt**.

AN EARLY LIFE OF PRIVILEGE

Roosevelt was born in 1882 into a patrician family, descended on his father's side from Dutch gentry who in the 17th century had built large estates on the fertile land along the Hudson River. His mother's family—the Delanos—traced their ancestors back to the Mayflower. His education at Groton, Harvard College, and Columbia Law School was typical of the path followed by the sons of America's elite.

In 1921, at age 39, Roosevelt was stricken by polio and permanently lost the use of his legs. Before becoming paralyzed, he had not distinguished himself either at school or in the practice of law, nor could he point to many significant political achievements. He owed his political ascent more to his famous name—Theodore Roosevelt was his older cousin—than to actual accomplishments. He was charming, gregarious, and popular among his associates in the New York Democratic Party. He enjoyed a good time and devoted a great deal of energy to sailing, partying, and enjoying the company of women other than his wife, **Eleanor Roosevelt.** But the polio attack changed him, and he seemed to acquire a new determination and seriousness.

Roosevelt's physical debilitation also transformed his relationship with Eleanor, with whom he had shared a testy and increasingly loveless marriage. Eleanor's dedication to nursing Franklin back to health forged a new bond between them. More conscious of his dependence on others, he now welcomed her as a partner in his career. Eleanor soon displayed a talent for political organization and public speaking. She would become an active, eloquent First Lady and an architect of American liberalism.

ROOSEVELT LIBERALISM

As governor of New York (1929–1933), Roosevelt had initiated various reform programs, and his success made him the front-runner in the contest for the 1932 Democratic presidential nomination. It was by no means certain, however, that he would be the party's choice. Since 1924 the Democrats had been divided between Southern and Midwestern agrarians on the one hand and Northeastern ethnics on the

Franklin D. Roosevelt *President from 1933 to 1945, and the creator of the New Deal.*

Eleanor Roosevelt *A politically engaged and effective First Lady and an architect of American liberalism.*

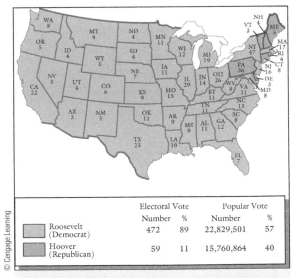

	Electoral Vote		Popular Vote	
	Number	%	Number	%
Roosevelt (Democrat)	472	89	22,829,501	57
Hoover (Republican)	59	11	15,760,864	40

© Cengage Learning

Map 25.1 PRESIDENTIAL ELECTION, 1932. *The trauma of the Great Depression can be gauged by the shifting fortunes of President Herbert Hoover. In 1928, he had won 444 electoral votes and carried all but eight states (see Map 24.2, p. 653). In 1932, by contrast, he won only 59 electoral votes and carried only seven states. His Democratic opponent, Franklin D. Roosevelt, was the big winner.*

FROM HERBERT HOOVER TO FRANKLIN D. ROOSEVELT. *This 1933 photograph shows the outgoing and incoming presidents on the way to FDR's inauguration. By this time, the two men detested each other, a sentiment that, in this photograph, FDR concealed better than his predecessor.*

The Art Archive/Culver Pictures/Picture Desk

other. The agrarians favored government regulation—both of the nation's economy and of the private affairs of its citizens. Their support of government intervention in the pursuit of social justice marked them as economic progressives, while their advocacy of Prohibition revealed cultural conservatism as well as a nativistic strain. By contrast, urban ethnics opposed Prohibition and other forms of government interference in the private lives of its citizens. Urban ethnics were divided over whether the government should regulate the economy, with former New York governor Al Smith increasingly committed to a laissez-faire policy and Senator Robert Wagner of New York and others supporting more federal control.

Roosevelt sought to carve out a middle ground. As governor of New York, and then as a presidential candidate in 1932, he surrounded himself with men and women who embraced the new reform movement called liberalism. Liberals shared with the agrarians and Wagner's supporters a desire to regulate capitalism, but agreed with Al Smith that the government had no business telling people how to live their lives. Roosevelt managed to unite the party behind him at the 1932 Democratic Party convention. In a rousing call to action, he declared: "Ours must be the party of liberal thought, of planned action, of enlightened international outlook, and of the greatest good for the greatest number of citizens." He promised "a new deal for the American people."

Roosevelt liberalism *New reform movement that sought to regulate capitalism but not the morals of private citizens. This reform liberalism overcame divisions between Southern agrarians and Northeastern ethnics.*

THE FIRST NEW DEAL, 1933–1935

FOCUS QUESTION
What do you consider to be the three or four most important pieces of legislation in the First New Deal? Why?

By the time Roosevelt assumed office, the economy lay in shambles. From 1929 to 1932 industrial production fell by 50 percent, while new investment declined from $16 billion to less than $1 billion. The nation's banking system was on the verge of collapse. In 1931 alone, more than 2,000 banks had shut their doors. Unemployment was soaring. Some Americans feared that the opportunity for reform had already passed.

But not Roosevelt. In his first "Hundred Days," from early March through early June 1933, Roosevelt persuaded Congress to pass 15 major pieces of legislation to help bankers, farmers, industrialists, workers, homeowners, the unemployed, and the hungry (see Table 25.1). He also prevailed on Congress to repeal Prohibition. Not all the new laws helped to relieve distress and promote recovery. But, in the short term, that seemed not to matter. Roosevelt had brought energy and hope to the nation. He was confident, decisive, and defiantly cheery. "The only thing we have to fear is fear itself," he declared. On the second Sunday after his inaugural, he launched a series of radio addresses known as "fireside chats," speaking in a plain, friendly, and direct voice to Americans throughout the country.

Many who heard the president speaking warmly and conversationally to them "in their homes" found the experience riveting. Millions wrote letters to him and to Eleanor Roosevelt over the next few years. Many of the letters were simply addressed to "Mr. or Mrs. Roosevelt, Washington, D.C."

SAVING THE BANKS

Roosevelt's first order of business was to save the nation's financial system. By inauguration day, several states had already shut their banks. Roosevelt immediately ordered all the nation's banks closed—a bold move he brazenly called a "bank holiday." He then had Congress rush through an Emergency Banking Act (EBA) that made federal loans available to private bankers. He followed that with an Economy Act (EA) that committed the government to balancing the budget.

Both the EBA and the EA were fiscally conservative programs first proposed by Hoover. The EBA made it possible for private bankers to retain financial control of

TABLE 25.1

LEGISLATION ENACTED DURING THE "HUNDRED DAYS," MARCH 9–JUNE 16, 1933		
Date	**Legislation**	**Purpose**
March 9	Emergency Banking Act	Provide federal loans to private bankers
March 20	Economy Act	Balance the federal budget
March 22	Beer-Wine Revenue Act	Repeal Prohibition
March 31	Unemployment Relief Act	Create the Civilian Conservation Corps
May 12	Agricultural Adjustment Act	Establish a national agricultural policy
May 12	Emergency Farm Mortgage Act	Provide refinancing of farm mortgages
May 12	Federal Emergency Relief Act	Establish a national relief system, including the Civil Works Administration
May 18	Tennessee Valley Authority Act	Promote economic development of the Tennessee Valley
May 27	Securities Act	Regulate the purchase and sale of new securities
June 5	Gold Repeal Joint Resolution	Cancel the gold clause in public and private contracts
June 13	Home Owners Loan Act	Provide refinancing of home mortgages
June 16	National Industrial Recovery Act	Set up a national system of industrial self-government and establish the Public Works Administration
June 16	Glass-Steagall Banking Act	Create Federal Deposit Insurance Corporation; separate commercial and investment banking
June 16	Farm Credit Act	Reorganize agricultural credit programs
June 16	Railroad Coordination Act	Appoint federal coordinator of transportation

Source: Arthur M. Schlesinger Jr., *The Coming of the New Deal* (Boston: Houghton Mifflin, 1959), pp. 20–21.

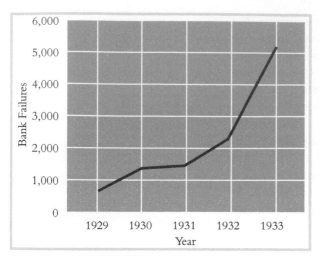

BANK FAILURES, 1929–1933
Source: From C. D. Bremer, *American Bank Failures* (New York: Columbia University Press, 1935), p. 42.

their institutions, and the EA announced the government's intention to pursue a fiscally prudent course. Only after the financial crisis had eased did Roosevelt turn to the structural reform of banking. A second Glass-Steagall Act (1933) separated commercial banking from investment banking. It also created the Federal Deposit Insurance Corporation (FDIC), which assured depositors that the government would protect up to $5,000 of their savings. The Securities Act (1933) and the Securities Exchange Act (1934) imposed long-overdue regulation on the New York Stock Exchange, both by reining in buying on margin and by establishing the Securities and Exchange Commission to enforce federal law.

ECONOMIC RELIEF

Roosevelt understood the need to temper financial prudence with compassion. Congress responded swiftly in 1933 to Roosevelt's request to establish the Federal Emergency Relief Administration (FERA), granting it $500 million for relief to the poor. To head it, Roosevelt appointed a brash young reformer, Harry Hopkins. Roosevelt then won congressional approval for the Civilian Conservation Corps (CCC), which put more than 2 million single young men to work planting trees, halting erosion, and otherwise improving the environment. The following winter, Roosevelt launched the Civil Works Administration (CWA), an ambitious work-relief program, also under Harry Hopkins's direction, that hired 4 million unemployed at $15 a week and put them to work on 400,000 government projects. For middle-class Americans threatened with the loss of their homes, Roosevelt won congressional approval for the Homeowners' Loan Corporation (1933) to refinance mortgages. These direct subsidies to millions of jobless and home-owning Americans lent credibility to Roosevelt's claim that the New Deal would set the country on a new course.

AGRICULTURAL REFORM

In 1933 Roosevelt expected economic recovery to come not from relief but through agricultural and industrial cooperation. He regarded the Agricultural Adjustment Act, passed in May, and the National Industrial Recovery Act (NIRA), passed in June, as the most important legislation of his Hundred Days. Both were based on the idea that curtailing production would trigger economic recovery. By shrinking the supply of agricultural and manufactured goods, Roosevelt's economists reasoned, these laws would restore the balance of normal market forces. Then, as demand for scarce goods exceeded supply, prices would rise and revenues would climb. Farmers and industrialists, earning a profit once again, would increase their investment in new technology and hire more workers.

To curtail farm production, the **Agricultural Adjustment Administration (AAA)**, set up by the Agricultural Adjustment Act, began paying farmers to keep a portion of their land out of cultivation and to reduce the size of their herds. The program was controversial; many farmers did not readily accept the idea that they were to be paid more money for working less land and husbanding fewer livestock. But few refused the government payments.

The AAA had made no provision, however, for the countless tenant farmers and farm laborers who would be thrown out of work by the reduction in acreage. In the

Agricultural Adjustment Administration (AAA) *1933 attempt to promote economic recovery by reducing supply of crops, dairy, and meat produced by American farmers.*

South, the victims were disproportionately black. A Georgia sharecropper wrote Harry Hopkins of his misery: "I have Bin farming all my life But the man I live with Has Turned me loose taking my mule [and] all my feed.... I can't get a Job so Some one said Rite you."

The programs of the AAA also proved inadequate to Great Plains farmers, whose economic problems had been compounded by ecological crisis. Just as the Depression rolled in, the rain stopped falling on the plains. The land, stripped of its native grasses by decades of plowing, dried up and turned to dust. And then the dust began to blow, sometimes traveling 1,000 miles across open prairie. Dust became a fixed feature of daily life on the plains (which soon became known as the "Dust Bowl"), covering furniture, floors, and stoves, and accumulating in people's hair and lungs.

The government responded to this calamity by establishing the Soil Conservation Service (SCS) in 1935. Recognizing that the soil problems of the Great Plains could not be solved simply by taking land out of production, SCS experts urged plains farmers to plant soil-conserving grasses and legumes in place of wheat. They taught them how to plow along contour lines and how to build terraces. Bolstered by the new assistance, which included government subsidies, Great Plains agriculture began to recover.

Still, the government offered little to the rural poor—the tenant farmers and sharecroppers. Nearly 1 million had left their homes by 1935, and another 2.5 million would leave after 1935. Most headed west, piling their belongings onto their jalopies, snaking along Route 66 until they reached California. They became known as Okies, because many, although not all, had come from Oklahoma.

In 1936 the Supreme Court ruled that AAA-mandated limits on farm production constituted illegal restraints of trade. Congress responded by passing the Soil Conservation and Domestic Allotment Act, which justified the removal of land from cultivation for reasons of conservation rather than economics. This new act also called upon landowners to share their government subsidies with sharecroppers and tenant farmers, although many landowners managed to evade this and subsequent laws.

The use of subsidies, begun by the AAA, did eventually bring stability and prosperity to agriculture. But the costs were high. Agriculture became the most heavily subsidized sector of the U.S. economy, and the Department of Agriculture grew into one of the government's largest bureaucracies. And the rural poor, black and white, never received a fair share of federal benefits.

INDUSTRIAL REFORM

American industry was so vast that paying individual manufacturers direct subsidies to reduce, or even halt, production was never contemplated. Instead, the government decided to limit production through persuasion and association. To head the **National Recovery Administration (NRA)**, authorized under the National Industrial Recovery Act, Roosevelt chose General Hugh Johnson. Johnson's first task was to convince industrialists and businessmen to raise employee wages to a minimum of 30 to 40 cents an hour and to limit employee hours to a maximum of 30 to 40 hours a week. The intent was to reduce the quantity of goods that any factory or business could produce.

Johnson distributed NRA pamphlets and pins throughout the country. He used the radio to exhort every American to do his or her part. He staged an NRA celebration in Yankee Stadium and organized a parade down New York City's Fifth

National Recovery Administration (NRA) *1933 attempt to promote economic recovery by persuading private groups of industrialists to decrease production, limit hours of work per employee, and standardize minimum wages.*

SELLING THE NRA THROUGH SEX AND SUNBURN. *Americans were asked to display their support for the NRA by pasting eagles onto their factory entrances, store fronts, and even clothes. The young women in this photo dispensed with pasting, choosing instead to allow the sun to burn their bare backs around a stenciled blue eagle and NRA lettering, which were being applied by the woman in the white gown.*

© Bettmann/CORBIS

Avenue. He sent letters to millions of employers asking them to place a "blue eagle"—the logo of the NRA—on storefronts, at factory entrances, and on company stationery to signal their participation in the campaign to limit production and restore prosperity. Blue eagles soon sprouted everywhere, usually accompanied by the slogan "We Do Our Part."

Johnson understood, however, that his propaganda campaign could not by itself guarantee recovery. So he brought together the largest producers in every sector of manufacturing and asked each group (or conference) to work out a code of fair competition that would specify prices, wages, and hours throughout the sector. He also asked each conference to restrict production.

In the summer and fall of 1933, the NRA codes drawn up for steel, textiles, coal mining, rubber, garment manufacture, and other industries seemed to be working. The economy picked up and people began to hope that an end to the Depression might be near. But in the winter and spring of 1934, economic indicators plunged downward once again and manufacturers began to evade the provisions of the codes. Government committees set up to enforce the codes turned out to be powerless to punish violators. By the fall of 1934, it was clear that the NRA had failed. When the Supreme Court declared the NRA codes unconstitutional in May 1935, the Roosevelt administration allowed the agency to die.

REBUILDING THE NATION'S INFRASTRUCTURE

The National Industrial Recovery Act also launched the Public Works Administration (PWA). The PWA was given a $3.3 billion budget to sponsor internal improvements that would strengthen the nation's infrastructure of roads, bridges, sewage systems, hospitals, airports, and schools. The PWA authorized the building of three major dams in the West—the Grand Coulee, Boulder, and Bonneville—that opened up large stretches of Arizona, California, and Washington to industrial and agricultural development. It funded the construction of the Triborough Bridge in New York City and the 100-mile causeway linking Florida to Key West. It also appropriated money to construct thousands of new schools.

QUICK REVIEW

THE FIRST NEW DEAL (1933–1935)

- Stabilized banking system, appropriated millions for relief of unemployed, and offered homeowners mortgage protection

- Attempted to repair agricultural and industrial economy through production cutbacks

- Vast water control projects (dams and canals), especially in the West and South, to expand nation's irrigation and drinking water supplies and electricity generation

- Criticized by some for favoring large economic interests and ignoring ordinary people

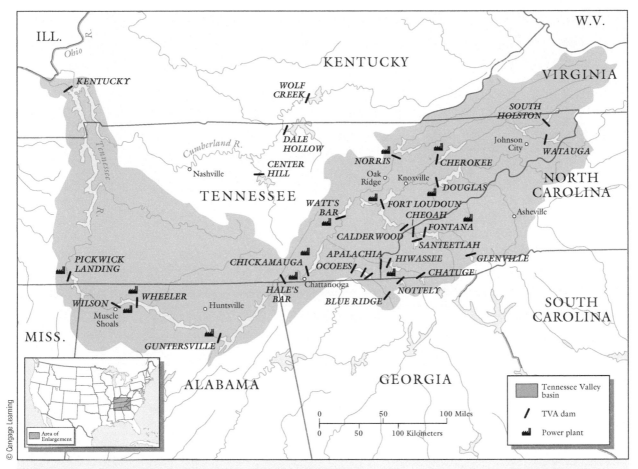

Map 25.2 TENNESSEE VALLEY AUTHORITY. *This map shows the vast scale of the TVA, and pinpoints the locations of 29 dams and 13 power plants that emerged from this project.*

THE TVA ALTERNATIVE

One piece of legislation specified a strategy for economic recovery very different from the one promoted by the NRA. The Tennessee Valley Authority Act (1933) called for the government itself—rather than private corporations—to promote economic development throughout the Tennessee Valley, a vast river basin winding through parts of Kentucky, Tennessee, Mississippi, Alabama, Georgia, and North Carolina. The **Tennessee Valley Authority (TVA)** built, completed, or improved more than 20 dams. The TVA built hydroelectric generators and soon became the nation's largest producer of electricity. Its low utility rates compelled private utility companies to reduce their rates as well. The TVA also constructed waterways to bypass unnavigable stretches of the river, reduced the danger of flooding, and taught farmers how to prevent soil erosion and use fertilizers.

Although the TVA was one of the New Deal's most celebrated successes, it did not become a model for nationwide experiments in public economic management. With the TVA, the government was bringing prosperity to an impoverished region. It would have been quite a different matter to assume control of established industries and banks. Neither Roosevelt, nor Congress, nor the public favored such a radical growth of governmental power. Thus, the New Deal never embraced the idea of the federal government as a substitute for private enterprise.

Tennessee Valley Authority (TVA) *Ambitious and successful use of government resources and power to promote economic development throughout the Tennessee Valley.*

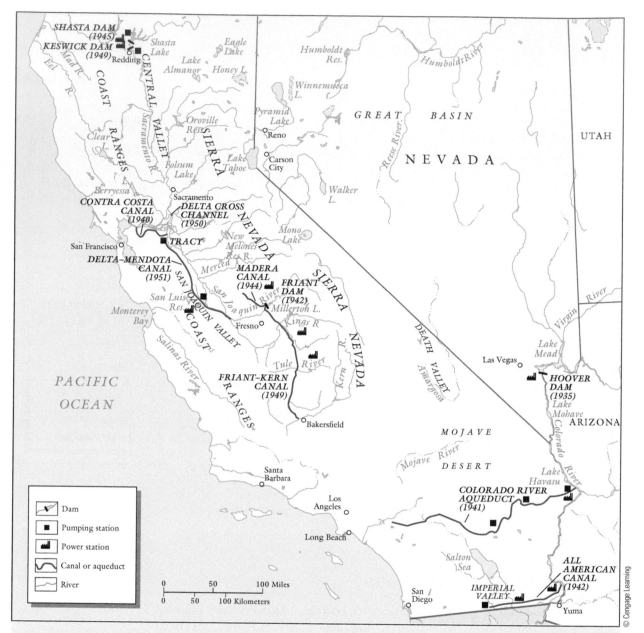

Map 25.3 **FEDERAL WATER PROJECTS IN CALIFORNIA BUILT OR FUNDED BY THE NEW DEAL.** *This map demonstrates how much California cities and agriculture benefited from water projects—dams, canals, aqueducts, pumping stations, and power plants—begun under the New Deal. The projects extended from the Shasta Dam in the northern part of the state to the All-American Canal that traversed the Imperial Valley south of San Diego, and included the Colorado River Aqueduct that would bring drinking water to Los Angeles.*

THE NEW DEAL AND WESTERN DEVELOPMENT

The West benefited most from the New Deal. Between 1933 and 1939, per-capita payments for public works projects, welfare, and federal loans in the Rocky Mountain and Pacific Coast states outstripped those of any other region.

Dam building was central to the New Deal's Western program. Western real estate and agricultural interests wanted to dam the West's major rivers to provide water and electricity for urban and agricultural development. They found a government ally in the Bureau of Reclamation, which became, under the New Deal, a prime dispenser of infrastructural funds. Drawing on PWA monies, the bureau oversaw the building of the Boulder Dam (later renamed Hoover Dam), which provided drinking water for southern California, irrigation water for California's Imperial Valley, and electricity for Los Angeles and southern Arizona. The Central Valley Project and the All-American Canal provided irrigation, drinking water, and electricity to California farmers and towns. The greatest construction project of all was the Grand Coulee Dam on the Columbia River in Washington, which created a lake 150 miles long. Together with the Bonneville Dam (also on the Columbia), the Grand Coulee gave the Pacific Northwest the cheapest electricity in the country and created the potential there for economic and population growth.

These developments did not attract as much attention in the 1930s as did the TVA. The benefits were not fully realized until after the Second World War. Also, dam building in the West was not seen as a radical experiment in government planning and management. Unlike the TVA, the Bureau of Reclamation hired private contractors to do the work. Moreover, the benefits of these dams were intended to flow first to large agricultural and real estate interests, not to the poor. They were intended to aid private enterprise rather than bypass it. In political terms, then, dam building in the West was more conservative than it was in the Tennessee Valley.

Western development
Disproportionate amount of New Deal funds sent to Rocky Mountain and Pacific Coast areas to provide water and electricity for urban and agricultural development.

POLITICAL MOBILIZATION, POLITICAL UNREST, 1934–1935

Although Roosevelt and the New Dealers dismantled the NRA in 1935, they could not stop the political forces it had set it in motion. Americans now believed that they themselves could make a difference. If the New Dealers could not achieve economic recovery, the people would find others who could.

POPULIST CRITICS OF THE NEW DEAL

Some critics were disturbed by what they perceived as the conservatism of New Deal programs. Banking reforms, the AAA, and the NRA, they alleged, all seemed to favor large economic interests. Ordinary people had been ignored.

In the South and Midwest, millions listened to the radio addresses of Louisiana senator **Huey Long**, a former governor of that state and a spellbinding orator. In attacks on New Deal programs, he alleged that "not a single thin dime of concentrated, bloated, pompous wealth, massed in the hands of a few people, has been raked down to relieve the masses." Long offered a simple alternative: "Break up the swollen fortunes of America and . . . spread the wealth among all our people."

Long's rhetoric inspired hundreds of thousands of Americans to join Share the Wealth clubs. A majority came from middle-class ranks. They worried that the New Deal's big-business orientation was undermining their economic and social status. Many Share the Wealth club members also came from skilled and white-collar sections of the working class. By 1935 Roosevelt regarded Long as the man most likely to unseat him in the presidential election of 1936. But before that campaign began, Long was assassinated.

Meanwhile, in the Midwest, **Father Charles Coughlin,** the "radio priest," delivered a message similar to Long's. Like Long, Coughlin appealed to anxious middle-class Americans and to once-privileged groups of workers who believed that middle-class status was slipping from their grasp. A former Roosevelt

Huey Long *Democratic senator and former governor of Louisiana who used the radio to attack the New Deal as too conservative. FDR regarded him as a major rival.*

Father Charles Coughlin *The "radio priest" from the Midwest who alleged that the New Deal was being run by bankers. His growing anti-Semitism discredited him by 1939.*

supporter, Coughlin had become a critic. The New Deal was run by bankers, he claimed. The NRA was a program to resuscitate corporate profits. Coughlin called for a strong government to compel capital, labor, agriculture, professionals, and other interest groups to do its bidding. He founded the National Union of Social Justice (NUSJ) in 1934 as a precursor to a political party that would challenge the Democrats in 1936.

As Coughlin's disillusionment with the New Deal deepened, a strain of anti-Semitism appeared in his radio talks; he accused Jewish bankers of masterminding a world conspiracy to dispossess the toiling masses. Although Coughlin was a compelling speaker, he failed to build the NUSJ into an effective force. Its successor, the Union Party, attracted only a tiny percentage of voters in 1936. Embittered, Coughlin moved further to the political right. By 1939 his denunciations of democracy and Jews had become so extreme that some radio stations refused to carry his addresses. Still, millions of Americans continued to be drawn to the "radio priest."

Another popular figure was Francis E. Townsend, a California doctor who claimed that the way to end the Depression was to give every senior citizen $200 a month. The Townsend Plan briefly garnered the support of an estimated 20 million Americans.

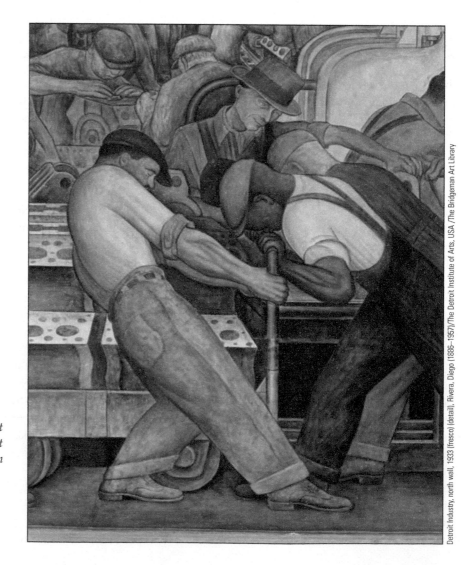

MEN AT WORK. *This is a detail from the huge mural that the Mexican artist Diego Rivera painted for the walls of the Detroit Art Museum in 1932–1933. The strong, confident pose of Rivera's workers reveals his conviction (one he shared with other 1930s artists) that industrial workers stood at the heart of American civilization and that they would play a key role in rehabilitating a society devastated by depression.*

LABOR PROTESTS

The attacks by Long, Coughlin, and Townsend on New Deal programs deepened popular discontent and helped to legitimate other insurgent movements. The most important was the labor movement. Workers began joining unions in response to the National Industrial Recovery Act, and especially its clause granting them the right to join labor organizations of their own choosing and obligating employers to bargain with them in good faith. Union members' demands were modest at first: they wanted to be treated fairly by their foremen, and they wanted employers to observe the provisions of the NRA codes and to recognize their unions. But few employers were willing to grant workers any say in their working conditions. Many ignored the NRA's wage and hour guidelines altogether and even used their influence with NRA code authorities to get worker requests for wage increases and union recognition rejected.

Workers flooded Washington with protest letters and then began to take matters into their own hands. In 1934 they staged 2,000 strikes in virtually every industry and region of the country. A few of those strikes escalated into armed confrontations between workers and police that shocked the nation. In Toledo in May, 10,000 workers surrounded the Electric Auto-Lite plant, declaring that they would block all exits and entrances until the company agreed to shut down operations and negotiate a union contract. Two strikers were killed in an exchange of gunfire. In San Francisco in July, longshoremen fought employers and police in street skirmishes in which two were killed and scores wounded. In September, 400,000 textile workers at mills from Maine to Alabama walked off their jobs. Attempts by employers to bring in replacement workers triggered violent confrontations that caused several deaths, hundreds of injuries, and millions of dollars in property damage.

ANGER AT THE POLLS

In the fall of 1934, workers took their anger to the polls. In Rhode Island, they broke the Republican Party's 30-year domination of state politics. In the country as a whole, Democrats won 70 percent of the contested seats in the Senate and House. The Democrats increased their majority, from 310 to 319 (out of 432) in the House, and from 60 to 69 (out of 96) in the Senate. But the victory was not an unqualified one for Roosevelt. The 74th Congress would include the largest contingent of radicals ever sent to Washington. Their support for the New Deal depended on whether Roosevelt delivered more relief, more income security, and more political power to farmers, workers, the unemployed, and the poor.

RADICAL THIRD PARTIES

Radical critics of the New Deal also made an impressive showing in state politics in 1934 and 1936. They were particularly strong in states gripped by labor unrest. In Wisconsin, Philip La Follette, the son of Robert La Follette (see Chapter 21), was elected governor in 1934 and 1936 as the candidate of the radical Wisconsin Progressive Party. In Minnesota, discontented agrarians and urban workers organized the Minnesota Farmer-Labor Party and elected their candidate to the governorship in 1930, 1932, 1934, and 1936. And in California, the socialist and novelist Upton Sinclair and his organization, End Poverty in California (EPIC), came closer to winning the governorship than anyone had expected.

The growing appeal of the **Communist Party** offered further evidence of voter volatility. The American Communist Party (CP) had emerged in the early 1920s with

Communist Party *Radical group that wanted America to follow the Soviet Union's path to socialism. The CP organized some of the country's poorest workers into unions and pushed the New Deal leftward, but was never popular enough to bid for power itself.*

AP/Wide World Photos

ELEANOR ROOSEVELT, REFORMER. *Eleanor Roosevelt traveled extensively in the 1930s, meeting with many different groups of Americans, including the miners depicted in this photo, seeking to learn more about their condition and ways that the New Deal might assist them. Through such travels and reports, she helped shape the New Deal agenda.*

the support of radicals who wanted to adopt the Soviet Union's path to socialism. It began to attract attention in the early 1930s. CP organizers spread out among the poorest and most vulnerable populations in America—homeless urban blacks in the North, black and white sharecroppers in the South, Chicano and Filipino agricultural workers in the West—and mobilized them in unions and unemployment leagues. CP members also played significant roles in the strikes described earlier, and they were influential in the Minnesota Farmer-Labor Party. Once they stopped preaching world revolution in 1935 and began calling instead for a "popular front" of democratic forces against fascism, their ranks grew even more. By 1938, approximately 80,000 Americans were thought to have been members of the CP. Although the CP proclaimed its allegiance to democratic principles beginning in 1935, it remained a dictatorial organization that took its orders from the Soviet Union. Many Americans, fearing the growing strength of the CP, began to call for its suppression. The CP, however, was never strong enough to gain power for itself. Its chief role in 1930s politics was to channel popular discontent into unions and political parties that would, in turn, force New Dealers to respond to the demands of the nation's dispossessed.

THE SECOND NEW DEAL, 1935–1937

FOCUS QUESTION

What was "underconsumptionism" and how did it inform the legislation of the Second New Deal? How was the Second New Deal different from the first?

The labor unrest of 1934 had taken Roosevelt by surprise, and for a time he kept his distance from the protesters. But in the spring of 1935, with the 1936 presidential election coming up, he decided to place himself at their head. He called for the "abolition of evil holding companies," attacked the wealthy for their profligate ways, and called for new programs to aid the poor and downtrodden. Roosevelt had not become a socialist, as his critics charged. Rather, he sought to reinvigorate his appeal among poorer Americans and turn them away from radical solutions.

PHILOSOPHICAL UNDERPINNINGS

To point the New Deal in a more populist direction, Roosevelt turned to a relatively new economic theory, **underconsumptionism**. Advocates held that a chronic weakness in consumer demand had caused the Great Depression. The path to recovery lay, therefore, not in restricting the output of producers but in boosting consumer expenditures through government support for strong labor unions (to force up wages), higher social welfare expenditures (to put more money in the hands of the poor), and public works projects (to create hundreds of thousands of new jobs).

Underconsumptionists did not worry that new welfare and public works programs might strain the federal budget. If the government found itself short of revenue, it could always borrow additional funds from private sources. Government borrowing, in fact, was viewed as a crucial antidepression tool. Those who lent the government money would receive a return on their investment; those

underconsumptionism *Theory that underconsumption, or a chronic weakness in consumer demand, had caused the Depression. This theory guided the Second New Deal, leading to the passage of laws designed to stimulate consumer demand.*

who received government assistance would have additional income to spend on consumer goods; and manufacturers would profit from increases in consumer spending. Government borrowing, in short, would stimulate the circulation of money through the economy and would put an end to the Depression.

Many politicians and economists rejected the notion that increased government spending and the deliberate buildup of federal deficits would lead to prosperity. Roosevelt himself remained committed to fiscal restraint and balanced budgets. But in 1935, as the nation entered its sixth year of the Depression, he was willing to give the new ideas a try. Reform-minded members of the 1934 Congress were themselves eager for a new round of legislation directed more to the needs of ordinary Americans than to the needs of big business.

LEGISLATION

Congress passed much of that legislation in January to June 1935, a period that came to be known as the Second New Deal. The **Social Security Act** required the states to set up welfare funds from which money would be disbursed to the elderly poor, the unemployed, unmarried mothers with dependent children, and the disabled. It also enrolled a majority of working Americans in a pension program that guaranteed them a steady income upon retirement. A federal system of employer and employee taxation was set up to fund the pensions.

Equally historic was the passage of the National Labor Relations Act (NLRA). This act delivered what the NRA had only promised: the right of every worker to join a union of his or her own choosing, and the obligation of employers to bargain with that union in good faith. The **NLRA**, also called the **Wagner Act** after its Senate sponsor, Robert Wagner of New York, set up a National Labor Relations Board (NLRB) to supervise union elections and to investigate claims of unfair labor practices. The NLRB was to be staffed by federal appointees, who would have the power to impose fines on employers who violated the law.

Congress also passed the Holding Company Act to break up the 13 utility companies that controlled 75 percent of the nation's electric power. It passed the Wealth Tax Act, which increased tax rates on the wealthy from 59 to 75 percent, and on corporations from 13.75 to 15 percent; and it passed the Banking Act, which strengthened the power of the Federal Reserve Board over its member banks. It created the Rural Electrification Administration (REA) to bring electric power to rural households. Finally, it passed the $5 billion Emergency Relief Appropriation Act. Roosevelt funneled part of this sum to the PWA and the CCC and used another part to create the National Youth Administration (NYA), which provided work and guidance to the nation's youth.

Roosevelt directed most of the new relief money, however, to the **Works Progress Administration** (WPA). The WPA built or improved thousands of schools, playgrounds, airports, and hospitals. WPA crews were put to work raking leaves, cleaning streets, and landscaping cities. In the process, the WPA provided jobs to approximately 30 percent of the nation's jobless.

By the time the decade ended, the WPA, in association with an expanded Reconstruction Finance Corporation, PWA, and other agencies, had built 500,000 miles of roads, 100,000 bridges, 100,000 public buildings, and 600 airports. The New Deal had transformed America's urban and rural landscapes. The awe generated by these public works projects helped Roosevelt retain popular support at a time when the success of the New Deal's economic policies was uncertain. The WPA also funded a program of public art, supporting the work of thousands of painters, architects,

Social Security Act *Centerpiece of the welfare state (1935) that instituted the first federal pension system and set up funds to take care of groups (such as the disabled and unmarried mothers with children) unable to support themselves.*

The Wagner Act (NLRA) *Named after its sponsor, Senator Robert Wagner (D-NY), this 1935 act gave every worker the right to join a union and compelled employers to bargain with unions in good faith.*

Works Progress Administration *Federal relief agency established in 1935 that disbursed billions to pay for infrastructure improvements and funded a vast program of public art.*

TABLE 25.2

SELECTED WPA PROJECTS IN NEW YORK CITY, 1938		
Construction and Renovation	**Education, Health, and Art**	**Research and Records**
East River Drive	Adult education: homemaking, trade and technical skills, and art and culture	Sewage treatment, community health, labor relations, and employment trends surveys
Henry Hudson Parkway	Children's education: remedial reading, lip reading, and field trips	Museum and library catalogs and exhibits
Bronx sewers	Prisoners' vocational training, recreation, and nutrition	Municipal office clerical support
Glendale and Queens public libraries	Dental clinics	Government forms standardization
King's County Hospital	Tuberculosis examination clinics	
Williamsburg Housing Project	Syphilis and gonorrhea treatment clinics	
School buildings, prisons, and firehouses	City hospital kitchen help, orderlies, laboratory technicians, nurses, doctors	
Coney Island and Brighton Beach boardwalks	Subsistence gardens	
Orchard Beach	Sewing rooms	
Swimming pools, playgrounds, parks, drinking fountains	Central Park sculpture shop	

Source: John David Millet, *The Works Progress Administration in New York City* (Chicago: Public Administration Service, 1938), pp. 95–126.

writers, playwrights, actors, and intellectuals. Beyond extending relief to struggling artists, it fostered the creation of art that spoke to the concerns of ordinary Americans, adorned public buildings with colorful murals, and boosted public morale (see Table 25.2).

QUICK   REVIEW

THE SECOND NEW DEAL (1935–1938)

- Prompted by failure of First New Deal and widespread political unrest

- Wanted to boost consumer demand through support for labor unions, social welfare, and public works

- Social Security, Wagner Act, and emergency relief appropriations were most important acts

- Democrats and FDR rode Second New Deal to electoral victory in 1936

- Anticorporate rhetoric was more powerful than the reality of the laws

VICTORY IN 1936: THE NEW DEMOCRATIC COALITION

Roosevelt described his Second New Deal as a program to limit the power and privilege of the wealthy few and to increase the security and welfare of ordinary citizens. He called on voters to limit corporate power and "save a great and precious form of government for ourselves and the world." American voters responded by handing Roosevelt a landslide victory. He received 61 percent of the popular vote; Alf Landon of Kansas, his Republican opponent, received only 37 percent (See Map 25.4).

The 1936 election won for the Democratic Party its reputation as the party of reform and the party of the "forgotten American." Of the 6 million Americans who went to the polls for the first time, 5 million voted for Roosevelt. Among the poorest Americans, Roosevelt received 80 percent of the vote. Black voters in the North deserted the Republican Party, calculating that their interests would best be served by the "Party of the Common Man." Roosevelt also did well among white middle-class voters, many of whom were grateful to him for pushing through the Social Security Act. These constituencies would constitute the "Roosevelt coalition" for most of the next 40 years.

RHETORIC VERSUS REALITY

Roosevelt's anticorporate rhetoric in 1935 and 1936 was more radical than the laws he supported. The Wealth Tax Act took less out of wealthy incomes and estates than was advertised, and the utility companies that were to have been broken up by the

HISTORY THROUGH FILM

MR. DEEDS GOES TO TOWN (1936)

Directed by Frank Capra; starring Gary Cooper (Longfellow Deeds), Jean Arthur (Babe Bennett), Lionel Stander (Cornelius Cobb), George Bancroft (McWade), and H. B. Warner (Judge Walker)

Frank Capra, the most popular movie director of the 1930s, made several films featuring simple, small-town heroes who vanquish the evil forces of wealth and decadence. In *Mr. Deeds Goes to Town*, the heroic ordinary American is Longfellow Deeds of Mandrake Falls, Vermont, who goes to New York City to claim a fortune left him by his uncle. Deciding to give the fortune away, he becomes the laughingstock of slick city lawyers, hardboiled newspapermen and women, cynical literati, and self-styled aristocrats. He also becomes a hero to the unemployed and downtrodden to whom he wishes to give the money. By making the conflict between the wealthy and ordinary Americans central to this story, Capra illuminated convictions popular in 1930s New Deal politics.

The movie delivers its serious message, however, in a hilarious style. Capra was a master of what became known as "screwball" comedy. Longfellow Deeds slides down banisters, locks his bodyguards in a closet, uses the main hall of his inherited mansion as an echo chamber, punches a famous intellectual in the "kisser" (face), and turns his own trial for insanity into a delightful attack on the pretensions and peculiarities of corporate lawyers, judges, and psychiatrists. Central to the story, too, is an alternately amusing and serious love story between Deeds and a newspaperwoman, Babe Bennett (Jean Arthur). Bennett insinuates herself into Deeds's life by pretending to be a destitute woman without work, shelter, family, or friends. Deeds, who has long dreamed about rescuing a "lady in distress," falls for the beautiful Bennett. Bennett, in turn, uses her access to Deeds to learn about his foibles and then mock them (and him) in newspaper stories written for a ruthless and scandal-hungry public. But Deeds's idealism, honesty, and virtue overwhelm Bennett's cynicism. By movie's end, she has proclaimed her love and is ready to return with Deeds to Mandrake Falls, to become, it seems likely, his devoted wife and the nurturing mother of his children.

In Babe Bennett's conversion from tough reporter to female romantic we can detect the gender conservatism of 1930s culture. The movie suggests that Bennett's early cruelty toward Deeds was a consequence of her inappropriate involvement in the rough, masculine world of newspaper work. Only by abandoning this realm and returning to the "natural" female realm of hearth and home can she recover her true and soft womanly soul. Thus, this movie is as rich a document for exploring attitudes toward male and female behavior as it is for examining the relations between rich and poor.

© The Granger Collection, New York

Gary Cooper as Longfellow Deeds (center of photo with hand on cheek) during his hilarious insanity trial. Cooper's bodyguard, Lionel Stander (Cobb) sits to the left of Cooper, and Cooper is looking at H. B. Warner (Judge Walker), who is presiding at the trial.

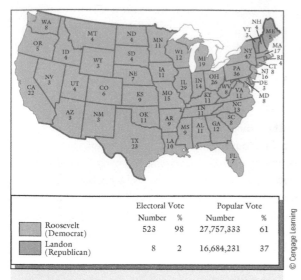

	Electoral Vote		Popular Vote	
	Number	%	Number	%
Roosevelt (Democrat)	523	98	27,757,333	61
Landon (Republican)	8	2	16,684,231	37

© Cengage Learning

Map 25.4 **PRESIDENTIAL ELECTION, 1936**. *In 1936, Franklin D. Roosevelt's reelection numbers were overwhelming: 98 percent of the electoral vote, and more than 60 percent of the popular vote. No previous election in American history had been so one-sided.*

Frances Perkins *Secretary of labor under Roosevelt and the first female Cabinet member.*

Holding Company Act remained largely intact. Moreover, Roosevelt promised more than he delivered to the nation's poor. Farmworkers, for example, were not covered by the Social Security Act or by the National Labor Relations Act. Consequently, thousands of African American sharecroppers in the South, along with substantial numbers of Chicano farm workers in the Southwest, were excluded from these acts' protections and benefits. Moreover, the New Deal made little effort to restore voting rights to Southern blacks or to protect their basic civil rights.

Roosevelt's populist stance in 1935 and 1936 also obscured the support that some capitalists were giving the Second New Deal. In the West, Henry J. Kaiser headed a consortium of six companies that built the Hoover, Bonneville, and Grand Coulee dams. In the Midwest and the East, Roosevelt's corporate supporters included real estate developers, mass merchandisers, clothing manufacturers, and the like. These firms, in turn, had financial connections with newer investment banks and with consumer-oriented banks such as the Bank of America. They were willing to tolerate strong labor unions, welfare programs, and high levels of government spending. But they had no intention of surrendering their wealth or power. The Democratic Party had become, in effect, the party of the masses and one section of big business. The conflicting interests of these two constituencies would create tensions within the Democratic Party throughout the years of its political domination.

MEN, WOMEN, AND REFORM

For the academics, policymakers, and bureaucrats who designed and administered the rapidly growing roster of New Deal programs and agencies, 1936 and 1937 were heady years. Fired by idealism and dedication, they were confident they could make the New Deal work. They won congressional approval for the Farm Security Administration (FSA), an agency designed to improve the economic lot of tenant farmers, sharecroppers, and farm laborers. They got passed laws that outlawed child labor, set minimum wages and maximum hours for adult workers, and committed the federal government to building low-cost housing. They tried to regulate concentrations of corporate power.

Who were these reformers? The men among them often had earned advanced degrees in law and economics at elite universities such as Harvard, Columbia, and Wisconsin. Not all had been raised among wealth and privilege, however, as was generally the case with earlier generations of reformers. To his credit, Franklin Roosevelt was the first president since his cousin Theodore Roosevelt to welcome Jews and Catholics into his administration. These men had had to struggle to make their way, first on the streets and then in school and at work. They brought to the New Deal intellectual aggressiveness, quick minds, and mental toughness.

The profile of New Deal women was different. Although a few, notably Eleanor Roosevelt and Secretary of Labor **Frances Perkins**, were more visible than women in previous administrations had been, many of the female New Dealers worked in relative obscurity, in agencies like the Women's Bureau or the Children's Bureau (both in the Department of Labor). And women who worked on major legislation or directed major programs received less credit than men in comparable positions. Moreover, female New Dealers tended to be a generation older than their male colleagues and were more likely to be Protestant than Catholic or Jewish.

The New Deal offered these women little opportunity to advance the cause of female equality. Demands for greater economic opportunity, sexual freedom, and full equality for women and men were heard less often in the 1930s than they had been in the preceding two decades. One reason was that the women's movement had fragmented after suffrage had been achieved. Another was that prominent New Deal women did not vigorously pursue a campaign for equal rights. They concentrated instead on "protective legislation"—laws that safeguarded female workers, who were thought to be more fragile than men. Those who insisted that women needed special protections could not easily argue that women were the equal of men in all respects.

But feminism was also hemmed in on all sides by a male hostility that the Depression had only intensified. Men had built their identities on the value of hard work and the ability to provide for their families. The loss of work made them feel inadequate, and the fact that the unemployment rates of men tended to be higher than those of women exacerbated their vulnerability (see Table 25.3). Many fathers and husbands resented wives and daughters who had taken over their breadwinning roles.

This male anxiety had consequences. Several states passed laws outlawing the hiring of married women. The labor movement made the protection of the male wage earner one of its principal goals. The Social Security pension system did not cover waitresses, domestic servants, and other largely female occupations. Artists glorified strong men in their paintings and created images of muscled male workers for public murals and sculptures. Boys and male adolescents, meanwhile, found a new hero in Superman, the "man-of-steel" comic-book figure who debuted in 1938. Superman's strength, unlike that of so many men in the 1930s, could not be taken away—except by Kryptonite and Lois Lane, that "dangerous" working woman.

LABOR IN POLITICS AND CULTURE

In 1935 John L. Lewis of the United Mine Workers, Sidney Hillman of the Amalgamated Clothing Workers, and the leaders of six other unions that had seceded from the

CIO *The Committee and then Congress for Industrial Organization, founded in 1935 to organize the unskilled and semi-skilled workers ignored by the AFL. The CIO reinvigorated the labor movement.*

sit-down strike *Labor strike strategy in which workers occupied their factory and refused to do any work until the employer agreed to recognize the workers' union. This strategy succeeded against General Motors in 1937.*

Frank Capra *Popular 1930s filmmaker who celebrated the decency, honesty, and patriotism of ordinary Americans in such films as Mr. Deeds Goes to Town and Mr. Smith Goes to Washington.*

TABLE 25.3

RATES OF UNEMPLOYMENT IN SELECTED MALE AND FEMALE OCCUPATIONS, 1930		
Male Occupations	**Percentage Male**	**Percentage Unemployed**
Iron and steel	96%	13%
Forestry and fishing	99	10
Mining	99	18
Heavy manufacturing	86	13
Carpentry	100	19
Laborers (road and street)	100	13
Female Occupations	**Percentage Female**	**Percentage Unemployed**
Stenographers and typists	96%	5%
Laundresses	99	3
Trained nurses	98	4
Housekeepers	92	3
Telephone operators	95	3
Dressmakers	100	4

Source: U.S. Department of Commerce, Bureau of the Census, *Fifteenth Census of the United States, 1930, Population* (Washington, D.C.: Government Printing Office, 1931).

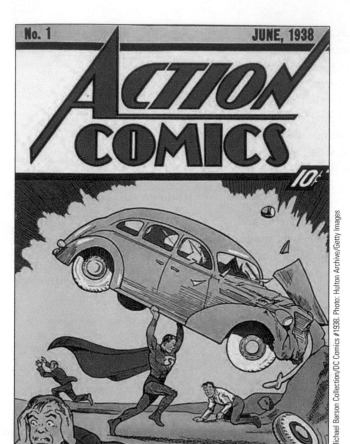

No. 1   JUNE, 1938

ACTION COMICS   10¢

The Michael Barson Collection/DC Comics #1938. Photo: Hulton Archive/Getty Images

SUPERMAN. *This male hero was one of many muscled men to appear in comics, murals, and sculptures in the 1930s—at the very moment when the vulnerability of real men to unemployment and poverty was extreme.*

American Federation of Labor (AFL) cobbled together a new labor organization. The Committee for Industrial Organization (**CIO**), later renamed the Congress of Industrial Organizations, took as its goal the organization of nonunion workers into effective unions that would strengthen labor's influence in the workplace. In 1936 Lewis and Hillman created a second organization, Labor's Non-Partisan League (LNPL), to develop a labor strategy for the 1936 elections. Although professing the league's nonpartisanship, Lewis intended from the start that LNPL's role would be to channel labor's money, energy, and talent into Roosevelt's reelection campaign. Roosevelt welcomed the league's help, and labor would become one of the most important constituencies of the new Democratic coalition. The passage of the Wagner Act and the creation of the NLRB in 1935 enhanced the labor movement's status and credibility. Membership in labor unions climbed steadily, and in short order union members began flexing their new muscle.

In late 1936 the United Auto Workers (UAW) took on General Motors, widely regarded as the mightiest corporation in the world. Workers occupied key GM factories in Flint, Michigan, vowing to continue their **sit-down strike** until GM agreed to recognize the UAW and negotiate a collective-bargaining agreement. Frank Murphy, the pro-labor governor of Michigan, refused to use National Guardsmen to evict the strikers, and Roosevelt also declined to send federal troops. GM capitulated after a month of resistance. Soon, the U.S. Steel Corporation, which had defeated unionists in the bloody strike of 1919 (see Chapter 23), announced that it was ready to negotiate a contract with the newly formed CIO steelworkers union.

The labor movement's public stature grew along with its size. Many writers and artists depicted the labor movement as the voice of the people and the embodiment of the nation's values. Murals appeared in public buildings featuring portraits of blue-collar Americans at work. Broadway's most celebrated play in 1935 was Clifford Odets's *Waiting for Lefty*, a raw drama about taxi drivers who confront their bosses and organize an honest union.

Many of the most popular novels and movies of the 1930s celebrated the decency, honesty, and patriotism of ordinary Americans. In *Mr. Deeds Goes to Town* (1936) and *Mr. Smith Goes to Washington* (1939), **Frank Capra** delighted movie audiences with fables about simple men who vanquish the evil forces of wealth and decadence. John Steinbeck's 1939 bestseller, *The Grapes of Wrath*, told an epic tale of an Oklahoma family's fortitude in surviving eviction from their land, migrating westward, and suffering exploitation in the "promised land" of California. In themselves and in one another, writers like

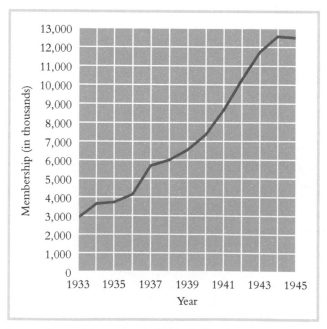

LABOR UNION MEMBERSHIP, 1933–1945
Source: From Christopher Tomlins, "AFL Unions in the 1930s," in Melvyn Dubofsky and Stephen Burwood, eds., *Labor* (New York: Garland, 1990), p. 1023.

Steinbeck seemed to be saying, Americans would discover the resolve they needed to rebuild a culture that had surrendered its identity to corporations and business.

The Okie migrants to California included a writer and musician named Woody Guthrie. Born in 1913 in Okemah, Oklahoma, Guthrie grew up in nearby Pampa, Texas. He wasn't born poor—his father was a small businessman and a local politician—but by the time he reached his 20s, Guthrie had known a great deal of hardship: his father's business failed, three family homes burned down, one sister died from burns, and then the drought and dust storms struck. In the 1930s, Guthrie joined the Okie migration to California. Emerging from a country music tradition in Texas and Oklahoma, Guthrie found a radio audience among the many Texans and Okies in California. But casting himself as the bard of ordinary Americans everywhere, Guthrie quickly developed a broader appeal. He loved America for the beauty of its landscape and its people, sentiments evident in "This Land Is Your Land," written in 1940 in response to Irving Berlin's "God Bless America" (a song Guthrie disliked because he thought it encouraged a false sense of complacency). Guthrie did not have a refined singing voice, but his "hillbilly" lyrics, melodies, and humor were inventive and often inspiring. He would have a powerful influence on subsequent generations of musicians, including Bob Dylan and Bruce Springsteen.

Guthrie traveled everywhere in the 1930s, from Los Angeles to New York and from Texas to Washington state. The more he learned about the hardships of individual Americans, the closer he drew to the labor movement and to the Communist Party. Increasingly, his writings and songs criticized the industrialists, financiers, and their political agents who, he believed, had brought on the calamity of the Depression. But Guthrie always associated his criticism with the hope that the working people of America, united, could take back their land—the message he meant to convey with "This Land Is Your Land"—and restore its greatness. Guthrie's optimism underscored how much the cultural mood had changed since the early 1930s. In his focus on ordinary working Americans, in his hope for the future, and in his fusion of dissent and patriotism, Guthrie was emblematic of the dominant stream of culture and politics in the late 1930s.

Library of Congress Prints and Photographs Division [LC-USZ62-120588]

WOODY GUTHRIE. *A bard from Okemah, Oklahoma, embraced by millions for his homespun melodies and lyrics and for his hopeful message that Americans could survive the depression with their dignity and sense of humor intact.*

AMERICA'S MINORITIES AND THE NEW DEAL

Reformers believed that issues of capitalism's viability, economic recovery, and the inequality of wealth and power outweighed problems of racial and ethnic discrimination. Because they were disproportionately poor, most minority groups did profit from the populist and pro-labor character of New Deal reforms. But the gains were distributed unevenly. Eastern and southern European ethnics benefited the most, while African Americans and Mexican Americans advanced the least.

FOCUS QUESTION
Which minority groups in American society benefited most from the New Deal and which benefited least?

EASTERN AND SOUTHERN EUROPEAN ETHNICS

Eastern and southern European immigrants and their children had begun mobilizing politically in the 1920s in response to religious and racial discrimination (see Chapter 24). By the early 1930s, they had made themselves into a political force in the Democratic Party. Roosevelt understood their importance well. He made sure that a significant portion of New Deal monies for welfare, infrastructure improvements, and unemployment relief reached the urban areas where most European ethnics lived. As a result, Jewish and Catholic Americans voted for Roosevelt in large numbers. The New Deal did not eliminate anti-Semitism and anti-Catholicism from American society, but it did allow millions of European ethnics to believe, for the first time, that they would overcome the second-class status they had long endured.

Southern and eastern European ethnics also benefited from their presence in the working class and their contributions to labor's gains. Roosevelt accommodated himself to their wishes in part because he respected the power they wielded through their labor organizations.

AFRICAN AMERICANS

The New Deal did more to reproduce patterns of racial discrimination than to advance the cause of racial equality. African Americans who belonged to CIO unions or who lived in Northern cities benefited from New Deal programs, but the vast majority of blacks lived in rural areas of the South where they were barred from voting, largely excluded from AAA programs, and denied federal protection in their efforts to form agricultural unions. The TVA hired few blacks. Those enrolled in the CWA and other work-relief programs were often paid less than whites doing the same jobs. Roosevelt consistently refused to support legislation to make lynching a federal crime.

This failure to push a strong civil rights agenda did not mean that New Dealers were themselves racist. Eleanor Roosevelt spoke out frequently against racial injustice. In 1939 she resigned from the Daughters of the American Revolution when the organization refused to allow black opera singer **Marian Anderson** to perform in its concert hall. She then pressured the federal government into granting Anderson permission to sing from the steps of the Lincoln Memorial. On Easter Sunday in 1939, 75,000 people gathered to hear Anderson and to demonstrate their support for racial equality.

Franklin Roosevelt eliminated segregationist practices in the federal government that had been in place since Woodrow Wilson's presidency. He appointed African Americans to second-level posts in his administration. Working together in what came to be known as the "Black Cabinet," these officials fought hard against discrimination in New Deal programs.

But Roosevelt was never willing to make the fight for racial justice a priority. He refused to support the Black Cabinet if it meant alienating white Southern senators who controlled key congressional committees. This refusal reflected Roosevelt's belief that economic issues were more important than racial ones. It revealed, too, Roosevelt's pragmatism. His decisions to support particular policies often depended on his calculation of their potential political cost or gain. Roosevelt believed pushing for civil rights would cost him the support of the white South. Meanwhile, African Americans and their supporters were not yet strong enough as an electoral constituency or as a reform movement to force Roosevelt to accede to their wishes.

Marian Anderson *Black opera singer who broke a color barrier in 1939 when she sang to an interracial audience of 75,000 from the steps of the Lincoln Memorial.*

MUSICAL LINK TO THE PAST

AN AFRICAN AMERICAN RHAPSODY

Songwriter: Duke Ellington
Title: "Creole Rhapsody Parts One and Two"
(1931—the second recording)
Performers: Duke Ellington and His Orchestra

By 1931, Duke Ellington was the premier African American bandleader, his hit songs airing nightly through a live national radio hook-up (the first for any black act) from Harlem's Cotton Club. But Ellington was not satisfied with mere popularity and fame. "I have always been a firm believer in musical experimentation," he proclaimed. "To stand still musically is equivalent to losing ground." Ellington was a serious artist and composer, and "Creole Rhapsody" represented one of his first major bids to cultivate this image. Most pop records seldom broke the three-minute barrier, but "Creole" lasted nine minutes, spanning two sides of a 78-RPM record. While jazz and blues artists generally composed within 8-, 12-, and 16-bar forms, Ellington experimented with different phrase lengths. In an era when blacks were primarily associated with "torrid" dance records, the shifting tempos of "Creole" marked it as a record for concentrated listening. Ellington also composed the solos to ensure that they jelled with his elaborate arrangement, which did away with musical improvisation, a trademark of jazz and blues performances. Ellington was more involved with recording technique than most artists, sometimes placing microphones far away from his players to achieve a more evocative sound.

"Creole Rhapsody" reached only minor hit status, but Ellington and his manager Irving Mills took advantage of the event of this unprecedented recording to bolster Ellington's image as a serious artist, a status that no other African American had achieved in the segregated and white-dominated popular music marketplace of the period. In contrast to the denigrating stereotypes that accompanied the appearance of most blacks in the mass media, Ellington was respectfully portrayed in the manner of a classical conductor, usually clad in a tuxedo and tails, baton in his hand.

Not all contemporary observers endorsed the idea of Ellington as a major composer. The English critic Constant Lambert wrote in 1934 that "Ellington is definitely a petit maitre," a "small master" incapable of extended composition. Many music lovers, however, embraced "Creole Rhapsody." The New York School of Music named it the best composition of the year because "it portrayed Negro life as no other piece had." Ellington kept the critics, both the laudatory and castigating ones, at a distance and continued to search for musical innovation. He almost never took a formal political stand or made a speech demanding civil rights for blacks during the 1930s, choosing to let his music and his reputation as an innovative bandleader speak for themselves.

1. From listening to "Creole Rhapsody," can you discern what the New York School of Music meant in celebrating this composition as a unique portrait of Negro life?

 Listen to an audio recording of this music on the Musical Links to the Past CD.

MEXICAN AMERICANS

The experience of Mexicans during the Great Depression was harsh. In 1931, Hoover's secretary of labor, William N. Doak, announced a plan for repatriating illegal aliens (returning them to their land of origin) and giving their jobs to American citizens. The federal campaign quickly focused on **Mexican repatriation** in California and the Southwest. The U.S. Immigration Service staged a number of publicized raids, rounded up large numbers of Mexicans and Mexican Americans, and demanded that each detainee prove his or her legal status. Those who failed to produce the necessary documentation were deported.

Mexican repatriation *Secretary of Labor William Doak's plan to deport illegal Mexican aliens to Mexico. By 1935, over 500,000 Mexicans had left the United States.*

John Collier *Activist head of the Bureau of Indian Affairs who improved U.S. policy toward Native Americans and guided the landmark Indian Reorganization Act through Congress.*

Local governments pressured many more into leaving. The combined efforts of federal, state, and local governments created a climate of fear in Mexican communities; by 1935, 500,000 had returned to Mexico, the same number as had come to the United States in the 1920s. Among these were legal immigrants unable to produce their immigration papers, the American-born children of illegals, and some Mexican Americans who had lived in the Southwest for generations.

The advent of the New Deal in 1933 eased but did not eliminate pressure on Chicano communities. New Deal agencies made more money available for relief, thereby lightening the burden on state and local governments. Some federal programs, moreover, prohibited the removal of illegal aliens from relief rolls. But federal laws, more often than not, failed to dissuade local officials from continuing their campaign against Mexican immigrants. Where Mexicans gained access to relief rolls, they received payments lower than those given to "Anglos" (whites) or were compelled to accept tough agricultural jobs that did not pay living wages.

Life grew harder in other ways for Mexicans who stayed in the United States. The Mexican cultural renaissance that had arisen in 1920s Los Angeles (see Chapter 24) could not sustain itself. Hounded by government officials, Mexicans everywhere sought to escape public attention and scrutiny. In Los Angeles, they retreated into the separate community of East Los Angeles.

Mexicans and Mexican Americans who lived in urban areas and worked in blue-collar industries did benefit from New Deal programs. In Los Angeles, Chicanos joined unions in large numbers and won concessions from their employers. These Mexicans and Mexican Americans shared the belief of southern and eastern Europeans that the New Deal would bring them economic improvement and cultural acceptance. But most Chicanos lived in rural areas and labored in agricultural jobs. The National Labor Relations Act did not protect their right to organize unions, and the Social Security Act excluded them from the new federal welfare system.

QUICK REVIEW

MINORITIES AND THE NEW DEAL

- Eastern and southern Europeans benefited because of growing power in Democratic Party and in organized labor

- African Americans supported New Deal but FDR never made civil rights a priority issue

- Government pressured 500,000 Mexicans to return to Mexico

- New Deal reversed harsh policy toward Native Americans through Indian Reorganization Act

AMERICAN INDIANS

From the 1880s until the early 1930s, federal policy had contributed to the elimination of Native Americans as a distinctive population. The Dawes Act of 1887 (see Chapter 18) had called for tribal lands to be broken up and allotted to individual owners in the hope that Indians would adopt the work habits of white farmers. But Native Americans had proved loyal to their languages, religions, and cultures. Few of them succeeded as farmers, and many lost land to white speculators.

The shrinking land base in combination with a growing population deepened Native American poverty. The assimilationist pressures on Native Americans, meanwhile, reached a climax in the 1920s when the Bureau of Indian Affairs (BIA) outlawed Indian religious ceremonies, forced children from tribal communities into federal boarding schools, banned polygamy, and imposed limits on the length of men's hair.

Government officials working in the Hoover administration began to question this harsh policy, but its reversal had to await the New Deal and Roosevelt's appointment of **John Collier** as BIA commissioner. Collier pressured New Deal agencies to employ Indians on projects that improved reservation land and trained Indians in land conservation methods. He prevailed on Congress to pass the Pueblo Relief Act of 1933, which compensated Pueblos for land taken from them in the 1920s, and the Johnson-O'Malley Act of 1934, which offered federal funds to states to provide Indians with health care, welfare, and education.

Collier also took steps to abolish federal boarding schools, encourage enrollment in local public schools, and establish community day schools. He insisted that Native Americans be allowed to practice their traditional religions, and he created the Indian Arts and Crafts Board in 1935 to nurture traditional Indian artists and to help them market their works.

The centerpiece of Collier's reform strategy was the Indian Reorganization Act (IRA, also known as the Wheeler-Howard Act) of 1934, which revoked the allotment provisions of the Dawes Act. This landmark act recognized the rights of Native American tribes to chart their own political, cultural, and economic futures. It reflected Collier's commitment to "cultural pluralism," a doctrine that celebrated the diversity of peoples and cultures in American society and sought to protect that diversity against the pressures of assimilation. Specifically, the IRA restored land to tribes, granted Indians the right to establish constitutions and bylaws for self-government, and provided support for new tribal corporations that would regulate the use of communal lands.

Collier encountered opposition everywhere: from Protestant missionaries and cultural conservatives who wanted to continue an assimilationist policy; from white farmers and businessmen who feared that the new legislation would restrict their access to Native American land; and even from a sizable number of Indian groups, some of which had embraced assimilation while others viewed the IRA as one more attempt by the federal government to impose "the white man's will" on the Indian peoples.

In fact, a vocal minority of Indians continued to oppose the act even after its passage. The Navajo, along with 76 other tribes, voted to reject its terms. Still, a large majority of tribes began to organize new governments under the IRA. Although their quest for independence would suffer setbacks, these tribes were able to enhance their freedom and autonomy.

THE NEW DEAL ABROAD

When he entered office, Roosevelt seemed to favor a nationalist approach to international relations. The United States, he believed, should pursue foreign policies to benefit its domestic affairs, without regard for the effects of those policies on world trade and international stability. Thus, in June 1933, Roosevelt pulled the United States out of the World Economic Conference in London, a meeting called by leading nations to strengthen the gold standard and thereby stabilize the value of their currencies. Roosevelt feared that the other nations would force the United States into an agreement designed to keep the gold content of the dollar high and commodity prices in the United States low, which would frustrate New Deal efforts to inflate the prices of agricultural and industrial goods.

Soon after his withdrawal from the London conference, however, Roosevelt put the United States on a more internationalist course. In November 1933, he became the first president to establish diplomatic ties with the Soviet Union. In December 1933, he inaugurated a **Good Neighbor Policy** toward Latin America by formally renouncing the right of the United States to intervene in the affairs of Latin American nations. To back up his pledge, Roosevelt ordered home the Marines stationed in Haiti and Nicaragua, scuttled the Platt Amendment that had given the United States control over the Cuban government since 1901, and granted Panama more political autonomy and a greater administrative role in operating the Panama Canal.

Good Neighbor Policy
Roosevelt's foreign policy initiative that formally renounced the right of the United States to intervene in Latin American affairs, leading to improved relations between the United States and Latin American countries.

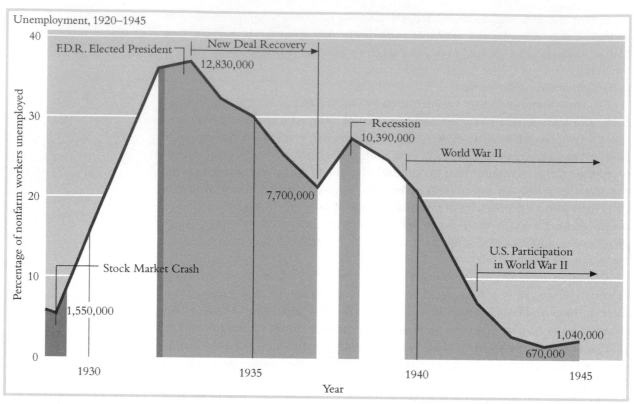

Unemployment, 1920–1945

UNEMPLOYMENT IN THE NONFARM LABOR FORCE, 1929–1945
Source: Data from *Historical Statistics of the United States, Colonial Times to 1970* (White Plains, NY: Kraus International, 1989), p. 126.

None of this, however, meant that the United States had given up its influence over Latin America. When a 1934 revolution brought a radical government to power in Cuba, the United States ambassador there worked with conservative Cubans to put a regime more favorable to U.S. interests in its place. The United States did refrain from sending troops to Cuba. It also kept its troops at home in 1936 when a radical government in Mexico nationalized several U.S.- and British-owned petroleum companies. The United States merely demanded that the new Mexican government compensate the oil companies for their lost property, which Mexico eventually did.

The Roosevelt administration's recognition of the Soviet Union and embrace of the Good Neighbor Policy can be seen as an international expression of the liberal principles that guided its domestic policies. But these diplomatic initiatives also reflected Roosevelt's interest in stimulating international trade. American businessmen wanted access to the Soviet Union's market. Latin America was already a huge market for the United States, but one in need of greater stability.

Roosevelt's interest in building international trade was also evident in his support for the Reciprocal Trade Agreement, passed by Congress in 1934. This act allowed his administration to lower U.S. tariffs by as much as 50 percent in exchange for similar reductions by other nations. By the end of 1935, the United States had negotiated reciprocal trade agreements with 14 countries.

Actually increasing the volume of international trade turned out to be more difficult than passing legislation to encourage it. Free-trade supporters encountered opposition both within the United States and abroad. In Germany and Italy, Adolf Hitler and Benito Mussolini told their people that the solution to their ills lay not in trade but in military strength and conquest. Throughout the world, similar appeals to national pride proved more popular than calls for tariff reductions and international trade.

STALEMATE, 1937–1940

By 1937 and 1938 the New Deal had begun to lose momentum. One reason was an emerging split between working-class and middle-class Democrats. After the UAW's victory over General Motors in 1937, other workers began to stage sit-down strikes. Many middle-class Americans, meanwhile, were becoming disturbed by labor's growing power.

THE COURT-PACKING FIASCO

The president's proposal on February 5, 1937, to alter the makeup of the Supreme Court exacerbated middle-class fears. Roosevelt asked Congress to give him the power to appoint one new Supreme Court justice for every member of the court who was over the age of 70 and who had served for at least 10 years. His stated reason was that the current justices were too old and feeble to handle the large volume of cases coming before them. But his real purpose was to prevent the conservative justices on the court from dismantling his New Deal. Roosevelt had not minded when, in 1935, the court had declared the NRA unconstitutional, but he was not willing to see the Wagner Act and the Social Security Act invalidated. His proposal would have given him the authority to appoint six additional justices, thereby securing a pro–New Deal majority.

The president seemed genuinely surprised by the outrage that greeted his **court-packing plan**. Roosevelt's political acumen had apparently been dulled by his 1936 victory. His inflated sense of power infuriated many previous New Deal enthusiasts. Although working-class support for Roosevelt remained strong, many middle-class voters turned away. In 1937 and 1938 a conservative opposition took shape, uniting Republicans, conservative Democrats, and civil libertarians determined to protect private property and government integrity.

Ironically, Roosevelt's court-packing scheme was probably unnecessary. In March 1937, just one month after he proposed his plan, Supreme Court Justice Owen J. Roberts, who had formerly opposed New Deal programs, decided to support them. In April and May, the Court upheld the constitutionality of the Wagner Act and Social Security Act, both by a five-to-four margin. Roosevelt allowed his court-reform proposal to die in Congress that summer. Within three years, five of the aging justices had retired, giving Roosevelt the opportunity to fashion a court more to his liking. Nonetheless, Roosevelt's reputation had suffered.

THE RECESSION OF 1937–1938

A sharp recession struck the country in late 1937 and 1938. The New Deal programs of 1935 had stimulated the economy, prompting Roosevelt to begin to scale back relief programs. New payroll taxes took $2 billion from wage earners' salaries to finance the Social Security pension fund. That withdrawal would not have hurt the economy had the money been returned to circulation as pensions for retirees. But no Social Security pensions were scheduled to be paid until 1941. Once again, the economy became starved for money, and once again the stock market crashed. By March 1938, the unemployment rate had soared to 20 percent. In the off-year elections later that year, voters elected many conservative Democrats and Republicans opposed to the New Deal. These conservatives were not strong enough to dismantle the New Deal reforms already in place, but they were able to block the passage of new ones.

court-packing plan *1937 attempt by Roosevelt to appoint one new Supreme Court justice for every sitting justice over the age of 70 who had served for at least 10 years. Roosevelt's purpose was to prevent conservative justices from dismantling the New Deal, but the plan died in Congress and inflamed opponents of the New Deal.*

C O N C L U S I O N

The New Deal reinvigorated American democracy. Some feared that Roosevelt, by accumulating more power into the hands of the federal government than had ever been done in peacetime, aspired to autocratic rule. But nothing of the sort happened. The New Dealers inspired millions of Americans who had never before voted to go to the polls. Groups that had been marginalized now felt that their political activism could make a difference.

Not everyone benefited to the same degree from the broadening of American democracy. Northern factory workers, farm owners, European ethnics, and middle-class consumers were among the groups that benefited most. In contrast, the socialist and communist elements of the labor movement failed to achieve their radical demands. Southern industrial workers, black and white, benefited little from New Deal reforms; farm laborers also realized few gains. Feminists made no headway. African Americans and Mexican Americans gained meager influence over public policy.

Of course, New Deal reforms might not have mattered to any group had not the Second World War rescued the New Deal economic program. With government war orders flooding factories from 1941 on, the economy grew vigorously, unemployment vanished, and prosperity finally returned. The architects of the Second New Deal, who had argued that large government expenditures would stimulate consumer demand and trigger economic recovery, were vindicated.

The war also solidified the political reforms of the 1930s: an increased role for the government in regulating the economy and in ensuring the social welfare of those unable to help themselves; strong state support for unionization, agricultural subsidies, and progressive tax policies; and the use of government power and money to develop the West and Southwest. Voters returned Roosevelt to office for unprecedented third and fourth terms. And these same voters remained wedded for the next 40 years to Roosevelt's central idea: that a powerful state would enhance the pursuit of liberty and equality.

QUESTIONS FOR REVIEW AND CRITICAL THINKING

Review

1. What caused the crash of 1929, and why did the ensuing depression last so long?
2. What do you consider to be the three or four most important pieces of legislation in the First New Deal? Why?
3. What was "underconsumptionism" and how did it inform the legislation of the Second New Deal? How was the Second New Deal different from the first?
4. Which minority groups in American society benefited most from the New Deal and which benefited least?

Critical Thinking

1. How did the Great Depression and New Deal shape the literature and art of the 1930s?
2. Why did the New Deal prove so popular given that, in the 1930s, it failed to solve the problem of unemployment?

ONLINE RESOURCES

 Visit the companion website to access flashcards, crossword puzzles, exercises, and quizzes related to this chapter: www.cengage.com/history/murrin/libertyequalconc5e.

See our interactive ebook for map and primary source activities.

ISCOVERY   *Why did the New Deal prove so popular even though it did not immediately solve the problem of unemployment?*

GOVERNMENT AND LAW Think about what you read in this chapter and study the information in the table below. The legislation of the First Hundred Days was numerous and varied, as it attempted to repair the economic damage suffered by various sectors of the economy: banks, farmers, businessmen, and the unemployed. Which of the programs established by this legislation were most successful in repairing the economy? Which programs were least successful? Was this legislation successful in remedying the Great Depression? Roosevelt's popularity increased between 1932 and 1936. Was this the result of the legislation of the First Hundred Days or legislation passed in subsequent years? Or both?

In thinking about this question, begin by breaking it down into the components shown below. A discussion of the significance of each component should appear in your answer.

ECONOMICS AND TECHNOLOGY The New Deal placed major emphasis on harnessing water to generate electricity, irrigate fields, and supply drinking water to urban areas. Two of the major areas in which the New Deal underwrote these projects were the Tennessee Valley and central and southern California. Study the maps on pages 671 and 672. How successful were these projects? In what ways were the projects in the Tennessee Valley and California similar? In what ways were they different? How do you explain the differences in approach? Which of the two projects brought more lasting support and credit to the New Deal?

TABLE 25.1

LEGISLATION ENACTED DURING THE "HUNDRED DAYS," MARCH 9–JUNE 16, 1933		
Date	**Legislation**	**Purpose**
March 9	Emergency Banking Act	Provide federal loans to private bankers
March 20	Economy Act	Balance the federal budget
March 22	Beer-Wine Revenue Act	Repeal Prohibition
March 31	Unemployment Relief Act	Create the Civilian Conservation Corps
May 12	Agricultural Adjustment Act	Establish a national agricultural policy
May 12	Emergency Farm Mortgage Act	Provide refinancing of farm mortgages
May 12	Federal Emergency Relief Act	Establish a national relief system, including the Civil Works Administration
May 18	Tennessee Valley Authority Act	Promote economic development of the Tennessee Valley
May 27	Securities Act	Regulate the purchase and sale of new securities
June 5	Gold Repeal Joint Resolution	Cancel the gold clause in public and private contracts
June 13	Home Owners Loan Act	Provide refinancing of home mortgages
June 16	National Industrial Recovery Act	Set up a national system of industrial self-government and establish the Public Works Administration
June 16	Glass-Steagall Banking Act	Create Federal Deposit Insurance Corporation; separate commercial and investment banking
June 16	Farm Credit Act	Reorganize agricultural credit programs
June 16	Railroad Coordination Act	Appoint federal coordinator of transportation

Source: Arthur M. Schlesinger Jr., *The Coming of the New Deal* (Boston: Houghton Mifflin, 1959), pp. 20–21.

26

AMERICA DURING THE SECOND WORLD WAR

T he Second World War vastly changed American life. The United States abandoned isolationism, moved toward military engagement on the side of the Allies, and emerged triumphant in a global war.

The mobilization for war finally lifted the nation out of the Great Depression. The nation's productive capacity—spurred by innovative technologies and by a new working relationship among government, business, labor, and scientific researchers—dwarfed that of all other nations and provided the economic basis for military victory.

At home, Americans reconsidered the meanings of liberty and equality. Although a massive publicity campaign initially stressed how wartime sacrifices would protect and preserve an "American way of life," the war raised questions. How would the nation, while striving for victory, reorder its economy, its politics, and the cultural and social patterns that had shaped racial, ethnic, and gender relationships during the 1930s? What processes of reconstruction, at home and abroad, might be required to build a prosperous and lasting peace?

TIMELINE

1931	1933	1935	1937	1939	1941	1943	1945

■ **1931**
Japanese forces seize Manchuria

■ **1933**
Hitler takes power in Germany

■ **1936**
Spanish Civil War begins • Germany and Italy agree to cooperate as the Axis Powers

■ **1937**
Neutrality Act broadens provisions of Neutrality Acts of 1935 and 1936
• Roosevelt makes "Quarantine" speech • Japan invades China

■ **1938**
France and Britain appease Hitler at Munich

■ **1939**
Hitler and Stalin sign Soviet-German nonaggression pact • Hitler invades Poland;
war breaks out in Europe • Congress amends Neutrality Act to assist Allies

1940 ■
Paris falls after German *blitzkreig* (June) • Battle of Britain carried
to U.S. by radio broadcasts • Roosevelt makes "destroyers-for-bases"
deal with Britain • Selective Service Act passed • Roosevelt wins third term

1941 ■
Lend-Lease established • Roosevelt creates Fair Employment Practices Commission
• Roosevelt and Churchill proclaim the Atlantic Charter • U.S. engages in undeclared
naval war in North Atlantic • Congress narrowly repeals Neutrality Act
• Japanese forces attack Pearl Harbor (December 7)

1942 ■
Rio de Janeiro Conference (January) • President signs Executive Order 9066 for internment
of Japanese Americans (February) • General MacArthur driven from Philippines (May)
• U.S. victorious in Battle of Midway (June) • German army defeated at Battle of Stalingrad
(August) • Operation TORCH begins (November)

1943 ■
Axis armies in North Africa surrender (May) • Allies invade Sicily (July) and
Italy (September) • "Zoot suit" incidents in Los Angeles; racial violence in Detroit
• Allies begin drive toward Japan through South Pacific islands

1944 ■
Allies land at Normandy (D-Day, June 6) • Allied armies reach Paris (August) • Allies turn back Germans
at Battle of the Bulge (September) • Roosevelt reelected to fourth term • Bretton Woods Conference
creates IMF and World Bank • Dumbarton Oaks Conference establishes plan for United Nations

1945 ■
U.S. firebombs Japan • Yalta Conference (February) • Roosevelt dies; Truman becomes president (April)
• Germany surrenders (May) • Hiroshima and Nagasaki hit with atomic bombs (August)
• Japan surrenders (September) • United Nations established (December)

THE ROAD TO WAR: AGGRESSION AND RESPONSE

The road to the Second World War began at least a decade before U.S. entry in 1941.
In Japan, Italy, and Germany, economic stagnation created political conditions that
nurtured ultranationalist movements. Elsewhere in Europe and in the United
States, economic problems made governments turn inward, concentrating on
domestic recovery and avoiding foreign entanglements.

FOCUS QUESTION
*How did events in Asia and in
Europe affect debate within
the United States over whether
or not to embrace more interventionist policies overseas?*

THE RISE OF AGGRESSOR STATES

On September 18, 1931, Japanese military forces seized Manchuria and created Manchukuo, a puppet state. This action violated the League of Nations charter, the Washington naval treaties, and the Kellogg-Briand Pact (see Chapter 24). Focused on domestic matters, the international community hesitated to oppose Japan's move. The Hoover-Stimson Doctrine (1931) announced a U.S. policy of "nonrecognition" toward Manchukuo, and the League of Nations condemned Japan's action. Japan simply ignored these rebukes.

Meanwhile, ultranationalist states in Europe also sought to alleviate domestic ills through military aggression. **Adolf Hitler's** National Socialist (Nazi) Party came to power in Germany in 1933 and instituted a **fascist** regime, a one-party dictatorial state. Hitler denounced the Versailles peace settlement of 1919, blamed Germany's problems on a Jewish conspiracy, claimed a genetic superiority for the "Aryan race" of German-speaking peoples, and promised a new Germanic empire, the **Third Reich**. The regime withdrew from the League of Nations in 1933 and, in a blatant violation of the Versailles treaty, dramatically boosted Germany's military budget. Another fascist government in Italy, headed by Benito Mussolini, also launched a military buildup and dreamed of empire. In October 1935 Mussolini's armies took over Ethiopia.

U.S. NEUTRALITY

Many Americans wished to isolate their nation from these foreign troubles. Antiwar movies, such as *All Quiet on the Western Front* (1931), implicitly portrayed the First World War as a power game played by business and governmental elites, who used appeals to nationalism to dupe young soldiers into serving as cannon fodder. During the mid-1930s a Senate investigating committee headed by Republican Gerald P. Nye of North Dakota held well-publicized hearings and concluded that the United States had been maneuvered into the First World War to preserve the profits of American bankers and munitions makers. By 1935, opinion polls suggested that Americans overwhelmingly opposed involvement in foreign conflicts.

To prevent a repetition of the circumstances that had supposedly drawn the United States into the First World War, Congress enacted neutrality legislation. The **Neutrality Acts of 1935 and 1936** mandated an arms embargo against **belligerents,** prohibited loans to them, and curtailed travel by Americans on ships belonging to nations at war. The Neutrality Act of 1937 extended the embargo to include all trade with any belligerent, unless the nation paid in cash and carried the goods away in its own ships.

Critics charged that foreswearing U.S. intervention actively aided expansionist powers such as Nazi Germany. In March 1936 Nazi troops seized the Rhineland. A few months later, Hitler and Mussolini began assisting General Francisco Franco, a fellow fascist seeking to overthrow Spain's republican government. Republicans in Spain appealed to nonfascist nations for assistance, but only the Soviet Union responded. Britain, France, and the United States, fearing that the conflict would flare into world war if more nations took sides, remained uninvolved.

Although the United States remained officially uninvolved, the Spanish Civil War precipitated a major debate. Conservative groups generally hailed Franco as a staunch anticommunist who supported religion and social stability in Spain. In contrast, the political left championed republican Spain and denounced the fascism sweeping Europe. Cadres of Americans, including the famed "Abraham Lincoln

Adolph Hitler *German fascist dictator whose aggressive policies touched off the Second World War in Europe.*

fascism *Type of highly centralized government that used terror and violence to suppress opposition. Its rigid social and economic controls often incorporated strong nationalism and racism. Fascist governments were dominated by strong authority figures or dictators.*

Third Reich *New empire Adolph Hitler promised the German people would bring glory and unity to the nation.*

Neutrality Acts of 1935 and 1936 *Legislation that restricted loans, trade, and travel with belligerent nations in an attempt to avoid the entanglements that had brought the United States into the First World War.*

belligerent *Country actively engaged in a war.*

Brigade," crossed the Atlantic to fight alongside republican forces in Spain. American peace groups differed over how to avoid a wider war. Some continued to advocate neutrality and isolation, but others argued for intervention against the spread of fascism.

In October 1937 Roosevelt called for international cooperation to "quarantine" aggressor nations. Still suspicious of foreign entanglements, a majority of legislators refused to budge, even if this meant a victory by Franco in Spain's civil war.

THE MOUNTING CRISIS

As Americans debated how to deal with foreign aggression, Japan attacked China. In summer 1937, after an exchange of gunfire between Japanese and Chinese troops at the Marco Polo Bridge near Beijing, Japanese armies invaded and captured Shanghai, Nanjing, Shandong, and Beijing. Japan demanded that China become subservient to Tokyo. It also proposed an East Asian Co-Prosperity Sphere that would supposedly liberate Asian nations from Western colonialism and create a self-sufficient economic zone under Japanese leadership. In late 1937 Japanese planes sank the American gunboat *Panay* as it evacuated Americans from Nanjing. Japan's quick apology defused a potential crisis. Still, the Panay incident and Japan's brutality in occupying Nanjing, where perhaps 300,000 Chinese civilians were killed, alarmed Roosevelt.

Meanwhile, in Europe, Germany continued on the march. In March 1938 Hitler annexed Austria to the Third Reich and announced his intention to seize the Sudetenland, a portion of Czechoslovakia inhabited by 3.5 million people of German descent. In May FDR began a program of naval rearmament. French and British leaders, still hoping to avoid war, met with Hitler in Munich in September 1938. They acquiesced to Germany's seizure of the Sudetenland in return for Hitler's promise to seek no more territory. Hailed by Britain's prime minister as a guarantee of "peace in our time," the arrangement soon became a symbol of what interventionists called the "appeasement" of aggression.

In March 1939 Germans marched into Prague and, within a few months, annexed the rest of Czechoslovakia. In August 1939 Hitler signed a nonaggression pact with the Soviet Union. In a secret protocol, Hitler and Soviet leader Joseph Stalin agreed on a plan to divide up Poland and the Baltic States.

THE OUTBREAK OF WAR IN EUROPE

When Hitler's armies stormed into Poland on September 1, 1939, the Second World War officially began. Britain and France declared war but could not mobilize in time to help Poland, which fell within weeks. Then an eerie calm settled over Europe during the winter.

In April 1940 a full-scale German **blitzkrieg**, or "lightning war," began moving swiftly, overrunning Denmark, Norway, the Netherlands, Belgium, Luxembourg, and France. The speed of the Nazi advance shocked Allied leaders in Paris and London. Britain barely managed to evacuate its troops, but not its equipment, from the French coastal town of Dunkirk, just before it fell to a German onslaught. Early in June, Italy joined Germany by declaring war on the Allies. Later in June, France fell, and Hitler installed a pro-Nazi government at Vichy in southern France. In only 6 weeks, Hitler's army had seized complete control of Europe's Atlantic coastline, from the North Sea south to Spain, where Franco remained officially neutral but decidedly pro-Axis.

blitzkrieg *A "lightning war;" a coordinated and massive military strike by German army and air forces.*

Map 26.1 GERMAN EXPANSION AT ITS HEIGHT. *This map shows the expansion of German power from 1938 through 1942. Which countries fell to German control? Why might Americans have differed over whether these moves by Germany represented a strategic threat to the United States?*

THE U.S. RESPONSE TO WAR IN EUROPE

cash and carry U.S. foreign policy prior to American entry into World War II that required belligerents to pay cash and carry products away in their own ships. This arrangement minimized risks to American exports, loans, and shipping.

Meanwhile, alarmed at the Nazi surge, Roosevelt pressured Congress to modify its neutrality legislation and called for other measures, "short of war," to help Britain and France. Late in 1939 Congress did lift the ban on selling military armaments to either side and substituted a **cash-and-carry** provision that permitted arms sales to belligerents who could pay cash and use their own ships for transport. Because its naval forces dominated the Atlantic sea lanes, Britain primarily benefited from this change in policy. Congress also passed the Selective Training and Service Act of 1940, the first peacetime draft in U.S. history. Abandoning any pretense of neutrality, the United States also began supplying war materiel directly to Great Britain.

Meanwhile, from August through October 1940, Germany's **Luftwaffe** conducted daily raids on British air bases and nearly knocked out its Royal Air Force (RAF). On the verge of a KO, however, Hitler suddenly changed strategy and ordered, instead, the bombing of London and other cities. The use of airpower against civilians in the Battle of Britain, as it was called, shocked and aroused sympathy among Americans, who heard of events during dramatic radio broadcasts from London.

In September 1940 Roosevelt agreed to transfer 50 First World War–era naval destroyers to the British navy. In return, the United States gained the right to build eight naval bases in British territories in the Western Hemisphere. This "destroyers-for-bases" deal infuriated isolationists. The America First Committee, organized by General Robert E. Wood, head of Sears, Roebuck, and Company, launched a campaign to sway Congress and public opinion in an isolationist direction.

Although those who favored staying out of the war were generally lumped together as "isolationists," this single term obscures their ideological diversity. Some pacifists opposed all wars as immoral, even those against fascist regimes. Some political progressives disliked fascism but feared even more the centralization of governmental power that conducting a war would require in the United States. Some conservatives sympathized with the anticommunism of fascist states, and some Americans shared Hitler's anti-Semitism.

A current of anti-Jewish sentiment existed in the United States. In 1939 congressional leaders had quashed the Wagner-Rogers bill, which would have boosted immigration quotas in order to allow for the entry of 20,000 Jewish children otherwise slated for Hitler's concentration camps. Bowing to anti-Semitic prejudices, the United States adopted a restrictive refugee policy. The consequences of these policies became especially grave after June 1941, when Hitler established the death camps that would systematically exterminate millions of Jews, gypsies, homosexuals, and anyone else whom the Nazis deemed unfit for life in the Third Reich and its occupied territories. In September 1941 Burton K. Wheeler of Montana created a special Senate committee to investigate whether Hollywood movies were being used to promote prowar views. Some isolationists, pointing out that many Hollywood producers were Jewish, expressed blatantly anti-Semitic views.

To counteract the isolationists, those who favored supporting the Allies also organized. The Military Training Camps Association lobbied on behalf of the Selective Service Act. The Committee to Defend America by Aiding the Allies, headed by William Allen White, a well-known Republican newspaper editor, organized more than 300 local chapters in just a few weeks. Similar to the isolationists, interventionist organizations drew from a diverse group of supporters. All, however, sounded alarms that fascist brutality, militarism, and racism might overrun Europe as Americans watched passively.

Presidential electoral politics in 1940 forced Roosevelt, nominated for a third term, to tone down his pro-Allied rhetoric. The Republicans nominated Wendell Willkie, a lawyer and business executive with ties to the party's liberal, internationalist wing. To differentiate his policies from Willkie's, the president played to the popular opposition to war, promising not to send American troops to fight in "foreign wars." Once he had won an unprecedented third term, however, Roosevelt unveiled his most ambitious plan yet to support Britain's war effort.

AN "ARSENAL OF DEMOCRACY"

Britain was nearly out of money, so the president proposed that the United States would now "lend-lease," or loan rather than sell, munitions to the Allies. Making the United States a "great arsenal of democracy," FDR claimed, would "keep war away from our country and our people." Congressional debate over the

Luftwaffe *German air force.*

QUICK   REVIEW

THE SECOND WORLD WAR APPROACHES

- Germany occupied Czechoslovakia and invaded Poland

- Britain and France declared war on Germany and appealed for U.S. aid

- Japan invaded Manchuria and China, and bombed Pearl Harbor

- U.S. gradually terminated neutrality for "measures short of war" and ultimately entered war

Lend-Lease Act *A 1941 act by which the United States "loaned" munitions to the Allies, hoping to avoid war by becoming an "arsenal" for the Allied cause.*

Joseph Stalin *Soviet communist dictator who worked with Allied leaders during Second World War.*

wolfpacks *German submarine groups that attacked enemy merchant ships or convoys.*

Pearl Harbor *Japan's December 7, 1941, attack on this U.S. base in Hawaii brought the United States into the Second World War.*

Lend-Lease Act was bitter, but it passed as House Resolution 1776 on March 11, 1941. When Germany turned its attention away from Britain and suddenly attacked its recent ally, the Soviet Union, in June, Roosevelt extended lend-lease assistance to the communist regime of **Joseph Stalin**.

Roosevelt next began coordinating military strategy with Britain. He secretly pledged to follow a Europe-first approach if the United States was drawn into a two-front war against both Germany and Japan. Publicly, Roosevelt deployed U.S. Marines to Greenland and Iceland to free up the British forces that had protected these strategic Danish possessions after Germany's 1940 conquest of Denmark. In August 1941 Roosevelt and British Prime Minister Winston Churchill met on the high seas off the coast of Newfoundland to work toward a formal wartime alliance. They agreed to an eight-point Atlantic Charter that disavowed territorial expansion, endorsed protection of human rights and self-determination, and pledged the postwar creation of a new world organization that would ensure "general security." Roosevelt also agreed to Churchill's request that the U.S. Navy convoy American goods as far as Iceland. Soon, in an undeclared naval war, Germany's formidable **wolfpacks** began attacking U.S. ships.

By this time Roosevelt and his advisors believed that defeating Hitler would require U.S. entry into the war, but public support still lagged. Privately, the president likely hoped that Germany would commit some provocative act in the North Atlantic that would jar public opinion. The October 1941 sinking of the U.S. destroyer *Reuben James* did just that. Congress repealed the Neutrality Act, but the vote was so close and debate so bitter that Roosevelt knew he could not yet seek a formal declaration of war.

PEARL HARBOR

As it turned out, Japan, rather than Germany, sparked America's involvement. In response to Japan's 1937 invasion of China, the United States extended economic credits to China and curtailed sales of equipment to Japan. In 1939 the United States abrogated its Treaty of Commerce and Navigation with Japan, an action that meant further restrictions on U.S. exports to the island nation. A 1940 ban on the sale of aviation fuel and high-grade scrap iron to Japan was also intended to slow Japan's military advances.

These measures did not halt Japanese expansion. As the European war sapped the strength of France, the Netherlands, and Great Britain, Japanese militarists hoped to grab Europe's Asian colonies and incorporate them into Japan's own East Asian Co-Prosperity Sphere. Japan therefore pushed deep into French Indochina, seeking the raw materials it could no longer buy from the United States, and prepared to launch attacks on Singapore, the Netherlands, East Indies (Indonesia), and the Philippines.

Roosevelt expanded the trade embargo against Japan, promised further assistance to China, and accelerated the U.S. military buildup in the Pacific. In mid-1941 he froze all Japanese assets in the United States, effectively bringing under presidential control all commerce between the two countries, including trade in petroleum, which was vital to the Japanese economy and war effort. Faced with impending economic strangulation, Japanese leaders did not reassess their plan to create an East Asian empire. Instead, they began planning a preemptive attack on the United States. With limited supplies of raw materials, especially oil, Japan had little hope of winning a prolonged war. Japanese military strategists gambled that a surprise, crippling blow would limit U.S. capabilities and force U.S. concessions.

On December 7, 1941, Japanese bombers swooped down on **Pearl Harbor**, Hawaii, and destroyed much of the U.S. Pacific Fleet. Altogether, 19 ships were sunk or severely damaged; nearly 200 aircraft were destroyed or disabled; and 2,200 Americans were killed. The attack could have been worse. U.S. aircraft carriers, out to sea at the time, were spared, as were the base's fuel storage tanks and repair facilities. In a dramatic message broadcast by radio on December 8, Roosevelt decried the attack and labeled December 7 as "a date which will live in infamy," a phrase that served as a battle cry throughout the war. Japan had rallied Americans, not brought them to terms.

A few Americans charged that Roosevelt had intentionally provoked Japan in order to open a "back door" to war. They pointed out that the fleet at Pearl Harbor lay vulnerable, not even in a state of full alert. The actions and inactions of leaders, however, were more confused than devious. Intelligence experts expected Japan to move toward Singapore or other British or Dutch possessions in Asia. Intercepted messages, along with visual sightings of Japanese ships, seemed to confirm preparations for a strike in Southeast Asia (which did occur). American leaders doubted that Japan would risk a direct attack and discounted the skill of Japan's military planners.

On December 8, 1941, Congress declared war against Japan. Japan's allies, Germany and Italy, declared war on the United States three days later. Hitler mistakenly assumed that the fight against Japan would keep the United States preoccupied in the Pacific. The three Axis Powers drastically underestimated America's ability to mobilize swiftly and effectively.

FIGHTING THE WAR IN EUROPE

Initially, the war went badly for the Allies. German forces controlled most of Europe from Norway to Greece and had pushed eastward into the Soviet Union. Now they rolled across North Africa, and German submarines endangered Allied supply lines in the Atlantic. Japan seemed unstoppable in the Pacific, overrunning Malaya, the Dutch East Indies, and the Philippines and moving against the British in Burma and the Australians in New Guinea.

The United States had been unprepared for war, but new bureaucracies and technologies quickly guided a crash program for mobilization. The newly formed Joint Chiefs of Staff, consisting of representatives from each of the armed services, guided Roosevelt's strategy. The War Department's Pentagon complex, a giant, five-story, five-sided building, was completed in January 1943 after 16 months of around-the-clock work. In 1942 aircraft equipped with radar, a new technology developed in collaboration with Britain, proved effective against submarines, and during 1943 Germany's U-boat threat faded "from menace to problem," in the words of one U.S. naval strategist. Perhaps most critical, a massive Allied codebreaking operation, based at Bletchley Park in England, perfected decryption machines. Decrypted German messages, called "Ultra" for "ultrasecret," gave the Allies a crucial advantage. Throughout the war, Germans never discovered that many of their decoded radio communications were being forwarded to Allied commanders—sometimes even before they had reached their German recipients.

FOCUS QUESTION
What military strategies did the United States and the Allies ultimately adopt when fighting in both the European and Asian theaters of the Second World War?

CAMPAIGNS IN NORTH AFRICA AND ITALY

Military strategy divided the Allied Powers. All agreed that their primary focus would be on Europe, and Roosevelt and his military strategists established a unified command with the British. The Soviet Union pleaded with Roosevelt and

Churchill to open a second front in Western Europe by way of an invasion across the English Channel into France, to relieve pressure on the USSR. Many of Roosevelt's advisers agreed: If German troops succeeded in knocking the Soviet Union out of the war, Hitler could turn his full attention toward Britain. Churchill, however, urged instead the invasion of French North Africa, in order to nibble away at the edges of enemy power.

At a meeting in Casablanca, Morocco, in January 1943, Roosevelt sided with Churchill. To assuage Stalin's fear that his two allies might sign a separate peace with Hitler, Roosevelt and Churchill promised to remain in the fight until Germany agreed to an "unconditional surrender."

The North African operation, code-named TORCH, began with Anglo-American landings in Morocco and Algeria in November 1942. As TORCH progressed, the Soviets suddenly turned the tide of battle on the eastern front with a decisive victory at Stalingrad.

Hitler poured reinforcements into North Africa but could stop neither TORCH nor the British drive westward from Egypt. In the summer of 1943 the Allies followed up their successful North African campaign by overrunning the island of Sicily and then fighting their way, slowly, northward through Italy's mountains.

Some U.S officials worried about the postwar implications of wartime strategy. Secretary of War Henry Stimson, for example, warned that the Allied campaigns through Africa and Italy might leave the Soviets dominant in most of Europe. Acting on their advice, Roosevelt finally agreed to set a date for the cross-Channel invasion that Stalin had long been promised.

Operation Overlord

Operation OVERLORD, directed by General **Dwight D. Eisenhower**, began on June 6, 1944, D-Day. During the preceding months, probably the largest invasion force in history had assembled in England. Disinformation and diversionary tactics fooled the Germans into expecting a landing at the narrowest part of the English Channel rather than in the Normandy region. After several delays, because of the Channel's unpredictable weather, nervous commanders finally ordered the daring plan to begin. The night before, as naval guns pounded the Normandy shore, three divisions of paratroopers dropped behind enemy lines to disrupt German communications. Then, at dawn, more than 4,000 Allied ships landed troops and supplies on Normandy's beaches. The first American forces to come ashore at Omaha Beach met especially heavy German fire and took enormous casualties, but the waves of invading troops continued. Only three weeks after D-Day, more than a million Allied personnel controlled the French coast and opened the long-awaited Second Front.

Just as the 1943 Battle of Stalingrad had reversed the course of the war in the East, so OVERLORD changed the momentum in the West. Within three months, U.S., British, and Free French troops entered Paris. After repulsing a desperate German counteroffensive in Belgium, at the Battle of the Bulge in December and January, Allied armies swept eastward, crossing the Rhine, and headed toward Berlin to meet up with westward-advancing Soviet troops.

As the war in Europe drew to a close, the horrors perpetrated by the Third Reich became fully visible to the world. Hitler's campaign of extermination, now called the Holocaust, killed more than 5 million Jews out of Europe's prewar population of 10 million. Hundreds of thousands more from various other groups were also murdered, especially gypsies, homosexuals, intellectuals, communists, and the physically and mentally challenged. Although only a military victory put an end to

Dwight D. Eisenhower
Supreme Commander of the Allied Forces in Europe, orchestrator of the Normandy invasion, and President of the United States (1953–1961).

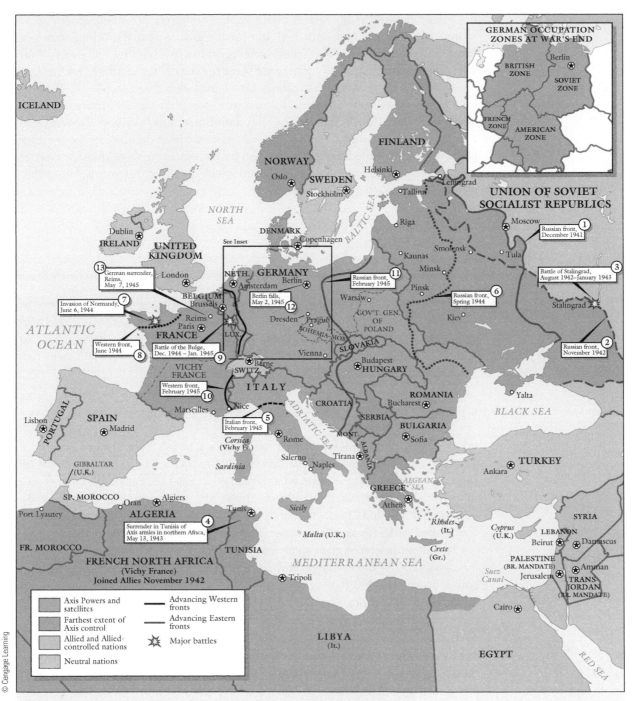

Map 26.2 ALLIED ADVANCES AND COLLAPSE OF GERMAN POWER. *This map depicts the final Allied advances and the end of the war in Germany. Through what countries did Soviet armies advance, and how might their advance have affected the postwar situation? How was Germany divided by occupying powers, and how might that division have affected postwar politics?*

German death camps, the Allies might have saved thousands of Jews by helping them escape and emigrate. Allied leaders, however, worried about how to deal with large numbers of Jewish refugees, and they also claimed they could not spare scarce ships to transport them to sanctuary. The Allies would, in 1945 and 1946, bring 24 German high officials to trial at Nuremberg for "crimes against humanity." Large quantities of money, gold, and jewelry that Nazi leaders stole from victims of the Holocaust and deposited in Swiss banks, however, remained concealed for more than 50 years. Not until 1997 did Jewish groups and the U.S. government force an investigation of the Swiss banking industry's holdings of stolen "Nazi gold," an inquiry that finally prompted some restitution for victims' families.

With Hitler's suicide in April and Germany's surrender on May 8, 1945, the military foundations for peace in Europe were complete. Soviet armies controlled Eastern Europe; British and U.S. forces predominated in Italy and the rest of the Mediterranean; Germany and Austria fell under divided occupation. Governmental leaders now needed to work out a plan for transforming these military arrangements into a comprehensive political settlement for the postwar era. Meanwhile, the war in the Pacific was far from over.

The Pacific Theater

For six months after Pearl Harbor, Japan's forces steadily advanced. Singapore fell easily. Japan overwhelmed U.S. naval garrisons in the Philippines and on Guam and Wake islands. Filipino and American troops surrendered at Bataan and Corregidor in the Philippines. Other Japanese forces headed southward to menace Australia and New Zealand.

SEIZING THE OFFENSIVE IN THE PACIFIC

When Japan finally suffered its first naval setback at the Battle of the Coral Sea in May 1942, Japanese naval commanders decided to hit back hard. They amassed 200 ships and 600 planes to destroy what remained of the U.S. Pacific fleet and to take Midway Island. U.S. Naval Intelligence, however, was monitoring Japanese codes and warned Admiral Chester W. Nimitz of the plan. Surprising the Japanese armada, U.S. planes sank four Japanese carriers and destroyed a total of 322 planes.

Two months later, American forces splashed ashore at Guadalcanal in the Solomon Islands. The bloody engagements in the Solomons continued for months on both land and sea, but they accomplished one major objective: seizing the military initiative in the Pacific. According to prewar plans, the war in Europe was to have received highest priority, but by 1943 the two theaters were receiving roughly equal resources.

The bloody engagements in the Pacific reinforced racial prejudices and brutality on both sides. Japanese leaders hoped the war would confirm the superiority of the divine Yamato race. Prisoners taken by the Japanese, particularly on the Asian mainland, were brutalized in almost unimaginable ways. The Japanese army's Unit 731 tested bacteriological weapons in China and conducted horrifying medical experiments on live subjects. American propaganda images played on themes of racial superiority, portraying the Japanese people as animalistic subhumans. American troops often rivaled Japan's forces in their disrespect for the enemy dead and sometimes killed the enemy rather than take prisoners.

CHINA POLICY

U.S. policymakers hoped that China would fight effectively against Japan and emerge after the war as a strong, united nation. Neither hope seemed realized. China was beset by civil war.

Jiang Jieshi's Nationalist government was incompetent and unpopular. It avoided engaging the Japanese invaders and still made extravagant demands for U.S. assistance. A growing communist movement led by Mao Zedong fought more effectively against the Japanese invaders, but U.S. policy continued to support Jiang as China's future leader. Meanwhile, Japan's advance into China continued, and in 1944 its forces captured seven key U.S. air bases in China.

U.S. STRATEGY IN THE PACIFIC

In contrast to the European Theater, no unified command guided the war in the Pacific. Consequently, military actions often emerged from compromise. General Douglas MacArthur, commander of the army in the South Pacific, favored an offensive launched from his headquarters in Australia through New Guinea and the Philippines and on to Japan. After Japan had driven him out of the Philippines in May 1942, he promised to return. Admiral Nimitz disagreed. He favored an advance across the smaller islands of the central Pacific, bypassing the Philippines. Unable to decide between the two strategies, the Joint Chiefs of Staff authorized both.

Both offensives moved forward, marked by fierce fighting and heavy casualties. MacArthur took New Guinea. Nimitz's forces liberated the Marshall Islands and the Marianas in 1943 and 1944. An effective radio communication system conducted by a Marine platoon of Navajo Indians, the **Navajo Signal Corps**, made a unique contribution to success. Navajo, a language unfamiliar to Japanese intelligence officers, provided a secure medium for sensitive communications.

In late 1944 the fall of Saipan brought American bombers within range of Japan. The capture of the islands of Iwo Jima and Okinawa during spring 1945 further shortened that distance. Okinawa illustrated the ferocity of the campaigns: 120,000 Japanese and 48,000 American soldiers died. Given these numbers, U.S. military planners dreaded the prospect of invading Japan's home islands.

Airpower looked more and more enticing. The results of the Allies' strategic bombing of Germany, including the destruction of such large cities as Hamburg and Dresden, were ambiguous, and military historians continue to debate whether the damage against military targets really offset the huge civilian casualties and the unsustainable losses of American pilots and aircraft. Nonetheless, U.S. strategists continued to believe that strategic bombing might provide the crucial advantage in the Pacific. In February 1944 General Henry Harley ("Hap") Arnold devised a plan for firebombing major Japanese cities. Bombers added to the horror of war, Arnold conceded, but when used "with the proper degree of understanding" could become "the most humane of all weapons." Arnold's air campaign, operating from bases in China, turned out to be cumbersome. It was replaced by a more effective and lethal operation run by General Curtis LeMay from Saipan.

The official position on the incendiary raids against Japanese cities was that they constituted "precision" rather than "area" bombing. In actuality, the success of a mission was measured by the number of square miles it left scorched. The number of Japanese civilians killed in the raids is estimated to have been greater than Japanese soldiers killed in battle. Air attacks on Tokyo during the night of March 9/10, 1945, inaugurated the new policy. They leveled nearly a quarter of the city and incinerated more than 100,000 people. LeMay summarized his strategy: "Bomb and burn them until they quit."

By the winter of 1944–45, a combined sea and air strategy had emerged: The United States sought "unconditional surrender" by blockading Japan's seaports,

Navajo Signal Corps *Navajo Indians who conveyed military intelligence in their native language to preserve its secrecy.*

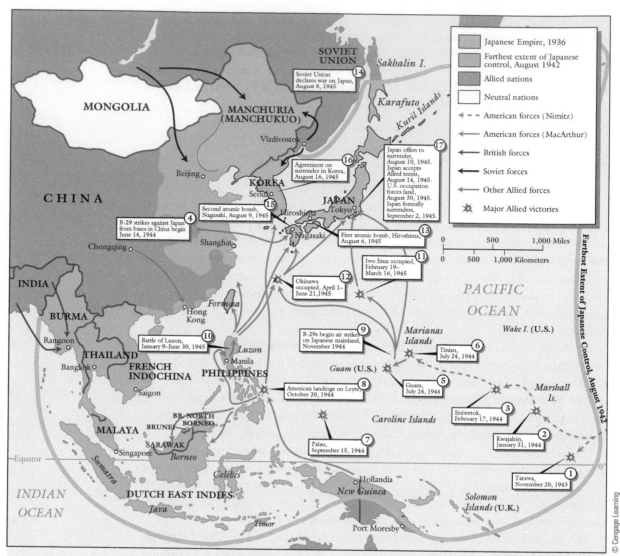

Map 26.3 PACIFIC THEATER OFFENSIVE STRATEGY AND FINAL ASSAULT AGAINST JAPAN. *This map suggests the complicated nature of devising a war strategy in the vast Pacific region. What tactics did the United States use to advance upon and finally prevail over the island nation of Japan?*

bombarding its cities from the air, and, perhaps, by invading Japan. Critics of the policy of unconditional surrender, which most Japanese assumed meant the death of their emperor, later suggested that it may have hardened Japan's determination to fight even after defeat had become inevitable. Defenders of the policy suggest that any softening of U.S. terms would have only encouraged Japanese resistance. Whatever the case, American leaders believed that victory would only come through massive destruction.

A NEW PRESIDENT, THE ATOMIC BOMB, AND JAPAN'S SURRENDER

On April 13, 1945, newspaper headlines across the country read "President Roosevelt Dead." Sorrow and shock spread through the armed forces, where many young men and women had hardly known any other president. Through diplomatic conference halls, Roosevelt's personal magnetism had often brought unity, if not always clarity; and among his many supporters, he had symbolized optimism and unity through depression and war. Roosevelt had also accumulated a host of critics and enemies. He had defeated Republican Thomas E. Dewey in the 1944 presidential election by the smallest popular-vote margin in nearly 30 years. Politically and physically weakened, Roosevelt fought to retain his dominant place in the political spotlight. Unaware of Roosevelt's precarious health, both Republican and Democrats assumed FDR would lead the United States into the postwar world.

Emerging from Roosevelt's shadow, the new president, **Harry S Truman**, seemed an unimposing presence. Born on a farm near Independence, Missouri, Truman served in France during the First World War, became a U.S. Senator in 1934, and was tabbed as Roosevelt's running mate in 1944. Roosevelt offered an upper-class image of well-practiced and worldly charm. The blunt-spoken Truman proudly presented himself as a "little man from Missouri." He knew little about international affairs or about any informal understandings that Roosevelt may have made with foreign leaders.

Only after succeeding Roosevelt did Truman learn about events at Los Alamos, New Mexico. There, since the late 1930s, scientists from all across the world had been secretly working on a new weapon. Advances in theoretical physics had suggested that splitting the atom (fission) would release a tremendous amount of energy. Fearful that Germany was racing ahead of the United States in this research, Albert Einstein, a Jewish refugee from Germany, had urged Roosevelt to launch a secret program to build a bomb based on the latest atomic research. The government subsequently enlisted top scientists in the Manhattan Project, a huge, secret military operation. On July 16, 1945, the first atomic weapon was successfully tested at Trinity Site, near Alamogordo, New Mexico.

Truman and his top policymakers assumed that the weapon would be put to immediate use. They were eager to end the war, both because a possible land invasion of Japan might prove so costly in American lives and because the Soviet Union was planning to enter the Pacific Theater, where Truman wished to limit Soviet power. Churchill called the bomb a "miracle of deliverance" and a peace-giver. Truman later publicly claimed that he had never lost a night's sleep over its use.

Privately, he and other U.S. officials admitted to more qualms. There was disagreement over where and how the bomb should be deployed. A commission of atomic scientists recommended a "demonstration" that would impress Japan with the bomb's power yet cause no loss of life. General George C. Marshall suggested using it on purely military installations or only on manufacturing sites, after first warning away Japanese workers. Ultimately, the Truman administration discarded these options. The bomb, Secretary of War Henry Stimson said, had to make "a profound psychological impression on as many inhabitants as possible."

In the context of the earlier aerial bombardment of Japanese cities, dropping atomic bombs on the previously unbombed cities of **Hiroshima** and Nagasaki on August 6 and 9, 1945, seemed only a small departure from existing policy. "Fat Man" and "Little Boy," as the two bombs were nicknamed, came to be viewed as merely bigger, more effective firebombs. Atomic weapons did, however, produce a new level of violence. Colonel Paul Tibbets, who piloted the U.S. plane that dropped the first bomb, reported that "the shimmering city became an ugly smudge . . . a pot

Harry S Truman *Franklin Roosevelt's vice president who became president when Roosevelt died on April 12, 1945.*

Hiroshima *Japanese city destroyed by atomic bomb on August 6, 1945.*

TOTAL WAR: DRESDEN AND HIROSHIMA. *The effects of "total war" are graphically illustrated in these photographs—of the devastation of Dresden, Germany (top), by the British Bomber Command and the U.S. 8th Air Force on February 13 and 14, 1945, and that of Hiroshima, Japan (bottom), by the U.S. 509th Composite Group on August 6, 1945. In the initial attack on Dresden, 786 aircraft dropped 5,824,000 pounds (2,600 long tons) of bombs on the city, killing an estimated 60,000 people and injuring another 30,000. An area of more than 2.5 square miles in the city center was demolished, and some 37,000 buildings were destroyed. To critics, the bombing of Dresden, a target that many argued was of little strategic value, exemplified the excessive use of airpower.*

In sobering comparison, Hiroshima was devastated by one bomb weighing only 10,000 pounds (4.4 long tons)—an atomic bomb—dropped from one aircraft. The single U-235 bomb killed 68,000 people outright, injured another 30,000, and left 10,000 missing. (These figures do not include those who later developed diseases from deadly gamma rays.) The bomb obliterated almost 5 square miles of the city's center and destroyed 40,653 buildings. Truman reported the strike as "an overwhelming success." Many hailed the atomic bomb as a necessary step toward military victory; others worried about the dawn of the "nuclear age."

© UPI/Bettmann/Corbis

© UPI/Bettmann/Corbis

VJ Day *August 15, 1945; day on which the war in the Pacific was won by the Allies.*

of bubbling hot tar." Teams of U.S. observers who entered Hiroshima and Nagasaki in the aftermath were stunned at the instantaneous incineration of both human beings and manmade structures, and shocked to contemplate the longer-lasting horror of radiation disease.

The mushroom clouds over Hiroshima and Nagasaki inaugurated a new "atomic age" in which dreams of peace mingled with nightmares of global destruction. But in those late summer days of 1945 most Americans sighed with relief. News reports of August 15 proclaimed Japan's surrender, **VJ Day.**

THE WAR AT HOME: THE ECONOMY

The success of the U.S. military effort depended on economic mobilization at home. This effort ultimately brought the Great Depression of the 1930s to an end and transformed the nation's government, its business and financial institutions, and its labor force.

FOCUS QUESTION
How did mobilizing for war produce political, economic, and social changes in the United States?

GOVERNMENT'S ROLE IN THE ECONOMY

The federal bureaucracy nearly quadrupled in size during the war. New economic agencies proliferated. The most powerful of these, the War Production Board, oversaw the conversion and expansion of factories, allocated resources, and enforced production priorities and schedules. The War Labor Board adjudicated labor-management disputes. The War Manpower Commission allocated workers to various industries. The Office of Price Administration regulated prices to control inflation and rationed such scarce commodities as gasoline, rubber, steel, shoes, coffee, sugar, and meat. Although most of the controls were abandoned after the war, the concept of greater governmental oversight of the economy survived.

From 1940 to 1945 the U.S. economy expanded rapidly, and the gross national product (GNP) rose, year-by-year, by 15 percent or more. When Roosevelt called for the production of 60,000 planes shortly after Pearl Harbor, skeptics jeered. Yet within a few years the nation produced nearly 300,000 planes. The Maritime Commission oversaw the construction of millions of tons of new ships. A once stagnant economy spewed out prodigious quantities of other supplies, including 2.5 million trucks and 50 million pairs of shoes.

Striving to increase production, industry entered into a close relationship with government to promote scientific and technological research and development (**R&D**). Government money subsidized new industries, such as electronics, and transformed others, such as rubber and chemicals. Eventually, an Office of Scientific Research and Development contracted with universities and scientists for a variety of projects. Under this program, radar and penicillin (both British discoveries), rocket engines, and other new products were perfected for wartime use. Refugees from Nazi tyranny contributed significantly to this scientific innovation.

BUSINESS AND FINANCE

To finance the war effort, government spending rose from $9 billion in 1940 to $98 billion in 1944. In 1941 the national debt stood at $48 billion; by V-J Day it was $280 billion. With few goods to buy, Americans invested in war bonds, turning their savings into tanks and planes. Although war bonds provided a relatively insignificant contribution to overall defense spending, they did help raise personal saving to record levels and gave those who purchased them a direct psychological and economic stake in victory.

As production shifted from autos to tanks, and from refrigerators to guns, consumer goods became scarce. Essentials such as food, fabrics, and gasoline were rationed and, consequently, were shared more equitably than before the war. Higher taxes on wealthier Americans redistributed income and narrowed the gap in wealth between the well-to-do and other citizens. War bonds, rationing, and progressive taxation encouraged a sense of shared sacrifice and helped ease the class tensions of the 1930s.

R&D *Research and development.*

Even as the war fostered personal savings and some income redistribution, however, it also facilitated the dismantling of some New Deal agencies most concerned with the poor. A Republican surge in the off-year elections of 1942—the GOP gained 44 seats in the House and 7 in the Senate—helped strengthen an anti–New Deal coalition in Congress. In 1943 legislators abolished the job-creation programs of the Works Progress Administration (WPA), the Civilian Conservation Corps (CCC), and the National Youth Administration (NYA) (see Chapter 25). It also shut down the Rural Electrification Administration (REA) and Farm Security Administration (FSA), agencies that had assisted impoverished rural areas. As business executives flocked to Washington, D.C., to run the new wartime agencies, the Roosevelt administration adopted a relatively cooperative stance toward big business.

Big businesses considered essential to wartime victory flourished under governmental subsidies. What was essential, of course, became a matter of definition. Coca-Cola and Wrigley's chewing gum won precious sugar allotments by arguing that GIs overseas "needed" to enjoy these products. Both companies prospered. The Kaiser Corporation, whose spectacular growth during the 1930s had been spurred by federal dam contracts, now turned its attention to building ships, aircraft, and military vehicles. Federal subsidies and tax breaks enabled factories to expand and retool.

The war concentrated power in the largest corporations. After Roosevelt ordered his justice department to postpone enforcement of antitrust laws, government lawyers tucked away long-planned legal cases, such as one against America's great oil cartel. Congressional efforts to investigate possible collusion in the awarding of large government contracts and to increase assistance to small businesses similarly made little headway. The top 100 companies, which had provided 30 percent of the nation's total manufacturing output in 1940, were providing 70 percent by 1943.

braceros *Guest workers from Mexico allowed into the United States because of labor shortages from 1942 to 1964.*

THE WORKFORCE

During the early years of the military buildup, people who had scrounged for jobs during the Great Depression found work. Employment in heavy industry invariably went to men, and most of the skilled jobs went to whites. But as military service depleted the ranks of white males, women and minorities became more attractive candidates for production jobs. Soon, both private employers and public officials were encouraging women to go to work; southern African Americans to move to northern industrial cities; and Mexicans to enter the United States under the **bracero** guest farm worker program.

Hired for jobs never before open to them, women became welders, shipbuilders, lumberjacks, and miners. Women won places in prestigious symphony orchestras, and one Major League Baseball owner financed the creation of a women's league to give new life to the national pastime. Many employers hired married women, who before the war would have been lucky to obtain a position even in traditionally female occupations such as teaching. Minority women moved into clerical and sales jobs, where they had not previously been welcome. Most workplaces, however, continued to be segregated by sex.

© Bettmann/CORBIS

WOMEN JOIN THE WAR EFFORT. *Women employees at the Convair Company in California use a rivet gun and bucking bar, tools traditionally used only by men.*

CHILDREN ARE ENLISTED IN THE WAR EFFORT. *These children, flashing the "V-for-Victory" sign, stand atop a pile of scrap metal. Collecting scrap of all kinds for war production helped to engage millions of Americans on the home front.*

The scope of unpaid labor, long provided primarily by women, also expanded. Volunteer activities such as Red Cross projects, civil defense work, and recycling drives claimed more and more of the time of women, children, and older people. Government publications exhorted homemakers: "Wear it out, use it up, make it do, or do without." Both in the home and in the workplace, women's responsibilities and workloads increased.

The new labor market improved the general economic position of African Americans. By executive order in June 1942, Roosevelt created the Fair Employment Practices Commission (FEPC), which aimed to ban discrimination in hiring. In 1943 the government announced that it would not recognize as collective bargaining agents any unions that discriminated on the basis of race. The War Labor Board outlawed the practice of paying different wages to whites and nonwhites doing the same job. Before the war, the African American population had been mainly southern, rural, and agricultural; within a few years, a substantial percentage of African Americans had become northern, urban, and industrial. Although employment discrimination was hardly eliminated, twice as many African Americans held skilled jobs at the end of the war as at the beginning.

For both men and women, the war brought higher wages and longer work hours. Although the government tried to limit wage increases during the war, overtime often raised paychecks. During the war, average weekly earnings for industrial workers rose nearly 70 percent. Farmers, who had suffered through many years of low prices and overproduction, doubled their income and then doubled it again.

THE LABOR FRONT

The scarcity of labor during the war substantially strengthened the union movement. Union membership rose by 50 percent. Although women and workers of color joined unions in unprecedented numbers, the main beneficiaries of labor's new clout were the white males who still comprised the bulk of union workers.

Especially on the national level, the commitment of organized labor to female workers was weak. Not a single woman served on the executive boards of either the American Federation of Labor (AFL) or the Congress of Industrial Organizations (CIO). The International Brotherhood of Teamsters even required women to sign a statement that their union membership could be revoked when the war was over. Unions did fight for contracts stipulating equal pay for men and women who worked in the same job, but these benefited women only as long as they held "male" jobs. The unions' primary purpose in advocating equal pay was to maintain wage levels for the men who would return to their jobs after the war. During the first year of peace, as employers trimmed their workforces, both businesses and unions gave special preference to returning veterans and worked to ease women and minority workers out of their wartime positions. Unions based their policies on seniority and their wage demands on the goal of securing male workers a "family wage," one sufficient to support an entire family.

Some union leaders feared that hiring traditionally lower-paid workers (women and minorities) would jeopardize the wage gains and recognition that unions had won during the hard-fought labor struggles of the 1930s. As growing numbers of African Americans were hired, racial tensions in the workplace increased. All across the country—at a defense plant in Lockland, Ohio; at a transit company in Philadelphia; at a shipbuilding company in Mobile—white workers walked off the job to protest the hiring of African Americans, fearing that management might use the war as an excuse to erode union power.

The labor militancy of the 1930s, although muted by a wartime no-strike pledge, persisted into the 1940s. Wildcat strikes erupted among St. Louis bus drivers, Detroit assembly-line workers, and Philadelphia streetcar conductors. In the Motor City, a group of aircraft workers, angry at the increasing regimentation of the production process, fanned out across a factory floor and cut off the neck ties worn by their supervisors. Despite the no-strike assurances, the United Mine Workers called a walkout in the bituminous coal fields in 1943. When the War Labor Board took a hard line against the union's demands, the strike was prolonged. The increasingly conservative Congress responded with the Smith-Connally Act of 1943, which empowered the president to seize plants or mines if strikes interrupted war production. Even so, the war helped to strengthen organized labor's place in American life.

Assessing Economic Change

Overall, the economic impact of the war proved substantial. Most workplaces became more inclusive, in terms of gender and race, than ever before. So did labor unions. More people entered the paid labor force, and many earned more money than rationing restrictions on consumer goods allowed them to spend. In a remarkable reversal of conditions during the Great Depression, jobs were plentiful and savings piled up.

More than anything else, the institutional scale of American life was transformed. Big government, big business, and big labor all grew even bigger during the war years. Science and technology forged new links of mutual interest among these three sectors. The old America of family farms, family-run businesses, and small towns did not disappear, but urban-based, bureaucratized institutions increasingly organized life in postwar America.

A New Role for Government?

The growth of governmental power during the war years prompted debates over the role of government in a postwar world. During the heyday of the New Deal, a broad view of governmentally guaranteed "security" had resulted in programs such as the Social Security System and federal agencies to secure home mortgages and personal savings accounts. At the same time, community-based groups and labor unions had begun to build a set of cooperative social welfare and health institutions they hoped would create a vast, nonprofit security-safety net.

As military victory began to seem likely, President Roosevelt and his advisers talked of harnessing the national government's power behind expanded efforts to enhance security in everyday life. Some dreamed of extending wartime health-care and day-care programs into a more comprehensive social welfare system.

In 1944 FDR introduced a "Second Bill of Rights" calling for measures to ensure that Americans could enjoy the "right" to a wide range of liberties, including regular employment, adequate food and shelter, appropriate educational opportunities, and guaranteed health care. Translating this vision into reality, its proponents generally assumed, would require the government to continue the kind of economic and social planning it was doing in wartime.

Large insurance companies, and some private businesses, recognizing the popularity of security-focused proposals, came forward with private alternatives to governmental programs. Insurers expanded earlier efforts to market their own programs, directed toward individual policyholders, for providing security against sickness, disability, and unexpected death. At the same time, insurance companies worked with large corporations to develop group insurance plans as substitutes, and also as supplements, for the kind of governmental programs already provided by the New Deal and imagined in the controversial Second Bill of Rights.

THE WAR AT HOME: SOCIAL ISSUES AND SOCIAL MOVEMENTS

Dramatic social changes accompanied the wartime mobilization. Many people, ordered by military service or attracted by employment, moved away from the communities where they had grown up. The war demanded sacrifice from all, and Americans willingly obliged. Yet, for many, wartime ideals also spotlighted everyday inequalities.

SELLING THE WAR

During the First World War, government propagandists had asked Americans to fight for a more democratic and peaceful world. Such idealistic goals, however, had little appeal for the skeptical generation that had witnessed the failures of Woodrow Wilson's promises. Sensitive to popular attitudes, the Roosevelt administration asked Americans to fight to preserve the "American way of life"—not to save the world.

Hollywood studios and directors eagerly answered the government's call. The film factory produced both commercial movies with military themes, such as *Destination Tokyo* (1943), and documentaries, such as the *Why We Fight* series, directed by Frank Capra. Capra contrasted Norman Rockwell-like characters with harrowing portrayals of the tightly regimented lifestyles in the military-dominated dictatorships of Germany, Italy, and Japan. Hollywood personalities sold war bonds, entertained the troops, and worked on documentaries for the Army's Pictorial Division.

The advertising industry also contributed. Roosevelt encouraged advertisers to sell the benefits of freedom. Most obliged, and "freedom" often appeared in the form of new washing machines, improved kitchen appliances, streamlined automobiles, a wider range of lipstick hues, and other consumer products. As soon as the fighting ended, wartime ads promised, technological know-how would transform the United States into a consumer's paradise.

In the spring of 1942 Roosevelt created the Office of War Information (OWI) to coordinate propaganda and censorship. Many New Deal Democrats saw it catering to advertisers who preferred imagery extolling the future joys of consumerism to ones promoting broader visions of liberty and equality. Republicans blasted the

Office of War Information, 1943. Courtesy, the American Legion Poster Collection

"Food is a Weapon." *This 1943 poster shows the Office of War Information skillfully extending its major theme: that the war was not a crusade to change the world but to preserve and protect what Americans already enjoyed. Employing ordinary words and everyday imagery, it suggests that people at home could assist the war by watching what they ate. Moreover, the poster's final directive suggests how the war made better nutrition both a personal and patriotic goal.*

agency for cranking out crass political appeals for causes favored by Roosevelt's New Dealers. Despite such criticism, the OWI established branch offices throughout the world, published a magazine called *Victory*, and produced hundreds of films, posters, and radio broadcasts.

GENDER ISSUES

The gap between Rockwell-type imagery and daily demands became apparent in the range of social issues affecting women.

The wartime United States called on women to serve their country as more than wives and mothers. Some 350,000 women volunteered for military duty during the war, and more than a thousand became pilots for the Women's Airforce Service Pilots (WASPs). Not everyone approved, but most in Congress supported a woman's corps in each branch of the military—an innovation proposed but never adopted during the First World War.

Even as the war narrowed gender differences in employment, widespread imagery frequently framed the changes as temporary. Women's expanded participation in the workplace was often portrayed as a temporary sacrifice intended, ultimately, to preserve and protect their "natural" sphere in the home. Stereotypes abounded. A typical ad suggesting that women take on farm work declared: "A woman can do anything if she knows she looks beautiful doing it."

In some ways, the war may have even widened the symbolic gap between notions of femininity and masculinity. Military culture fostered a "pin-up" mentality toward women. Tanks and planes were decorated with images of female sexuality, and the home-front entertainment industry, led by Hollywood, promoted its glamorous female stars as anxious to "please" their "boys" in the military. Wartime popular culture often associated masculinity with misogyny. After the war, tough-guy fiction, on display in Mickey Spillane's "Mike Hammer" series of detective novels, portrayed female sexuality as both alluring and threatening to men.

Public policymaking sometimes worked to reinforce gender divisions. The military assigned most of the women who joined the armed services to stateside clerical and supply jobs. Day care programs for mothers working outside their homes received reluctant and inadequate funding. The thousands of centers set up during the conflict filled only a fraction of the need and were swiftly shut down after the war. Meanwhile, social scientists oftentimes blamed mothers for an apparent spike in rates of juvenile delinquency and divorce during the war years.

RACIAL ISSUES

Messages about race were as ambiguous as those related to gender. Before the war, America had been a sharply segregated society. Disenfranchised in the South, African Americans in the rest of the country experimented with how best to use the

MUSICAL LINK TO THE PAST

SONGS OF THE SECOND WORLD WAR

Songwriter: Cole Porter
Title: "Don't Fence Me In" (1944)
Artist: Bing Crosby

Harry Lillis ("Bing") Crosby (1903–77) displayed musical talent at an early age, but his years at Gonzaga University during the 1920s set the stage for the multimedia stardom he would later enjoy, especially during the Second World War. College broadened Crosby's musical tastes; deepened his cultural literacy; and provided, as a student-musician, his introduction to show business. His academic education also far exceeded that of most other pop artists of his era. Dropping out of college during his senior year and abandoning plans to become a lawyer, Crosby joined up with band director Paul Whiteman and performed as a member of a vocal trio, the Rhythm Boys. Crosby struck out on his own in 1930.

Crosby's way of doing a song, which came to be called "crooning," departed from earlier styles. It modified the bombastic approaches of the blues "shouters," such as Bessie Smith, and the "belters," including Irish tenors such as John McCormick and vaudevillians such as Al Jolson. Crooners put over songs in a relaxed, sometimes conversational manner. Crosby was not the first to embrace crooning, but his attention to intonation, phrasing, and pacing distinguished him from others and provided a model for subsequent vocal stylists, including Frank Sinatra, Tony Bennett, and Peggy Lee. Crosby also seamlessly melded a wide range of musical influences, such as the "scat-singing" jazz vocals of Louis Armstrong, into his own singing. The bandleader-musical critic Artie Shaw later called Crosby "the first hip white person born in the United States."

During the Second World War, Crosby dominated the pop music industry, starred in motion pictures (winning the Academy Award for Best Actor in 1944), headlined a popular program on network radio, and tirelessly toured the European theater, entertaining U.S. troops. According to students of his more than 1,600 recordings, this demanding schedule took a toll on the suppleness of his voice. It also extended Crosby's range

of material and swelled his popularity. According to *Yank* magazine, service personnel ranked Crosby ahead of FDR and General Dwight D. Eisenhower as the person most responsible for maintaining their morale.

Crosby's war-year recordings spanned nearly the entire range of that era's diverse musical genres, especially those connected to the swing sound of the Big Bands, including the one led by his younger brother, Bob. Bing performed uptempo morale boosters, sentimental ballads, patriotic numbers, and the like; for his willingness to tackle novelty ditties, in German, he earned the affectionate title of "der Bingle." Bing Crosby's most memorable and bestselling songs of the war period—"White Christmas" (1942) and "I'll Be Home for Christmas" (1943)—seemingly spoke to a widespread hope that fighting the Second World War would ultimately allow military personnel and their families to re-embrace, during happier days to come, traditional values and practices.

Crosby's version of "Don't Fence Me In" (1944)—written by Cole Porter, one of the era's most sophisticated musical talents—goes in a somewhat different direction. It resembles the sound of western-swing bands (such as that of Bob Wills and the Texas Playboys). Roy Rogers, a singer-actor who starred in B-cowboy pictures, introduced the number in the 1943 motion picture *Stagedoor Canteen*. Another version by The Andrews Sisters, a trio known for their upbeat energy, reached the charts even before Crosby released a competing, ultimately better-selling rendition of the same song.

1. Can you hear Crosby's recording of "Don't Fence Me In" display not only his crooning but his ability to blend together, in the same number, different musical styles? What might some of these be?

2. Compare and contrast Crosby's version of "Don't Fence Me In" with his iconic renderings of "White Christmas" and "I'll Be Home for Christmas." How do these tunes seem to express, in different ways, wartime desires and hopes? How might the last-recorded of these three songs suggest a popular willingness to consider the possibility that war might do more than simply safeguard the "American Way of Life"? In what ways, though, might "Don't Fence Me In" seem entirely in synch with traditional American values?

CHAPTER 26

HISTORY THROUGH FILM

CASABLANCA (1942)

Directed by Michael Curtiz; starring Humphrey Bogart (Rick Blaine), Ingrid Bergman (Ilsa Lund), Paul Henreid (Victor Lazlo), Conrad Veidt (Major Strasser), Claude Rains (Captain Renault), and Dooley Wilson (Sam)

Casablanca began as a modest wartime collaboration between Warner Brothers and the OWI. The studio provided the stars, the script, and the crew. The OWI offered guidance on how best to portray the Allied cause. It successfully urged, for example, that the role of Sam, an African American piano man, be related more specifically to contemporary civil-rights issues.

Released at the same time that Allied forces were pursing their TORCH campaign in North Africa, in November 1942, *Casablanca* contains numerous references to the war. Most powerfully and pointedly, the film's own placement in cinematic time, December 1941, offers opportunities to disparage "isolationism." On several occasions, dialogue in the movie alludes to a real-life incident, the Japanese attack on Pearl Harbor, that will not happen until after *Casablanca's* own narrative timeframe ends. This technique (used in virtually every Hollywood film about familiar historical events) encourages viewers to take pride in their ability to spot historical references. Most important to *Casablanca's* political agenda, these allusions underscore its support for the necessity of U.S. involvement—and victory—in the Second World War.

More often, though, *Casablanca* conceals its political messages by entangling them in a set of personal dilemmas faced by its male lead, Rick Blaine, memorably played by Humphrey Bogart.

One of Classical Hollywood's most powerful motion pictures, Casablanca *(1943) highlighted the personal and political dilemmas raised by U.S. entry into the Second World War. Here, Rick (Humphrey Bogart), Ilsa (Ingrid Bergman), and Sam (Dooley Wilson) uneasily recall their past in prewar Paris and ponder their wartime futures.*

Everett Collection

Once an antifascist activist who had "run guns to Ethiopia" and fought against Franco in Spain, Rick now only wants to isolate himself from larger causes and preside over Rick's American Café in Casablanca. Remaining personally aloof from global politics, he watches refugees from fascism stream through this North African city on their way, they hope, to freedom in the United States. For mysterious reasons, Blaine himself cannot or will not return home.

There seems little mystery, however, about the root cause of Rick's personal isolationism: the beautiful Ilsa Lund, portrayed by Ingrid Bergman. Before the Nazis stormed into Paris in 1939, Rick and Ilsa had planned to flee the city together, but she deserted him at the train station. Only when Ilsa unexpectedly resurfaces, two years later in Casablanca, does Rick learn why she had abandoned him. As she was preparing to leave Paris, news arrived that her husband, Victor Lazlo, an antifascist crusader, had not perished, as she had thought, at the hands of the Nazis. Respecting her marriage vows, Ilsa had reluctantly forsaken Rick, rushed to the injured Victor, and nursed him back to health.

Trapped in Casablanca with a now-recovered Lazlo, Ilsa presents Rick with a series of personal and political dilemmas. She pleads with him, after her own husband's entreaties go unheeded, to help Victor escape to the United States, where he can resume his antifascist activism. As long as Lazlo stays in Casablanca—nominally under the legal control of Vichy France but effectively under the thumb of a murderous Nazi officer, Major Strasser—his political reputation presumably protects him from immediate danger. At the same time, though, Lazlo's continued presence in North Africa makes him of little value to the Allied cause, which the brooding Rick refuses to assist. Although Rick claims that his noninterventionist policy stems from a commitment to political neutrality, the movie makes clear that personal considerations dominate his politics: Lazlo will only leave Casablanca with Ilsa, whom Rick discovers remains as romantically attracted to him as he is to her.

Casablanca's script conveniently provides Rick with the means to help Ilsa and Lazlo—or Ilsa and himself—flee together: two blank "letters of transit," which have been hidden in Rick's Café. These documents, according to the movie's shaky legal logic, permit anyone, even Lazlo, to depart from Casablanca on the next plane flight. If Rick gives the letters to Lazlo, he stands to lose Ilsa for a second time and to compromise his noninterventionist political principles. If he uses the documents to flee Casablanca with Ilsa, he will harm the Allied cause by preventing Lazlo from actively rejoining it. Can Rick, once a heroic activist himself, continue to remain uninvolved? Is there any way he can reconcile the conflicting demands he now confronts?

Casablanca frames the fictional Rick Blaine's personal-political problems as symbolically parallel to those that the United States and its citizens faced before their own real-life entry into the Second World War. Seeing Humphrey Bogart make all the "correct" decisions, presumably, helped convince *Casablanca*'s wartime viewers that they and their political leaders had also made appropriate decisions. Watching *Casablanca* today, perhaps, helps convince viewers that people such as the fictional Rick Blaine really did make up America's "greatest generation."

political power they had gained during the 1930s. In California and throughout the Southwest, residents who traced their ancestry back to Mexico, including many who had long resided in the United States, worked to address a wide range of discriminatory policies in employment, education, and housing.

President Roosevelt refused to abandon the policy of segregation in the armed forces. Although the Army integrated Latino and American Indian soldiers, along with those from various European ethnic groups, into its combat units, military leaders refused to do the same for people of African and Japanese ancestry. The National Association for the Advancement of Colored People (NAACP) and others pressed for integration, but Roosevelt's top advisers remained opposed to change. The army even adopted the scientifically absurd practice of segregating donated blood into separate stores of "white" and "black" plasma. African Americans were relegated to inferior jobs and excluded from combat duty. Toward the end of the

UNITED WE WIN

"UNITED WE WIN." *Government posters created during the Second World War attempted to mute class and racial divisions and to offer images of all Americans united against fascism.*

war, when troop shortages forced the administration to put African American units into combat, they performed with distinction.

Meanwhile, on the home front, volatile social issues continued to simmer. As the wartime production system created more jobs, vast numbers of people from the rural South, including several hundred thousand African Americans, moved to cities such as Los Angles and Detroit. People already living in these areas often chafed at the influx of newcomers, who competed with them for jobs and housing and placed greater demands on public services such as transportation, education, and recreational facilities.

Social strains began to flare into violence. This escalation most often occurred in overcrowded urban spaces, where diverse populations and cultures already competed and clashed. In Detroit, in June 1943, conflict between white and black youth at an amusement park rapidly spiraled into a multiple-day riot. The violence left nearly 40 people, most of them African American, dead, injured hundreds, and inflicted millions of dollars worth of damage to property.

Racial disturbances were not restricted to confrontations between whites and blacks. In Los Angeles, the "Zoot Suit Riots" of 1943 erupted when soldiers and sailors from nearby military bases attacked young Mexican American and African American men wearing **zoot suits**—flamboyant outfits featuring oversized coats and trousers. Violence only escalated as the city's police force entered the fray, often beating and arresting Mexican Americans. A military order restricting servicemen to their bases finally helped quell the disorder.

Even when wartime tensions did not produce the kind of violence seen in Detroit and Los Angeles, the Second World War highlighted longstanding social issues. For many Native Americans, for instance, the wartime years increased the pressures associated with longer-term patterns of migration and assimilation. Approximately 25,000 Indian men and several hundred Indian women served in the armed forces. Tens of thousands of other Indian men and women, many leaving their reservations for the first time, found wartime work in urban areas. Many Indians moved back and forth between city and reservation, seeking to live in two significantly different worlds.

People of Japanese descent faced a unique situation. Shortly after the attack on Pearl Harbor, fear of sabotage by pro-Japanese residents engulfed West Coast communities. One military report claimed that a "large, unassimilated, tightly knit racial group, bound to an enemy nation by strong ties of race, culture, custom, and religion . . . constituted a menace" that justified extraordinary action.

zoot suits *Flamboyant outfits that featured oversized trousers; commonly worn by young Mexican-American men as a symbol of ethnic and cultural rebellion.*

internment *Removal of first- and second-generation Japanese-Americans into secured camps, a 1942 action then justified as a security measure but since deemed unjustified by evidence.*

Although lacking evidence of disloyalty, the president in February 1942 issued Executive Order 9066, directing the relocation and **internment** of first-and second-generation Japanese Americans (called Issei and Nisei, respectively) at inland camps. Significantly, in Hawaii, where the presumed danger of subversion should have been much greater, no such internment took place. There, people of Japanese ancestry constituted nearly 40 percent of the population and were essential to the economy.

Forced to abandon their possessions or sell them for a pittance, nearly 130,000 Japanese Americans were confined in flimsy barracks, enclosed by barbed wire and under armed guard. Two-thirds of the detainees were native-born U.S. citizens. Many left behind thriving agricultural enterprises vital to wartime production. In December 1944 a divided U.S. Supreme Court upheld the constitutionality of Japanese relocation in *Korematsu* v. *U.S.* (1944). In 1988 Congress officially apologized for the internment and authorized a cash indemnity for anyone who had been confined in the camps.

INTERNMENT. *Uniformed officials check the baggage of people of Japanese descent as they are being evacuated to internment camps.*

FDR Library

SOCIAL MOVEMENTS

The global fight against fascism proved helpful to movements that were working for social change in America. Nazism, based on the idea of racial inequality, exposed the racist underpinnings of older social-science research. The view that racial difference was not the result of biology but of culture gained wider acceptance during the war. The idea that a democracy could bridge racial differences provided a basis for the postwar struggle against discrimination.

Northward migration of African Americans accelerated demands for equality. Drawn by the promise of wartime jobs, nearly 750,000 African Americans relocated to northern cities, where many sensed the possibility of political power for the first time in their lives. They found an outspoken advocate of civil rights within the White House. First Lady Eleanor Roosevelt repeatedly antagonized southern Democrats and members of her husband's administration by her advocacy of civil rights and her participation in integrated social functions.

The *Amsterdam News*, a Harlem newspaper, called for a "Double V" campaign—victory at home as well as abroad. In January 1941 the labor leader A. Philip Randolph promised to lead tens of thousands of black workers in a march on Washington to demand more defense jobs and integration of the military forces. President Roosevelt feared the event would embarrass his administration and urged that it be canceled. Randolph's persistence ultimately forced Roosevelt to create the FEPC. Although this new agency gained little effective power, its very existence helped advance the ideal of nondiscrimination.

In California and throughout the Southwest during the war years, Latino organizations highlighted the irony of fighting overseas for a nation that denied equality at home and challenged the United States to live up to its democratic rhetoric. Approximately 500,000 Mexican Americans served, often with great distinction, in the military. Not wishing to anger this constituency, the Roosevelt administration, also feared harm to its Good Neighbor Policy in Latin America (see Chapter 25). The president's coordinator of Inter-American affairs allocated federal money to train Spanish-speaking workers for wartime employment, improve education in barrios, and provide high school graduates with new opportunities to enter college. Organizations such as the League of United Latin American Citizens (LULAC) mounted several drives against discrimination.

Particularly in urban areas, civil rights groups emerged from the wartime years with a strong base from which to fight for jobs and political power. Founded in 1942, the interracial Committee (later, Congress) on Racial Equality (CORE) devised new ways of opposing discrimination. CORE activists staged sit-ins to integrate restaurants, theaters, and other public facilities, especially in Washington, D.C.

People of Japanese descent, despite the internment, also laid the basis for postwar campaigns for equality. The courage and sacrifice of Japanese American soldiers became legendary. The 100th Battalion and the 442nd Regimental Combat Team, segregated units, suffered stunning casualties, often while undertaking extremely dangerous combat missions in Europe. In the Pacific theater, 6,000 members of the Military Intelligence Service provided invaluable service.

In the face of divisive issues and new social movements, wartime propaganda stressed national unity and contrasted America's "melting pot" ethos with German and Japanese obsessions about racial "purity." Wartime movies, plays, radio dramas, and music fostered a sense of national community by expressing pride in cultural diversity. As members of each of America's racial and ethnic groups distinguished themselves in the military, the claim of equality—"Americans All," in the words of a wartime slogan—took on greater moral force. Imagery extolling social solidarity and freedom provided a foundation for the antidiscrimination movements of the decades ahead.

SHAPING THE PEACE

FOCUS QUESTION
What major institutions and policies did the United States and the Allies adopt in their effort to shape the reconstruction of the postwar world?

Even before the war ended, U.S. policymakers began considering postwar peace arrangements. The Truman administration built on Roosevelt's wartime conferences and agreements to shape the framework of international relations for the next half-century.

INTERNATIONAL ORGANIZATIONS

In the Atlantic Charter of 1941, and at a conference in Moscow in October 1943, the Allied Powers had pledged to create a replacement for the defunct League of Nations. Internationalist-minded Americans saw the new United Nations (UN) offering a more realistic version of Woodrow Wilson's vision of the United States leading a world body that could deter aggressor nations and promote peaceful political change. At the Dumbarton Oaks Conference in Washington in August 1944, and at a subsequent meeting in San Francisco in April 1945, the Allies worked out the UN's organizational structure. It included a General Assembly, in which each member nation would be represented and cast one vote. A smaller body, the Security Council, would include five permanent members from the Allied Coalition—the United States, Great Britain, the Soviet Union, France, and Nationalist China—and six rotating members. The Security

Council would have primary responsibility for maintaining peace, but permanent members could veto any council decision. A UN Secretariat, headed by a Secretary General, would handle day-to-day business, and an Economic and Social Council would sponsor measures to improve living conditions throughout the world.

The U.S. Senate, with only two dissenting votes, approved joining the UN in July 1945. This victory for internationalism contrasted sharply with the Senate's 1919 rejection of membership in the League of Nations. Opponents of Wilson's dream had worried that internationalist policies might limit the ability of the United States to pursue its own national interests. Following the Second World War, however, a newly powerful United States appeared able to dominate international organizations such as the UN. It seemed unlikely that decisions by it or other international bodies could hamstring U.S. foreign policy. In addition, most U.S. leaders recognized that the war had partly resulted from the lack of a coordinated, international response to aggression during the 1930s.

Eleanor Roosevelt, the former first lady and a committed social activist, played a prominent role in building the new postwar internationalist ethos. A delegate to the first meeting of the UN's General Assembly, she chaired its Commission on Human Rights and guided the drafting of a Universal Declaration of Human Rights, adopted by the UN in 1948. The document set forth "inalienable" human rights and freedoms as cornerstones of international law.

Economic agreements also illustrated a growing acceptance of international organizations. At the Bretton Woods (New Hampshire) Conference of 1944, assembled nations created the International Monetary Fund (IMF), which was designed to maintain stable exchange by ensuring that each nation's currency could be converted into any other national currency at a fixed rate. The U.S. dollar, initially pegged at a value of $32 dollars for an ounce of gold, would provide the lynchpin. Exchange rates could be altered only with the agreement of the IMF.

The International Bank for Reconstruction and Development, later renamed the World Bank, was also created to provide loans to war-battered countries and promote the resumption of world trade. In 1948 the General Agreement on Tariffs and Trade (GATT) established the institutional groundwork for breaking up closed trading blocs and implementing free and fair trade agreements.

SPHERES OF INTEREST AND POSTWAR SETTLEMENTS

In wartime negotiations, Stalin, Churchill, and Roosevelt all had assumed that powerful nations—their own—would enjoy special "spheres of influence" in the postwar world. As early as January 1942 the Soviet ambassador to the United States reported to Stalin that Roosevelt had tacitly assented to Soviet postwar control over the Baltic states of Lithuania, Latvia, and Estonia. In 1944 Stalin and Churchill agreed, informally and secretly, that Britain would continue its sway over Greece and that the Soviets could control Romania and Bulgaria. U.S. leaders, meanwhile, assumed that Latin America would remain within their sphere of influence. Roosevelt sometimes seemed to imply that he accepted Stalin's goal of having states friendly to the USSR on his vulnerable western border, but at the Tehran Conference of November 1943 he also told Stalin that U.S. voters of Eastern European descent expected their homelands to be independent after the war.

Historians continue to differ on precisely how Roosevelt might have intended to reconcile his contradictory positions on the postwar Soviet sphere of influence. As long as the Soviet military remained essential to Germany's defeat—and Roosevelt also wanted the USSR to join the war against Japan—the president struck a conciliatory tone with Stalin. After Roosevelt's death, however, the Soviets' powerful position in Eastern Europe became a focus of bipolar tensions.

Early in the war, both nations had urged the dismemberment and deindustrialization of a defeated Nazi Germany. At a conference held at Yalta, in Ukraine, in February 1945, the three Allied powers agreed to divide Germany into four zones of occupation (with France as the fourth occupying force). Later, as relations among the victors worsened, this temporary division of Germany hardened into a Soviet-dominated zone in the East and the other three zones to its west. Berlin, the German capital, also was divided, even though the city itself lay totally within the Soviet zone.

Postwar differences also involved Poland. At Yalta, the Soviets agreed to permit free elections in postwar Poland and to create a government "responsible to the will of the people," but Stalin believed that the other Allied leaders had tacitly accepted Soviet dominance over Poland. The agreement at Yalta was ambiguous at best. The war was still at a critical stage, and the western Allies chose to sacrifice clarity in order to encourage cooperation with the Soviets. After Yalta, the Soviets assumed that Poland would be in their sphere of influence, but many Americans charged the Soviets with bad faith for failing to hold free elections and for not relinquishing control.

In Asia, military realities likewise influenced postwar settlements. At Tehran in November 1943 and again at Yalta, Stalin pledged to send troops to Asia as soon as Germany surrendered. The first U.S. atomic bomb fell on Hiroshima, however, just one day before the Soviets were to enter the Pacific Theater of the war, and the United States assumed total charge of the occupation and postwar reorganization of Japan. The Soviet Union and the United States divided Korea, which had been controlled by Japan, into separate zones of occupation. Here, as in Germany, these zones would later emerge as two antagonistic states (see Chapter 27).

The fate of the European colonies seized by Japan in Southeast Asia was another contentious issue. Most U.S. officials preferred to see the former British and French colonies become independent nations, but they also worried about the left-leaning politics of many anticolonial nationalist movements. As the United States developed an anticommunist foreign policy, it moved to support British and French efforts to reassemble their colonial empires.

In the Philippines, the United States honored its longstanding pledge to grant independence. A friendly government that agreed to respect American economic interests and military bases took power in 1946 and enlisted American advisers to help suppress leftist rebels. In 1947 the United Nations designated the Mariana, Caroline, and Marshall Islands as the "Trust Territories of the Pacific" and authorized the United States to administer their affairs.

Although the nations of Latin America had been only indirectly involved in military conflict and peace negotiations, the war directly affected U.S. relations with them. During the 1930s the Roosevelt administration's Good Neighbor Policy had helped improve U.S.–Latin American relations. The Office of Inter-American Affairs (OIAA), created in 1937, further expanded cultural and economic ties. After the German invasion of Poland in 1939, Latin American leaders stood nearly united behind the Allies. After U.S. entry into the war, at a conference in Rio de Janeiro in January 1942, every Latin American country except Chile and Argentina broke diplomatic ties with the Axis governments. When naval warfare in the Atlantic severed commercial connections between Latin America and Europe, Latin American countries became critical suppliers of raw materials to the United States.

Wartime conferences avoided clear decisions about creating a Jewish homeland in the Middle East. The Second World War prompted survivors of the Holocaust and Jews from around the world to take direct action. **Zionism**, the movement to found a Jewish state in Palestine, the ancient homeland of Jewish people, attracted thousands of Jews to the Middle East. They began to carve out, against the wishes of Palestinians and other Arab people, the new nation of Israel.

Zionism *Movement to establish a Jewish state in Palestine.*

C O N C L U S I O N

The world changed dramatically during the Second World War. For the United States, wartime mobilization ended the Great Depression and focused most of the government's attention on international concerns. The war brought victory over dictatorial, expansionist regimes, and the United States emerged as the world's preeminent power.

At home, a more powerful national government, concerned with preserving national security, assumed nearly complete power over the economy. New, cooperative ties were forged among government, business, and scientific researchers. These sectors worked together to provide the seemingly miraculous growth in productivity that ultimately won the war.

The early 1940s sharpened debates over liberty and equality. Many Americans saw the Second World War as a struggle to protect and preserve the liberties they already enjoyed. Others, inspired by a struggle against racism and injustice abroad, insisted that a war for freedom abroad should help secure equal rights at home.

News of Japan's 1945 surrender prompted joyous celebrations throughout the United States. Still, Americans remained uncertain about postwar reconstruction policies and about future relations with their wartime ally, the Soviet Union. Domestically, the wrenching dislocations of war took their toll. And, of course, the nation now faced the future without the charismatic leadership of Franklin D. Roosevelt.

QUESTIONS FOR REVIEW AND CRITICAL THINKING

Review

1. How did events in Asia and in Europe affect debate within the United States over whether or not to embrace more interventionist policies overseas?
2. What military strategies did the United States and the Allies ultimately adopt when fighting in both the European and Asian theaters of the Second World War?
3. How did mobilizing for war produce political, economic, and social changes in the United States?
4. What major institutions and policies did the United States and the Allies adopt in their effort to shape the reconstruction of the postwar world?

Critical Thinking

1. In what ways had the United States already moved, even before the attack on Pearl Harbor, toward intervention in the Second World War?
2. How did Franklin Roosevelt's domestic policies during the Second World War both fulfill and retreat from the aspirations of his New Deal?

ONLINE RESOURCES

 Visit the companion website to access flashcards, crossword puzzles, exercises, and quizzes related to this chapter: www.cengage.com/history/murrin/libertyequalconc5e.

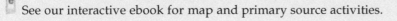

See our interactive ebook for map and primary source activities.

ᴅISCOVERY

How did World War II affect citizens both in America and elsewhere, thus making it a true "total" war?

WARFARE Examine the destruction to the cities of Dresden and Hiroshima shown in these photos. Were these areas densely populated? From your examination of these photos and your reading in this chapter, what observations can you make about how World War II impacted civilians? Do you think civilians had become a bigger target in the Second World War than they had been in the First? If so, why?

ECONOMICS, TECHNOLOGY, AND SOCIETY Compare the images on pages 708, 709, and 716. Do they suggest that war overcame traditional prejudices about the role of women and racial minorities in the workplace? What does the second picture suggest about the economic role of children in the Second World War? What caused these changes to occur? What fears might these changes have created within society? What does the "United We Win" poster convey about the effects of the war on racial divisions? Did wartime attitudes and changes have lasting effects on gender roles and race relations in the country?

In thinking about this question, begin by breaking it down into the components shown below. A discussion of the significance of each component should appear in your answer.

TOTAL WAR: DRESDEN AND HIROSHIMA

27

THE AGE OF CONTAINMENT, 1946–1953

The Second World War, portrayed as a struggle to preserve the "American way of life," ended up transforming it. The fight against fascism had propelled foreign-policy issues to the center of domestic politics, and postwar international tensions kept them there. As the Second World War gave way to a Cold War between the United States and the Soviet Union, U.S. leaders overhauled military strategy. They claimed a broad authority for the nation's commander in chief and called for a global stand against communism. An aggressive campaign to shore up "national security" came to affect many areas of domestic life.

The Cold War years, between 1946 and 1953, raised questions about governmental power. What role should Washington play in the postwar economy? Could a more powerful national government help people enjoy greater "security" in their own lives? How might such a government affect liberty and equality? Debate over these issues marked the presidency of Democrat Harry Truman (1945–1953), who struggled to implement his anticommunist agenda and to define his Fair Deal programs.

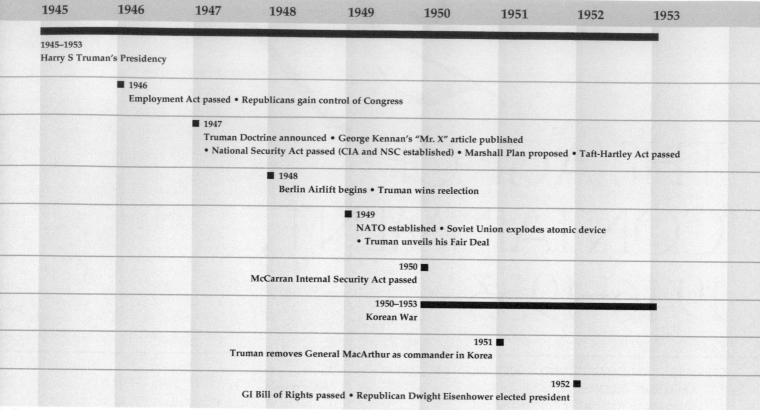

1945–1953
Harry S Truman's Presidency

■ **1946**
Employment Act passed • Republicans gain control of Congress

■ **1947**
Truman Doctrine announced • George Kennan's "Mr. X" article published
• National Security Act passed (CIA and NSC established) • Marshall Plan proposed • Taft-Hartley Act passed

■ **1948**
Berlin Airlift begins • Truman wins reelection

■ **1949**
NATO established • Soviet Union explodes atomic device
• Truman unveils his Fair Deal

1950 ■
McCarran Internal Security Act passed

1950–1953
Korean War

1951 ■
Truman removes General MacArthur as commander in Korea

1952 ■
GI Bill of Rights passed • Republican Dwight Eisenhower elected president

CREATING A NATIONAL SECURITY STATE, 1945–1949

FOCUS QUESTION

What major conflicts between the United States and the Soviet Union shaped the Cold War, and what were the principal elements of the foreign policy called containment?

Cold War *The political, military, cultural, and economic rivalry between the United States and the Soviet Union that developed after the Second World War and lasted until the disintegration of the Soviet State after 1989.*

The wartime alliance between the United States and the Soviet Union proved little more than a marriage of convenience. Defeating the Axis had forced these two nations to cooperate, but collaboration scarcely lasted beyond victory. Relations between the two deteriorated into a **Cold War** of suspicion and tension.

ONSET OF THE COLD WAR

Historians have dissected the beginning of the Cold War from many perspectives. The traditional interpretation focuses on Soviet expansionism, stressing a historical Russian appetite for new territory, an ideological zeal to spread communism, or some interplay between the two. According to this view, the United States needed to take as hard a line as possible. Other historians—generally called revisionists— argue that the Soviet Union's obsession with securing its borders was an understandable response to the invasion of its territory during both world wars. The United States, in this view, should have tried to reassure the USSR, pursing conciliatory policies instead of ones that intensified Soviet fears. Still other scholars maintain that assigning blame obscures how clashing interests and different political cultures made postwar tensions between the two superpowers inevitable.

In any view, Harry Truman's role was central. Truman initially hoped that he could somehow deal with Soviet Premier Joseph Stalin. As differences between the former allies emerged, however, Truman turned to his more hard-line advisers.

The atomic bomb provided an immediate source of friction. At the Potsdam Conference of July 1945, Truman had casually told Stalin, without mentioning the atomic bomb, about a new U.S. weapon of "unusual destructive force." Well informed by Soviet intelligence operations about the Manhattan Project, Stalin ordered his scientists to intensify the Soviet Union's own nuclear weapons program. Truman likely hoped that the bomb would scare the Soviets, and it did. Historians debate whether it frightened the Soviets into more cautious behavior or made them more aggressive.

As atomic warfare against Japan gave way to atomic diplomacy with the Soviet Union, U.S. leaders clashed among themselves over how to proceed. One group, predicting the Soviets would soon possess their own atomic weapons, urged Truman to share technology with the USSR in hopes of forestalling a nuclear arms race. Hard-liners, fearing Soviet intentions and doubting their nuclear knowledge, rejected this approach.

In 1946 Truman authorized Bernard Baruch, a special representative at the United Nations, to explore ways of controlling, rather than sharing, atomic power. The Baruch Plan proposed that the United States would abandon its nuclear weapons if the USSR met certain conditions. The Soviets would have to agree to a process for outside monitoring and verification of their atomic energy program and to surrender veto power in the UN in cases regarding nuclear issues. Soviet leaders, rejecting the Baruch Plan, counter-proposed that the United States destroy its atomic weapons as the first step toward any final bargain. The United States rejected this idea. Both nations used the deadlock to justify a stepped-up arms race.

Other sources of friction involved U.S. loan policies and Soviet domination of Eastern Europe. Truman ended lend-lease assistance to the Soviet Union at the end of the war and linked future reconstruction loans to Soviet cooperation with the United States over the future of Europe. This linkage strategy never worked. Lack of capital and suspicions about Western intentions provided the Soviets with excuses for an aggressive, hard-line stance. A Soviet sphere of influence in Eastern Europe, which Stalin called defensive and Truman labeled expansionist, solidified. By 1946, the former allies seemed ready to become bitter adversaries.

Truman pledged to stop the campaign of communist expansionism he claimed Moscow directed. Truman's anticommunist initiatives, in both foreign and domestic affairs, extended the reach and power of the executive branch.

Containment Abroad: The Truman Doctrine

In March 1947, the president announced what became known as the Truman Doctrine in a speech to Congress about the civil war in Greece, where communist-led insurgents appeared ready to topple a pro-Western government. Truman's advisers claimed that a leftist victory in Greece would expose Turkey, a nation considered critical to the U.S. strategic position, to Soviet expansionism. Seeking to justify U.S. aid to Greece and Turkey, Truman asserted that U.S. security interests now spanned the globe, and the fate of "free peoples" everywhere hung in the balance. Unless the United States aided those who were "resisting attempted subversion by armed minorities or by outside pressures," totalitarian communism would spread and, ultimately, threaten the United States itself.

The Truman Doctrine's global vision of national security encountered some skepticism. Henry Wallace, the most visible Democratic critic, chided Truman for exaggerating the Soviet threat. Conservative Republicans were suspicious of the increase of executive power and the vast expenditures the Truman Doctrine seemed to imply. If Truman wanted to win support for his position, Republican Senator Arthur Vandenberg had already advised, he should "scare hell" out of people, something Truman proved quite willing to do. With backing from both Republicans and Democrats, Congress approved Truman's request for $400 million in assistance to Greece and Turkey, most of it for military aid, in the spring of 1947. This vote signaled broad, bipartisan support for a national security policy that came to be called **containment.**

The term containment first appeared in a 1947 article in the journal *Foreign Affairs* by George Kennan, the State Department's premier Soviet expert. Writing under the pseudonym "X," Kennan argued that the "main element" in any U.S. policy "must be that of a long-term, patient but firm and vigilant containment of Russian expansive tendencies." The article quickly became associated with the urgent tone of the Truman Doctrine.

Containment thus became a catchphrase for a global, anticommunist national security policy. In the popular view, containment linked all leftist insurgencies, wherever they occurred, to a **totalitarian movement** controlled from Moscow that directly threatened the United States. Even a small gain by the Soviets in one part of the globe would, in this view, encourage them to extend their aggressive initiatives. Although foreign policy debates regularly included sharp disagreements over how to pursue containment, few Americans questioned the need for a global and activist foreign policy.

TRUMAN'S LOYALTY PROGRAM

Nine days after proclaiming the Truman Doctrine, the president issued Executive Order 9835. It called for a system of loyalty boards empowered to determine if there were "reasonable grounds" for concluding that any government employee belonged to an organization or held political ideas that might pose a "security risk" to the United States. People judged to be security risks would lose their government jobs. The loyalty program also authorized the attorney general's office to identify organizations it deemed **subversive** and place them on a special Attorney General's List.

The Truman Loyalty Program rested on its assessment of Soviet espionage activity in the United States. Although few people ever doubted that Soviets were conducting spy operations in the United States during the 1940s, sharp disagreement has persisted regarding their scope and threat. Such debates now take place in light of recently declassified evidence from communist archives and U.S. surveillance agencies' files indicating that both nations engaged in a wide range of spying activities. By 1943, for instance, a super-secret Army counterintelligence unit had begun intercepting transmissions between Moscow and the United States. Called the VENONA files and finally released in 1995, these intercepted messages showed that the USSR had helped finance America's Communist Party; placed informants in governmental agencies; and begun obtaining secret information about U.S. atomic work as early as 1944. The issue of Soviet espionage, in short, was a legitimate concern. Still, historians remain divided over the significance and reliability of specific pieces of the VENONA evidence.

There is little doubt, though, that the case Truman made on behalf of his loyalty policy failed to satisfy a diverse group of critics. The president justified the program by claiming that the United States faced relatively few security risks but that their potential to do harm demanded a response unprecedented in peacetime. Truman's position, however, angered both fervent anticommunists, who accused the

containment *Label used to describe the global anticommunist national security policies adopted by the United States to stop the expansion of communism during the late 1940s.*

totalitarian movement *Movement in which the individual is subordinated to the state and all areas of life are subjected to centralized, total control— usually by force*

subversive *Systematic, deliberate attempt to overthrow or undermine a government or society by people working secretly within the country.*

MARSHALL PLAN. *This poster, by an artist from the Netherlands, was the winning entry in a contest run in Marshall Plan countries. It suggests how the plan encouraged a united Europe to transcend the divisions that had led to two world wars.*

·ALL OUR COLOURS TO THE MAST·

president of doing too little to fight subversion at home, and civil libertarians, who charged him with whipping up fears that far exaggerated any actual threat.

THE NATIONAL SECURITY ACT, THE MARSHALL PLAN, AND THE BERLIN CRISIS

Shaking off criticism, the Truman administration pursued its anticommunist initiatives. The **National Security Act** of 1947 created several new bureaucracies. The old Navy and War Departments were transformed, by 1949, into a unified Department of Defense. Another new arm of the executive branch, the National Security Council, was given broad authority over planning foreign policy. The Air Force was established as a separate service equal to the Army and Navy. Finally, the act created the Central Intelligence Agency (CIA) to gather information and conduct covert activities. The CIA proved to be the most flexible arm of the national security bureaucracy. Shrouded from public scrutiny, its secret operations crisscrossed the globe. The CIA cultivated ties with anti-Soviet groups in Eastern Europe and within the Soviet Union. It helped finance pro-U.S. labor unions in Western Europe to curtail the influence of leftist organizations. It orchestrated covert campaigns to prevent the Italian Communist Party from winning an electoral victory in 1948 and to bolster anticommunist parties in France, Japan, and elsewhere.

Truman's White House also linked its economic policies in Western Europe to the doctrine of containment. Concerned that Western Europe's economic problems might benefit communist movements, Secretary of State George C. Marshall sought to strengthen the region's economies. Under his 1947 plan, funds provided by the United States would allow governments in Western Europe to coordinate a broad program of postwar economic reconstruction. Between 1946 and 1951, the United States provided nearly $13 billion in assistance to 17 Western European nations.

The **Marshall Plan**, enacted by Congress in early 1948, proved a success. The plan helped brighten the economic scene in Western Europe, where industrial production quickly rebounded. Improved standards of living enhanced political stability and helped undermine the appeal of communist-led movements. When conservatives called it a "giveaway" program, supporters emphasized how it expanded both markets and investment opportunities for American businesses.

U.S. policymakers viewed the future of postwar Germany, initially divided into four zones of occupation, as crucial to the security of Western Europe. In June 1948, the United States, Great Britain, and France announced a currency-reform program as the first step toward integrating their separate sectors into the Federal Republic of Germany or West Germany. Soviet leaders expressed alarm. Having twice been invaded by Germany during the preceding 35 years, they wanted that country reunited but weak. Hoping to sidetrack Western plans, in June 1948 the Soviets cut off all highways, railroads, and water routes linking West Berlin, which was located within their zone, to West Germany.

National Security Act (1947) *Reorganized the U.S. military forces within a new Department of Defense, and established the National Security Council and the Central Intelligence Agency.*

Marshall Plan *Plan of U.S. aid to Europe that aimed to contain communism by fostering postwar economic recovery. Proposed by Secretary of State George C. Marshall in 1947, it was known formally as the European Recovery Program.*

This Soviet blockade of Berlin failed. American and British pilots, in what became known as the Berlin Airlift, delivered virtually all of the items Berliners needed to continue their daily routines. Truman, hinting at a military response, sent two squadrons of B-29 bombers to Britain. Stalin abandoned the blockade in May 1949, and the Soviets then created the German Democratic Republic out of their East German sector. West Berlin survived as an enclave inside East Germany but tied to the West.

THE ELECTION OF 1948

National security issues helped Harry Truman win the 1948 election, a victory that capped a remarkable political comeback. Truman had been losing the support of those Democrats, led by his secretary of commerce, Henry A. Wallace, who thought his containment policies too militant. After Wallace continued to criticize U.S. policy toward the Soviet Union, Truman ousted him from the cabinet. Two months later, in the off-year national elections of November 1946, voters had given the Republicans control of Congress for the first time since 1928. Although Truman's political fortunes seemed somewhat improved by late 1947, few political handicappers liked his chances in 1948. Challenged from the left by a new Progressive Party, which nominated Wallace, and from the right by both Thomas E. Dewey, the Republican nominee, and Strom Thurmond, the pro-segregationist candidate of the new States' Rights Party, or Dixiecrats, Truman waged a vigorous campaign. He called the GOP-controlled Congress into special session, presented it with domestic policy proposals abhorrent to most Republicans, and then denounced "that do-nothing, good-for-nothing, worst Congress."

Dewey aided Truman's cause by running an exceedingly cautious campaign. A pro-Democratic newspaper caricatured Dewey's standard speech as four "historic sentences: Agriculture is important. Our rivers are full of fish. You cannot have freedom without liberty. The future lies ahead." By contrast, Truman mounted an energetic, tub-thumping campaign. It featured blunt and caustic attacks on his opponents, most famously delivered from the back of his own campaign train. Dewey was plotting "a real hatchet job on the New Deal," he charged, and the GOP, controlled by a cabal of "cunning men," was preparing for "a return of the Wall Street economic dictatorship." "Give 'em hell, Harry!" shouted his supporters. In November, Truman won just under 50 percent of the popular vote but secured a solid majority in the electoral college. Democrats also regained control of Congress.

Truman's victory now seems less surprising to historians than it did to analysts in 1948. Despite Republican victories in the 1946 congressional elections, the Democratic Party was hardly enfeebled. The Democratic congressional candidates who identified themselves with Franklin Roosevelt rather than with Truman generally polled a higher percentage of the vote in their districts than did Truman. Voter loyalty to the memory of Roosevelt and his New Deal coalition helped bring the Democrats their victory.

After accepting his party's call for new civil rights measures, Truman survived the revolt of the Dixiecrats, whose candidate, Strom Thurmond, denounced Truman for backing a "civil wrongs" program and charged that "radicals, subversives, and reds" now

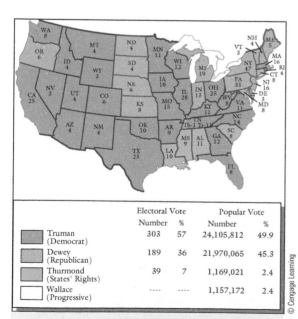

	Electoral Vote		Popular Vote	
	Number	%	Number	%
Truman (Democrat)	303	57	24,105,812	49.9
Dewey (Republican)	189	36	21,970,065	45.3
Thurmond (States' Rights)	39	7	1,169,021	2.4
Wallace (Progressive)	----	----	1,157,172	2.4

© Cengage Learning

Map 27.1 **PRESIDENTIAL ELECTION, 1948.** *This electoral map shows how, in this close election, Truman won the presidency despite gaining less than 50 percent of the popular vote.*

controlled the Democratic Party. The Dixiecrat movement did portend political changes among Southern whites, who had loyally voted Democratic since the late 19th century. In 1948, however, Truman carried all but four states of the old Confederacy.

Truman's hard-line anticommunist rhetoric proved crucial to sidetracking Henry Wallace. Hampered by the Progressive Party's refusal to reject support from the U.S. Communist Party, Wallace received less than 3 percent of the popular tally and no electoral votes. The 1948 election suggested a lesson for elections to come: Successful presidential candidates could never appear "soft" on national security issues.

THE ERA OF THE KOREAN WAR, 1949–1952

To carry out his containment policy, Truman marshaled the nation's economic and military resources. A series of Cold War crises in 1949 and the outbreak of war on the Korean peninsula heightened anticommunist fervor.

NATO, CHINA, AND THE BOMB

In April 1949 the United States, Canada, and 10 European nations formed the **North Atlantic Treaty Organization (NATO)**. They pledged that an attack against one would automatically be treated as a strike against all. Republican Senator Robert Taft called NATO a provocation to the Soviet Union, an "entangling alliance" that violated traditional U.S. foreign policy, and a threat to Congress's constitutional power to declare war. Still, the NATO concept prevailed, and the idea of pursuing containment through such "mutual defense" pacts expanded during the 1950s.

Meanwhile, events in China heightened Cold War tensions. Although the United States had extended Jiang Jieshi's incompetent National government billions in military aid and economic assistance, Jiang had steadily lost ground to the forces of Mao Zedong. Experienced U.S. diplomats privately predicted Jiang's downfall, but the Truman administration continued publicly to portray Jiang as the respected leader of "free China."

In 1949, when Mao's armies forced Jiang off the mainland to the nearby island of Formosa (Taiwan), many Americans wondered how communist forces could have triumphed. Financed by conservative business leaders, the powerful "China lobby" excoriated Truman and his new secretary of state, Dean Acheson, for having "lost" China to the communists. New international tensions and domestic political pressures ultimately convinced the Truman administration to embrace Jiang's regime on Taiwan. For more than 20 years, even after the friction between China and the Soviet Union became evident, the United States refused to recognize or deal with Mao's "Red China."

The communist threat seemed even more alarming when, in 1949, the Soviets exploded a crude atomic device, marking the end of the U.S. nuclear monopoly. Already besieged by critics who saw a world filled with Soviet gains and U.S. losses, Truman authorized the development of a new and far more deadly weapon, the hydrogen bomb.

North Atlantic Treaty Organization (NATO)
Established by treaty in 1949 to provide for the collective defense of noncommunist European and North American nations against possible aggression from the Soviet Union and to encourage political, economic, and social cooperation.

The cold war split Europe into two opposing alliances. Germany was divided into two countries: The Federal Republic of Germany (West Germany) and the German Democratic Republic (East Germany). Berlin, the former capital of Germany, was also divided. In 1949 NATO was formed, and in 1955 the Warsaw Pact came into existence.

THE DIVISION OF BERLIN

- American Zone
- British Zone
- French Zone
- Soviet Zone

(The American, British, and French zones were consolidated as West Berlin)

- NATO Countries
- Warsaw Pact Countries
- Nonaligned Countries

© Cengage Learning

Map 27.2 DIVIDED GERMANY AND THE NATO ALLIANCE. *This map shows the geopolitics of the Cold War. Which countries aligned with the United States through NATO? Which aligned with the Soviet Union through the Warsaw Pact? Note how Berlin became a divided city, although it was located within East Germany.*

NSC-68 AND THE KOREAN WAR

NSC-68 *National Security Council Document number 68 (1950) that provided the rationale and comprehensive strategic vision for U.S. policy during the Cold War.*

Prompted by events of 1949, the Truman administration reviewed its foreign policy assumptions. The task of conducting this review fell to Paul Nitze, who produced a policy paper identified as **NSC-68** (National Security Council Document 68). It opened with an alarming account of a global ideological clash between "freedom," spread by U.S. power, and "slavery," promoted by the Soviet Union, the center of an international communist movement. Despairing of fruitful negotiations with the Soviets, NSC-68 urged a full-scale effort to enlarge U.S. power. It endorsed covert action, economic pressure, propaganda campaigns, and a massive military buildup. Because Americans might oppose larger military spending and budget deficits, the report cautioned, U.S. actions should be labeled as "defensive" and be presented as a stimulus to the economy rather than as a drain on national resources.

The dire warnings of NSC-68 seemed to be confirmed in June 1950 when communist North Korea invaded South Korea. Truman characterized the attack as a simple case of Soviet-inspired aggression against a free state and invoked the rhetoric of containment: "If aggression is successful in Korea, we can expect it to spread through Asia and Europe to this hemisphere." The Korean situation, however, defied such simplistic analysis. Japanese military forces had occupied Korea between 1905 and 1945, and after Japan's defeat in the Second World War, Koreans had expected to reestablish their own independent nation. Instead, the Soviet and U.S. zones of occupation resulting from the war became two states, split at the 38th parallel. The Soviet Union supported North Korea's communist government, headed by the dictatorial Kim Il-sung. The United States backed Syngman Rhee to head an unsteady and autocratic government in South Korea.

On June 25, 1950, after consulting with Soviet and Chinese leaders and receiving their approval, Kim moved troops across the 38th parallel to attempt unification. Rhee appealed to the United States for military assistance.

The situation in Korea escalated into an international conflict. The Soviets, unaware of the details of Kim's plans, were boycotting the UN on the day the invasion was launched and could not veto a U.S. proposal to send a UN peacekeeping force to Korea. Under UN auspices, the United States rushed assistance to Rhee, who moved to quell dissent in the South as well as to repel the armies of the North.

U.S. goals in Korea were unclear. Should the United States seek to contain communism by driving North Korea's forces back over the 38th parallel? Or should it try to reunify Korea under Rhee's leadership? This option seemed somewhat fanciful when North Korean forces pushed rapidly southward. Within three months, they took Seoul, the capital of South Korea, and reached the southern tip of the Korean Peninsula. UN troops, most of them from the United States, seemed unprepared. American firepower, however, gradually took its toll on North Korea's elite troops and on the untrained recruits sent to replace them.

General Douglas MacArthur then devised a plan that most other commanders considered crazy: an amphibious landing behind enemy lines. Those stunned by his audacious proposal were even more astounded by its results. On September 15, 1950, Marines landed at Inchon, suffered minimal casualties, and recaptured Seoul in less than two weeks.

The shifting tide of battle devastated Korea. The **Korean War** was called a "limited" war because it never spread off the Korean Peninsula or involved nuclear weapons, but intense bombing preceded every military move, and neither side seemed concerned about civilian casualties. The number of estimated dead and wounded reached perhaps one tenth of Korea's total population. As rival armies battled for control of Seoul, the city became rubble, with only the capitol building and a train station left standing.

As MacArthur's troops drove northward, Truman faced a crucial decision. Emboldened by success, MacArthur urged moving beyond containment to an all-out war of "liberation" and reunification. Other advisers warned that China would retaliate if U.S. forces approached its border. Truman allowed MacArthur to carry the war into the North but cautioned against provoking China.

General Douglas MacArthur *Supreme commander of Allied forces in the southwest Pacific during the Second World War; leader of the occupation forces in the reconstruction of Japan; and head of UN forces during the Korean War.*

Korean War *Conflict lasting from 1950 to 1953 between communist North Korea, aided by China, and South Korea, aided by UN forces consisting primarily of U.S. troops.*

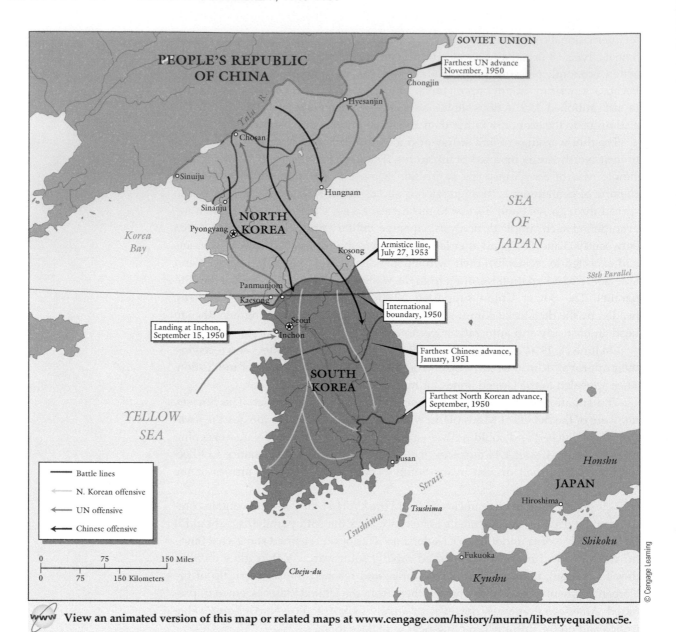

Map 27.3 KOREAN WAR. *This map shows the lines of battle and the armistice line that still divides the two Koreas. Note the advances made first by North Korea and then by UN (United States–led) troops.*

MacArthur pushed too far, advancing toward the Chinese–Korean border. China responded by sending troops into North Korea and driving MacArthur back across the 38th parallel. With China now in the war, Truman pondered his options. When MacArthur's troops regained the initiative, Truman ordered the general to negotiate a truce at the 38th parallel. MacArthur, challenging the president, argued publicly for all-out victory over North Korea—and over China, too. Truman thereupon relieved MacArthur from his post in April 1951, pointing out that the Constitution made military officers subordinate to the president, the nation's commander in chief.

MacArthur returned home a war hero. Opinion polls reported overwhelming opposition to Truman's decision to dump the popular general. Yet during Senate hearings on MacArthur's dismissal, other military strategists dismissed his scenario for Korea as the "wrong war in the wrong place." MacArthur's once luminous image, along with his political ambitions, soon faded.

Truman now set out to arrange a peace settlement for Korea. As negotiations stalled, another military hero, Dwight Eisenhower, the Republican candidate for president in 1952, promised to go to Korea, if elected, and accelerate the peace process. Harry Truman would leave office in 1953 without securing a formal end to the Korean War.

KOREA AND CONTAINMENT

The Korean War, by seeming to justify the global anticommunist offensive that NSC-68 had recommended, spurred the Truman administration to expand its containment initiatives. It announced plans to rearm West Germany, scarcely five years after Germany's defeat, and to increase NATO's military forces. A proposal for direct military aid to Latin American governments, which had been rejected in the past, slid through Congress. In the Philippines, the United States stepped up military assistance to suppress the leftist Huk rebels. In 1951, the United States signed a formal peace treaty with Japan and a security pact that granted the United States a military base on Okinawa. The United States acquired similar bases in the Middle East, bolstering its strategic position in that oil-rich area. The ANZUS mutual defense pact of 1952 linked the United States strategically to Australia and New Zealand. And in French Indochina, Truman began assisting French efforts against a communist-led independence movement.

Fearful of communist gains, U.S. policy-makers opposed any movement whose political orientation seemed left-leaning. The U.S. occupation government in Japan, for example, increasingly restricted the activities of labor unions, suspended an antitrust program that American officials had earlier implemented, and barred communists from posts in the government and in the universities. As in Germany, the United States tried to contain communism by strengthening pro-U.S. elites and by promoting economic growth.

Anticommunism also prompted the United States to ally with South Africa. In 1949 the all-white (and militantly anticommunist) Nationalist Party instituted a legal-social system, called **apartheid**, based on elaborate rules of racial separation and subordination of blacks. Some State Department officials warned that any pact with South Africa, by implying support for apartheid, would damage U.S. prestige, but the Truman administration nonetheless concluded an alliance with South Africa's white supremacist regime.

The Truman administration's anticommunist stance, again in line with NSC-68, included more than military moves. Throughout the world, economic pressure, CIA covert activities, and propaganda campaigns helped advance anticommunist objectives. Truman's global "Campaign of Truth," an intensive informational and psychological offensive, used mass media imagery and cultural exchanges to counter Soviet propaganda. A rhetoric of defensiveness took hold: the Defense Department replaced the War Department; "national security" replaced "national interest." Meanwhile, the United States extended its power into Iran, Greece, and Turkey, all once inside Britain's sphere of influence; initiated the Marshall Plan and NATO; transformed former enemies—Italy, Germany, and Japan—into anti-Soviet bulwarks; assumed control of hundreds of Pacific islands; launched research to develop the H-bomb; winked at apartheid to win an anticommunist ally in South Africa; solidified its sphere of influence in Latin America; acquired bases around the world; and devised a master plan for using military, economic, and covert

apartheid *Legal system practiced in South Africa and based on elaborate rules of racial separation and subordination of blacks.*

think tank *Group or agency organized to conduct intensive research or engage in problem solving, especially in developing new technology, military strategy, or social planning.*

RAND *Think tank developed by the U.S. military to conduct research and development.*

action to achieve its goals. Beginning with the Truman Doctrine of 1947, the United States reinvented itself as a global superpower.

While the Truman administration fortified the U.S. strategic position overseas, its policies produced what the historian Michael Sherry has called "the militarization of American life." With strong bipartisan support in Congress, the White House accelerated what would become a massive military buildup and an increasing merger between military and economic policy-making. Congress granted a new Atomic Energy Commission broad powers to oversee development of a U.S. nuclear power industry. To develop both the weaponry and the policies implied by a global security strategy, Congress created a **think tank**—RAND, an acronym for Research and Development. Expensive contracts for military materials worried cost-conscious members of Congress, but the prospect of new jobs in their home districts helped mute opposition.

PURSUING NATIONAL SECURITY AT HOME

FOCUS QUESTION
How did the foreign policy of containment affect domestic policy and American life?

Although containment abroad generally gained bipartisan support, the president's programs for containing subversive influences at home encountered bitter, sustained opposition. Militant anticommunists, taking their cue from Truman's own rhetoric, leveled increasingly alarming allegations of internal communist subversion. Civil libertarians, on the other hand, complained about "witch-hunts" against people whose only sin was dissent from prevailing policies. Many people, even dedicated anticommunists, began to worry that irresponsible smear campaigns and wild goose chases after unlikely subversives could discredit the government's effort to identify authentic Soviet agents. The search for supposed subversives eventually touched many areas of postwar life.

ANTICOMMUNISM AND THE U.S. LABOR MOVEMENT

The issue of anticommunism helped unsettle the U.S. labor movement. After the end of the Second World War, workers had struck for increased wages and a greater voice in workplace routines and production decisions. Strikes had brought both the auto and the electronics industries to a standstill. In Stamford, Connecticut, and Lancaster, Pennsylvania, general strikes had led to massive work stoppages that later spread to other large cities. After Truman threatened to seize mines and railroads shut down by work stoppages and to order strikers back to work, labor militancy began to subside.

Unimpressed, in 1947 the Republican-controlled Congress effectively tapped anticommunist sentiment to pass the Labor-Management Relations Act, popularly known as the Taft-Hartley Act. The law negated some of the gains made by organized labor during the 1930s by limiting a union's power to conduct boycotts, to compel employers to accept "closed shops" in which only union members could be hired, and to conduct any strike that the president judged harmful to national security. In addition, the measure required union officials to sign affidavits stating that they did not belong to the Communist Party or any other "subversive" organization. A union that refused to comply was effectively denied protections under national labor laws. Truman vetoed Taft-Hartley, but Congress overrode him. By the end of the Truman era, some type of loyalty-security check had been conducted on about 20 percent of the U.S. workforce, more than 13 million people.

Anticommunism also affected both internal union politics and labor–management relations. Some union members had long charged that communist organizers were more loyal to the Communist Party than to their own unions or to the nation. Differences over whether to support the Democratic Party or Henry Wallace's Progressive effort in 1948 had embittered relations within many unions. In the years following Truman's victory, the Congress of Industrial Organizations (CIO) expelled 13 unions—a full third of its membership. Meanwhile, many workers found their own jobs at risk because of their political ideas.

HUAC AND THE LOYALTY PROGRAM

Anticommunists carefully scrutinized the entertainment industry. In 1947, the **House Un-American Activities Committee** (**HUAC**) opened hearings into communist influences in Hollywood. Basking in the glare of newsreel cameras, committee members seized on the refusal of ten screenwriters, producers, and directors—all current or former members of the American Communist Party—to testify about their own politics and that of others in the film community. "The Hollywood Ten" claimed that the First Amendment barred HUAC from scrutinizing their political activities. The federal courts upheld HUAC's investigative powers, however, and the Hollywood Ten eventually went to prison for contempt of Congress.

Meanwhile, studio heads drew up a **blacklist** of alleged subversives whom they agreed not to hire. Leaders in other sectors of the entertainment industry, particularly television, adopted a similar policy. Although prominent celebrities dominated media accounts of blacklisting activities, many anonymous labor union members, who worked behind the scenes in technical and support positions, also lost their source of livelihood.

By the mid-1950s hundreds of people were unable to find jobs unless they agreed to appear as "friendly witnesses" before HUAC to provide the names of people they had seen at some "communist meeting" sometime in the increasingly distant past. Some of those called to testify, such as the writer Lillian Hellman, refused to answer any questions. Others, such as the director Elia Kazan, cooperated. Individual decisions over whether or not to "name names" would divide members of the entertainment business and labor union movement for decades.

The search for subversives also created new political celebrities. Ronald Reagan, who was president of the Screen Actors Guild *and* a secret informant for the FBI (identified as "T-10"), testified about communist influences in Hollywood. Richard Nixon, then an obscure member of Congress from California, began his political ascent in 1948 when Whittaker Chambers, a journalist formally active in communist circles, came before HUAC to charge **Alger Hiss** with having been a party member and with passing classified information to Soviet agents during the late 1930s.

The Hiss-Chambers-Nixon affair instantly sparked controversy. Hiss, a prominent Democrat with a lengthy career

House Un-American Activities Committee (HUAC) *Congressional committee (1938–1975) that zealously investigated suspected Nazi and Communist sympathizers.*

blacklist *In the postwar years, a list of people who could no longer work in the entertainment industry because of alleged contacts with communists.*

Alger Hiss *High-level State Department official who was accused, in a controversial case, of being a communist and a Soviet spy.*

"IT'S OKAY --- WE'RE HUNTING COMMUNISTS"

IT'S OKAY—WE'RE HUNTING COMMUNISTS. *This 1947 "Herblock" (Herbert Block) cartoon presents a critical view of the impact of HUAC's communist-hunting.*

"It's okay – We're hunting Communists," October 31, 1947 Ink, graphite, and opaque white over graphite underdrawing on layered paper. Published in the Washington Post [18]. © Herb Block. Library of Congress Prints and Photographs Division [LC-USZ62-127327]

in public service, maintained that he had been framed. Although legal technicalities prevented his indictment for espionage, he was charged with lying to Congress and went to prison. To Nixon and his supporters, the case of Alger Hiss, who had advised FDR during the Yalta Conference (see Chapter 26), demonstrated the need for greater vigor in hunting down subversives. During the mid-1990s, the availability of long-classified documents prompted an extensive re-airing of the Hiss controversy. Some scholars continued to see the Hiss case, as with that of the Hollywood Ten, as more hype than substance, but most historians have concluded that Hiss (along with several other high-ranking government officials) had likely passed at least some information to Soviet agents during the 1930s and 1940s.

Meanwhile, pursuing its own anticommunist course, the Truman administration implemented its loyalty program and dismissed hundreds of federal employees. Truman's attorney general, Tom Clark, authorized J. Edgar Hoover, head of the FBI, to compile a secret list of alleged subversives whom the government could then detain, without any legal hearing, during a time of national emergency.

Fears that subversives might immigrate to the United States helped shape the McCarran-Walter Act of 1952. This congressional statute empowered immigration officials to deny entry to persons they determined could endanger national security by bringing dangerous ideas into the country. The law also authorized the deportation of immigrants, even U.S. citizens, who belonged to organizations on the Attorney General's List.

At the same time, Hoover's FBI compiled its own confidential dossiers on a wide range of artists and intellectuals, including some, such as Ernest Hemingway and John Steinbeck, with no ties to the Communist Party. Prominent African Americans became special targets. The FBI kept close tabs, for instance, on civil rights activist Bayard Rustin. Richard Wright (author of the acclaimed novel *Native Son*), W. E. B. Du Bois (the nation's most celebrated African American historian), and Paul Robeson (a well-known entertainer-activist) were singled out by the State Department and immigration officials because of their links to the U.S. Communist Party and their identification with anti-imperialist and antiracist organizations throughout the world. In addition, suspicions of homosexuality could make people, including the nominally closeted Rustin, into targets for governmental surveillance and discrimination.

TARGETING DIFFERENCE

Public signs of homosexual behavior, as the stance adopted by Bayard Rustin suggested, increased during the postwar era. During the Second World War, more visible and assertive gay and lesbian subcultures emerged, particularly in larger cities such as New York and San Francisco. After the war, Dr. Alfred Kinsey's research on sexual behavior—his first volume, on male sexuality, appeared in 1948—claimed that homosexual behavior could be found throughout American society, and that people pursued a wide range of sexual behaviors, from exclusively heterosexual to exclusively homosexual. In 1952, the issue of transsexuality hit the headlines when the press revealed that, after a series of "sex-change" operations in Europe, George W. Jorgensen, Jr. had become a "blonde beauty," Christine Jorgensen.

By this time, a small "homophile" movement, aimed at combating legal discrimination, had emerged. Gays formed the Mattachine Society (in 1950), and lesbians later founded the Daughters of Bilitis, organizations that began to advocate rights for homosexuals.

The Kinsey Report's implicit claim that homosexuality was simply another form of sexuality, alongside the discreet militancy of the "homophile" organizations, produced a backlash that became connected to the broader antisubversion crusade. The fact that several founders of the Mattachine Society had also been members of the Communist Party, coupled with the claim that homosexuals could be black-mailed by Soviet agents more easily than heterosexuals, helped link homosexuality with threats to national security. "One homosexual can pollute a Government office," a Senate report claimed.

Today, historians of sexuality see a "Lavender Scare" about homosexuality accompanying the "Red Scare" about communism. Popular imagery portrayed both homosexuality and communism as subversive "diseases" that inwardly "sick" people, who seemed outwardly little different than other Americans, could spread throughout the body politic. Only knowledgeable experts could uncover all of the subversive communists and homosexuals working in sensitive positions inside the U.S. government. Suspicion of "sexual deviance" became an acceptable basis for subjecting government employees to loyalty board hearings and, ultimately, deny-ing them the same legal and constitutional protections enjoyed by heterosexuals.

THE "GREAT FEAR"

Some cultural historians view the search for subversives during the late 1940s and early 1950s unfolding in an atmosphere of anxiety they call the "Great Fear." The real events that energized the Truman administration, such as atomic tests by the Soviets, also heightened the impact of stories about communist agents having sto-len U.S. nuclear secrets or about gay subversives shaping foreign policy. A growing sense of insecurity, in turn, spurred efforts to safeguard national security.

As this feeling of anxiety began to settle over U.S. politics, the Justice Depart-ment arrested, in 1950, several members of an alleged spy ring. Julius and Ethel Rosenberg, both members of the American Communist Party, became the central characters in this case.

The Rosenberg case became a Cold War melodrama. Their trial, the verdicts of guilty, the sentences of death, the numerous legal appeals, the worldwide protests, and their 1953 executions at Sing Sing Prison all provoked intense controversy. Could the Rosenbergs, the parents of two young children, have been involved in the theft of nuclear secrets? And if so, were their death sentences, on the charge of espionage, the constitutionally appropriate punishment? To their supporters, the Rosenbergs (who died maintaining their innocence) had fallen victim to anticom-munist hysteria. Federal officials seemed primarily interested in finding scapegoats. To others, the evidence showed that information had been channeled to the Soviets.

Documents released since the 1990s convinced most historians that Julius Rosenberg had been involved in some kind of espionage (although the usefulness of his information is still at issue) and that Ethel Rosenberg had known of his activities. Yet the government declined to prosecute others who almost certainly had been atomic spies. Only Julius and Ethel Rosenberg faced a charge that carried the death penalty.

The courts' response to the Great Fear became another matter for sustained debate. During the 1949 prosecution of leaders of the American Communist Party, the trial judge accepted the Justice Department's claim that, by definition, this political party was part of an international conspiracy against the "free world." Its Marxist ideology and its publications, even in the absence of any proof of subversive *acts,* justified convicting the party's leaders of sedition. In contrast, civil libertarians insisted that the government lacked evidence that Communist Party publications and speeches, by themselves, posed a "clear and present danger" to national security. In this view, the beliefs of any political group, including a communist one, enjoyed the protection of the First Amendment, and only actions could be put on trial. When the convictions of the Communist Party leaders were appealed to the Supreme Court, in the landmark case of *Dennis* v. *U.S.* (1951), the High Court modified the "clear and present danger" doctrine and upheld the lower courts.

The Truman administration was itself drawing increased scrutiny from zealous red-hunters. In Congress, Republicans and conservative Democrats denounced Truman's anticommunist initiatives as too limited and had passed the McCarran Internal Security Act in 1950. It authorized the detention, during any national emergency, of alleged subversives in special camps and created the Subversive Activities Control Board (SACB) to investigate organizations suspected of links to the Communist Party and to oversee registration of groups allegedly controlled by communists.

The Truman administration responded ambiguously to the McCarran Act. Although the president vetoed the law, a futile gesture that Congress quickly overrode, his administration authorized the FBI to devise a secret detention program, which contained even fewer safeguards than the one created by Congress, and continued to enforce its own loyalty program. Still, Truman could never defuse doubts about his anticommunist credentials.

QUICK   REVIEW

MCCARTHYISM

- Named after Republican Senator Joseph McCarthy of Wisconsin

- Targeted Truman's State Department, Democrats, and alleged subversives

- Term came to connote any demagogic use of exaggerated and unsubstantiated charges against one's political opponents

MCCARTHYISM

Republican Senator Joseph McCarthy of Wisconsin became Truman's prime accuser, charging in 1950 that communists were at work in the State Department. People rightly feared the future, according to McCarthy, "not because our only powerful potential enemy has sent men to invade our shores, but rather because of the traitorous actions of those who have been treated so well by this Nation." Among those people, McCarthy named Secretary of State Dean Acheson and his predecessor, General George C. Marshall.

A master of political imagery and sexual innuendo, McCarthy subtly linked the Lavender and Red Scares. He portrayed anticommunists in Truman's administration as both overly privileged and insufficiently manly. People such as Acheson, who had been "born with silver spoons in their mouths," had degenerated into effete "enemies from within." McCarthy derided Acheson as the "Red Dean of fashion" and as the leader of the "lace handkerchief crowd." By the final years of Truman's presidency, McCarthy seemed unstoppable. Although McCarthy failed to substantiate most of his charges, he lacked neither imagination nor targets. In the summer of 1950 a Senate subcommittee, after examining government files, concluded that McCarthy's charges against the state department amounted to "the most nefarious campaign of half-truths and untruths in the history of this republic." McCarthy simply charged that the files had been "raped," and he went after Millard Tydings, the senator who had chaired the subcommittee. In the November 1950 elections, Tydings was defeated, in part because of a fabricated photograph that linked him to communist activities.

Despite McCarthy's recklessness, influential people tolerated, even encouraged, him. Conservative, anticommunist leaders of the Roman Catholic Church embraced McCarthy, himself a Catholic. Leading Republicans welcomed McCarthy's assaults on their Democratic rivals. In contrast, the historically minded among the senator's opponents saw him as the latest personification of a form of populist-style demagoguery, which became labeled **McCarthyism**.

THE NATIONAL SECURITY CONSTITUTION

Too much attention on the theatrics of McCarthyism, however, can obscure long-term political and constitutional changes during the era of the Great Fear. Concern about national security altered the nation's structure of governance. Except for the 22nd Amendment, adopted in 1951, which barred future presidents from following FDR's example and serving more than two terms, the written Constitution was not modified during this era. But congressional legislation, especially the National Security Act of 1947, and the growing power of executive branch agencies such as the CIA, the FBI, and the Pentagon significantly changed the nation's constitutional structure and its approach to governance. The view that the presidency possessed only limited powers gave way to the view that greatly extending the power of the national government, especially of the executive branch, was justified in the name of protecting national security.

Truman encountered few obstacles when he took the United States into an undeclared war in Korea. The idea of constitutional limitations arose only after he asserted his presidential authority and, in 1952, ordered his commerce secretary to seize control of the domestic steel industry in order to prevent a threatened strike. Although Truman could have invoked the Taft-Hartley Act to obtain a 60-day "cooling off" period, instead he claimed, in effect, that the Cold War had changed constitutional practice. The president, as commander-in-chief, possessed virtually unlimited power whenever emergency action was required to safeguard national security.

When the "steel seizure case" (officially known as *Youngstown Sheet & Tube Company* v. *Sawyer*) reached the Supreme Court, three justices, all Truman appointees, agreed with the president's claims of emergency executive powers. Six others, for differing reasons, rejected Truman's position, but all expressed support for somewhat less expansive views of presidential authority when national security was at issue. Constitutional scholars would come to see this case as a short-term defeat for Truman but hardly a long-term setback for national security powers.

McCarthyism *Public accusations of disloyalty made with little or no regard for actual evidence. Named after Senator Joseph McCarthy, these accusations and the scandal and harm they caused came to symbolize the most virulent form of anticommunism.*

TRUMAN'S FAIR DEAL

Truman claimed to share much of Franklin Roosevelt's domestic vision, and many supporters of FDR's New Deal still endorsed the Second Bill of Rights that Roosevelt had announced in 1944 (see Chapter 26). According to this vision, all Americans had the "right" to a wide range of substantive liberties, including employment, food and shelter, education, and health care. Whenever people could not obtain these "rights," the national government was responsible for providing access to them. Following the Second World War, most Western European nations were creating or expanding their own "welfare states." These systems of governance required ongoing economic and social planning and an aggressive use of state power.

In the United States, however, proposals for government planning and for new social welfare measures stalled. Critics had assailed wartime Washington's use of

FOCUS QUESTION
What were the guiding assumptions of the Fair Deal, and which of its major initiatives seemed likely to pass through Congress? Which proposals seemed likely to stall there—and why?

governmental power to regulate economic relationships. During Truman's presidency, opposition to FDR's Second Bill of Rights grew stronger. Any attempt to update the New Deal, insisted most Republicans and some Democrats, threatened unconstitutional intrusions into people's rights and posed a threat to individual initiative and responsibility. Dixiecrat Democrats joined conservative Republicans to block any legislation that they believed might dismantle white supremacy in the South. The National Association of Manufacturers (NAM) denounced the Truman administration as a menace to the nation's free-enterprise system.

THE EMPLOYMENT ACT OF 1946 AND THE PROMISE OF ECONOMIC GROWTH

The Truman administration, faced with intense opposition to Roosevelt's agenda, sought a fresh approach to domestic policy-making. The 1946 debate over the Full Employment Bill provided it. This measure, as conceived, would have empowered Washington to ensure employment for all citizens seeking work. To the bill's opponents, the phrase "full employment" implied a step toward a European-style of welfare state, even socialism.

As the effort to enact this measure stalled, a scaled-back approach emerged. The law that Congress finally passed, renamed the Employment Act of 1946, called for "maximum" (rather than full) employment and specifically declared that private enterprise, not government, bore primary responsibility for economic decision making. The act nonetheless created a new executive branch body, the Council of Economic Advisers, to formulate long-range policy recommendations and signaled that government would assume some responsibility for the performance of the economy.

A crucial factor in the gradual acceptance of Washington's new role was a growing faith that *advice* from economic experts, as an alternative to government *planning*, could guarantee a constantly expanding economy. An influential group of economists, many of them disciples of Britain's John Maynard Keynes, insisted that their expertise could temper the boom-and-bust cycles that had afflicted the nation's economy.

The promise of economic expansion dazzled postwar leaders. Using the relatively new measure of gross national product (GNP), economists could actually calculate the nation's growing economic bounty. Developed in 1939, GNP—defined as the total dollar value of all goods and services produced in the nation during a given year—became the standard gauge of economic health. Corporate executives, who had feared that the end of the war would bring long-term labor unrest and trigger a deep recession, viewed a rising GNP as a guarantor of social stability. The Truman administration welcomed the prospect of an expanding economy, which would increase federal tax revenues and, in turn, finance Washington's domestic agenda.

Truman and his advisers spread the gospel of governmentally stimulated economic growth. This new faith nicely dovetailed with the spending levels their national security plans required. The Cold War could serve as "an automatic pump primer" for the U.S. economy. Sharp increases in military rearmament signaled an economic policy observers began to call "military Keynesianism." Moreover, Cold War assistance programs such as the Marshall Plan were designed to create markets and investment opportunities overseas. Economic growth at home was linked to development in the world at large—and to the all-pervasive concern with national security.

SHAPING THE FAIR DEAL

In 1949, Truman unveiled his "Fair Deal." He proposed extending popular New Deal programs such as Social Security and minimum wage laws; enacting legislation dealing with civil rights, national health care, and federal aid for education; and repealing the Taft-Hartley Act of 1947. The president also urged substantial spending on public housing projects, and his secretary of agriculture called for new governmental subsidies to support farm prices. The core assumption on which Truman built his entire Fair Deal—that sustained economic growth could finance enlarged government programs—came to dominate policy planning.

Two prominent programs illustrate the approach to domestic social policy that emerged during the Fair Deal years. The first, the so-called **GI Bill** (officially titled the Serviceman's Readjustment Act of 1944), provided comprehensive benefits for those who had served in the armed forces. The Bill provided vets with financial assistance for college and job-training programs. By 1947, the year of peak enrollment, roughly half of the entire college and university population was receiving aid under the GI Bill. In other provisions, veterans received preferential treatment when applying for government jobs; favorable financial terms when purchasing homes or businesses; and, eventually, comprehensive medical care in veterans' hospitals. The Veterans Readjustment Assistance Act of 1952, popularly known as the "GI Bill of Rights," extended these programs to veterans of the Korean War. In essence, although the Truman administration never enacted all of FDR's Second Bill of Rights, the Fair Deal did ensure that veterans would enjoy some of its key provisions.

The Social Security program expanded under Truman's Fair Deal. Rebutting attacks against this New Deal measure by conservatives opposed to what they regarded as an unwarranted extension of federal power, Social Security's supporters defended its provisions for the disabled and the blind and argued that older people had earned the "income security" through years of work and monetary

GI Bill *Officially called the Serviceman's Readjustment Act of 1944, it provided veterans with college and job-training assistance, preferential treatment in hiring, and subsidized home loans, and was later extended to Korean War veterans in 1952.*

© Margaret Bourke-White/Time Life Pictures/Getty Images

THE POSTWAR COLLEGE SCENE. *This picture by the famed photojournalist Margaret Bourke-White shows veterans of the Second World War dominating available space in a classroom at the University of Iowa. Tapping financial support offered under the GI Bill (1944), more than 600 vets enrolled in 1946 at Iowa. Returning servicemen, who represented more than 60 percent of this university's total enrollment, often taxed existing facilities here and at other universities throughout the country.*

contributions withheld from their paychecks. Under the Social Security Act of 1950, the level of benefits increased significantly; the retirement portions of the program expanded; and coverage was extended to more than 10 million people, including agricultural workers.

More expansive (and expensive) Fair Deal proposals, however, either failed or were scaled back. For instance, Truman's plan for a comprehensive national health insurance program faced opposition from several different quarters. Consumer groups and labor unions, intent on creating nonprofit community-run health plans, saw Truman's proposal for a centralized system as a blueprint for unnecessarily bureaucratizing medical care. The American Medical Association (AMA) and the American Hospital Association (AHA) opposed any governmental intervention in the traditional fee-for-service medical system and steered Congress toward a less intrusive alternative—federal financing of new hospitals under the earlier Hill-Burton Act (1946). Large insurance companies, which were continuing to push their own private plans, also opposed the Truman plan. Opinion polls suggested that many voters, many of whom were enrolling in private health insurance plans such as Blue Cross and Blue Shield, found Truman's health proposals confusing.

The Fair Deal's housing proposals met a similarly mixed reception. Continued shortage of affordable housing in urban areas after the war stirred some support for home-building programs. Conservatives recognized the housing shortage, and some supported the Housing Act of 1949. This law authorized construction of 810,000 public housing units and provided federal funds for "urban renewal" zones, areas to be cleared of rundown dwellings and rebuilt with new construction. The Housing Act proclaimed ambitious goals but provided relatively modest funding, especially for its public-housing component. Private construction firms and real estate agents welcomed funding for federal home loan guarantee programs—such as those established under the GI Bill and through the Federal Housing Administration (FHA)—but they lobbied effectively against publicly financed housing projects.

Fair Deal policy-making ultimately focused on specific groups, such as veterans and older Americans, rather than on more extensive programs such as a national health care plan or an extensive housing program. With opponents dismissing the broader Fair Deal proposals as "welfare schemes," the White House found it easier to defend more narrowly targeted programs that could be hailed as economic security measures.

CIVIL RIGHTS

The Truman administration also struggled to place the national government's power behind a growing civil rights movement. After returning to the home front, few African, Latino, and Native American service personnel wished to remain passive bystanders when laws reduced them to second-class citizens. Moreover, the people of color who had moved to cities, seeking to escape discrimination and find wartime employment, wanted to build on the social and economic gains they had made during the earlier 1940s. Drives to translate the vision of liberty and equality in FDR's Second Bill of Rights into reality animated grassroots activists in the postwar period.

During his 1948 presidential campaign, Truman strongly endorsed the proposals of a civil rights committee he had established in 1946. The report, entitled "To Secure These Rights," called for federal legislation against lynching; a special civil rights division within the Department of Justice; antidiscrimination initiatives in

---

QUICK   REVIEW

TRUMAN'S FAIR DEAL

- Marked by faith that postwar economic growth could fund new governmental social welfare programs

- Major initiatives aimed at creating "maximum" employment opportunities, extending Social Security and GI Bill benefits, easing the housing shortage, and providing national health insurance

- Also included Truman's endorsement of a number of civil rights measures, including antilynching legislation and integration of the military

employment, housing, and public facilities; and desegregation of the military. These proposals helped prompt the Dixiecrat revolt of 1948, but they also gained Truman significant support from African Americans and Latinos.

Truman continued to support the civil rights cause. When successive Congresses failed to enact any civil rights legislation—including a law against lynching and a ban on the poll taxes that prevented most Southern blacks from voting—leaders of the movement turned to the White House and to the federal courts. After labor leader A. Philip Randolph threatened to organize a protest campaign, Truman issued an executive order, in 1948, calling for desegregation of the armed forces.

Truman spoke candidly of how segregation tarnished America's image in a Cold War world "which is 90 percent colored." Although Cold War anxiety could help justify harassment of African American leaders with links to communism, it also made legalized segregation into a foreign policy liability by highlighting the limits of America's claim to represent liberty and equality.

Truman's Justice Department also appeared in court to support litigants who contested government-backed public school segregation and "restrictive covenants" (legal agreements that prevented racial or religious minorities from acquiring real estate). In 1946 the Supreme Court declared restrictive covenants unconstitutional and began chipping away at the "separate-but-equal" principle used since *Plessy* v. *Ferguson* (1896) to justify segregated schools. A federal court in California, ruling on a case brought the previous year in Orange County by LULAC and the NAACP, held that segregating students of Mexican descent in separate, and unequal, schools violated their constitutional rights. In 1948, a second federal court—with the case now entitled *Westminster School District* v. *Mendez*—agreed with the first. In 1950 the Supreme Court ruled that, under the 14th Amendment, racial segregation in state-financed graduate and law schools was unconstitutional. The familiar arguments used to legitimize racial segregation in public education seemed ripe for a successful challenge.

The years immediately after the Second World War, in sum, marked a turning point in domestic policy-making. The New Deal's vision of comprehensive socioeconomic planning gave way to the Fair Deal's view: The nation could expect uninterrupted economic growth, enabling Washington to finance, through rising tax revenues, programs designed to assist specific groups. As one supporter of this new approach argued, postwar policy-makers were sophisticated enough to embrace "partial remedies," such as the GI Bill, rather than to wait for fanciful "cure-alls," such as FDR's Second Bill of Rights.

Signs of a Changing Culture

The postwar years accelerated the pace of cultural change. Encouraged by the advertising industry, Americans seemed, at one level, to view anything new as "progress." Yet, at another level, the speed and scope of change during these years brought a feeling of uneasiness and anxiety into everyday life.

The Baseball "Color Line"

The interplay between celebrating and fearing change could be seen in the integration of organized baseball during the 1940s and early 1950s. In 1947 Major League

FOCUS QUESTION
How did a resurgent civil rights movement and a new suburban culture help to signal changes in American life during the immediate postwar era?

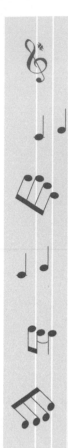

MUSICAL LINK TO THE PAST

BIG BAND TO BEBOP

Songwriter: Charlie Parker
Title: "Koko" (1946)
Performers: Charlie Parker's Ri Bop Boys

Charlie "Bird" Parker, the most important jazz musician in the mid-1940s, introduced a new kind of jazz called "bebop" with his recording of "Koko." Black bebop musicians broke the old big band formulas by performing at a faster, near-anarchic tempo with more notes per bar, playing songs far beyond the usual three minutes. Disdaining formal arrangements, reducing the number of players in ensembles, and stressing individual expression through extended solos, the music required a technical proficiency beyond the reach of most musicians.

Artists like Parker refused to play dance music or entertain audiences as previous jazz figures did. They emphasized their own musical preferences and played a harsh, challenging, intellectual music. Some historians suggest that bebop's sound symbolized the increasing anger and rebellion among African Americans during the postwar years.

Bebop's initial recordings appeared on small record labels such as Savoy (owned by an electronics retailer who also released music) and Dial (opened by a Hollywood record store entrepreneur to give beboppers wider exposure). Independent labels have played a leading role in introducing new American musical movements. Other examples include 1950s rock and roll (spearheaded by labels such as Sun and Chess) and hip-hop (by labels including Tommy Boy and Sugar Hill).

1. What recent changes in American popular music seem analogous to the transition from big band to bebop?
2. Has the widespread popularity of hip-hop induced major record companies to change what they release? Explain.

Listen to an audio recording of this music on the Musical Links to the Past CD.

Baseball's policy of racial segregation finally cracked when **Jackie Robinson,** who had played baseball in the Negro National League, became the Brooklyn Dodgers' first baseman. Some ballplayers, including several on Robinson's own club, considered a boycott. Baseball's leadership, seeking new sources of players and seeing a steady stream of African American fans coming through the turnstiles, threatened to suspend any player who refused to play with or against Robinson.

Officially, organized baseball became desegregated. The Cleveland Indians acquired center fielder Larry Doby, and other top-flight players abandoned the Negro leagues for clubs in the American and National circuits. Eventually, the skills of Robinson—named Rookie of the Year in 1947 and the National League's Most Valuable Player in 1949—and other players of African descent carried the day. Although light-skinned Latinos had long passed through the racial barrier, Orestes ("Minnie") Minoso, a Cuban-born veteran of the Negro circuits, became the first Afro-Latino to break into the big leagues in 1949. Major League teams began fielding greater numbers of African American and Latino players, and some began recruiting in Mexico and the Caribbean. During the 50th anniversary of Robinson's debut, Major League Baseball staged elaborate memorial ceremonies for Robinson, who had died in 1972, and congratulated the sport for having led the fight against racial prejudice during the Cold War years.

As cultural historians note, however, baseball's leadership had unofficially limited its own desegregation effort. Several teams waited years before integrating their rosters, claiming that they could find no talented African American or Latino prospects. More commonly, clubs restricted the number of nonwhite players they

Jackie Robinson *African American whose addition to the Brooklyn Dodgers in 1947 began the lengthy process of integrating Major League Baseball.*

JACKIE ROBINSON. *In 1947 Jackie Robinson joined the Brooklyn Dodgers and became the first African American since the 19th century to play major league baseball. He had served as a lieutenant in the Army during the Second World War. Racial integration of the national pastime of baseball became a powerful symbol of progress in race relations.*

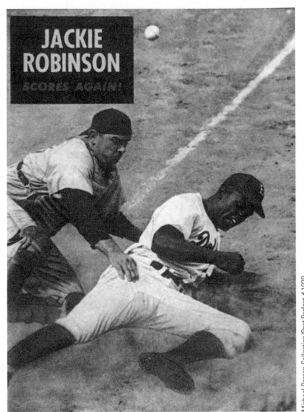

Michael Barson Collection/Past Perfect # 1938

would take on and kept their managers, coaches, and front-office personnel solidly white.

The African American and Latino players who followed in Robinson's footsteps confronted continuing obstacles. They often encountered overt, off-the-field discrimination during spring training in the South and Southwest. Young prospects playing for minor league teams in small towns endured similar problems. Spanish-speaking players struggled to convince managers, sportswriters, and teammates that they could "understand" the subtleties of either baseball or North American culture.

NEW SUBURBAN DEVELOPMENTS

In suburbia, too, change was both celebrated and feared. Suburban living had long been a feature of the "American dream." The new Long Island town of Levittown, New York, which welcomed its first residents in October 1947, seemed to make that dream a reality, at affordable prices, for middle-income families.

Nearly everything about Levittown seemed unprecedented. Levitt & Sons, a construction company that had mass-produced military barracks during the Second World War, claimed to be completing a five-room bungalow every 15 minutes. Architectural critics sneered at these "little boxes," but potential buyers stood in long lines hoping to purchase one. By 1950, Levittown contained more than 10,000 homes and 40,000 residents, and bulldozers and construction crews were sweeping through other suburban developments across the country.

To help potential buyers, the government offered an extensive set of programs. The FHA, established during the New Deal, helped underwrite an elaborate lending system. Typically, people who bought FHA-financed homes needed only 5 percent of the purchase price as a down payment; they could finance the rest with a long-term, government-insured mortgage. Military veterans enjoyed even more favorable terms under the GI loan program. These government programs made it cheaper to purchase a suburban house than to rent an apartment in most cities. Moreover, homeowners could deduct the interest payments on their mortgages from their federal income tax.

The postwar suburbs gained a reputation for being ideal places to raise children, and families were having babies in unprecedented numbers. Toward the end of the war, a number of factors, including earlier marriages and rising incomes, fueled a **baby boom** that would last until the mid-1960s. With houses occupying only about 15 percent of suburban lots, large lawns served as private playgrounds. Suburban schools were as new as the homes, and their well-appointed facilities attracted both skilled, enthusiastic teachers and the children of other middle-income families.

In many respects, suburbia symbolized new possibilities, confidence in the future, and acceptance of change. As contemporary observers noted, however, suburbia also appeared to offer a material and psychological refuge. Buying a suburban home seemed a way of cushioning the impact of the social and demographic

baby boom *Dramatic increase in births during the years after World War II, 1946–1964.*

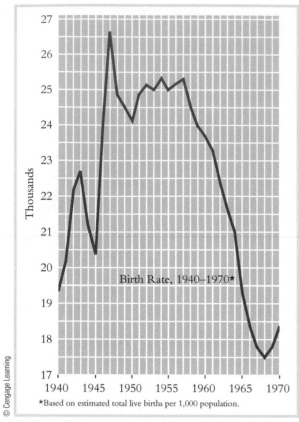

*Based on estimated total live births per 1,000 population.

THE BABY BOOM

changes ushered in by the war. As African American families migrated to Northern and Western cities, in search of jobs and greater opportunity, whites began to see moving to the new suburbs as a way to avoid living in integrated communities. Governmental policies contributed to this trend through the financial incentives provided to homebuyers. After the Supreme Court declared restrictive covenants unconstitutional, local officials rarely enforced the decision. Various informal and extralegal arrangements prevented, until well into the 1960s, any African American from buying a home in Levittown.

Other policies and practices helped to segregate the new postwar suburbs. Local groups vetoed public housing projects in their communities. Although land and building costs would have been cheaper in the suburbs, public housing projects were concentrated on relatively expensive, high-density urban sites. At the same time, the lending industry channeled government-guaranteed loans away from most urban neighborhoods, and private lenders routinely denied credit to African Americans and Latinos seeking to buy new suburban housing.

No one in the postwar housing industry admitted intentional racial discrimination. William Levitt could identify his private housing projects with the public crusade against communism. "No man who owns his house and lot can be a Communist," he remarked in 1948. "He has too much to do." Even as Levitt claimed he could help solve the problem of housing—and perhaps even that of communist subversion—he also resisted any suggestion that his construction choices had anything to do with race.

Similarly, the architects of this new suburbia saw nothing problematic with postwar gender patterns. The financial industry extended the vast majority of its loan guarantees to white men. Only rarely could single women, from any ethnic background, obtain loans. The FHA, a governmental agency, justified the policy on the grounds that men were the family breadwinners and that women seldom made enough money to qualify as good credit risks.

POSTWAR HOLLYWOOD

Hollywood turned out powerful symbols of the Cold War era's fascination with—and fear of—cultural change. Hollywood dominated the entertainment business at the start of the postwar era. As the overseas markets reopened and their male stars returned from military service, the major studios expected to prosper, and Hollywood expected to cheer the nation through the Cold War much as it had through the Depression and the Second World War. The Hollywood musical, filled with lively stars, upbeat tunes, and flashy dance sequences, seemed to be the perfect expression of optimism. MGM's *On the Town* (1949) epitomized the early postwar musical. It saturated movie screens with hopeful imagery. During 24 hours of shore leave, three U.S. sailors sing and dance their way through New York City, sample the fruits of both elite and popular culture, and fall in love with three equally vibrant young women. Ending with a title card proudly proclaiming it had been filmed in "Hollywood, USA," this musical also seemed to herald the American film industry's own bright future.

Even as *On the Town* arrived in movie theaters, however, Hollywood's fortunes were changing. By 1949, attendance figures—along with profits—began to plummet. The same year MGM shot *On the Town*, the Supreme Court ruled that antitrust laws required the major studios to give up their highly profitable ownership of local movie theaters. This decision rocked Hollywood just as it faced labor strife, internal

HISTORY THROUGH FILM

HIGH NOON (1952)

Directed by Fred Zinnemann;
starring Gary Cooper (Will Kane),
Grace Kelly (Amy Fowler Kane),
Katy Jurado (Helen Ramirez)

During the early Cold War era, no Hollywood western gained as much popular and critical acclaim—and created as much controversy—as the movie *High Noon*.

Montana-born Gary Cooper, one of those iconic Hollywood stars who seem to embody idealized versions of "everyman," played Will Kane, an aging, Old West lawman, whose dream of retiring as town marshal and settling down with his young bride, portrayed by Grace Kelly, is suddenly shattered. News arrives that Frank Miller, a vicious outlaw who had once run the town, has been released from prison and is returning on the noontime train. Miller and his henchmen pledge to kill Kane and regain power. Will the marshal strap on his gun and defend

the town? Or will he respect his new wife's pacifist faith, abandon his violent ways, and escape harm's way with her at his side?

Although the rules of the western genre require Kane not to flee, the script of *High Noon* greatly complicated his course. Kane had earlier saved the town by vanquishing Miller, but now the townspeople refuse to help him defend their community. If Kane will simply leave, they hope to cut a deal with Miller. As images of clocks ticking toward high noon fill the screen, Kane prepares for the final showdown.

Viewers during the Cold War era invariably saw *High Noon* as offering political statements about their own time but disagreed about what the movie might actually be trying to say. While viewers sympathetic to leftist politics embraced the movie as a commentary on McCarthyism, right-leaning viewers condemned that as simplistic allegory. Other commentators viewed *High Noon* as a morality tale about the choices the United States faced in a Cold War world. Most saw the movie's climactic gunfight—during which Kane (with the crucial help of his loyal wife) dispatches the Miller gang—as symbolic affirmation for the U.S. policy of forcefully containing, rather than passively negotiating with, communist aggressors.

High Noon's final scene further complicated debates and sparked its own bitter contests: A victorious Will Kane contemptuously throws his marshal's badge into the dirt. Disgusted with the townspeople's cowardice, he leaves town for good, on a buckboard, with his wife.

Although film critics and cultural historians might continue to debate, the people who ran Hollywood could hardly miss the movie's most obvious message. Gaining four Academy Awards, *High Noon* showed how familiar elements of the western genre could represent the complexities of the times. During the rest of the fifties and early 1960s, Hollywood and network television deluged audiences with actual and "disguised" westerns. Still rerun frequently on television, *High Noon* demonstrates how popular iconography can supply powerful portrayals of national anxieties.

© Sunset Boulevard/Corbis Sygma

Gary Cooper as Marshal Will Kane.

The Everett Collection

DEADLY IS THE FEMALE. *Also called* Gun Crazy *(1949), this film noir played on fears of social breakdown and inspired the later movie* Bonnie and Clyde *(1967).*

conflict over blacklisting, and soaring production costs. The rise of television delivered another blow to an industry already reeling backward.

Meanwhile, Hollywood released a cycle of motion pictures that came to be called *films noirs,* or "dark cinemas." Nearly always filmed in black and white and often set at night in large cities, *films noirs* peeked into the dark corners of postwar America. Noir characters continued to pursue dreams and hopes but with little chance of ever succeeding. Failure and loss seemed to be the rule rather than the exception.

Many *films noirs* featured alluring *femme fatales,* beautiful but dangerous women who challenged the prevailing order, particularly its gender hierarchies. The *femme fatale* represented the opposite of the faithful, nurturing wife and mother. Usually unmarried and childless, she threatened both men and women.

In *The File on Thelma Jordan* (1949), for instance, Barbara Stanwyck's title character cynically destroys the marriage of a weak-willed district attorney. Neither love nor even lust drives her illicit affair with him; instead, she seduces him as part of a cleverly ambitious—but ultimately unsuccessful—scheme to manipulate the criminal justice system. The postwar era's most prominent female stars—including Stanwyck, Joan Crawford, Rita Hayworth, and Lana Turner—achieved both popular and critical acclaim playing *femme fatales.*

Although the fear of communism during the years from 1946 to 1953 accentuated pressures for conformity, the growing prosperity, new expectations stemming from the war, and demographic shifts inevitably transformed many social and cultural patterns. The everyday lives of Americans—racial patterns and living arrangements and social expectations—were changing.

FROM TRUMAN TO EISENHOWER

Harry Truman declined to run for another term in 1952. His tumultuous years in the public spotlight put his Democratic Party on the defensive, and denunciations of communism and of Truman fueled an energetic Republican campaign.

THE ELECTION OF 1952

Adlai Stevenson of Illinois, the Democratic presidential candidate in 1952, warned that "Soviet secret agents and their dupes" had "burrowed like moles" into governments throughout the world. "We cannot let our guard drop for even a moment," he claimed. A solidly anticommunist stance, however, could not save Stevenson or his party. The Republicans first linked Stevenson to the unpopular Truman presidency. Their vice presidential nominee, Senator Richard Nixon of California, called Stevenson "Adlai the appeaser." The GOP's formula for electoral victory could be reduced to a simple equation, "K1C2": "Korea, corruption, and communism."

A SOLDIER-POLITICIAN

For their presidential candidate, Republicans looked to a hero of the Second World War, General Dwight David Eisenhower, popularly known as "Ike." Eisenhower grew up in Kansas, graduated from West Point, ascended through Army ranks, and directed the Normandy invasion of 1944 as Supreme Allied Commander. He served as Army Chief of Staff from 1945 to 1948 and, after an interim period as president of Columbia University, became the commander of NATO, a post he held until May 1952. Eisenhower had never sought elective office, but a half-century of military service had made him a skilled politician.

Eisenhower's personal appeal dazzled political insiders and commentators. Although his partisan affiliations had always been so hazy that some Democrats had courted him in 1948, he eventually emerged as the GOP's savior. Key Republicans convinced Eisenhower that Robert Taft, his main GOP rival, leaned too far to the right on domestic issues and lacked a firm commitment to containment policies overseas. Perceived as a middle-of-the-road candidate, Ike appeared ready to direct the nation through a cold war as skillfully as he had led it through a hot one. The Republican effort in 1952, perhaps the first to experiment with the possibilities of televised appeals, relied on its candidate's overwhelming charisma. A GOP campaign button simply announced "I Like IKE!"

The first military leader to gain the presidency since Ulysses S. Grant (1869–1877), Eisenhower achieved a great personal victory in 1952. The Eisenhower–Nixon ticket rolled up almost 7 million more popular votes than the Democrats and dominated the electoral college by a margin of 442 to 89. The Republican Party itself made modest gains. It managed a single-vote majority in the Senate and an eight-vote edge in the House of Representatives. The Democratic coalition FDR had forged during the 1930s still survived, even though it showed signs of fraying, especially in the South. There, some of the white Southern votes that had gone to the Dixiecrats in 1948 began moving toward the Republicans, and Eisenhower carried four states in the Democratic Party's once "solid South."

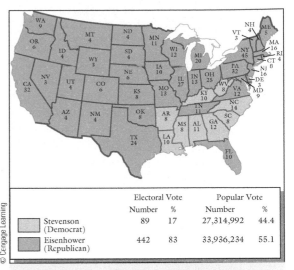

	Electoral Vote		Popular Vote	
	Number	%	Number	%
Stevenson (Democrat)	89	17	27,314,992	44.4
Eisenhower (Republican)	442	83	33,936,234	55.1

Map 27.4 **PRESIDENTIAL ELECTION, 1952.** *In this overwhelming victory for Eisenhower, Stevenson carried only a few states. Note that the so-called "solid South" remained largely Democratic. This trend would shift substantially over the next two decades.*

C O N C L U S I O N

An emphasis on aggressively safeguarding national security helped reshape national life during the years after the Second World War. As worsening relations between the United States and the Soviet Union developed into a Cold War, the Truman administration pursued policies that expanded the power of the government, particularly the executive branch. The militarization of foreign policy intensified when the United States went to war in Korea in 1950.

On the home front, Americans debated how best to protect national security, combat subversion, and calm cultural anxieties. The New Deal vision faded, but Truman's Fair Deal promised that new economic wisdom would be able to guarantee economic growth and thereby provide the tax revenues to expand domestic programs. Truman also pressed for national measures against racial discrimination.

The 1952 election of Dwight D. Eisenhower gave the Republicans the presidency for the first time in 20 years. Eisenhower's personal appeal, however, did not signal an end to the power of the Democratic coalition that had held sway since the 1930s.

QUESTIONS FOR REVIEW AND CRITICAL THINKING

Review

1. What major conflicts between the United States and the Soviet Union shaped the Cold War, and what were the principal elements of the U.S. foreign policy called containment?

2. How did the foreign policy of containment affect domestic policy and American life?

3. What were the guiding assumptions of the Fair Deal, and which of its major initiatives seemed likely to pass through Congress? Which proposals seemed likely to stall there, and why?

4. How did a resurgent civil rights movement and a new suburban culture help signal changes in American life during the immediate postwar era?

Critical Thinking

1. In what ways was U.S. policy during the Korean War consistent or inconsistent with the policy of containment?

2. How did Truman's Fair Deal seek both to fulfill and depart from Roosevelt's New Deal vision?

ONLINE RESOURCES

 Visit the companion website to access flashcards, crossword puzzles, exercises, and quizzes related to this chapter: www.cengage.com/history/murrin/libertyequalconc5e.

 See our interactive ebook for map and primary source activities.

How did the Cold War affect American politics and culture?

GOVERNMENT AND LAW Examine the cartoon "It's Okay—We're Hunting Communists." Who are the people in the street who have been run over? Who is driving the car? What was the Committee on Un-American Activities and what was it attempting to do in early Cold War America? Why did it claim that its actions were justified? Does the cartoonist think that the actions of this committee were legitimate? From reading this chapter, how do you assess the threat that communists posed to America during these years and the work of the Committee on Un-American Activities, and then Senator McCarthy, in containing this threat?

In thinking about this question, begin by breaking it down into the components shown below. A discussion of the significance of each component should appear in your answer.

CULTURE AND SOCIETY Look at the *film noir* poster on page 748 in light of the material in this chapter. What is suggested by the woman's dress, pose, expression, and size compared to the man? What was the social significance of the *femme fatale*? How was this image of women seen to threaten both men and women and represent social breakdown? How might these movies have both challenged the conformity of the late 1940s and 1950s and underscored the threats posed by those who broke the law or stepped outside traditional gender roles?

"It's okay - We're hunting Communists," October 31, 1947 Ink, graphite, and opaque white over graphite underdrawing on layered paper. Published in the Washington Post (18). © Herb Block. Library of Congress Prints and Photographs Division [LC-US262-127327]

IT'S OKAY—WE'RE HUNTING COMMUNISTS

28

AFFLUENCE AND ITS DISCONTENTS, 1953–1963

With the end of the fighting in Korea in 1953, Cold War tensions began to abate. President Dwight David Eisenhower modulated the pitch of the anticommunist rhetoric coming from the White House, although he and his successor, John F. Kennedy, still pledged a determined anticommunist foreign policy.

At home, Ike and JFK supported, with differing degrees of enthusiasm, efforts to extend some of the domestic programs initiated during the 1930s and 1940s. Sustained economic growth during the late 1950s and early 1960s encouraged talk about an age of "affluence." It also generated concern about conformity, the behavior of young people, and the impact of commercial mass culture. At the same time, concern about the distribution of the nation's economic bounty and a movement to end racial discrimination renewed debates over the use of governmental power—and the meanings of liberty and equality.

TIMELINE

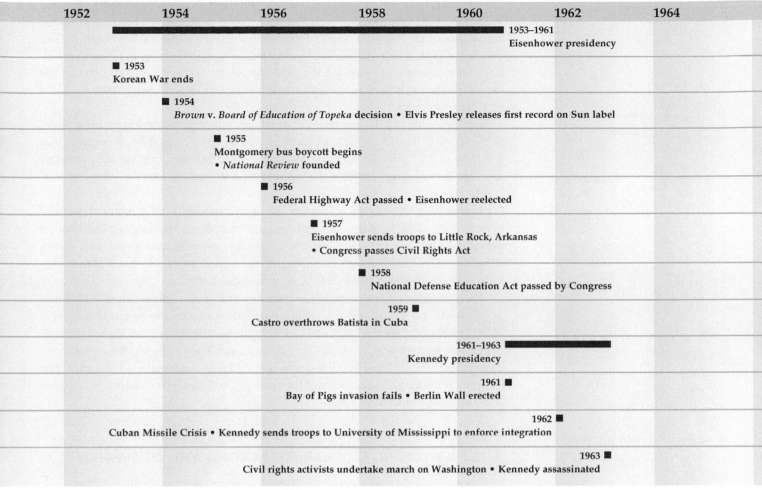

1952	1954	1956	1958	1960	1962	1964

1953–1961
Eisenhower presidency

■ **1953**
Korean War ends

■ **1954**
Brown v. *Board of Education of Topeka* decision • Elvis Presley releases first record on Sun label

■ **1955**
Montgomery bus boycott begins
• *National Review* founded

■ **1956**
Federal Highway Act passed • Eisenhower reelected

■ **1957**
Eisenhower sends troops to Little Rock, Arkansas
• Congress passes Civil Rights Act

■ **1958**
National Defense Education Act passed by Congress

1959 ■
Castro overthrows Batista in Cuba

1961–1963
Kennedy presidency

1961 ■
Bay of Pigs invasion fails • Berlin Wall erected

1962 ■
Cuban Missile Crisis • Kennedy sends troops to University of Mississippi to enforce integration

1963 ■
Civil rights activists undertake march on Washington • Kennedy assassinated

FOREIGN POLICY, 1953–1960

The U.S. strategy for containing communism shifted during the 1950s. Bipolar confrontations between the United States and the Soviet Union over European issues gave way to greater reliance on nuclear deterrence and on directing more subtle power plays in the **Third World:** the Middle East, Asia, Latin America, and Africa.

FOCUS QUESTION
In what ways did the "New Look" reorient the foreign policy of containment?

EISENHOWER TAKES COMMAND

Eisenhower honored a campaign pledg to travel to Korea to end U.S. military involvement there. Negotiations temporarily broke down, however, over whether North Korean and Chinese prisoners of war (POWs) could choose to remain in South Korea. Anxious to conclude matters, Eisenhower began to hint about using nuclear weapons if diplomacy failed. Talks resumed, and on July 27, 1953, both sides signed a truce that established a commission of neutral nations to handle the POW issue. (The POWs themselves were subsequently allowed to determine whether they wished to be repatriated.) A conflict in which more than 2 million Asians, mostly noncombatants, and 53,000 Americans died finally ended. A formal peace treaty remained unsigned, however, and the 38th parallel became one of the most heavily fortified borders in the world.

Third World *Less economically developed areas of the world, primarily the Middle East, Asia, Latin America, and Africa.*

At home, Ike gradually wrested control of the national security issue from more militant anticommunists, including Senator Joseph McCarthy. Congress exceeded the wishes of the Eisenhower administration when it passed the Communist Control Act of 1954, which barred the American Communist Party from running candidates in elections and extended the 1950 McCarran Act. With a GOP president in the White House, however, most Republicans began to reject confrontational styles of anticommunism.

Joe McCarthy finally careened out of control when he began to speculate about subversives in the U.S. Army. A Senate committee investigated his charges. Under the glare of TV lights, McCarthy appeared as a crude bully, hurling wild slanders in every direction. In late 1954 the Senate voted to censure him for "unbecoming" conduct.

Meanwhile, the Eisenhower administration crafted its own national security agenda, extending Truman's earlier programs of domestic surveillance and covert action overseas. It also backed a secret program to develop new aerial surveillance capabilities; by 1956 intelligence photographs taken from new **U-2 spy planes** provided U.S. strategists with a clear view of the Soviet arsenal.

Most historians have come to see Eisenhower as a skilled president who could aggressively use the power of his office while often seeming to be doing relatively little. Eisenhower, in the words of one scholar, conducted a "hidden hand presidency." In foreign policy, he usually allowed John Foster Dulles, his secretary of state from 1953 to 1959, to take center stage. Ike also encouraged the idea that George Humphrey, his secretary of the treasury, and Sherman Adams, his chief of staff, handled domestic matters.

THE NEW LOOK, GLOBAL ALLIANCES, AND SUMMITRY

Generally working behind the scenes, Eisenhower refashioned the nation's anticommunist foreign policy. To begin, he allowed Secretary of State Dulles to warn, repeatedly, that Washington would consider adopting measures to "roll back," rather than simply to contain, communism.

Meanwhile, the Eisenhower administration reviewed U.S. military policy. The head of the Joint Chiefs of Staff urged cutting back the military budget and emphasizing nuclear weaponry and air power. This "New Look" reflected Eisenhower's concern that spiraling military expenditures might eventually strangle economic growth. The new approach would rely less on costly ground forces and more on advanced nuclear capabilities, airpower, covert action, cultural outreach, and economic pressure.

The Eisenhower administration elevated psychological warfare and "informational" programs into major Cold War weapons. The government-run Voice of America extended its radio broadcasts globally. Washington secretly funded Radio Free Europe, Radio Liberty (beamed to the Soviet Union), and Radio Asia. In 1953 Eisenhower persuaded Congress to create the United States Information Agency (USIA) to coordinate anticommunist propaganda campaigns.

The Eisenhower administration's doctrine of **massive retaliation** gambled that the threat of U.S. nuclear weaponry would check Soviet expansion. To make the U.S. nuclear umbrella more effective, Eisenhower expanded NATO to include West Germany in 1955 and added two other mutual defense pacts with noncommunist nations in Central and Southeast Asia. The Southeast Asia Treaty Organization (SEATO), formed in 1954, linked the United States to Australia, France, Great Britain, New Zealand, Pakistan, the Philippines, and Thailand. The Central Treaty

U-2 spy plane *Aircraft specializing in high-altitude reconnaissance.*

massive retaliation *Assertion by the Eisenhower administration that the threat of U.S. atomic weaponry would hold Communist powers in check.*

Organization (CENTO), created in 1959, included Pakistan, Iran, Turkey, Iraq, and Great Britain.

The United States and the USSR, hoping to improve relations, began holding high-level "summit meetings." In May 1955 U.S. and Soviet leaders agreed to end the postwar occupation of Austria and to transform it into a neutral nation. Two months later, the United States, the Soviet Union, Britain, and France met in Geneva, Switzerland, and inaugurated cultural exchanges. Some optimistic observers began to talk about the "spirit of Geneva." In fall 1959, to heal rifts over the future of divided Berlin, Khrushchev toured the United States, visiting a farm in Iowa and Disneyland in California. Although a 1960 Paris summit meeting fell apart after the Soviets shot down a U-2 spy plane over their territory, the tone of Cold War rhetoric seemed to grow less strident during Eisenhower's presidency.

The superpowers even began to consider reducing their stockpiles of nuclear weapons. Eisenhower's **Open Skies** initiative of 1955 proposed mutual reconnaissance flights over each other's territory to verify disarmament efforts. The Soviets balked, but some progress was made in limiting atomic testing. Responding to the health hazards of radioactive fallout, both nations slowed aboveground testing and discussed a broader test-ban agreement.

For some Americans, these efforts came too late. Government documents finally declassified in the 1980s confirmed that people who had lived "downwind" from nuclear test sites during the 1940s and 1950s suffered a number of atomic-related illnesses. Subsequent revelations showed that the government had covertly experimented with radioactive materials on unsuspecting citizens.

Events in Eastern Europe tested the likelihood that the United States and the USSR would square off, militarily, there. Many Soviet-dominated "satellite" countries resented their badly managed communist economies and detested their police-state regimes. Seizing on hints of what appeared to be a post-Stalin relaxation of the USSR's heavy hand, insurgents in Poland staged a three-day rebellion in June 1956. They forced the Soviets to accept Wladyslaw Gomulka, an old foe of Stalin, as Poland's head of state. Hungarians then rallied in support of Imre Nagy, another anti-Stalinist communist, who pledged to create a multiparty political system. After attempts at finding some accommodation failed, Soviet military forces moved against the new Hungarian government.

Hungarian insurgents appealed to the United States for assistance. They apparently took seriously earlier U.S. rhetoric about "rolling back" Soviet power. U.S. military strategists, however, recognized the danger of mounting a military operation so close to Soviet territory. Soviet armies crushed the uprising and killed thousands, including Nagy.

COVERT ACTION AND ECONOMIC LEVERAGE

Meanwhile, the U.S. campaign to contain communism shifted toward the Third World, with covert action and economic pressure the primary tools. These tactics, less visible and less expensive than military deployments, also seemed less likely to provoke political controversies at home or showdowns with the Soviets abroad.

The CIA, headed by Allen Dulles, brother of the secretary of state, played a key role in U.S. policy. In 1953 the CIA helped engineer the election of the anticommunist Ramón Magsaysay as president of the Philippines. That same year, the CIA facilitated a coup in Iran, which overthrew Mohammed Mossadegh's constitutional

Open Skies *Eisenhower's proposal that U.S. and Soviet disarmament be verified by reconnaissance flights over each other's territory.*

QUICK REVIEW

EISENHOWER'S FOREIGN POLICY

- Negotiated truce in Korean War

- Provided surveillance of Soviet military capabilities with U-2 spy planes

- Emphasized air power and nuclear capabilities in his "New Look" military posture

- Used covert action, economic pressure, and informational diplomacy as techniques of containment

- Lowered Cold War tensions at summit meetings and atomic test-ban talks

(and left-leaning) government and restored Shah Reza Pahlavi to power. The increasingly dictatorial shah remained a firm ally of Washington and a friend to American oil interests until he was ousted by Islamic fundamentalists in 1979. In 1954 the CIA secretly helped topple President Jacobo Arbenz Guzmán's elected government in Guatemala. Officials in Washington and executives of the United Fruit Company wanted Arbenz, whose broad support included that of Guatemala's communist party, ousted.

Impressed by the potential of these covert operations, the National Security Council widened the CIA's mandate. By 1960 the CIA deployed approximately 15,000 agents around the world.

Eisenhower also employed economic strategies—trade and aid—to fight communism and win allies. Governmental initiatives sought to open new opportunities for U.S. enterprises overseas, discourage other countries from adopting state-directed economic systems, and encourage expanded trade ties. Supporters of these efforts credited U.S. policy with encouraging greater stability in recipient countries. Military aid to the Third World rose sharply as well. The buildup of armaments in Third World nations provided the United States with stronger anticommunist allies but also contributed to the development of military dictatorships.

AMERICA AND THE THIRD WORLD

In pursuing its policies, the Eisenhower administration employed a broad definition of "communist." In many nations, groups advocating labor rights and land redistribution had allied with local communist movements. Such groups' opponents could hope to win U.S. support by mentioning the word "communist" to policymakers in Washington.

LATIN AMERICA

In Latin America, the White House gravitated toward dictatorial regimes that welcomed U.S. economic investment and opposed leftist movements. Eisenhower publicly honored dictators in Peru and Venezuela and privately confessed admiration for the anticommunism of Paraguay's General Alfredo Stroessner, a tyrant who sheltered ex-Nazis and ran his country as if it were a private fiefdom. Eisenhower's administration cultivated its close ties with Cuban dictator Fulgencio Batista, and the CIA secretly trained Batista's repressive security forces.

Such policies encouraged anti-American sentiment in much of Latin America. Events in Cuba dramatized the growing hostility. After Fidel Castro toppled Batista's pro-U.S. regime in December 1959 and promised to reduce Cuba's dependence on the United States, the Eisenhower administration imposed an economic boycott. Castro turned to the Soviet Union, declared himself a communist, squashed dissent at home, and pledged to support Cuban-style insurgencies throughout Latin America.

The Eisenhower administration ordered a review of the U.S. policies that seemed to be generating animosity and sparking anti-U.S. political movements throughout Latin America. This review ultimately recommended greater emphasis on encouraging democratic political processes, human rights, and economic growth in Latin America. Meanwhile, the CIA pondered how best to hamstring, and then eliminate, Castro.

NASSERISM AND THE SUEZ CRISIS OF 1956

In the Middle East, distrust of nationalism and neutralism shaped U.S. policy. In 1954 when Colonel Gamal Abdel Nasser led a successful military coup in Egypt against a corrupt monarchy, he promised to help rescue other Arab nations from European domination and guide them toward "positive neutralism" in the Cold War. Nasser denounced Israel; boosted Egypt's economic and military power; extended diplomatic recognition to the People's Republic of China; and purchased advanced weapons from communist Czechoslovakia.

The Eisenhower administration viewed these policies as neither positive nor neutral. It cancelled loans to build the Aswan Dam, a project designed to improve agriculture along the Nile River and provide power for new Egyptian industries. Nasser responded, in July 1956, by seizing the British-controlled Suez Canal. Suez was of economic and symbolic importance to Britain, and its forces, joined by those of France and Israel, attacked Egypt in October and seized back the canal.

Eisenhower distrusted Nasser, but he opposed Britain's blatant attempt to retain its imperial position. Denouncing the Anglo-French-Israeli action, he threatened to destabilize Britain's currency unless the invasion ended. Eventually, a plan supported by the United States and the UN gave Egypt control over to the Suez Canal, but U.S. influence in the area suffered as the Soviet Union took over financing of the Aswan Dam.

With Nasser-style nationalism now seeming to lean toward the USSR, the Eisenhower administration feared the spread of "Nasserism" throughout the energy-rich Middle East. In spring 1957 the **Eisenhower Doctrine** pledged to defend Middle Eastern countries "against overt armed aggression from any nation controlled by international communism." When ruling elites in Lebanon and Jordan faced revolts by domestic forces friendly to Nasser, Eisenhower dispatched U.S. Marines to Lebanon, and Britain helped Jordan's King Hussein retain his throne.

The Eisenhower administration tried to squelch left-leaning political movements throughout the Third World. In 1958 the CIA furnished planes and pilots to rebels trying to overthrow Achmed Sukarno, leader of Indonesia, who drew support from that nation's large Communist Party. The rebellion failed, and Sukarno tightened his grip on power. CIA operatives also became involved in a plot against Patrice Lumumba, a popular black nationalist in the Congo. Lumumba's opponents killed him in 1961, and scholars still debate the CIA's role in his death.

VIETNAM

Eisenhower's effort to thwart communism and neutralism in the Third World set the stage for a more permanent commitment—in Vietnam. There, communist-nationalist forces led by Ho Chi Minh sought independence from France. At the end of the Second World War, Ho had appealed in vain to the United States to forestall the return of French colonial administration over all Indochina. But U.S. leaders supported French rule. In 1946 Ho Chi Minh and his Vietminh forces went to war against France and its ally, Bao Dai. After a stunning defeat at Dien Bien Phu in 1954, France decided to withdraw from Indochina. The Geneva Peace Accords of 1954, which the United States refused to sign, divided the old Indochina into three sovereign nations: Laos, Cambodia, and Vietnam. The accords further split Vietnam into two jurisdictions—North Vietnam and South Vietnam—until an election could unify the country under a single government.

Eisenhower's advisers feared that events in Vietnam, where Ho Chi Minh stood poised to win any electoral contest, could set off a geopolitical chain reaction that

Eisenhower Doctrine *Policy that stated that the United States would use armed force to respond to imminent or actual communist aggression in the Middle East.*

might ultimately "endanger the stability and security" of Europe and Japan, a formulation known as the "domino theory." As Ho Chi Minh's communist government consolidated control over North Vietnam, Eisenhower supported a noncommunist South Vietnam and ordered covert operations to prevent Ho Chi Minh from becoming head of a unified Vietnam. Ngo Dinh Diem, an anticommunist Catholic who led the South, renounced the Geneva Peace Accords and refused to hold elections to establish a unified government. Diem redistributed French-owned land, augmented his military forces, and launched an industrialization program. But Diem alienated much of South Vietnam's predominantly Buddhist population, and, as time passed, he grew increasingly isolated from his own people. The United States sent billions of dollars and hundreds of military advisers to prop up Diem's government.

Although Eisenhower feared that U.S. military involvement there would be a "tragedy," he increased aid to South Vietnam and tied America's policy to Diem's shaky political fortunes. The decision of whether Eisenhower's commitments would lead to military action by the United States itself would fall to Ike's successors.

AFFLUENCE—A "PEOPLE OF PLENTY"

FOCUS QUESTION
How could economic growth be seen as both an opportunity and a problem during the 1950s?

In his farewell address of 1961, the former general warned that the greatest danger to the United States was not communism but the nation's own "military-industrial complex." This complex, he said, threatened to so accelerate the costs of Cold-War containment that the burden of military expenditures would eventually harm the U.S. domestic economy.

Eisenhower's warning contained several ironies. Most obviously, his administration, while trying to contain costs, had watched ever-larger sums of money flow to the national-security establishment. Moreover, his selection of businessmen to head the Department of Defense seemingly dramatized the same linkage Ike decried. In addition, Eisenhower's warnings about possible dangers came after eight years during which his White House had praised the nation's continued economic growth. In 1940 the United States had still teetered on the brink of economic depression. By 1960 it could claim a GNP more than five times that of Great Britain and at least 10 times that of Japan.

ECONOMIC GROWTH

The 1950s marked the midpoint of a period of steady economic growth that began during the Second World War and continued until the early 1970s. At the time, historian David Potter called Americans a "people of plenty." Corporations turned out vast quantities of consumer goods and enjoyed rising profits.

Newer industries, such as chemicals and electronics, dominated world markets. Corning Glass reported that most of its sales in the mid-1950s came from products that had been unknown in 1940. General Electric proclaimed that "progress is our most important product." National security policies helped sustain this economic growth by facilitating global access to raw materials and energy. Government spending on defense also pumped money into the economy; in 1955 military expenditures accounted for about 10 percent of the GNP.

The new suburbs and their residents exemplified this age of consumer abundance. Because these outlying areas lacked, at best, adequate mass transit, life revolved around the automobile. Car-buying expanded during the 1950s as the two-car family and new suburban shopping malls became tangible symbols of economic growth. Widespread ownership of kitchen appliances, television sets, and automobiles supported the claim that Americans were a people of plenty. In 1955 *Fortune* magazine hailed "The Rich Middle-Income Class."

Harvard economist John Kenneth Galbraith topped the bestseller lists with his book *The Affluent Society* (1958). The ideal of **affluence** fit nicely with the dominant vision that celebrated constant economic growth and steady improvement of living standards as a uniquely American way of life. The gulf between rich and poor no longer seemed to be between people with cars and those without them, but between people with Cadillacs and Lincolns and those with Fords. "Luxury has reached the masses," proclaimed *Fortune* magazine.

Many economists claimed that greater government expenditures would generate even faster growth, but the Eisenhower administration demurred. Fearing that increased spending would fuel inflation, it kept nonmilitary expenditures under tight control and remained committed, at least rhetorically, to restraining even the Pentagon's budget. By the late 1950s the federal government ran balanced budgets.

HIGHWAYS AND WATERWAYS

Eisenhower did, however, endorse several costly new programs. He supported the **Highway Act of 1956**, citing national-security considerations. Financed largely by a national tax on gasoline, the act funded a national system of limited-access expressways. Touted as the largest public works project in world history, this program delighted the oil, concrete, and tire industries; provided steady work for construction firms and labor unions; and boosted the interstate trucking business. It also confirmed the victory of the automobile over competing modes of surface transportation.

The White House also supported expensive water-diversion projects in the West. The Army Corps of Engineers and the Bureau of Reclamation spent billions of dollars on dams, irrigation canals, and reservoirs. Irrigation turned desert into cropland, and elaborate pumping systems even forced rivers to flow uphill. By 1960 much of the West had access to trillions of gallons of water per year, and governmental expenditures laid the basis for new economic growth in Texas, California, and Arizona.

These water projects came at a price. Technologically complicated and costly, they needed similarly complex bureaucracies to sustain them. As a consequence, local communities lost power to government agencies and large-scale entrepreneurs, who pushed aside smaller farmers and ranchers. American Indian tribes, especially, found portions of their land being flooded for reservoirs or purchased by agribusinesses. Moreover, these vast projects—which diverted surface waters, tapped into groundwater tables, and dotted the West with dams and reservoirs—produced ecological problems. They degraded habitats and contributed to the buildup of salt byproducts in the water and the soil. Some scientists began to warn about the overuse of pesticides such as DDT.

LABOR–MANAGEMENT ACCORD

Most corporate leaders, supportive of the kind of government involvement required to build highways and water projects, were learning to live with labor unions as well. The auto industry showed the way.

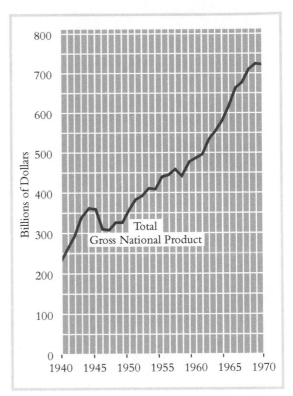

STEADY GROWTH OF GROSS NATIONAL PRODUCT, 1940–1970

affluence *Abundance of material goods or wealth.*

Highway Act of 1956 *Act that appropriated $25 billion for the construction of more than 40,000 miles of interstate highways over a 10-year period.*

Refrigerator-Freezers!

THE FINAL FROST BARRIER!

IT'S HERE!
A FROST-PROOF
FOOD FREEZER!
NO FROST!
NO FROST-LOCKED
FOODS!
NO DEFROSTING!

You'll feel like a queen . . .
- Trim Upright Freezer with award-winning Sheer Look and embossed white-bright Lacework Styling.
- Takes so little floor space – only 32 inches wide – yet this 16 cu. ft. Frost-Proof Imperial Freezer shown, stores 560 lbs. of food.

- Serve family meals in minutes. Be always ready for guests.
- Shop once a week. Enjoy bulk buying that cuts food bills.
- Cook and bake in quantity. Enjoy "free" days.
- Freeze leftovers, like stew, turkey, cake, enjoy them weeks later.
- Have fun freezing your own fruits and vegetables; fish and game, too.

DESIGNED WITH YOU IN MIND!

A REFRIGERATOR OF PLENTY. *As new jet planes were breaking the sound barrier, new refrigerators broke the "frost barrier." Advertising celebrated abundance and progress.*

Union leaders recognized that closer cooperation with corporate management could guarantee employment stability and political influence for their unions. Taking their cue from the United Auto Workers (UAW), one of the most militant unions during the 1930s, labor agreed to bargain aggressively on issues that immediately affected worker paychecks and benefits But also to abide by their union contracts and disavow the wildcat tactics used during the 1930s and 1940s. To police this new labor-management détente, both sides looked to the federal government's National Labor Relations Board (NLRB). Meanwhile, in 1955, the American Federation of Labor (AFL) and the Congress of Industrial Organizations (CIO), long at odds, merged.

Some activists expressed concern about the new direction of the labor movement. Although membership rolls stood at record highs, nearly two-thirds of all unionized workers lived in only 10 states. Worse, there were clear signs in some areas of union strength, such as the Northeast, of companies beginning to move jobs elsewhere, especially to states in the South, where the union movement lacked strong roots.

Business leaders, on the other hand, judged the new direction in labor-management relations as a victory for their side. *Fortune* magazine noted that General Motors had paid a price in terms of more costly employee benefits and higher wages, but that it "got a bargain" on the larger issue of labor peace.

Many nonunionized businesses also expanded benefits for their workers. Companies such as Sears and Eastman Kodak encouraged a cooperative corporate culture by offering health and pension plans, profit-sharing arrangements, and social programs. Some created private recreational parks for the exclusive use of their employees. Satisfying workers, executives reasoned, would reduce the appeal of both unionization and governmental welfare measures.

During the 1950s and early 1960s real wages (what workers make after adjusting their paychecks for inflation) rose steadily, and jobs were plentiful. The frequency of industrial accidents dropped; fringe benefits (health insurance, paid vacation time, and retirement plans) improved; and job security was generally high.

POLITICAL PLURALISM

Economic growth also appeared to help sustain a stable political system. Observers of the domestic scene could not help but see their own times in terms of memories of the past and visions of the future. After the conflicts of the 1930s, the disruptions during the Second World War, and the Great Fear of the early Cold War period, the 1950s seemed an era of relative tranquility. Moreover, domestic life in the United States seemed less troubled and chaotic than that in other parts of the Cold War world. An increasingly prosperous nation worked, fairly effectively, to mute conflict and solve domestic problems.

According to the dominant viewpoint, which political scientists called "pluralism" (or "interest-group pluralism"), U.S. politics featured a roughly equal bargaining process among well-organized interest groups. John Kenneth Galbraith coined the term "countervailing power" to claim that labor unions, consumer lobbies, farm organizations, and other groups could check the desires of giant corporations. No single group could hope to dictate to the others, celebrants of pluralism claimed, because so many interests felt so securely empowered. Pluralists shrugged off signs of decline in political participation, clearly evident in how few citizens went to the polls on election days, by arguing that low voter turnouts showed widespread satisfaction with how well existing processes worked.

In addition to praising the process, pluralists praised the results. Public leaders, it seemed, could find a "realistic" solution to virtually every political problem. Short-term conflicts over specific issues might never disappear, but supporters of the pluralist vision pointed out how affluence could moderate political passions and point warring interests toward viable long-term agreements on fundamental arrangements. As a professor at Harvard Law School put it, constant economic growth meant that "in any conflict of interest," it was "always possible to work out a solution" because continuing affluence guaranteed that any settlement would leave all interests "better off than before."

A RELIGIOUS PEOPLE

The celebration of political pluralism accompanied the exaltation of religion's role in American life. Congress, as part of the crusade against "atheistic communism," constructed a nondenominational prayer room on Capitol Hill; added the phrase "under God" to the Pledge of Allegiance; and declared the phrase "In God We Trust," emblazoned on U.S. currency for nearly a century, the official national motto.

At the same time, observers claimed that intense religious allegiances no longer divided people as much as in the past. President Eisenhower declared that "our government makes no sense unless it is founded in a deeply felt religious faith—and I don't care what it is."

Religious leaders echoed this theme of religious pluralism and toleration. Will Herberg's *Protestant-Catholic-Jew* (1955) argued that these three faiths were really "saying the same thing" in affirming the "spiritual ideals" and "moral values" of the American way of life. Rabbi Morris Kretzer, head of the Jewish Chaplain's Organization, reassured Protestants and Catholics that they and their Jewish neighbors shared "the same rich heritage of the Old Testament . . . the sanctity of the Ten Commandments, the wisdom of the prophets, and the brotherhood of man." A 1954 survey claimed that more than 95 percent of the population identified with one of the three major faiths, and religious commentators talked about the "Judeo-Christian tradition."

Several religious leaders became celebrities. The Baptist evangelist Billy Graham achieved superstar status during the 1950s. Norman Vincent Peale, a

Protestant minister, sold millions of books declaring that belief in a Higher Power could bring "health, happiness, and goodness" to daily life. His *The Power of Positive Thinking* (1952) remained a bestseller throughout the 1950s. The Catholic Bishop Fulton J. Sheen hosted the prime-time television program *Life Is Worth Living*.

Peale, Sheen, and Graham identified with conservative, anticommunist causes, but an emphasis on religious faith could be found all across the political spectrum. Dorothy Day, who had been involved in religiously based community activism since the early 1930s, continued to crusade for world peace and for a program aimed at redistributing wealth. Church leaders and laypeople from all three major religions provided leadership in the civil rights movement.

Discontents of Affluence

These celebrations of affluence, political pluralism, and religious faith existed alongside a vibrant body of social criticism. The 1950s produced a diverse body of literature that looked critically at conformity, young people, mass culture, discrimination, and inequality.

Conformity in an Affluent Society

In *The Organization Man* (1956), sociologist William H. Whyte, Jr., indicted corporate culture for contributing to an unwanted byproduct of affluence: conformity. Whyte saw ordinary corporate employees deferring to the wishes and values of their bosses, at the expense of their own individuality. David Riesman, another sociologist, offered an even broader critique in *The Lonely Crowd* (1950). He wrote of a shift from an "inner-directed" culture, in which people looked to themselves and their immediate families for their sense of identity and self-worth, to an "other-directed" one, in which people looked to others for approval and measured their worth against mass-mediated images. An other-directed society emphasized "adjustment" to the expectations of others rather than individual "autonomy."

Riesman pointed to *Tootle, the Engine*, a popular children's book, to show how baby boomers learned conformist values. After "Tootle" shows a preference for jumping the rails and frolicking in the fields, peer pressure from his community gets him "back on the tracks." If he remains on the straight-and-narrow and follows lines laid down by others, Tootle learns, his future as a powerful and fast-moving streamliner seems assured.

The critique of social conformity reached its widest audience through the best-selling books of journalist Vance Packard. *The Hidden Persuaders* (1957) argued that advertising—especially its calculated appeals to the insecurities of consumers—encouraged conformity. His book, Packard claimed, could help its readers "to achieve a creative life in these conforming times" when so many people "are left only with the roles of being consumers or spectators."

Critics such as Whyte, Riesman, and Packard generally highlighted signs of conformity and loss of selfhood supposedly evident among middle-class men, but writers such as **Betty Friedan** warned about an analogous malaise among women. Business corporations expected middle-class wives to help their husbands deal with the demands of corporate life, and many women found themselves entrapped in a stultifying sphere of domestic obligations. Women's individuality and power, Friedan wrote, was stifled within a conformist "feminine mystique."

Betty Friedan *Author of* The Feminine Mystique *(1963) and founder of the National Organization for Women (1966).*

QUICK   REVIEW

CHARACTERISTICS OF "AGE OF AFFLUENCE" IN THE 1950s

- New consumer products, youth culture, and expanded mass culture

- Rising wages, benefits, and living standards, and steady employment for most male workers

- New system of interstate highways

- New lands for development opened by massive government-funded irrigation projects

- Emphasis on political and religious "pluralism"

- New concerns about conformity

The affluent cultural climate of the 1950s, then, hardly discouraged social criticism, some of it quite pointed. The much-vaunted American way of life, in the view of sociologist C. Wright Mills, featured increasingly regimented work routines and meaningless leisure-time activities that could rarely produce any true sense of satisfaction. Meanwhile, a "power elite" set the agenda for all public policy discussions, especially those involving national security and domestic spending priorities.

RESTIVE YOUTH

Concerns about young people intensified during the 1950s. At one point, criminologists linked a rise in juvenile delinquency to the sale of comic books. The *Seduction of the Innocent* (1954), by the psychologist Frederick Wertham, blamed comics featuring images of sex and violence for "mass-conditioning" children and stimulating social unrest. Responding to legislation by some U.S. cities and to calls for federal regulations, the comic book industry embraced self-censorship. Publishers who followed new guidelines for portraying violence and deviant behavior could display a seal of approval. The "great comic book scare" faded away.

Other worrisome signs persisted, however. In 1954 Elvis Presley, a former truck driver from Memphis, rocked the pop music scene with a string of hits on the tiny Sun record label. Presley's sensual, electric stage presence thrilled his young admirers and outraged critics. Presley and other youthful exponents of rock and roll music—including Buddy Holly from West Texas, Richard Valenzuela (Richie Valens) from East Los Angeles, Frankie Lymon

ELVIS PRESLEY. *A former truck driver from Memphis, "Elvis the Pelvis" drew upon blues, gospel, hillbilly, and pop music traditions to become the premier rock 'n' roll star of the 1950s.*

from Spanish Harlem, and "Little Richard" Penniman from Georgia—leaped over cultural and ethnic barriers and shaped new musical forms from older ones, especially African American rhythm and blues and the "hillbilly" music of southern whites. Rock 'n' rollers spoke to the hopes and fears of millions of young fans. They sang about the joy of "having a ball tonight"; the pain of the "summertime blues"; the torment of being "a teenager in love"; and the hope of deliverance, through the power of rock, from "the days of old." Songs such as "Roll over Beethoven" by Chuck Berry became powerful teen anthems.

Guardians of older, family-oriented forms of commercial culture found rock music far more frightening than comic books. They denounced its lyrics, pulsating guitars, and screeching saxophones as an assault on the very idea of music. Even its name, it seemed obvious, played to raging teenage hormones. Religious groups denounced rock as the "Devil's music;" anticommunists detected a clever Red strategy to corrupt youth; and segregationists saw it as part of a plot to encourage "race-mixing." Even the FBI's J. Edgar Hoover weighed in, calling rock music "repulsive to right-thinking people" and a social force that would soon have "serious effects on our young people." The danger of rock 'n' roll seemed abundantly evident in The *Blackboard Jungle* (1955), a hit movie about a racially mixed group of sexually active students who, for good measure, terrorize teachers and mock adult authority.

Rock 'n' roll music spoke to the concerns of its young audience. The satirical "Charlie Brown" contrasted pieties about staying in school with the bleak educational opportunities open to many students. Chuck Berry sang of a terminally bored teenager riding around "with no particular place to go." This kind of implied social criticism in songs anticipated the more overtly rebellious music of the 1960s.

At the same time, rock music and the larger youth culture of the 1950s also merged into that era's mass-consumption ethic. Sun Records, lacking capital, sold Presley's contract to RCA. Record companies and Top-40 radio stations saw middle-class teenagers as a market segment worth targeting. In "Sweet Little Sixteen," Berry sang about an affluent teenager chasing after the latest fashions, the next rock 'n' roll show, and "about half-a million framed autographs." Record companies promoted performers who exalted the pursuit of "fun, fun, fun," which apparently required the latest clothes, late-model automobiles, and rock 'n' roll records.

THE MASS CULTURE DEBATE

Concern about social conformity and youth-oriented styles merged into a wider debate over mass culture. Much of the anxiety about the decline of individualism and the rise of disruptive young people stemmed from fears that "hidden persuaders" might reach millions of people with standardized imagery and messages. Cosmopolitan cultural critics worried that "bad" art—such as comics and rock 'n' roll—would soon purge anything "good" from the cultural marketplace. Moreover, they warned that the mass media would obscure local cultural differences underneath a blur of superficial imagery.

Television, dominated by three large corporations (NBC, CBS, and ABC) and sustained by advertisers, provided a prominent target in the mass-culture debate. Picturing millions of passive viewers gathered around "the boob tube," critics decried both the quality and the presumed impact of mass-produced programming. Network television, according to its critics, encouraged viewers to retreat into unrealities such as a mythical Old West or the fake competition of TV quiz shows. By the late 1950s the television networks filled many of their prime-time hours with western-themed series (such as *Gunsmoke*) and quiz programs (such as the *64,000 Question*) (whose contestants had been supplied the answers they pretended to be puzzling over). The head of the Federal Communications Commission (FCC) would soon denounce TV as a "vast wasteland."

Critics also worried about television's effect on the fabric of everyday life. Architects rearranged living space so that the TV set could become the focal point of family gatherings. New products—such as the frozen TV dinner, the TV tray, the recliner chair, and the influential magazine *TV Guide*—became extensions of television culture.

The mass culture that critics decried, however, was embedded within the economic system that these same observers generally celebrated. Was it possible to eliminate the curse of mass culture without sacrificing liberty and affluence? If, for example, Congress legislated against "dangerous" cultural products, censorship might end up curtailing free expression. If local communities were to step in, as some had done with comics, the results might be even worse. The prospect of southern segregationists confiscating civil rights literature, or local censorship boards banning books by celebrated authors, hardly appealed to the cosmopolitan, well-educated critics of mass culture. Their extensive critique seemed short on solutions; most important, it did nothing to halt the flood of products and programs aimed at an ever-expanding audience.

CHANGING GENDER POLITICS

The 1950s saw significant changes in how and where people lived and worked. This era particularly challenged ideas about the nature of gender relationships.

THE NEW SUBURBS AND GENDER IDEALS

In middle-class homes, especially in the new suburbs, women discovered just how "liberating" consumer technology might be. Modern conveniences—automatic clothes washers, more powerful vacuum cleaners, home freezers—eased old burdens but created new ones. The time that women spent on domestic duties was not reduced so much as shifted to new activities requiring new household gadgets.

Life in the new suburbs was structured by a broad pattern of "separate spheres: a public sphere of work and politics dominated by men, and a private sphere of housework and child care reserved for women. Because few businesses located in these suburbs, men commuted from home to work, while women found employment opportunities about as scarce as child-care facilities. Mothers spent a great deal of time taking care of their baby-boomer children. In contrast to the urban neighborhoods or the rural communities where many suburban housewives had grown up, suburbs of the 1950s contained few older relatives or younger single women who could help with household and child-care duties.

Without mothers or grandmothers living close by, young suburban mothers turned to child-care manuals for advice. **Dr. Benjamin Spock**'s *Baby and Child Care*, first published in 1946, sold millions of copies. Like earlier advice books, Spock's assigned virtually all child-care duties to women and implied that the family and the nation itself depended on how well mothers performed.

The alarmist tone of many of these books reflected—and helped generate—widespread concern about juvenile delinquency. A problem teen, according to one 1950s study, sprang from a "family atmosphere not conducive to development of emotionally well-integrated, happy youngsters, conditioned to obey legitimate authority." The ideal mother devoted herself to rearing her children. Women who sought careers outside of the home and marriage risked being labeled as maladjusted and deviant—real-life versions of the *femme fatales* who populated films noirs (see Chapter 27).

Versions of this message appeared nearly everywhere. Even the nation's prestigious women's colleges assumed their graduates would pursue men and marriage. In a 1955 commencement address at Smith College, Adlai Stevenson, the Democratic Party's urbane presidential contender, reminded graduates that it was the duty of each to keep her husband "truly purposeful, to keep him whole." Popular magazines, psychology literature, and pop-culture imagery suggested that wives and mothers held the keys to social stability. In addition, almost by definition, women who desired alternative arrangements, either in their work or their sexual preferences, needed to be pressured, much as Tootle the Engine, to return to the straight and narrow.

Competing portraits, however, painted a more complicated picture of gender arrangements. Most men told researchers that they preferred an active partner to a "submissive, stay-at-home" wife. Popular TV shows, such as "Father Knows Best"

Dr. Benjamin Spock *Pediatrician who wrote* Baby and Child Care *(1946), the most widely used childrearing book during the baby-boom years.*

and "Leave It to Beaver," suggested that fathers should be more engaged in family life than they seemed to be. Advice manuals, while envisioning suburban husbands earning their family's entire income, increasingly urged them to be "real fathers" at home. Parenting literature emphasized "family togetherness," and institutions such as the Young Men's Christian Association (YMCA) offered courses on how to achieve it.

This call for family togetherness was partly a response to what cultural historians have seen as an incipient "male revolt" against "the "male breadwinner role." Hugh Hefner's *Playboy* magazine, which debuted in 1953, epitomized this trend. It ridiculed men who neglected their own happiness in order to support a wife and children as suckers rather than saints. *Playboy*'s first issue proclaimed: "We aren't a 'family magazine.'" In Hefner's version of the good life, a man rented a "pad" rather than owned a home, drove a sports car rather than a station wagon, and courted the Playmate of the Month rather than the Mother of the Year.

SIGNS OF WOMEN'S CHANGING ROLES

Despite media images of homebound wives and mothers, greater numbers of women worked outside the house. Female employment, even among married women, rose steadily as jobs expanded in the clerical and service sectors. In 1948 about 25 percent of married mothers held jobs outside the home; at the end of the 1950s nearly 40 percent did. With the introduction of a new method of oral contraception, the birth control pill, in 1960 women could enjoy greater control over family planning and career decisions—and over decisions about their own sexual behavior. By 1964 one-quarter of the couples who used contraception relied on "The Pill." At the same time, activists began to press for an end to anti-abortion laws that restricted the ability of women to find legal and relatively safe ways to terminate pregnancies.

Employment opportunities remained limited. Virtually all of the nation's nurses, telephone operators, secretaries, and elementary school teachers were women. Historically, pay scales in these areas lagged behind those for men in comparable fields; union jobs remained rare; and chances for advancement were limited. As the number of low-paid jobs for women expanded during the 1950s, better-paid professional opportunities actually narrowed. Medical, law, and other professional schools admitted few, if any, women. When Sandra Day (who would later become U.S. Supreme Court Justice Sandra Day O'Connor) graduated with honors from a prestigious law school during the 1950s, not a single private firm offered her a job. She worked, without pay, in the public sector. The number of women on college faculties shrank even from the low levels of earlier decades.

Although employers still invoked the "family wage" to justify higher wages for men, more women were supporting a family on their own paychecks. This was especially true for women of color. Recognizing that images of domesticity hardly fit the lives of many African American women, *Ebony* magazine celebrated black women who combined success in parenting and at work.

Mass-circulation magazines aimed at women of European descent also carried mixed messages about gender roles. Although many social commentators continued to label a woman's pursuit of activities outside the home as "unnatural," popular magazines also featured stories about women in public life and in business. The 1950s, in short, saw growing diversity in both the social roles that women were assuming and the ways in which mass culture represented them.

THE FIGHT AGAINST DISCRIMINATION, 1953–1960

When Dwight Eisenhower took office, the Supreme Court was preparing to rehear a legal challenge to racially segregated educational systems. The NAACP and its chief legal strategist, Thurgood Marshall, spearheaded the challenge. Before the rehearing took place, Eisenhower appointed Earl Warren, a former Republican governor of California, as chief justice. The Supreme Court, with Warren as its "Chief," entered the widening struggle against discrimination.

THE *BROWN* CASES, 1954–1955

The Supreme Court case popularly known as "the *Brown* decision" actually included a series of constitutional challenges to school segregation. In 1954 Chief Justice Warren wrote a unanimous opinion (in ***Brown* v. *Board of Education*** of Topeka) declaring that state-mandated segregation of public schools violated the constitutional right of African American students to equal protection of the law. A companion case decided the same day (*Bolling* v. *Sharpe*) outlawed segregated schools in the District of Columbia. Although these decisions technically applied only to schools, they suggested that other segregated public facilities now lay open to constitutional challenge. In 1955, though, yet another Supreme Court decision, known as "*Brown II*," decreed that school desegregation should not go into effect immediately; it could, instead, move forward "with all deliberate speed."

Carrying out the broader implications of the *Brown* cases challenged the nation's political, social, and cultural institutions. The crusade for civil rights sometimes seemed focused on the 16 states that the Census Bureau officially called "the South," but demographic changes helped make the civil rights movement much more than a regional force.

During the 1950s the South became more like the rest of the country. New cultural forces, such as network television, penetrated the region. Machines were displacing the region's predominantly black field workers. The absence of strong labor unions, and the presence of favorable tax laws, attracted national chain stores and northern-based businesses. Meanwhile, the racial composition of cities in the West, Midwest, and Northeast became more like that of the South. In 1940 more than three-quarters of the nation's African Americans lived in the South. After the Second World War, many African Americans left the rural South and became important political constituencies in northern urban areas, where most Democrats and many Republicans generally supported efforts to end racial discrimination. As more African Americans voted Democratic, however, the GOP gained ground among white voters in what had long been the Democratic Party's "solid South" and in the new suburban neighborhoods, especially in the Middle and Far West.

The most familiar stories about the civil rights crusade during the 1950s have long concentrated on the South, but it had nationwide scope. A relatively broad movement to end segregation and racial discrimination emerged, especially among African Americans, in virtually every Northern and Western city. These urban-based movements employed a variety of tactics, such as "shop where you can work" campaigns, which urged African American consumers to patronize only businesses that would employ them. They tried to bring more black workers into the union movement and the public-service sector, so that they could find jobs in police and fire departments as well as in all of the agencies of state and local government. Increasingly, though, gaining political leverage seemed crucial to making gains in other areas.

FOCUS QUESTION
How did the fight against discrimination raise new political issues and visions during the 1950s and early 1960s? How did the nation's political and social institutions respond to these issues?

Brown* v. *Board of Education *1954 case in which the U.S. Supreme Court unanimously overruled the "separate but equal" doctrine and held that segregation in the public schools violated the principle of equal protection under the law.*

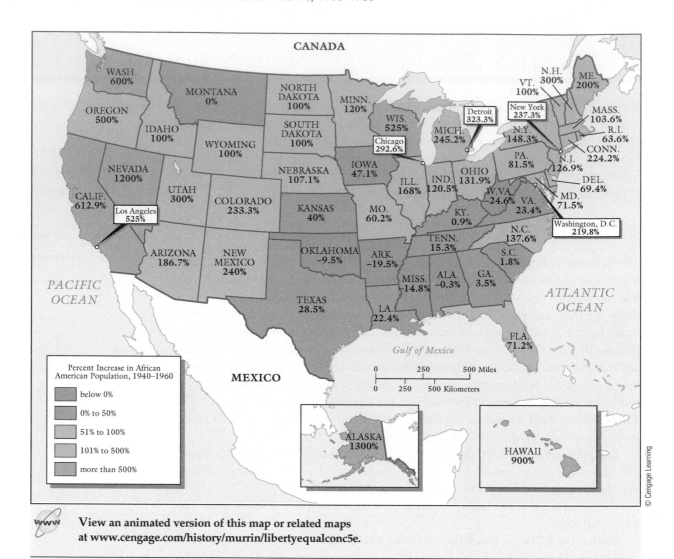

www **View an animated version of this map or related maps at www.cengage.com/history/murrin/libertyequalconc5e.**

Map 28.1 SHIFTS IN AFRICAN AMERICAN POPULATION PATTERNS, 1940–1960. *During and after the Second World War, large numbers of African Americans left the rural South and migrated to new locations. Which states had the largest percentage of outmigration? Which saw the greatest percentage of population increase? How might this migration have affected American life?*

As African Americans mounted new attacks on segregation and discrimination in the South, white segregationists pledged "massive resistance" to the *Brown* decisions and went to court with delaying tactics. One hundred members of Congress signed a "Southern Manifesto" in 1956 that condemned the Court's desegregation rulings as a "clear abuse of judicial power" and pledged support for any state that intended "to resist forced integration by any lawful means."

Defiance went beyond the courtroom. White vigilantes unfurled the banners of the Ku Klux Klan and formed new racist organizations, such as the White Citizens Council. Those who joined the civil rights cause constantly risked injury and death. Racial tensions escalated. In August 1955 two white Mississippians murdered 14-year-old Emmett Till, a visitor from Chicago, because they thought he had acted "disrespectful" toward a white woman. Mamie Till Bradley insisted that her son's death not remain a private incident. She demanded that his maimed corpse be displayed for "the whole world to see" and that his killers be punished. When their case came to trial, an all-white Mississippi jury quickly found the two men—who would subsequently confess their crime to a magazine reporter—not guilty.

THE MONTGOMERY BUS BOYCOTT AND MARTIN LUTHER KING, JR.

The southern civil rights movement increasingly supplemented legal maneuvering with direct action. Following an earlier, partially successful 1953 campaign to desegregate the transportation system in Baton Rouge, Louisiana, activists in Montgomery, Alabama, raised their own sights. After police arrested **Rosa Parks** for defying a local segregation ordinance, Montgomery's black community demanded complete desegregation, boycotted public transportation, and organized carpools as alternative transit. Joining with Rosa Parks, a longtime bastion of the local NAACP chapter, many other black women in Montgomery helped coordinate the complicated, months-long boycott. Responding to events in Montgomery, the Supreme Court extended the premise of the *Brown* decisions on education and specifically declared segregation of public buses to be unconstitutional.

After a campaign lasting more than a year, the **Montgomery bus boycott** succeeded. City officials, saddled with financial losses and legal defeats, agreed to end Montgomery's separatist transit policy. Events in Montgomery suggested that black activists, even in the segregated South, could effectively mobilize—and then organize—community resources to fight against racial discrimination.

The bus boycott vaulted **Dr. Martin Luther King, Jr.,** one of its leaders, into the national spotlight. Born and educated in Atlanta, with a doctorate in theology from Boston University, King and other black ministers followed up the victory in Montgomery by forming the Southern Christian Leadership Conference (SCLC). In addition to demanding desegregated public facilities, the SCLC sought to organize an ongoing sociopolitical movement that would work for permanent change.

The young, male ministers in SCLC sought advice across generational and gender divides. With tactical advice from Bayard Rustin, who had been involved in civil rights activism since the 1940s, and the organizational skills of Ella Baker, another veteran organizer, Dr. King led the SCLC's effort to register African American voters throughout the South.

King and the SCLC relied on **civil disobedience** to obtain social change. According to Dr. King, nonviolent direct action would dramatize, through both word and deed, the evil of racial discrimination. King's powerful presence and religiously rooted rhetoric carried the message of civil rights to most parts of the United States and the world.

THE POLITICS OF CIVIL RIGHTS: FROM THE LOCAL TO THE GLOBAL

All across the country, civil rights activites went forward. Shortly after the conclusion of the Montgomery bus boycott, New York City passed the nation's first "open housing"

Rosa Parks *African American seamstress in Montgomery, Alabama, who, after refusing to give up her bus seat to a white man, was arrested and fined. Her protest sparked a subsequent bus boycott that attracted national sympathy for the civil rights cause and put Martin Luther King, Jr., in the national spotlight.*

Montgomery bus boycott *Political protest campaign mounted in 1955 to oppose the city's policy of racial segregation on its public transit system. The Supreme Court soon declared segregation on public transit unconstitutional.*

Martin Luther King, Jr. *African American clergyman who advocated nonviolent social change and shaped the civil rights movement of the 1950s and 1960s.*

civil disobedience *Nonviolent refusal to obey a law in an attempt to call attention to government policies considered unfair.*

ROSA PARKS IS FINGERPRINTED. *Parks, whose refusal to move to the back of the bus touched off the Montgomery bus boycott, was among some 100 people charged with violating segregation laws.*

AP Photos

ordinance, a model for other local and state measures intended to end racial discrimination in the sale and rental of homes and apartments. Efforts to end discrimination in housing faced tough going, however. Typically, white homeowners in those urban and older suburban neighborhoods where African Americans or Latinos might hope to buy or rent adopted the same exclusionary strategies used so effectively by their counterparts in the new suburbs.

In cities and states outside the South, civil rights groups won legislation to outlaw discrimination in hiring, sometimes working with sympathetic allies. In 1958, for example, a labor-civil rights coalition in California, joining under slogans such as "Fight Sharecropper Wages," defeated an anti-union right-to-work proposal they said threatened to drive down pay for all workers. Buoyed by this success, the same coalition began lobbying members of the legislature to enact a California-wide open housing measure. Political institutions in Washington, D.C., felt pressure to act on civil rights. The Supreme Court lent its support at crucial times, such as during the Montgomery bus boycott, but Congress, with the ability to enact legislation, remained deeply divided on racial issues. With southern segregationists, all members of the Democratic majority, holding key posts on Capitol Hill, antidiscrimination measures faced formidable obstacles.

Even so, Congress did pass its first civil rights measure in more than 80 years. The **Civil Rights Act of 1957** expedited lawsuits by African Americans who claimed abridgement of their right to vote. It also created a Commission on Civil Rights, an advisory body empowered to study alleged violations and recommend remedies. In 1960, with the crucial support of Lyndon Johnson of Texas, the Democratic leader in the Senate, a second civil rights act added more procedures to safeguard voting rights. These civil rights measures became law against fierce opposition from southern Democrats.

President Eisenhower initially appeared reluctant to tackle racial discrimination. He supported the Civil Rights Act of 1957 but held back when some Republicans urged a dramatic presidential step—such as barring racial discrimination on construction projects financed by federal funds. A confirmed gradualist, Eisenhower saw the fight against segregation as primarily a local matter, and he expressed doubts that federal power could change the attitudes of people opposed to integration.

In 1957, however, events in Little Rock, Arkansas, forced Eisenhower to tap his executive power and enforce a federal court decree ordering the desegregation of the city's Central High School. Orval Faubus, the state's segregationist governor, promised to prevent black students from entering the school building and deployed his state's National Guard to block them. Confronting this direct challenge to national authority, Eisenhower took command of the Arkansas National Guard and augmented it with members of the U.S. Army. Black students, escorted by armed troops, finally entered Central High. The primary issue at stake, Eisenhower insisted, was a state's defiance of the law rather than school desegregation.

The confrontation in Little Rock also underscored the international dimension of civil-rights politics in the United States. Washington often found itself on the defensive when foreign critics pointed to the U.S. record on civil rights. The Soviet Union delighted in telling people, particularly in the Third World, how racial discrimination showed "the façade of the so-called 'American democracy.'" When the U.S. Supreme Court, in *Cooper* v. *Aaron* (1958), unanimously invalidated an Arkansas law intended to block integration, the world press highlighted the decision, and the Eisenhower administration's global informational campaign stressed America's support for liberty and equality.

Civil Rights Act of 1957 *First civil rights act since Reconstruction; aimed at securing voting rights for African Americans in the South.*

AMERICAN INDIAN POLICY

The Eisenhower administration struggled with its policy toward American Indians. It attempted to implement two programs, **termination and relocation**, already underway before it took office. The first called for an end to the status of Indians as "wards of the United States" and a grant of all the "rights and privileges pertaining to American citizenship." The goals of termination, to be pursued on a tribe-by-tribe basis, were to abolish reservations, liquidate tribal assets, and curtail the social services offered by the Bureau of Indian Affairs (BIA).

Under the relocation program, which had begun in 1951, Indians were encouraged to leave rural reservations and seek jobs in urban areas. In 1954 the BIA intensified its relocation efforts, with Minneapolis, St. Louis, Dallas, and several other cities joining Denver, Salt Lake City, and Los Angeles as relocation sites. Both relocation and termination assumed that American Indians could easily be assimilated into the mainstream of U.S. life.

The initiatives quickly failed. As several tribes were terminated during the 1950s almost 12,000 people lost their status as tribal members, and the bonds of communal life for many Indians grew weaker. Land formally held by tribes fell into the hands of commercial, non-Indian developers. Indians from terminated tribes also lost both their exemption from state taxation and the social services provided by the BIA. They gained little in return. Relocation went no better. Most relocated Indians found only low-paying, dead-end jobs and racial discrimination.

Native American activists and their supporters soon mobilized against termination and relocation. By 1957 their efforts forced the government to scale back the initial timetable, which had called for liquidating every tribe within five years. In 1960 the party platforms of both the Republicans and Democrats repudiated termination, and in 1962 the policy was stopped. The relocation program continued, however, and by 1967 almost half of the nation's Indians lived in relocation cities. This policy neither touched the deep-rooted problems that many Indians confronted, including a life expectancy only two-thirds that of whites, nor provided significantly better employment or education opportunities.

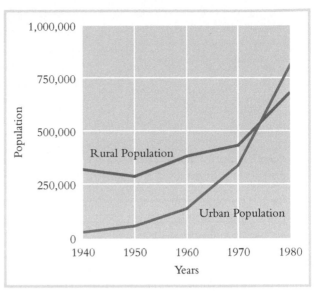

TOTAL URBAN AND RURAL INDIAN POPULATION IN THE UNITED STATES, 1940–1980

THE GROWTH OF SPANISH-SPEAKING POPULATIONS

Millions of Spanish-speaking people, many recently arrived in the United States, also began mobilizing in hopes of realizing the nation's commitments to liberty and equality. Puerto Ricans began moving in larger numbers from their island commonwealth to the mainland in the 1950s. By 1960 New York City's Puerto Rican population was nearly 100 times greater than it had been before the Second World War. Large numbers of Puerto Ricans also settled in Chicago, Boston, and Hartford, Connecticut. Officially U.S. citizens, most of the newcomers spoke only Spanish; social and cultural clubs helped them connect with the Puerto Rican communities they had left behind. At the same time, Puerto Ricans began to organize against the discrimination they faced in housing and jobs. The Puerto Rican-Hispanic Leadership Forum, organized in 1957, presaged the emergence of groups that looked more to social and economic conditions—and, ultimately, greater political clout—in the United States than to cultural affinities with Puerto Rico.

termination and relocation
Policies designed to assimilate American Indians by terminating tribal status and relocating individuals to cities removed from their reservations.

Meanwhile, Spanish-speaking people from Mexico were moving to California and the Southwest, where they joined established Mexican American communities. In 1940 Mexican Americans had been the most rural of all the major ethnic groups; by 1950, in contrast, more than 65 percent of Mexican Americans were living in urban areas, a figure that would climb to 85 percent by 1970. Mexican Americans began to become an important political force in many southwestern cities.

Beginning in 1942 and continuing until 1967 the U.S. government sponsored the *bracero* (or farmhand) program, which brought nearly 5 million Mexicans northward to fill agricultural jobs. Many *braceros* and their families remained in the United States after their work contracts expired. Legal immigrants from Mexico joined them, as did undocumented immigrants, who became targets of a government dragnet called "Operation Wetback." ("Wetback" was a term of derision, implying a swim across the Rio Grande River to reach the United States.) During a five-year period the government claimed to have rounded up and deported to Mexico nearly 4 million undocumented immigrants. This operation, critics charged, helped stigmatize even U.S. citizens of Mexican heritage and justify discriminatory treatment.

Groups representing Mexican Americans mobilized against discrimination. Labor organizers sought higher wages and better working conditions in the factories and fields, even as the FBI labeled their efforts "communist inspired" and harassed unions with large Mexican American memberships, such as the United Cannery, Agricultural, Packing and Allied Workers of America (UCAPAWA). A lengthy mining strike in New Mexico became the subject of the independent motion picture *Salt of the Earth* (1954). Pressure from Washington, the film industry, and anticommunist labor unions throughout the 1950s prevented distribution of this collaboration among blacklisted filmmakers, striking miners, and their families.

Middle-class organizations such as the League of United Latin American Citizens (LULAC) and the Unity League sought to desegregate schools and other public facilities throughout the Southwest. Lawyers for these groups faced a strategic dilemma. Legal challenges brought on behalf of plaintiffs of African descent, as in the *Brown* cases, relied on the claim that state laws separating "whites" and "coloreds" violated guarantees of legal equality. Most states, though, classified persons whose ancestors came from Mexico as legally "white." As earlier cases such as *Westminster* had shown (see Chapter 27), school officials in states such as California and Texas segregated students of Mexican-descent on the basis of real and alleged "language deficiencies" rather than on "race." The "other white" legal status of Mexican Americans, in other words, complicated the ability of organizations such as LULAC to frame court challenges. In practice, it also prevented lawyers from automatically relying on precedents involving "white-against-black" discrimination.

URBAN-SUBURBAN ISSUES

The growth of suburbia during the 1950s helped to highlight urban issues, many of them related to race. Throughout this period, both public and private institutions were shifting resources away from cities, especially away from neighborhoods in which Latinos and African Americans lived. Adopting a policy called **redlining**, many banks and loan institutions denied funds for homebuyers and businesses in areas that were labeled "decaying" or "marginal" because they contained aging buildings, dense populations, and growing numbers of people of non-European descent. The Federal Housing Administration (FHA) and other governmental agencies channeled most lending toward the newer suburbs. In 1960, for example, the FHA failed to put up a single dollar for home loan guarantees in Camden or Paterson, New

redlining *Refusal by banks and loan associations to grant loans for home buying and business expansion in neighborhoods that contained aging buildings, dense populations, and growing numbers of nonwhites.*

Jersey—cities in which minority populations were growing—while it poured millions of dollars into surrounding, largely all-white suburbs.

"Urban renewal" programs, authorized by the Housing Act of 1949 (see Chapter 27), often seemed aimed at "urban removal." Although the law called for "a feasible method for the temporary relocation" of persons displaced, developers generally ignored the requirement. Throughout the 1950s Robert Moses, who directed New York City's vast construction projects, simply concealed the number of people dislocated by his urban renewal and highway building programs.

Plans for federally built public housing quickly faltered in most areas of the United States. Although suburban areas, where land was abundant and inexpensive, seemed the obvious place to locate affordable housing, middle-income homeowners used their political clout and zoning laws to freeze out government-sponsored housing projects. At the same time, private housing interests lobbied to limit the number of public units actually constructed and to ensure that they would offer tenants few amenities, such as closets with doors. Originally conceived as short-term alternatives for families who would soon move to their own homes, publicly built facilities became stigmatized as "the projects," permanent housing of last resort for people with chronically low incomes.

The urban-suburban policies of the 1950s, in short, came to look in need of major repair. In 1960 both the Democratic and Republican Parties pledged to create a new cabinet office for urban affairs and to reconsider Washington's role in addressing the cycle of continued suburban growth and onrushing urban decay.

DEBATING THE ROLE OF GOVERNMENT

Discussion of urban-suburban issues accompanied a broader debate over the power of the federal government. Although Eisenhower sometimes hinted that he favored rolling back the New and Fair Deals, he actually presided over a modest expansion of earlier initiatives: a larger Social Security system, a higher minimum wage, better unemployment benefits, and a new Department of Health, Education, and Welfare (HEW). Still, Eisenhower insisted his approach represented that of a "modern Republicanism."

THE NEW CONSERVATIVES

Eisenhower's self-professed moderation angered a group who became known as the "new conservatives." Eisenhower was popular—and the first Republican president since Herbert Hoover—but did his administration really represent conservative GOP principles?

Not according to Arizona's Barry Goldwater, who won a U.S. Senate seat in 1952. Goldwater quickly emerged as the spokesperson for those Republicans who viewed Eisenhower's policies as insufficiently conservative and too indebted to GOP constituencies on the East Coast.

The Conscience of a Conservative (1960) summarized Goldwater's critique. By refusing to take stronger military measures against the Soviet Union and by not making "victory the goal" of U.S. policy, Eisenhower had likely endangered national security. Goldwater portrayed almost all domestic programs, including federal civil rights legislation, as grave threats to individual liberty.

While Goldwater was pressing the GOP to reject Eisenhower's modern Republicanism, the publisher William F. Buckley, Jr., was framing a new conservative message for the 1960s. In *God and Man at Yale* (1952), the devoutly Roman Catholic Buckley attacked what he saw as a "collectivist" and antireligious tilt in higher education. In 1955 Buckley helped found the *National Review,* which avoided the anti-Semitism of some old-line conservatives and the hysterical anticommunism of groups such as the John Birch Society and adopted strategies for the long run. To this end, conservatives established Young Americans for Freedom (YAF) in 1960, several years before similar college-based political organizations emerged on the political left.

Adopting another long-term approach, called "fusionism," to building a conservative movement, Buckley's group avoided litmus tests. The *National Review*—and the movement it hoped to create—came to feature a creative tension among three broad constituencies: "traditionalist" conservatives, who insisted that social stability depended on allowing the educated, talented few, such as themselves, to dominate the nation's institutions; "libertarians," who favored reducing the power of government and enlarging personal freedoms; and staunch anticommunists, who insisted that national power be used aggressively to oppose the Soviets.

Meanwhile, Barry Goldwater's brand of conservatism proved especially appealing to the fiercely anticommunist "suburban warriors" from the Sunbelt states. Their militant agenda focused on making sure that "outside" authorities, both state and national, could not infringe on their local liberties.

ADVOCATES OF A MORE ACTIVE GOVERNMENT

While the new conservative movement mobilized to scale back domestic social policies, an even more eclectic group pressed for expanding governmental programs. Social activists criticized Eisenhower's reluctance to use the power of his office to attack racial discrimination, and when unemployment rose in an economic downturn in 1958–59, many economists ridiculed Eisenhower's commitment to a balanced budget. Even after economic conditions improved, economists such as John Kenneth Galbraith urged significant deficit spending. Other critics, while avoiding the rhetoric of conservatives such as Goldwater, found Eisenhower's national security policies to be insufficient. The 1957 Gaither Report, prepared by foreign policy analysts with ties to the defense industry, urged an immediate increase of about 25 percent in the Pentagon's budget and programs for building fallout shelters, developing intercontinental ballistic missiles (ICBMs), and expanding conventional military forces.

Eisenhower reacted cautiously. Keeping his defense budget well below the levels critics had proposed, he actually reduced the size of several army and air force units. Through super-secret U-2 surveillance flights over the USSR, Eisenhower knew that the Soviets were lagging behind, rather than outpacing, the United States in military capability.

Concerns about national security and calls for greater government spending also affected U.S. educational policies. Throughout the 1950s some critics complained about schools imparting "life-adjustment" skills instead of teaching traditional academic subjects. Rudolf Flesch's bestselling *Why Johnny Can't Read* (1956) anticipated books that asked why Johnny and his classmates couldn't add or subtract very well either, and why they lagged behind their counterparts in the Soviet Union in science. These critics pressed for more funding for public schools. Simultaneously, the nation's leading research universities sought greater federal aid for higher education; in summer 1957 prominent scientists implored the Defense Department to expand its support for basic scientific research. The case for increased spending throughout much of national life suddenly became more compelling when, in October 1957, the Soviets launched the world's first artificial satellite—the 22-inch sphere, *Sputnik.*

Sputnik First Soviet satellite sent into orbit around the earth in 1957.

U.S. Scientists Plot Orbit. *In the United States in October of 1957, all eyes turned toward* Sputnik, *the first satellite to orbit the earth and a major achievement for the Soviet Union. American scientists took measure of the feat, magazines featured the story that "Reds got it first," and many people scanned the night skies for a glimpse of the light refracted by the large rocket that had propelled* Sputnik *into space. A sense of fear that the United States might lose the "space race" gripped the nation.*

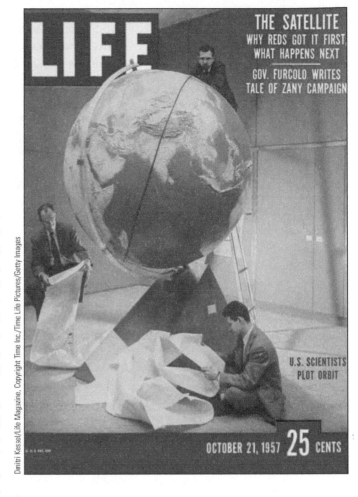

Dmitri Kessel/Life Magazine, Copyright Time Inc./Time Life Pictures/Getty Images

After *Sputnik*, phrases such as "national security" and "national defense" cleared the way for resources to flow more freely out of Washington. The National Defense Education Act of 1958 funneled aid to college-level programs in science, engineering, foreign languages, and the social sciences. This act marked a milestone in overcoming congressional opposition, especially from southerners who feared that federal aid could increase pressure for racial integration, to federal funding of education. The Soviets' apparent superiority in satellite technology fueled an R&D effort overseen by a new National Aeronautics and Space Administration (NASA).

Many hoped that domestic social welfare programs would also become the beneficiaries of increased federal spending. Galbraith's *The Affluent Society* (1958) saw a dangerous tilt in the "social balance," away from "public goods." Affluent families could vacation in their new automobiles, but they needed to pass through shabby cities along litter-filled roadsides.

Michael Harrington wrote passionate essays insisting that the need to address economic inequality remained as urgent as it had been during the 1930s. At least one-third of the nation's people—living in rural areas, small towns, and cities—barely subsisted in a land of supposed abundance. Avoiding the usual trappings of economic analysis, Harrington crafted dramatic stories about how poverty ravaged the health and spirit of people whose lives had been largely untouched by the economic growth of the 1940s and 1950s.

Several years later, when addressing social and economic issues became a priority, critics such as Galbraith and Harrington became political celebrities. Their critiques, however, grew out of the political culture of the late 1950s. The presidential agenda of **John F. Kennedy** was rooted in the calls for more active foreign and domestic policies that had emerged during the 1950s.

John F. Kennedy *President from 1961 to 1963; noted for youthful charm and vigor, and his "New Frontier" vision for America.*

The Kennedy Years: Foreign Policy

A wealthy, politically ambitious father had groomed John Fitzgerald Kennedy for the White House. The young Kennedy graduated from Harvard in 1940, won military honors while serving in the navy during the Second World War, became a representative from Massachusetts in 1946, and captured a Senate seat in 1952. Kennedy became better known for his social life than his command of legislative details, but he quickly parlayed his charm and youthful good looks into political stardom. His 1953 marriage

FOCUS QUESTION
What foreign and domestic policies did the Kennedy administration champion?

flexible response *Kennedy's approach to the Cold War that aimed to provide a wide variety of military and nonmilitary methods to confront communist movements.*

to Jacqueline Bouvier added another dash of glamour. A favorite of the media herself, Jackie won plaudits for her good taste, stylish dress, and fluency in several languages. After John Kennedy narrowly missed winning the vice presidential nomination in 1956, he took aim at the top spot on the 1960 Democratic ticket.

THE ELECTION OF 1960

John F. Kennedy (JFK), often accompanied by Jackie and by his brothers, Robert and Ted, barnstormed across the country. This early presidential campaigning, along with a talented staff and his family's vast wealth, helped Kennedy overwhelm his Democratic challengers, Senators Hubert Humphrey of Minnesota and Lyndon Johnson of Texas. By pledging to separate his Catholic religion from his politics and by confronting those who appealed to anti-Catholic prejudice, Kennedy defused the religious issue that had doomed the candidacy of Al Smith in 1928 (see chapter 24).

Vice President Richard Nixon, running for the Republicans, spent much of the 1960 presidential campaign on the defensive. Nixon seemed notably off-balance during the first of several televised debates in which a cool, tanned Kennedy emerged, according to surveys of TV viewers, with a clear victory over a pale, nervous Nixon. Despite chronic and severe health problems which his entourage concealed, Kennedy projected vigor and energy, if not experience.

Kennedy's 1960 campaign highlighted issues from the 1950s that, taken together, became his "New Frontier" agenda. Although Senator Kennedy's civil rights record had been mixed, candidate Kennedy declared his support for new legislation and, in an important symbolic act, dispatched aides to Georgia to assist Martin Luther King, Jr., who was facing jail time for a minor traffic violation. He also endorsed new social programs to rebuild rural communities, increase educational opportunities, and improve urban conditions.

Kennedy's New Frontier included two other central issues: promoting greater economic growth and conducting a more aggressive foreign policy. Dismissing Eisenhower's policies as timid, Kennedy suggested using tax cuts and deficit spending to juice the economy. He criticized Eisenhower for failing to rid the hemisphere of Castro in Cuba and for allowing a "missile gap" to develop in the arms race with the Soviet Union. By spending more on defense, Kennedy claimed, he would create a **flexible response** against communism, especially in the Third World. The "American people are tired of the drift in our national course . . . and . . . they are ready to move again," Kennedy proclaimed.

The 1960 election defied easy analysis. Kennedy defeated Nixon by only about 100,000 popular votes, and his victory in the Electoral College rested on razor-thin margins in several states, including Illinois. Many Republicans urged Nixon to challenge Kennedy's suspicious vote total there, but the vice president chose to accept the disputed result. JFK's triumph owed a great debt to his vice presidential running mate, Lyndon Baines Johnson, whose regional appeal helped the Democratic ticket carry the Deep South and his home state of Texas.

JFK and Jackie riveted media attention on the White House. They hobnobbed with movie stars and hosted prominent intellectuals. Kennedy's inaugural featured designer clothing, a poignant appearance by the aged poet Robert Frost, and an oft-quoted speech in which JFK challenged people to "ask not what your country can do for you; ask what you can do for your country." The "best and the brightest," the name

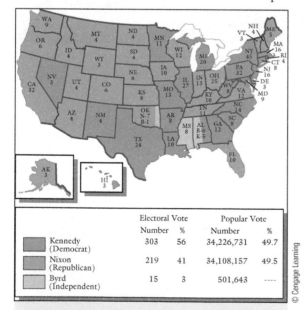

	Electoral Vote		Popular Vote	
	Number	%	Number	%
Kennedy (Democrat)	303	56	34,226,731	49.7
Nixon (Republican)	219	41	34,108,157	49.5
Byrd (Independent)	15	3	501,643	----

Map 28.2 **PRESIDENTIAL ELECTION, 1960.** *In one of the closest elections in American history in terms of the popular vote, Kennedy narrowly outpolled Nixon. Kennedy's more commanding victory in the electoral vote produced some discussion about the consequences if the electoral college one day produced a president who had failed to carry the popular vote—a situation that did indeed occur in the election of 2000.*

© Cengage Learning

later given to the hard-driving people who joined Kennedy's administration, promised to launch exciting and difficult crusades, even to the frontier of outer space.

KENNEDY'S FOREIGN POLICY GOALS

Kennedy promised an emphasis on flexible response in his foreign policy. Although Secretary of Defense Robert McNamara quickly found that the alleged missile gap did not exist, the Kennedy administration boosted the defense budget anyway. It supported military assistance programs, propaganda agencies, and covert-action plans. In one of his most popular initiatives, the president created the Peace Corps, a volunteer program that sent Americans, especially young people, to nations around the world to work on development projects that might undercut communism's appeal.

Eisenhower's effort to reorient U.S. Latin American policy away from reliance on dictators and toward socioeconomic programs was repackaged as Kennedy's "Alliance for Progress." Unveiled in spring 1961 in hopes of checking the spread of Castro-like insurgencies, the Alliance promised $20 billion in loans over a 10-year period to Latin American countries that would undertake land reform and economic development measures. Most Latin Americans judged Kennedy's Alliance, which underestimated obstacles to social and economic change, as more symbolic than substantive.

CUBA AND BERLIN

The worst fiasco of the Kennedy presidency, an ill-conceived 1961 CIA mission against Cuba, also had its roots in the Eisenhower administration. The CIA had been planning a secret invasion to oust Fidel Castro, and Kennedy, overriding the doubts of some of his advisers, supported this plan. On April 17, 1961, however, when U.S.-trained forces (mainly anticommunist Cuban exiles) landed at the Bahia de Cochinas (**Bay of Pigs**) on the southern coast of Cuba, the expected popular uprising failed to materialize. Instead, forces loyal to Castro quickly surrounded and captured the invaders. Kennedy rejected any additional steps, including the air strikes the Cuban exiles had expected, and, initially, denied any U.S. involvement in the invasion. The CIA's role quickly became public knowledge, however, and anti-U.S sentiment swept across much of Latin America. Castro tightened his grip over Cuban life and strengthened his ties to the Soviet Union.

Kennedy responded to the Bay of Pigs by admitting error and by devising a new covert program, "Operation Mongoose." It aimed to destabilize Cuba's economy and, in concert with organized crime figures, to kill the Cuban leader.

Meanwhile, two other dramatic confrontations began unfolding, more slowly, in Berlin and in Cuba. In June 1961 Nikita Khrushchev and Kennedy met in Vienna, Austria, where the Soviets proposed ending the Western presence in Berlin and reuniting the city as part of East Germany. Kennedy refused to abandon West Berlin, but in August 1961 the communist regime began to erect first a barbed-wire fence and then a concrete barrier to separate East from West Berlin. This "Berlin Wall" became a symbol of communist repression. Kennedy's assertion, *"Ich bin ein Berliner,"* delivered in front of the wall to a cheering crowd of West Berliners, provided a memorable image of JFK's presidency.

Superpower confrontation escalated to a potentially lethal level during the **Cuban Missile Crisis** of October 1962. The Soviet Union, responding to pleas from

Bay of Pigs *Site of an ill-fated 1961 invasion of Cuba by a U.S.-trained force that attempted to overthrow the government of Fidel Castro.*

Cuban Missile Crisis (1962) *Serious Cold War confrontation between the United States and the Soviet Union over the installation of Soviet missiles in Cuba.*

Castro, sent armaments to Cuba. After U-2 spy-planes showed missile-launching sites in Cuba, the Kennedy administration announced it would never allow the Soviet Union to place nuclear warheads so close to U.S. soil. It demanded that the Soviets dismantle the missile silos and turn back supply ships heading for Cuba. After tense strategizing sessions with his top advisers, Kennedy rejected a military strike against Cuba, fearing it might lead to war with the Soviet Union. Instead, he ordered the Navy to "quarantine" Cuba. The Strategic Air Command went on full alert for a possible nuclear conflict. Meanwhile, both sides engaged in secret diplomatic maneuvers to forestall such a catastrophe.

Delicate maneuvering by both governments finally ended the standoff. On October 28, 1962, Khrushchev ordered the Soviet missiles in Cuba dismantled and the supply ships brought home; Kennedy promised not to invade Cuba and secretly assured Khrushchev that he would complete a previously ordered withdrawal of U.S. missiles from Turkey. When Soviet archives opened in the mid-1990s, Americans learned that the confrontation had been even more dangerous than imagined. Unknown to the Kennedy administration in 1962, the Soviets had already placed tactical nuclear weapons, which could have reached U.S. targets, in Cuba.

The Cuban Missile Crisis underscored the risk of nuclear conflict and made the superpowers more cautious. To prevent a future confrontation or an accident, they established a direct telephone "hot-line" between Moscow and Washington, D.C.

SOUTHEAST ASIA AND FLEXIBLE RESPONSE

In Southeast Asia, Kennedy continued earlier U.S. attempts to preserve a non-communist state in South Vietnam. After the Bay of Pigs fiasco, in which the overthrow of an already established communist government had failed, JFK became determined to prevent any communist-led "war of national liberation" from succeeding.

Even so, the odds against preserving a pro-U.S. government in South Vietnam seemed to grow longer as Kennedy's own presidency lengthened. Opposition to the regime of Ngo Dinh Diem, in power since 1954, had now coalesced in the National Liberation Front (NLF). Formed in December 1960, the NLF included groups that resented Diem's dependence on the United States; communists who demanded more extensive land reform; an array of political leaders fed up with Diem's corruption and cronyism; and groups beholden to Ho Chi Minh's communist government in the North. North Vietnam began sending supplies, then thousands of troops, to the South to support the NLF.

Kennedy saw Vietnam as a test case for flexible response. Elite U.S. troops, the Green Berets, were trained in "counterinsurgency" tactics, and teams of social scientists, charged with "nation building," were sent to give advice on social-economic reforms and internal security. Finally, JFK deployed nearly 11,000 U.S. troops who would supposedly only advise, rather than actively fight alongside, South Vietnamese forces.

When these efforts were met only with greater corruption in the Diem government, U.S. officials gave disgruntled South Vietnamese military officers the green light to orchestrate its overthrow. In November 1963 Diem was routed from his presidential palace and murdered. This coup, which brought a military regime to power in Saigon, bred even greater political instability. The NLF and North Vietnam, in turn, ratcheted up the military pressure.

QUICK   REVIEW

KENNEDY AND THE COLD WAR

- Emphasized foreign affairs over domestic issues

- Projected image of a young and vigorous new leader

- Authorized ill-fated Bay of Pigs invasion

- Denounced construction of Soviet wall dividing Berlin

- Steered careful diplomatic responses during Cuban Missile Crisis

- Developed "flexible response" as new way of fighting communism abroad

- Entangled the United States in South Vietnam

After nearly three years, JFK's Southeast Asian policy seemed no more coherent than Eisenhower's. The overall goal remained consistent: prevent communist forces from toppling any anticommunist government in Saigon. The United States could not afford to "lose" South Vietnam. Kennedy's presidency ended with its policy in Vietnam in a state of flux, perhaps even disarray.

THE KENNEDY YEARS: DOMESTIC POLICY

Despite his pledge to increase federal spending to speed economic growth, Kennedy hesitated to follow up on this campaign promise. He feared that federal budget deficits might cost him support among fiscal conservatives and business leaders. Relations with corporate leaders nevertheless turned ugly in 1962, when Kennedy clashed with the president of U.S. Steel over that company's decision to raise prices beyond the guidelines suggested by the White House.

POLICYMAKING DURING THE EARLY 1960s

In 1962 the White House asked Congress to lower tax rates as a means of promoting economic growth. The economy had nicely rebounded from its downturn of 1957–58, but Kennedy argued that lower tax rates for everyone, along with special deductions for businesses that invested in new plants and equipment, would spur jobs and growth. Despite opposition from Democrats who thought these changes tilted toward corporations and the wealthy, the tax bill seemed headed for passage in fall 1963.

On social welfare, the Kennedy administration proposed a higher minimum wage and new urban rebuilding programs. It also supported the Area Redevelopment Bill of 1961, which called for directing federal grants and loans to impoverished areas such as **Appalachia**. Meanwhile, under the urban renewal programs begun in the 1940s, bulldozers continued to raze parts of urban America, often displacing affordable housing.

THE CIVIL RIGHTS MOVEMENT, 1960–1963

Although JFK had talked about new civil rights legislation, he initially tried to placate the segregationist wing of his Democratic Party. The president and his brother, Robert, whom he had appointed attorney general, listened sympathetically when J. Edgar Hoover, director of the FBI, falsely warned of continuing communist ties to Martin Luther King, Jr. To monitor King's activities, the FBI illegally wiretapped his conversations.

In early 1960 African American students at North Carolina A & T College in Greensboro sat down at a drugstore lunch counter and politely asked to be served in the same manner as white customers. This was the beginning of the **sit-in movement,** a new phase of civil rights activism. In both the South and the North, young demonstrators staged nonviolent sit-ins at restaurants, bus and train stations, and other public facilities. With anthems such as "We Shall Overcome" inspiring solidarity, the courage of these demonstrators reenergized the antidiscrimination movement. In 1961 interracial activists from CORE and the **Student Nonviolent Coordinating Committee (SNCC)**, a student group that emerged from the sit-in movement, risked racist retaliation by conducting "freedom rides" across the South. The **freedom riders** were challenging the Kennedy administration to enforce

Appalachia *13-state region, running along the Appalachian Mountain chain, from southern New York to northern Mississippi.*

sit-in movement *Activity that challenged legal segregation by demanding that blacks have the same access to public facilities as whites. These nonviolent demonstrations were staged at restaurants, bus and train stations, and other public places.*

Student Nonviolent Coordinating Committee (SNCC) *Interracial civil rights organization formed by young people involved in the sit-in movement that later adopted a direct-action approach to fighting segregation.*

freedom riders *Members of interracial groups who traveled the South on buses to test a series of federal court decisions declaring segregation on buses and in waiting rooms to be unconstitutional.*

federal court decisions that had declared state laws requiring segregation on interstate buses (and in bus stations) to be unconstitutional.

This grassroots activism forced the Kennedy administration into action of its own. It dispatched U.S. marshals and National Guard troops to protect the freedom riders and to help integrate educational institutions in the Deep South, including the Universities of Mississippi and Alabama. In November 1962 Kennedy issued the long-promised executive order that banned racial discrimination in federally financed housing. The following February he sent Congress a civil rights bill that called for faster trials in cases involving challenges to racial discrimination in voting.

Events in the South, however, grew more violent. In 1963 racial conflict convulsed Birmingham, Alabama. White police officers unleashed dogs and turned high-pressure water hoses on African Americans, including young children, who were seeking to desegregate public facilities. Four young girls were later murdered (and 20 people injured) when white supremacists bombed Birmingham's Sixteenth Street Baptist Church, a center of the local civil rights campaign. After thousands of African Americans rallied in protest—and two more children were killed, this time by police officers—the Kennedy administration moved to staunch the bloodletting.

The determination of civil rights activists created a real-life drama that played to the entire world on television. Using the same medium, Kennedy made an emotional plea for a national commitment to the battle against discrimination. Recent events had raised "a moral issue . . . as old as Scriptures and . . . as clear as the Constitution." Racial violence was "weakening the respect with which the rest of the world regards us," the president insisted. The issue of civil rights dominated national politics during the last six months of Kennedy's presidency.

The White House still hoped it might influence the direction and pace of change. It crafted legislation designed to dampen the enthusiasm for civil rights demonstrations. It called for a ban against racial discrimination in public facilities and housing, and for new measures to protect the voting rights of African Americans in the South. When the administration recognized that its legislative proposals would not derail a "March on Washington for Jobs and Freedom" sponsored by a coalition of civil rights and labor organizations planned for the late summer of 1963, it belatedly endorsed the event.

RACIAL CONFLICT IN BIRMINGHAM. *Images such as this 1963 photograph of a confrontation in Birmingham, Alabama, in which segregationists turned dogs on youthful demonstrators, helped rally public support for civil rights legislation. Events in Birmingham, however, also presaged the increasingly violent clashes that would punctuate the efforts to end racial discrimination.*

AP Photo/Bill Hudson

On August 28, 1963, an integrated group of more than 200,000 people marched through the nation's capital to the Lincoln Memorial. There, Martin Luther King, Jr., delivered his famous "I Have a Dream" speech. Speakers generally applauded Kennedy's latest initiatives but urged a broader agenda, including a higher minimum wage and a federal program to guarantee new jobs. Well-organized and smoothly run, this one-day demonstration received overwhelmingly favorable coverage from the national media and put even greater political pressure on the White House and Congress to lend their assistance to the movement.

WOMEN'S ISSUES

The seeds of a resurgent women's movement were also being sown, although more quietly, during the Kennedy years. All across the political spectrum, women began speaking out on contemporary issues. The energy of women such as Phyllis Schlafly, whose book *A Choice, Not an Echo* (1964) became one of the leading manifestos on the political right, helped fuel the new conservatism. African American activists such as Bernice Johnson Reagon (whose work with the Freedom Singers combined music and social activism) and Fannie Lou Hamer (who spearheaded the organization of a racially integrated Freedom Democratic Party in Mississippi) fought discrimination based on both race and gender. Women union leaders pushed for greater employment opportunities and more equitable work environments, and Chicana farm workers became key figures in union-organizing efforts in California. Women also played an important role in protests, through the Committee for a Sane Nuclear Policy (SANE) and the Women's Strike for Peace, against the U.S.–Soviet arms race. During Kennedy's final year in office, Betty Friedan published *The Feminine Mystique*. Widely credited with helping to revive organized feminist activity in the United States, Friedan's book drew on her own social criticism from the late 1950s and articulated the dissatisfactions that many middle-class women felt about the narrow confines of domestic life and the lack of public roles available to them.

To address women's concerns, Kennedy appointed a Presidential Commission on the Status of Women, chaired by Eleanor Roosevelt. After negotiating differences between moderate and more militant members, the commission issued a report that documented discrimination against women in employment and wages. Kennedy responded with a presidential order to eliminate gender discrimination within the federal civil service. He also supported the Equal Pay Act of 1963, which made it a federal crime for employers to pay lower wages to women who did the same work as men.

THE ASSASSINATION OF JOHN F. KENNEDY

By fall 1963 the Kennedy White House, although still struggling to reframe both its domestic and foreign policies, expected JFK would easily win re-election in 1964. Then, on November 22, 1963, John F. Kennedy was shot dead as his presidential motorcade moved through Dallas, Texas. Vice President Lyndon Johnson, who had accompanied Kennedy to Texas, took the oath of office and rushed back to Washington. Equally quickly, the Dallas police arrested Lee Harvey Oswald and pegged him as JFK's assassin. Oswald had loose ties to organized crime; had once lived in the Soviet Union; and had a bizarre set of political affiliations, including shadowy ones with groups interested in Cuba. Oswald, who declared his innocence, never faced trial. Jack Ruby, whose Dallas nightclub catered to underworld figures, killed Oswald, on national television, while the alleged gunman was in police custody. An

HISTORY THROUGH FILM

JFK (1991)

*Directed by Oliver Stone; starring
Kevin Costner (Jim Garrison), Tommy Lee
Jones (Clay Shaw), Donald Sutherland ("Mr. X"),
and Joe Pesci (David Ferrie)*

JFK addressed two issues that have long intrigued the historical profession and the general public: Did John F. Kennedy fall victim to a lone assassin or a larger conspiracy? How might the course of U.S. history, including the nation's involvement in Vietnam, have been different if Kennedy's presidency had not ended in November 1963?

This movie restages the 1967 criminal prosecution by Jim Garrison, then the district attorney of New Orleans, against Clay Shaw, a local business leader. This real-life court case provides the vehicle for speculating that a shadowy conspiracy—involving government officials, military officers, and business executives—killed Kennedy because of fears that he planned to end the U.S. commitment to South Vietnam.

To dramatize its claims, JFK employs overtly cinemtaic techniques. When the Garrison character screens the famous "Zapruder film," the home movie that provides the only visual record of Kennedy's shooting, JFK inserts simulated, black-and-white images of sharpshooters catching the

president in a deadly cross-fire. Later, the movie shows a mysterious figure planting the "magic bullet," a nearly pristine projectile the Warren Commission insisted came from the rifle of Lee Harvey Oswald and passed through Kennedy's body, on a hospital gurney.

JFK is vintage Oliver Stone. The most prolific and controversial filmmaker-historian of his time, Stone delights in disrupting dominant narratives about the past. His most successful historical movies—JFK, Platoon (1986), Born on the Fourth of July (1989), The Doors (1991), and Nixon (1995)—all feature stories riddled by disjuncture and uncertainty. When the Garrison character in JFK decides to challenge the official story of the Kennedy assassination, he warns his staff, ". . . we're through the looking glass . . . white is black, and black is white."

Resembling Stone's equally controversial Natural Born Killers (1994), JFK focuses less on telling a coherent tale than using the movie to suggest tangled relationships between visual imagery and popular perception. The opening sequence bombards the screen with quick-moving, seemingly disconnected imagery. Viewers, as if they themselves are passing "through the looking glass," must struggle to connect the disjointed visual pieces contained in the cinematic puzzle that is JFK.

The movie, in this sense, seems more interested in posing, rather than settling, historical questions. Viewers might compare and contrast, for example, how JFK uses two very differently composed sequences, featuring performances by two very different character actors (Donald Sutherland and Joe Pesci), to explain Kennedy's death. Sutherland's "Mr. X," an entirely fictive operative who supposedly works in the national security bureaucracy, sees Kennedy's assassination as only one in a long line of "dirty tricks," orchestrated by a military-industrial complex. During a scene shot against the iconography of the nation's capital—which recalls Frank Capra's classic *Mr. Smith Goes to Washington* (1939)—Sutherland calmly

Kevin Costner portrays New Orleans District Attorney Jim Garrison in JFK.

WARNER BROS/THE KOBAL COLLECTION

offers Garrison (and film viewers) a logically ordered, tightly packaged analysis of Kennedy's assassination. In contrast, the brief sequence featuring Joe Pesci's frenetic David Ferrie—a real-life foot soldier in organized crime and Cuban-exile circles, whom some investigators link to JFK's assassination—lacks any coherent center. This character, in contrast to Sutherland's, warns Garrison that he will never puzzle out Kennedy's death.

JFK, the movie, raised such a popular furor that it led to a massive, congressionally ordered project to safeguard all government documents that might relate to Kennedy's assassination. Will these traditional sources bring historians any closer to solving, beyond reasonable doubts, Kennedy's assassination? Or, as Joe Pesci's character warns in JFK, do historians confront "a mystery, inside a riddle, wrapped in an enigma"?

investigation by a special commission headed by Chief Justice Earl Warren concluded that both Oswald and Ruby had acted alone.

Kennedy's life and presidency remain topics of historical debate and tabloid-style speculation. Researchers have provided new details about his poor health, reliance on exotic medications, and dalliances with women—all of which were kept from the public at the time. As historians speculate about how such revelations might have affected Kennedy's ability to make crucial decisions, they continue to debate what JFK might have done in Vietnam and on the domestic front had he won the 1964 presidential election. The passage of time, in short, has diminished neither scholarly nor popular interest in John F. Kennedy and in his thousand-day presidency.

C O N C L U S I O N

After 1953 tensions with the Soviet Union eased a bit, especially after the Cuban Missile Crisis in 1962 brought them to the brink of nuclear war. Still, the United States continued to pursue determinedly anticommunist policies that featured the continued buildup of nuclear weapons, new forms of economic pressure, and expanded covert activities. Developments in the Third World, particularly in Cuba and Southeast Asia, became of growing concern to policymakers.

At home, the years between 1953 and 1963 were ones of steady economic growth. A cornucopia of new consumer products encouraged talk about an age of affluence but also produced apprehension about conformity, unruly youth, and the impact of mass culture. At the same time, the millions of people whom economic prosperity bypassed, and those who faced racial and ethnic discrimination, saw their causes move to the center of public debates over the meaning of liberty and equality. The Eisenhower administration, critics charged, seemed too reluctant to use the power of government to fight discrimination and push economic programs designed to spread the benefits of affluence more widely. The policy initiatives of the early 1960s, associated with Kennedy's New Frontier, grew out of the criticism of the 1950s. More quietly, in both the political and cultural arenas, a new conservative movement was also taking shape.

Although Kennedy preferred to focus on foreign policy, the press of domestic events, particularly those associated with the civil rights movement, forced him to consider how presidential power might be used to address the issues of liberty and equality at home.

The post-Kennedy era would continue to highlight questions about liberty, equality, and power. Was the United States spreading liberty in Vietnam? Was it sufficiently active in pursuing equality at home? The troubled era of "America's longest war," 1963–74, would turn on how different people attempted to respond to these questions.

QUESTIONS FOR REVIEW AND CRITICAL THINKING

Review

1. In what ways did the "New Look" reorient the foreign policy of containment?
2. How could economic growth be seen as both an opportunity and a problem during the 1950s?
3. How did the fight against discrimination raise new political issues and visions during the 1950s and early 1960s? How did the nation's political and social institutions respond to these issues?
4. What foreign and domestic policies did the Kennedy administration champion?

Critical Thinking

1. How did the policies of the Eisenhower and the Kennedy administrations toward the Cold War, discrimination, and economic growth show both differences and similarities?
2. Why does the relatively brief presidency of JFK loom so large in popular memory?

ONLINE RESOURCES

 Visit the companion website to access flashcards, crossword puzzles, exercises, and quizzes related to this chapter: www.cengage.com/history/murrin/libertyequalconc5e.

See our interactive ebook for map and primary source activities.

 DISCOVERY

How did images of America as an "affluent society" generate a critique of conformity and focus attention on the situation of African Americans in the 1950s and 1960s?

ECONOMICS AND TECHNOLOGY How does the below advertisement represent the growing "affluent society" of the 1950s? What evidence can you point to in the picture that the country's economic growth and improvements in transportation and technology had major effects on the everyday life of ordinary people? How broadly accessible were consumer items such as refrigerators in 1950s America? Did their accessibility shape perceptions about equality in America and the gap separating rich from poor? If so, how? What connections, if any, can be drawn between the "affluent society" of the 1950s and the protest movements that emerged in the 1960s?

In thinking about this question, begin by breaking it down into the components shown below. A discussion of the significance of each component should appear in your answer.

CULTURE AND SOCIETY Look at the map on page 768 and reflect on what you read in this chapter about racial discrimination and the civil rights movement. Which areas of the country gained the largest African American population between 1940 and 1960? Which areas lost the most? What do you think were the main causes for these shifts?

Examine the photo of Rosa Parks, taken when she was arrested for her participation in the Montgomery Bus Boycott of 1955 (page 769), and the photo of the civil rights conflict in Birmingham in 1963 (page 780). What do the two photos suggest about continuities in the Civil Rights movement between 1955 and 1963? What do they suggest about changes in the movement during that time? Which of the two protests do you think was more important in terms of attracting national support to the civil rights movement? Why?

The Granger Collection, New York

A REFRIGERATOR OF PLENTY

29

AMERICA DURING ITS LONGEST WAR, 1963–1974

Lyndon Baines Johnson promised to finish what John F. Kennedy's New Frontier had begun. Ultimately, though, LBJ's troubled presidency bore little resemblance to Kennedy's. In Southeast Asia, Johnson faced a critical decision: Should the United States deploy its own forces to prop up its beleaguered South Vietnamese ally? At home, Johnson mobilized the federal government's power to promote greater equality. But was his "Great Society" a realizable vision? Many Americans, particularly young people, came to oppose Johnson's policies. By 1968, the United States was politically polarized and awash in both foreign and domestic controversies.

The polarization so much in evidence during 1968 seemed to grow worse during the years that followed. By the end of America's longest war and the Watergate crisis that caused President Richard Nixon's resignation, the nation's political culture and social fabric looked very different from those of 1963.

TIMELINE

| 1963 | 1965 | 1967 | 1969 | 1971 | 1973 | 1975 |

1963–1969
Johnson presidency

■ **1964**
Civil Rights Act of 1964 and Economic Opportunity Act passed • Gulf of Tonkin Resolution gives Johnson authority to conduct undeclared war • Johnson defeats Barry Goldwater

■ **1965**
Plans for the Great Society announced • Congress passes Voting Rights Act • Violence rocks Los Angeles and other urban areas

■ **1966**
Black Power movement emerges • *Miranda* v. *Arizona* decision guarantees rights of criminal suspects • U.S. begins massive air strikes in North Vietnam

■ **1967**
Large antiwar demonstrations begin

■ **1968**
Tet offensive launched (January) • Martin Luther King, Jr. assassinated (April) • Robert Kennedy assassinated (June) • Civil Rights Act of 1968 passed

1969–1974
Nixon presidency

■ **1969**
Nixon announces "Vietnamization" policy • My Lai massacre becomes public

■ **1970**
U.S. troops enter Cambodia • Student demonstrators killed at Kent State and Jackson State • Environmental Protection Agency created

1971 ■
"Pentagon Papers" published • Military court convicts Lieutenant Calley in connection with My Lai incident

1972 ■
Nixon crushes McGovern in presidential election

1973 ■
Paris peace accords signed • *Roe* v. *Wade* upholds women's right to abortion

1974 ■
House votes impeachment, and Nixon resigns• Ford assumes presidency

1975 ■
Saigon falls to North Vietnamese forces

THE GREAT SOCIETY

Lyndon B. Johnson lacked Kennedy's charisma, but he possessed other political assets. As a member of the House of Representatives during the late 1930s and early 1940s and as majority leader of the U.S. Senate during the 1950s, Johnson mastered the art of interest-group horse trading. Few issues, it appeared, defied an LBJ-forged solution. Nearly everyone could be flattered, cajoled, or threatened into lending him their support. During Johnson's time in Congress, his wealthy Texas benefactors gained valuable oil and gas concessions and lucrative construction contracts, while Johnson acquired a personal fortune. Cities such as Dallas and Houston and much of the Southwest also benefited from Johnson's skill in gaining federal funding for building projects.

FOCUS QUESTION
How did the Johnson administration define Great Society goals, and how did it approach problem-solving? Why did the Great Society produce so much controversy?

George Tames/NYT Pictures

THE PRESENCE OF LYNDON B. JOHNSON. *As both senator and president, Lyndon Johnson employed body language—the "Johnson treatment"—as a favored means of lining up support for his policies.*

Kennedy's death gave Johnson the opportunity to display his political skills on the presidential stage. Confident that he could forge a national consensus behind a bold program for social and economic change, Johnson urged Congress to honor JFK's memory by passing legislation that Kennedy's administration had proposed. Johnson concentrated on three domestic issues: tax cutting, civil rights, and economic inequality.

CLOSING THE NEW FRONTIER

Johnson quickly achieved the major domestic goals of JFK's New Frontier. Working behind the scenes, he secured passage of JFK's $10 billion tax cut, a measure intended to stimulate the economy. Although economists still differ on how much this tax measure contributed to the economic boom of the mid-1960s, it *appeared* to work. GNP rose 7 percent in 1964 and 8 percent the following year, unemployment dropped, and inflation remained low.

In his January 1964 State of the Union address, Johnson had called for "an unconditional war on poverty in America." Constantly prodded by the White House, Congress created the Office of Economic Opportunity (OEO) to coordinate a multipart program. First headed by R. Sargent Shriver, brother-in-law of John Kennedy, the OEO was charged with eliminating "the paradox of poverty in the midst of plenty." The Economic Opportunity Act of 1964, in addition to establishing the OEO, mandated loans for rural and small-business development; established a work-training program called the Jobs Corps; created Volunteers in Service to

America (VISTA), a domestic version of the Peace Corps; provided low-wage, public service jobs for young people; began a work-study program to assist college students; and authorized the creation of federally funded social programs to be planned in concert with local community groups.

In addition, Johnson took special pride in helping to push a more extensive version of Kennedy's civil rights proposal through Congress. Championing the measure as a memorial to Kennedy, he fully recognized that Southerners in their own Democratic Party would try to block it. Consequently, he successfully sought Republican support.

The **Civil Rights Act of 1964**, passed in July 1964, strengthened federal remedies, monitored by a new Equal Employment Opportunity Commission (EEOC), against job discrimination. The act also prohibited racial discrimination in all public accommodations connected to interstate commerce, such as motels and restaurants. Moreover, Title VII, a provision added during congressional debate, barred discrimination based on sex and was extremely important to the reviving women's movement.

Meanwhile, that same summer, a coalition of civil rights groups enlisted young volunteers for a voter registration campaign in Mississippi—an operation called **Freedom Summer**. During that tension-filled time, segregationists murdered six civil rights workers, but others pressed forward, only to see their grassroots work frustrated by the national Democratic Party. Pressured by LBJ, the 1964 Democratic convention voted to seat Mississippi's "regular" all-white delegates rather than members of the alternative, racially diverse Freedom Democratic Party (FDP). This rebuff prompted people such as Fannie Lou Hamer of the FDP to recall earlier suspicions about Lyndon Johnson. Although LBJ seemed more committed to civil rights than John Kennedy had been, would Johnson—and Hubert Humphrey, his handpicked vice presidential running mate—continue to press for legislation after the 1964 election?

THE ELECTION OF 1964

The Republicans nominated Senator Barry Goldwater of Arizona, the hero of conservatives, to challenge Johnson. Strategists for Goldwater predicted that a campaign based on a conservative platform would attract the millions of voters who rejected both Democratic policies and Dwight Eisenhower's modern Republican ones. Goldwater denounced Johnson's foreign policy for tolerating communist expansion and attacked his domestic agenda, including civil rights, for destroying individual liberties. One of only eight Republican senators who had opposed the 1964 Civil Rights Act, Goldwater denounced the measure as an unconstitutional extension of national power.

A few ill-considered remarks haunted Goldwater's candidacy. Goldwater suggested that people who feared nuclear war were "silly and sissified." He wondered, out loud, if Social Security might become a voluntary program. His proclamation, at the 1964 Republican convention, that "extremism in the pursuit of liberty is no vice" and "moderation in the pursuit of justice is no virtue," fed fears that Goldwater himself might be an "extremist."

Even many Republican voters deserted Goldwater, and he led the GOP to a spectacular defeat in November. Johnson carried 44 states and won more than 60 percent of the popular vote; Democrats also gained 38 seats in Congress. On the surface the 1964 election seemed a triumph for Lyndon Johnson's views.

In retrospect, however, the 1964 election signaled important political changes that would soon rebound against Johnson and, in time, the Democratic Party.

Civil Rights Act of 1964 *Bipartisan measure that denied federal funding to segregated schools and barred discrimination by race and sex in employment, public accommodations, and labor unions.*

Freedom Summer *Summer of 1964, when nearly a thousand volunteers went to Mississippi to aid in voter registration and other civil rights projects.*

Indeed, during the Democratic primaries, Alabama's segregationist governor, George Wallace, had run strongly against the president in several states. Already well positioned as an opponent of the civil rights movement, Wallace denounced any "meddling" by Washington in local affairs. The 1964 election proved the last until that of 2008 in which the Democratic Party would capture the White House by proposing to expand the domestic reach of the national government.

Goldwater's defeat invigorated rather than discouraged his supporters. His staff pioneered several innovative campaign tactics, such as direct-mail fundraising. By refining these techniques during future campaigns, conservative strategists helped make 1964 the beginning, not the end, of the Republican Party's movement to the right. Goldwater's stand against the Civil Rights Act of 1964 helped him carry five Southern states. These victories—along with Wallace's earlier appeal to "white backlash" voters—suggested that opposition to new civil rights measures could woo Southern whites who had once been solidly Democratic.

Finally, the Goldwater campaign introduced a new group of conservative activists to national politics. Ronald Reagan, an actor and corporate spokesperson, proved such an effective campaigner in 1964 that conservative Republicans began grooming him for a political career. Younger conservatives, such as William Rehnquist and Newt Gingrich, entered the national arena. Historians now credit Goldwater for his role in helping to refashion American conservatism.

LYNDON JOHNSON'S GREAT SOCIETY

Lyndon Johnson hoped to capitalize quickly on his electoral victory. Enjoying broad support in Congress, Johnson unveiled plans for a **Great Society**, an array of federal programs designed to "enrich and elevate our national life." Some of the programs fulfilled the dreams of his Democratic predecessors. Nationally funded medical coverage for the elderly (Medicare) and for low-income citizens (Medicaid) culminated efforts begun during the New and Fair Deals. Similarly, an addition to the president's cabinet, the Department of Housing and Urban Development (HUD), built on earlier plans for coordinating urban revitalization programs. And the **Voting Rights Act of 1965**, which created federal oversight of local elections in the South, capped a long-term effort to end racial discrimination at the ballot box.

In 1965, Congress enacted another milestone measure, addressing matters long discussed—and long avoided. A new immigration law finally abolished the discriminatory "national origins" quota system established in 1924 (see Chapter 24). Henceforth, people wishing to immigrate to the United States faced roughly the same set of hurdles, a change that, in practice, primarily assisted people from Asia and Latin America.

Many Great Society proposals rested on the prosperity of the 1960s, which seemed destined to go on forever. Even a costly war in Southeast Asia could not dampen Johnson's optimism: continuing prosperity would underwrite his bold expansion of national power.

The array of Johnson-sponsored initiatives that rolled through Congress heartened his supporters and appalled his critics. The Model Cities Program offered smaller-scale alternatives to urban renewal efforts; rent supplements and an expanded food stamp program went to help low-income families; and Head Start provided educational opportunities for disadvantaged children. New federal educational programs aimed to upgrade classroom instruction, especially in low-income neighborhoods, and a legal services initiative would assist those who could not afford private attorneys. These measures were meant to help people fight their own

Great Society *Series of domestic initiatives announced in 1964 by President Lyndon Johnson to "end poverty and racial injustice." They included the Voting Rights Act of 1965, establishment of the Department of Housing and Urban Development, Head Start, job-training programs, Medicare and Medicaid expansion, and various community action programs.*

Voting Rights Act of 1965 *Law that provided new federal mechanisms to help guarantee African Americans the right to vote.*

way out of economic distress. This service-based approach to social policy, Johnson insisted, would give people a "hand up" rather than a "handout."

The Great Society's Community Action Program (CAP) took a significantly different tack. It authorized grassroots activists, working through neighborhood organizations, to design community-based projects that could gain funding from Washington. By promoting "maximum feasible participation" by ordinary citizens rather than relying on social planners, the architects of CAP hoped to grow new varieties of grassroots democracy that could revitalize American politics.

EVALUATING THE GREAT SOCIETY

Why did the Great Society become so controversial? Most obviously, the dramatic extension of Washington's influence rekindled old debates about the use, as both an issue of constitutional law and pragmatic policy-making, of the power of the national government. In addition, Johnson's extravagant rhetoric, promising an "unconditional" victory over poverty, raised expectations that could not be met during a single presidency. Most importantly, the expectation that continued economic growth would generate tax revenues sufficient to finance new social programs faded as the economy began to sputter during the 1970s. Facing financial worries of their own, many of people who had initially been inclined to accept the Great Society during the 1960s became receptive to the argument, first popularized by George Wallace and the Goldwater campaign, that bureaucrats in Washington were taking their hard-earned dollars and wasting them on flawed social experiments. Worsening economic conditions, exacerbated by the escalating cost of the war in Vietnam, made federal expenditures on domestic social welfare measures increasingly controversial.

Historians still disagree on the impact of Johnson's Great Society programs. Charles Murray's *Losing Ground* (1984) charged that LBJ's social programs encouraged antisocial behavior. It argued that too many people, lured by welfare payments, abandoned the goals of marrying, settling down, and seeking jobs. In this view, the money given over to Great Society programs created government deficits that slowed economic growth. Had ill-advised social spending not undermined personal initiative and disrupted the nation's economy, continued economic growth could have provided virtually everyone with a comfortable lifestyle. This conservative argument portrayed the Great Society as the cause of, not the remedy for, economic distress.

Others rejected this view. They found scant evidence for the claim that most people preferred welfare to meaningful work. Moreover, spending for the military sector outstripped that for social programs and seemed the principal cause of the burgeoning budget deficit. Funds actually spent on Great Society programs, in this view, neither matched Johnson's promises nor reached the lavish levels claimed in studies such as *Losing Ground.*

Many antipoverty activists faulted the Great Society for not seriously challenging the prevailing distribution of political and economic power. The Johnson administration, they argued, remained closely wedded to large-scale bureaucratic solutions, forged by people connected to Washington elites. The White House quickly jettisoned, for example, the CAP model of grassroots empowerment. In addition, the Great Society, by assuming that economic growth would continue to finance federal initiatives, rejected measures that might redistribute income and wealth, such as a revised tax code. The Johnson administration never seriously tried to fulfill its promises, this critique concluded.

QUICK   REVIEW

JOHNSON'S "GREAT SOCIETY"

- Introduced or expanded a wide range of programs to help alleviate poverty

- Launched or enhanced services such as Medicare, Medicaid, legal aid, job training, and work-study programs

- Assumed that continued economic growth would fund social service programs

- Barred discrimination on the basis of race and gender

- Created controversy and contributed to a major realignment in U.S. politics

Although historians disagree on the Great Society's impact, there is broad agreement that Johnson's domestic program signaled a break with the past. Washington's financial outlay increased more than 10 percent during every year of LBJ's presidency. In 1960, federal spending on social welfare constituted 28 percent of total governmental outlays; by 1970, this figure had risen to more than 40 percent. Moreover, Great Society programs such as Medicaid, legal services, and job training permitted many low-income families to have services that more affluent ones had long taken for granted.

From perhaps the most important perspective, though, the Great Society proved a political failure. Over time, a highly critical view of the Great Society's flaws and failures helped to energize the conservative wing of the GOP, and fewer and fewer Democrats would risk defending Lyndon Johnson's vision. After boldly extending national power, in short, Johnson's domestic policies inflamed political passions. Controversy over social spending policies would reshape political life during the years that followed LBJ's presidency.

ESCALATION IN VIETNAM

FOCUS QUESTION
Through what incremental steps did the Johnson administration involve the United States ever more deeply in the war in Vietnam? What seemed to be the goal of its policies?

Johnson's divisive crusade to build a Great Society at home found its counterpart abroad in the **Vietnam War**. His pledge to protect South Vietnam demanded ever more of the nation's resources. Johnson's policies in Vietnam further polarized the nation and strained its economy.

THE GULF OF TONKIN RESOLUTION

Immediately after John Kennedy's assassination, Johnson had hesitated to widen the war in Southeast Asia. He did not wish, however, to appear "soft" on communism, and he soon accepted the recommendation of his military advisers to order air strikes against North Vietnam. He prepared a congressional resolution authorizing such an escalation of hostilities.

Events in the Gulf of Tonkin, off the coast of North Vietnam, provided the rationale for taking this resolution to Capitol Hill. On August 1, 1964, the U.S. destroyer *Maddox*, while on an intelligence-gathering mission, exchanged gunfire with North Vietnamese ships. Three days later, the *Maddox* returned with the *Turner Joy* and, during severe weather, reported what could have been signs of a failed torpedo attack. Although the *Maddox*'s commander radioed that the episode needed further analysis, Johnson immediately denounced "unprovoked aggression" by North Vietnam against the United States. (A later study concluded that there had never been a North Vietnamese attack.) Congress overwhelmingly authorized Johnson to take "all necessary measures to repel armed attack." Johnson treated this **Gulf of Tonkin Resolution** as tantamount to a congressional declaration of war and cited it as legal justification for all subsequent military action in Vietnam.

Despite his own aggressive response to events in the Gulf of Tonkin, Johnson successfully positioned himself as a cautious moderate during the presidential campaign of 1964. When Barry Goldwater demanded stronger measures against North Vietnam and even hinted at possible use of tactical nuclear weapons, Johnson's campaign managers portrayed Goldwater as a threat to the survival of civilization. Johnson himself seemed to promise not to commit U.S. troops to any land war in Southeast Asia.

Soon after the election, however, Johnson decisively deepened U.S. involvement there. More than a year after the 1963 coup against Diem (see Chapter 28), South

Vietnam War *Conflict lasting from 1946 to 1975, with direct U.S. military involvement from 1964 to 1973. Highly controversial, the war devastated the Vietnam countryside, spilled into all of Indochina, and ended in a victory for communist North Vietnam, which then united the country under its rule.*

Gulf of Tonkin Resolution
Measure passed by Congress in August 1964 that provided authorization for an air war against North Vietnam after U.S. destroyers were allegedly attacked by North Vietnamese torpedoes. Johnson invoked it as authority for expanding the Vietnam War.

Vietnam faced continued political chaos. The incompetence of successive governments in Saigon was fueling popular discontent, and South Vietnamese troops were deserting at an alarming rate. In January 1965, another Saigon regime collapsed, and factionalism stalled the emergence of any viable alternative.

Lacking an effective ally in South Vietnam, Johnson pondered his options. His aides offered conflicting advice. National Security Adviser McGeorge Bundy predicted Saigon's defeat unless the United States greatly increased its military role. Walt W. Rostow assured Johnson that, once North Vietnam recognized that the United States would never abandon its commitment, it would give up its plans to overrun the South. Undersecretary of State George Ball, by contrast, warned that U.S. troops would never preserve South Vietnam. He wrote that "no one has demonstrated that a white ground force of whatever size can win a guerrilla war . . . in jungle terrain in the midst of a population that refuses cooperation to the white forces." Senate Majority Leader Mike Mansfield urged Johnson to find some way of reuniting Vietnam as a neutral country. The Joint Chiefs of Staff, afflicted by interservice rivalries, provided conflicting military assessments and no clear guidance.

Although privately doubting the chances for success, Johnson became obsessed about the political and diplomatic consequences of a U.S. pullout. He feared that domestic criticism of any communist victory would endanger his Great Society programs. Moreover, he accepted the familiar Cold War proposition that a U.S. withdrawal would set off a "domino effect" in Asia and encourage communist-leaning insurgencies in Latin America, increase Soviet pressure on West Berlin, and damage U.S. credibility around the world. Both Eisenhower and Kennedy had staked U.S. prestige on a noncommunist South Vietnam. Johnson either had to abandon that commitment or chart an uncertain course by ordering a massive infusion of American troops.

Ultimately, Johnson decided to expand U.S. military involvement in Southeast Asia. He ordered a sustained campaign of bombing in North Vietnam, code-named "Rolling Thunder." He also deployed U.S. ground forces to regain lost territory in the South, expanded covert operations, and stepped up economic aid to the beleaguered South Vietnamese government. Only six months after the 1964 election, with his advisers still divided, Johnson committed the United States to a wider war.

napalm *Incendiary and toxic chemical contained in bombs used by the United States in Vietnam.*

THE WAR CONTINUES TO WIDEN

The war grew more intense during 1965. Hoping to break the enemy's will, U.S. military commanders sought to inflict more casualties. The Johnson administration authorized the use of **napalm,** a chemical that charred both foliage and people, and allowed the Air Force to bomb new targets. Additional U.S. combat troops arrived, but every escalation seemed to require a further one. After North Vietnam rejected a Johnson peace plan that it viewed as surrender, the United States again stepped up its military effort. North Vietnam's leader, Ho Chi Minh, who was pursuing a long-term strategy of attrition, became convinced that Johnson had little public or congressional support for continuing the costly war.

In April 1965, Johnson applied his Cold War, anticommunist foreign policy closer to home. Responding to exaggerated reports about a communist threat to the Dominican Republic, Johnson sent U.S. troops to unseat a left-leaning, elected president and to install a government eager to support U.S. interests. This incursion violated a longstanding "good neighbor" pledge not to intervene militarily in the Western Hemisphere. Although the action angered critics throughout Latin America, the overthrow of a leftist government in the Dominican Republic seemed to steel Johnson's determination to hold the line against communism in Vietnam.

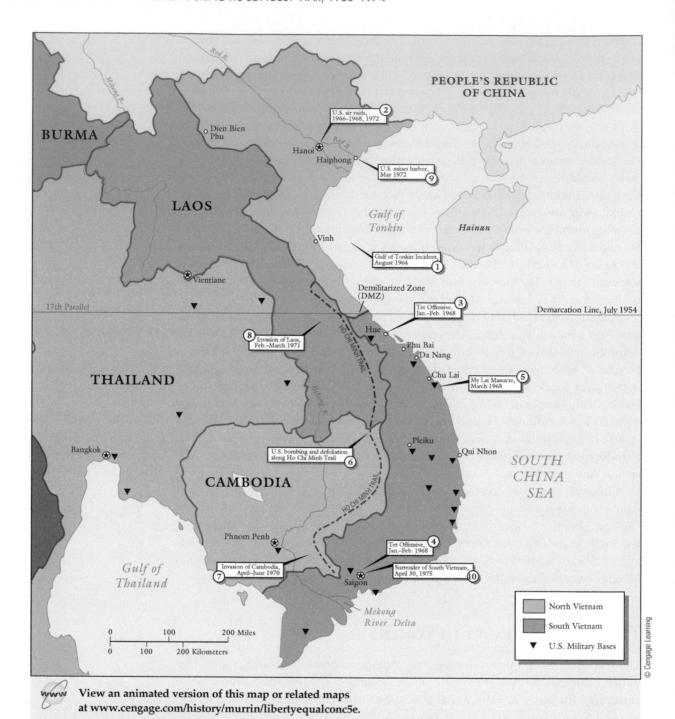

Map 29.1 VIETNAM WAR. *The war in Vietnam spread into neighboring countries as the North Vietnamese ran supplies southward along a network called the Ho Chi Minh Trail and the United States tried to disrupt their efforts. Unlike the Korean War (see map on p. 732), this guerrilla-style war had few conventional "fronts" of fighting.*

www   **View an animated version of this map or related maps at www.cengage.com/history/murrin/libertyequalconc5e.**

Later that spring, as the fifth government since Diem's 1963 murder was taking office in Saigon, U.S. strategists continued to wonder how to stabilize South Vietnam. General William Westmoreland, who directed the U.S. effort, recommended aggressively sending his troops on "search and destroy" missions against communist forces. In July 1965, Johnson publicly agreed to send 50,000 additional military personnel to Vietnam. Privately, LBJ pledged to send another 50,000, and he left open the possibility of sending even more. He also approved **saturation bombing** in the South Vietnamese countryside and intensified bombardment of the North.

Some advisers urged Johnson to admit candidly the greatly expanded scope of the U.S. effort. They recommended an outright declaration of war by Congress or at least legislation allowing the president to wield the economic and informational controls that previous presidential administrations had used during wartime. But Johnson worried about arousing greater protests from Congress and a growing antiwar movement. Rather than risk debates that could ramp up dissent, Johnson decided to stress the administration's willingness to negotiate and to act as if the war was not really a war. As the Johnson administration talked of seeing "light at the end of the tunnel," it apparently hoped that most people in the United States would remain largely in the dark about events in Vietnam.

Over the next three years, U.S. involvement steadily increased. The number of U.S. troops in Vietnam grew to 535,000. Operation RANCHHAND scorched South Vietnam's croplands and defoliated half its forests in an effort to eliminate the natural cover for enemy troop movements. Approximately 1.5 million tons of bombs— more than all the tonnage dropped during the Second World War—pounded North Vietnamese cities and pummeled the villages and hamlets of the South. Still, Johnson carefully avoided bombing close to the Chinese border or doing anything else that might provoke either Chinese or Soviet entry into the war.

Despite the escalating violence, Vietnam remained a "limited" war. The U.S. strategy was to contain the NLF and North Vietnam by continually escalating the cost they would pay, in lost lives and bombed-out infrastructure. The weekly "body count" of enemy dead remained the measure for gauging progress. Estimates that a kill ratio of 10 to 1 would force North Vietnam and the NLF to pull back encouraged the military to unleash more firepower and further inflate enemy casualty figures. This same calculation provided an automatic justification for more U.S. troops: Whenever the number of enemy forces seemed to increase, the Pentagon required additional troops to maintain the desired kill ratio. Johnson, whose notorious temper flared at the first hint of bad news, welcomed kill statistics as a sign that "victory was around the corner." But North Vietnam, assisted by the Soviet Union and China, could match every U.S. escalation. The North Vietnamese funneled supplies into the South through a shifting network of roads and paths called the **Ho Chi Minh Trail**. By the end of 1967, several of Johnson's key aides, most notably Secretary of Defense Robert McNamara, decided that the United States could not sustain its seemingly open-ended commitment to South Vietnam. The majority of Johnson's advisors, however, refused to accept such an assessment.

The destruction wreaked by U.S. forces was giving North Vietnamese, Chinese, and Soviet leaders a decided propaganda advantage. Critics around the world condemned the ferocity of U.S. bombardments. In Western Europe, demonstrations against the United States became prominent features of political life. The president and members of his administration were hounded by antiwar protesters everywhere they went, and LBJ complained of being a prisoner in his own White House.

Meanwhile, the United States failed to find an effective ally in Saigon. The devastation of the countryside, the economic destabilization caused by the flood of U.S. dollars, and corruption took their toll. The "pacification" and "strategic hamlet" programs, which gathered Vietnamese farmers into tightly guarded villages, sounded viable in Washington but created greater chaos by uprooting at least a quarter of South Vietnamese from their villages and ancestral lands. Buddhist priests persistently demonstrated against foreign influence. When, in 1967, two generals, Nguyen Van Thieu and Nguyen Cao Ky, who had headed the government in Saigon tried to

QUICK   REVIEW

JOHNSON'S DECISION TO ESCALATE THE WAR IN VIETNAM

- Containment policy and domino theory warned against allowing communist expansion

- Civilian and military advisers gave conflicting advice about major military involvement

- Danger of direct involvement by China or the Soviet Union limited U.S. military options

- Dubious attack in the Gulf of Tonkin prompted a Congressional resolution authorizing the escalation of military action against North Vietnam

saturation bombing *Intensive bombing designed to destroy everything in a targeted area.*

Ho Chi Minh Trail *U.S. name for the various routes, primarily through Laos, the North Vietnamese used to bring troops and supplies into South Vietnam.*

legitimize their rule with elections, the effort fell short. A voting process marked by corruption only highlighted their precarious position.

THE MEDIA AND THE WAR

Johnson lectured the American public about upholding the nation's honor and diplomatic commitments, but dissent continued to mount. In previous wars, Washington had restricted media coverage. Hoping to avoid the controversy that overt censorship would surely cause, the Johnson administration employed informal ways of managing information. With television making Vietnam a **"living room war"**—one that people could watch in their own homes—Johnson kept three sets playing in his office in order to monitor what viewers were seeing. Most of what he saw, early on, he liked.

Antiwar activists assailed what they considered the media's uncritical reporting on the war. Too many journalists, they claimed, accepted story frames constructed by the White House. Especially in the early years, few reporters wrote critical stories that dissected either the U.S. military effort or the travails of its South Vietnamese ally.

In time, however, the tone and content of media coverage changed. Images of unrelenting destruction came across TV screens. After gazing at his TV sets, LBJ began telephoning network executives, castigating them for critical broadcasts. A few journalists, such as David Halberstam, challenged the reassuring reports handed out by U.S. officials in Saigon. Gloria Emerson's grim reports portrayed the war as one in which poor and disproportionately nonwhite troops fought and died so that wealthy families, with draft-exempt "fortunate sons," might reap war-related profits. Harrison Salisbury sent stories from North Vietnam that detailed the destructive impact of U.S. bombing missions.

As the conflict dragged on, the media began to talk about a "war at home" between **"hawks"** and **"doves."** Johnson insisted his administration was following time-tested containment policies. Secretary of State Dean Rusk warned of the dangers of "appeasement." But influential U.S. politicians—led by J. William Fulbright of Arkansas, chair of the powerful Senate Foreign Relations Committee—warned of misplaced priorities and of an "arrogance of power." Meanwhile, antiwar protesters began to challenge the entire structure of U.S. politics and culture.

living room war *Phrase suggesting that television coverage had brought the Vietnam War into the living rooms of Americans and may have led many to question the war.*

hawks *Supporters of intensified military efforts in the Vietnam War.*

doves *Opponents of military action, especially those who wanted quickly to end U.S. involvement in the Vietnam War.*

THE WAR AT HOME

FOCUS QUESTION
What domestic social movements emerged during America's longest war? How did they seek to change U.S. political culture and the direction of public policy? What role did commercial media play in the "movement of movements"?

Millions came to oppose the war in Southeast Asia, and support for the Great Society at home began to erode. By 1968, tensions escalated into confrontation, violence, and one of the most divisive presidential election campaigns in U.S. history.

THE MOVEMENT OF MOVEMENTS

During the 1960s, groups of young people, most of them college students, protested against the war in Vietnam and in favor of social change, especially in race relations, at home. They urged Americans to "expand their minds," often with a little help from drugs and rock music, and to seek alternative ways of living their lives. Iconic images from the 1960s provide a kaleidoscopic panorama of what one historian calls a "movement of movements." All across the political and cultural spectrum—not simply on the New Left or among the young or African

MUSICAL LINK TO THE PAST

THE FOLK-ROCK MOMENT

Songwriter: Bob Dylan
Title: "Subterranean Homesick Blues" (1965)

In the early 1960s, Bob Dylan emerged from an acoustic folk music revival with stirring protest songs such as "Blowin' in the Wind." In 1965, however, Dylan adopted an amplified rock-and-roll sound, with electric guitar and drums; for the next year, folk fans around the world booed when Dylan arrived onstage with his electric band.

The 1965 recording of "Subterranean Homesick Blues" displayed Dylan's revamped musical style. He dropped the relatively straightforward protest lyrics, which he dismissed as "finger-pointing songs," for a more free-form approach that used "chains of flashing images" in a manner reminiscent of 1950s Beat Generation writers Allen Ginsberg and Jack Kerouac. The words did not always immediately make sense, but many of the phrases entered national consciousness ("Don't follow leaders, watch the parking meters"; "You don't need a weatherman to know which way the wind blows"). Dylan's new compositions combined alienation with humor. As "Dylanologist" Paul Williams has written: "Some reacted by calling Dylan a 'sell-out,' not realizing, at least at first, that he was now making the most anti-establishment, revolutionary music of his or anyone's career." A new style of popular song took hold and swept across the world.

1. Why do you think that stylistic turning points in musical history (such as Dylan's embrace of a rock sound or the arrival of the waltz in the 1850s) prompt public resistance? Why do people view music as threatening, as something more than mere entertainment?

2. Do you think that Dylan's new songwriting style influenced hip-hop songwriting in the 1980s, such as "The Message" (see Chapter 31)? If so, how? If not, why not?

 Listen to an audio recording of this music on the Musical Links to the Past CD.

Americans or cultural dissenters—Americans joined movements that challenged the established order.

The energy produced by this movement of movements tended to tilt against two dominant ideals of the 1950s and early 1960s: the faith in political (or interest) group pluralism and the parallel conviction that deeply held spiritual beliefs ultimately united, rather than divided, the nation and its diverse people (see Chapter 28). As the war in Vietnam dragged on, people increasingly doubted that the existing political system could solve problems. At the same time, disparate movements based on deeply held values—involving issues such as war and peace, race relationships, gender politics, the environment, and sexuality—appeared headed in different directions.

Ultimately, this movement of movements produced political, social, and cultural polarization. No single group could lay exclusive claim to the historical era often called "the Sixties," the period from roughly 1963 to 1975, which coincided with America's longest war. Numerous social movements sought to redirect national life down different paths, often with no clear maps.

Media imagery did not create or manufacture, for popular consumption, this movement of movements. Activists recognized, however, that time in the media spotlight helped demonstrate both their deep commitment and their equally passionate disdain for the policies they opposed. Often beginning with posters and

AMERICAN ATTITUDES TOWARD THE VIETNAM WAR
Responses to the question: "Do you think that the United States made a mistake in sending troops to fight there?"

pamphlets, movement activists produced increasingly sophisticated imagery and eye-catching public demonstrations.

Four of the earliest and most prominent of the movements that accompanied America's longest war involved the New Left, the counterculture, Black Power, and antiwar protest.

MOVEMENTS ON COLLEGE CAMPUSES: A NEW LEFT

While relatively few college students actually became active in social movements, their activities set the tone for campus politics, attracted extensive media attention, and, in time, generated popular controversy.

In 1962, two years after conservatives had formed Young Americans for Freedom (YAF) (see Chapter 28), students on the left established Students for a Democratic Society (SDS). Although SDS endorsed familiar political causes, such as civil rights, it attracted more attention for the spiritual and personalized style of its politics. Its "Port Huron Statement" of 1962 pledged to fight the "loneliness, estrangement, isolation" that supposedly afflicted so many people. Charging that the dominant insider culture valued bureaucratic expertise over citizen engagement and economic growth over meaningful work, SDS spoke for alternative visions. In politics, it called for "participatory democracy"—grassroots activism and institutions responsive to local needs.

Indeed, localized struggles in communities throughout the South, such as those waged during Freedom Summer in Mississippi, seemed tangible examples of participatory democracy. They seemed to promise the chance to reenergize the nation's politics and reorient its moral compass. Organizing efforts in the Deep South thus attracted idealistic white students from Northern colleges. Risking racist violence, they went to the South to work alongside local political activists, trying to register African American voters and then organizing them for political action. Some of these students remained there, working for civil rights; others returned to the North and joined neighborhood-based political projects.

New Left activists had a constantly expanding view of what counted as "politics." Although voter registration drives in the South did seek greater access to the political process, for example, New Left activists placed far greater emphasis on alternative political forms, such as sit-ins and demonstrations. They viewed their generation as uniquely situated to confront a political system dominated by powerful and entrenched interests.

On campus, young people chafed at courses that seemingly ignored the relevant issues of the day and college administrators who imposed restrictions such as sex-segregated living arrangements and dorm hours. Far worse, these dissenters argued, giant universities, accepting funding from the Pentagon and corporations, seemed oblivious to the social and moral implications of their war-related research. During the "Berkeley Revolt" of 1964 and 1965, students and sympathetic faculty protested restrictions on political activity on campus and then began speaking out against the Vietnam War and racial discrimination. The long-running drama at Berkeley, which disrupted classes and polarized the university, came to symbolize the turmoil that the media called "the war on campus."

THE COUNTERCULTURE

Berkeley also came to symbolize the interrelationship between the political movements of the New Left and the vertiginous energies of the **counterculture**. The alternative counterculture of the 1960s is a difficult "movement" to identify, especially since one of its self-defining slogans proclaimed "Do Your Own Thing." The counterculture elected no officers, held no formal meetings, and maintained no central office to issue manifestos. It burst into view in low-income neighborhoods, such as San Francisco's Haight-Ashbury area, and along the streets bordering college campuses, such as Berkeley's Telegraph Avenue. People who claimed to speak for it espoused values, styles, and institutions hailed as both "utopian" *and* as "realistic" alternatives to those of the prevailing "straight" culture.

Dissenting cultural ventures did not spring up spontaneously but drew on earlier models, such as the "Beat movement" of the 1950s. A loosely connected group of writers and poets, the Beats had denied that either the material abundance or conventional spiritual ideals of the 1950s fulfilled the promise of liberty. Rejecting the "people of plenty" credo (see Chapter 28), the Beats claimed that an excess of consumer goods and oppressive technologies condemned most people to wander through alienated lives feeling oppressed, emotionally crippled, or just plain bored. Beat writers such as Jack Kerouac, author of *On the Road* (1957), praised the rebels of their generation, nonconformists like themselves, for challenging settled routines and seeking more instinctual, sensual, and authentic ways of living. The Beat poet Allen Ginsberg, in works such as *Howl* (1956), decried soulless materialism and puritanical moral codes and celebrated the kind of liberty that drugs, Eastern mysticism, and same-sex love affairs could supposedly provide.

The counterculture of the 1960s left its imprint on a wide range of social movements, including the urban cooperative movement, radical feminism, **environmentalism**, and the fight against restrictions on lifestyle choices. It also affected culture. The mass media invariably highlighted the flamboyant clothing, hairstyles, and uninhibited sexuality. They liked to portray countercultural **hippies** as being on the cutting edge of a massive, fun-filled "youth rebellion" and focused on use of drugs, such as marijuana and LSD, communal living arrangements, and new forms of music, such as the folk rock of the Byrds and the acid rock of the Grateful Dead. The singer-songwriter Bob Dylan was hailed as the counterculture's prophet-laureate.

counterculture *Antiestablishment movement that symbolized the youthful social upheaval of the 1960s. Ridiculing traditional attitudes toward such matters as clothing, hairstyles, and sexuality, the counterculture urged a more open and less regimented approach to daily life.*

environmentalism *Movement with roots in earlier conservation, preservation, and public health movements that grew in power after 1970, when concern mounted over the disruption of ecological balances and critical habitats.*

hippies *People who identified with the 1960s counterculture. They were often depicted as embracing mind-altering drugs, communal living arrangements, and new forms of music.*

Fusing musical idioms used by African American blues artists such as Muddy Waters with poetic touches indebted to the Beats, Dylan's "Like a Rolling Stone" (1965) exploded onto both the Top 40 charts of AM radio and the freewheeling playlists of the new alternative FM stations. New publications, including the magazine *Rolling Stone,* dispatched youthful journalists to report on—and participate in—the countercultural "scene."

Images and products from the counterculture soon found a ready market. The ad agency for Chrysler Motors urged car buyers to break away from older patterns, purchase a youthful-looking 1965 model, and thereby join the "Dodge Rebellion." Recognizing the appeal of bands such as San Francisco's Jefferson Airplane, the music industry, too, saw profits to be made. An early countercultural happening, the Human Be-In, organized by community activists from San Francisco in early 1967, provided a model for subsequent, commercially dominated music festivals such as Monterrey Pop (later in 1967) and Woodstock (in 1969).

Back on college campuses, however, some of the students and faculty attracted to New Left political movements seemed initially baffled by the counterculture. The novelist Ken Kesey shocked a 1965 political demonstration at Berkeley with a style of politics indebted to the theatrics of the counterculture. Accompanied by veterans from the Beat movement and youthful members of his communal group, "the Merry Pranksters," Kesey alternated between singing choruses of "Home on the Range" and urging students to focus on revolutionizing, especially through drugs such as LSD, how they lived their own lives.

AFRICAN AMERICAN SOCIAL MOVEMENTS

The movement of movements also reshaped efforts to achieve freedom and equality for African Americans. Early on, leaders such as Dr. King recognized the value of media coverage. TV images of the violence in Selma, Alabama, in 1965 had helped galvanize support for federal voting-rights legislation. At one point, ABC television interrupted the anti-Nazi film *Judgment at Nuremberg* to show white Alabama state troopers beating peaceful, mostly African American, voting-rights marchers. Lyndon Johnson used television to promise that "we shall overcome" the nation's "crippling legacy of bigotry and injustice."

At the same time, conservatives insisted that activists were provoking conflict and violence and that only a renewed commitment to law and order would ease racial tensions. Movement activists who looked to Dr. King replied that racism, lack of opportunity, and inadequate government remedies produced the frustration that spawned violence. Other voices within this broad movement of movements, however, doubted that governmental power could ever solve race-related issues.

This debate intensified in 1965 in the wake of a devastating racial conflict in Los Angeles. An altercation between a white highway patrol officer and a black motorist escalated into six days of violence, centered in the largely African American community of Watts in south-central Los Angeles. Thirty-four people died; hundreds of businesses and homes were burned; heavily armed National Guard troops patrolled the streets; and television camera crews carried images across the nation and around the world. Violence erupted in many other American cities during the remainder of the 1960s.

What should be the response to events such as those in Watts? Most local politicians blamed civil rights "agitators" for the troubles. Dr. King rushed to the scene, preaching the politics of nonviolence, while some black activists insisted that only aggressive political action could draw attention to racial inequalities in jobs, housing, and law enforcement.

HISTORY THROUGH FILM

MALCOLM X (1992)

*Directed by Spike Lee; starring Denzel Washington
(Malcolm X), Angela Bassett (Betty Shabbaz),
Al Freeman, Jr. (Elijah Muhammad)*

For more than 25 years, Hollywood failed to make a movie portraying the foremost advocate of Black Power, Malcolm X, whose *Autobiography* is a literary classic. Delays in obtaining financing, crafting a script, and finding a director always stymied production plans. Spike Lee, America's best-known African American film director, insisted that only he could do

Everett Collection

Denzel Washington stars as Malcolm X.

justice to the story of Malcolm X, who was assassinated by rivals at a speaking engagement in Harlem in 1965 at the age of 40. Finally, in 1992, with a budget of $34 million, Lee's independent production company (named "Forty Acres and a Mule," after the land-distribution program for former slaves advocated after the Civil War) released a movie starring Denzel Washington that argues for Malcolm X's continuing relevance.

The film montages that begin and end the movie underscore the film director's outlook. Against the backdrop of the Warner Brothers logo, the soundtrack introduces the actual voice of Malcolm X decrying examples of racism in U.S. history. Malcolm X's accusations continue as a giant American flag appears on screen and is cut into pieces by jagged images from the amateur video of Los Angeles police officers beating Rodney King, a notorious instance of police brutality that took place in 1991. Next, the flag begins to burn until, revealed behind it, a giant "X," adorned with remnants of the flag, fills the frame. The ending of the movie presents archival footage of Malcolm X, along with images of South African freedom fighter Nelson Mandela, while the voice of Ozzie Davis, the celebrated African American actor, gives a eulogy.

When first released, the film opened to packed movie houses. Despite a multimedia publicity blitz, however, box-office revenues steadily declined. Viewers said that the lengthy, episodic movie taxed their patience and attention span.

Watching *Malcolm X* on video or DVD today, however, allows us to concentrate on its best sequences, speeding by ones that seem to drag, and returning to those that are unclear at first. In spite of being more than three hours long, *Malcolm X* offers a complex account of the early Black Power movement and the social ferment that gripped the nation during the 1960s.

Even before Watts, a new **Black Power** movement, which had been heralded by a charismatic leader named **Malcolm X,** was emerging. A minister in the Nation of Islam, a North American–based group popularly known as the "Black Muslims," Malcolm X initially denounced the civil rights movement. He saw Dr. King's gradual, nonviolent approach as irrelevant to the everyday problems of most African Americans and proclaimed that integration was unworkable. Although he never advocated initiating confrontation, Malcolm X did endorse self-defense "by any means necessary."

Malcolm X offered more than angry rhetoric. He urged African Americans to "recapture our heritage and identity" and "launch a cultural revolution to unbrainwash an entire people." Seeking a broad movement, Malcolm X eventually broke from the Black Muslims and established his own Organization of Afro-American Unity. Murdered in 1965 by enemies from the Nation of Islam, Malcolm X remained, especially after the posthumous publication of his *Autobiography* (1965), a powerful symbol of militant politics and a source for renewed pride in African American cultural visions.

These visions increasingly diverged from the political perspectives that dominated LBJ's administration. Officially committed to additional civil rights legislation, the president privately sensed that many federal laws bypassed the root causes of the current conflicts. He began listening to advisors who suggested social programs, later called "affirmative action," specifically to assist African Americans. In fall 1965, the president invited several hundred black leaders to the White House for a "racial summit." Two veteran activists, A. Philip Randolph and Bayard Rustin, used the occasion to lobby for their Freedom Budget, which called for spending $100 billion on infrastructure projects in low-income neighborhoods.

Meanwhile, events in the South highlighted the increasingly frenetic movement-of-movements phenomenon. SNCC and Dr. King's SCLC pressed forward, often along separate paths. Their movements faced the constant threat of violence, and state and local legal systems seemingly unable to restrain or punish vigilantes who attacked, or even killed, civil rights workers. White Southern legal officials appeared no better at overseeing electoral contests. Charging that vote-counters had robbed an SNCC-sponsored slate of victory in a local election in Lowndes County, Alabama, Stokely Carmichael began to organize activists in that locale. To symbolize the militancy of this third-party movement, SNCC commissioned a special logo: a coiled black panther.

In June 1966, a KKK gunman shot James Meredith, who was conducting a one-person "March against Fear" from Memphis, Tennessee, to Jackson, Mississippi. Activists hastily gathered in Mississippi. An enlarged March against Fear to complete Meredith's walk became the first large-scale movement project—in contrast to the 1963 March on Washington or the 1965 voting-rights campaign in Alabama—that did not seek new civil right legislation. In this sense, it seemed an effort to demonstrate that movements for liberty and equality now also emphasized struggles for dignity, pride, and empowerment. Moreover, symbolic political activities relied on media visibility, and Meredith's shooting had already focused national news coverage on Mississippi.

As Stokely Carmichael played to the omnipresent TV cameras, Dr. King, an old hand at this political art form, admiringly acknowledged the younger activist's shrewd grasp of media routines. Carmichael now explicitly urged that struggle not remain just one for "Freedom," the byword of the SCLC, but for "Black Power," insisting that Black Power best described the kind of politics that direct-action movements such as SNCC should now embrace.

Black Power *Mid-1960s movement that called for modifying integrationist goals in favor of gaining political and economic power for separate black-directed institutions and emphasizing pride in African American heritage.*

Malcolm X *Charismatic African American leader who criticized integration and urged the creation of separate black economic and cultural institutions. He became a hero to members of the Black Power movement.*

Black Power provided a sometimes inflammatory label for an often pragmatic set of claims. At different times and places during the 1960s, African American activists determined that they should seek greater on-the-ground power both in and for their own communities. Operating from this perspective, in 1966, several college students from Oakland announced a new Black Power organization. The Black Panther Party's platform employed militant rhetoric on behalf of 10 objectives, including greater opportunities for housing, education, and employment; legal protections, especially against police misconduct; and improved health and nutrition in low-income black neighborhoods.

The Panthers quickly became a media phenomenon. Adapting quasi-military symbols and organizational forms from Third World revolutionary movements, a trio of media-savvy young men—Huey Newton, Bobby Seale, and Eldridge Cleaver—gained national attention. A 1967 rally on behalf of the Second Amendment right to use firearms for self-defense, against what armed demonstrators called "fascist pig" police officers, attracted the notice of the FBI's J. Edgar Hoover, who made destroying the Black Panther Party a key goal.

Other groups and movements extended Black Power ideals to a wide range of issues. Fully embracing the word *black* and a political-cultural agenda based on their racial identity, they asserted their power to pursue separate, African American–directed routes not just toward liberty and equality but, sometimes, "liberation" from the prevailing political culture. "Black Is Beautiful" became a watchword. James Brown, the "Godfather of Soul," captured this new spirit with his song, "Say It Loud, I'm Black and I'm Proud" (1968).

Within this context, Congress passed the **Civil Rights Act of 1968**. One provision of this omnibus measure, popularly known as the Fair Housing Act, sought to eliminate racial discrimination in the real estate market, but the act also provided exemptions that enfeebled its own enforcement. Moreover, another section in the law declared it a crime to cross state lines in order to incite a "riot." Supporters hailed this provision as a law-and-order measure, while critics countered that it targeted political activists, especially those in the Black Power movement.

THE ANTIWAR MOVEMENT

Meanwhile, one movement began to overshadow all others: the movement to end the war in Vietnam.

The antiwar movement never fell into neat categories. Some of the strongest "antiwar" sentiment, for example, blamed LBJ for not prosecuting the war *aggressively enough*. At the other end of the spectrum, small movements called for a North Vietnam-NLF victory. The chant, "Ho, Ho, Ho Chi Minh/NLF is Gonna Win" enraged Johnson and distressed many in the antiwar coalition.

While a diverse constituency opposed the war, the antiwar movement faced the same questions as all the other movements of the 1960s. What kind of politics best expressed the ethical and spiritual values of its supporters? And how might mass-mediated images of this movement's activities and performances represent its politics to a broader audience?

On college campuses, supporters and opponents of the war debated at **teach-ins**, which later gave way to street demonstrations. A draft-resistance movement emerged, often symbolized by the burning of draft cards and sometimes marked by the flight to Canada. In August 1967, campus protests passed a crucial threshold when a pitched, bloody battle broke out between antiwar demonstrators and police at the University of Wisconsin in Madison.

Civil Rights Act of 1968
Measure that banned racial discrimination in housing and made interference with a person's civil rights a federal crime. It also stipulated that crossing state lines to incite a riot was a federal crime.

teach-ins *Forums, usually on college campuses, at which supporters and opponents of Johnson's policies in Vietnam debated one another.*

Dr. Martin Luther King, Jr., a long-time critic of the war, now faced intensive pressure, especially from antiwar clergy, to spell out his moral-spiritual position. Speaking at New York's Riverside Church in April 1967, Dr. King bitterly noted a black-and-white truth. African American troops, mostly from low-income communities, served and died in numbers far greater than their proportion of the U.S. population "for a nation that has been unable to seat them together in the same schools" with the white soldiers now at their side in Vietnam. The immoral "madness" in Vietnam "must cease," Dr. King thundered.

This speech provided a gauge of both the growing antiwar movement and the expanding polarization in the United States. Voices from across the political-media spectrum condemned King's address. Although the *New York Times* did not, as some commentators did, call King a "traitor," it read his antiwar pronouncement through the familiar frame of narrow interest groups. The *Times* charged Dr. King with seeking media attention and with damaging the civil rights cause by expounding on a matter about which he lacked the political credentials to comment intelligently. The same issues raised by King's speech—the nature of politics and the role of the media—surrounded popular discussion of a massive 1967 antiwar demonstration in Washington. This event underscored how the politics of the New Left and the spirit of the counterculture marched together, at least when in opposition to Lyndon Johnson's policies in Vietnam. Noting the visual media's voracious appetite for pictures of dissent, a small group of experienced activists invented a kind of "non-movement movement" that bypassed the hard work of mobilization and organization in favor of hoping that media images would do the work for them. Two members of this group, Abbie Hoffman and Jerry Rubin, proclaimed themselves leaders of a (nonexistent) Youth International Party (the "Yippies") and simply waited for media coverage to surround their activities, as they knew it would.

Hoffman and Rubin raised the curtain on a neo-vaudevillian, countercultural style of politics. In one famous incident, they tossed fake money onto the floor of the New York Stock Exchange. Invoking the sit-in movement, they joked about staging department store "loot-ins." Their contribution to the 1967 antiwar march, they announced, would be a separate trek to the Pentagon, where marchers chanting mystical incantations would levitate the building.

Although the Pentagon remained firmly planted, the Pentagon march generated eye-catching TV footage. It also won novelist Norman Mailer a National Book Award for *Armies of the Night* (1968), his account of the event.

1968

But the media's relationship to deepening antiwar sentiment seemed uncertain. Might not media images of colorful quipsters such as Hoffman and Rubin help fuel cultural polarization rather than political action? Was the media's taste for spectacular demonstrations trivializing underlying issues? Such questions became even more pressing during the tumultuous 12 months of 1968.

TURMOIL IN VIETNAM

At the end of January 1968, during a supposed truce in observance of Tet, the Vietnamese lunar new year celebration, NLF and North Vietnamese forces suddenly went on the attack throughout South Vietnam, even seizing the grounds of the U.S. embassy in Saigon temporarily.

Militarily, this **Tet offensive** ended with the NLF and the North gaining relatively little territory at considerable cost. Supporters of the war blamed media imagery for exaggerating the effect of the early attacks, ignoring NLF and North Vietnamese losses, and thereby turning "victory" into "defeat." Critics countered that the Tet offensive had caught the U.S. military ill prepared to take advantage of badly mauled enemy forces.

More importantly, Tet proved a defeat for the Johnson administration. After CBS-TV anchor Walter Cronkite returned from a post-Tet tour of Vietnam and told a national audience that the United States would never prevail there, Lyndon Johnson reportedly mused that if he had lost "the most trusted person in America," as Cronkite was known, he had lost the rest of the country.

When General Westmoreland requested an additional 206,000 U.S. troops, most of Johnson's advisers insisted, instead, that South Vietnamese troops shoulder more of the military burden. Johnson conceded that another large increase in U.S troops, even if forces could have been spared from other duties, would have further fanned antiwar opposition.

The Tet offensive threw Lyndon Johnson's own political future into stark relief. Faced with open revolt by antiwar Democrats, led by Senator Eugene McCarthy of Minnesota, Johnson surprised all but his closest aides and announced, on March 31, 1968, that he would not run for reelection. He limited the bombing of North Vietnam and announced that he would begin peace negotiations. McCarthy, campaigning on a peace platform, continued his quest for the Democratic nomination, now running against Johnson's ever-loyal vice president, Hubert H. Humphrey.

TURMOIL AT HOME

One former LBJ supporter gladdened by Johnson's withdrawal was Dr. Martin Luther King., Jr. He hoped that the Democratic Party would embrace an antiwar candidate, possibly Senator Robert Kennedy (RFK) of New York, JFK's younger

Tet offensive *Surprise National Liberation Front (NLF) attack during the lunar new year holiday in early 1968 that brought high casualties to the NLF but fuelled pessimism about the war's outcome in the United States.*

THE FUNERAL PROCESSION OF DR. MARTIN LUTHER KING, APRIL 9, 1968. *Martin Luther King, Jr.'s assassination in 1968 sparked both violent protests and solemn mourning for the slain civil rights leader. Thousands of his grieving supporters followed the cart, drawn by mules, that carried King's body through the streets of his native Atlanta.*

© Bettmann/CORBIS

brother. But on April 4, 1968, while visiting Memphis, Tennessee, in support of a strike by African American sanitation workers, King was assassinated. A lone shooter named James Earl Ray was charged with the murder. Ray quickly pleaded guilty and received a 99-year prison sentence. Subsequently, though, he recanted, claiming to have been a pawn in a larger white supremacist conspiracy. Ray died in 1998, still insisting on his innocence, a claim that intrigued members of the King family but convinced few legal observers.

As news of King's murder spread, violence swept through more than 100 cities and towns. Thirty-nine people died; 75,000 regular and National Guard troops were called to duty. When President Johnson proclaimed Sunday, April 7, a day of national mourning for the slain civil rights leader, parts of the nation's capital city remained ablaze.

Meanwhile, Robert Kennedy joined the race for the Democratic presidential nomination. Promising to end violence at home and the war in Vietnam, he asserted that only another Kennedy could win the presidency in November.

Then, on June 5, minutes after winning California's Democratic primary, Robert Kennedy fell victim to an assassin's bullets. Bystanders grabbed Sirhan Sirhan, a Palestinian immigrant, who was later convicted of the killing. Television coverage of Kennedy's funeral was a disturbing reminder of King's recent murder and of the assassination of RFK's own brother five years earlier.

The violence of 1968 continued. During the Republican national convention in Miami, as presidential candidate Richard Nixon was promising to restore law and order, racial violence broke out in that city; four people lost their lives. Later that summer, in Chicago, thousands of antiwar demonstrators converged on the Democratic Party's convention to protest the nomination of Hubert Humphrey, who was still supporting Johnson's policy in Vietnam. Responding to provocative acts by some demonstrators, including Abbie Hoffman and Jerry Rubin, police officers indiscriminately attacked antiwar forces and journalists. Although an official report later talked about a "police riot," opinion polls showed that most people supported the use of force in Chicago. Humphrey easily captured the Democratic presidential nod, but disagreements over Johnson's Vietnam policy and the meaning of the violence in Chicago left his party bitterly divided.

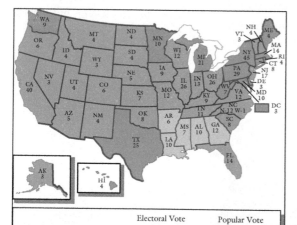

	Electoral Vote		Popular Vote	
	Number	%	Number	%
Humphrey (Democrat)	191	35.5	31,275,166	42.9
Nixon (Republican)	301	56.0	31,785,480	43.6
Wallace (American Independent)	46	8.5	9,906,473	13.5

Map 29.2 **PRESIDENTIAL ELECTION, 1968.** *George Wallace's independent, third-party candidacy influenced the election of 1968. Compare this map with ones of earlier and later election years to see how the southern states gradually left the Democratic column and, in time, became a base of Republican power.*

THE ELECTION OF 1968

Both Humphrey and Nixon worried about the candidacy of Alabama's George Wallace, a Southern Democrat who ran for president as a third-party candidate in 1968. He chose a militant hawk, retired Air Force General Curtis LeMay, as his running mate. With his opposition to civil rights well established, Wallace could concentrate his fire on the counterculture and the antiwar movement. If any "hippie" protestor ever blocked his motorcade, Wallace once announced, "It'll be the last car he'll ever lay down in front of." Declaring his independence from the interest groups that supposedly controlled the political process, Wallace also courted voters who saw themselves as captive to "tax-and-spend" bureaucracies in Washington. Wallace never expected to gain the presidency. But if neither major-party candidate won a majority of the electoral votes, the presidential election would rest with the House of Representatives, where Wallace might act as a power broker.

Nixon narrowly prevailed in November. Although he won 56 percent of the electoral vote, Nixon outpolled Humphrey in the popular vote by less than 1 percent. Humphrey had benefited when Johnson ordered a temporary halt in the bombing of North Vietnam and pledged to begin peace talks in Paris. Still, Humphrey carried only Texas in the South. George Wallace picked up 46 electoral votes, all from the Deep South, and 13.5 percent of the popular vote nationwide. Nixon won five crucial Southern states and attracted, all across the country, those whom he called "the forgotten Americans, the non-shouters, the non-demonstrators."

THE NIXON YEARS, 1969–1974

Raised in a modest Quaker home in southern California, Richard Nixon had campaigned for the presidency as the kind of leader who would restore tranquility. His presidency, however, coincided with more, rather than less, turmoil.

FOCUS QUESTION
What new domestic and foreign policies did the Nixon administration initiate?

LAWBREAKING AND VIOLENCE

A handful of people on the political fringe embraced violence, generally through bomb attacks. There were nearly 200 actual and attempted bombings on college campuses during the 1969–1970 academic year; an explosion at the University of Wisconsin claimed the life of a late-working grad student. Nonlethal attacks rocked other targets, including the Bank of America, Chase Manhattan Bank, and even the U.S. Congress. On one highly publicized occasion in 1970, three members of the Weather Underground blew themselves apart when their own bomb factory exploded.

At the same time, government officials stepped up their use of force. Fred Hampton of the Black Panthers and prison activist George Jackson died under circumstances their supporters called political assassination and public officials considered normal law enforcement. Agents of J. Edgar Hoover's FBI harassed activists, planted damaging rumors, and even operated as *agent provocateurs*, urging protestors to undertake actions that officials might later prosecute as criminal offenses.

State and local officials stepped up their own efforts to restore order. During the fall of 1971, New York's Governor Nelson Rockefeller suddenly broke off negotiations with inmates at Attica State Prison, who had seized several cell blocks and taken guards hostage in a protest over what they considered intolerable living conditions. He then ordered heavily armed state troopers and National Guard forces into the complex. When this "Attica Uprising" finally ended, 29 prisoners and 11 guards lay dead. On college campuses, too, local officials and administrators were increasingly less hesitant to employ force against demonstrators.

A NEW PRESIDENT

Richard Nixon insisted that his vast public experience made him the ideal president for such troubled times. After graduating from Whittier College in California, Nixon studied law at Duke University and served in the Navy during the Second World War. He then began a meteoric political career that took him to the House of Representatives in 1946, the Senate in 1950, and the vice presidency in 1952.

Nixon seemed to thrive on confronting personal challenges. He entitled an early memoir of his political life *Six Crises*. After his narrow loss to Kennedy in 1960 and his failure, in 1962, to win the California governorship, Nixon denounced the media and announced his retirement from politics. Johnson's problems resurrected Nixon's political fortunes. He emerged from the 1968 elections more confident than ever, it seemed, of his leadership abilities.

THE ECONOMY

Nixon's presidency coincided with economic problems that had been unthinkable only a decade earlier. No single cause can account for them, but most analyses begin with the war in Vietnam. This expensive military commitment, along with increased domestic spending and a volatile international economy, began to curtail economic growth.

Lyndon Johnson, determined to stave off defeat in Indochina without cutting Great Society programs or raising taxes, had concealed the true costs of the war. Nixon inherited a deteriorating (although still favorable) balance of trade and rising rate of inflation. Between 1960 and 1965, consumer prices grew only about 1 percent per year; by 1968, this figure exceeded 4 percent.

By 1971, the unemployment rate topped 6 percent. According to conventional wisdom, expressed in a technical economic concept called "the Phillips curve," when unemployment increases, prices should remain constant or even decline. Yet *both* unemployment and inflation remained on the rise. Economists coined the term **stagflation** to describe this puzzling convergence of economic stagnation and price inflation. Along with stagflation, U.S. exports were becoming less competitive in international markets, and in 1971, for the first time in the 20th century, the United States ran a trade deficit, importing more products than it exported.

Long identified as an opponent of governmental regulation of the economy but now fearful of the political consequences of stagflation and trade imbalances, Nixon needed a quick cure for the nation's economic ills. Suddenly he proclaimed his belief in governmental remedies and announced, in August 1971, a "new economic policy" that included a 90-day freeze on any increases in both wages and prices, to be followed by government monitoring to detect "excessive" increases in either.

To try to reverse the trade deficit, Nixon revised the United States' relationship to the world monetary structure. Dating from the 1944 Bretton Woods agreement (see Chapter 26), the value of the U.S. dollar had been tied to the value of gold at $35 for every ounce. This meant that the United States would exchange its dollars for gold at that rate if any other nation's central bank requested it to do so. Other countries had fixed their own exchange rates against the dollar. But U.S. trade deficits undermined the value of the dollar, enabling foreign banks to exchange U.S. dollars for gold at highly favorable rates. In response, the Nixon administration abandoned the fixed gold-to-dollar ratio in August 1971. Henceforth, the U.S. dollar would "float" in value against the prevailing market price in gold and against all other currencies. Nixon could then devalue the dollar in hopes of making American goods more competitive in global markets. The strategy fundamentally altered the international economic order. In 1973, oil-producing nations in the Middle East, citing a cheaper dollar and U.S. military aid to Israel as justification, further changed the world economy by temporarily embargoing certain countries, lowering petroleum exports, and raising prices. For the United States, the days of "cheap oil" came to an end.

stagflation *Condition of simultaneous economic stagnation and price inflation.*

SOCIAL POLICY

At the urging of Daniel Patrick Moynihan, a special presidential adviser on domestic issues, Nixon also proposed an equally dramatic overhaul of welfare policy. His proposed Family Assistance Plan (FAP) would replace most existing welfare measures, including the controversial Aid to Families with Dependent Children (AFDC). AFDC provided government payments to cover basic costs of care for low-income children who had lost the support of a bread-winning parent. Under FAP, every family would be guaranteed an annual income of $1,600. Moynihan touted FAP as advancing equality since it replaced existing arrangements, which assisted *only* those with special circumstances (such as low-income mothers with small children), with a system that aided *all* low-income families.

FAP debuted to tepid reviews. Conservatives claimed that income supplements for families with regularly employed, albeit low-paid, wage earners would be too costly. Proponents of more generous governmental assistance programs argued that FAP's income guarantee was too miserly. The House of Representatives approved a modified version of FAP in 1970, but a curious alliance of senators who opposed Nixon's proposal for very different reasons blocked its passage. Nixon abandoned FAP, and the nation's welfare system would not be overhauled until the 1990s.

Some changes in domestic policy were enacted, however. In an important move, Congress passed the president's revenue-sharing plan, part of his "new federalism," which returned a portion of federal tax dollars to state and local governments in the form of **block grants.** Instead of Washington specifying how these funds could be used, the block grant concept allowed state and local officials, within general guidelines, to spend the funds as they saw fit.

A Democratic-controlled Congress and a Republican White House also cooperated to increase funding for many Great Society initiatives: Medicare, Medicaid, rent subsidies for low-income people, and Supplementary Security Insurance (SSI) payments to those who were elderly, blind, or disabled. In 1972, Social Security benefits were "indexed," which meant they would increase along with the inflation rate.

Indeed, the reach of federal social welfare programs actually expanded during Nixon's presidency, and the percentage of people living below the "poverty line" dropped during Nixon's first term.

ENVIRONMENTALISM

A new environmental movement became a significant force during Nixon's presidency. Landmark legislation of the 1960s—such as the Wilderness Act of 1964, the National Wild and Scenic Rivers Act of 1968, and the National Trails Act of 1968—had already protected large areas of the country from commercial development. In the 1970s, a broader environmental movement focused on people's health and on ecological balances. Accounts such as **Rachel Carson**'s *Silent Spring* (1962) had raised concerns that the pesticides used in agriculture, especially DDT, threatened bird populations. Air pollution in cities such as Los Angeles had become so toxic that simply breathing became equivalent to smoking several packs of cigarettes per day. Industrial processes, atomic weapons testing, and nuclear power plants prompted fear of cancer-causing materials. The Environmental Defense Fund, a private organization formed in 1967, went to court to try to limit DDT and other dangerous toxins. Earth Day, a festival first held in 1970, aimed to raise awareness about the hazards of environmental degradation.

block grants *Part of Nixon's new economic plan in which a percentage of federal tax dollars would be returned to state and local governments to spend as they deemed fit.*

Rachel Carson *American environmentalist best known for* Silent Spring *(1962), a widely read book that questioned the use of chemical pesticides and helped stimulate the modern environmental movement.*

The Nixon administration, although not a sponsor of Earth Day, did take environmental issues seriously. Nixon supported creation of the **Environmental Protection Agency (EPA)** and signed major pieces of congressional legislation: the Resources Recovery Act of 1970 (dealing with waste management), the Clean Air Act of 1970, the Water Pollution Control Act of 1972, the Pesticides Control Act of 1972, and the Endangered Species Act of 1973. National parks and wilderness areas were expanded, and a new law required that "environmental impact statements" be prepared in advance of any major government project.

The new environmental standards brought both unanticipated problems and significant improvements. The Clean Air Act's requirement for taller factory smokestacks, for example, moved pollutants higher into the atmosphere, where they produced a dangerous byproduct, "acid rain." Still, the act's restrictions on auto and smokestack emissions cleared smog out of city skies and helped people with respiratory ailments. It reduced six major airborne pollutants by one third in a single decade. Lead emissions into the atmosphere declined by 95 percent.

CONTROVERSIES OVER RIGHTS

New legislation on social and environmental concerns accompanied debates over the federal government's responsibility to protect citizens' rights. The struggle to define these rights embroiled the U.S. Supreme Court in controversy.

A majority of justices, supporters of the Great Society's political vision, sought to bring an expanding list of rights under constitutional protection. As this group charted the Court's path during the 1960s, two Eisenhower appointees, Chief Justice Earl Warren and Associate Justice William Brennan, often led the way. Although nearly all of the Warren Court's decisions involving rights issues drew critical fire, perhaps the most emotional cases involved handling criminal suspects. *Miranda* v. *Arizona* (1966) held that the Constitution required police officers to advise persons suspected of having committed a felony offense of their constitutional right to remain silent and to consult an attorney, including one provided to indigents by the government. Defenders of this decision, which established the famous "Miranda warning," saw it as the logical extension of settled precedents; the Court's critics, in contrast, accused its majority of "inventing" liberties not found in the Constitution. Amid rising public concern over crime, political conservatives made *Miranda* a symbol of the judicial "coddling" of criminals and the Warren Court's supposed disregard for constitutional law.

Richard Nixon had campaigned for president as an opponent of the Warren Court and promised to appoint federal judges who would "apply" rather than "make" the law. Before the 1968 election, Chief Justice Warren announced his retirement, but Lyndon Johnson's plan to anoint his close confidante, Associate Justice Abe Fortas, stalled. Consequently, the victorious Nixon could appoint a Republican loyalist, Warren Burger, as chief justice. Subsequent vacancies allowed Nixon to appoint three other Republicans to the High Court.

This new Burger Court faced controversial rights-related cases of its own. Lawyers sympathetic to the Great Society vision advanced the argument that access to adequate economic assistance from the federal government was a constitutionally protected right. The Supreme Court, however, rejected this claim when deciding *Dandridge* v. *Williams* (1970). It held that states could limit the amount they paid to welfare recipients. Payment schedules that varied from state to state did not violate the constitutional requirement of equal protection of the law.

Environmental Protection Agency (EPA) *Organization established in 1970 that brought under a single institutional umbrella the enforcement of laws intended to protect environmental quality.*

Rights-related claims involving health-and-safety legislation generally fared better. A vigorous consumer movement, drawing inspiration from Ralph Nader's exposé about auto safety (*Unsafe at Any Speed,* 1965), joined with environmentalists to bolster rights to workplace safety, consumer protection, and nontoxic environments. Their efforts, overcoming opposition from many business groups, found expression in such legislation as the Occupational Safety Act of 1973 and stronger consumer and environmental protection laws. The Burger Court invariably supported the constitutionality of these measures.

At the same time, a newly energized women's rights movement pressed another set of issues. The **Equal Rights Amendment (ERA)**, initially proposed during the 1920s, promised to explicitly guarantee women the same legal rights as men. Easily passed by Congress in 1972 and quickly ratified by more than half the states, the ERA suddenly stalled. Conservative women's groups, such as Phyllis Schlafly's "Stop ERA," charged that this constitutional change would undermine traditional "family values" and expose women to new dangers, such as military service. The ERA failed to attain approval from the three quarters of states needed for ratification. Ultimately, women's groups abandoned the ERA effort in favor of using the courts to adjudicate equal rights claims on a case-by-case, issue-by-issue basis.

Equal Rights Amendment (ERA) *Proposed amendment to the Constitution providing that equal rights could not be abridged on account of sex. It won congressional approval in 1972 but failed to gain ratification by the states.*

AP Photo/Eddie Acams

WOMEN'S RIGHTS DEMONSTRATORS, AUGUST 16, 1970. *Activists gathered in Washington, D.C., to demonstrate on behalf of women's rights take time to rest. Symbolically, they effectively "occupy" a statue erected in honor of a 19th-century military hero, Admiral David G. Farragut.*

Roe v. Wade *Supreme Court decision in 1973 that ruled that blanket state prohibitions against abortion violated a woman's right to privacy. The decision prompted decades of political controversy.*

One of these issues, whether a woman possessed a constitutional right to terminate a pregnancy, became far more controversial than the ERA. In **Roe v. Wade** (1973), the Burger Supreme Court narrowly ruled that a state law making abortion a criminal offense violated a woman's "right to privacy." The *Roe* decision outraged antiabortion groups, who rallied under the "Right-to-Life" banner on behalf of the unborn fetus, providing new support for the already expanding conservative wing of the Republican Party. On the other side, feminist groups made the issue of individual choice in reproductive decisions a central rallying point.

Meanwhile, with little controversy, the president signed an extension of the Voting Rights Act of 1965. Another measure, popularly known as Title IX, banned sexual discrimination in higher education. In time, it became the legal basis for pressing colleges to adopt "gender equity" in all areas, including athletics. The Nixon administration also refined the "affirmative action" concept, which had surfaced during Lyndon Johnson's presidency, and required that all hiring and contracting that depended on federal funding take "affirmative" steps to enroll greater numbers of African Americans as union apprentices.

FOREIGN POLICY UNDER NIXON AND KISSINGER

Even as it wrestled with divisive domestic concerns, the Nixon White House was far more interested in international affairs. Henry Kissinger, Nixon's national security adviser and then secretary of state, laid out a grand strategy: **détente** with the Soviet Union, normalization of relations with China, and disengagement from direct military involvement in South Vietnam.

DÉTENTE

Although Nixon had built his career on hard-line anticommunism, he and Kissinger worked to ease tensions with the two major communist nations: the Soviet Union and China. The Nixon–Kissinger team expected that improved relations might lead these nations to reduce their support for North Vietnam, increasing chances for a successful U.S. pullback from the war.

Arms control talks took top priority in U.S.–Soviet relations. In 1969, the two superpowers opened the Strategic Arms Limitation Talks (SALT); after several years of high-level diplomacy, they signed an agreement (SALT I) that limited further development of both antiballistic missiles (ABMs) and offensive intercontinental ballistic missiles (ICBMs). SALT I's impact on the arms race was limited because it said nothing about the number of nuclear warheads that a single missile might carry. Still, the ability to conclude any arms-control pact signaled improving relations.

Nixon's overtures toward the People's Republic of China brought an even more dramatic break with the Cold War past. Secret negotiations, often conducted personally by Kissinger, led to a slight easing of U.S. trade restrictions and, then, to an invitation from China for Americans to compete in a table-tennis match. This much-celebrated "ping-pong diplomacy" presaged more significant exchanges. Most spectacularly, in 1972, Nixon visited China, posing for photos with Mao Zedong

détente *An easing of tensions, particularly between the United States and the Soviet Union.*

and strolling along the Great Wall. A few months later, the UN admitted the People's Republic as the sole representative of China, and in 1973 the United States and China exchanged informal diplomatic missions.

VIETNAMIZATION

In Vietnam, the Nixon administration decided to speed withdrawal of U.S. ground forces, a policy called **Vietnamization.** In July 1969, the "Nixon Doctrine" pledged that the United States would extend military assistance to anticommunist governments in Asia but would require them to supply their own combat forces. From the outset, Vietnamization imagined the removal of U.S. ground troops without accepting compromise or defeat. While officially adhering to Johnson's 1968 bombing halt over the North, Nixon and Kissinger accelerated both the ground and air wars by launching new offensives and by approving a military invasion of Cambodia, an ostensibly neutral country.

The 1970 Cambodian invasion set off a new wave of domestic protest. Campuses exploded in angry demonstrations, and bomb threats prompted some institutions to begin the summer vacation early. White police officers fatally shot two students at the all-black **Jackson State** College in Mississippi, and National Guard troops at **Kent State** University in Ohio fired on unarmed protestors, killing four students. As antiwar demonstrators descended on Washington, Nixon seemed personally unnerved by the furor.

The continuing controversy over the "My Lai" incident further polarized sentiment over the war. Shortly after the 1968 Tet episode, troops had entered the small South Vietnamese hamlet of My Lai and murdered more than 200 civilians, most of them women and children. This massacre became public in 1969 and refocused debate over U.S policy. Military courts convicted only one officer, Lieutenant William Calley, of any offense. Many charged that the military was using Calley as a scapegoat for a failed strategy that emphasized body counts and lax rules of engagement. Injecting the White House into this controversy, Nixon ordered that the young lieutenant be confined to his officer's quarters pending the results of his appeal. Ultimately, Calley was ordered released based on procedural irregularities.

Meanwhile, the Nixon administration widened military operations to include Laos as well as Cambodia. Although it denied waging any such campaign, large areas of those agricultural countries were ravaged. As the number of Cambodian refugees swelled and food supplies dwindled, the communist guerrilla force there—the Khmer Rouge—became a well-disciplined army. The Khmer Rouge

Vietnamization *Policy whereby the South Vietnamese were to assume more of the military burdens of the war and allow the United States to withdraw combat troops.*

Jackson State (incident) *Killing of two students on May 13, 1970, after an escalation in tensions between students at Jackson State University, a historically black institution, and National Guard troops in Mississippi.*

Kent State (incident) *Killing of four students on May 4, 1970, by the National Guard at a Kent State University protest against the U.S. incursion into neutral Cambodia.*

AP Photos

John Filo/Premium Archive/Getty Images

IMAGES THAT SHOCKED. *The war in Indochina produced a spiral of violence that also found its way back to the United States. In the photo at left, a military officer in the South Vietnamese Army summarily executes a prisoner suspected of being a member of the Viet Cong. At right, an anguished young woman bends over the body of a college student killed by Ohio National Guard troops at Kent State University in 1970.*

eventually came to power and, in a murderous attempt to eliminate dissent, turned Cambodia into a "killing field." It slaughtered more than 1 million Cambodians. While Nixon continued to talk about U.S. troop withdrawals and peace negotiations with North Vietnam proceeded in Paris, the Vietnam War broadened into a conflict that destabilized all of Indochina.

Even greater violence was yet to come. In spring 1972, a North Vietnamese offensive approached within 30 miles of Saigon, and U.S. generals warned of imminent defeat. Nixon responded by resuming the bombing of North Vietnam and by mining its harbors. Just weeks before the November 1972 election, Kissinger again promised peace and announced a cease-fire. After Nixon's reelection, however, the United States unleashed even greater firepower. During the "Christmas bombing" of December 1972, the heaviest bombardment in history, B-52 planes pounded military and civilian targets in North Vietnam around the clock.

By this time, however, much of the media, Congress, and the public wanted an end to the bloodshed. Many were sickened by the violence in Asia and condemned the administration's effort to expand its power to stem dissent at home. Perhaps most importantly, sagging morale among troops in the field began to undermine the U.S. effort. Soldiers questioned the purpose of their sacrifices; some refused to engage the enemy; and a few openly defied their own superiors. At home, Vietnam Veterans Against the War (VVAW), a new organization, joined the antiwar coalition.

Running out of options, Nixon proceeded with full-scale Vietnamization. In January 1973, the United States signed peace accords in Paris that provided for the withdrawal of U.S. troops. As ground forces departed, the South Vietnamese government, headed by Nguyen Van Thieu, continued to fight, increasingly demoralized and ineffectual. In spring 1975, nearly two years after the Paris accords, South Vietnam's army and Thieu's government collapsed as North Vietnamese armies entered the capital of Saigon. America's longest war ended in defeat.

© Paul Conklin/PhotoEdit

THE AFTERMATH OF WAR

Between 1960 and 1973, approximately 3.5 million American men and women served in Vietnam: 58,000 died, 150,000 were wounded, and 2,000 were classified as missing. In the aftermath of this costly, divisive war, Americans struggled to understand why their country failed to prevail over a small, barely industrialized nation. Those still supporting the war argued that it had been lost on the home front. They blamed an irresponsible media, a disloyal antiwar movement, and a Congress afflicted by a "failure of will." The war, they insisted, had been for a laudable cause. Politicians, setting unrealistic limits on the Pentagon, had prevented strategists from attaining victory. By contrast, those who had opposed the war stressed the overextension of U.S. power, the misguided belief in national omnipotence, and the miscalculations of decision makers. For them, the United States had waged a war in the wrong place for the wrong reasons. The human costs in both the United States and Indochina outweighed any possible gain.

THE VIETNAM WAR MEMORIAL. *This memorial, a kind of wailing wall that bears the names of all Americans who were killed in action in Vietnam, was dedicated on the Mall in Washington, D.C., in 1982.*

Regardless of their positions on the war, most Americans seemed to agree on a single proposition: There should be "no more Vietnams." The United States should not undertake another military operation that lacked clear and compelling political objectives, sustained public support, and realistic means to accomplish the goal. Eventually, the people who wanted to aggressively reassert U.S. power in the world dismissed this widely held position as "the Vietnam syndrome."

EXPANDING THE NIXON DOCTRINE

Although the Nixon Doctrine initially applied to the Vietnamization of the war in Indochina, Nixon and Kissinger extended its premise to the entire world. The White House made clear that the United States would not dispatch its troops to quash insurgencies but would generously aid anticommunist regimes or factions willing to fight their own battles.

During the early 1970s, U.S. Cold War strategy came to rely on supporting staunchly anticommunist regional powers. These included nations such as Iran under Shah Reza Pahlavi, South Africa with its apartheid regime, and Brazil with its repressive military dictatorship. All of these countries built large, U.S.-trained military establishments. U.S. military assistance, together with covert CIA operations, also incubated and protected anticommunist dictatorships in South Korea, the Philippines, and much of Latin America. U.S. arms sales to the rest of the world skyrocketed. In one of its most controversial foreign policies, the Nixon administration employed covert action against the elected socialist government of Salvador Allende Gossens in Chile in 1970. After Allende took office, Kissinger pressed for the destabilization of his government. In 1973 the Chilean military overthrew Allende, immediately suspended democratic rule, and announced that Allende had committed suicide.

Critics charged that the United States, in the name of anticommunism, too often wedded its diplomatic fortunes to questionable covert actions and unpopular military governments. Later, Democratic Senator Frank Church conducted Senate hearings into abuses of power by the executive branch, especially the CIA's actions in Chile. Supporters of Nixon and Kissinger, however, gave them high marks for a pragmatic foreign policy that combined détente toward the communist giants with containment directed toward the spread of revolutionary regimes.

THE WARS OF WATERGATE

Nixon's presidency ultimately collapsed as a result of fateful decisions made in the Oval Office. Long known as a political loner who ruminated about taking revenge against his enemies, Nixon often seemed his own greatest foe. He ordered the Internal Revenue Service (IRS) to harass prominent Democrats with expensive audits; placed antiwar and Black Power activists under surveillance; and conducted risky covert activities on the domestic front that even rattled the constitutional sensibilities of an old ally, J. Edgar Hoover. Isolated with a close-knit group of advisers, Nixon eventually created his own secret intelligence unit, which set up shop in the White House. This group quickly acted on the president's behalf.

During the summer of 1971, Daniel Ellsberg, an antiwar activist who had once worked in the national security bureaucracy, leaked to the press a top-secret history of U.S. involvement in the Vietnam War, subsequently known as the "Pentagon

FOCUS QUESTION
What political and legal controversies entrapped the Nixon administration, and how did Watergate-related events ultimately force Nixon's resignation?

Papers." Nixon responded by seeking, unsuccessfully, a court injunction to stop publication and, more ominously, by unleashing his secret intelligence unit, dubbed the **Plumbers,** to stop leaks to the media. Seeking something that might discredit Ellsberg, the Plumbers burglarized his psychiatrist's office. Thus began a series of **dirty tricks** and outright crimes, sometimes financed by funds solicited for Nixon's 1972 reelection campaign, which would culminate in the constitutional crisis known as **Watergate.**

THE ELECTION OF 1972

Nixon's political strategists worried that domestic troubles and the war in Vietnam might deny the president another term. Creating a campaign organization separate from that of the Republican Party, with the ironic acronym of CREEP (Committee to Re-elect the President), they secretly raised millions of dollars, much of it from illegal contributions.

As the 1972 campaign took shape, Nixon's chances for reelection dramatically improved. An assassin's bullet crippled George Wallace. Senator Edmund Muskie of Maine, initially Nixon's leading Democratic challenger, made a series of blunders (some of them, perhaps, precipitated by Republican "dirty tricksters") that derailed his campaign. Eventually, Senator George McGovern of South Dakota, an outspoken opponent of the Vietnam War but a lackluster campaigner, won the Democratic nomination.

McGovern never seriously challenged Nixon. He called for higher taxes on the wealthy, a guaranteed minimum income for all Americans, amnesty for Vietnam War draft resisters, and the decriminalization of marijuana. In foreign policy, McGovern urged deep cuts in defense spending and peace in Vietnam—proposals that Nixon successfully portrayed as signs of weakness. Nixon won an easy victory in November, receiving the electoral college votes of all but one state and the District of Columbia. Although the 26th Amendment, ratified one year before the election, had lowered the voting age to 18, relatively few of the newly enfranchised voters cast ballots.

NIXON PURSUED

In achieving victory, however, the president's supporters left a trail of crime and corruption. In June 1972, a surveillance team with links to both CREEP and the White House had been arrested while fine-tuning eavesdropping equipment in the Democratic Party's headquarters in Washington's Watergate office complex. In public, Nixon's spokespeople dismissed the Watergate break-in as a "third-rate burglary;" privately, the president and his inner circle launched a cover-up. They paid hush money to the Watergate burglars and ordered CIA officials to misinform the FBI that any investigation into the burglary would jeopardize national security. Nixon succeeded in containing the political damage through the 1972 election, but events soon overtook him.

While reporters from the *Washington Post* pursued the taint of scandal around the White House, Congress and federal prosecutors sought evidence of illegal activities during the 1972 campaign. In 1973, Judge John Sirica, a Republican appointee presiding over the trial of the Watergate burglars, pushed for additional information, and Senate leaders convened a special, bipartisan Watergate Committee, headed by North Carolina's conservative Democratic senator Sam Ervin, to investigate. Federal prosecutors uncovered

Plumbers *Nixon's secret intelligence unit designed to stop information leaks to the media.*

dirty tricks *Actions designed to destroy the reputation and effectiveness of political opponents of the Nixon administration, especially during 1972 election.*

Watergate *Business and residential complex in Washington, D.C., that came to stand for the political espionage and cover-ups directed by the Nixon administration. The complicated web of Watergate scandals brought about Nixon's resignation in 1974.*

evidence that seemed to link key administration figures, including John Mitchell, Nixon's former attorney general and later the head of CREEP, to illegal activities.

In May 1973, one of the Watergate burglars and other witnesses testified before the Senate's Watergate Committee about illegal activities committed by CREEP and the White House. Senator Ervin called Nixon's closest aides before the committee, and the televised hearings became a daily political drama that much of the country watched. Testimony from John Dean, who had been the president's chief legal counsel, linked Nixon himself to attempts to cover up Watergate and to other illegal activities. The president steadfastly denied Dean's charges.

Along the way, though, Senate investigators discovered that a voice-activated taping machine had recorded every conversation in Nixon's Oval Office. These tapes made it possible to determine whether the president or Dean, Nixon's primary accuser, was lying. While claiming he was not "a crook," Nixon also claimed an "executive privilege" to keep the tapes from being released to either Congress or federal prosecutors, but Judge Sirica, Archibald Cox (a special, independent prosecutor in the Watergate case), and Congress all demanded access to them.

If Nixon's own problems were not enough, his vice president Spiro Agnew resigned in October 1973 after pleading no contest to income-tax evasion. He agreed to a plea-bargain arrangement to avoid prosecution for having accepted illegal kickbacks while in Maryland politics. Acting under the 25th Amendment (ratified in 1967), Nixon appointed—and both houses of Congress confirmed—Representative **Gerald Ford** of Michigan, a Republican Party stalwart, as the new vice president.

NIXON'S FINAL DAYS

Nixon's clumsy efforts to protect himself backfired. During the fall of 1973, Nixon fired Archibald Cox, hoping to prevent him from gaining access to the tapes. When this firing prompted an outcry, the president appointed an equally tenacious independent replacement, Leon Jaworski. Nixon's own release of edited transcripts of some Watergate-related conversations merely strengthened demand for the original recordings. Finally, by proclaiming that he would obey only a "definitive" Supreme Court decision, Nixon all but invited the justices to deliver a unanimous ruling on the question of the tapes. On July 24, 1974, the Court did just that in the case of *U.S. v. Nixon*. No claim of executive privilege could justify the refusal to release evidence in a criminal investigation.

After televised deliberations, a bipartisan majority of the House Judiciary Committee voted three formal articles of impeachment against the president for obstruction of justice, violation of constitutional liberties, and refusal to produce evidence. Nixon promised to rebut these accusations before the Senate, the body authorized by the Constitution (Article I, Section 3) to render a verdict of guilty or not guilty after impeachment by the House.

Nixon's aides, however, were already orchestrating his departure. One of his own attorneys had discovered that a tape Nixon had been withholding contained the long-sought "smoking gun," clear evidence of a criminal offense. It confirmed that during a 1972 conversation, Nixon had helped hatch the plan by which the CIA would advance a fraudulent claim of national security in order to stop the FBI from investigating the Watergate break-in. At this point, Nixon's own secretary of defense ordered military commanders to ignore any order from the president, the

Gerald Ford *A GOP member of the House of Representatives, Gerald Ford became the first person to be appointed vice president of the United States. When Richard Nixon resigned in 1974, Ford became president.*

constitutional commander-in-chief, unless the secretary had countersigned it. Abandoned by almost every prominent Republican and confronted by a Senate prepared to vote him guilty on the impeachment charges, Nixon went on television on August 8, 1974, to announce his resignation. On August 9, Gerald Ford became the nation's 38th president.

In 1974, most people told pollsters that Watergate was one of the gravest crises in the history of the republic and that the Nixon administration had posed a serious threat to constitutional government. As time passed, though, the details of Watergate faded away. Opinion polls conducted on the 20th anniversary of Nixon's resignation suggested that most Americans only dimly recalled the Watergate episode.

What specific forces might account for this change? One may be that although nearly a dozen members of his administration—including its chief law enforcement officer, John Mitchell—were convicted of criminal activities, Nixon avoided prosecution. Gerald Ford granted him an unconditional pardon. The nation was spared the spectacle of a former president undergoing trial, but it was also denied an authoritative accounting, in a court of law, of Nixon's misdeeds.

Another reason for fading memories may be the media's habit of attaching the Watergate label to nearly every political scandal of the post-Nixon era. The suffix -*gate* became attached to grave constitutional episodes and to obviously trivial political events. Many people came to consider "Watergate" a synonym for "politics as usual." Finally, images of what historian Stanley Kutler calls the "wars of Watergate" have tended to blend into broader pictures of the political, social, economic, and cultural turmoil that accompanied U.S. involvement in the nation's longest war.

C O N C L U S I O N

The power of the national government grew steadily in the years between 1963 and 1974. Lyndon Johnson's Great Society provided a blueprint for waging a War on Poverty, and his administration dramatically escalated the war in Vietnam.

This growth of government power prompted divisive debates that polarized the country. During Johnson's administration, both his war strategy and his Great Society faltered, top leaders became discredited, and his presidency collapsed. Johnson's Republican successor, Richard Nixon, let loose an abuse of power that ultimately drove him from office in disgrace. The hopes of the early 1960s—that the U.S. government could promote liberty and equality both at home and throughout the rest of the world—ended in frustration.

The era of America's longest war was a time of high political passion, of cultural and racial conflict, of differing definitions of patriotism. It saw the slow convergence of an antiwar movement, along with the emergence of youthful dissent, Black Power, women's activism, and contests over what constituted Americans' basic rights. Different groups invoked different explanations for the fates of both the Great Society and the war effort, and divisions from this era shaped politics and culture for years to come. Many Americans became skeptical, many even cynical, about expanding the power of the federal government in the name of expanding liberty and equality.

QUESTIONS FOR REVIEW AND CRITICAL THINKING

Review

1. How did the Johnson administration define Great Society goals, and how did it approach problem-solving? Why did the Great Society produce so much controversy?

2. Through what incremental steps did the Johnson administration involve the United States ever more deeply in the war in Vietnam? What seemed to be the goal of its policies?

3. What domestic social movements emerged during America's longest war? How did they seek to change U.S. political culture and the direction of public policy? What role did commercial media play in the "movement of movements"?

4. What new domestic and foreign policies did the Nixon administration initiate?

5. What political and legal controversies entrapped the Nixon administration, and how did Watergate-related events ultimately force Nixon's resignation?

Critical Thinking

1. What long-term repercussions did America's longest war exact on the U.S. economy, social fabric, political culture, and foreign policy?

2. Great Society proposals prompted growing debates over the extension of government power and over definitions of civil and personal liberties. How did issues of race, gender, and the distribution of wealth and income figure in these debates?

3. Why were the Sixties marked by so much protest and unrest? How would the polarization of views during that era continue to affect how people saw the history and future of the United States?

ONLINE RESOURCES

 Visit the companion website to access flashcards, crossword puzzles, exercises, and quizzes related to this chapter: www.cengage.com/history/murrin/libertyequalconc5e.

 See our interactive ebook for map and primary source activities.

ISCOVERY   *How did American involvement in the Vietnam War affect American government and society?*

CULTURE AND SOCIETY Think about the reading in this chapter and examine the graph on American attitudes toward the Vietnam War. What happened between March of 1966 and January of 1971 to change people's feelings so dramatically?

Look at the "Images that Shocked" on page 813. How are these pictures similar? What feelings do they convey? Was the increase in violence in American society in the late 1960s and early 1970s connected to the violence that Americans were seeing unfold in Vietnam? Did the war influence the civil rights movement and the student movement? If so, how? More broadly, how do you think the visual media—most notably television and photographs—influenced American politics during the 1960s?

In thinking about this question, begin by breaking it down into the components shown below. A discussion of the significance of each component should appear in your answer.

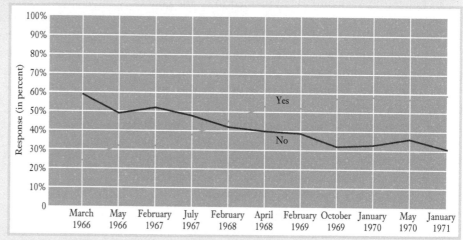

AMERICAN ATTITUDES TOWARD THE VIETNAM WAR

30

POWER AND POLITICS, 1974–1992

The national government continually expanded its power following the onset of the Second World War. Most Americans supported increasing military and intelligence capabilities and using domestic programs to cushion against economic downturns and assist needy families.

Events of the 1960s and early 1970s, particularly Vietnam and Watergate, shook faith in government. Secrecy, corruption, and economic problems bred further disillusionment. During the 1970s and 1980s Americans debated how to respond to an aging industrial economy, a ballooning federal deficit, and a beleaguered social welfare system. Did the country need new governmental programs, or might conditions improve if Washington reduced its role? Emotional issues such as abortion, environmental regulation, and taxation policy also created controversy over the use of governmental power.

Disagreement extended to foreign policy. Should the United States set aside anticommunism to pursue other goals, as Democratic president Jimmy Carter (1977–1981) initially urged, or should it wage the Cold War even more

TIMELINE

1968	1972	1976	1980	1984	1988	1992

■ **1968**
Indian Bill of Rights enacted by Congress

■ **1969**
The Stonewall Inn raid inaugurates new phase in gay and lesbian activism

■ **1970**
Congressional Black Caucus organized

■ **1973**
Roe v. *Wade* decision upholds women's right to abortion

■ **1974**
Nixon resigns and Ford becomes president; Ford soon pardons Nixon

■ **1975**
South Vietnam falls to North Vietnam • Ford asserts U.S. power in *Mayaguez* incident
• National Conservative Action Political Committee formed

■ **1976**
Jimmy Carter elected president

■ **1978**
Carter helps negotiate Camp David peace accords on Middle East

■ **1979**
Soviet Union invades Afghanistan • *Sandinistas* come to power in Nicaragua
• U.S. hostages seized in Iran

■ **1980**
Reagan elected president • U.S. hostages in Iran released

■ **1981**
Reagan tax cut passed

■ **1983**
U.S. troops removed from Lebanon • U.S. troops invade Grenada
• Reagan announces SDI ("Star Wars") program

■ **1984**
Reagan defeats Walter Mondale

■ **1986**
Tax Reform Act passed • Reagan administration
rocked by revelation of Iran-*Contra* affair

1988 ■
George H. W. Bush defeats Michael Dukakis in presidential election
• Congress enacts Indian Gaming Regulation Act

1989 ■
Communist regimes in Eastern Europe collapse;
Berlin Wall falls • Cold War, in effect, ends

1990 ■
Bush angers conservative Republicans by agreeing to a tax increase

1991 ■
Bush orchestrates Persian Gulf War against Iraq • Clarence Thomas
confirmation hearings highlight issue of sexual harassment

1992 ■
Bill Clinton defeats Bush and third-party candidate Ross Perot in presidential race

vigorously, as his successor, Republican Ronald Reagan (1981–1989), advocated? After 1989, when the Cold War ended unexpectedly, the United States needed to find a foreign policy for a post-Cold War world, a task that fell to the post-Reagan generation of national leaders.

Meanwhile, the "movement of movements," a legacy of the 1960s, refused to fade away. Along with a "New Right" movement, social movements associated with women's rights, gay rights, and racial and ethnic identities affected how Americans saw themselves and their nation's future.

THE CARETAKER PRESIDENCY OF GERALD FORD (1974–1977)

When Richard Nixon resigned in August 1974, Gerald R. Ford, his vice president, moved from one office to which voters had never elected him to another, the presidency. Emphasizing his long career in the House of Representatives, Ford promised to "heal the land," but he achieved limited success. A genial, unpretentious former college football star who preferred that his public appearances be accompanied by the fight song of his alma mater, the University of Michigan, rather than "Hail to the Chief," Ford seemed a weak, indecisive leader.

FOCUS QUESTION
How did the legacies of the Vietnam War and Watergate help shape U.S. politics in the decade that followed?

TRYING TO WHIP INFLATION

Ford's plan to present his administration as an updated version of the modern Republicanism of the 1950s quickly foundered. His appointment of Nelson Rockefeller as vice president infuriated GOP conservatives, and his pardoning of former president Nixon, in September 1974, angered almost everyone. Ford's approval rating skidded downward.

Economic problems dominated the domestic side of the 865-day Ford presidency. Ford touted a program called "Whip Inflation Now" (WIN), which included a one-year surcharge on income taxes and cuts in federal spending as solutions. After both unemployment and prices still crept higher, Ford conceded WIN to be a loser. During 1975 unemployment reached 8.5 percent, and the inflation rate topped 9 percent.

Meanwhile, Ford clashed with the Democratic-controlled Congress over how to deal with **stagflation**. Ford, who vetoed nearly 40 spending bills while in office, finally agreed to a congressional economic package that included a tax cut, an increase in unemployment benefits, an unbalanced federal budget, and limited controls on oil prices. Democrats charged that Ford could not implement coherent programs of his own. Many Republicans complained that he could not stand up to congressional Democrats.

FOREIGN POLICY

Upon assuming office, Ford pledged a renewal of U.S. military support to the government in South Vietnam, if North Vietnam ever directly threatened its survival. The antiwar mood in the United States and battlefield conditions in Vietnam, however, made fulfilling this commitment impossible. North Vietnam's armies stormed across the South in March 1975, and Congress, relieved that U.S. troops had finally been withdrawn after the 1973 Paris peace accords, refused any new American involvement.

Spring 1975 brought new communist victories. In early April, Khmer Rouge forces in Cambodia drove a U.S.-backed government from the capital of Phnom Penh, and on April 30, 1975, North Vietnamese troops overran the South Vietnamese capital of Saigon, renaming it Ho Chi Minh City. Debate over U.S. policy in Indochina became especially heated in the months that followed.

Within this charged atmosphere, Ford tried to demonstrate U.S military power. In May 1975 a contingent of Khmer Rouge boarded a U.S. ship, the *Mayaguez*, taking its crew hostage. Secretary of State Henry Kissinger declared that it was time to "look ferocious" and convinced Ford to order bombing strikes against Cambodia and a rescue

stagflation *Condition of simultaneous economic stagnation and price inflation.*

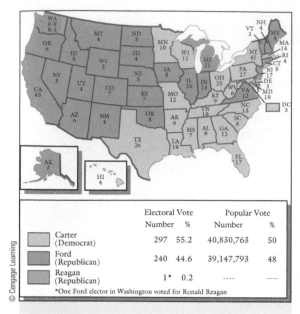

	Electoral Vote		Popular Vote	
	Number	%	Number	%
Carter (Democrat)	297	55.2	40,830,763	50
Ford (Republican)	240	44.6	39,147,793	48
Reagan (Republican)	1*	0.2	----	----

*One Ford elector in Washington voted for Ronald Reagan

Map 30.1 **PRESIDENTIAL ELECTION, 1976.**
This map shows the low voter turnout and the very close election that made Jimmy Carter president. Notice how Carter, from Georgia, drew votes from Southern states.

operation for the crew. This military response, coupled with Chinese pressure on the Khmer Rouge, secured the release of the *Mayaguez* and its crew. Although the *Mayaguez* rescue cost more lives than it saved, Ford's approval ratings briefly shot up. His other foreign policy initiatives, which included extending Nixon's policy of détente with the Soviet Union and pursuing peace negotiations in the Middle East, achieved little. Gerald Ford increasingly appeared a caretaker president.

THE ELECTION OF 1976

Ford nearly lost the GOP presidential nomination in 1976. Conservative Republicans rallied behind Ronald Reagan, who ignited his effort by campaigning as a "true conservative" who, unlike Ford, owed nothing to Washington insiders. Ford had already won just enough delegates in the early primaries, however, to eke out a narrow first-ballot victory at the Republican Party's national convention.

The Democrats did turn to an outsider, James Earl (Jimmy) Carter. A retired naval officer, engineer, peanut farmer, and former governor of Georgia, Carter campaigned by stressing personal character. He highlighted his small-town roots and his Southern Baptist faith. To balance the ticket, he picked Senator Walter Mondale of Minnesota as his running mate. In November Carter won a narrow victory over Ford.

Carter's election rested on a transitory coalition. He carried every southern state except Virginia, running well among both whites who belonged to fundamentalist and evangelical churches and African Americans. Carter also courted former antiwar activists by promising to pardon most Vietnam-era draft resisters. Walter Mondale's appeal helped capture the Democratic strongholds of New York, Pennsylvania, and Ohio. The election was close, however, and voter turnout hit its lowest mark (54 percent) since the end of the Second World War.

JIMMY CARTER'S ONE-TERM PRESIDENCY (1977–1981)

Jimmy Carter's lack of a popular mandate and his outsider status proved serious handicaps. After leaving government, Carter reflected on his difficulties: "I had a different way of governing. . . . I was a southerner, a born-again Christian, a Baptist, a newcomer." Moreover, Carter was caught between advisers who claimed that the national government exercised too much power and those who argued that Washington did too little to address domestic and foreign problems. His policies often seemed hesitant and inconsistent.

WELFARE AND ENERGY INITIATIVES

Carter puzzled over welfare policy. His staff differed over whether to increase monetary assistance to low-income families or to create several million public service jobs, underwritten by additional federal spending. Carter proposed a compromise that failed in Congress, and the impulse to overhaul the nation's social welfare system continued to flounder.

The president pushed harder on energy issues. The United States obtained 90 percent of its energy from fossil fuels, much of it from imported petroleum. In 1978, as in 1973, the Organization of Petroleum Exporting Countries (OPEC), a cartel dominated by oil-rich nations in the Middle East, dramatically raised the price of crude oil and precipitated acute worldwide shortages. As gasoline became expensive and scarce, drivers denounced high prices and long lines at the pumps. Carter promised to make the United States less dependent on imported fossil fuel.

The president had earlier charged James Schlesinger, head of a new Department of Energy, with developing a plan. Schlesinger outlined ambitious goals to decrease U.S. reliance on foreign sources: (1) expand domestic energy production through tax incentives and deregulation; (2) levy new taxes to discourage consumption; (3) foster conservation; and (4) promote nonpetroleum energy sources, especially coal and nuclear power. Neither Carter nor Schlesinger consulted Congress or even some members of the president's own administration. Instead, in April 1977, Carter announced that the energy crisis represented "the moral equivalent of war," and he advanced a plan that included more than 100 interrelated provisions.

Congress quickly rejected it. Gas and oil interests opposed higher taxes. Consumer activists blocked deregulation. Environmentalists charged that greater use of coal would increase air pollution. Carter continued to press for energy conservation; for development of renewable sources, such as solar and wind-generated energy; and for greater use of nuclear power.

The nuclear option generated sharp controversy. In theory, nuclear reactors could provide inexpensive, almost limitless amounts of energy. The cost of building and maintaining them, however, far exceeded original estimates and posed safety risks. In 1979 a serious reactor malfunction at Three Mile Island, Pennsylvania, produced fears of a nuclear-reactor meltdown. Responding to growing concerns, power companies canceled orders for new reactors, and the nuclear power industry's expansion halted. Meanwhile, OPEC oil prices continued to rise, from about $3.60 a barrel in 1971 to nearly $36 a decade later, at the end of Carter's presidency.

A FALTERING ECONOMY

Rising oil prices and a lingering case of stagflation, legacies of the Nixon and Ford years, heightened the nation's economic woes. Carter pledged to lower both unemployment and inflation, rekindle economic growth, and balance the federal budget (which showed a deficit of about $70 billion in 1976). He pushed for tax cuts, increased public-works spending, and pro-growth Federal Reserve Board policies. These measures, however, only further aggravated matters. By 1980 the economy had virtually stopped expanding; unemployment (after temporarily dipping) continued to rise; and inflation topped 13 percent. Voters told pollsters that their economic fortunes had deteriorated while Carter was in office.

Economic distress spread beyond individuals. New York City, beset by long-term economic problems and short-term fiscal mismanagement, faced bankruptcy. Private bankers and public officials had to secure congressional "bailout" legislation that granted special loan guarantees to America's largest city. Its troubles were hardly unique. According to one estimate, Chicago lost 200,000 manufacturing jobs during the 1970s. Bricks from demolished buildings in St. Louis became one of that city's leading products. Soaring unemployment, rising crime rates, deteriorating downtowns, and shrinking tax revenues afflicted most urban areas, even as inflation further eroded the buying power of city budgets.

Conservative economists and business interests charged that domestic programs favored by most congressional Democrats contributed to economic distress. Increasing the minimum wage and enforcing unnecessary safety and antipollution regulations, they argued, drove up the cost of doing business and forced companies to raise prices to consumers. During his last two years in office, Carter seemed to agree with some of this analysis. Defying many Democrats in Congress, he cut spending for social programs, sought to reduce capital-gains taxes to encourage investment, and inaugurated the process of "deregulating" various industries, beginning with the financial and transportation sectors.

Negotiating Disputes Overseas

In foreign as in domestic policy, Carter promised new directions. On his first day in office, he granted amnesty to most Vietnam-era draft resisters. He soon declared that he would not display an "inordinate fear of Communism" and would press human-rights issues. After four years, however, his foreign policy initiatives were also in disarray.

Carter had little background in foreign policy. Furthermore, his top aides—Cyrus Vance as secretary of state and Zbigniew Brzezinski as national security adviser—pursued contradictory agendas. Vance preferred quiet diplomacy and avoidance of confrontations, while Brzezinski favored a hard-line, anti-Soviet policy with an emphasis on military muscle. Pulled in divergent directions, Carter's foreign policy seemed to waffle. Carter himself favored settling disputes through negotiation, and he made human rights a priority.

Carter's faith in negotiation and in his own skills as a facilitator yielded some successes. On the issue of the Panama Canal, the object of diplomatic negotiations for 13 years, Carter secured treaties that granted Panama increasing authority over the waterway and full control in 2000. Carter convinced skeptical senators, whose votes he needed to ratify any treaty, that the canal was no longer an economic or strategic necessity.

Carter's personal touch also emerged during the Camp David Peace Talks of 1978. Relations between Egypt and Israel had been strained since the Yom Kippur War of 1973, when Israel repelled an Egyptian attack and seized the Sinai Peninsula and territory along the West Bank (of the Jordan River). Reviving earlier Republican efforts to broker a peace settlement, Carter brought Menachem Begin and Anwar Sadat, leaders of Israel and Egypt, respectively, to the presidential retreat at Camp David. After 13 days of difficult bargaining, the three leaders announced a framework for further negotiations and a peace treaty. Middle East tensions hardly vanished, but these Camp David Accords kept alive high-level discussions, lowered the level of acrimony between Egypt and Israel, and bound both nations to the United States through Carter's promises of economic aid.

In Asia, the Carter administration built on Nixon's initiative, expanding economic and cultural relations with China. The United States finally established formal diplomatic ties with the People's Republic on New Year's Day 1979.

Campaigning for Human Rights Abroad

Carter's foreign policy became best known for its emphasis on human rights. Carter argued that Cold War alliances with repressive dictatorships, even in the name of anticommunism, undermined U.S. influence in the world.

Carter's human rights policy, however, proved difficult to orchestrate. His administration continued to support some harsh dictators, such as Ferdinand Marcos in the Philippines. Moreover, rhetoric about human rights helped justify uprisings against longstanding dictator-allies in Nicaragua and Iran. Revolutions in these countries, fueled by resentment against the United States, brought anti-American regimes to power and presented Carter with difficult choices.

In Nicaragua, the *Sandinista* movement toppled the dictatorship of Anastasio Somoza, whom the United States had long supported. The *Sandinistas*, initially a coalition of moderate democrats and leftists, soon tilted toward a militant Marxism and began to expropriate private property. Republican critics charged that Carter's policies had given a green light to Communism throughout Central America, and some pledged to oust the *Sandinistas*.

CONFRONTING PROBLEMS IN IRAN AND AFGHANISTAN

If events in Nicaragua eroded Carter's standing, those in Iran and Afghanistan all but shattered it. The United States had steadfastly supported the dictatorial Shah Reza Pahlavi, who had reigned in oil-rich Iran since an American-supported coup in 1953. The shah's overthrow in January 1979, by a revolutionary movement dominated by Islamic fundamentalists, signaled a massive repudiation of U.S. influence. When the White House allowed the deposed shah to enter the United States for medical treatment in November 1979, Iranians seized the U.S. embassy in Tehran and 66 American hostages. Iran demanded the return of the shah in exchange for the hostages' release.

In response, Carter replaced human-rights rhetoric with tough talk, levied economic sanctions against Iran, and—over the objections of Cyrus Vance (who subsequently resigned)—sent a combat team to rescue the hostages. This military effort ended in an embarrassing failure. Carter's critics cited this "hostage crisis" as conclusive proof of his incompetence. After Carter's defeat in the 1980 presidential election, diplomatic efforts finally freed the hostages, but the United States and Iran remained at odds.

AMERICAN HOSTAGES IN IRAN. *The Iranian government presents American hostages to the press under a banner protesting Carter's decision to admit the shah into the United States to obtain medical treatment.*

© Bettman/CORBIS

Criticism of Carter also focused on the Soviet Union's 1979 invasion of Afghanistan, a move primarily sparked by Soviet fear of the growing influence of Islamic fundamentalists along its borders. Carter responded in a nonmilitary manner. He halted grain exports to the Soviet Union (angering his farm constituency), organized a boycott of the 1980 Summer Olympic Games in Moscow, withdrew a new Strategic Arms Limitation Treaty (SALT) from the Senate, and revived registration for the military draft. Still, Republicans (along with some Democrats) charged Carter with allowing U.S. power and prestige to decline.

For a time, after Senator Edward Kennedy of Massachusetts entered the 1980 presidential primaries, it seemed as if Carter's own Democratic Party might deny him a second term. Although Kennedy's challenge eventually fizzled, it popularized anti-Carter themes that Republicans would gleefully embrace. "It's time to say no more hostages, no more high interest rates, no more high inflation, and no more Jimmy Carter," was Kennedy's standard stump speech.

A NEW RIGHT

In the mid-1970s a diverse coalition of "New Right" activists began to mobilize. Their vision of conservatism attracted support from several different constituencies. Older activists, who had rallied around William F. Buckley's *National Review* during the 1950s and Barry Goldwater during the mid-1960s, provided continuity (see Chapter 28). Buckley's interview show, *Firing Line*, became one of public television's most successful programs during the 1970s and 1980s.

Established activists such as Buckley teamed up with a group of intellectuals called the **neoconservatives,** or neocons. Many neoconservatives had been anticommunist Democrats during the 1950s and early 1960s. Unsettled by the rebelliousness of the 1960s, they believed that the Democratic Party was abandoning an anticommunist foreign policy and catering to social activists who sought to enlarge government entitlement programs. Many embraced the Republican Party during the 1980s and offered intellectual sustenance to a new generation of conservative thinkers.

A new militancy among conservative business leaders also helped build the New Right. Some business spokespeople claimed that health and safety regulations and environmental legislation endangered "economic freedom." They urged rededication to the idea of limited government. Generous funding by corporations and philanthropic foundations helped staff conservative research institutions such as the American Enterprise Institute and The Heritage Foundation, and finance new lobbying organizations such as The Committee on the Present Danger. Conservatism also gained considerable ground on college campuses, which had been incubators of the New Left and the counterculture during the 1960s.

The New Right attracted additional grassroots support from Protestants in **fundamentalist** and **evangelical** churches. Since the 1920s, fundamentalists and evangelical Protestants had generally stayed clear of partisan politics, but the Supreme Court's abortion decision in *Roe* v. *Wade* (1973) mobilized their leaders. Arguing that religious values should actively shape political policymaking, leaders of a new **religious right** sought to join religious faith and political action. The insistence of a clear separation between church and state, a guiding constitutional principle during the era of Earl Warren's Supreme Court, struck the religious right as a violation of the right to the "free exercise of religion." Particularly in the South, conservatives embarked on a lengthy legal crusade to prevent the Internal Revenue Service from denying tax-exempt status to the private Christian colleges and academies that opposed racial integration. Challenging older constitutional precedents against state

neoconservatives *Group of intellectuals, many of whom had been anti-Communist Democrats during the 1950s and 1960s, who came to emphasize hard-line foreign policies and conservative social stances.*

fundamentalists *Religious groups that preach the necessity of fidelity to a strict moral code, individual commitment to Christ, and faith in the literal truth of the Bible.*

evangelicals *Religious groups that generally place an emphasis on conversion of non-Christians.*

religious right *Christians who wedded their religious beliefs to a conservative political agenda and gained growing influence in Republican party politics during the late 1970s.*

aid to religious institutions, they also urged that government should use tax monies to help fund church-centered education and "faith-based" social programming.

It soon became apparent that opposition to existing federal social programs and cultural appeals could energize millions of voters. In 1975 New Right activists formed the National Conservative Political Action Committee (NCPAC), the first of many similar organizations, including the Conservative Caucus and Jerry Falwell's Moral Majority. These organizations lobbied in Washington, backed conservative Republican candidates, and developed political positions on a wide range of "family values." They particularly opposed policies, such as legalized abortion, that feminists tended to favor, and they condemned gay and lesbian lifestyles. On the local level, the religious right tried to influence school boards, charging that liberal educators promoted dangerous, antibiblical ideas such as feminism, multiculturalism, and evolution. Many rallied behind the ideas of "vouchers" and charter schools, both methods by which financing could be withdrawn from the public schools and used to create educational alternatives. Conservative activists wanted tax dollars to directly support the religious and cultural values held by their churches and families.

The New Right also opposed changes associated with the 1960s in college curricula and cultural life. It saw colleges contributing to "the closing of the American mind" (the title of a bestselling 1987 book by Allan Bloom) by exposing students only to what was trendy and "politically correct" (or PC). Educational conservatives such as William Bennett and Lynn Cheney warned about identity politics and the alleged debasement of intellectual traditions. The government-funded National Endowment for the Humanities (NEH) and the National Endowment for the Arts (NEA) came under the New Right's fire when they backed nontraditional projects.

The New Right adeptly publicized its positions. Well-funded conservative organizations sponsored academic conferences, popular gatherings, and media programming. Pat Robertson, for example, built a multimedia empire, including his popular *700 Club*, a program that merged evangelical religion with New Right politics. Conservative broadcasters such as Rush Limbaugh drew huge audiences to the talk-radio genre. Other conservative activists eagerly embraced the Internet. By the end of the 20th century, the Fox News Channel (FNC) was cultivating conservative viewers by tilting its coverage toward New Right perspectives.

The New Right, much like other activist groups, hardly moved in lockstep. More traditional members of the New Right coalition denounced the free-trade policies and the global military strategy that other conservatives promoted. However, while remaining a coalition of disparate parts, the New Right became a powerful force. It successfully challenged the once-dominant political agenda of the Democratic Party, propelled the mainstream of the Republican Party decidedly rightward, established a strong foothold in public-policy and media discussions, and succeeded in remapping the nation's cultural and informational landscape.

Ronald Reagan

Ronald Reagan courted the New Right on both economic and social issues. A taxpayer revolt that had swept through California politics during the late 1970s provided a model for Reagan's attack on "tax-and-spend" policymaking at the federal level. (The situation was ironic, however, because California's tax revolt had emerged in response to tax increases adopted while Reagan was the state's governor.) Across the country, people increasingly responded to the tax-reduction message. In addition to urging large tax cuts, Regan also opposed abortion rights, advocated prayer in school, extolled conservative family values, and offered new

FOCUS QUESTION
To what extent did Ronald Reagan's administration represent a victory for the New Right agenda in both domestic and foreign policy?

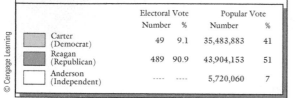

	Electoral Vote		Popular Vote	
	Number	%	Number	%
Carter (Democrat)	49	9.1	35,483,883	41
Reagan (Republican)	489	90.9	43,904,153	51
Anderson (Independent)	----	----	5,720,060	7

© Cengage Learning

***Map 30.2* PRESIDENTIAL ELECTION, 1980.**
Compare this map with the one showing the election of Jimmy Carter four years earlier. What factors might explain such a sudden downturn in Democratic fortunes?

approaches to affirmative action and energy policy. Conservative religious figures, including Jerry Falwell and Pat Robertson, former Democrats, joined Reagan's new Republican coalition. Even Jimmy Carter's own Southern Baptists, who had rallied behind him in 1976, along with born-again Christians across the country, began flocking to Reagan.

THE ELECTION OF 1980

Easily capturing the Republican nomination, and anointing one of his defeated rivals, George H.W. Bush, as a running mate, Ronald Reagan exuded confidence and advanced an optimistic vision of a rejuvenated America. Punctuating his speeches with quips inspired by Hollywood movies, he stressed his opposition to domestic social spending and high taxes while promising support for a stronger national defense. To underscore the nation's economic problems under Carter, Reagan asked repeatedly, "Are you better off now than you were four years ago?" Quickly offering his own answer, Reagan cited what he called a "misery index," which added the rate of inflation to the rate of unemployment.

Reagan also seized issues that the Democratic Party had long regarded its own: economic growth and increased personal consumption. In 1979 one of Jimmy Carter's advisers had gloomily portrayed the nation's economic problems as so severe that there was "no way we can avoid a decline in our standard of living. All we can do is adapt to it." In contrast, Reagan promised that sharp tax cuts and budget trimming would restore robust economic expansion.

The Reagan-Bush team swept to victory. Although it gained only slightly more than 50 percent of the popular vote (John Anderson, a middle-of-the-road Republican who ran as an independent, won about 7 percent), the GOP ticket captured the Electoral College tally by a 489 to 49 margin. Moreover, Republicans took away 12 Democratic Senate seats, gaining control of the Senate, though not the House of Representatives.

A "NEW MORNING IN AMERICA"

Although conservative think tanks deluged the Reagan administration with policy suggestions, the president focused on three major priorities: cutting federal taxes, reducing the governmental regulatory structure, and boosting national-security capabilities.

TAXES, SUPPLY-SIDE ECONOMICS, AND THE "REAGAN REVOLUTION"

To justify cutting taxes, Reagan touted **supply-side economics**. This economic theory held that sizeable tax reductions would stimulate growth by putting more money in the hands of both producers and investors, thereby curing the economic stagnation of the 1970s. Reagan pushed a tax-reduction plan through Congress in 1981. Many Democrats, who had supported more limited tax cuts during Carter's presidency, endorsed Reagan's plan. At the same time, the Federal Reserve Board under Paul Volker, a Carter appointee, kept interest rates high in hopes of driving down inflation.

supply-side economics

Economic theory that tax reductions targeted toward investors and businesses would stimulate production and eventually create jobs.

After a severe economic downturn in 1981 and 1982, the economy rebounded and entered a period of noninflationary growth. According to one study, the economy added nearly 17 million new jobs; figures on real income, after having declined throughout the 1970s, began to rise; and inflation dropped from double digits to around 2 percent. Although unemployment figures did not fall as sharply, Reagan's supporters hailed a "Reagan Revolution."

This revival and its causes, however, were controversial. Critics complained that Reagan had not matched tax cuts with budget reductions, and budget deficits soared. Reagan constantly inveighed against deficits and "big spenders," but his eight years in Washington, even after he rolled back some of the tax reduction, saw annual deficits triple to nearly $300 billion. To finance such deficit spending, the United States borrowed abroad and piled up the largest foreign debt in the world. Reagan's "revolution," critical economists charged, brought short-term recovery for some people, courted a long-term deficit problem, and harmed people who truly needed governmental programs.

Although partisans of the Reagan Revolution argued that its effects would ultimately "trickle down" and benefit everyone, its detractors countered that too many groups fell through the holes of Reagan's "Swiss-cheese" economy. Farmers in the Midwest watched falling crop prices hamper their repayment of high-interest loans they had contracted during the inflation-ridden 1970s. Mortgage foreclosures, reminiscent of the 1930s, hit the farm states, and the ripple effect decimated the economies of small towns. In urban areas, many jobs created during the 1980s came in the service sector and offered low wages with limited benefits. The minimum wage, when adjusted for inflation, declined in value during Reagan's presidency.

The surge of the Reagan era, then, brought upward mobility for some but growing disadvantage for others. People with educational credentials and marketable skills could make significant economic gains. The number of African American families earning a solid middle-class income, for example, more than doubled between 1970 and 1990. African American college graduates could expect incomes comparable to those of their white classmates, partly as a result of affirmative action hiring plans put in place by the Nixon and Carter administrations, and many could, therefore, afford to leave problem-plagued inner-city neighborhoods.

The situation looked very different, however, for those who remained persistently unemployed, perhaps trapped in declining urban centers. At the end of the 1980s one-third of all African American families lived in poverty, and the number earning less than $15,000 per year had doubled since 1970. In inner cities, fewer than half of African American children were completing high school, and more than 60 percent were unemployed. The gap between the well-off and the disadvantaged widened during the 1980s.

CUTTING REGULATIONS AND WELFARE MEASURES

Meanwhile, Reagan pursued his second major goal: cutting back on the federal regulatory structure. In 1981 Reagan fired the nation's air traffic controllers after their union refused to halt a nationwide strike. The action portended more aggressive anti-union strategies that both his administration and business interests would pursue during the 1980s. The percentage of unionized workers fell to just 16 percent by the end of Reagan's presidency. Recognizing the balance of power tilting against them, workers increasingly turned away from strikes as an economic weapon.

Reagan had entered office promising to break OPEC's oil monopoly by encouraging the development of new sources of supply. Ignoring environmentalists' calls to decrease U.S. dependence on fossil fuels by promotion of renewable sources, Reagan and his successor, George H.W. Bush, pursued a "cheap oil" policy. The tapping of new oil fields at home and abroad, together with rivalries among OPEC's members, weakened the cartel's hold on the world market and reduced energy costs.

The Reagan administration also placed its New Right stamp on the federal legal system. Almost immediately, Reagan nominated a Supreme Court justice, Sandra Day O'Connor (the first woman to sit on the Court), who appeared a staunch conservative. With the Republican Party controlling the Senate until 1986, Reagan also named prominent conservative jurists, such as Robert Bork and Antonin Scalia, to lower federal courts. The New Right, which had decried the "rights revolution" of the Supreme Court, welcomed the influx of conservative judges. Civil libertarians, by contrast, complained that the federal courts were becoming less hospitable to legal arguments made by criminal defendants, labor unions, and political dissenters. By 1990, because of retirements, about half of all federal judges had reached the bench during Ronald Reagan's presidency. Reagan also sought out staunch conservatives for nonjudicial appointments. He staffed the justice department with young attorneys, such as John Roberts and Samuel Alito, who expressed a desire to help conservative judges whittle back Warren-era judicial precedents.

To oversee environmental issues, Reagan appointed James Watt, an outspoken critic of governmental regulation, as secretary of the interior. Watt supported the so-called "sagebrush rebellion," in which western states demanded fewer restrictions on the use of public land within their borders. Particularly in the timber states of the Pacific Northwest, people hotly debated protection of endangered species, such as rare bird populations, if it interfered with lumber-related opportunities. Reagan's first two appointees to the Department of Energy actually proposed eliminating the cabinet office they headed—an idea that Congress blocked. In both the interior and energy departments, the White House relaxed enforcement of federal safety and environmental regulations.

The Reagan administration decreased funding for various kinds of public-benefit programs, particularly Aid to Families with Dependent Children (AFDC). Reductions in food stamps and other programs increased poverty rates and fell disproportionately on female-headed households and on children. By the end of the 1980s one of every five children was being raised in a household whose income fell below the official poverty line.

Reagan steadfastly rejected suggestions of eliminating the basic set of New-Deal programs that he called a "social safety net," and he rejected calls for revising the Social Security system. During the 1970s Social Security payments had been "indexed" to automatically increase along with the rate of inflation. Larger Social Security checks, along with Medicare benefits, enabled millions of Americans over 65 to do relatively well during the Reagan years.

Despite sometimes sharp debate, especially over the soaring federal deficit and the widening gap between rich and poor, Reagan remained popular. His genial optimism seemed unshakable. He even appeared to rebound quickly—although close observers noted a clear decline in his energies—after being shot by a would-be assassin in March 1981. No matter what problems beset his administration, criticism rarely stuck to Reagan, whom one frustrated Democrat dubbed the "Teflon president."

ROUTING THE DEMOCRATS, 1984

Democrats continually underestimated Reagan's appeal—a miscalculation that doomed their 1984 presidential effort. Walter Mondale, Jimmy Carter's vice president, ran on a platform calling for "the eradication of discrimination in all aspects of American life" and for an expansion of social welfare programs. Mondale proposed higher taxes to fund this agenda and chose as his running mate Representative Geraldine Ferraro of New York, the first woman to stand for president or vice president on a major party ticket.

Republican campaign ads—often framed by the slogan "It's Morning Again in America"—portrayed a glowing landscape of bustling small towns and lush farmlands. They attacked Mondale's support from labor unions and civil-rights groups as a vestige of the "old politics" of "special interests" and his tax proposal as a return to the "wasteful" policies popularly associated with the stagflation of the 1970s. The 1984 presidential election ended with Mondale carrying only his home state of Minnesota and the District of Columbia.

REAGAN'S SECOND TERM

Although economic growth continued during Reagan's second term, corruption and mismanagement in the financial industry increasingly appeared as toxic byproducts of Reaganomics. The deregulation of financial institutions had allowed savings and loan (S&L) officers to venture into risky loans, particularly in real estate. By 1985 alarmed observers foresaw an impending S&L meltdown, but both the Reagan administration and Congress, hoping to duck the matter until after the 1988 election, ignored the warning.

Finally, in 1989, Congress did create a bailout plan designed to save some S&Ls and to transfer assets from already failed institutions to solvent ones. The plan proved astronomically expensive, and taxpayers footed the bill. Meanwhile, the process by which large, well-connected commercial banks purchased the remaining assets of bankrupt S&Ls at bargain-basement prices reeked of corruption and scandal. As a result of the S&L debacle of the 1980s, the banking industry went through a sudden, unplanned consolidation, and many people lost savings.

The White House and Congress struggled to deal with two other much-debated domestic issues: reduction of the federal deficit and overhaul of the social welfare system. The Gramm-Rudman-Hollings Act, passed in 1985, mandated a balanced federal budget by 1991. The goal was not met, however, and the government deficit continued to soar. The Family Support Act of 1988 pressured states to inaugurate work-training programs and to begin moving people, including mothers receiving AFDC payments, off the welfare rolls. Despite their own limited impact, Gramm-Rudman-Hollings and the Family Support Act set policymakers on a course that culminated in comprehensive budget-reduction and welfare-overhaul packages nearly a decade later.

Conservatives would eventually hail Ronald Reagan as a giant of their movement, but during his second term, even some of his supporters looked balefully at his domestic record. The 1986 resignation of Warren Burger allowed Reagan to elevate William Rehnquist to the position of chief justice and appoint Antonin Scalia, a staunch conservative, to replace Rehnquist as an associate justice. In 1987, however, the Senate, now with a Democratic majority following the 1986 elections, rebuffed Reagan's attempt to place Robert Bork, a particular favorite of the New Right, on the High Court. Bork's rejection enraged conservatives, some of whom blamed Reagan for not working hard enough on Bork's behalf. Meanwhile, the religious wing of the New Right chafed at what it considered Reagan's tepid support of its crusades against abortions and in favor of sectarian prayers in public schools.

Although never lacking for critics, the conservative Reagan Revolution succeeded in advancing much of the New Right's agenda and significantly changed

S&L *financial institution, earlier called a "thrift" or "building and loan," that traditionally specialized in home mortgages but could move into new ventures after deregulatory legislation of the 1970s and early 1980s.*

HISTORY THROUGH FILM

The First Movie-Star President

Ronald Reagan began his presidency in Hollywood. The political career of the "Great Communicator" built on, rather than broke away from, his days in the entertainment industry. His media advisers could count on directing a seasoned professional. Reagan always knew where to stand; how to deliver lines effectively; how to convey emotions through both body language and dialogue; and when to melt into the background so that other players in the cast of his presidency might carry a crucial scene.

Ronald Reagan, a master of both imagery and rhetoric, could casually and effectively adopt poses indebted to the Hollywood westerns in which he had once appeared. Here, the septuagenarian president, decked out in denim, stars in a western-themed parade.

Several of Reagan's movies provided rehearsals for roles he would play in the White House. Initially, Reagan's opponents thought that his old film parts, particularly in *Bedtime for Bonzo* (1947), where he co-starred with a chimpanzee, would be a political liability. Instead of disavowing his days in Hollywood, Reagan accentuated his fluency with film-related imagery. His efforts to cheer on the nation during the 1980s consciously invoked his favorite film role, that of the 1920s Notre Dame football star, George Gipp, whom Reagan played in *Knute Rockne, All American* (1940). Similarly, when tilting with a Democratic-controlled Congress over tax policy, Reagan invoked Clint Eastwood's famous screen character Dirty Harry, promising to shoot down any tax increase. "Go ahead, make my day," he taunted. On another occasion, he cited *Rambo* (1982), an action thriller set in post-1975 Vietnam as a possible blueprint for dealing with countries that had seized U.S. hostages. As he freely drew from Hollywood motion pictures, Reagan occasionally seemed unable to separate "reel" from "real" life. During one session with reporters, he referred to his own dog as "Lassie," the canine performer who had been Reagan's Hollywood contemporary during the 1940s and 1950s.

Life in Hollywood also provided a prologue to President Reagan's conservative policies. Early in his film career, Reagan appeared in four films as the same character, a government agent named "Brass Bancroft." In these B-grade thrillers, Reagan developed an image that he later deployed in politics: the action-oriented character who could distinguish (good) friends from (evil) foes. *Murder in the Air* (1940), one of the Brass Bancroft movies, even featured a science-fiction-style "death ray" that resembled the SDI ("Star Wars") armaments that President Reagan would champion more than 40 years later.

Subsequent film roles refined his Hollywood image. Poor eyesight kept Reagan out of combat during the Second World War, but he served long hours as an Army Air Corps officer, making movies in support of the war effort. He appeared in several films, such as *For God and Country* (1943), and more often provided upbeat voiceovers, once even sharing a soundtrack with President Franklin Roosevelt. He also starred, on loan from the Air Corps, in *This Is the Army* (1943), one of the most successful of wartime Hollywood's military-oriented musicals. After the war, Reagan increasingly directed his energies toward Cold War politics in the film capital. His tenure as the anticommunist president of the Screen Actors Guild—and as a secret FBI informant—likely speeded his conversion from New Deal Democrat to right-leaning Republican. In his final onscreen roles Reagan usually portrayed the kind of independent, rugged individualist—often in westerns such as *Law and Order* (1953)—whom he would later lionize in his political speeches.

Nancy Reagan, who costarred with her husband in *Hellcats of the Navy* (1957) and later as the nation's First Lady, offered her close-up view of the relationship between Reagan the actor and Reagan the politician: "There are not two Ronald Reagans." During the 1980s Hollywood and Washington, D.C., became embodied in the same character, Ronald Wilson Reagan.

the nation's political vocabulary. "Liberalism" no longer suggested governmental initiatives to stimulate the economy, promote greater equality, and advance liberty for all. Instead, Republicans turned "liberal" into a code word for wasteful social programs devised by a bloated federal government that gouged hardworking people and squandered their dollars. The term "conservative," as used by New Right Republicans, came to stand for economic growth through the curtailment of governmental power and support for traditional sociocultural values. The once-dominant Democratic Party of the New Deal, Fair Deal, and Great Society confronted an uncertain future.

RENEWING THE COLD WAR

In foreign policy, Reagan promised to reverse what he derided as Carter's passivity. He declared that the Vietnam War had been a "noble cause" that politicians had refused to win. Renewing the rhetoric of the Cold War, Reagan denounced the USSR as an "evil empire" and promised a military buildup to confront the Soviets.

THE DEFENSE BUILDUP

Dramatic increases in military spending followed, even while tax cuts were reducing federal revenues. The Pentagon enlarged the Navy and expanded strategic nuclear forces, deploying new missiles throughout Western Europe. At the height of Reagan's military buildup, which produced gaping budget deficits, the Pentagon was purchasing about 20 percent of the nation's manufacturing output.

In 1983 Reagan proposed the most expensive defense system in history: a space-based shield against incoming missiles. Beginning as a vague hope, this **Strategic Defense Initiative (SDI)** soon had its own Pentagon agency, which sought $26 billion, over five years, in research costs alone. Controversy swirled around SDI.

Strategic Defense Initiative (SDI) *Popularly termed "Star Wars," a proposal to develop technology for creation of a space-based defensive missile shield around the United States.*

Skeptics dubbed it "Star Wars" and shuddered at its astronomical costs. Although most scientists dismissed the plan as impossible to implement, Congress voted appropriations for SDI, and Reagan steadfastly insisted that a defensive shield could work. Reagan also suggested that, as the Soviets increased the burden on their own fragile economy in order to compete in the accelerating arms race, the USSR might collapse under the economic strain. SDI dominated both strategic debates at home and arms talks with the Soviet Union.

Reagan's foreign policy agenda included numerous nonmilitary initiatives. In a new "informational" offensive, the administration funded conservative groups around the world and established Radio Martí, a Florida station beamed at Cuba and designed to discredit Fidel Castro's communist government. When the **United Nations Educational, Scientific, and Cultural Organization (UNESCO)** adopted an allegedly anti-American tone, Reagan cut off U.S. contributions to this agency. The White House also championed free markets, pressing other nations to minimize tariffs and restrictions on foreign investment. The Caribbean Basin Initiative, for example, rewarded small nations in the Caribbean region that adhered to free-market principles with U.S. aid packages.

The CIA, headed by William Casey, stepped up its covert activities. Some became so obvious they hardly qualified as covert. It was no secret, for instance, that the United States sent aid to anticommunist forces in Afghanistan, many of them radical Islamic fundamentalist groups, and to the opponents of the *Sandinista* government in Nicaragua, the *contras*.

DEPLOYING MILITARY POWER

In renewing the global Cold War, Reagan promised military support to "democratic" revolutions anywhere, a move designed to contain the Soviet Union's sphere of influence. Reagan's UN ambassador, Jeane Kirkpatrick, wrote that "democratic" forces included almost any movement, no matter how autocratic, that was anticommunist. The United States thus funded opposition forces in countries aligned with the Soviet Union: Ethiopia, Angola, South Yemen, Cambodia, Guatemala, Grenada, Afghanistan, and Nicaragua. Reagan called the participants in such anticommunist insurgencies "freedom fighters," although few displayed any visible commitment to democratic values or institutions.

The Reagan administration also deployed U.S. military power, initially in southern Lebanon in 1982. Here, Israeli troops faced off against Islamic groups supported by Syria and Iran. Alarmed by radical Islamic influence within Lebanon, the Reagan administration convinced Israel to withdraw and sent 1,600 U.S. marines as part of an international "peacekeeping force" to restore stability. Islamic militias, however, turned against the U.S. forces. After a massive truck bomb attack against a military compound killed 241 U.S. troops, mostly Marines, in April 1983, Reagan decided to end this ill-defined undertaking. In February 1984 Reagan ordered the withdrawal of U.S. troops and disengaged from Lebanon. Another military intervention seemed more successful. In October 1983 Reagan sent 2,000 U.S. troops to the tiny Caribbean island of Grenada, whose socialist leader was forging ties with Castro's Cuba. U.S. troops swept aside Grenada's government and installed one friendlier to U.S. policies.

Buoyed by Grenada, the Reagan administration fixed its sights on Nicaragua. Here, the Marxist-leaning *Sandinista* government was trying to break Nicaragua's dependence on the United States. The Reagan administration responded with economic pressure, an informational campaign, and greater assistance to the *contras*.

United Nations Educational, Scientific, and Cultural Organization (UNESCO) *UN organization intended to create peace and security through collaboration among member nations.*

contras *Military force in Nicaragua, trained and financed by the United States, that opposed the Nicaraguan Marxist government led by the* Sandinista *Party.*

These early initiatives stirred considerable controversy. Mounting evidence of the *contras'* corruption and brutality fueled growing criticism. Finally, Democrats in Congress broke with the president's policy and barred additional military aid to the *contras*, a group Reagan, escalating his freedom-fighter rhetoric, had once compared to America's own "Founding Fathers." The Reagan administration encouraged wealthy American conservatives and foreign governments to help fund the *contra* cause.

Meanwhile, violence continued to escalate throughout the Middle East. Militant Islamic groups increased attacks against Israel and Western powers. Bombings and kidnappings of Westerners became more frequent. Apparently, Libya's Muammar al-Qaddafi and Iranian leaders encouraged such activities. In the spring of 1986 the United States launched an air strike into Qaddafi's personal compound. It killed his young daughter, but Qaddafi and his government survived. Despite what looked like a long-range assassination attempt against a foreign leader, an action outlawed by Congress. Americans generally approved of using strong measures against sponsors of terrorism and hostage taking.

THE IRAN-*CONTRA* CONTROVERSY

In November 1986 a magazine in Lebanon reported that the Reagan administration was selling arms to Iran in order to secure the release of Americans being held hostage by Islamic militants. These alleged deals violated the Reagan administration's own pledges against selling arms to Iran or rewarding hostage taking by negotiating for the release of captives. During the 1980 campaign, of course, Reagan had made hostages in Iran a symbol of U.S. weakness under Carter. When Iranian-backed groups continued to kidnap Americans during Reagan's own presidency, it seemed that Reagan had begun seeking clandestine ways to recover hostages.

As Congress began to investigate, the story became more bizarre. It appeared that the Reagan administration had not only sold arms to Iran but had funneled profits from these back-channel deals to the *contra* forces in Nicaragua, thereby circumventing the congressional ban on U.S. military aid. Oliver North, an aide in the office of the national security adviser, had directed the effort, working with international arms dealers and private go-betweens. North's covert machinations seemingly violated both the stated policy of the White House and an act of Congress.

The **Iran-*contra* affair** never reached the proportions of the Watergate scandal. In contrast to Richard Nixon, Ronald Reagan stepped forward and testified, through a deposition, that he could not recall any details about either the release of hostages or the funding of the *contras*. His management skills might deserve criticism, Reagan admitted, but he had never intended to break any laws or violate any presidential promise. Vice President George H. W. Bush, whom investigators initially inked to some of North's machinations, also claimed ignorance. Oliver North and several others in the Reagan administration were convicted of felonies, including falsification of documents and lying to Congress, but appellate courts later overturned these verdicts. North destroyed so many documents and left so many false paper trails that congressional investigators struggled even to compile a simple narrative of events. Finally, in 1992, just a few days before the end of his presidency, George H. W. Bush pardoned six former Reagan-era officials connected to the Iran-*contra* controversy.

Iran-*contra* affair *Reagan administration scandal in which the United States secretly sold arms to Iran, a country implicated in holding American hostages, and diverted the money to finance the* contras. *Both transactions raised serious legal issues.*

QUICK   REVIEW

MAJOR FEATURES OF THE REAGAN PRESIDENCY

- Tax cuts and growing government deficits

- Attempts to roll back some government welfare programs

- Huge increases in military spending and eventual easing of U.S.–Soviet tensions

- Prolonged expansion in many but not all economic sectors

- Appointment of conservative judges to federal courts

THE BEGINNING OF THE END OF THE COLD WAR

After six years of renewed Cold War confrontations, Reagan's last two years saw a sudden thaw in U.S.–Soviet relations. The economic cost of superpower rivalry was burdening both nations. Moreover, political change swept the Soviet Union and eliminated reasons for confrontation. Mikhail Gorbachev, who became general secretary of the Communist Party in 1985, promised a new style of Soviet leadership. He understood that his isolated country faced economic stagnation and environmental problems brought on by decades of poorly planned industrial development. To redirect the Soviet Union's course, he withdrew troops from Afghanistan, reduced commitments to Cuba and Nicaragua, proclaimed a policy of *glasnost* ("openness"), and began to implement *perestroika* ("economic liberalization") at home.

Gorbachev's policies gained him acclaim throughout the West, and summit meetings with the United States yielded breakthroughs in arms control. At Reykjavik, Iceland, in October 1986, Reagan shocked both Gorbachev and his own advisers by proposing a wholesale ban on nuclear weapons. Although negotiations at Reykjavik stumbled over Soviet insistence that the United States abandon SDI, Gorbachev later dropped that condition. In December 1987, Reagan and Gorbachev signed a major arms treaty that reduced each nation's supply of intermediate-range missiles and allowed for on-site verification, which the Soviets had never before permitted. The next year, Gorbachev scrapped the policy that forbade nations under Soviet influence from renouncing Communism.

In effect, Gorbachev declared an end to the cold war. Within the next few years, the Soviet sphere of influence—and the Soviet Union itself—would cease to exist.

glasnost Russian term describing increased openness in Soviet Union under Mikhail Gorbachev.

perestroika Russian term describing economic liberalization that began in the late 1980s.

THE FIRST BUSH PRESIDENCY (1989–1993)

FOCUS QUESTION
What forces and events contributed to the end of the Cold War?

The Reagan presidency, particularly its initiatives in foreign policy, boosted the 1988 electoral prospects of Reagan's heir-apparent, Vice President George H. W. Bush. He easily secured the Republican presidential nomination.

THE ELECTION OF 1988

Born into a wealthy Republican family and educated at Yale, Bush had prospered in the oil business, served in the House of Representatives, and headed the CIA. To court the New Right, decidedly lukewarm to his candidacy, he chose Senator J. Danforth (Dan) Quayle, a youthful conservative from Indiana, as a running mate. Quayle would soon delight political comedians who highlighted his verbal blunders.

Governor Michael Dukakis of Massachusetts emerged as the Democratic presidential candidate. Hoping to distance himself from the disastrous Democratic effort in 1984, Dukakis avoided talk of new domestic programs and higher taxes. Instead, he spoke about bringing competence and honesty to the White House.

Bush emerged the winner, but Democrats retained control of both houses of Congress. The turnout was the lowest for any national election since 1924, and polls suggested that many voters remained unimpressed with either Bush or Dukakis.

Once in the White House, Bush began to lose crucial support. He angered New Right Republicans by agreeing to an increase in the minimum wage and by failing to veto a seemingly noncontroversial civil rights measure, a law that critics charged with establishing "quotas" for the "preferential hiring" of women and people of color. Moreover, in 1990 he broke his "no new taxes" pledge, an issue on which New Right leaders came to judge his worthiness as Reagan's successor. When Bush agreed to an upward revision in tax rates in order to deal with the still-rising federal deficit, the New Right bitterly denounced his decision.

Meanwhile, the Democratic-controlled Congress and the Republican-occupied White House deadlocked over how to address key domestic issues such as reorganization of the health care and social welfare systems. Worse for the president's political future, the economic growth of the Reagan years began slowing, while the budget deficit continued to grow. George H. W. Bush's chances for a second term seemed to depend on his record in foreign, rather than domestic, policy.

THE END OF THE COLD WAR

During the first Bush presidency, communist states began to topple like dominoes. In 1989 Poland's anticommunist labor movement, Solidarity, ousted the pro-Soviet regime. The pro-Moscow government in East Germany fell in November 1989. Both West and East Germans hacked down the Berlin Wall and, then, began the difficult process of reunification. Popular movements similarly forced out communist governments throughout Eastern Europe. Yugoslavia quickly disintegrated, and warfare ensued as rival ethnic groups re-created separate states in Slovenia, Serbia, Bosnia, and Croatia. Latvia, Lithuania, and Estonia, which had been under Soviet control since the Second World War, declared their independence.

Most dramatically, the major provinces that had anchored the Soviet Union assumed self-government. The president of the new state of Russia, Boris Yeltsin, put down a coup by hard-line communists in August 1991, and he soon solidified his political position. In December 1991 Yeltsin brokered a plan to abolish the Soviet Union and replace it with 11 separate republics, loosely joined in a commonwealth arrangement.

© Owen Franker/CORBIS

BERLIN WALL, 1989. *Berliners celebrated the end of the Cold War by chiseling away at the Berlin Wall, which the communist East German state had erected in 1962 to prevent the flow of refugees to West Berlin. Pieces of the Berlin Wall became coveted symbols of the fall of communism.*

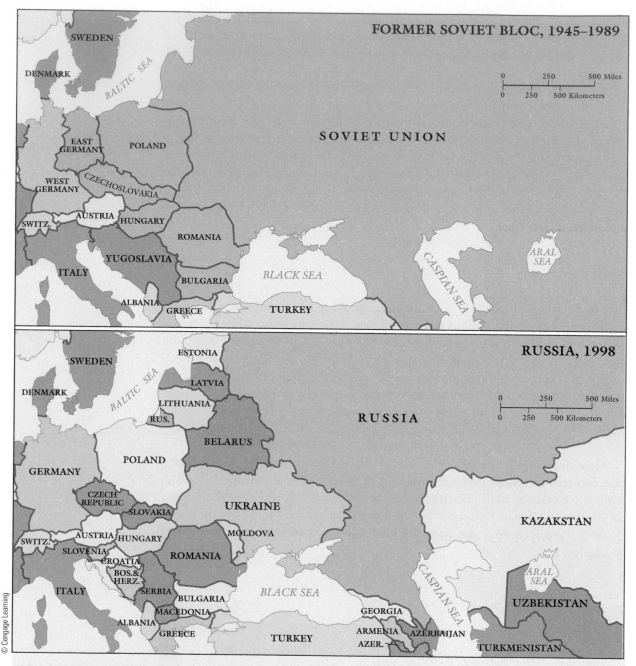

Map 30.3 COLLAPSE OF THE SOVIET BLOC. *These contrasting maps show the Soviet Union and the countries it dominated before and after the fall of communist governments. What countries in Eastern Europe escaped Russian control after 1989? What new countries emerged out of the old Soviet Union?*

In response, the Bush administration set about redefining U.S. national security in a post-Cold War era. The collapse of the Soviet Union weakened support for the leftist insurgencies in Central America that had so preoccupied the Reagan administration. Nicaraguans voted out the *Sandinistas,* who became just another political party in a multiparty system. The Pentagon pondered new military missions, imagining rapid, sharply targeted strikes rather than lengthy, conventional campaigns. The armed forces might even serve in the "war against drugs," an effort that Bush had suggested during his 1988 presidential campaign.

General Manuel Noriega, the president of Panama, was deeply involved in the drug trade, and the Reagan administration had secured an indictment against him for international narcotics trafficking. Confronting Noriega posed a potentially embarrassing problem for the Bush administration. The anticommunist general had been recruited as a CIA "asset" during the mid-1970s, when Bush had headed the Agency. Nevertheless, the United States needed a friendly and a stable government in Panama in order to complete the transfer of the Panama Canal to Panamanian sovereignty in 2000. Bush finally decided to topple the mercurial Noriega. During "Operation Just Cause," U.S. Marines landed in Panama in December 1989 and laid siege to the president's headquarters. Noriega soon surrendered, was extradited to Florida, and went to prison after a 1992 conviction for trafficking in cocaine.

The Panamanian operation carried major implications. Deposing the leader of a foreign government by unilateral military action raised questions of international law, but this operation, which involved 25,000 U.S. troops and few casualties, provided a new model for post-Cold War strategy. The Pentagon firmed up plans for creating highly mobile, rapid deployment forces. A test of its new strategy came during the Persian Gulf War of 1991.

THE PERSIAN GULF WAR

On August 2, 1990, Iraq's Saddam Hussein ordered his troops to occupy the neighboring oil-rich emirate of Kuwait. U.S. intelligence analysts had been caught off guard, and they now warned that Iraq's next target might be Saudi Arabia, the largest oil exporter in the Middle East and a longtime U.S. ally.

Moving swiftly, Bush orchestrated a multilateral, international response. Four days after Iraq's invasion of Kuwait, he launched Operation Desert Shield by sending several hundred thousand U.S. troops to Saudi Arabia. Bush convinced the Saudi government, concerned about allowing Western troops on sacred Islamic soil, to accept a U.S. military presence in Saudi Arabia. After consulting with European leaders, Bush approached the UN, which denounced Iraqi aggression, ordered economic sanctions against Iraq, and authorized the United States to lead an international force to Kuwait if Saddam Hussein's troops did not withdraw.

Bush assembled a massive coalition force, ultimately nearly 500,000 troops from the United States and some 200,000 from other countries. He claimed a moral obligation to rescue Kuwait, and his policymakers also spoke frankly about the economic threat that Hussein's aggression posed for the oil-dependent economies of the United States and its allies. These arguments persuaded Congress to approve a resolution backing the use of force.

In mid-January 1991 the United States launched an air war on Iraq and, after a period of devastating aerial bombardment, began a ground offensive in late February. Coalition forces, enjoying air supremacy, decimated Saddam Hussein's armies in a matter of days. U.S. casualties were relatively light (148 deaths in battle). Estimates of Iraqi casualties ranged from 25,000 to 100,000 deaths. Although the conflict had lasted scarcely six weeks, it took an enormous toll on highways, bridges, communications, and other infrastructure facilities in both Iraq and Kuwait.

In a controversial decision, Bush stopped short of ousting Saddam Hussein, a goal that the UN had never approved and that U.S military planners had considered too costly and risky. Instead, the United States, backed by the UN,

QUICK REVIEW

FOREIGN POLICY UNDER GEORGE HERBERT WALKER BUSH

- End of Cold War and collapse of communist regimes in Eastern Europe

- Emphasis on economic globalization

- Persian Gulf War in response to Iraq's move into Kuwait

- Perceived by critics as failing to project "vision" for post–Cold War world order

maintained its economic pressure, ordered the dismantling of Iraq's nuclear and bacteriological capabilities, and enforced "no-fly" zones over northern and southern Iraq to help protect the Kurds and Shi'a Muslims from Hussein's continued persecution. The Persian Gulf War temporarily boosted George H. W. Bush's popularity.

Bush's economic foreign policy, although less visible than his leadership during the Iraq war, was of considerable importance. The president pressed a program of international economic integration. During the mid-1980s huge debts that Third World nations owed to U.S. institutions had threatened the international banking system, but most of these obligations had been renegotiated by the early 1990s. Market economies, which replaced centrally planned ones, began to emerge in former communist states; Western Europe moved toward economic integration; and most nations of the Pacific Rim experienced steady economic growth. The president also supported (but was unable to pass) a North American Free Trade Agreement (NAFTA), which would eliminate tariff barriers and join Canada, the United States, and Mexico together in the largest free-market zone in the world.

Ultimately, however, voters judged Bush's record on foreign affairs as something of a muddle. He had organized an international coalition against Iraq, assisted post-Cold War Russia and Eastern Europe, and embraced global economic integration. On other issues, the president seemed indecisive. The United States remained on the sidelines as full-scale warfare erupted among the states of the former Yugoslavia, with Serbs launching a brutal campaign of territorial aggrandizement and "ethnic cleansing" against Bosnian Muslims. In Africa, when severe famine wracked Somalia, Bush ordered U.S. troops to secure supply lines for humanitarian aid, but the American public remained wary of this military mission. As the old goals of containing the Soviet Union became irrelevant, George H. W. Bush failed to effectively articulate new ones.

THE ELECTION OF 1992

The inability to portray coherence in either domestic or foreign policy threatened Bush's reelection and forced concessions to the New Right. Dan Quayle, although clearly a liability with voters outside his conservative constituency, returned as Bush's running mate. The president allowed New Right activists, who talked about "a religious war" for "the soul of America" and pictured Democrats as the enemy of family values, to dominate the 1992 Republican National Convention. Conservative Democrats and independents, who had supported Ronald Reagan and Bush in the previous three presidential elections, found this rhetoric unsettling.

Bush's Democratic challenger, Governor William Jefferson Clinton of Arkansas, stressed economic issues. Campaigning as a "New Democrat," Bill Clinton promised job creation, deficit reduction, and an overhaul of the nation's health care system. Sounding almost like a Republican, Clinton pledged to shrink the size of government and to "end this [welfare] system as we know it." "People who can work ought to go to work, and no one should be able to stay on welfare forever," he insisted. This rhetoric made it difficult for Bush to label Clinton as a "big government liberal."

Clinton's focus on the economy helped deflect attention from the sociocultural issues on which he was vulnerable. As a college student, he had avoided service in Vietnam and, while in England as a Rhodes Scholar, had demonstrated against the war. When Bush, a decorated veteran of the Second World War, challenged the patriotism of his Democratic challenger, Clinton countered by emphasizing, rather than repudiating, his roots in the 1960s. He appeared on MTV and touted his devotion to (relatively soft) rock music. In addition, he chose Senator Albert Gore of Tennessee, a Vietnam veteran, as his running mate.

The 1992 election brought Clinton a surprisingly easy victory. The quixotic campaign of Ross Perot, a Texas billionaire who spent more than $60 million of his own money on a third-party run, likely hurt insider Bush more than outsider Clinton. With Perot in the race, Clinton garnered only 43 percent of the popular vote but won 370 electoral votes by carrying 32 states and the District of Columbia. Bush won a majority only among white Protestants in the South. In contrast, Clinton carried the Jewish, African American, and Latino vote by large margins and even gained a plurality among people who had served in the Vietnam War. He also ran well among independents who had supported Reagan and Bush during the 1980s. Perhaps most surprising, about 55 percent of eligible voters went to the polls, a turnout that reversed 32 years of steady decline in voter participation.

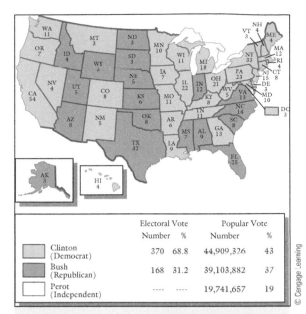

		Electoral Vote		Popular Vote	
		Number	%	Number	%
	Clinton (Democrat)	370	68.8	44,909,326	43
	Bush (Republican)	168	31.2	39,103,882	37
	Perot (Independent)	----	----	19,741,657	19

Map 30.4 PRESIDENTIAL ELECTION, 1992. *Notice the substantial number of votes cast for an independent candidate, Ross Perot. How did Perot's vote totals affect Bill Clinton's mandate as president?*

MOVEMENT ACTIVISM

The activism associated with the 1960s became firmly embedded in most areas of American life in the decades that followed. The proliferation of locally based activism, often focused on neighborhood-related projects, such as safer streets and cleaner parks, prompted one historian to see a "backyard revolution" taking place during the 1970s and 1980s. Even the U.S. Congress, hardly an institution inclined to fund domestic revolutions, recognized the value of locally based activism and created, in 1978, the National Consumer Cooperative Bank. Legislators charged it with providing loans to support grass-roots enterprise. By the early 21st century, virtually every public forum featured the influence, and the clash, of activists who claimed to represent some particular constituency or goal.

Mass demonstrations reminiscent of those against the Vietnam War remained one tool of advocacy and protest. Both anti-abortion and pro-choice forces, for example, regularly demonstrated in Washington, D.C. During the 1980s, the Clamshell Alliance conducted a campaign of civil disobedience against a nuclear reactor being built in Seabrook, New Hampshire, and a coalition of West Coast activists waged a lengthy, unsuccessful struggle to close the University of California's Lawrence Livermore National Laboratory, which was developing nuclear weapons. In nearly every major city and many smaller towns, women's groups staged annual Take Back the Night rallies to call attention to the danger of sexual assault.

The media tended to ignore most mass demonstrations unless they sparked violent conflict. In 1991, for example, 30,000 Korean Americans staged a march for racial peace in Los Angeles. Although it was the largest demonstration ever conducted by any Asian American group, even the local media failed to cover it. Only C-Span, a niche network devoted to public-affairs programming, provided minimal coverage of events of social and political protest.

FOCUS QUESTION
How did social movements of the post-1960s era affect social life, culture, and the ways people saw their own personal identities during the 1970s and 1980s?

MUSICAL LINK TO THE PAST

NOT FOR WOMEN ONLY

Songwriter: Joni Mitchell
Title: "Hejira" (1976)

Except for the blues queens of the 1920s, American women held relatively little sway in 20th century popular music. Even though Ella Fitzgerald, Billie Holiday, and Barbra Streisand gained fame as singers, few women wrote songs, became known for their expertise on an instrument, supervised studio production and arrangements, or worked in the upper echelon of record companies.

With a string of groundbreaking, bestselling albums in the 1970s, Joni Mitchell changed all that. Mitchell wrote songs that detailed her inner life. With her unique tunings and playing style on the acoustic guitar, she had an immediately recognizable sound. And as the producer of her own recordings, she enjoyed full control in the studio.

In "Hejira," as in many of her songs, Mitchell sings with yearning about the benefits, adventures, and struggles of being an independent career woman. Like many women of her time, she found that asserting her autonomy and bypassing traditional roles was not easy, personally or professionally.

Nevertheless, throughout her career, Joni Mitchell stubbornly resisted being pigeonholed as a "women's artist." In 1991 she said: "For a while it was assumed that I was writing women's songs. Then men began to notice that they saw themselves in the songs, too. A good piece of art should be androgynous. I'm not a feminist. That's too divisional for me."

WOMEN'S ISSUES

In this environment, women's groups adopted a range of methods to rally new supporters and re-energize their core constituencies. Struggles over gender-related issues had emerged within the labor movement and the civil-rights and antiwar movements of the 1960s. Initially, many of the men involved in these causes complained that issues of gender equality interfered with broader fights to redirect labor, racial, or foreign policies, but women themselves insisted on calling attention to their second-class status in movements that claimed to be egalitarian. The spread of the birth control pill during the 1960s gave women greater control over reproductive choices but also complicated the meaning of "sexual freedom." Throughout the 1970s women promoted "consciousness-raising" sessions to discuss how *political* empowerment was inseparable from *personal* power relationships involving housework, child rearing, sexuality, and economic independence. "The personal is political" became a watchword for the new women's movement.

MS. DEBUTS. Ms. *magazine, created by an all-woman staff, debuted in January 1972 and sold out 300,000 copies in eight days. Editor Gloria Steinem stated that the magazine would help teach women "not how to make jelly, but how to seize control of your life."*

The number of groups addressing issues of concern to women continually expanded. As part of the new activism, the National Organization for Women (NOW) became generally identified with the rights-based agenda of the mainstream of the Democratic Party. African American women often formed separate organizations that emphasized issues of cultural and ethnic identity. Chicana groups coalesced within the UFW movement and alongside many Mexican American organizations. Lesbians also organized their own groups, often allying with an emerging gay rights movement. Many U.S. feminist organizations joined with groups in other nations on behalf of international women's rights.

With agendas often varying along lines of class, race, ethnicity, and religion, the women's movement remained highly diverse, but women from different backgrounds often cooperated to build new institutions and networks. Their efforts included battered-women's shelters; health and birthing clinics specializing in women's medicine; rape crisis centers; economic development counseling for women-owned businesses; union-organizing efforts led by women; organizations of women in specific businesses or professions; women and gender studies programs in colleges and universities; and academic journals and popular magazines devoted to women's issues. Pressure for gender equity also affected existing institutions. Country clubs and service organizations began admitting women members. Many Protestant denominations came to accept women into the ministry, and Reform Judaism placed women in its pulpits. Educational institutions adopted "gender-fair" hiring practices and curricula. American women by the beginning of the 21st century lived in an environment significantly different from that of their mothers.

One pressing issue for women was economic self-sufficiency. Increases in AFDC payments and an expansion of the Food Stamp program had boosted social welfare payments for single mothers with children during the 1960s, but the economic dislocations of the following decades undercut the value, measured in constant dollars, of these benefits. Homeless shelters, which once catered almost exclusively to single men, began taking in women and children. Activists highlighted the feminization of poverty and the growing number of children reared in low-income, female-headed families. Proposals for reshaping the pattern of governmental support through welfare reform in the 1990s increasingly sought to limit direct governmental payments and to emphasize moving women, even those with young children, into the workforce.

The job market, however, remained laced with inequalities. Women constituted 30 percent of the labor force in 1950 and more than 45 percent in 2001. Although women increasingly entered the professions and gained unionized positions (by 2000 nearly 45 percent of union members were women, compared with 18 percent in 1960), the average female worker still earned around 75 cents for every dollar taken home by men. "Glass ceilings" limited women's chances for promotion, and childcare expenses often fell disproportionately on women who worked outside the home.

Sexual harassment on the job became a highly charged issue. Most women's groups pressed government and private employers to curtail sexually charged behaviors that they saw demeaning women and exploiting their lack of power vis-à-vis male supervisors and coworkers. In 1986 the U.S. Supreme Court ruled that sexual harassment constituted a form of discrimination under the Civil Rights Act of 1964.

In 1991 the issue gained national attention when Anita Hill, an African American law professor, accused Clarence Thomas, an African American nominee for the U.S. Supreme Court, of having sexually harassed her when both worked for the federal government. Feminists denounced the all-male Senate Judiciary Committee, which was responsible for considering Thomas's nomination, for failing even to understand, let alone investigate seriously, the issue of sexual harassment. Although the Senate narrowly approved Thomas for the High Court, women's groups mobilized female voters and elected four women as U.S. senators in 1992.

Sexual harassment also became a controversial issue within the U.S. military, which began to recruit women more actively. The service academies accepted female cadets, and women found places within the military hierarchy. Soon, however, revelations about harassment and even sexual assaults against female naval officers by male comrades revealed problems. Attempts by Navy officials to cover up sexual harassment during the 1991 "Tailhook" convention provoked outrage, and several high-ranking officers were forced to step down.

SEXUAL POLITICS

Issues involving gays and lesbians also became more public and political. In 1969 New York City police raided the Stonewall Inn, a bar in Greenwich Village with a largely homosexual clientele. Patrons resisted arrest, and the resultant confrontations pitted the neighborhood's gay and lesbian activists, who claimed to be the victims of police harassment, against law enforcement officials.

Historians of sexuality have come to criticize what they call "the Stonewall Narrative," in which events at a single Greenwich Village bar ignited what would become known as the Lesbian-Gay-Bisexual-Transgendered (LGBT) movement. Recent studies emphasize that LGBT activism did not suddenly emerge in 1969 but, instead, grew out of earlier movements, such as the Mattachine Society, and cultural communities, including that of the Beats (see Chapter 29).

Still, the 1969 events at the Stonewall Inn, because of the prominence they received in mainstream and alternative media, marked an important benchmark in sexual politics. Gay and lesbian activism became an important part of the larger "movement of movements" that continued during the 1970s and 1980s. Thousands of advocacy and support groups, such as New York City's Gay Activist Alliance (GAA), sprang up. As many individuals "came out of the closet," newspapers, theaters, nightspots, and religious groups proudly identified themselves as activists. LGBT communities emerged, particularly in larger cities, and benefited from a general relaxation of legal and cultural controls over the portrayal and practice of sexuality. They demanded that law enforcement officials treat attacks against them no less seriously than attacks against all other communities. They also asserted constitutional claims to equal access to housing, jobs, and benefits for domestic partners.

One issue, with international implications, was especially urgent. A human immunodeficiency virus produced an immune deficiency syndrome, **HIV-AIDS**, a contagious disease for which medical science offered virtually nothing in the way of cure. The disease could be transmitted through the careless use of intravenous drugs, tainted blood supplies, and unprotected sexual intercourse. At first, the incidence of HIV-AIDS in the United States was primarily limited to gay men, and activists charged that, as a consequence, cultural and religious conservatives placed a low priority on medical efforts to understand its causes, check its spread, or devise a cure. The resultant controversy over medical funding galvanized empowerment efforts among LGBT organizations, such as Aids Coalition to Unleash Power, or ACT UP. With the development of prevention programs and drugs that could combat HIV-AIDS, however, most public figures came to support new efforts both at home and overseas, particularly in Africa, to address HIV-AIDS. It remained a modern scourge that threatened advancement in many parts of the world, but its specific identification with LGBT rights faded.

HIV-AIDS *Acquired immune deficiency syndrome (AIDS) resulting from infection with the human immunodeficiency virus (HIV). It progressively impedes the body's ability to protect itself from disease.*

AIDS *ACT UP* CAMPAIGN. *Health care issues increasingly galvanized grassroots activists in the late 20th century. In 1989 members of ACT UP, a group that represents militant homosexuals, protested what they saw as the federal government's inattention to the issue of AIDS during the 1980s.*

LGBT activism met opposition from cultural and religious conservatives. In 2003, for instance, a divided U.S. Supreme Court declared that state laws criminalizing sodomy violated the Constitution. The court's opinion in *Lawrence v. Texas* hinted that the same reasoning might strike down state bans against same-sex marriages. After Vermont and then several other U.S. and Canadian jurisdictions formally authorized same-sex unions, conservative activists in the United States sponsored a constitutional amendment that would define marriage as a union between a man and a woman. The definition of marriage, like the abortion-rights controversy over when life began, increasingly polarized national and local politics.

RACE, ETHNICITY, AND SOCIAL ACTIVISM

The emphasis on group identity as the fulcrum for social activism became especially strong among racial and ethnic communities. Extending the activism of the 1960s, groups emphasized pride in their distinctive traditions and insisted cultural differences should be affirmed rather than feared. Especially with the influx of new immigrants, identity politics and multiculturalism took on growing importance.

ACTIVISM AMONG AFRICAN AMERICANS

African American activists had developed a strong sense of cultural identity during the civil rights and Black Power struggles of the 1960s (see Chapters 28 and 29), and activists during the following decades continued to stress pride in African American cultural life. The emphasis on racial pride showed in Spike Lee's film *Malcolm X* (1991), in rap and hip-hop music, and among educators who advocated an "Afrocentric" curriculum. The Black Entertainment Television network (BET) aimed its programming specifically to African American viewers, although it also attracted a multicultural audience.

Academics such as Henry Lewis Gates, Jr., who became head of Harvard's Afro-American Studies Department in 1991, deepened the study of the black experience. African American culture, in the view of Gates and others, was not "a thing apart, separate from the whole, having no influence on the shape and shaping of American culture." Gates insisted that African American authors, such as Toni Morrison (who won the Nobel Prize for Literature in 1993) and Alice Walker, be viewed as writers who take "the blackness of the culture for granted" and use this as "a springboard to write about those human emotions that we share with everyone else." The cultural works of African Americans, in short, could simultaneously be seen as unique and different, *and also* be viewed in relationship to broader cultural traditions.

Issues of equal treatment in the legal and criminal justice systems became an important part of the agenda for African American activists. **Racial profiling** was one prominent issue. Repeated studies suggested that police detained African Americans as criminal suspects and stopped black motorists far more often than members of any other ethnic group. Activists called this practice DWB, or "driving while black." (In Hispanic communities, DWB came to stand for "driving while brown.") Profiling seemed a reminder, both symbolic and real, of the days of legally sanctioned discrimination. Moreover, differences in the sentencing of convicted felons raised a broader concern. Courts imposed harsher sentences for crimes, for instance, involving crack cocaine, a drug consumed in some African American neighborhoods, than for those involving the more expensive varieties of cocaine favored by white, suburban drug users. Statistical evidence also indicated that African American men in their late twenties were about 10 times more likely than their white counterparts to be imprisoned. Similar statistics showed African Americans convicted of potential capital crimes were more likely to receive the death penalty than were prison inmates from other ethnic and racial backgrounds.

Other practices that symbolized racism of the past also became the target of activists. At the beginning of the 1990s several southern states and institutions still flew the Confederate flag. Groups that defended this practice insisted it merely honored those who had supported the Confederacy during the Civil War, not the system of chattel slavery. Activists, however, countered that the Confederate cause could not be separated from that of defending slavery and that the Confederate flag had long symbolized resistance to civil rights initiatives. The flag controversy flared throughout the 1990s, and most Confederate flags in public areas did start coming down.

By the beginning of the 21st century most African Americans embraced cultural pride but also worked within the country's dominant institutions. In 1970 13 African American members of Congress established the **Congressional Black Caucus (CBC)** as a means of providing a common front on a wide range of foreign and domestic issues. Picking up the mantle of A. Philip Randolph and Bayard Rustin's "Freedom Budget" of the 1960s, the CBC would issue a hypothetical "Alternative

racial profiling *Law-enforcement practice of using racial appearance to screen for potential wrongdoing.*

Congressional Black Caucus (CBC) *Congressional group formed in 1969, focused on eliminating disparities between African Americans and white Americans.*

Budget," which targets more money toward social initiatives; campaign on behalf of better relations between the United States and African nations; and take stands on issues, such as racial profiling and drug sentencing, that particularly affect African Americans.

ACTIVISM AMONG NATIVE AMERICANS

Native Americans mounted activist movements along two broad fronts. Indians had, of course, longstanding identities based on their tribal affiliation, and many issues, particularly those involving land and treaty disputes, turned on specific, tribal-based claims. Other questions, which seemed to require strategies that extended beyond a single tribe or band, became identified as "pan-Indian" in nature.

In 1969 people from several tribes began a two-year sit-in, designed to dramatize a history of broken treaty promises, at the former federal prison on Alcatraz Island in San Francisco harbor. Expanding on this tactic, the American Indian Movement (AIM), created in 1968 by young activists from several Northern Plains tribes, adopted even more confrontational approaches. Violent clashes, with both federal officials and older American Indian leaders, erupted in 1973 on the Pine Ridge Reservation in South Dakota. In response, federal officials targeted members of AIM with illegal surveillance and a series of controversial criminal prosecutions.

© Andre Jenny/The Image Works

GAMING AT POTAWATOMI CASINO. *During the 1980s casino-style gaming began to emerge as one of the nation's leading entertainment enterprises. Native Americans embraced casinos, such as this one located near Milwaukee, Wisconsin, as important ways to generate jobs and capital on Indian reservations. The Potawatomi complex, which opened in 1991, now juxtaposes traditional style sculptures, an Indian heritage center and gift shop, an imaginatively designed building, more than 1,000 slot machines, and a cabaret-style dinner theater patterned after those in Las Vegas.*

Meanwhile, important social and legal changes were taking place. In the Civil Rights Act of 1968, which contained several sections that became known as the "Indian Bill of Rights," Congress extended most of the provisions of the constitutional Bill of Rights to Native Americans living on reservations, while reconfirming the legitimacy of tribal laws. Federal legislation and several Supreme Court decisions in the 1970s subsequently reinforced the principle of "tribal self-determination." In 1978 Congress provided funds for educational institutions that would build job skills and preserve tribal cultures. Tribal identification itself required legal action. By the early 21st century, the federal government officially recognized nearly 600 separate tribes and bands.

Tapping the expertise of the Native American Rights Fund (NARF), tribes pressed demands that derived from old treaties with the U.S. government. Some sought recognition of fishing and agricultural rights, campaigns that often provoked resentment among non-Indians who argued that these claims, based on federal authority, should not take precedence over state and local laws. American Indians also sued to protect tribal water rights and traditional religious ceremonies, some of which included the ritualistic use of drugs such as peyote. In 1990, Congress passed the Native American Graves Protection and Repatriation Act, which required universities and museums to return human remains and sacred objects to tribes that requested them.

Claiming exemption from state gaming laws, Native Americans began to open bingo halls and then full-blown casinos. In 1988 the U.S. Supreme Court ruled that states could not prohibit gambling operations on tribal land, and Congress responded with the Indian Gaming Regulatory Act. Gambling emerged as one of the most lucrative sectors of the nation's entertainment business, and Indian-owned casinos thrived. Ironically, the glitzy, tribal-owned casinos often financed tribal powwows and other efforts to nurture older cultural practices. Sometimes the competition to establish casinos in prime locations prompted intertribal political and legal conflict.

To forestall the disappearance of native languages, American Indian activists urged bilingualism and renewed attention to tribal rituals. Indian groups also denounced the use of stereotypical nicknames, such as "Chiefs" and "Redskins," and Indian-related logos in amateur and professional sports. The federal government assisted this cultural-pride movement by funding two National Museums of the American Indian, one in New York and the other in Washington, D.C. The National Park Service changed the name of "Custer Battlefield" in Montana to "Little Bighorn Battlefield," redesigning its exhibits to honor American Indian culture.

ACTIVISM IN SPANISH-SPEAKING COMMUNITIES

Spanish-speaking Americans, who constituted the fastest-growing ethnic group in the United States, highlighted the diversity and complexity of identity. Many Spanish-speaking people, especially in the Southwest, prefer the umbrella term "Latino," whereas others, particularly in Florida, use the term "Hispanic." At the same time, people whom the U.S. Census began (in 1980) labeling Hispanic more frequently identified themselves according to the specific Spanish-speaking country or commonwealth from which they or their ancestors had immigrated.

Chicanismo *Populist pride in the Mexican American heritage that emerged in the late 1960s. Chicano, once a term of derision, became a rallying cry among activists.*

Mexican Americans, members of the oldest and most numerous Spanish-speaking group, could tap a long tradition of social activism. The late 1960s saw an emerging spirit of **Chicanismo,** a populist-style pride in a heritage that could be traced back to the ancient civilizations of Middle America. Young activists made "Chicano/a," terms of derision that older Mexican Americans had generally avoided in the past, into a rallying cry.

In cities in the Southwest during the 1970s, advocates of *Chicanismo* gained considerable cultural influence. Members of **La Raza Unida**, a political party founded in 1967, began to win local elections. At the same time, Mexican American communities experienced a cultural flowering. New Spanish-language newspapers and journals reinforced a growing sense of pride, and many churches sponsored festivals with ethnic dancing, mural painting, poetry, and literature. Mexican Americans successfully pushed for programs in Chicano/a Studies at colleges and universities.

Developments in San Antonio, Texas, a city with a large Mexican American population, suggested the potential fruits of grassroots political organizing. In the 1970s Ernesto Cortes, Jr., took the lead in founding Communities Organized for Public Service (COPS), a group that brought the energy and talents of Mexican Americans, particularly women, into the city's public arena for the first time. Mexican American activists worked with Anglo business leaders and Democratic politicians such as Henry Cisneros, who became the city's mayor in 1981.

By the early 21st century Mexican American activism was becoming increasingly diverse. The Mexican American Legal Defense and Education Fund (MALDEF), established in 1968, emerged as a highly visible national group ready to lobby or litigate. At the local level, organizations formed on the model of COPS, such as United Neighborhood Organization (UNO) in Los Angeles, worked on community concerns. Mexican Americans, both women and men, often spearheaded labor-organizing efforts, particularly in the rapidly expanding service sector. Professional women could join organizations such as the National Network of Hispanic Women.

Social activism among Puerto Ricans in the United States emerged more slowly. Some stateside Puerto Ricans focused their political energy on the persistent "status" question—that is, whether Puerto Rico should seek independence, strive for statehood, or retain a commonwealth connection to the mainland. New York City's Puerto Rican Day Parade became the city's largest ethnic celebration and an important focus of cultural pride. A 1976 report by the U.S. Commission on Civil Rights, however, concluded that Puerto Ricans remained "the last in line" for government-funded benefits and opportunity programs. Over time, the Puerto Rican Legal Defense and Education Fund and allied groups helped Puerto Ricans surmount obstacles to the ballot box and political office. In 2000 these groups organized a well-publicized, ultimately successful campaign to stop the U.S. Navy from using the small island of Vieques as a target range, a practice that created health and ecological hazards for Puerto Rico.

Cuban Americans who had begun immigrating in large numbers to south Florida during the 1960s generally enjoyed greater access to education and higher incomes than did most Latinos who came later, even from Cuba. This initial wave of Cuban immigrants also tended to be more politically conservative, generally voted Republican, and lobbied for a hard line toward Castro's communist government back in Cuba. Cuban Americans became active in Florida politics and civic affairs, and a new generation born in the United States increasingly questioned the persistent "exile mentality" that revolved around anti-Castro activities.

Beneath a common Spanish language, then, lay great diversity in terms of economic status, national and cultural identification, political affiliation, and activist goals and organizations. Established communities that identified with Mexico, Puerto Rico, and Cuba developed a wide range of mobilizing and organizing styles. More recent immigrants from the Dominican Republic and Central America, who were the most economically deprived and least organized, also began to add their voices and concerns.

La Raza Unida *Mexican American–based movement that scored some political successes in the Southwest in the late 1960s and early 1970s.*

ACTIVISM AMONG ASIAN AMERICANS

Americans of Chinese, Japanese, Korean, Filipino, and other backgrounds began to create an Asian American movement. Organizations such as the Asian Pacific Planning Council (APPCON), founded in 1976, lobbied to obtain government funding for projects that benefited Asian American communities. The Asian Law Caucus, founded during the early 1970s by opponents of U.S. intervention in Vietnam, and the Committee against Anti-Asian Violence, created a decade later in response to a wave of racially motivated attacks, mobilized for a wide range of legal battles. During the 1970s Asian American studies programs also took shape at colleges and universities, particularly on the West Coast. By the early 1980s Asian American political activists enjoyed growing influence, especially within the Democratic Party, and began getting elected to public office. Beginning in 1997 the National Asian Pacific American Network Council, the first civil-rights group to be formed by Asian Americans, began to lobby on issues related to immigration and education.

Emphasizing this broad, Asian American identity, however, raised questions of inclusion, exclusion, and rivalry. Filipino American activists, members of the second largest Asian American group in the United States in 1990, often resisted the Asian American label because they believed that Chinese Americans or Japanese Americans dominated groups such as APPCON. Many people of Filipino descent focused on specific goals, particularly an effort to obtain citizenship and veteran's benefits for former soldiers of the Second World War who had fought against Japan in the Philippines. Japanese American groups also lobbied on behalf of specific issues, and in 1988 Congress formally apologized and voted to a reparations payment of $20,000 to every living Japanese American who had been confined in internment camps during the Second World War. Similarly, Hmong and Vietnamese groups pursued their own concerns. In 2000, for instance, Hmong and their allies succeeded in obtaining the Hmong Veterans Naturalization Act, which allowed Hmong immigrants (and their spouses and widows) to use an interpreter when taking the test to obtain U.S. citizenship.

Socioeconomic differences often made it difficult to frame a single Asian American agenda. Although many groups showed remarkable upward educational and economic mobility during the late 1980s and early 1990s, for example, others such as Hmong immigrants and Chinese American garment workers struggled to find jobs that paid more than the minimum wage.

As a result of combined pressure from different ethnic groups, the federal government finally decided to designate "Asian or Pacific Islanders" (API) as a single pan-ethnic category in the censuses of 1990 and 2000. It also provided, however, nine specifically enumerated subcategories (such as Hawaiian or Filipino) and allowed other API groups (such as Hmong or Samoan) to write in their respective ethnic identifications. Thus, the term Asian American—which by the beginning of the 21st century applied to more than 10 million people and dozens of different ethnicities—both reflected, and was challenged by, the new emphasis on ethnic identity.

THE DILEMMAS OF ANTIDISCRIMINATION EFFORTS

How might governmental power best advance the cause of equality? Between the end of the Second World War and about 1970, antidiscrimination movements and the courts had argued that the governments not categorize individuals according to group identities based on race or ethnicity. On matters such as education, housing, or employment, the law must remain "color-blind" and treat people equally.

Gradually, however, new social-activist agendas envisioned that governmental power should do more than simply eliminate discriminatory barriers to *individual* opportunity. It should take **affirmative action** so that *groups* that had historically faced discrimination could begin to receive an equitable share of the nation's jobs, public spending, and educational programs. Affirmative action, supporters argued, would help compensate for past discrimination and for continued, perhaps hidden, prejudices.

Affirmative action sparked controversy. Critics charged that any program to "set aside" jobs or openings in educational institutions for certain racial or ethnic groups smacked of "quotas." Moreover, was not affirmative action *on behalf of* some groups inevitably also "reverse discrimination" *against* others? The claim of reverse discrimination became particularly emotional when members of one ethnic group received jobs or entry to educational institutions despite lower scores on qualifying exams. Even some beneficiaries of compensatory programs complained that the label of "affirmative action hire" could demean their individual talents. Courts struggled to square affirmative action programs with antidiscrimination precedents. They tended to strike down as unconstitutional affirmative action plans that contained inflexible quotas and to uphold less rigid plans that made group identity only one of many criteria that influenced hiring or educational decisions.

In 1996, after a hotly contested referendum campaign, voters in California passed Proposition 209, which aimed at ending most affirmative action measures in California by abolishing racial or gender preference in state hiring, contracting, and college admissions. Proposition 209 remained controversial, and proponents of affirmative action in California, over the next decade, challenged its constitutionality in federal and state courts.

Ironically, the debates over identity politics and affirmative action coincided with a rise in racial and ethnic intermarriage—a trend that might, in time, change the discussion. The 2000 census suggested that growing numbers of people identified themselves as "mixed race" and could not, or would not, claim a single ethnic-racial identity. In 1997 the media hailed Eldrick ("Tiger") Woods as the first African American golfer to win the prestigious Masters tournament, but Woods, whose mother was from Thailand, resisted the label. In an official statement, Woods said he was "equally proud" to be "both African American and Asian" but hoped that he could also "be just a golfer and a human being."

QUICK   REVIEW

CULTURAL DIGNITY MOVEMENTS

- Pressure for cultural recognition and antidiscrimination measures by feminist, racial and ethnic, and LGBT activists

- Controversy over affirmative action

- Critique of identity politics by the conservative movement

affirmative action *Programs or policies that attempt to compensate for past injustice or discrimination by promoting employment and educational opportunities.*

C O N C L U S I O N

The "Reagan Revolution" of the 1980s rested on a conservative movement that had been taking shape for several decades. New Right Republicans distrusted extending federal government power, advocated sharp tax cuts, and stressed a sociocultural agenda emphasizing "traditional" values. The dozen years of Republican dominance of the White House, from 1980 to 1992, helped shift the terms of political debate in the United States. The "liberal" label became one that most Democrats sought to avoid. In foreign policy, Reagan's military buildup coincided with—and contributed to, according to his admirers—the last years of the Cold War.

Meanwhile, American society seemed to fragment into specialized identifications. Social activism often organized around sexual, ethnic, and racial identities. Celebrants of multiculturalism celebrated this trend, while supporters of the New Right argued that identity politics was dividing the nation. The New Right's stress on limiting the power of government and promoting conservative values increasingly set the terms for public debate, reconfiguring discussions about how government power could best promote liberty and equality.

QUESTIONS FOR REVIEW AND CRITICAL THINKING

Review

1. How did the impact of the Vietnam War and Watergate eras help to shape the presidencies of Gerald Ford and Jimmy Carter?
2. To what extent did Ronald Reagan's eight years in the White House represent a victory for the New Right agenda, in both domestic and foreign policy?
3. What international forces and events contributed to the end of the Cold War?
4. How did social movements of the post-Sixties era affect social life, culture, and the ways people saw their own personal identities?

Critical Thinking

1. In what ways was the Reagan presidency simply *not* the Ford and Carter presidencies? In what other ways did the Reagan presidency establish a more forceful record, one indebted to the New-Right movement of the 1970s and 1980s?
2. In what ways did social movements continue to play such an important role in post-Sixties politics and culture?

ONLINE RESOURCES

 Visit the companion website to access flashcards, crossword puzzles, exercises, and quizzes related to this chapter: www.cengage.com/history/murrin/libertyequalconc5e.

 See our interactive ebook for map and primary source activities.

What were some of the key issues that helped shape American elections in the 25 years between 1974 and 1992?

FOREIGN POLICY Study this map and Map 23.2 on page 621. Examine the effects of the Soviet Union's 1989 collapse on the geography of Europe and Asia. How many independent nations in Europe and Asia emerged after 1989 from lands that had either been part of the Soviet Union or under Soviet control? What happened after 1989 to Czechoslovakia, Yugoslavia, Lithuania, Latvia, and Estonia, countries that the Treaty of Versailles had first brought into being in 1919? From your examination of the map on this page, what conclusions might you draw about the likely effects of the Soviet Union's collapse on politics in Europe, the Middle East, and Asia? Do you think the power of the Soviet Union is likely to be broadly dispersed among the many nations that once made it up, or do you think it will flow to and be reconsolidated by Russia? From your reading of this map, what would you identify as the likely geopolitical implications of the Soviet Union's collapse for the United States?

In thinking about this question, begin by breaking it down into the components shown below. A discussion of the significance of each component should appear in your answer.

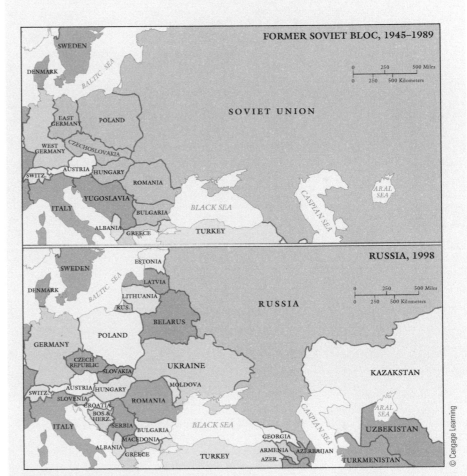

Map 30.3 COLLAPSE OF THE SOVIET BLOC

THE DECLARATION OF INDEPENDENCE

The Unanimous Declaration of the Thirteen United States of America

When in the Course of human events it becomes necessary for one people to dissolve the political bands which have connected them with another, and to assume among the Powers of the earth, the separate and equal station to which the Laws of Nature and of Nature's God entitle them, a decent respect to the opinions of mankind requires that they should declare the causes which impel them to the separation.

We hold these truths to be self-evident, that all men are created equal, that they are endowed by their Creator with certain unalienable Rights, that among these are Life, Liberty and the pursuit of Happiness. That to secure these rights, Governments are instituted among Men, deriving their just Powers from the consent of the governed. That whenever any Form of Government becomes destructive of these ends, it is the Right of the People to alter or to abolish it, and to institute new Government, laying its foundation on such principles and organizing its Powers in such form, as to them shall seem most likely to effect their Safety and Happiness. Prudence, indeed, will dictate that Governments long established should not be changed for light and transient causes; and accordingly all experience hath shewn, that mankind are more disposed to suffer, while evils are sufferable, than to right themselves by abolishing the forms to which they are accustomed. But when a long train of abuses and usurpations, pursuing invariably the same Object evinces a design to reduce them under absolute Despotism, it is their right, it is their duty, to throw off such Government, and to provide new Guards for their future security. Such has been the patient sufferance of these Colonies; and such is now the necessity which constrains them to alter their former Systems of Government. The history of the present King of Great Britain is a history of repeated injuries and usurpations, all having in direct object the establishment of an absolute Tyranny over these States. To prove this, let Facts be submitted to a candid world.

He has refused his Assent to Laws, the most wholesome and necessary for the public good.

He has forbidden his Governors to pass Laws of immediate and pressing importance, unless suspended in their operation till his Assent should be obtained; and when so suspended, he has utterly neglected to attend to them.

He has refused to pass other Laws for the accommodation of large districts of people, unless those people would relinquish the right of Representation in the Legislature, a right inestimable to them and formidable to tyrants only.

He has called together legislative bodies at places unusual, uncomfortable, and distant from the depository of their Public Records, for the sole Purpose of fatiguing them into compliance with his measures.

He has dissolved Representative Houses repeatedly, for opposing with manly firmness his invasions on the rights of the People.

He has refused for a long time, after such dissolutions, to cause others to be elected; whereby the Legislative Powers, incapable of Annihilation, have returned to the People at large for their exercise; the State remaining in the mean time exposed to all the dangers of invasion from without, and convulsions within.

He has endeavoured to prevent the Population of these States; for that purpose obstructing the Laws for Naturalization of Foreigners; refusing to pass others to encourage their migrations hither, and raising the conditions of new Appropriations of Lands.

He has obstructed the Administration of Justice, by refusing his Assent to Laws for establishing Judiciary Powers.

He has made Judges dependent on his Will alone, for the tenure of their offices, and the amount and payment of their salaries.

He has erected a multitude of New Offices, and sent hither swarms of Officers to harass our People, and eat out their substance.

He has kept among us, in times of peace, Standing Armies without the Consent of our legislatures.

He has affected to render the Military independent of and superior to the Civil Power.

He has combined with others to subject us to a jurisdiction foreign to our constitution, and unacknowledged by our laws; giving his Assent to their Acts of pretended Legislation: For Quartering large bodies of armed troops among us: For protecting them, by a mock Trial, from Punishment for any Murders which they should commit on the Inhabitants of these States: For cutting off our Trade with all parts of the world: For imposing Taxes on us without our Consent: For depriving us in many cases, of the benefits of Trial by Jury: For transporting us beyond Seas to be tried for pretended offences: For abolishing the free System of English Laws in a neighbouring Province, establishing therein an Arbitrary government, and enlarging its Boundaries so as to render it at once an example and fit instrument for introducing the same absolute rule into these Colonies: For taking away our Charters, abolishing our most valuable Laws, and altering fundamentally the Forms of

---

Text is reprinted from the facsimile of the engrossed copy in the National Archives. The original spelling, capitalization, and punctuation have been retained. Paragraphing has been added.

our Governments: For suspending our own Legislatures, and declaring themselves invested with Power to legislate for us in all cases whatsoever.

He has abdicated Government here, by declaring us out of his Protection, and waging War against us.

He has plundered our seas, ravaged our Coasts, burnt our towns, and destroyed the lives of our people.

He is at this time transporting large Armies of foreign Mercenaries to compleat the works of death, desolation and tyranny, already begun with circumstances of Cruelty and perfidy scarcely paralleled in the most barbarous ages, and totally unworthy the Head of a civilized nation.

He has constrained our fellow Citizens taken Captive on the high Seas to bear Arms against their Country, to become the executioners of their friends and Brethren, or to fall themselves by their Hands.

He has excited domestic insurrections amongst us, and has endeavoured to bring on the inhabitants of our frontiers, the merciless Indian Savages, whose known rule of warfare, is an undistinguished destruction of all ages, sexes and conditions.

In every stage of these Oppressions We have Petitioned for Redress in the most humble terms: Our repeated Petitions have been answered only by repeated injury. A Prince, whose character is thus marked by every act which may define a Tyrant, is unfit to be the ruler of a free People.

Nor have We been wanting in attentions to our British brethren. We have warned them from time to time of attempts by their legislature to extend an unwarrantable jurisdiction over us. We have reminded them of the circumstances of our emigration and settlement here. We have appealed to their native justice and magnanimity, and we have conjured them by the ties of our common kindred to disavow these usurpations, which, would inevitably interrupt our connections and correspondence. They too have been deaf to the voice of justice and of consanguinity. We must, therefore, acquiesce in the necessity, which denounces our Separation, and hold them, as we hold the rest of mankind, Enemies in War, in Peace Friends.

We, therefore, the Representatives of the United States of America, in General Congress, Assembled, appealing to the Supreme Judge of the world for the rectitude of our intentions, do, in the Name, and by Authority of the good People of these Colonies, solemnly publish and declare, That these United Colonies are, and of Right ought to be Free and Independent States; that they are Absolved from all Allegiance to the British Crown, and that all political connection between them and the State of Great Britain, is and ought to be totally dissolved; and that, as Free and Independent States, they have full Power to levy War, conclude Peace, contract Alliances, establish Commerce, and to do all other Acts and Things which Independent States may of right do. And for the support of this Declaration, with a firm reliance on the protection of divine Providence, we mutually pledge to each other our Lives, our Fortunes and our sacred Honor.

THE CONSTITUTION OF THE UNITED STATES OF AMERICA

We the People of the United States, in Order to form a more perfect Union, establish Justice, insure domestic Tranquility, provide for the common defence, promote the general Welfare, and secure the Blessings of Liberty to ourselves and our Posterity, do ordain and establish this Constitution for the United States of America.

Article I.

SECTION 1. All legislative Powers herein granted shall be vested in a Congress of the United States, which shall consist of a Senate and House of Representatives.

SECTION 2. The House of Representatives shall be composed of Members chosen every second Year by the People of the several States, and the Electors in each State shall have the Qualifications requisite for Electors of the most numerous Branch of the State Legislature.

No Person shall be a Representative who shall not have attained to the Age of twenty five Years, and been seven Years a Citizen of the United States, and who shall not, when elected, be an Inhabitant of that State in which he shall be chosen.

Representatives and direct Taxes[1] shall be apportioned among the several States which may be included within this Union, according to their respective Numbers, which shall be determined by adding to the whole Number of free Persons, including those bound to Service for a Term of Years, and excluding Indians not taxed, three fifths of all other Persons.[2]

The actual Enumeration shall be made within three Years after the first Meeting of the Congress of the United States, and within every subsequent Term of ten Years, in such Manner as they shall by Law direct. The Number of Representatives shall not exceed one for every thirty Thousand, but each State shall have at Least one Representative; and until such enumeration shall be made, the State of New Hampshire shall be entitled to chuse three; Massachusetts eight; Rhode Island and Providence Plantations one; Connecticut five; New York six; New Jersey four; Pennsylvania eight; Delaware one; Maryland six; Virginia ten; North Carolina five; South Carolina five; and Georgia three.

When vacancies happen in the Representation from any State, the Executive Authority thereof shall issue Writs of Election to fill such Vacancies.

The House of Representatives shall chuse their Speaker and other Officers; and shall have the sole Power of Impeachment.

SECTION 3. The Senate of the United States shall be composed of two Senators from each State, chosen by the Legislature thereof, for six Years; and each Senator shall have one Vote.[3]

Immediately after they shall be assembled in Consequence of the first Election, they shall be divided as equally as may be into three Classes. The Seats of the Senators of the first Class shall be vacated at the Expiration of the second Year, of the second Class at the Expiration of the fourth Year, and of the third Class at the Expiration of the sixth Year, so that one third may be chosen every second Year; and if Vacancies happen by Resignation, or otherwise, during the Recess of the Legislature of any State, the Executive thereof may make temporary Appointments until the next Meeting of the Legislature, which shall then fill such Vacancies.[4]

No Person shall be a Senator who shall not have attained to the Age of thirty Years, and been nine Years a Citizen of the United States, and who shall not, when elected, be an Inhabitant of that State for which he shall be chosen.

The Vice President of the United States shall be President of the Senate, but shall have no Vote, unless they be equally divided.

The Senate shall chuse their other Officers, and also a President pro tempore, in the Absence of the Vice President, or when he shall exercise the Office of President of the United States.

The Senate shall have the sole Power to try all Impeachments. When sitting for that Purpose, they shall be on Oath or Affirmation. When the President of the United States is tried, the Chief Justice shall preside: And no Person shall be convicted without the Concurrence of two thirds of the Members present.

Judgment in Cases of Impeachment shall not extend further than to removal from Office, and disqualification to hold and enjoy any Office of honor, Trust or Profit under the United States: but the Party convicted shall nevertheless be liable and subject to Indictment, Trial, Judgment and Punishment, according to Law.

SECTION 4. The Times, Places and Manner of holding Elections for Senators and Representatives, shall be prescribed in each State by the Legislature thereof, but the Congress may at any time by Law make or alter such Regulation, except as to the Places of chusing Senators.

The Congress shall assemble at least once in every Year, and such Meeting shall be on the first Monday in December, unless they shall by Law appoint a different Day.[5]

Text is from the engrossed copy in the National Archives. Original spelling, capitalization, and punctuation have been retained.
[1]Modified by the Sixteenth Amendment.
[2]Replaced by the Fourteenth Amendment.
[3]Superseded by the Seventeenth Amendment.
[4]Modified by the Seventeenth Amendment.
[5]Superseded by the Twentieth Amendment.

SECTION 5. Each House shall be the Judge of the Elections, Returns and Qualifications of its own Members, and a Majority of each shall constitute a Quorum to do Business; but a smaller Number may adjourn from day to day, and may be authorized to compel the Attendance of absent Members, in such Manner, and under such Penalties as each House may provide.

Each House may determine the Rules of its Proceedings, punish its Members for disorderly Behaviour, and, with the Concurrence of two thirds, expel a Member.

Each House shall keep a Journal of its Proceedings, and from time to time publish the same, excepting such Parts as may in their Judgment require Secrecy; and the Yeas and Nays of the Members of either House on any question shall, at the Desire of one fifth of those Present, be entered on the Journal.

Neither House, during the Session of Congress, shall, without the Consent of the other, adjourn for more than three days, nor to any other Place than that in which the two Houses shall be sitting.

SECTION 6. The Senators and Representatives shall receive a Compensation for their Services, to be ascertained by Law, and paid out of the Treasury of the United States. They shall in all Cases, except Treason, Felony and Breach of the Peace, be privileged from Arrest during their Attendance at the Session of their respective Houses, and in going to and returning from the same; and for any Speech or Debate in either House, they shall not be questioned in any other Place.

No Senator or Representative shall, during the Time for which he was elected, be appointed to any civil Office under the Authority of the United States, which shall have been created, or the Emoluments whereof shall have been encreased during such time; and no Person holding any Office under the United States, shall be a Member of either House during his Continuance in Office.

SECTION 7. All Bills for raising Revenue shall originate in the House of Representatives; but the Senate may propose or concur with Amendments as on other Bills.

Every Bill which shall have passed the House of Representatives and the Senate shall, before it become a Law, be presented to the President of the United States; If he approve he shall sign it, but if not he shall return it, with his Objections to that House in which it shall have originated, who shall enter the Objections at large on their Journal, and proceed to reconsider it. If after such Reconsideration two thirds of that House shall agree to pass the Bill, it shall be sent, together with the Objections, to the other House, by which it shall likewise be reconsidered, and if approved by two thirds of that House, it shall become a Law. But in all such Cases the Votes of both Houses shall be determined by yeas and Nays, and the Names of the Persons voting for and against the Bill shall be entered on the Journal of each House respectively. If any Bill shall not be returned by the President within ten Days (Sundays excepted) after it shall have been presented to him, the Same shall be a Law, in like Manner as if he had signed it, unless the Congress by their Adjournment prevent its Return, in which Case it shall not be a Law.

Every Order, Resolution, or Vote to which the Concurrence of the Senate and House of Representatives may be necessary (except on a question of Adjournment) shall be presented to the President of the United States; and before the Same shall take Effect, shall be approved by him, or being disapproved by him shall be repassed by two thirds of the Senate and House of Representatives, according to the Rules and Limitations prescribed in the Case of a Bill.

SECTION 8. The Congress shall have power To lay and collect Taxes, Duties, Imposts and Excises, to pay the Debts and provide for the common Defence and general Welfare of the United States; but all Duties, Imposts and Excises shall be uniform throughout the United States; To borrow Money on the credit of the United States; To regulate Commerce with foreign Nations, and among the several States, and with the Indian Tribes; To establish an uniform Rule of Naturalization, and uniform Laws on the subject of Bankruptcies throughout the United States; To coin Money, regulate the Value thereof, and of foreign Coin, and fix the Standard of Weights and Measures; To provide for the Punishment of counterfeiting the Securities and current Coin of the United States; To establish Post Offices and post Roads; To promote the Progress of Science and useful Arts, by securing for limited Times to Authors and Inventors the exclusive Right to their respective Writings and Discoveries; To constitute Tribunals inferior to the supreme Court; To define and punish Piracies and Felonies committed on the high Seas, and Offences against the Law of Nations;

To declare War, grant Letters of Marque and Reprisal, and make Rules concerning Captures on Land and Water; To raise and support Armies, but no Appropriation of Money to that Use shall be for a longer Term than two Years; To provide and maintain a Navy; To make Rules for the Government and Regulation of the land and naval Forces; To provide for calling forth the Militia to execute the Laws of the Union, suppress Insurrections and repel Invasions; To provide for organizing, arming, and disciplining, the Militia, and for governing such Part of them as may be employed in the Service of the United States, reserving to the States respectively, the Appointment of the Officers, and the Authority of training the Militia according to the discipline prescribed by Congress; To exercise exclusive Legislation in all Cases whatsoever, over such District (not exceeding ten Miles square) as may, by Cession of particular States, and the Acceptance of Congress, become the Seat of the Government of the United States, and to exercise like Authority over all Places purchased by the Consent of the Legislature of the State in which the Same shall be, for the Erection of Forts, Magazines, Arsenals, dock-Yards, and other needful Buildings;—And To make all Laws which shall be necessary and proper for carrying into Execution the foregoing Powers, and all other Powers vested by this Constitution in the Government of the United States, or in any Department or Officer thereof.

SECTION 9. The Migration or Importation of such Persons as any of the States now existing shall think proper to admit, shall not be prohibited by the Congress prior to the Year one thousand eight hundred and eight, but a Tax or duty may be imposed on such Importation, not exceeding ten dollars for each Person.

The Privilege of the Writ of Habeas Corpus shall not be suspended, unless when in Cases of Rebellion or Invasion the public Safety may require it.

No Bill of Attainder or ex post facto Law shall be passed.

No Capitation, or other direct, Tax shall be laid, unless in Proportion to the Census or Enumeration herein before directed to be taken.

No Tax or Duty shall be laid on Articles exported from any State.

No Preference shall be given by any Regulation of Commerce or Revenue to the Ports of one State over those of another: nor shall Vessels bound to, or from, one State, be obliged to enter, clear, or pay Duties in another.

No Money shall be drawn from the Treasury, but in Consequence of Appropriations made by Law, and a regular Statement and Account of the Receipts and Expenditures of all public Money shall be published from time to time.

No Title of Nobility shall be granted by the United States: And no Person holding any Office of Profit or Trust under them, shall, without the Consent of the Congress, accept of any present, Emolument, Office, or Title, of any kind whatever, from any King, Prince, or foreign State.

SECTION 10. No State shall enter into any Treaty, Alliance, or Confederation; grant Letters of Marque and Reprisal; coin Money; emit Bills of Credit; make any Thing but gold and silver Coin a Tender in Payment of Debts; pass any Bill of Attainder, ex post facto Law, or Law impairing the Obligation of Contracts, or grant any Title of Nobility.

No State shall, without the Consent of the Congress, lay any Imposts or Duties on Imports or Exports, except what may be absolutely necessary for executing its inspection Laws: and the net Produce of all Duties and Imposts, laid by any State on Imports or Exports, shall be for the Use of the Treasury of the United States; and all such Laws shall be subject to the Revision and Controul of the Congress.

No State shall, without the Consent of Congress, lay any Duty of Tonnage, keep Troops, or Ships of War in time of Peace, enter into any Agreement or Compact with another State, or with a foreign Power, or engage in War, unless actually invaded, or in such imminent Danger as will not admit of delay.

Article II.

SECTION 1. The executive Power shall be vested in a President of the United States of America. He shall hold his Office during the Term of four Years, and, together with the Vice President, chosen for the same Term, be elected, as follows: Each State shall appoint, in such Manner as the Legislature thereof may direct, a Number of Electors, equal to the whole Number of Senators and Representatives to which the State may be entitled in the Congress: but no Senator or Representative, or Person holding an Office of Trust or Profit under the United States, shall be appointed an Elector.

The Electors shall meet in their respective States, and vote by Ballot for two Persons, of whom one at least shall not be an Inhabitant of the same State with themselves. And they shall make a List of all the Persons voted for, and of the Number of Votes for each; which List they shall sign and certify, and transmit sealed to the Seat of the Government of the United States, directed to the President of the Senate. The President of the Senate shall, in the Presence of the Senate and House of Representatives, open all the Certificates, and the Votes shall then be counted. The Person having the greatest Number of Votes shall be the President, if such Number be a Majority of the whole Number of Electors appointed; and if there be more than one who have such Majority, and have an equal Number of Votes, then the House of Representatives shall immediately chuse by Ballot one of them for President; and if no Person have a Majority, then from the five highest on the List the said House shall in like Manner chuse the President. But in chusing the President, the Votes shall be taken by States, the Representation from each State having one Vote; A quorum for this Purpose shall consist of a Member or Members from two thirds of the States, and a Majority of all the States shall be necessary to a Choice. In every Case, after the Choice of the President, the Person having the greatest Number of Votes of the Electors shall be the Vice President. But if there should remain two or more who have equal Votes, the Senate shall chuse from them by Ballot the Vice President.[6]

The Congress may determine the Time of chusing the Electors, and the Day on which they shall give their Votes; which Day shall be the same throughout the United States.

No Person except a natural born Citizen, or a Citizen of the United States, at the time of the Adoption of this Constitution, shall be eligible to the Office of President, neither shall any Person be eligible to that Office who shall not have attained to the Age of thirty five Years, and been fourteen Years a Resident within the United States.

In Case of the Removal of the President from Office, or of his Death, Resignation, or Inability to discharge the Powers and Duties of the said Office, the Same shall devolve on the Vice President, and the Congress may by Law provide for the Case of Removal, Death, Resignation or Inability, both of the President and Vice President, declaring what Officer shall then act as President, and such Officer shall act accordingly, until the Disability be removed, or a President shall be elected.[7]

The President shall, at stated Times, receive for his Services, a Compensation, which shall neither be encreased nor diminished during the Period for which he shall have been elected, and he shall not receive within that Period any other Emolument from the United States, or any of them.

Before he enter on the Execution of his Office, he shall take the following Oath or Affirmation:—"I do solemnly swear (or affirm) that I will faithfully execute the Office of President of the United States, and will to the best of my Ability, preserve, protect and defend the Constitution of the United States."

SECTION 2. The President shall be Commander in Chief of the Army and Navy of the United States, and of the Militia of the several States, when called into the actual Service of the United States; he may require the Opinion, in writing, of the principal Officer in each of the executive Departments, upon any Subject relating to the Duties of their respective Offices, and he shall have Power to grant Reprieves and Pardons for Offences against the United States, except in Cases of Impeachment.

He shall have Power, by and with the Advice and Consent of the Senate, to make Treaties, provided two thirds of the Senators present concur; and he shall nominate, and by and with the Advice and Consent of the Senate, shall appoint Ambassadors, other public Ministers and Consuls, Judges of the supreme Court, and all other Officers of the United States,

---

[6]Superseded by the Twelfth Amendment.
[7]Modified by the Twenty-fifth Amendment.

whose Appointments are not herein otherwise provided for, and which shall be established by Law; but the Congress may by Law vest the Appointment of such inferior Officers, as they think proper, in the President alone, in the Courts of Law, or in the Heads of Departments.

The President shall have Power to fill up all Vacancies that may happen during the Recess of the Senate, by granting Commissions which shall expire at the End of their next Session.

SECTION 3. He shall from time to time give the Congress Information of the State of the Union, and recommend to their Consideration such Measures as he shall judge necessary and expedient; he may, on extraordinary Occasions, convene both Houses, or either of them, and in Case of Disagreement between them, with Respect to the Time of Adjournment, he may adjourn them to such Time as he shall think proper; he shall receive Ambassadors and other public Ministers; he shall take Care that the Laws be faithfully executed, and shall Commission all the Officers of the United States.

SECTION 4. The President, Vice President and all civil Officers of the United States, shall be removed from Office on Impeachment for, and Conviction of, Treason, Bribery, or other high Crimes and Misdemeanors.

Article III.

SECTION 1. The judicial Power of the United States, shall be vested in one supreme Court, and in such inferior Courts as the Congress may from time to time ordain and establish.

The Judges, both of the supreme and inferior Courts, shall hold their Offices during good Behaviour, and shall, at stated Times, receive for their Services, a Compensation, which shall not be diminished during their Continuance in Office.

SECTION 2. The judicial Power shall extend to all Cases, in Law and Equity, arising under this Constitution, the Laws of the United States, and Treaties made, or which shall be made, under their Authority;—to all Cases affecting Ambassadors, other public Ministers and Consuls;—to all Cases of admiralty and maritime Jurisdiction;—to Controversies to which the United States shall be a Party;—to Controversies between two or more States;—between a State and Citizens of another State;[8]—between Citizens of different States,—between Citizens of the same State claiming Lands under Grants of different States, and between a State, or the Citizens thereof, and foreign States, Citizens or Subjects.

In all Cases affecting Ambassadors, other public Ministers and Consuls, and those in which a State shall be Party, the supreme Court shall have original Jurisdiction. In all the other Cases before mentioned, the supreme Court shall have appellate Jurisdiction, both as to Law and Fact, with such Exceptions, and under such Regulations as the Congress shall make.

The Trial of all Crimes, except in Cases of Impeachment, shall be by Jury; and such Trial shall be held in the State where the said Crimes shall have been committed; but when not committed within any State, the Trial shall be at such Place or Places as the Congress may by Law have directed.

SECTION 3. Treason against the United States, shall consist only in levying War against them, or in adhering to their Enemies, giving them Aid and Comfort. No Person shall be convicted of Treason unless on the Testimony of two Witnesses to the same overt Act, or on Confession in open Court.

The Congress shall have Power to declare the Punishment of Treason, but no Attainder of Treason shall work Corruption of Blood, or Forfeiture except during the Life of the Person attainted.

Article IV.

SECTION 1. Full Faith and Credit shall be given in each State to the public Acts, Records, and judicial Proceedings of every other State. And the Congress may by general Laws prescribe the Manner in which such Acts, Records and Proceedings shall be proved, and the Effect thereof.

SECTION 2. The Citizens of each State shall be entitled to all Privileges and Immunities of Citizens in the several States.

A Person charged in any State with Treason, Felony, or other Crime, who shall flee from Justice, and be found in another State, shall on Demand of the executive Authority of the State from which he fled, be delivered up, to be removed to the State having Jurisdiction of the Crime.

No Person held to Service or Labour in one State, under the Laws thereof, escaping into another, shall, in Consequence of any Law or Regulation therein, be discharged from such Service or Labour, but shall be delivered up on Claim of the Party to whom such Service or Labour may be due.

SECTION 3. New States may be admitted by the Congress into this Union; but no new State shall be formed or erected within the Jurisdiction of any other State, nor any State be formed by the Junction of two or more States, or Parts of States, without the Consent of the Legislatures of the States concerned as well as of the Congress.

The Congress shall have Power to dispose of and make all needful Rules and Regulations respecting the Territory or other Property belonging to the United States; and nothing in this Constitution shall be so construed as to Prejudice any Claims of the United States, or of any particular State.

SECTION 4. The United States shall guarantee to every State in this Union a Republican Form of Government, and shall protect each of them against Invasion; and on Application of the Legislature, or of the Executive (when the Legislature cannot be convened) against domestic Violence.

Article V.

The Congress, whenever two thirds of both Houses shall deem it necessary, shall propose Amendments to this Constitution, or, on the Application of the Legislatures of two thirds of the several States, shall call a Convention for proposing Amendments, which, in either Case, shall be valid to all Intents and Purposes, as Part of this Constitution, when ratified by the Legislatures of three fourths of the several States, or by

[8]Modified by the Eleventh Amendment.

Conventions in three fourths thereof, as the one or the other Mode of Ratification may be proposed by the Congress; Provided that no Amendment which may be made prior to the Year One thousand eight hundred and eight shall in any Manner affect the first and fourth Clauses in the Ninth Section of the first Article; and that no State, without its Consent, shall be deprived of its equal Suffrage in the Senate.

Article VI.

All Debts contracted and Engagements entered into, before the Adoption of this Constitution, shall be as valid against the United States under this Constitution, as under the Confederation.

This Constitution, and the Laws of the United States which shall be made in Pursuance thereof; and all Treaties made, or which shall be made, under the Authority of the United States, shall be the supreme Law of the Land; and the Judges in every State shall be bound thereby, any Thing in the Constitution or Laws of any State to the Contrary notwithstanding.

The Senators and Representatives before mentioned, and the Members of the several State Legislatures, and all executive and judicial Officers, both of the United States and of the several States, shall be bound by Oath or Affirmation, to support this Constitution; but no religious Test shall ever be required as a Qualification to any Office or public Trust under the United States.

Article VII.

The Ratification of the Conventions of nine States, shall be sufficient for the Establishment of this Constitution between the States so ratifying the Same.

Done in Convention by the Unanimous Consent of the States present the Seventeenth Day of September in the Year of our Lord one thousand seven hundred and Eighty seven and of the Independence of the United States of America the Twelfth. In witness whereof We have hereunto subscribed our Names,

Articles in Addition to, and Amendment of, the Constitution of the United States of America, Proposed by Congress, and Ratified by the Legislatures of the Several States, Pursuant to the Fifth Article of the Original Constitution.

Amendment I[9]

Congress shall make no law respecting an establishment of religion, or prohibiting the free exercise thereof; or abridging the freedom of speech, or of the press; or the right of the people peaceably to assemble, and to petition the Government for a redress of grievances.

Amendment II

A well regulated Militia, being necessary to the security of a free State, the right of the people to keep and bear Arms shall not be infringed.

Amendment III

No Soldier shall, in time of peace, be quartered in any house, without the consent of the Owner, nor in time of war, but in a manner to be prescribed by law.

Amendment IV

The right of the people to be secure in their persons, houses, papers, and effects, against unreasonable searches and seizures, shall not be violated, and no Warrants shall issue, but upon probable cause, supported by Oath or affirmation, and particularly describing the place to be searched, and the persons or things to be seized.

Amendment V

No person shall be held to answer for a capital or otherwise infamous crime, unless on a presentment or indictment of a Grand Jury, except in cases arising in the land or naval forces, or in the Militia, when in actual service in time of War or public danger; nor shall any person be subject for the same offence to be twice put in jeopardy of life or limb; nor shall be compelled in any criminal case to be a witness against himself, nor be deprived of life, liberty, or property, without due process of law; nor shall private property be taken for public use, without just compensation.

Amendment VI

In all criminal prosecutions, the accused shall enjoy the right to a speedy and public trial, by an impartial jury of the State and district wherein the crime shall have been committed, which district shall have been previously ascertained by law, and to be informed of the nature and cause of the accusation; to be confronted with the witnesses against him; to have compulsory process for obtaining witnesses in his favor, and to have the Assistance of Counsel for his defence.

Amendment VII

In suits at common law, where the value in controversy shall exceed twenty dollars, the right of trial by jury shall be preserved, and no fact tried by a jury, shall be otherwise reexamined in any Court of the United States, than according to the rules of the common law.

Amendment VIII

Excessive bail shall not be required, nor excessive fines imposed, nor cruel and unusual punishments inflicted.

Amendment IX

The enumeration in the Constitution, of certain rights, shall not be construed to deny or disparage others retained by the people.

Amendment X

The powers not delegated to the United States by the Constitution; nor prohibited by it to the States, are reserved to the States respectively, or to the people.

[9]The first ten amendments were passed by Congress September 25, 1789. They were ratified by three-fourths of the states December 15, 1791.

Amendment XI[10]

The Judicial power of the United States shall not be construed to extend to any suit in law or equity, commenced or prosecuted against one of the United States by Citizens of another State, or by Citizens or Subjects of any Foreign State.

Amendment XII[11]

The Electors shall meet in their respective States and vote by ballot for President and Vice-President, one of whom, at least, shall not be an inhabitant of the same State with themselves; they shall name in their ballots the person voted for as President, and in distinct ballots the person voted for as Vice-President, and they shall make distinct lists of all persons voted for as President, and of all persons voted for as Vice-President, and of the number of votes for each, which lists they shall sign and certify, and transmit sealed to the seat of the government of the United States, directed to the President of the Senate;—The President of the Senate shall, in the presence of the Senate and House of Representatives, open all the certificates and the votes shall then be counted;—The person having the greatest number of votes for President, shall be the President, if such number be a majority of the whole number of Electors appointed; and if no person have such majority, then from the persons having the highest numbers not exceeding three on the list of those voted for as President, the House of Representatives shall choose immediately, by ballot, the President.

But in choosing the President, the votes shall be taken by states, the representation from each state having one vote; a quorum for this purpose shall consist of a member or members from two-thirds of the states, and a majority of all the states shall be necessary to a choice. And if the House of Representatives shall not choose a President whenever the right of choice shall devolve upon them, before the fourth day of March next following, then the Vice-President shall act as President, as in the case of the death or other constitutional disability of the President.—The person having the greatest number of votes as Vice-President, shall be the Vice-President, if such number be a majority of the whole number of Electors appointed, and if no person have a majority, then from the two highest numbers on the list, the Senate shall choose the Vice-President; a quorum for the purpose shall consist of two-thirds of the whole number of Senators, and a majority of the whole number shall be necessary to a choice. But no person constitutionally ineligible to the office of President shall be eligible to that of Vice-President of the United States.

Amendment XIII[12]

SECTION 1. Neither slavery nor involuntary servitude, except as a punishment for crime whereof the party shall have been duly convicted, shall exist within the United States, or any place subject to their jurisdiction.

SECTION 2. Congress shall have power to enforce this article by appropriate legislation.

Amendment XIV[13]

SECTION 1. All persons born or naturalized in the United States, and subject to the jurisdiction thereof, are citizens of the United States and of the State wherein they reside. No State shall make or enforce any law which shall abridge the privileges or immunities of citizens of the United States; nor shall any State deprive any person of life, liberty, or property, without due process of law; nor deny to any person within its jurisdiction the equal protection of the laws.

SECTION 2. Representatives shall be apportioned among the several States according to their respective numbers, counting the whole number of persons in each State, excluding Indians not taxed. But when the right to vote at any election for the choice of electors for President and Vice-President of the United States, Representatives in Congress, the Executive and Judicial officers of a State, or the members of the Legislature thereof, is denied to any of the male inhabitants of such State, being twenty-one years of age, and citizens of the United States, or in any way abridged, except for participation in rebellion, or other crime, the basis of representation therein shall be reduced in the proportion which the number of such male citizens shall bear to the whole number of male citizens twenty-one years of age in such State.

SECTION 3. No person shall be a Senator or Representative in Congress, or elector of President and Vice-President, or hold any office, civil or military, under the United States, or under any State, who, having previously taken an oath, as a member of Congress, or as an officer of the United States, or as a member of any State legislature, or as an executive or judicial officer of any State, to support the Constitution of the United States, shall have engaged in insurrection or rebellion against the same, or given aid or comfort to the enemies thereof. But Congress may by a vote of two-thirds of each House, remove such disability.

SECTION 4. The validity of the public debt of the United States, authorized by law, including debts incurred for payment of pensions and bounties for services in suppressing insurrection or rebellion, shall not be questioned. But neither the United States nor any State shall assume or pay any debt or obligation incurred in aid of insurrection or rebellion against the United States, or any claim for the loss or emancipation of any slave; but all such debts, obligations, and claims shall be held illegal and void.

SECTION 5. The Congress shall have the power to enforce, by appropriate legislation, the provisions of this article.

Amendment XV[14]

SECTION 1. The right of citizens of the United States to vote shall not be denied or abridged by the United States or by any State on account of race, color, or previous conditions of servitude—

---

[10]Passed March 4, 1794. Ratified January 23, 1795.
[11]Passed December 9, 1803. Ratified June 15, 1804.
[12]Passed January 31, 1865. Ratified December 6, 1865.
[13]Passed June 13, 1866. Ratified July 9, 1868.
[14]Passed February 26, 1869. Ratified February 2, 1870.

SECTION 2. The Congress shall have power to enforce this article by appropriate legislation.

Amendment XVI[15]

The Congress shall have power to lay and collect taxes on incomes, from whatever source derived, without apportionment among the several States, and without regard to any census or enumeration.

Amendment XVII[16]

The Senate of the United States shall be composed of two Senators from each State, elected by the people thereof, for six years; and each Senator shall have one vote. The electors in each State shall have the qualifications requisite for electors of the most numerous branch of the State legislatures.

When vacancies happen in the representation of any State in the Senate, the executive authority of such State shall issue writs of election to fill such vacancies: Provided, That the legislature of any State may empower the executive thereof to make temporary appointments until the people fill the vacancies by election as the legislature may direct.

This amendment shall not be so construed as to affect the election or term of any Senator chosen before it becomes valid as part of the Constitution.

Amendment XVIII[17]

SECTION 1. After one year from the ratification of this article the manufacture, sale, or transportation of intoxicating liquors within, the importation thereof into, or the exportation thereof from the United States and all territory subject to the jurisdiction thereof for beverage purposes is hereby prohibited.

SECTION 2. The Congress and the several States shall have concurrent power to enforce this article by appropriate legislation.

SECTION 3. This article shall be inoperative unless it shall have been ratified as an amendment to the Constitution by the legislatures of the several States, as provided in the Constitution, within seven years from the date of the submission hereof to the States by the Congress.

Amendment XIX[18]

The right of citizens of the United States to vote shall not be denied or abridged by the United States or by any State on account of sex.

Congress shall have power to enforce this article by appropriate legislation.

Amendment XX[19]

SECTION 1. The terms of the President and Vice-President shall end at noon on the 20th day of January, and the terms of Senators and Representatives at noon on the 3d day of January, of the years in which such terms would have ended if this article had not been ratified; and the terms of their successors shall then begin.

SECTION 2. The Congress shall assemble at least once in every year, and such meeting shall begin at noon on the 3d day of January, unless they shall by law appoint a different day.

SECTION 3. If, at the time fixed for the beginning of the term of the President, the President elect shall have died, the Vice-President elect shall become President. If a President shall not have been chosen before the time fixed for the beginning of his term, or if the President elect shall have failed to qualify, then the Vice-President elect shall act as President until a President shall have qualified; and the Congress may by law provide for the case wherein neither a President elect nor a Vice-President elect shall have qualified, declaring who shall then act as President, or the manner in which one who is to act shall be selected, and such person shall act accordingly until a President or Vice-President shall have qualified.

SECTION 4. The Congress may by law provide for the case of the death of any of the persons from whom the House of Representatives may choose a President whenever the right of choice shall have devolved upon them, and for the case of the death of any of the persons from whom the Senate may choose a Vice-President whenever the right of choice shall have devolved upon them.

SECTION 5. Sections 1 and 2 shall take effect on the 15th day of October following the ratification of this article.

SECTION 6. This article shall be inoperative unless it shall have been ratified as an amendment to the Constitution by the legislatures of three-fourths of the several States within seven years from the date of its submission.

Amendment XXI[20]

SECTION 1. The eighteenth article of amendment to the Constitution of the United States is hereby repealed.

SECTION 2. The transportation or importation into any State, Territory, or possession of the United States for delivery or use therein of intoxicating liquors, in violation of the laws thereof, is hereby prohibited.

SECTION 3. This article shall be inoperative unless it shall have been ratified as an amendment to the Constitution by

---

[15]Passed July 12, 1909. Ratified February 3, 1913.
[16]Passed May 13, 1912. Ratified April 8, 1913.
[17]Passed December 18, 1917. Ratified January 16, 1919.
[18]Passed June 4, 1919. Ratified August 18, 1920.
[19]Passed March 2, 1932. Ratified January 23, 1933.
[20]Passed February 20, 1933. Ratified December 5, 1933.

conventions in the several States, as provided in the Constitution, within seven years from the date of the submission hereof to the States by the Congress.

Amendment XXII[21]

No person shall be elected to the office of the President more than twice, and no person who has held the office of President, or acted as President, for more than two years of a term to which some other person was elected President shall be elected to the office of the President more than once.

But this Article shall not apply to any person holding the office of President when this Article was proposed by the Congress, and shall not prevent any person who may be holding the office of President, or acting as President, during the term within which this Article becomes operative from holding the office of President or acting as President during the remainder of such term.

Amendment XXIII[22]

SECTION 1. The District constituting the seat of Government of the United States shall appoint in such manner as the Congress may direct: A number of electors of President and Vice President equal to the whole number of Senators and Representatives in Congress to which the District would be entitled if it were a State, but in no event more than the least populous State; they shall be in addition to those appointed by the States, but they shall be considered, for the purposes of the election of President and Vice President, to be electors appointed by the State; and they shall meet in the District and perform such duties as provided by the twelfth article of amendment.

SECTION 2. The Congress shall have power to enforce this article by appropriate legislation.

Amendment XXIV[23]

SECTION 1. The right of citizens of the United States to vote in any primary or other election for President or Vice President, or for Senator or Representative in Congress, shall not be denied or abridged by the United States or any State by reason of failure to pay any poll tax or other tax.

SECTION 2. The Congress shall have power to enforce this article by appropriate legislation.

Amendment XXV[24]

SECTION 1. In case of the removal of the President from office or of his death or resignation, the Vice President shall become President.

SECTION 2. Whenever there is a vacancy in the office of the Vice President, the President shall nominate a Vice President who shall take office upon confirmation by a majority vote of both Houses of Congress.

SECTION 3. Whenever the President transmits to the President pro tempore of the Senate and the Speaker of the House of Representatives his written declaration that he is unable to discharge the powers and duties of his office, and until he transmits them a written declaration to the contrary, such powers and duties shall be discharged by the Vice President as Acting President.

SECTION 4. Whenever the Vice President and a majority of either the principal officers of the executive department or of such other body as Congress may by law provide, transmit to the President pro tempore of the Senate and the Speaker of the House of Representatives their written declaration that the President is unable to discharge the powers and duties of his office, the Vice President shall immediately assume the powers and duties of the office of Acting President

Thereafter, when the President transmits to the President pro tempore of the Senate and the Speaker of the House of Representatives his written declaration that no inability exists, he shall resume the powers and duties of his office unless the Vice President and a majority of either the principal officers of the executive department or of such other body as Congress may by law provide, transmit within four days to the President pro tempore of the Senate and the Speaker of the House of Representatives their written declaration that the President is unable to discharge the powers and duties of his office. Thereupon Congress shall decide the issue, assembling within forty-eight hours for that purpose if not in session. If the Congress, within twenty-one days after receipt of the latter written declaration, or, if Congress is not in session, within twenty-one days after Congress is required to assemble, determines by two-thirds vote of both Houses that the President is unable to discharge the powers and duties of his office, the Vice President shall continue to discharge the same as Acting President; otherwise, the President shall resume the powers and duties of his office.

Amendment XXVI[25]

SECTION 1. The right of citizens of the United States, who are eighteen years of age or older, to vote shall not be denied or abridged by the United States or by any State on account of age.

SECTION 2. The Congress shall have power to enforce this article by appropriate legislation.

Amendment XXVII[26]

No law, varying the compensation for the service of the Senators and Representatives, shall take effect, until an election of Representatives shall have intervened.

[21]Passed March 12, 1947. Ratified March 1, 1951.
[22]Passed June 16, 1960. Ratified April 3, 1961.
[23]Passed August 27, 1962. Ratified January 23, 1964.
[24]Passed July 6, 1965. Ratified February 11, 1967.
[25]Passed March 23, 1971. Ratified July 5, 1971.
[26]Passed September 25, 1789. Ratified May 7, 1992.

1919 steel strike Walkout by 300,000 steelworkers in the Midwest demanding union recognition and an 8-hour day. It was defeated by employers and local and state police forces, who sometimes resorted to violence.

40 acres and a mule Largely unfulfilled hope of many former slaves that they would receive free land from the confiscated property of ex-Confederates.

9th and 10th U.S. Cavalry African-American army units that played pivotal roles in the Spanish-American war.

abolitionism Movement begun in the North about 1830 to abolish slavery immediately and without compensation to owners.

abolitionist A person who wanted to abolish slavery.

abrogating a treaty Process of abolishing a treaty so that it is no longer in effect.

affirmative action Program or policy that attempted to compensate for past injustice or discrimination to ensure more employment and educational opportunities.

affluence Abundance of material goods or wealth.

Agricultural Adjustment Administration (AAA) 1933 attempt to promote economic recovery by reducing supply of crops, dairy, and meat produced by American farmers.

Aguinaldo, Emilio Anticolonial leader who fought for independence of the Philippines first from Spain and then from the United States.

Alamo Battle between Texas revolutionaries and the Mexican army at the San Antonio mission called the *Alamo* on March 6, 1836, in which all 187 Texans were killed.

Albany Congress An intercolonial congress that met in Albany, New York, in June 1754. The delegates urged the Crown to assume direct control of Indian relations beyond the settled boundaries of the colonies, and they drafted a plan of confederation for the continental colonies. No colony ratified it, nor did the Crown or Parliament accept it.

Algonquians Indian peoples who spoke some dialect of the Algonquian language family.

alien Person from another country who is living in the United States.

American Anti-Slavery Society Organization created by northern abolitionists in 1833 that called for immediate, uncompensated emancipation of the slaves.

American Colonization Society Established by elite gentlemen of the middle and upper-south states in 1816, this organization encouraged voluntary emancipation of slaves, to be followed by their emigration to the West African colony of Liberia.

American System Program proposed by Henry Clay and others to foster national economic growth and interdependence among the geographical sections. It included a protective tariff, a national bank, and internal improvements.

Amerind The forerunner of the vast majority of Indian languages in the Americas.

amnesty General pardon granted to a large group of people.

anarchist Activist who calls for the violent destruction of the capitalist system so that a new socialist order can be built.

Anasazi An advanced pre-Columbian cliff-dwelling culture that flourished for two centuries in what are now the states of Arizona, New Mexico, Utah, and Colorado before abandoning these sites in the late 13th century A.D.

Anderson, Marian Black opera singer who broke a color bar in 1939 when she sang to an interracial audience of 75,000 from the steps of the Lincoln Memorial.

Anglican A member of the legally established Church of England, or that church itself.

Anglos English-speaking people.

anxious bench Bench at or near the front of a religious revival meeting where the most likely converts were seated.

apartheid Legal system practiced in South Africa and based on elaborate rules of racial separation and subordination of blacks.

armistice A temporary stop in fighting. Often in effect before a final peace treaty is signed.

Article X of the Covenant Addendum to the Treaty of Versailles that empowered the League of Nations to undertake military actions against aggressor nations.

artisan A skilled laborer who works with his hands. In early America, artisans often owned their own shops and produced goods either for general sale or for special order.

Association Groups created by the First Continental Congress in local committees to enforce its trade sanctions against Britain. The creation of these groups was an important sign that Congress was beginning to act as a central government.

associationalism Herbert Hoover's approach to managing the economy. Firms and organizations in each economic sector would be asked to cooperate with each other in the pursuit of efficiency, profit, and the public good.

astrolabe A device that permitted accurate calculation of latitude or distances north and south.

Atlantic slave trade A European commerce that led to the enslavement of millions of people who were shipped from their African homelands to European colonies in the Americas.

attrition A type of warfare in which an effort is made to exhaust the manpower, supplies, and morale of the other side.

Auburn system Prison system designed to reform criminals and reduce expenses through the sale of items produced in workshops. Prisoners slept in solitary cells, marched in military formation to meals and workshops, and were forbidden to speak to one another at any time.

Australian ballot (secret ballot) Practice that required citizens to vote in private rather than in public and required the government (rather than political parties) to supervise the voting process.

Aztec The last pre-Columbian high culture in the Valley of Mexico. It was conquered by the Spaniards in 1519–1521.

baby boom Sudden increase in births in the years after World War II.

backcountry Term used in the 18th and early 19th centuries to refer to the western settlements and the supposed misfits who lived in them.

Bacon's Rebellion The most serious challenge to royal authority in the English mainland colonies prior to 1775. It erupted in Virginia in 1676 after the governor and Nathaniel Bacon, the principal rebel, could not agree on how best to wage war against frontier Indians.

balance of trade The relationship between imports and exports. The difference between exports and imports is the balance between the two. A healthy nation should export more than it imports. This is known as a favorable balance of trade.

bandeirantes Brazilian frontiersmen who traveled deep into South America to enslave Indians. The slaves then were worked to death on the sugar plantations.

banknotes Paper money, issued by banks, that circulated as currency.

barrios Spanish-speaking urban areas, usually separate districts in southwestern towns and cities.

bateau A light, flat-bottomed boat with narrow ends that was used in Canada and the northeastern part of the colonies.

Battle of Lexington The first military engagement of the Revolutionary War. It occurred on April 19, 1775, when British soldiers fired into a much smaller body of minutemen on Lexington green.

Battle of Little Big Horn A battle in eastern Montana Territory on the bluffs above Little Big Horn River on June 25, 1876.

Bay of Pigs Site of an ill-fated 1961 invasion of Cuba by a U.S.-trained force that attempted to overthrow the government of Fidel Castro.

Beatles Preeminent musical group associated with the "British invasion" in the 1960s.

belligerent Country actively engaged in a war.

Beringia A land bridge during the last ice age across the Bering Strait between Siberia and Alaska. It was once an area where plants, animals, and humans could live.

bicameral legislature A legislature with two houses or chambers.

Bill of Rights First ten amendments to the Constitution, which protect the rights of individuals from abuses by the federal government.

Black Codes Laws passed by southern states that restricted the rights and liberties of former slaves.

Black Power Mid-1960s movement that called for modifying integrationist goals in favor of gaining political and economic power for separate black-directed institutions and emphasized pride in African-American heritage.

Black Republicans Label coined by the Democratic Party to attack the Republican Party as believers in racial equality. The Democrats used this fear to convince many whites to remain loyal to them.

blacklist In the postwar years, a list of people who could no longer work in the entertainment industry because of alleged contacts with communists.

blitzkrieg A "lightning war"; a coordinated and massive military strike by German army and air forces.

block grants Part of Nixon's new economic plan in which a percentage of federal tax dollars would be returned to state and local governments to spend as they deemed fit.

blockade runner A ship designed to run through a blockade.

blockade The closing of a country's harbors by enemy ships to prevent trade and commerce, especially to prevent traffic in military supplies.

blockhouse A wooden fort with an overhanging second floor. The white settlers of Kentucky used blockhouses to defend themselves against Indians.

blood sports Sporting activities emphasizing bloodiness that were favored by working-class men of the cities. The most popular in the early 19th century were cockfighting, ratting, dogfights, and various types of violence between animals.

bonanza farms Huge wheat farms financed by eastern capital and cultivated with heavy machinery and hired labor.

Bonus Army Army veterans who marched on Washington, D.C., in 1932 to lobby for economic relief but who were rebuffed by Hoover.

Boone, Daniel A pioneer settler of Kentucky, Boone became the most famous American frontiersman of his generation.

border ruffians Term used to describe pro-slavery Missourians who streamed into Kansas in 1854, determined to vote as many times as necessary to install a proslavery government there.

Boston Massacre The colonial term for the confrontation between colonial protestors and British soldiers in front of the customs house on March 5, 1770. Five colonists were killed and six wounded.

Boston Tea Party In December 1773, Boston's Sons of Liberty threw 342 chests of East India Company tea into Boston harbor rather than allow them to be landed and pay the hated tea duty.

bounty jumpers Men who enlisted in the Union army to collect the bounties offered by some districts to fill military quotas; these men would enlist and then desert as soon as they got their money.

Boxers Chinese nationalist organization that instigated an uprising in 1900 to rid China of all foreign influence.

braceros Guest workers from Mexico allowed into the United States because of labor shortages from 1942 to 1964.

Brown v. Board of Education 1954 case in which the U.S. Supreme Court unanimously overruled the "separate but equal"

doctrine and held that segregation in the public schools violated the principle of equal protection under the law.

"broad" wives Wives of slave men who lived on other plantations and were visited by their husbands during off hours.

Brown, John Prominent abolitionist who fought for the antislavery cause in Kansas (1856) and led a raid to seize the Harpers Ferry arsenal in 1859.

Bryan, William Jennings A two-term Democratic congressman from Nebraska who won the party's presidential nomination in 1896 after electrifying delegates with his "Cross of Gold" speech. Bryan was twice more nominated for president (1900 and 1908); he lost all three times.

Bull Moosers Followers of Theodore Roosevelt in the 1912 election.

bulldozing Using force to keep African Americans from voting.

Burr, Aaron Vice President under Thomas Jefferson who killed Alexander Hamilton in a duel and eventually hatched schemes to detach parts of the west from the United States.

Bush, George H. W. Republican President (1989–1993) who directed an international coalition against Iraq in the Persian Gulf War.

Bush Doctrine Foreign policy principles, announced by Bush administration, that emphasized possibility of preemptive military strikes and goal of fostering "democratic" regime change.

bushwhackers Confederate guerrilla raiders especially active in Missouri. Jayhawkers were the Union version of the same type of people. Both groups did a tremendous amount of damage with raids, arson, ambush, and murder.

Butternuts Democrats from the southern river-oriented counties of the Northwest region whose name came from the yellow vegetable dye with which they colored their homespun clothing.

Cahokia The largest city created by Mississippian mound builders. Located in Illinois near modern St. Louis, it thrived from A.D. 900 to 1250 and then declined.

californios Spanish-speaking people whose families had resided in California for generations.

camp meeting Outdoor revival often lasting for days; a principal means of spreading evangelical Christianity in the United States.

Capra, Frank Popular 1930s filmmaker who celebrated the decency, honesty, and patriotism of ordinary Americans in such films as *Mr. Deeds Goes to Town* and *Mr. Smith Goes to Washington*.

caravel A new type of ocean-going vessel that could sail closer to a head wind than any other sailing ship and make speeds of from three to twelve knots per hour.

Carnegie, Andrew A Scottish immigrant who became the most efficient entrepreneur in the U.S. steel industry and earned a great fortune.

carpetbaggers Northerners who settled in the South during Reconstruction.

Carson, Rachel American marine biologist and author best known for *Silent Spring* (1962), a widely read book that questioned

the use of chemical pesticides and helped stimulate the modern environmental movement.

Carter, Jimmy Democratic president (1977–1981) whose single term in office was marked by inflation, fuel shortages, and a hostage crisis.

cash and carry U.S. foreign policy prior to American entry into World War II that required belligerents to pay cash and carry products away in their own ships. This arrangement minimized risks to American exports, loans, and shipping.

Cavaliers Supporters of the Stuart family of Charles I during the civil wars.

changing system Elaborate system of neighborhood debts and bartering used primarily in the South and West where little cash money was available.

Chavez, Cesar Political activist, leader of the United Farm Workers of America, and the most influential Mexican American leader during the 1970s.

Cherokee War Between December 1759 and December 1761, the Cherokee Indians devastated the South Carolina backcountry. The British army intervened and in turn inflicted immense damage on the Cherokee.

Chicanismo Populistic pride in the Mexican-American heritage that emerged in the late 1960s. Chicano, once a term of derision, became a rallying cry among activists.

chinampas The highly productive gardens built on Lake Taxcoco by the Aztecs.

CIO The Committee, and then Congress, for Industrial Organization, founded in 1935 to organize the unskilled and semi-skilled workers ignored by the AFL. The CIO reinvigorated the labor movement.

circuit court Court that meets at different places within a district.

circuit-riding preachers Methodist ministers who traveled from church to church, usually in rural areas.

Civil Rights Act of 1957 First civil rights act since Reconstruction, aimed at securing voting rights for African Americans in the South.

Civil Rights Act of 1964 Bipartisan measure that denied federal funding to segregated schools and barred discrimination by race and sex in employment, public accommodations, and labor unions.

Civil Rights Act of 1968 Measure that banned racial discrimination in housing and made interference with a person's civil rights a federal crime. It also stipulated that crossing state lines to incite a riot was a federal crime.

Clay, Henry Speaker of the House, senator from Kentucky, and National Republican presidential candidate who was the principal spokesman for the American System.

Clinton, Bill Democratic president (1993–2001) whose two-term presidency witnessed rapid economic growth but also a sexual scandal that fueled an impeachment effort, which he survived.

close-order assault Military tactic of attacking with little space between men. In the face of modern weapons used during the Civil War, such fighting produced a high casualty rate.

Clovis tip A superior spear point developed before 9000 B.C. It was in use nearly everywhere in North and South America and produced such an improvement in hunting ability that it contributed to the extinction of most large mammals.

Coercive (Intolerable) Acts Four statutes passed by Parliament in response to the Boston Tea Party, including one that closed the port of Boston until the tea was paid for, and another that overturned the Massachusetts Charter of 1691. The colonists called them the Intolerable Acts and included the Quebec Act under that label.

Cold War The political, military, cultural, and economic rivalry between the United States and the Soviet Union that developed after the Second World War and lasted until the disintegration of the Soviet State after 1989.

collective bargaining Negotiations between representatives of workers and employers on issues such as wages, hours, and working conditions.

Collier, John Activist head of the Bureau of Indian Affairs who improved U.S. policy toward Native Americans and guided the landmark Indian Reorganization Act through Congress.

colonial economy Economy based on the export of agricultural products and the import of manufactured goods; sometimes used to describe the dependence of the South on the North.

Columbus, Christopher The Genoese mariner who persuaded Queen Isabella of Spain to support his voyage of discovery across the Atlantic in 1492. Until his death in 1506, he believed he had reached East Asia. Instead he had discovered America.

Committee on Public Information U.S. Government agency established in 1917 to arouse support for the war and, later, to generate suspicion of war dissenters.

committees of correspondence Bodies formed on both the local and colonial levels that played an important role in exchanging ideas and information. They spread primarily anti-British material and were an important step in the first tentative unity of people in different colonies.

common law The heart of the English legal system was based on precedents and judicial decisions. Common-law courts offered due process through such devices as trial by jury, which usually consisted of local men.

common schools Tax-supported public schools built by state and local governments.

Communist Party Radical group that wanted America to follow the Soviet Union's path to socialism. The CP organized some of the country's poorest workers into unions and pushed the New Deal leftward, but was never popular enough to bid for power itself.

commutation fee $300 fee that could be paid by a man drafted into the Union army to exempt him from the current draft call.

compensated emancipation Idea that the federal government would offer compensation or money to states that voluntarily abolished slavery.

competence Understood in the early republic as the ability to live up to neighborhood economic standards while protecting the

long-term independence of the household.

Compromise of 1850 Series of laws enacted in 1850 intended to settle all outstanding slavery issues.

Congressional Black Caucus (CBC) Congressional group formed in 1969 that focused on eliminating disparities between African Americans and white Americans.

congressional caucus In the early republic, the group of congressmen that traditionally chose the party's presidential candidates. By the 1820s, the American public distrusted the caucus as undemocratic because only one party contested for power. The caucus was replaced by the national nominating convention.

conquistadores The Spanish word for conquerors.

Conscience Whigs A group of antislavery members of the Whig Party.

Conservation Movement that called for managing the environment to ensure the careful and efficient use of the nation's natural resources.

consumer durable Consumer goods that were meant to last, such as washing machines and radios.

containment Label used to describe the global anticommunist national-security policies adopted by the United States to stop the expansion of communism during the late 1940s.

contraband of war Term used to describe slaves who came within the Union lines.

contras Military force in Nicaragua, trained and financed by the United States, that opposed the Nicaraguan socialist government led by the Sandinista Party.

convention In England, a meeting, usually of the houses of Parliament, to address an emergency, such as the flight of James II to France in 1688. The convention welcomed William and Mary, who then restored the traditional parliamentary system. In the United States by the 1780s, conventions had become the purest expression of the popular will, superior to the legislature, as in the convention that drafted the Massachusetts Constitution of 1780.

cooperatives Marketing groups established by such groups as the Farmers Alliance that eliminated "middlemen" and reduced prices to farmers. The idea also was tried by some labor groups and included other types of businesses such as factories.

Copperheads Term used by some Republicans to describe Peace Democrats to imply that they were traitors to the Union.

corrupt bargain Following the election of 1824, Andrew Jackson and his supporters alleged that, in a "corrupt bargain," Henry Clay sold his support during the House vote in the disputed election of 1824 of John Quincy Adams in exchange for appointment as Secretary of State.

Cortés, Hernán The Spanish conquistador who vanquished the Aztecs.

cotton Semitropical plant that produces white, fluffy fibers that can be made into textiles.

Coughlin, Father Charles The "radio priest" from the Midwest who alleged that the New Deal was being run by

bankers. His growing anti-Semitism discredited him by 1939.

counterculture Anti-establishment movement that symbolized the youthful social upheaval of the 1960s. Ridiculing traditional attitudes toward such matters as clothing, hair styles, and sexuality, the counterculture urged a more open and less regimented approach to daily life.

coureur de bois A French phrase interpreted as "a roamer of the woods," referring to French colonists who participated in the fur trade with the Indians and lived part of the year with them.

court-packing plan 1937 attempt by Roosevelt to appoint one new Supreme Court justice for every sitting justice over the age of 70 and who had sat for at least 10 years. Roosevelt's purpose was to prevent conservative justices from dismantling the New Deal, but the plan died in Congress and inflamed opponents of the New Deal.

Covenant Chain of Peace An agreement negotiated by Governor Edmund Andros in 1677 that linked the colony of New York to the Iroquois Five Nations and was later expanded to include other colonies and Indian peoples.

covenant theology The belief that God made two personal covenants with humans: the covenant of works and the covenant of grace.

coverture A common-law doctrine under which the legal personality of the husband covered the wife, and he made all legally binding decisions.

Crazy Horse War chief of the Oglala Lakota (Sioux) Indians who forged an alliance with Cheyenne chiefs to resist white expansion into the Black Hills in 1874–1875; led the attack on Custer's 7th Cavalry at Little Big Horn.

Credit Mobilier Construction company for the Union Pacific Railroad that gave shares of stock to some congressmen in return for favors.

crisis conversion Understood in evangelical churches as a personal transformation that resulted from directly experiencing the Holy Spirit.

crop lien system System of credit used in the poor rural South whereby merchants in small country stores provided necessary goods on credit in return for a lien on the crop. As the price of crops fell, small farmers, black and white, drifted deeper into debt.

Cuban Missile Crisis (1962) Serious Cold War confrontation between the United States and the Soviet Union over the installation of Soviet missiles in Cuba.

Custer, George A. Civil War hero and postwar Indian fighter who was killed at Little Big Horn in 1876.

Davis, Jefferson Mississippi planter and prominent leader of the Southern Democrats in the 1850s, who later served as president of the Confederacy.

Dawes Plan 1924 U.S. backed agreement to reduce German reparation payments by more than half. The plan also called on banks to invest $200 million in the German economy.

Debs, Eugene V. Leader of the Socialist Party who received almost a million votes in the election of 1912.

Declaration of Independence A document drafted primarily by Thomas Jefferson of Virginia; this document justified American independence to the world by affirming "that all men are created equal" and have a natural right to "life, liberty, and the pursuit of happiness." The longest section of the Declaration condemned George III as a tyrant.

deflation Decline in consumer prices or a rise in the purchasing power of money.

Deism Belief that God created the universe but did not intervene in its affairs.

Denmark Vesey Leader of a slave conspiracy in and around Charleston, South Carolina in 1822.

deskilling Process in which the employment market produces jobs requiring fewer skill (and offering less income) than in the past.

détente An easing of tensions, particularly between the United States and the Soviet Union.

Dewey, John Philosopher who believed that American technological and industrial power could be made to serve the people and democracy.

direct election of senators Constitutional amendment that mandated the election of senators by the people rather than by selection by state legislatures.

dirty tricks Actions designed to destroy the reputation and effectiveness of political opponents of the Nixon administration.

disfranchisement Process of barring groups of adult citizens from voting.

dissenter Person who disagrees openly with the majority opinion.

Dix, Dorothea Boston reformer who traveled throughout the country campaigning for humane, state-supported asylums for the insane.

dollar diplomacy Diplomatic strategy formulated under President Taft that focused on expanding American investments abroad, especially in Latin America and East Asia.

domestic fiction Sentimental literature that centered on household and domestic themes that emphasized the toil and travails of women and children who overcame adversity through religious faith and strength of character.

Douglas, Stephen A. Senator from Illinois who emerged as a leading Democrat in 1850 and led efforts to enact the Compromise of 1850.

doves Opponents of military action, especially those who wanted quickly to end U.S. involvement in the Vietnam War.

dower rights The right of a widow to a portion of her deceased husband's estate (usually one third of the value of the estate). It was passed to their children upon her death.

dowry The cash or goods a woman received from her father when she married.

drawbacks Form of rebate offered to special customers by the railroads.

Dred Scott Missouri slave who sued for freedom on grounds of prolonged residence in a free state and free territory; in 1857, the Supreme Court found against his case, declaring the Missouri Compromise unconstitutional.

Du Bois, W. E. B. Leader of the NAACP, the editor of its newspaper, *The Crisis*, and an outspoken critic of Booker T. Washington and his accomodationist approach to race relations.

Earned Income Tax Credit (EITC) First adopted in 1975 and modeled after similar programs in other countries, the federal EITC allows a tax credit for families and individuals with children—and with incomes below a specified level; some states have similar arrangements.

economy of scale Term used in both industry and agriculture to describe the economic advantages of concentrating capital, units of production, and output.

Eisenhower Doctrine Policy that stated that the United States would use armed force to respond to imminent or actual communist aggression in the Middle East.

Eisenhower, Dwight D. Supreme Commander of the Allied Forces in Europe, orchestrator of the Normandy Invasion, and President of the United States (1953–1961).

elect Those selected by God for salvation.

Electoral College The group that elects the president. Each state receives as many electors as it has congressmen and senators combined and can decide how to choose its electors. Every elector votes for two candidates, one of whom has to be from another state.

emancipation Refers to release from slavery or bondage. Gradual emancipation was introduced in Pennsylvania and provided for the eventual freeing of slaves born after a certain date when they reached age 28.

embargo Government order prohibiting the movement of merchant ships or goods in or out of its ports.

encomienda A system of labor introduced into the Western Hemisphere by the Spanish. It permitted the holder, or *encomendero*, to claim labor from Indians in a district for a stated period of time.

enfranchise To grant the right to vote.

Enlightenment The new learning in science and philosophy that took hold, at least in England, between 1660 and the American Revolution. Nearly all of its spokesmen were religious moderates who were more interested in science than religious doctrine and who favored broad religious toleration.

entail A legal device that required a landowner to keep his estate intact and pass it on to his heir.

enumerated commodities A group of colonial products that had to be shipped from the colony of origin to England or another English colony. The most important commodities were sugar and tobacco.

Environmental Protection Agency (EPA) Organization established in 1970 that brought under a single institutional umbrella the enforcement of laws intended to protect environmental quality.

environmentalism Movement with roots in earlier conservation, preservation, and public health movements that grew in power after 1970, when concern mounted over the disruption of ecological balances and critical habitats.

Equal Rights Amendment (ERA) Proposed amendment to the Constitution providing that equal rights could not be abridged on account of sex. It won congressional approval in 1972 but failed to gain ratification by the states.

Erie Canal Canal linking the Hudson River at Albany with the Great Lakes at Buffalo that helped to commercialize the farms of the Great Lakes watershed and to channel that commerce into New York City.

Espionage, Sabotage, and Sedition Acts Laws passed in 1917 and 1918 that gave the federal government sweeping powers to silence and even imprison dissenters.

established church The church in a European state or colony that was sustained by the government and supported by public taxes.

evangelical A style of Christian ministry that includes much zeal and enthusiasm. Evangelical ministers emphasized personal conversion and faith rather than religious ritual.

evangelicals Religious groups that generally placed an emphasis on conversion of non-Christians.

excise tax Internal tax on goods or services.

external taxes Taxes based on oceanic trade, such as port duties. Some colonists thought of them more as a means of regulating trade than as taxes for revenue.

factories A term used to describe small posts established for the early slave trade along the coast of Africa or on small offshore islands.

fall line A geographical landmark defined by the first waterfalls encountered when going up-river from the sea. These waterfalls prevented oceangoing ships from sailing further inland and thus made the fall line a significant early barrier. Land between the falls and the ocean was called the tidewater. Land above the falls but below the mountains was called the piedmont.

fascism Type of highly centralized government that used terror and violence to suppress opposition. Its rigid social and economic controls often incorporated strong nationalism and racism. Fascist governments were dominated by strong authority figures or dictators.

favorite son Candidate for president supported by delegates from his home state.

Federal Reserve Act Act that brought private banks and public authority together to regulate and strengthen the nation's financial system.

Federalists Supporters of the Constitution during the ratification process. Anti-Federalists resisted ratification.

feudal revival The reliance on old feudal charters for all of the profits that could be extracted from them. It took hold in several colonies in the mid-eighteenth century and caused serious problems between many landowners and tenants.

fiat money Paper money backed only by the promise of the government to accept it in payment of taxes. It originated in Massachusetts after a military emergency in 1690.

filibuster Congressional delaying tactic involving lengthy speeches that prevent legislation from being enacted.

filibustering A term used to describe several groups that invaded or attempted to invade various Latin American areas to attempt to add them to the slaveholding regions of the United States. The word originated from *filibustero*, meaning a freebooter or pirate.

fire-eaters Southerners who were eager, enthusiastic supporters of southern rights and later of secession.

First Continental Congress This intercolonial body met in Philadelphia in September and October 1774 to organize resistance against the Coercive Acts by defining American rights, petitioning the king, and appealing to the British and American people. It created the Association, local committees in each community to enforce nonimportation.

Five-Power Treaty 1922 treaty in which the United States, Britain, Japan, France, and Italy agreed to scrap more than 2 million tons of their warships.

flappers Rebellious middle-class young women who signaled their desire for independence and equality through style and personality rather than through politics.

flexible response Kennedy's approach to the Cold War that aimed to provide a wide variety of military and non-military methods to confront communist movements.

Ford, Gerald A GOP member of the House of Representatives, Gerald Ford became the first person to be appointed Vice President of the United States. When Richard Nixon resigned in 1974, Ford became President.

Fort Sumter Fort in Charleston's harbor occupied by United States troops after the secession of South Carolina.

Fourteen Points Plan laid out by Woodrow Wilson in January 1918 to give concrete form to his dream of a "peace without victory" and a new world order.

free silver Idea that the government would purchase all silver offered for sale and coin it into silver dollars at the preferred ratio between silver and gold of 16 to 1.

Freedmen's Bureau Federal agency created in 1865 to supervise newly freed people. It oversaw relations between whites and blacks in the South, issued food rations, and supervised labor contracts.

freedom riders Members of interracial groups who traveled the South on buses to test a series of federal court decisions declaring segregation on buses and in waiting rooms to be unconstitutional.

Freedom Summer Summer of 1964 when nearly a thousand white volunteers went to Mississippi to aid in voter registration and other civil rights projects.

free-labor ideology Belief that all work in a free society is honorable and that manual labor is degraded when it is equated with slavery or bondage.

Free-Soilers A term used to describe people who opposed the expansion of slavery into the territories. It came from the name of a small political party in the election of 1848.

French and Indian War Popular name for the struggle between Britain and France for the control of North America, 1754 to 1763, in which the British conquered New France. It merged into Europe's Seven Years' War (1756–1763) that pitted Britain and Prussia against France, Austria, and Russia.

Friedan, Betty Author of *The Feminine Mystique* (1963) and founder of the National Organization for Women (1966).

frontier An area on the advancing edge of American civilization.

fugitive slaves Runaway slaves who escaped to a free state.

Fulton, Robert Builder of the *Clermont*, the first practical steam-driven boat.

fundamentalists Religious groups that preached the necessity of fidelity to a strict moral code, individual commitment to Christ, and faith in the literal truth of the Bible.

funded national debt The state agreed to pay the interest due to its creditors before all other obligations.

Gabriel's rebellion Carefully planned but unsuccessful rebellion of slaves in Richmond and the surrounding area in 1800.

gang labor A system where planters organized their field slaves into gangs, supervised them closely, and kept them working in the fields all day. This type of labor was used on tobacco plantations.

Garvey, Marcus Jamaican-born black nationalist who attracted millions of African Americans in the early 1920s to a movement calling for black separatism and self-sufficiency.

gas and water socialists Term used to describe evolutionary socialists who focused their reform efforts on regulating municipal utilities in the public interest.

gentleman Term used to describe a person of means who performed no manual labor.

gentlemen's agreement (1907) Agreement by which the Japanese government promised to halt the immigration of its adult male laborers to the United States in return for President Theodore Roosevelt's pledge to end the discriminatory treatment of Japanese immigrant children in California's public schools.

GI Bill Officially called the Serviceman's Readjustment Act of 1944. It provided veterans with college and job-training assistance, preferential treatment in hiring, and subsidized home loans, and was later extended to Korean War veterans in 1952.

girdled trees Trees with a line cut around them so sap would not rise in the spring.

glasnost Russian term describing increased openness in Russian society under Mikhail Gorbachev.

Globalization Term used to describe process of removing national barriers to free flow of trade, financial investment, culture, and people throughout the world.

Glorious Revolution The overthrow of King James II by Whigs and Tories, who invited William of Orange to England. William landed in November 1688, the army defected to him, James fled to France, and in early 1689 Parliament offered the throne to William and his wife Mary, a daughter of James. Contemporaries called the event "glorious" because almost no blood was shed in England.

gold bugs "Sound money" advocates who wanted to keep the United States on the international gold standard and believed the expanded coinage of silver was foolhardy.

Gompers, Samuel F. America's most famous trade unionist while serving as president of the AFL (1896–1924). He achieved his greatest success organizing skilled workers.

Good Neighbor Policy Roosevelt's foreign policy initiative that formally renounced the right of the United States to intervene in Latin American affairs, leading to improved relations between the United States and Latin American countries.

governor-general The French official responsible for military and diplomatic affairs and for appointment of all militia officers in a colony.

graduated income tax Tax based on income with rates that gradually rise as the level of income rises.

Grangers Members of the Patrons of Husbandry (a farmers' organization) and a contemptuous name for farmers used by ranchers in the West.

Grant, Ulysses S. General-in-chief of Union armies who led those armies to victory in the Civil War.

Great American Desert The treeless area in the plains most Americans considered unsuitable for settlement. It generally was passed over by settlers going to the Pacific Coast areas.

Great Awakening An immense religious revival that swept across the Protestant world in the 1730s and 1740s.

Great Depression Economic downturn triggered by the stock market crash in October 1929 and lasting until 1941.

Great Society Series of domestic initiatives announced in 1964 by President Lyndon Johnson to "end poverty and racial injustice." They included the Voting Rights Act of 1965; the establishment of the Department of Housing and Urban Development, Head Start, and job-training programs; Medicare and Medicaid expansion; and various community action programs.

Great White Fleet Naval ships sent on a 45,000-mile world tour by President Roosevelt (1907–1909) to showcase American military power.

Greeley, Horace Editor of the *New York Tribune,* one of the most influential newspapers in the country.

greenbacks Paper money issued by the federal government during the Civil War to help pay war expenses. They were called greenbacks because of their color.

Greene, Nathanael A general from Rhode Island whose superb strategy of irregular war reclaimed the Lower South for the American cause in 1780–1781.

Greenwich Village Community of radical artists and writers in lower Manhattan that provided a supportive environment for various kinds of radical ideals.

Grenville, George As head of the British government from 1763 to 1765, Grenville passed the Sugar Act, Quartering Act, Currency Act, and the Stamp Act, provoking the imperial crisis of 1765–1766.

Grimke, Sarah Along with her sister Angelina, this elite South Carolina woman moved north and campaigned against slavery and for temperance and women's rights.

gross national product (GNP) Total value of all goods and services produced during a specific period.

Gulf of Tonkin Resolution Measure passed by Congress in August 1964 that provided authorization for an air war against North Vietnam after U.S. destroyers were allegedly attacked by North Vietnamese torpedoes. Johnson invoked it as authority for expanding the Vietnam War.

Gullah A language spoken by newly imported African slaves. Originally, it was a simple second language for everyone who spoke it, but gradually evolved into modern black English.

habeas corpus Right of an individual to obtain a legal document as protection against illegal imprisonment.

haciendas Large, landed estates established by the Spanish.

Hale, Sarah Josepha Editor of *Godey's Ladies Book* and an important arbiter of domesticity and taste for middle-class housewives.

Half-Way Covenant The Puritan practice whereby parents who had been baptized but had not yet experienced conversion could bring their children before the church and have them baptized.

Hamilton, Alexander Secretary of the Treasury under Washington who organized the finances of the new government and led the partisan fight against the Democratic Republicans.

Hard Money Democrats Democrats who, in the 1830s and 1840s, wanted to eliminate paper money and regarded banks as centers of trickery and privilege.

Harlem Renaissance 1920s African-American literary and artistic awakening that sought to create works rooted in black culture instead of imitating white styles.

Harpers Ferry Site of John Brown's 1859 raid on a U.S. armory and arsenal for the manufacture and storage of military rifles.

hawks Supporters of intensified military efforts in the Vietnam War.

Haywood, William Labor organizer known as "Big Bill" who led the radical union Industrial Workers of the World.

headright A colonist received 50 acres of land for every person whose passage to America he financed, including himself. This system was introduced in Virginia.

heathen A term used sometimes by Christians to refer to anyone who was not a Christian or a Jew.

herrenvolk **democracy** Concept that emphasized the equality of all who belonged to the master race—not all mankind.

Hessians A term used by Americans to describe the 17,000 mercenary troops hired by Britain from various German states, especially Hesse.

hidalgos The minor nobility of Spain. Many possessed little wealth and were interested in improving their position through the overseas empire.

High Federalists A term used to describe Alexander Hamilton and some of his less-moderate supporters. They wanted the naval war with France to continue and also wanted to severely limit the rights of an opposition party.

Highway Act of 1956 Act that appropriated $25 billion for the construction of more than 40,000 miles of interstate highways over a 10-year period.

hippies People who identified with the 1960s counterculture. They were often depicted as embracing mind-altering drugs, communal living arrangements, and new forms of music.

Hiroshima Japanese city destroyed by an atomic bomb on August 6, 1945.

Hiss, Alger High-level State Department employee who was accused, in a controversial case, of being a communist and Soviet spy.

Hitler, Adolph German fascist dictator whose aggressive policies touched off the Second World War.

HIV-AIDS Acquired immune deficiency syndrome (AIDS) resulting from infection with the human immunodeficiency virus (HIV). It progressively impedes the body's ability to protect itself from disease.

Hmong Ethnically distinct people who inhabited lands extending across the borders of the Indochinese countries of Vietnam, Cambodia, and Laos.

House of Burgesses The assembly of early Virginia that settlers were allowed to elect. Members met with the governor and his council and enacted local laws. It first met in 1619.

House Un-American Activities Committee (HUAC) Congressional committee (1938–1975) that zealously investigated suspected Nazi and Communist sympathizers.

household industry Work such as converting raw materials into finished products done by women and children to provide additional household income.

Howe, William (General) Howe commanded the British army in North America from 1776 to 1778. He won major victories in New York and northern New Jersey in 1776, but Washington regained control of New Jersey after his Trenton-Princeton campaign. Howe took Philadelphia in September 1777 but was recalled in disgrace after Britain's northern army surrendered at Saratoga.

Huguenots French Protestants who followed the beliefs of John Calvin.

Hull House First American settlement house established in Chicago in 1889 by Jane Addams and Ellen Gates Starr.

Human Genome Project Program launched in 1985 to map all genetic material in the twenty-four human chromosomes. It sparked ongoing debate over potential consequences of genetic research and manipulation.

Hurricane Katrina Severe Atlantic storm that slammed into the Gulf Coast in August 2005 and caused massive damage, particularly in New Orleans, and significant loss of life; inadequate preparation for and response to Katrina sparked debate over how state and local governments should address such "natural" disasters.

Hutchinson, Anne A religious radical who attracted a large following in Massachusetts, especially in Boston. She warned that nearly all of the ministers were preaching a covenant of works instead of the covenant of grace. Convicted of the Antinomian heresy after claiming that she received direct messages from God, she and her most loyal followers were banished to Rhode Island in 1638.

hydraulic mining Use of high-pressure streams of water to wash gold or other minerals from soil.

Immigration Act of 1924 (Johnson-Reed Act) Limited immigration to the United States to 165,000 a year, shrank immigration from southern and eastern Europe to insignificance, and banned immigration from East and South Asia.

Immigration Act of 1965 Law eliminating the national-origins quota system for immigration and substituting preferences for people with certain skills or with relatives in the United States.

Immigration Restriction Act of 1917 Measure that denied any adult immigrant who failed a reading test entry into the United States, and banned immigration from the "Asiatic Barred Zone."

impeach To charge government officeholders with misconduct in office.

impeachment Act of charging a public official with misconduct in office.

imperialists Those who wanted to expand their nation's world power through military prowess, economic strength, and control of foreign territory (often organized into colonies).

impressment Removal of sailors from American ships by British naval officers.

Inca The last and most extensive pre-Columbian empire in the Andes and along the Pacific coast of South America.

indentured servants People who had their passage to America paid by a master or ship captain. They agreed to work for their master for a term of years in exchange for cost of passage, bed and board, and small freedom dues when their terms were up. The number of years served depended on the terms of the contract. Most early settlers in the English colonies outside of New England arrived as indentured servants.

Indian Removal Act (1830) Legislation that offered the native peoples of the lower South the option of removal to federal lands west of the Mississippi. Those who did not take the offer were removed by force in 1838.

indigo A blue dye obtained from plants that was used by the textile industry. The British government subsidized the commercial production of it in South Carolina.

information revolution Acceleration of the speed and availability of information due to computer and satellite systems.

initiative Reform that gave voters the right to propose and pass a law independently of their state legislature.

Inns of Court England's law schools.

intendant The officer who administered the system of justice in New France.

interchangeable parts Industrial technique using machine tools to cut and shape a large number of similar parts that can be fitted together with other parts to make an entire item such as a gun.

internal improvements Nineteenth-century term for transportation facilities such as roads, canals, and railroads.

internal taxes Taxes that were imposed on land, on people, on retail items (such as excises), or on legal documents and newspapers (such as the Stamp Act). Most colonists thought that only their elective assemblies had the constitutional power to impose internal taxes.

Iran-*contra* affair Reagan administration scandal in which the U.S. secretly sold arms to Iran, a country implicated in holding American hostages, and diverted the money to finance the attempt by the *contras* to overthrow the Sandinista government of Nicaragua. Both transactions violated acts of Congress, which had prohibited funding the *contras* and selling weapons to Iran.

Iroquois League A confederation of five Indian nations centered around the Mohawk Valley who were very active in the fur trade. They first worked with the Dutch and then the English. They were especially successful in using adoption as a means of remaining strong.

irreconcilables Group of fourteen midwestern and western senators who opposed the Treaty of Versailles.

irregular war A type of war using men who were not part of a permanent or professional regular military force. It also can apply to guerilla-type warfare, usually against the civilian population.

itinerant preachers Ministers who lacked their own parishes and who traveled from place to place.

Jackson State (incident) Killing of two students on May 13, 1970, after an escalation in tensions between students at Jackson State University, a historically black institution, and National Guard troops in Mississippi.

Jackson, Andrew President of the United States (1829–1837) who founded the Democratic Party, signed the Indian Removal Act, vetoed the Second Bank, and signed the Force Bill.

Jackson, Thomas J. A native of Virginia, he emerged as one of the Confederacy's best generals in 1861–1862.

Jamestown Founded in 1607, Jamestown became England's first permanent settlement in North America. It served as the capital of Virginia for most of the 17th century.

Japanese internment Removal of first- and second-generation Japanese-Americans into secured camps, a 1942 action then justified as a security measure but since deemed unjustified by evidence.

Jim Crow laws Laws passed by southern states mandating racial segregation in public facilities of all kinds.

Johnson, Lyndon B. President (1963–1969) who undertook an ambitious Great Society program and a major military effort in Vietnam.

joint resolution An act passed by both houses of Congress with a simple majority rather than the two-thirds majority in the Senate.

joint-stock company A form of business organization that resembled a modern corporation. Individuals invested in the company through the purchase of shares. One major difference between then and today was that each stockholder had one vote regardless of how many shares he owned. The first permanent English

colonies in North America were established by joint-stock companies.

journeyman Wage-earning craftsman.

judicial review Supreme Court's power to rule on the constitutionality of congressional acts.

Kansas-Nebraska Act Law enacted in 1854 to organize the new territories of Kansas and Nebraska that effectively repealed the provision of the 1820 Missouri Compromise by leaving the question of slavery to the territories' settlers.

Kennan, George (Mr. X) American diplomat and historian who recommended the policy of containment toward Soviet aggression in a famous article published under the pseudonym "X."

Kennedy, John F. President from 1961 to 1963, noted for his youthful charm and vigor and his "New Frontier" vision for America.

Kent State (incident) Killing of four students on May 4, 1970, by the National Guard at a Kent State University protest against the U.S. incursion into neutral Cambodia.

King George's War Popular term in North America for the third of the four Anglo-French wars before the American Revolution (1744–1748). It is sometimes also applied to the War of Jenkins's Ear between Spain and Britain (1739–1748).

King, Martin Luther, Jr. African-American clergyman who advocated nonviolent social change and shaped the civil rights movement of the 1950s and 1960s.

Know-Nothings Adherents of nativist organizations and of the American party who wanted to restrict the political rights of immigrants.

Korean War Conflict lasting from 1950 to 1953 between communist North Korea, aided by China, and South Korea, aided by United Nations forces consisting primarily of U.S. troops.

Ku Klux Klan White terrorist organization in the South originally founded as a fraternal society in 1866. Reborn in 1915, it achieved popularity in the 1920s through its calls for Anglo-Saxon purity, Protestant supremacy, and the subordination of blacks, Catholics, and Jews.

La Raza Unida Mexican American–based movement that scored some political successes in the Southwest in the late 1960s and early 1970s.

lame-duck administration Period of time between an incumbent party's or officeholder's loss of an election and the succession to office of the winning party or candidate.

League of Women Voters Successor to National American Woman Suffrage Association, it promoted women's role in politics and dedicated itself to educating voters.

Lee, Robert E. U.S. army officer until his resignation to join the Confederacy as general-in-chief.

legal tender Any type of money that the government requires everyone to accept at face value.

Lend-Lease Act A 1941 act by which the United States "loaned" munitions to the

Allies, hoping to avoid war by becoming an "arsenal" for the Allied cause.

levee Earthen dike or mound, usually along the banks of rivers, used to prevent flooding.

Lewis and Clark Explorers commissioned in 1804 by President Jefferson to survey the Louisiana Purchase.

liberal Protestants Those who believed that religion had to be adapted to science and that the Bible was to be mined for its ethical values rather than for its literal meaning.

Liberty bonds Thirty-year government bonds with an annual interest rate of 3 1/2 percent sold to fund the war effort.

liberty tree A term for the gallows on which enemies of the people deserved to be hanged. The best known was in Boston.

limited liability Liability that protected directors and stockholders of corporations from corporate debts by separating those debts from personal liabilities.

Lincoln, Abraham Illinois Whig who became the Republican Party's first successful presidential candidate in 1860 and led the Union during the Civil War.

Lincoln-Douglas Debates Series of seven debates between Abraham Lincoln and Stephen Douglas in their contest for election to the U.S. Senate in 1858.

Lindbergh, Charles A. First individual to fly solo across the Atlantic (1927) and the greatest celebrity of the 1920s.

lintheads Term used by wealthier whites to describe poor whites who labored in southern cotton mills.

living room war Phrase suggesting that television coverage had brought the Vietnam War into the living rooms of Americans and may have led many to question the war.

lockout Act of closing down a business by the owners during a labor dispute.

Lodge, Henry Cabot Republican Senator from Massachusetts who led the campaign to reject the Treaty of Versailles.

logistics Military activity relating to such things as the transporting, supplying, and quartering of troops and their equipment.

long knives The term Indians used to describe Virginians.

Long, Huey Democratic senator and former governor of Louisiana who used the radio to attack the New Deal as too conservative. FDR regarded him as a major rival.

longhorn Breed of cattle introduced into the Southwest by the Spanish that became the main breed of livestock on the cattle frontier.

Lost Generation Term used by Gertrude Stein to describe U.S. writers and artists who fled to Paris in the 1920s after becoming disillusioned with America.

Louisiana Purchase Land purchased from France in 1803 that doubled the size of the United States.

Lowell, Francis Cabot Wealthy Bostonian who, with the help of the Boston Associates, built and operated integrated textile mills in eastern Massachusetts.

loyalists People in the 13 colonies who remained loyal to Britain during the Revolution.

Ludlow massacre Murder of 66 men, women, and children in April 1914 when company police of the Colorado Fuel and Iron Company fired randomly on striking United Mine Workers.

Luftwaffe German air force.

Lusitania British passenger ship sunk by a German U-boat on May 7, 1915, killing more than 1,000 men, women, and children.

MacArthur, Douglas Supreme commander of Allied forces in the southwest Pacific during the Second World War; leader of the occupation forces in the reconstruction of Japan; and head of United Nations forces during the Korean War.

magistrate An official who enforced the law. In colonial America, this person was usually a justice of the peace or a judge in a higher court.

Mahan, Alfred Thayer Influential imperialist who advocated construction of a large navy as crucial to the successful pursuit of world power.

Malcolm X Charismatic African-American leader who criticized integration and urged the creation of separate black economic and cultural institutions. He became a hero to members of the Black Power movement.

mandamus A legal writ ordering a person, usually a public official, to carry out a specific act. In Massachusetts in 1774, the new royal councilors were appointed by a writ of mandamus.

manifest destiny The belief that the United States was destined to grow from the Atlantic to the Pacific and from the Arctic to the tropics. Providence supposedly intended for Americans to have this area for a great experiment in liberty.

manumission of slaves The act of freeing a slave, done at the will of the owner.

Marbury v. Madison 1803 case involving the disputed appointment of a federal justice of the peace in which Chief Justice John Marshall expanded the Supreme Court's authority to review legislation.

maritime Of, or relating to, the sea.

Marshall Plan Plan of U.S. aid to Europe that aimed to contain communism by fostering postwar economic recovery. Proposed by Secretary of State George C. Marshall in 1947, it was known formally as the European Recovery Program.

Marshall, John Chief Justice of the United States Supreme Court from 1801 to 1835. Appointed by Federalist President John Adams, Marshall's decisions tended to favor the federal government over the states and to clear legal blocks to private business.

martial law Government by military force rather than by citizens.

mass production High-speed and high-volume production.

Massachusetts Bay Company A joint-stock company chartered by Charles I in 1629. It was controlled by Non-Separatists who took the charter with them to New England and, in effect, converted it into a written constitution for the colony.

massive retaliation Assertion by the Eisenhower administration that the threat of U.S. atomic weaponry would hold Communist powers in check.

matrilineal A society that determines inheritance and roles in life based on the female or maternal line.

Maya A literate, highly urbanized Mesoamerican civilization that flourished for more than a thousand years before its sudden collapse in the ninth century A.D.

McCarthyism Public accusations of disloyalty made with little or no regard to actual evidence. Named after Senator Joseph McCarthy, these accusations and the scandal and harm they caused came to symbolize the most virulent form of anti-communism.

McClellan, George B. One of the most promising young officers in the U.S. army, he became the principal commander of Union armies in 1861–1862.

McKinley, William A seven-term Republican congressman from Ohio whose signature issue was the protective tariff. He was the last Civil War veteran to be elected president.

Menéndez, Francisco An escaped South Carolina slave who fought with the Yamasee Indians against the colony, fled to Florida, was reenslaved by the Spanish, became a militia captain, was freed again, and was put in charge of the free-black town of Mose near St. Augustine in the late 1730s, the first community of its kind in what is now the United States.

merger movement Late-19th and early 20th-century effort to integrate different enterprises into single, giant corporations able to eliminate competition, achieve economic order, and boost profits.

Mesoamerica An area embracing Central America and southern and central Mexico.

Metacom's War (King Philip's War) A war that devastated much of southern New England in 1675–1676. It began as a conflict between Metacom's Wampanoags and Plymouth Colony but soon engulfed all of the New England colonies and most of the region's Indian nations.

Mexican repatriation Secretary of Labor William Doak's plan to deport illegal Mexican aliens to Mexico. By 1935, over 500,000 Mexicans had left the United States.

microchips Technological improvement that boosted the capability and reduced the size and cost of computer hardware.

middle class Social group that developed in the early nineteenth century comprised of urban and country merchants, master craftsmen who had turned themselves into manufacturers, and market-oriented farmers—small-scale entrepreneurs who rose within market society in the early nineteenth century.

Middle Ground The area of French and Indian cooperation west of Niagara and south of the Great Lakes. No one exercised sovereign power over this area, but the French used Indian rituals to negotiate treaties with their Algonquian trading partners, first against the Iroquois and later against the British.

midnight judges Federal judicial officials appointed under the Judiciary Act of 1801, in the last days of John Adams's presidency.

militia A community's armed force, made up primarily of ordinary male citizens rather than professional soldiers.

Millennium The period at the end of history when Christ is expected to return and rule with his saints for a thousand years.

minstrel show Popular form of theater among working men of the northern cities in which white men in blackface portrayed African Americans in song and dance.

missions Outposts established by the Spanish along the northern frontier to aid in Christianizing the native peoples. They also were used to exploit their labor.

Missouri Compromise Compromise that maintained sectional balance in Congress by admitting Missouri as a slave state and Maine as a free state and by drawing a line west from the 36°30' parallel separating future slave and free states.

modernists Those who believed in science rather than religion and in moving toward equality for men and women and for whites and nonwhites.

Monroe Doctrine Foreign policy doctrine proposed by Secretary of State John Quincy Adams in 1823 that denied the right of European powers to establish new colonies in the Americas while maintaining the United States' right to annex new territory.

Montgomery bus boycott Political protest campaign mounted in 1955 to oppose the city's policy of racial segregation on its public transit system. The Supreme Court soon declared segregation on public transit unconstitutional.

morale The general feeling of the people toward such events as a war. Good morale greatly enhances an ability to fight or sacrifice for a cause.

Mormons Members of the Church of Jesus Christ of Latter-day Saints, founded by Joseph Smith in 1830; the *Book of Mormon* supplemented the Bible.

Mourning War An Indian war often initiated by a widow or bereaved relative who insisted that her male relatives provide captives to repair the loss.

muckrakers Investigative journalists who propelled Progressivism by exposing corruption, economic monopolies, and moral decay in American society.

napalm Incendiary and toxic chemical contained in bombs used by the United States in Vietnam.

National American Women Suffrage Association Organization established in 1890 to promote woman suffrage; stressed that women's special virtue made them indispensable to politics.

National Association for the Advancement of Colored People (NAACP) Organization launched in 1910 to fight racial discrimination and prejudice and to promote civil rights for blacks.

National Recovery Administration (NRA) 1933 attempt to promote economic recovery by persuading private groups of industrialists to decrease production, limit hours of work per employee, and standardize minimum wages.

National Security Act (1947) Reorganized the U.S. military forces within a new Department of Defense, and established the National Security Council and the Central Intelligence Agency.

National War Labor Board U.S. government agency that brought together representatives of labor, industry, and the public to resolve labor disputes.

nativism Hostility of native-born Americans toward immigrants.

naturalization Process by which people born in a foreign country are granted full citizenship with all of its rights.

Navajo Signal Corps Navajo Indians who conveyed military intelligence in their native language to preserve its secrecy.

naval stores Items such as pitch, resin, and turpentine that were used to manufacture ships. Most of them were obtained from pine trees.

neoconservatives Group of intellectuals, many of whom had been anticommunist Democrats during the 1950s and 1960s, who came to emphasize hard-line foreign policies and conservative social stances.

neo-Federalists Nationalist Republicans who favored many Federalist economic programs such as protective tariffs and a national bank.

Neolithic The period known also as the late Stone Age. Agriculture developed, and stone, rather than metal, tools were used.

Neutrality Acts of 1935 and 1936 Legislation that restricted loans, trade, and travel with belligerent nations in an attempt to avoid the entanglements that had brought the United States into the First World War.

neutrality U.S. policy toward World War I from 1914 to 1917 that called for staying out of war but maintaining normal economic relations with both sides.

New Freedom Wilson's reform program of 1912 that called for temporarily concentrating government power so as to dismantle the trusts and return America to 19th-century conditions of competitive capitalism.

New Lights Term used to describe prorevival Congregationalists.

New Nationalism Roosevelt's reform program between 1910 and 1912, which called for establishing a strong federal government to regulate corporations, stabilize the economy, protect the weak, and restore social harmony.

New Sides Term used to describe evangelical Presbyterians.

New York's 369th Regiment Black army unit recruited in Harlem that served under French command and was decorated with the *Croix de Guerre* for its valor.

nickelodeons Converted storefronts in working-class neighborhoods that showed early short silent films usually lasting 15 minutes, requiring little comprehension of English, and costing only a nickel to view.

Nixon, Richard President of the United States (1969–1974) during the final years of the Vietnam War. He resigned the presidency when he faced impeachment for the Watergate scandals.

nonimportation agreements Agreements not to import goods from Great Britain. They were designed to put pressure on the British economy and force the repeal of unpopular parliamentary acts.

Non-Separatists English Puritans who insisted that they were faithful members of the Church of England while demanding that it purge itself of its surviving Catholic rituals and vestments.

normal schools State colleges established for the training of teachers.

North American Free Trade Agreement (NAFTA) 1994 agreement that aimed to lower or eliminate barriers restricting the trade of goods and services between the United States, Canada, and Mexico.

North Atlantic Treaty Organization (NATO) Established by treaty in 1949 to provide for the collective defense of noncommunist European and North American nations against possible aggression from the Soviet Union and to encourage political, economic, and social cooperation.

Northwest Ordinance This ordinance established the Northwest Territory between the Ohio River and the Great Lakes. Adopted by the Confederation Congress in 1787, it abolished slavery in the territory and provided that it be divided into 3 to 5 states that would eventually be admitted to the Union as full equals of the original 13.

NSC-68 National Security Council Document number 68 (1950) that provided the rationale and comprehensive strategic vision for U.S. policy during the Cold War.

nullification Beginning in the late 1820s, John C. Calhoun and others argued that the Union was a voluntary compact between sovereign states, that states were the ultimate judges of the constitutionality of federal law, that states could nullify federal laws within their borders, and that they had the right to secede from the Union.

Old Lights Antirevival Congregationalists.

Old Northwest The region west of Pennsylvania, north of the Ohio River, and east of the Mississippi River.

Old Sides Antirevival Presbyterians.

oligarchy A society dominated by a few persons or families.

Olmec The oldest pre-Columbian high culture to appear in what is now Mexico.

Onontio An Algonquian word that means "great mountain" and that was used by Indians of the Middle Ground to designate the governor of New France.

Open Door notes (1899–1900) Foreign policy tactic in which the United States asked European powers to respect China's independence and to open their spheres of influence to merchants from other nations.

Open Skies Eisenhower's proposal that U.S. and Soviet disarmament be verified by reconnaissance flights over each other's territory.

open-field agriculture A medieval system of land distribution used only in the New England colonies. Farmers owned scattered strips of land within a common field, and the town as a whole decided what crops to plant.

pacifist A person opposed to war or violence. The religious group most committed to pacifism is the Quakers.

Panama Canal An engineering marvel completed in 1914 across the new Central American nation of Panama. Connecting the Atlantic and Pacific Oceans, it shortened ship travel between New York and San Francisco by 8,000 miles.

parish A term used to describe an area served by one tax-supported church. The term was used primarily in regions settled by members of the Church of England.

Parks, Rosa African American seamstress in Montgomery, Alabama, who, after refusing to give up her bus seat to a white man, was arrested and fined. Her protest sparked a subsequent bus boycott that attracted national sympathy for the civil rights cause and put Martin Luther King, Jr., in the national spotlight.

parochial schools Schools associated with a church, usually Roman Catholic. The funding of these schools became a major political issue in the 1850s.

passive civil disobedience Nonviolent refusal to obey a law in an attempt to call attention to government policies considered unfair.

Patriot Act Also called USA Patriot Act and first limited to a four-year period, it contained numerous provisions for extending Washington's power to protect national security.

patronage The act of appointing people to government jobs or awarding them government contracts, often based on political favoritism rather than on abilities.

patronships Vast estates along the Hudson River that were established by the Dutch. They had difficulty attracting peasant labor, and most were not successful.

Peace of Paris The 1763 treaty that ended the war between Britain on the one side, and France and Spain on the other side. France surrendered New France to Britain. Spain ceded Florida to Britain, and France compensated its ally by ceding all of Louisiana to Spain.

peace without victory Woodrow Wilson's 1917 pledge to work for a peace settlement that did not favor one side over the other but ensured an equality among combatants.

Pearl Harbor Japan's December 7, 1941 attack on a U.S. base in Hawaii that brought the United States into the Second World War.

Penn, William A convert to the Society of Friends in the 1660s, Penn used his friendship with Charles II and James, Duke of York, to acquire a charter for Pennsylvania in 1681, and he then launched a major migration of Friends to the Delaware Valley.

people's capitalism An egalitarian capitalism in which all Americans could participate and enjoy the consumer goods that U.S. industry had made available.

per capita Term used to measure the wealth of a nation by dividing total income by population.

perestroika Russian term describing the economic liberalization that began in the late 1980s.

Perkins, Frances Secretary of Labor under Roosevelt and the first female Cabinet member.

Pershing, John J. Commander of the American Expeditionary Force that began landing in Europe in 1917 and that entered battle in the spring and summer of 1918.

personal liberty laws Laws enacted by nine northern states to prohibit the use of state law facilities such as jails or law officers in the recapture of fugitive slaves.

piedmont A term referring to the land above the fall line but below the Appalachian Mountains.

Pilgrims A pious, sentimental term used by later generations to describe the settlers who sailed on the Mayflower in 1620 and founded Plymouth Colony.

Pitt, William One of the most popular public officials in 18th-century Britain, he was best known as the minister who organized Britain's successful war effort against France in the French and Indian War.

placer mining Mining where minerals, especially gold, were found in glacial or alluvial deposits.

Platt Amendment Clause that the U.S. forced Cuba to insert into its constitution giving the U.S. broad control over Cuba's foreign and domestic policies.

plumbers Nixon's secret intelligence unit designed to stop information leaks to the media.

Plymouth Founded by Separatists in 1620, Plymouth was England's first permanent colony in New England.

political machines Organizations that controlled local political parties and municipal governments through bribery, election fraud, and support of urban vice while providing some municipal services to the urban poor.

politics of harmony A system in which the governor and the colonial assembly worked together through persuasion rather than through patronage or bullying.

politique A man who believed that the survival of the state took precedence over religious differences.

poll tax A tax based on people or population rather than property. It was usually a fixed amount per adult.

polygamy The act of having more than one wife.

Pontiac An Ottawa chief whose name has been attached to the great Indian uprising against the British in 1763–1764.

pools Technique used by railroads to divide up traffic and fix rates, thereby avoiding ruinous competition.

popular sovereignty The concept that settlers of each territory would decide for themselves whether to allow slavery.

postal campaign Abolitionist tactic to force the nation to confront the slavery question by flooding the mails, both North and South, with antislavery literature. Their hope was to raise controversy within an area that was the province of the federal government.

postmillennialism Belief (held mostly by middle-class evangelists) that Christ's Second Coming would occur when missionary conversion of the world brought about a thousand years of social perfection.

powwow Originally, a word used to identify tribal prophets or medicine men. Later it was used also to describe the ceremonies held by them.

praying Indians The Christian Indians of New England.

predestination A theory that states that God has decreed, even before he created the world, who will be saved and who will be damned.

Presbytery An intermediate level of organization in the Presbyterian church, above individual congregations but below the synod. One of its primary responsibilities was the ordination and placement of ministers.

presidios Military posts constructed by the Spanish to protect the settlers from hostile Indians. They also were used to keep non-Spanish settlers from the area.

Presley, Elvis Known as "the King" of Rock and Roll, he was the biggest pop star of the 1950s.

private fields Farms of up to five acres on which slaves working under the task system were permitted to produce items for their own use and sale in a nearby market.

privateers A privately owned ship that was authorized by a government to attack enemy ships during times of war. The owner of the ship got to claim a portion of whatever was captured. This practice damaged any enemy country that could not dramatically increase naval protection for its merchant ships.

Proclamation of 1763 It was issued by the Privy Council. Among other things, it tried to prevent the colonists from encroaching upon Indian lands by prohibiting settlement west of the Appalachian watershed unless the government first purchased those lands by treaty.

Progressive Party Political party formed by Theodore Roosevelt in 1912 when the Republicans refused to nominate him for president. The party adopted a sweeping reform program.

Prohibition Constitutional ban on the manufacture and sale of alcohol in the United States (1920–1933).

proprietary colony A colony owned by an individual(s) who had vast discretionary powers over the colony. Maryland was the first proprietary colony, but others were founded later.

protective tariff Tariff that increases the price of imported goods that compete with American products and thus protects American manufacturers from foreign competition.

Protestant Reformation A religious movement begun by Martin Luther in 1517 that led to the repudiation of the Roman Catholic Church in large parts of northern and central Europe.

provincial congress A type of convention elected by the colonists to organize resistance. They tended to be larger than the legal assemblies they displaced, and they played a major role in politicizing the countryside.

public Friends The men and women who spoke most frequently and effectively for the Society of Friends. They were as close as the Quakers came to having a clergy. They occupied special elevated seats in some meeting houses.

public virtue Meant, to the revolutionary generation, patriotism and the willingness of a free and independent people to subordinate their interests to the common good and even to die for their country.

Pueblo Revolt In the most successful Indian uprising in American history, the Pueblo people rose against the Spanish in 1680, killed most Spanish missionaries, devastated Spanish buildings, and forced the surviving Spaniards to retreat down the Rio Grande. The Pueblos maintained their autonomy for about a decade, but Spain reasserted control in the early 1690s.

Puritans An English religious group that followed the teachings of John Calvin. They wanted a fuller reformation of the Church of England and hoped to replace The Book of Common Prayer with sermons. They wanted to purify the Church of England of its surviving Catholic ceremonies and vestments.

Quakers A term of abuse used by opponents to describe members of the Society of Friends, who believed that God, in the form of the Inner Light, was present in all humans. Friends were pacifists who rejected oaths, sacraments, and all set forms of religious worship.

quasi-slavery Position that resembled slavery, such as that created by the Black Codes.

quitrent A relic of feudalism, a quitrent was a small required annual fee attached to a piece of land. It differed from other rents in that nonpayment did not lead to ejection from the land but to a suit for debt.

R&D Research and development.

racial profiling Law enforcement practice of using racial appearance to screen for potential wrongdoing.

railhead End of a railroad line, or the farthest point on the track.

railroad gauge Distance between the rails on which wheels of railroad cars fit.

"rainfall follows the plow" Erroneous belief that settlement and cultivation somehow changed the weather. It evolved due to heavier-than-normal precipitation during the 1870s and 1880s.

RAND Think tank developed by the U.S. military to conduct scientific research and development.

Reagan, Ronald Republican president (1981–1989) who steered domestic politics in a conservative direction and sponsored a huge military buildup.

real wages Relationship between wages and the consumer price index.

realism Form of thinking, writing, and art that prized detachment, objectivity, and skepticism.

rebates Practice by the railroads of giving certain big businesses reductions in freight rates or refunds.

recall Reform that gave voters the right to remove from office a public servant who had betrayed their trust.

Red Scare Widespread fear in 1919–1920 that radicals had coalesced to establish a communist government on American soil. In response, U.S. government and private citizens undertook a campaign to identify, silence, and, in some cases, imprison radicals.

redemptioners Servants with an indentured contract that allowed them to find masters after they arrived in the colonies. Many German immigrant families were redemptioners and thus were able to stay together while they served their terms.

redlining Refusal by banks and loan associations to grant loans for home buying and business expansion in neighborhoods that contained aging buildings, dense populations, and growing numbers of nonwhites.

referendum Procedure that allows the electorate to decide an issue through a direct vote.

Refugee Act of 1980 Law allowing refugees fleeing political persecution entry into United States.

religious bigotry Intolerance based on religious beliefs or practices.

religious right Christians who wedded their religious beliefs to a conservative political agenda and gained growing influence in Republican party politics after the late 1960s.

Republic of Texas Independent nation founded in 1836 when a revolution by residents in the Mexican province of Texas won their independence.

republics Independent Indian villages that were willing to trade with the British and remained outside the French system of Indian alliances.

Restoration era The period that began in 1660 when the Stuart dynasty under Charles II was restored to the throne of England. It ended with the overthrow of James II in 1688–1689.

restorationism Belief that all theological and institutional changes since the end of biblical times were man-made mistakes and that religious organizations must restore themselves to the purity and simplicity of the apostolic church.

restraint of trade Activity that prevented competition in the marketplace or free trade.

revival A series of emotional religious meetings that led to numerous public conversions.

revolving gun turret A low structure, often round, on a ship that moved horizontally and contained mounted guns.

rifling Process of cutting spiral grooves in a gun's barrel to impart a spin to the bullet. Perfected in the 1850s, it produced greater accuracy and longer range.

Robinson, Jackie African American whose addition to the Brooklyn Dodgers in 1947 began the lengthy process of integrating major league baseball.

rock 'n' roll Form of popular music that arose in the 1950s from a variety of musical styles, including rhythm and blues, country, and gospel. Its heavily accented beat attracted a large following among devotees of the emerging youth culture.

Rockefeller, John D. Founder of the Standard Oil Company whose aggressive practices drove many competitors out of business and made him one of the richest men in America.

Roe v. Wade Supreme Court decision in 1973 that ruled that a blanket prohibition against abortion violated a woman's right to privacy and prompted decades of political controversy.

rolling stock Locomotives, freight cars, and other types of wheeled equipment owned by railroads.

Roosevelt corollary 1904 corollary to the Monroe Doctrine, stating that the United States had the right to intervene in domestic affairs of hemispheric nations to quell disorder and forestall European intervention.

Roosevelt liberalism New reform movement that sought to regulate capitalism but not the morals or behavior of private citizens. This reform liberalism overcame divisions between southern agrarians and northeastern ethnics.

Roosevelt, Eleanor A politically engaged and effective First Lady, and an architect of American liberalism.

Roosevelt, Franklin D. President from 1933 to 1945 and the creator of the New Deal.

Rough Riders Much decorated volunteer cavalry unit organized by Theodore Roosevelt and Leonard Wood to fight in Cuba in 1898.

royal colony A colony controlled directly by the English monarch. The governor and council were appointed by the Crown.

Russo-Japanese War Territorial conflict between imperial Japan and Russia mediated by Theodore Roosevelt at Portsmouth, New Hampshire. The peace agreement gave Korea and other territories to Japan, ensured Russia's continuing control over Siberia, and protected China's territorial integrity.

Sacco and Vanzetti Case (1920) Controversial conviction of two Italian-born anarchists accused of armed robbery and murder.

sachem An Algonquian word that means "chief."

Safety-Fund Law New York state law that required banks to pool a fraction of their resources to protect both bankers and small stockholders in case of bank failures.

Salem witch trials About 150 people were accused of witchcraft in Massachusetts between March and September 1692. During the summer trials, 19 people were hanged and one was pressed to death after he refused to stand trial. All of those executed insisted they were innocent. Of the 50 who confessed, none was executed.

Saratoga A major turning point in the Revolutionary War. American forces prevented John Burgoyne's army from reaching Albany, cut off its retreat, and forced it to surrender in October 1777. This victory helped bring France into the war.

saturation bombing Intensive bombing designed to destroy everything in a target area.

scabs Strikebreakers who were willing to act as replacements for striking workers, thus undermining the effect of strikes as leverage against company owners.

scalawags Term used by southern Democrats to describe southern whites who worked with the Republicans.

scientific management Attempt to break down each factory job into its smallest components to increase efficiency, eliminate waste, and promote worker satisfaction.

secession The act of a state withdrawing from the Union. South Carolina was the first state to attempt to do this in 1860.

Second Continental Congress The intercolonial body that met in Philadelphia in May 1775 a few weeks after the Battles of Lexington and Concord. It organized the Continental Army, appointed George Washington commander-in-chief, and simultaneously pursued policies of military resistance and conciliation. When conciliation failed, it chose independence in July 1776 and in 1777 drafted the Articles of Confederation, which finally went into force in March 1781.

sedentary Societies that are rooted locally or are nonmigratory. Semisedentary societies are migratory for part of the year.

Seditious libel The common-law crime of openly criticizing a public official.

seigneurs The landed gentry who claimed most of the land between Quebec and Montreal. They were never as powerful as aristocrats in France.

Seneca Falls Convention (1848) First national convention of women's rights activists.

separation of powers The theory that a free government, especially in a republic, should have three independent branches capable of checking or balancing one another: the executive, the legislative (usually bicameral), and the judicial.

Separatists One of the most extreme English Protestant groups that were followers of John Calvin. They began to separate from the Church of England and form their own congregations.

September 11, 2001 Day on which U.S. airliners, hijacked by Al Qaeda operatives, were crashed into the World Trade Center and the Pentagon, killing around 3,000 people.

serfdom Early medieval Europe's predominant labor system, which tied peasants to their lords and the land. They were not slaves because they could not be sold from the land.

Seward, William H. Secretary of State under Abraham Lincoln and Andrew Jackson. He was best known for his purchase of Alaska from Russia.

share wages Payment of workers' wages with a share of the crop rather than with cash.

sharecropping Working land in return for a share of the crops produced instead of paying cash rent.

Shays's Rebellion An uprising of farmers in western Massachusetts in the winter of

1786–1787. They objected to high taxes and foreclosures for unpaid debts. Militia from eastern Massachusetts suppressed the rebels.

Sheppard-Towner Act Major social welfare program providing federal funds for prenatal and child health care, 1921–1929.

sickle cell A crescent- or sickle-shaped red blood cell sometimes found in African Americans. It helped protect them from malaria but exposed some children to the dangerous and painful condition of sickle cell anemia.

Sir Walter Raleigh An Elizabethan courtier who, in the 1580s, tried but failed to establish an English colony on Roanoke Island in what is now North Carolina.

sit-down strike Labor strike strategy in which workers occupied their factory but refused to do any work until the employer agreed to recognize the workers' union. This strategy succeeded against General Motors in 1937.

sit-in movement Activity that challenged legal segregation by demanding that blacks have the same access to public facilities as whites. These nonviolent demonstrations were staged at restaurants, bus and train stations, and other public places.

Sitting Bull Hunkapapa Lakota (Sioux) chief and holy man who led warriors against the U.S. Army in Montana Territory in 1876, culminating in the battle of Little Big Horn.

slash and burn A system of agriculture in which trees were cut down, girdled, or in some way destroyed. The underbrush then was burned, and a crop was planted. Men created the farms, and women did the farming. The system eventually depleted the fertility of the soil, and the entire tribe would move to a new area after 10 or 20 years.

Smith, Alfred E. Irish American, Democratic governor of New York who became in 1928 the first Catholic ever nominated for the presidency by a major party.

Smith, John (Captain) A member of the Virginia Council; his strong leadership from 1607 to 1609 probably saved the colony from collapse.

Smith, Joseph Poor New York farm boy whose visions led him to translate the *Book of Mormon* in late 1820s. He became the founder and the prophet of the Church of Jesus Christ of Latter-day Saints (Mormons).

Social Darwinism Set of beliefs explaining human history as an ongoing evolutionary struggle between different groups of people for survival and supremacy that was used to justify inequalities between races, classes, and nations.

Social Security Act Centerpiece of the welfare state (1935) that instituted the first federal pension system and set up funds to take care of groups (such as the disabled, and unmarried mothers with children) unable to support themselves.

socialism Political movement that called for the transfer of industry from private to public control, and the transfer of political power from elites to the laboring masses.

sodbuster Small farmer in parts of the West who adapted to the treeless plains and prairies, such as the construction of homes out of sod.

southern yeoman Farmer who owned relatively little land and few or no slaves.

sovereign power A term used to describe supreme or final power.

space shuttle Manned rocket that served as a space laboratory and could be flown back to the earth for reuse.

specie Also called "hard money" as against paper money. In colonial times, it usually meant silver, but it could also include gold coins.

spirituals Term later devised to describe the religious songs of slaves.

Spock, Dr. Benjamin Pediatrician who wrote *Baby and Child Care* (1946), the most widely used child-rearing book during the baby-boom generation.

spoils system System by which the victorious political party rewarded its supporters with government jobs.

Sputnik First Soviet satellite sent into orbit around the earth in 1957.

stagflation Condition of simultaneous economic stagnation and price inflation.

Stalin, Joseph Soviet communist dictator who worked with Allied leaders during Second World War.

Stamp Act Passed by the administration of George Grenville in 1765, the Stamp Act imposed duties on most legal documents in the colonies and on newspapers and other publications. Massive colonial resistance to the act created a major imperial crisis.

staple crop A crop grown for commercial sale. It usually was produced in a colonial area and was sold in Europe. The first staple crops were sugar and tobacco.

Starr, Kenneth Republican lawyer appointed as independent counsel to investigate possible wrongdoing by President Clinton.

States General The legislative assembly of the Netherlands.

stay laws A law that delays or postpones something. During the 1780s many states passed stay laws to delay the due date on debts because of the serious economic problems of the times.

Strategic Defense Initiative (SDI) Popularly termed "Star Wars," a proposal to develop technology for creation of a space-based defensive missile shield around the United States.

Student Nonviolent Coordinating Committee (SNCC) Interracial civil rights organization formed by young people involved in the sit-in movement that later adopted a direct-action approach to fighting segregation.

subtreasuries Plan to help farmers escape the ruinous interest rates of the crop lien system by storing their crops in federal warehouses until market prices were more favorable. Farmers could draw low-interest loans against the value of these crops.

subversive Systematic, deliberate attempt to overthrow or undermine a government or society by people working secretly within the country.

Sun Belt Southern rim of the United States running from Florida to California.

Sunday schools Schools that first appeared in the 1790s to teach working-class children to read and write but that by the 1820s and 1830s were becoming moral training grounds.

supply-side economics Economic theory that tax reductions targeted toward investors and businesses would stimulate production and eventually create jobs.

sweated Describes a type of worker, mostly women, who worked in her home producing items for subcontractors, usually in the clothing industry.

synod The governing body of the Presbyterian church. A synod was a meeting of Presbyterian ministers and prominent laymen to set policies for the whole church.

table a petition or bill Act of removing a petition or bill from consideration without debate by placing it at the end of the legislative agenda.

Taft, William Howard Roosevelt's successor as president (1909–1913) who tried but failed to mediate between reformers and conservatives in the Republican Party.

tariff A tax on imports.

task system A system of slave labor under which slaves had to complete specific assignments each day. After these assignments were finished, their time was their own. It was used primarily on rice plantations. Slaves often preferred this system over gang labor because it gave them more autonomy and free time.

Teapot Dome scandal Political scandal by which Secretary of Interior Albert Fall allowed oil tycoons access to government oil reserves in exchange for $400,000 in bribes.

Tecumseh Shawnee leader who assumed political and military leadership of the pan-Indian religious movement began by his brother Tenskwatawa.

tejanos Spanish-speaking settlers of Texas. The term comes from the Spanish word *Tejas* for Texas.

temperance Movement that supported abstaining from alcoholic beverages.

tenancy System under which farmers worked land that they did not own.

Tennessee Valley Authority (TVA) Ambitious and successful use of government resources and power to promote economic development throughout the Tennessee Valley.

Tenochtitlán The huge Aztec capital city destroyed by Cortés.

Tenskwatawa Brother of Tecumseh, whose religious vision of 1805 called for the unification of Indians west of the Appalachians and foretold the defeat and disappearance of the whites.

termination and relocation Policies designed to assimilate American Indians by terminating tribal status and relocating individuals off reservations.

Tet offensive Surprise National Liberation Front (NLF) attack during the lunar new year holiday in early 1968 that brought high casualties to the NLF but fuelled pessimism about the war's outcome in the United States.

The Man That Nobody Knows Bruce Barton's best-selling 1925 book depicting Jesus as a business executive.

think tank Group or agency organized to conduct intensive research or engage in problem solving, especially in developing new technology, military strategy, or social planning.

Third Reich New empire that Adolph Hitler promised the German people would bring glory and unity to the nation.

Third World Less economically developed areas of the world, primarily the Middle East, Asia, Latin America, and Africa.

Tierra del Fuego The region at the southern tip of South America.

tithe A portion of one's income that is owed to the church. In most places, it was one tenth.

toll roads Roads for which travelers were charged a fee for each use.

tories A term for Irish Catholic peasants who murdered Protestant landlords. It was used to describe the followers of Charles II and became one of the names of the two major political parties in England.

total war New kind of war requiring every combatant to devote virtually all his or her economic and political resources to the fight.

totalitarian movement Movement in which the individual is subordinated to the state and all areas of life are subjected to centralized, total control—usually by force.

Townshend Revenue Act Passed by Parliament in 1767, this act imposed import duties on tea, paper, glass, red and white lead, and painter's colors. It provoked the imperial crisis of 1767–1770. In 1770 Parliament repealed all of the duties except the one on tea.

traditionalists Those who believed that God's word transcended science and that America should continue to be guided by older hierarchies (men over women, whites over nonwhites, native-born over immigrants).

transcontinental railroad Railroad line that connected with other lines to provide continuous rail transportation from coast to coast.

treasury notes Paper money used by the Union to help finance the Civil War. One type of treasury note was known as a greenback because of its color.

Triangle Shirtwaist Company New York City site of a tragic 1911 industrial fire that killed 146 workers unable to find their way to safety.

Triple Alliance One set of combatants in World War I, consisting of Germany, Austria-Hungary, and Italy. When Italy left the alliance, this side became known as the Central Powers.

Triple Entente One set of combatants in World War I, consisting of Britain, France, and Russia. As the war went on, this side came to be known as the Allies or Allied Powers.

Truman, Harry S. Franklin Roosevelt's Vice President who became president when Roosevelt died on April 13, 1945.

trust Large corporations that controlled a substantial share of any given market.

Turner, Nat Baptist lay preacher whose religious visions encouraged him to lead a slave revolt in southern Virginia in 1831 in which 55 whites were killed—more than any other American slave revolt.

Turner's frontier thesis Theory developed by historian Frederick Jackson Turner, who argued that the frontier had been central to the shaping of American character and the success of the U.S. economy and democracy.

Twenty Negro Law Confederate conscription law that exempted from the draft one white man on every plantation owning 20 or more slaves. The law's purpose was to exempt overseers or owners who would ensure discipline over the slaves and keep up production but was regarded as discrimination by non-slaveholding families.

U-2 spy plane Aircraft specializing in high-altitude reconnaissance.

Ulster The northern province of Ireland that provided 70 percent of the Irish immigrants in the colonial period. Nearly all of them were Presbyterians whose fore-bears had moved to Ireland from Scotland in the previous century. They sometimes are called Scots-Irish today.

Uncle Tom's Cabin Published by Harriet Beecher Stowe in 1852, this sentimental novel told the story of the Christian slave Uncle Tom and became a best seller and the most powerful antislavery tract of the antebellum years.

underconsumptionism Theory that underconsumption, or a chronic weakness in consumer demand, had caused the depression. This theory guided the Second New Deal, leading to the passage of laws designed to stimulate consumer demand.

underground railroad A small group who helped slaves escape bondage in the South. It took on legendary status, and its role was much exaggerated.

UNESCO (United Nations Educational, Scientific, and Cultural Organization) UN organization intended to create peace and security through collaboration among member nations.

unicameral legislature A legislature with only one chamber or house.

Union Leagues Organizations that informed African-American voters of, and mobilized them to, support the Republican Party.

Unionists Southerners who remained loyal to the Union during the Civil War.

universal male suffrage System that allowed all adult males to vote without regard to property, religious, or race qualifications or limitations.

urban corridors Metropolitan strips of population running between older cities.

vestry A group of prominent men who managed the lay affairs of the local Anglican church, often including the choice of the minister, especially in Virginia.

vice-admiralty courts These royal courts handled the disposition of enemy ships captured in time of war, adjudicated routine maritime disputes between, for example, a ship's crew and its owner, and from time to time tried to decide cases involving parliamentary regulation of colonial commerce. This last category was the most controversial. These courts did not use juries.

Victorianism Moral code of conduct that advocated modesty, sexual restraint, and separate spheres of activity and influence for men and women.

Vietnam War Conflict lasting from 1946 to 1975, with direct U.S. military involvement from 1964 to 1973. Highly controversial, the war devastated the Vietnam countryside, spilled into all of Indochina, and ended in a victory for communist North Vietnam, which then united the country under its rule.

Vietnamization Policy whereby the South Vietnamese were to assume more of the military burdens of the war and allow the United States to withdraw combat troops.

virtual representation The English concept that Members of Parliament represented the entire empire, not just a local constituency and its voters. According to this theory, settlers were represented in Parliament in the same way that nonvoting subjects in Britain were represented. The colonists accepted virtual representation for nonvoting settlers within their colonies but denied that the term could describe their relationship with Parliament.

VJ Day August 15, 1945, day on which the war in the Pacific was won by the Allies.

Voting Rights Act of 1965 Law that provided new federal mechanisms to help guarantee African Americans the right to vote.

Wagner Act (NLRA) Named after its sponsor Senator Robert Wagner (D-NY), this 1935 act gave every worker the right to join a union and compelled employers to bargain with unions in good faith.

Walker, Madame C. J. Black entrepreneur who built a lucrative business from the hair and skin lotions she devised and sold to black customers throughout the country.

War Hawks Members of the Twelfth Congress, most of them young nationalists from southern and western areas, who promoted war with Britain.

War Industries Board U.S. government agency responsible for mobilizing American industry for war production.

war on terrorism Global effort, adopted after the attacks of September 11, 2001, by the United States and its allies to neutralize international groups deemed "terrorists," primarily radical Islamic groups such as Al Qaeda.

Washington, George A veteran of the French and Indian War, Washington was named commander in chief of the Continental Army by the Second Continental Congress in 1775 and won notable victories at Boston, Trenton, Princeton, and Yorktown, where Lord Cornwallis's army surrendered to him in 1781. His fellow delegates chose him to preside over the deliberations of the Philadelphia Convention in 1787, and after the federal Constitution was ratified, he was unanimously chosen the first president of the United States for two terms.

Watergate Business and residential complex in Washington, D.C., that came to stand for the political espionage and cover-ups directed by the Nixon administration. The complicated web of Watergate scandals brought about Nixon's resignation in 1974.

Western development Disproportionate amount of New Deal funds sent to Rocky Mountain and Pacific Coast areas to provide water and electricity for urban and agricultural development.

wheat blast A plant disease that affected wheat and first appeared in New England in the 1660s. There were no known remedies for the disease, and it gradually spread until wheat production in New England nearly ceased.

Wheatley, Phillis Eight-year-old Phillis Wheatley arrived in Boston from Africa in 1761 and was sold as a slave to wealthy John and Susannah Wheatley. Susannah taught her to read and write, and in 1767 she published her first poem in Boston. In 1773 she visited London to celebrate the publication there of a volume of her poetry, an event that made her a transatlantic sensation. On her return to Boston, the Wheatleys emancipated her.

Whigs The name of an obscure sect of Scottish religious extremists who favored the assassination of Charles and James of England. The term was used to denote one of the two leading political parties of late seventeenth-century England.

Whiskey Rebellion Revolt in Western Pennsylvania against the federal excise tax on whiskey.

whiskey ring Network of distillers and revenue agents that cheated the government out of millions of tax dollars.

Whitney, Eli The Connecticut-born tutor who invented the cotton gin.

wolfpacks German submarine groups that attacked enemy merchant ships or convoys.

Works Progress Administration Federal relief agency established in 1935 that disbursed billions to pay for infrastructural improvements and funded a vast program of public art.

Wounded Knee Site of a shootout between Indians and Army troops at the Pine Ridge Indian reservation in southwestern South Dakota.

XYZ Affair Incident that precipitated an undeclared war with France when three French officials (identified as X, Y, and Z) demanded that American emissaries pay a bribe before negotiating disputes between the two countries.

Yankee A Dutch word for New Englanders that originally meant something like "land pirate."

yankeephobia Popular term describing strong dislike of the United States, whose citizens were referred to as "yankees," in Latin America.

yellow dog contracts Written pledges by employees promising not to join a union while they were employed.

yellow journalism Newspaper stories embellished with sensational or titillating details when the true reports did not seem dramatic enough.

yeoman A farmer who owned his own farm.

"Young America" movement A group of young members of the Democratic Party who were interested in territorial expansion in the 1840s.

Yorktown The last major engagement of the Revolutionary War. Washington's army, two French armies, and a French fleet trapped Lord Cornwallis at Yorktown and forced his army to surrender in October 1781.

Zenger, John Peter Printer of the *New York Weekly Journal* who was acquitted in 1735 by a jury of the crime of seditious libel after his paper sharply criticized Governor William Cosby.

Zimmerman telegram Telegram from Germany's foreign secretary instructing the German minister in Mexico to ask that country's government to attack the United States in return for German assistance in regaining Mexico's "lost provinces" (Texas, New Mexico, and Arizona).

Zion A term used by the Mormons to describe their "promised land" where they could prosper and live without persecution.

Zionism Movement to establish a Jewish state in Palestine.

zoot suits Flamboyant outfits that featured oversized trousers; commonly worn by young Mexican-American men as a symbol of ethnic and cultural rebellion.

CHAPTER 1

Two recent general surveys of early American history provide excellent coverage up to Independence: **Alan Taylor, *American Colonies*** (2001); and **Richard Middleton, *Colonial America: A History, 1565–1776*,** 3rd ed. (2002). For a useful collection of essays, see **Stanley N. Katz, John M. Murrin,** and **Douglas Greenberg, eds., *Colonial America: Essays in Politics and Social Development*,** 5th ed. (2001).

Brian M. Fagan, *The Great Journey: The Peopling of Ancient America* (1987) is a fine introduction to pre-Columbian America. For the age of explorations, see **G. V. Scammell, *The First Imperial Age: European Overseas Expansion c. 1400–1715*** (1989); and **Alfred W. Crosby's** classic synthesis, *The Columbian Exchange: Biological and Cultural Consequences of 1492* (1972). For the slave trade, see **John Thornton, *Africa and Africans in the Making of the Modern World, 1400–1800*,** 2nd ed. (1998), which insists that Africans retained control of their affairs, including the slave trade, through the 17th century; and **Patrick Manning, *Slavery and African Life: Occidental, Oriental, and African Slave Trades*** (1990), which emphasizes the devastating impact of the slave trade in the 18th and 19th centuries. **Ira Berlin's *Many Thousands Gone: The First Two Centuries of Slavery in North America*** (1998) is an effective and comprehensive synthesis of a huge subject.

James Lockhart and **Stuart B. Schwartz, *Early Latin America: A History of Colonial Latin America and Brazil*** (1983) is an outstanding introduction to the Iberian empires. **J. H. Parry's *The Spanish Seaborne Empire*** (1966) retains great value. **David J. Weber's *The Spanish Frontier in North America*** (1992) is easily the best introduction to its subject.

CHAPTER 2

W. J. Eccles, *The French in North America, 1500–1783*, rev. ed. (1998) is a concise and authoritative survey. **C. R. Boxer, *The Dutch Seaborne Empire, 1600–1800*** (1965) is still the best synthesis of Dutch activity overseas. **Joyce E. Chaplin's *Subject Matter: Technology, the Body, and Science on the Anglo-American Frontier, 1500–1676*** (2001) and **Karen O. Kupperman's *Indians and English: Facing Off in Early America*** (2000) are efforts to keep Indians and the settlers of early Virginia and New England within a common focus. **Edmund S. Morgan's *American Slavery, American Freedom: The Ordeal of Colonial Virginia*** (1975) has become a classic, but **Thad W. Tate** and **David L. Ammerman, eds., *The Chesapeake in the Seventeenth-Century: Essays on Anglo-American Society*** (1979) is also indispensable. For the West Indies, see **Richard S. Dunn, *Sugar and Slaves: The Rise of the Planter Class in the English West Indies, 1624–1713*** (1972). **Winthrop Jordan's *White over Black: American Attitudes toward the Negro, 1550–1812*** (1968) retains its freshness and acuity.

Edmund S. Morgan's *Visible Saints: The History of a Puritan Idea* (1963) is a brief and accessible introduction to Puritan values in New England's first century. **Michael P. Winship's *Making Heretics: Militant Protestantism and Free Grace in Massachusetts, 1636–1641*** (2002) brings a challenging new perspective to the Antinomian controversy. **Carla G. Pestana's *Quakers and Baptists in Colonial Massachusetts*** (1991) deals with other dissenters from the New England Way. **Daniel Vickers, *Farmers and Fishermen: Two Centuries of Work in Essex County, Massachusetts, 1630–1850*** (1994) is the most helpful introduction to the New England economy.

For the Restoration colonies, see especially **Robert C. Ritchie, *The Duke's Province: A Study of New York Politics and Society, 1664–1691*** (1977); **Gary B. Nash, *Quakers and Politics: Pennsylvania Politics, 1681–1726*** (1968); **Barry J. Levy, *Quakers and the American Family: British Settlement in the Delaware Valley*** (1988); **Peter H. Wood, *Black Majority: Negroes in Colonial South Carolina from 1670 through the Stono Rebellion*** (1974), and **Alan Gallay, *The Indian Slave Trade: The Rise of the English Empire in the American South, 1670–1717*** (2002).

CHAPTER 3

The most comprehensive account of the Navigation Acts and England's instruments of enforcement is still **Charles M. Andrews, *The Colonial Period of American History*,** vol. 4 (1938). **Ian K. Steele's *The English Atlantic, 1675–1740: An Exploration of Communication and Community*** (1986) is original and imaginative.

Daniel K. Richter's *The Ordeal of the Long-house: The People of the Iroquois League in the Era of European Colonization* (1992); **Richard W. Cogley's *John Eliot's Mission to the Indians before King Philip's War*** (1999); **Jill Lepore's *The Name of War: King Philip's War and the Origins of American Identity*** (1998); and **Wilcomb Washburn, *The Governor and the Rebel: A History of Bacon's Rebellion in Virginia*** (1957) are all essential to understanding the crisis of the 1670s. For Virginia's transition to slavery after Bacon's Rebellion, see **Anthony S. Parent, Jr., *Foul Means: The Formation of a Slave Society in Virginia, 1660–1740*** (2003).

For the Dominion of New England and the Glorious Revolution in the colonies, see **Richard R. Johnson, *Adjustment to Empire: The New England Colonies, 1675–1715*** (1981); **John M. Murrin,** "The Menacing Shadow of Louis XIV and the Rage of Jacob Leisler: The Constitutional Ordeal of Seventeenth-Century New York," in **Stephen L. Schechter** and **Richard B. Bernstein, eds., *New York and the Union: Contributions to the American Constitutional Experience*** (1990), pp. 29–71; and **Lois G. Carr** and **David W. Jordan, *Maryland's Revolution of Government, 1689–1692*** (1974). The best study of Salem witchcraft, which is also a superb introduction to the Indian wars in northern New England, is **Mary Beth Norton, *In the Devil's Snare: The Salem Witchcraft Crisis of 1692*** (2002).

For the French and Spanish colonies in these critical decades, see especially **Richard White, *The Middle Ground: Indians, Empires, and Republics in the Great Lakes Region, 1650–1815*** (1991); and **Ramón Gutiérrez, *When Jesus Came, the Corn Mothers Went Away: Marriage, Sexuality, and Power in New Mexico, 1500–1846*** (1992), particularly on the Pueblo revolt.

On the householder economy in English North America, see **Laurel Thatcher Ulrich's *Good Wives: Images and**

Reality in the Lives of Women in Northern New England (1982), and **Mary M. Schweitzer**, *Custom and Contract: Household, Government, and the Economy in Colonial Pennsylvania* (1987).

CHAPTER 4

The best study of eighteenth-century immigration is **Bernard Bailyn**, *Voyagers to the West: A Passage in the Peopling of America on the Eve of the Revolution* (1986). **A. Roger Ekirch**, *Bound for America: The Transportation of British Convicts to the Colonies* (1987) is also important. For gentility and the Enlightenment, excellent studies include **Richard L. Bushman**, *The Refinement of America: Persons, Houses, Cities* (1992); **Ned Landsman**, *From Colonials to Provincials: Thought and Culture in America, 1680–1760* (1998); **David S. Shields**, *Civil Tongues and Polite Letters in British America* (1997); and **Charles E. Clark**, *The Public Prints: The Newspaper in Anglo-American Culture, 1665–1740* (1994). For early Georgia, see **Harold E. Davis**, *The Fledgling Province: Social and Cultural Life in Colonial Georgia, 1773–1776* (1976). **Mark A. Noll**, *The Rise of Evangelicalism: The Age of Edwards, Whitefield, and the Wesleys* (2003) provides an insightful overview of the Great Awakening. **Bernard Bailyn's** *The Origins of American Politics* (1968) has had a major impact.

For the renewal of imperial conflict after 1739, see **Jill Lepore**, *New York Burning: Liberty, Slavery, and Conspiracy in Eighteenth-Century Manhattan* (2005); **Fred Anderson**, *Crucible of War: The Seven Years War and the Fate of Empire in British North America, 1754–1766* (2000); **Timothy J. Shannon**, *Indians and Colonists at the Crossroads of Empire: The Albany Congress of 1754* (2000); **John Mack Faragher**, *A Great and Noble Scheme: The Tragic Story of the Expulsion of the French Acadians from their American Homeland* (2005); and **Ian K. Steele**, *Betrayals: Fort William Henry and the "Massacre"* (1990).

CHAPTER 5

The best one-volume narrative history of the coming of the Revolution remains **Merrill Jensen's** *The Founding of a Nation: A History of the American Revolution, 1763–1776* (1968). **Bernard Bailyn's** *The Ideological Origins of the American Revolution* (1967) has had an enormous impact. **Gregory Evans Dowd** provides a fresh perspective in *War Under Heaven: Pontiac, the Indian Nations, and the British Empire* (2002).

On the three imperial crises, **Edmund S. and Helen M. Morgan's** *The Stamp Act Crisis, Prologue to Revolution*, 3rd ed. (1953, 1995) has lost none of its saliency. **Pauline Maier's** *From Resistance to Revolution: Colonial Radicals and the Development of American Opposition to Britain, 1765–1776* (1972) and **Richard D. Brown's** *Revolutionary Politics in Massachusetts: The Boston Committee of Correspondence and the Towns* (1970) are both excellent on the process of disaffection. **David Ammerman's** *In the Common Cause: American Response to the Coercive Acts of 1774* (1974) is especially strong on the First Continental Congress and its aftermath. **David Hackett Fischer's** *Paul Revere's Ride* (1994) is a rare combination of exhaustive research and stirring prose. **Pauline**

Maier's *American Scripture: Making the Declaration of Independence* (1997) uses 90 local declarations of independence in the spring of 1776 to give context to Jefferson's famous text.

Important studies of internal tensions include **Gary B. Nash**, *The Urban Crucible: Social Change, Political Consciousness, and the Origins of the American Revolution* (1979); **Woody Holton's** imaginative *Forced Founders: Indians, Debtors, Slaves, and the Making of the American Revolution in Virginia* (1999); **James P. Whittenburg's** "Planters, Merchants, and Lawyers: Social Change and the Origins of the North Carolina Regulation," *William and Mary Quarterly*, 3d ser., 34 (1977): 214–238; and **Richard M. Brown**, *The South Carolina Regulators* (1963) explore the internal tensions in these colonies. **David Grimsted's** "Anglo-American Racism and Phillis Wheatley's 'Sable Veil,' 'Length'ned Chain,' and 'Knitted Heart,' " in Ronald Hoffman and Peter J. Albert, eds., *Women in the Age of the American Revolution* (1989) is a superb study of the emerging antislavery movement and women's role in it.

CHAPTER 6

Stephen Conway's *The War of American Independence, 1775–1783* (1995) is a strong and accessible history. **Charles Royster's** *A Revolutionary People at War: The Continental Army and American Character, 1775–1783* (1979) is the best study of its kind. The essays in **John Shy's** *A People Numerous and Armed: Reflections on the Military Struggle for American Independence*, rev. ed. (1990) have had a tremendous influence on other historians. **David Hackett Fischer's** *Washington's Crossing* (2004) is the most important book on the Revolutionary War to appear in several decades. **Walter Edgar's** *Partisans and Redcoats: The Southern Conflict That Turned the Tide of the American Revolution* (2001) is a fresh study of the bitter partisan war in the Lower South. For the war's impact on slavery, see **Sylvia R. Frey**, *Water from the Rock: Black Resistance in a Revolutionary Age* (1991). **Henry Wiencek's** *An Imperfect God: George Washington, His Slaves, and the Creation of America* (2003) is a superb study of how and why Washington chose to emancipate his slaves. Of the numerous studies of loyalism, **Paul H. Smith's** *Loyalists and Redcoats: A Study in British Revolutionary Policy* (1964) remains one of the best. The single most important book on emerging American constitutionalism remains **Gordon S. Wood**, *The Creation of the American Republic, 1776–1787* (1969). **Jackson Turner Main's** *Political Parties Before the Constitution* (1973) carefully investigates postwar divisions within the states. **Jack N. Rakove** won a Pulitzer Prize for *Original Meanings: Politics and Ideas in the Making of the Constitution* (1996). **Saul Cornell** provides a thoughtful approach to *The Other Founders: Anti-Federalism and the Dissenting Tradition in America* (1999).

CHAPTER 7

Stanley Elkins and **Eric McKitrick**, *The Age of Federalism: The Early American Republic, 1788–1800* (1993) is definitive. An insightful essay on the Jeffersonians is **Peter S. Onuf** and **Leonard J. Sadosky**, *Jeffersonian America* (2002). **Thomas G. Slaughter**, *The Whiskey Rebellion: Frontier Epilogue to the*

American Revolution (1986) is good on its subject. **Lance Banning, *The Jeffersonian Persuasion: Evolution of a Party Ideology* (1980) and **Drew R. McCoy, *The Elusive Republic: Political Economy in Jeffersonian America* (1980) are insightful studies of Jeffersonianism. On relations with other countries, see **Lawrence Kaplan, *Entangling Alliances with None: American Foreign Policy in the Age of Jefferson* (1987) and **Donald R. Hickey, *The War of 1812: A Forgotten Conflict* (1989). **Joseph J. Ellis, *Founding Brothers: The Revolutionary Generation* (2000) and **Joanne B. Freeman, *Affairs of Honor: National Politics in the New Republic* (2001) are fine studies of the political culture of the founding generation

CHAPTER 8

Douglas C. North, *The Economic Growth of the United States, 1790–1860* (1961) is an economic overview of these years, while **George Rogers Taylor**, *The Transportation Revolution, 1815–1860* (1951) remains the best single book on its subject. On rural society in the North, see **Christopher Clark**, *The Roots of Rural Capitalism: Western Massachusetts, 1780–1860* (1990); **Laurel Thatcher Ulrich**, *A Midwife's Tale: The Life of Martha Ballard, Based on Her Diary, 1785–1812* (1990); **Martin Bruegel**, *Farm, Shop, Landing: The Rise of a Market Society in the Hudson Valley, 1780–1860* (2002); **Jack Larkin**, *The Reshaping of Everyday Life, 1790–1840* (1988); and **Carolyn Merchant**, *Ecological Revolutions: Nature, Gender, and Science in New England* (1989). **John Mack Faragher**, *Sugar Creek: Life on the Illinois Prairie* (1986) treats settler societies. Solid studies of industrial communities include **Thomas Dublin**, *Women at Work: The Transformation of Work and Community in Lowell, Massachusetts, 1810–1860* (1979), and **Anthony F. C. Wallace**, *Rockdale: The Growth of an American Village in the Early Industrial Revolution* (1978). The best introduction to the seaports in these years is **Edwin G. Burrows** and **Mike Wallace**, *Gotham: A History of New York City to 1898* (1999). **Sean Wilentz**, *Chants Democratic: New York City and the Rise of the American Working Class* (1984) remains essential.

CHAPTER 9

On the plantation economy, see **Eugene D. Genovese**, *The Political Economy of Slavery: Studies in the Economy and Society of the Slave South*, 2d ed. (1989) and **R.W. Fogel**, *Without Consent or Contract: The Rise and Fall of American Slavery* (1994). **Walter Johnson**, *Soul by Soul: Life Inside the Antebellum Slave Market* (1999) analyzes ways in which planters made a white culture out of slavery. **Bertram Wyatt-Brown**, *Southern Honor: Ethics & Behavior in the Old South* (1982) is essential. On the southern yeomanry, see **Stephanie McCurry**, *Masters of Small Worlds: Yeoman Households, Gender Relations, & the Political Culture of the South Carolina Lowcountry* (1995) and **Steven Hahn**, *The Roots of Southern Populism: Yeoman Farmers and the Transformation of the Georgia Upcountry, 1850–1890* (1983). The social history of colonial and early national slavery is ably covered in **Ira Berlin**, *Many Thousands Gone: The First Two Centuries of Slavery in North America* (1998). Two pioneering works on slave culture are **Eugene D. Genovese**, *Roll, Jordan, Roll: The

World the Slaves Made (1974) and **Lawrence W. Levine**, *Black Culture and Black Consciousness: Afro-American Folk Thought from Slavery to Freedom* (1977).

CHAPTER 10

The early chapters of Paul Starr, **The Creation of the Media: Political Origins of Modern Communications** (2004) provide valuable introduction to the communications revolution. **Stuart M. Blumin**, *The Emergence of the Middle Class: Social Experience in the American City, 1760–1900* (1989) is a thorough study of work and material life among the urban middle class. Studies that treat religion, family, and sentimental culture include **Paul E. Johnson**, *A Shopkeeper's Millennium: Society and Revivals in Rochester New York, 1815–1837* (1978); **Mary P. Ryan**, *Cradle of the Middle Class: The Family in Oneida County, New York, 1790–1865* (1981); and **Jane Tompkins**, *Sensational Designs: The Cultural Work of American Fiction, 1790–1860* (1985). Nathan O. Hatch, **The Democratization of American Christianity** (1989) is a good introduction to plainfolk religion in these years. Studies of popular literature and entertainments include **Elliott J. Gorn**, *The Manly Art: Bare-Knuckle Prize Fighting in America* (1986); **Eric Lott**, *Love & Theft: Blackface Minstrelsy and the American Working Class* (1993); **David S. Reynolds**, *Beneath the American Renaissance: The Subversive Imagination in the Age of Emerson and Melville* (1988); and **Paul E. Johnson**, *Sam Patch, the Famous Jumper* (2003). Essential books on the culture of southern whites are **Bertram Wyatt-Brown**, *Southern Honor: Ethics & Behavior in the Old South* (1982); **Christine Leigh Heyerman**, *Southern Cross: The Beginnings of the Bible Belt* (1997); and Elizabeth Fox-Genovese and Eugene D. Genovese, *The Mind of the Master Class: History and Faith in the Southern Slaveholders' Worldview* (2005). An enlightening counterpoint between black and white understandings of the slave trade (and, by extension, of the slave South generally) is presented in **Walter Johnson**, *Soul by Soul: Life Inside the Antebellum Slave Market* (1999).

CHAPTER 11

Sean Wilentz, *The Rise of American Democracy: Jefferson to Lincoln* (2006) is a comprehensive and definitive political history, while **Harry L. Watson**, *Liberty and Power: The Politics of Jacksonian America* (1990) is an excellent shorter synthesis. **John Lauritz Larson**, *Internal Improvement: National Public Works and the Promise of Popular Government in the Early United States* (2001) is essential. On legal and constitutional issues, see **R. Kent Newmeyer**, *The Supreme Court under Marshall and Taney* (1968) and **Morton J. Horwitz**, *The Transformation of American Law, 1780–1860* (1977). *George Dangerfield*, *The Era of Good Feelings* (1953) and **Glover Moore**, *The Missouri Controversy, 1819–1821* (1953) are standard treatments of their subjects. On nullification, see **William W. Freehling**, *Prelude to Civil War: The Nullification Controversy in South Carolina, 1816–1836* (1965) and **Richard E. Ellis**, *The Union at Risk: Jacksonian Democracy, States' Rights and the Nullification Crisis* (1987).

Two important accounts of slavery in national politics are **William Lee Miller**, *Arguing About Slavery: The Great Battle in the United States Congress* (1996) and **Don E. Fehrenbacher**,

The Slaveholding Republic: An Account of the United States Government's Relations to Slavery (2001). On Jackson and Indian Removal, a good introduction is **Robert V. Remini, *Andrew Jackson and His Indian Wars* (2001). On the Bank War, see **Peter Temin, *The Jacksonian Economy* (1967). The making of the party system is the subject of **Richard Hofstadter, *The Idea of a Party System: The Rise of Legitimate Opposition in the United States, 1780–1840* (1969) and **Richard P. McCormick, *The Second American Party System: Party Formation in the Jacksonian Era* (1966).

CHAPTER 12

On party ideologies, see **John Ashworth, *Agrarians & Aristocrats: Party Political Ideology in the United States, 1837–1846* (1983), and **Daniel Walker Howe, *The Political Culture of the American Whigs* (1979). Constituencies and state-level issues are addressed in **Lee Benson, *The Concept of Jacksonian Democracy: New York as a Test Case* (1961); **Ronald P. Formisano, *The Transformation of Political Culture: Massachusetts Parties, 1790s–1840s* (1983); and **Lacy K. Ford, Jr., *Origins of Southern Radicalism: The South Carolina Upcountry, 1800–1860* (1988). **Richard J. Carwardine, *Evangelicals and Politics in Antebellum America* (1993) is an insightful study of religion and politics in these years. On the politics of schools, see **Carl F. Kaestle, *Pillars of the Republic: Common Schools and American Society, 1780–1860* (1983).

Influential studies of prisons and asylums include **David J. Rothman, *The Discovery of the Asylum: Social Order and Disorder in the New Republic* (1971) and **Michael Meranze, *Laboratories of Virtue: Punishment, Revolution, and Authority in Philadelphia, 1760–1835* (1996). Drinking and temperance are the subjects of **W. J. Rorabaugh, *The Alcoholic Republic: An American Tradition* (1979). The literature on reform movements is synthesized in **Steven Mintz, *Moralists & Modernizers: America's Pre–Civil War Reformers* (1995). Students might also consult **Robert H. Abzug, *Cosmos Crumbling: American Reform and the Religious Imagination* (1994); **Jean Fagan Yellin, *Women & Sisters: The Antislavery Feminists in American Culture* (1989); and **Lori D. Ginzberg, *Women and the Work of Benevolence: Morality, Politics, and Class in the 19th-Century United States* (1990). The cultural and moral underpinnings of reform are a subtext of **Karen Halttunen's subtle and important *Murder Most Foul: The Killer and the American Gothic Imagination* (1998).

CHAPTER 13

For the theme of Manifest Destiny, the best introduction is **Frederick Merk, *Manifest Destiny and Mission in American History* (1963). See also the essays in **Samuel W. Haynes and Christopher Morris, eds., *Manifest Destiny and Empire* (1997). Two good studies of the overland trails to California and Oregon and other points west are **John D. Unruh, Jr., *The Plains Across: The Overland Emigrants and the Trans-Mississippi West, 1840–1860* (1979), and **John Mack Faragher, *Women and Men on the Overland Trail* (1978). A fine introduction to the impact of American expansion on the Indians of the West is **Philip Weeks, *Farewell, My Nation: The American Indian and

the United States 1820–1890 (rev. ed., 2000). A good study of the relationship between American expansion and the coming of war with Mexico is **David Pletcher, *The Diplomacy of Annexation: Texas, Oregon, and the Mexican War* (1973). For the Mexican War, a good narrative is **John S. D. Eisenhower, *So Far from God: The U.S. War with Mexico 1846–1848* (1989). Opposition to and support for the war by different elements of the public are chronicled in **John H. Schroeder, *Mr. Polk's War: American Opposition and Dissent, 1846–1848* (1973) and **Robert W. Johannsen, *To the Halls of the Montezumas: The Mexican War in the American Imagination* (1985). For the conflict provoked by the issue of slavery's expansion into territory acquired from Mexico, see **David M. Potter, *The Impending Crisis 1848–1861* (1976); **Richard H. Sewell, *Ballots for Freedom: Antislavery Politics in the United States 1837–1860* (1976); **Michael A. Morrison, *Slavery and the American West: The Eclipse of Manifest Destiny and the Coming of the Civil War* (1997); and **Leonard D. Richards, *The Slave Power: The Free North and Southern Domination, 1780–1860* (2000). The best study of the Compromise of 1850 is **Holman Hamilton, *Prologue to Conflict: The Crisis and Compromise of 1850* (1964). The passage and enforcement of the Fugitive Slave Act is the subject of **Stanley W. Campbell, *The Slave Catchers* (1970). Still the best book on filibustering is Robert E. May, *The Southern Dream of a Caribbean Empire 1854–1861* (1971).

CHAPTER 14

For a detailed and readable treatment of the mounting sectional conflict in the 1850s, see **Allan Nevins, *Ordeal of the Union,* 2 vols. (1947), and *The Emergence of Lincoln,* 2 vols. (1950). The Kansas-Nebraska Act and its political consequences are treated in **Gerald W. Wolff, *The Kansas-Nebraska Bill: Party, Section, and the Coming of the Civil War* (1977). The conflict in Kansas itself is treated in **Nicole Etcheson, *Bleeding Kansas: Contested Liberty in the Civil War Era* (2004). For the cross-cutting issue of nativism and the Know-Nothings, see **William E. Gienapp, *The Origins of the Republican Party, 1852–1856* (1987), and **Tyler Anbinder, *Nativism and Politics: The Know-Nothing Party in the Northern United States* (1992). Two excellent studies of the role of Abraham Lincoln in the rise of the Republican Party are **Don E. Fehrenbacher, *Prelude to Greatness: Lincoln in the 1850s* (1962), and **Kenneth Winkle, *The Young Eagle: The Rise of Abraham Lincoln* (2003). The southern response to the growth of antislavery political sentiment in the North is the theme of **William J. Cooper, Jr., *The South and the Politics of Slavery 1828–1856* (1978).

The year 1857 witnessed a convergence of many crucial events; for a stimulating book that pulls together the threads of that year of crisis, see **Kenneth M. Stampp, *America in 1857: A Nation on the Brink* (1990). For economic developments during the era, an older classic is still the best introduction: **George Rogers Taylor, *The Transportation Revolution, 1815–1860* (1951). An important dimension of the southern economy is elucidated in **Fred Bateman and Thomas Weiss, *A Deplorable Scarcity: The Failure of Industrialization in the Slave Economy* (1981). Still the best study of the Republican free-labor ideology is **Eric Foner, *Free Soil, Free Labor, Free Men: The Ideology of the Republican Party before the Civil War* (2nd ed., 1995). For southern yeoman farmers, a good study is

Stephanie McCurry, *Masters of Small Worlds: Yeoman Households, Gender Relations, and the Political Culture of the Antebellum South Carolina Low Country* (1995). The best single study of the Dred Scott case is **Don E. Fehrenbacher, *The Dred Scott Case: Its Significance in American Law and Politics*** (1978), which was published in an abridged version with the title *Slavery, Law, and Politics: The Dred Scott Case in Historical Perspective* (1981).

CHAPTER 15

The most comprehensive one-volume study of the Civil War years is **James M. McPherson, *Battle Cry of Freedom: The Civil War Era*** (1988). The fullest and most readable narrative of the military campaigns and battles is **Shelby Foote, *The Civil War: A Narrative*,** 3 vols. (1958–1974). For the naval war, see **Ivan Musicant, *Divided Waters: The Naval History of the Civil War*** (1995). For the perspective of the soldiers and sailors who fought the battles, see **Bell I. Wiley's** two books: *The Life of Johnny Reb* (1943) and *The Life of Billy Yank* (1952). The motives of soldiers for enlisting and fighting are treated in **James M. McPherson, *For Cause and Comrades: Why Men Fought in the Civil War*** (1997).

For the home front in North and South, see **Phillip Shaw Paludan, *"A People's Contest": The Union and Civil War, 1861–1865*** (1988), and **Emory Thomas, *The Confederate Nation, 1861–1865*** (1979). For women and children, see **Elizabeth D. Leonard, *Yankee Women: Gender Battles in the Civil War*** (1994); **George C. Rable, *Civil Wards: Women and the Crisis of Southern Nationalism*** (1989); and **James Marten, *The Children's Civil War*** (1998).

For biographical studies of leaders on both sides, consult the following: **Phillip S. Paludan, *The Presidency of Abraham Lincoln*** (1994); **William C. Cooper, *Jefferson Davis, American*** (2000); **Brooks D. Simpson, *Ulysses S. Grant*** (2000); and **Emory M. Thomas, *Robert E. Lee*** (1995). For a study of the Fort Sumter crisis and the outbreak of the war that sets these events in their long-term context, see **Maury Klein, *Days of Defiance: Sumter, Secession, and the Coming of the Civil War*** (1997). For the guerrilla war in Missouri, the most useful of several books is **Michael Fellman, *Inside War: The Guerrilla Conflict in Missouri during the Civil War*** (1989). Of the many studies of diplomacy during the war, the most useful is **David P. Crook, *The North, the South, and the Powers 1861–1865*** (1974), an abridged version of which was published with the title *Diplomacy During the Civil War* (1975).

CHAPTER 16

Several studies offer important information and insights about questions of strategy and command in military operations: **Joseph G. Glatthaar, *Partners in Command: The Relationships between Leaders in the Civil War*** (1993); **Richard M. McMurry, *Two Great Rebel Armies*** (1989); **Michael C. Adams, *Our Masters the Rebels: A Speculation on Union Military Defeat in the East, 1861–1865*** (1978), reissued under the title *Fighting for Defeat* (1992); **Mark Grimsley, *The Hard Hand of War: Union Military Policy toward Southern Civilians, 1861–1865*** (1995); and **Gary W. Gallagher, *The Confederate War*** (1997). Of the many books about black soldiers in the Union Army, the most

useful is **Joseph T. Glatthaar, *Forged in Battle: The Civil War Alliance of Black Soldiers and White Officers*** (1990). The Confederate debate about enlisting and freeing slave soldiers is chronicled in **Robert Durden, *The Gray and the Black: The Confederate Debate on Emancipation*** (1972). Conscription in the Confederacy and Union is treated in **Albert B. Moore, *Conscription and Conflict in the Confederacy*** (1924), and **James W. Geary, *We Need Men: The Union Draft in the Civil War*** (1991).

For the draft riots in New York, see **Adrian Cook, *The Armies of the Streets: The New York Draft Riots of 1863*** (1974). The best study of the civil liberties issue in the North is **Mark E. Neely, Jr., *The Fate of Liberty: Abraham Lincoln and Civil Liberties*** (1990), and the same author has covered the same issue in the Confederacy in *Southern Rights: Political Prisoners and the Myth of Confederate Constitutionalism* (1999). For Civil War medicine, **Alfred Jay Bollet, *Civil War Medicine: Challenges and Triumphs*** (2002) is indispensable. A succinct account of the emancipation issue is **Ira Berlin, et al., *Slaves No More: Three Essays on Emancipation and the Civil War*** (1992).

The activities of women in the U.S. Sanitary Commission, as spies, and even as soldiers, are covered in **Jeanie Attie, *Patriotic Toil: Northern Women and the Civil War*** (1998); **Elizabeth D. Leonard, *All the Daring of a Soldier: Women of the Civil War Armies*** (1999); and **Deanne Blanton and Lauren M. Cook, *They Fought Like Demons: Women Soldiers in the American Civil War*** (2002).

CHAPTER 17

The most comprehensive and incisive history of Reconstruction is **Eric Foner, *Reconstruction: America's Unfinished Revolution 1863–1872*** (1988). For a skillful abridgement of this book, see **Foner, *A Short History of Reconstruction*** (1990). Also valuable is **Kenneth M. Stampp, *The Era of Reconstruction, 1865–1877*** (1965). Important for their insights on Lincoln and the Reconstruction question are **Peyton McCrary, *Abraham Lincoln and Reconstruction: The Louisiana Experiment*** (1978) and **LaWanda Cox, *Lincoln and Black Freedom: A Study in Presidential Leadership*** (1981). A superb study of the South Carolina Sea Islands as a laboratory of Reconstruction is **Willie Lee Rose, *Rehearsal for Reconstruction: The Port Royal Experiment*** (1964).

Three important studies of Andrew Johnson and his conflict with Congress over Reconstruction are **Eric L. McKitrick, *Andrew Johnson and Reconstruction*** (1960); **Hans L. Trefousse, *The Radical Republicans: Lincoln's Vanguard for Racial Justice*** (1969); and **Michael Les Benedict, *The Impeachment and Trial of Andrew Johnson*** (1973). Two books by **Michael Perman** connect events in the South and in Washington during Reconstruction: *Reunion without Compromise: The South and Reconstruction, 1865–1868* (1973) and *The Road to Redemption: Southern Politics 1868–1879* (1984). For counter-Reconstruction violence in the South, see **George C. Rable, *But There Was No Peace: The Role of Violence in the Politics of Reconstruction*** (1984). The evolution of sharecropping and other aspects of the transition from slavery to freedom are treated in **Roger L. Ransom and Richard Sutch, *One Kind of Freedom: The Economic Consequences of Emancipation*** (1977).

Of the many books on African Americans in Reconstruction, the following are perhaps the most valuable: **Thomas Holt**, *Black over White: Negro Political Leadership in South Carolina during Reconstruction* (1977) and **Laura F. Edwards**, *Gendered Strife and Confusion: The Political Culture of Reconstruction* (1997). An excellent collection of essays on the Freedmen's Bureau is **Paul A. Cimbala and Randall Miller, eds.**, *The Freedmen's Bureau and Reconstruction* (1999). Both black and white churches are the subject of **Daniel Stowell**, *Rebuilding Zion: The Religious Reconstruction of the South, 1863–1877* (1998).

CHAPTER 18

For general histories of the West, see **Robert V. Hine and John Mack Faragher**, *The American West: A New Interpretive History* (2000); **Richard White**, *"It's Your Misfortune and None of My Own": A New History of the American West* (1991); **William Deverell, ed.**, *A Companion to the American West* (2004); and **Patricia Nelson Limerick**, *The Legacy of Conquest: The Unbroken Past of the American West* (1987). For one of the "classics" of Western history, see **Henry Nash Smith**, *Virgin Land: The American West as Symbol and Myth* (1950).

On industrial ranching, see especially **David Igler**, *Industrial Cowboys: Miller & Lux and the Transformation of the Far West, 1850–1920* (2001). Influential and useful treatments of the industrial transformation of the West are **William Cronon**, *Nature's Metropolis: Chicago and the Great West* (1991), and **William G. Robbins**, *Colony and Empire: The Capitalist Transformation of the American West* (1994).

Histories that explore the Chinese in America include **Ronald Takaki**, *Strangers from a Different Shore: A History of Asian Americans* (1989, rev. 1998); **Yong Chen**, *Chinese San Francisco, 1850–1943: A Trans-Pacific Community* (2000); **Judy Yung**, *Unbound Feet: A Social History of Chinese Women in San Francisco* (1995); **Erika Lee**, *At America's Gates: Chinese Immigration during the Exclusion Era, 1882–1943* (2003); and **Sucheng Chan**, *This Bittersweet Soil: The Chinese in California Agriculture, 1860–1910* **(1986).** For a discussion of Southwest borderlands, see **Sarah Deutsch**, *No Separate Refuge: Culture, Class, and Gender on an Anglo-Hispanic Frontier in the American Southwest, 1880–1940* (1987). On mining, see **Elizabeth Jameson**, *All That Glitters: Class, Conflict, and Community in Cripple Creek* (1998). On women, see **Rebecca J. Mead**, *How the Vote Was Won: Woman Suffrage in the Western United States, 1868–1914* (2004); **Peggy Pascoe**, *Relations of Rescue: The Search for Female Moral Authority in the American West, 1974–1939* (1990); and **Sandra Myres**, *Western Women and the Frontier Experience, 1880–1915* (1982).

On the 19th- and 20th-century myths of the frontier, see **Richard White and Patricia Nelson Limerick**, *The Frontier in American Culture* (1994). The Indians' response to the reservation system after the 1860s is discussed in **Frederick Hoxie, Peter C. Mancall, and James H. Merrill, eds.**, *American Nations: Encounters in Indian Country, 1850 to the Present* (2001) and **Robert M. Utley**, *The Indian Frontier of the American West, 1846–1890* (1984). For a fascinating discussion of Buffalo Bill, see **Joy S. Kasson**, *Buffalo Bill's West: Celebrity, Memory, and Popular History* (2000).

On the New South, see especially **Edward I. Ayers**, *The Promise of the New South: Life after Reconstruction* (1992)

and the classic **C. Vann Woodward**, *Origins of the New South, 1877–1913* (1951). The Lost Cause ideology is examined in **Gaines M. Foster**, *Ghosts of the Confederacy: Defeat, the Lost Cause, and the Emergence of the New South* (1987). The rising tide of white racism is chronicled by **Joel Williamson**, *The Crucible of Race: Black-White Relations in the American South since Emancipation* (1984), which was also published in an abridged edition with the title *A Rage for Order: Black-White Relations in the American South since Emancipation* (1986).

On African American political action after the war, the best book is **Steven Hahn**, *A Nation under Our Feet: Black Political Struggles in the Rural South from Slavery to the Great Migration* (2003). On black experience after Reconstruction, see **Glenda Elizabeth Gilmore**, *Gender and Jim Crow: Women and the Politics of White Supremacy in North Carolina, 1896–1920* (1996); **Leon Litwack**, *Trouble in Mind: Black Southerners in the Age of Jim Crow* (1998); and **Michele Mitchell**, *Righteous Propagation: African Americans and the Politics of Racial Destiny after Reconstruction* (2004). On Ida B. Wells' anti-lynching campaign, a good place to start is **Gail Bederman**, *Manliness and Civilization: A Cultural History of Gender and Race in the United States, 1880–1917* (1995).

CHAPTER 19

General histories of the Gilded Age include **Rebecca Edwards**, *New Spirits: Americans in the Gilded Age, 1865–1905* (2006); and **Alan Trachtenberg**, *The Incorporation of America: Culture and Society in the Gilded Age* (1982).

For the impact of the railroad on the Gilded Age economy and culture, see **George R. Taylor and Irene D. Neu**, *The American Railroad Network, 1861–1890* (2003). For the rise of industry and "big business," the following are useful: **Walter Licht**, *Industrializing America* (1995) and **Glenn Porter**, *The Rise of Big Business, 1860–1910*, rev. ed. (1992). The best biography of Rockefeller is **Ron Chernow**, *Titan* (1998).

On the middle class and class hierarchy see **Sven Beckert**, *The Monied Metropolis: New York City and the Consolidation of the American Bourgeoisie, 1850–1896* (2001); **Stuart Blumin**, *The Emergence of the Middle Class: Social Experience in the American City, 1760–1900* (1989); and **Lawrence W. Levine**, *Highbrow/Lowbrow: the Emergence of Cultural Hierarchy in America* (1988).

For discussions of relation of class hierarchy to race, see **Gail Bederman**, *Manliness and Civilization: A Cultural History of Gender and Race in the United States, 1880–1917* (1995); and **Matthew Frye Jacobson**, *Barbarian Virtues: The United States Encounters Foreign Peoples at Home and Abroad, 1876–1917* (2000).

The effects of white-collar work on men and women are detailed in **Olivier Zunz**, *Making America Corporate, 1870–1920* (1990), and **Sue Porter Benson**, *Counter Cultures: Saleswomen, Managers, and Customers in American Department Stores, 1890–1940* (1986).

The rise of the department store is examined in **William Leach**, *Land of Desire: Merchants, Power, and the Rise of a New American Culture* (1993) and **Elaine S. Abelson**, *When Ladies Go A-Thieving: Middle-Class Shoplifters in the Victorian Department Store* (1989). Middle-class consumer culture is also discussed in **Ellen Gruber Garvey**, *The Adman in the Parlor:*

Magazines and the Gendering of Consumer Culture, 1880s to 1910s (1996), while the cultural development of American museums is the subject of **Steven Conn, *Museums and American Intellectual Life, 1876–1926*** (1998).

Conflicting visions of the Chicago World's Fair can be found in **Robert W. Rydell, *All the World's a Fair: Visions of Empire at the American International Expositions, 1876–1916*** (1984); **James Gilbert, *Perfect Cities: Chicago's Utopias of 1893*** (1991); and **Christopher Robert Reed, *"All the World Is Here": The Black Presence at the White City*** (2000).

On working-class and popular culture in cities, see **Nan Enstad, *Lades of Labor, Girls of Adventure: Working Women, Popular Culture, and Labor Politics at the Turn of the Century*** (1999); **John F. Kasson, *Amusing the Million: Coney Island at the Turn of the Century*** (1978); **David Nasaw, *Going Out: The Rise and Fall of Public Amusements*** (1993); and **Kathy Peiss, *Cheap Amusements: Working Women and Leisure in Turn-of-the Century New York*** (1986).

The labor movement is treated in **David Montgomery, *The Fall of the House of Labor: The Workplace, the State, and American Labor Activism*** (1987). For the Knights of Labor, see **Leon Fink, *Workingman's Democracy: The Knights of Labor and American Politics*** (1983), and **Robert E. Weir, *Beyond Labor's Veil: The Culture of the Knights of Labor*** (1996). On Homestead, see **Paul Krause, *The Battle for Homestead, 1880–1892*** (1992). For Haymarket and Pullman, see **Carl Smith, *Urban Disorder and the Shape of Belief: the Great Chicago Fire, the Haymarket Bomb, and the Model Town of Pullman*** (1995).

On the legacies of Populism see **Elizabeth Sanders, *Roots of Reform: Farmers, Workers and the American State, 1877–1917*** (1999). A fresh interpretation of several populist movements in American history is **Michael Kazin, *The Populist Persuasion: An American History*** (1995). For the beginnings of Progressive reform during this era, see the early chapters of **Michael McGerr, *A Fierce Discontent: Rise and Fall of the Progressive Movement in America, 1870–1920*** (2003).

CHAPTER 20

For a general overview of the period, see **Alan Dawley, *Struggles for Justice: Social Responsibility and the Liberal State*** (1991) and **Nell Irvin Painter, *Standing at Armageddon: The United States, 1877–1919*** (1987). On economic growth and corporate development, see **Harold G. Vatter, *The Drive to Industrial Maturity: The United States Economy, 1860–1914*** (1975), **Glenn Porter, *The Rise of Big Business, 1860–1910*** (1973), and **Robert Kanigel, *The One Best Way: Frederick Winslow Taylor and the Enigma of Efficiency*** (1997).

On immigration, consult **Roger Daniels, *Coming to America: A History of Immigration and Ethnicity in American Life*** (2002) and **Steven P. Erie, *Rainbow's End: Irish Americans and the Dilemmas of Urban Machine Politics, 1840–1945*** (1988). **David Montgomery, *The Fall of the House of Labor, 1865–1925*** (1987), offers a detailed portrait of labor during this period, and **John Hope Franklin** and **Alfred A. Moss Jr., *From Slavery to Freedom: A History of Negro Americans*,** 7th ed. (1994), offers a comprehensive account of African American life. On the rise of mass culture, see **David Nasaw, *Going Out: The Rise and Fall of Public Amusements*** (1993), and on the "new woman" and feminism, consult, **Nancy F. Cott, *The Grounding of Modern Feminism*** (1987).

CHAPTER 21

No topic in 20th-century American history has generated as large and rapidly changing a scholarship as has progressivism. Today, few scholars treat this political movement in the terms set forth by the progressives themselves: as a movement of "the people" against the "special interests." In *The Age of Reform: From Bryan to FDR* (1955), **Richard Hofstadter** argues that progressivism was the expression of a declining Protestant middle class at odds with the new industrial order. In *The Search for Order, 1877–1920* (1967), **Robert Wiebe** finds the movement's core in a rising middle class, closely allied to the corporations and bureaucratic imperatives that were defining this new order. **Gabriel Kolko, *The Triumph of Conservatism: A Reinterpretation of American History*** (1963), and **James Weinstein, *The Corporate Ideal in the Liberal State, 1900–1918*** (1969), both argue that progressivism was the work of industrialists themselves, who were eager to ensure corporate stability and profitability in a dangerously unstable capitalist economy. Without denying the importance of this corporate search for order, **Nell Irvin Painter, *Standing at Armageddon: The United States, 1877–1919*** (1987), and **Alan Dawley, *Struggles for Justice: Social Responsibility and the Liberal State*** (1991), insist on the role of the working class, women, and blacks in shaping the progressive agenda.

James T. Kloppenberg, *Uncertain Victory: Social Democracy and Progressivism in European and American Thought, 1870–1920* (1986), and **Thomas J. Knock, *To End All Wars: Woodrow Wilson and the Quest for a New World Order*** (1992), emphasize the influence of socialism on progressive thought, while **Martin J. Sklar, *The Corporate Reconstruction of American Capitalism, 1900–1916: The Market, the Law and Politics*** (1988), stresses the role of progressivism in "containing" or taming socialism. **Paul Boyer, *Urban Masses and Moral Order in America, 1820–1920*** (1978), treats progressivism as a cultural movement to enforce middle-class norms on an unruly urban and immigrant population. **Theda Skocpol, *Protecting Soldiers and Mothers: The Political Origins of Social Policy in the United States*** (1992), reconstructs the central role of middle-class Protestant women in shaping progressive social policy, while **Robert M. Crunden, *Ministers of Reform: The Progressives' Achievement in American Civilization, 1889–1920*** (1982), stresses the religious roots of progressive reform. Summaries of some of these various interpretations of progressivism—but by no means all—can be found in **Arthur S. Link** and **Richard L. McCormick, *Progressivism*** (1983). For the most recent synthesis of the progressive era, see **Michael McGerr, *A Fierce Discontent: The Rise and Fall of the Progressive Movement in America, 1870–1920*** (2003).

CHAPTER 22

General works on America's imperialist turn in the 1890s and early years of the 20th century include **John Dobson, *America's Ascent: The United States Becomes a Great Power, 1880–1914*** (1978), **Walter LaFeber, *The Cambridge History of Foreign Relations: The Search for Opportunity, 1865–1913*** (1993), and **Emily Rosenberg, *Spreading the American Dream: American Economic and Cultural Expansion, 1890–1945*** (1982). **David F. Trask, *The War with Spain in 1898*** (1981), is a comprehensive study of the Spanish-American War, but it should be supplemented with **Philip S. Foner,** *The Spanish-Cuban-American War and the Birth of American Imperialism,* 2 vols. (1972). **Stuart Creighton Miller,** *"Benevolent Assimilation": The American Conquest of the Philippines, 1899–1903* (1982), analyzes the Filipino-American war, **Louis A. Perez,** *Cuba Under the Platt Amendment, 1902–1934* (1986), examines the extension of U.S. control over Cuba, and **Marilyn B. Young,** *The Rhetoric of Empire: American China Policy, 1895–1901* (1968), explores the unfolding Open Door policy toward China.

   Howard K. Beale, *Theodore Roosevelt and the Rise of America to World Power* (1956), is still a crucial work on Roosevelt's foreign policy. Consult **Emily Rosenberg,** *Financial Missionaries to the World: The Politics and Culture of Dollar Diplomacy, 1900–1930* (1999) on the "dollar diplomacy" that emerged from the Taft Administration. On Wilson's foreign policy, see **Thomas J. Knock,** *To End All Wars: Woodrow Wilson and the Quest for a New World Order* (1992), and **Lloyd C. Gardner,** *Safe for Democracy: The Anglo-American Response to Revolution, 1913–1923* (1984).

CHAPTER 23

On America's neutrality and road to war, consult **Arthur S. Link,** *Woodrow Wilson: Revolution, War and Peace* (1979), and **John Milton Cooper Jr.,** *The Vanity of Power: American Isolationism and the First World War, 1914–1917* (1969). **David Kennedy,** *Over Here: The First World War and American Society* (1980), is a superb account of the effects of war on American society. For details on industrial mobilization, consult **Robert D. Cuff,** *The War Industries Board: Business–Government Relations during World War I* (1973). **David Montgomery,** *The Fall of the House of Labor: The Workplace, the State, and American Labor Activism, 1865–1925* (1987), expertly reconstructs the escalation of labor–management tensions during the war. **Stephen Vaughn,** *Holding Fast the Inner Lines: Democracy, Nationalism, and the Committee on Public Information* (1980), is an important account of the CPI, the government's central propaganda agency.

   Harry N. Scheiber, *The Wilson Administration and Civil Liberties, 1917–1921* (1960), analyzes the repression of dissent. On Wilson, Versailles, and the League of Nations, consult **Thomas J. Knock,** *To End All Wars: Woodrow Wilson and the Quest for a New World Order* (1992); **Arno Mayer,** *The Politics and Diplomacy of Peacemaking: Containment and Counterrevolution at Versailles, 1918–1919* (1967); and **Lloyd C. Gardner,** *Safe for Democracy: The Anglo-American Response to Revolution, 1913–1923* (1984). **Nell Irvin Painter,** *Standing at Armageddon: The United States, 1877–1919* (1987), offers a good overview of the class and racial divisions that convulsed American society in 1919. On the Red Scare, see **Robert K. Murray,** *Red Scare: A Study in National Hysteria* (1955). **William Tuttle Jr.,** *Race Riot: Chicago in the Red Summer of 1919* (1970), examines postwar race conflict, while **Judith Stein,** *The World of Marcus Garvey: Race and Class in Modern Society* (1986), explores the emergence of Marcus Garvey and the Universal Negro Improvement Association.

CHAPTER 24

William Leuchtenberg, *The Perils of Prosperity, 1914–1932* (1958), and **Ellis Hawley,** *The Great War and the Search for a Modern Order: A History of the American People and Their Institutions, 1917–1933* (1979), offer useful overviews of the 1920s. Important works on the consumer revolution include **Warren I. Susman,** *Culture as History: The Transformation of American Society in the Twentieth Century* (1984), **Roland Marchand,** *Advertising the American Dream: Making Way for Modernity, 1920–1940* (1985), and **Kathy Lee Peiss,** *Hope in a Jar: The Making of America's Beauty Culture* (1998). **John D. Hicks,** *Republican Ascendancy, 1921–1933* (1960), still serves as a good introduction to national politics, but consult, too, **Thomas B. Silver,** *Coolidge and the Historians* (1982) and **Ellis Hawley, ed.,** *Herbert Hoover as Secretary of Commerce: Studies in New Era Thought and Practice* (1974). On agricultural distress and protest, see **Theodore Saloutos** and **John D. Hicks,** *Twentieth Century Populism: Agricultural Discontent in the Middle West, 1900–1939* (1951).

   John Higham, *Strangers in the Land: Patterns of American Nativism, 1865–1925* (1955), remains an excellent work on the spirit of intolerance that gripped America in the 1920s. See also **Mae Ngai,** *Impossible Subjects: Illegal Aliens and the Making of Modern America* (2004). On the 1920s resurgence of the Ku Klux Klan, consult **Nancy MacLean,** *Behind the Mask of Chivalry: The Making of the Second Ku Klux Klan* (1994). **Irving Bernstein,** *The Lean Years: A History of the American Worker, 1920–1933* (1960), remains the most thorough examination of 1920s workers. On ethnic communities, Americanization, and political mobilization in the 1920s, see **Gary Gerstle,** *Working-Class Americanism: The Politics of Labor in a Textile City, 1914–1960* (1989), **George J. Sánchez,** *Becoming Mexican American: Ethnicity, Culture and Identity in Chicano Los Angeles, 1900–1945* (1993), and **Kristi Andersen,** *The Creation of a Democratic Majority, 1928–1936* (1979). On the Harlem Renaissance, see **Nathan Huggins,** *Harlem Renaissance* (1971). **Malcolm Cowley,** *Exile's Return: A Narrative of Ideas* (1934), is a marvelous account of the writers and artists who comprised the "Lost Generation."

CHAPTER 25

T. H. Watkins, *The Great Depression: America in the 1930s* (1993), provides a broad overview of society and politics during the 1930s. No work better conveys the tumult and drama of that era than **Arthur M. Schlesinger Jr.'s** three-volume *The Age of Roosevelt: The Crisis of the Old Order* (1957), *The Coming of the New Deal* (1958), and *The Politics of Upheaval* (1960). On Hoover's failure to restore prosperity and popular morale, see **David Burner,** *Herbert Hoover: A Public Life* (1979). The most complete biography of FDR, and one that is remarkably good at balancing Roosevelt's life and times, is **Kenneth S. Davis,** *FDR* (1972–1993), in four volumes. On Eleanor Roosevelt, see **Blanche Wiesen Cook,** *Eleanor Roosevelt,* vols. 1 and 2 (1992, 1999). On the New Deal, see **William E. Leuchtenberg,** *Franklin D. Roosevelt and the New Deal, 1932–1940* (1963); **Anthony J. Badger,** *The New Deal: The Depression Years, 1933–1940* (1989); and **Steve Fraser** and **Gary Gerstle, eds.,** *The Rise and Fall of the New Deal Order, 1930–1980* (1989). For the role of the labor movement in national politics, consult **Steven Fraser, *Labor Will Rule: Sidney Hillman and the Rise of American Labor*** (1991). The best work on the centrality of labor and the "common man" to literary and popular culture in the 1930s is **Michael Denning, *The Cultural Front: The Laboring of American Culture in the Twentieth Century*** (1996). **Harvard Sitkoff, *A New Deal for Blacks*** (1978), is a wide-ranging examination of the place of African Americans in New Deal reform. **Abraham Hoffman, *Unwanted Mexican Americans in the Great Depression: Repatriation Pressures, 1929–1939*** (1974), is the best introduction to the repatriation campaign, while **Mae Ngai, *Impossible Subjects: Illegal Aliens and the Making of Modern America*** (2004), expertly analyzes the problems of illegal alienage that this campaign caused. The importance of John Collier and the Indian Reorganization Act are treated well in **Lawrence C. Kelly, *The Assault on Assimilation: John Collier and the Origins of Indian Policy Reform*** (1983). **James T. Patterson, *Congressional Conservatism and the New Deal*** (1967), examines the growing opposition to the New Deal in the late 1930s, while **Alan Brinkley, *The End of Reform: New Deal Liberalism in Recession and War*** (1995), provocatively explores the efforts of New Dealers to adjust their beliefs and programs as they lost support, momentum, and confidence in the late 1930s.

Chapter 26

On the United States and the coming of World War II, see **Robert Dallek, *Franklin D. Roosevelt and American Foreign Policy, 1932–1945*** (1979), and **Waldo H. Heinrichs, *Threshold of War: Franklin D. Roosevelt and American Entry into World War II*** (1988). On the isolationist coalition, see **Justus Doenecke, *Storm on the Horizon: The Challenge to American Intervention, 1939–41*** (2003). For the war's military aspects, consult **John Keegan, *The Second World War*** (2005); **Gerhard L. Weinberg, *A World at Arms: A Global History of World War II*** (1994), and Gerald F. Linderman, *The World within War: America's Combat Experience in World War II* (1997). Few narrative histories can match the dramatic narrative sweep of **Stephen Ambrose's** many works, such as *D-Day: June 6, 1944: The Climactic Battle of World War II* (1994). **Michael Beschloss, *The Conquerors: Roosevelt, Truman and the Destruction of Hitler's Germany, 1941–1945*** (2002) is also highly readable. The decision to drop atomic bombs on Japan is adroitly analyzed in **J. Samuel Walker, *Prompt and Utter Destruction: Truman and the Use of the Atomic Bombs against Japan*** (2005).

David Kennedy's *The American People in World War II: Freedom from Fear, Part II* (2003) is a recent overview of the wartime years. See also **William L. O'Neill, *A Democracy at War: American's Fight at Home and Abroad in World War II*** (1993), and **Michael C. C. Adams, *The Best War Ever: America and World War II*** (1994). The superb synthesis by John Morton Blum, *V Was for Victory: Politics and American Culture during World War II* (1976) may be supplemented by the essays in **Lewis A. Erenberg and Susan E. Hirsch, eds., *The War in American Culture: Society and Consciousness During World War II*** (1996), and **Thomas Patrick Doherty, *Projections of War: Hollywood, American Culture, and World War II*** (1993). **Richard W. Steele, *Free Speech and the Good War*** (1999) examines governmental efforts to regulate dissent. **Karen Anderson, *Wartime Women: Sex Roles, Family Relations, and the Status of Women during World War II*** (1981) surveys women's roles during the war. **Ronald Takaki, *Double Victory: A Multicultural History of America in World War II*** (2000) is a good synthesis of issues related to race and ethnicity.

Chapter 27

David Reynolds, *One World Divisible: A Global History since 1945* (2001), provides an international context for the emerging Cold War; **Walter LaFeber, *America, Russia, and the Cold War, 1945–2002*** (9th rev. ed., 2002), offers an expert interpretive synthesis of U.S. policies; and **Melvyn P. Leffler and David Painter, eds., *The Origins of the Cold War: Rewriting Histories*** (2005), presents accessible essays on Cold War controversies. **Melvyn P. Leffler, *The Specter of Communism*** (1994), is a brief, critical account of the onset of the Cold War. **Leffler's *For the Soul of Mankind: The United States, The Soviet Union, and the Cold War*** (2007) offers more detail, as do **Michael J. Hogan, *A Cross of Iron: Harry S. Truman and the Origins of the National Security State, 1945–1954*** (1998), and **Arnold A. Offner, *Another Such Victory: President Truman and the Cold War, 1945–1953*** (2002). **John Lewis Gaddis, *The Cold War: A New History*** (2005), and his many other books present a less critical view. **Alonso L. Hamby, *Man of the People: A Life of Harry S. Truman*** (1995), provides an overview of Truman and his presidency.

On the Korean War, **William Stueck, Rethinking the Korean War: A New Diplomatic and Strategic History** (2004) and *The Korean War: An International History* (1995), provide overviews, while **Bruce Cumings's** many books, including *Korea: The Unknown War* (coauthored with Jon Halliday) (1988), provide a more critical view. Postwar reconstruction of former enemies is expertly treated in **John Dower, *Embracing Defeat: Japan in the Wake of World War II*** (2000), and **Marc Trachtenberg, *A Constructed Peace: The Making of the European Settlement, 1945–1963*** (1999).

On communism and anticommunism in America during this period, *Spies: The Rise and Fall of the KGB in America* (2009), by **John Earl Haynes, Harvey Klehr, and Alexander Vassiliev**, examines Soviet espionage. **Stanley I. Kutler, *American Inquisition: Justice and Injustice in the Cold War*** (1982), and **Ellen Schrecker, *The Age of McCarthyism*** (2001), stress the excesses of anticommunist crusading.

The effect of the Cold War and containment on American culture is the subject of many excellent studies. **Michael S. Sherry, *In the Shadow of War: The United States since the 1930s*** (1995), a broad synthesis, and **Stephen Whitfield, *The Culture of the Cold War*** (rev. ed., 1996), are good places to begin. **Tom Englehardt, *The End of Victory Culture and the Disillusioning of a Generation*** (1995), provides an influential interpretation. **Paul Boyer, *By the Bomb's Early Light*** (1985), and **Alan Nadel, *Containment Culture: American Narrative, Postmodernism, and the Nuclear Age*** (1995), examine diverse cultural effects of the atomic age. **Lary May, *The Big Tomorrow: Hollywood and the Politics of the American Way*** (2000), examines Hollywood film culture. **Jessica Wang, *American Science in an Age of Anxiety: Scientists, Anticommunism, and the Cold War*** (1999), stresses FBI pressure on scientists to support the Cold War. **Lizabeth Cohen, *A Consumer's Republic: Mass Consumption in Postwar America*** (2003), critically highlights the convergence of a number of important Cold War–era social and political forces.

CHAPTER 28

James T. Patterson, *Grand Expectations: The United States, 1945–1974* (1996) provides a good overview of the years from 1953 to 1963. For accounts of Eisenhower's presidential leadership, begin with Fred I. Greenstein, *The Hidden-Hand Presidency: Eisenhower as Leader* (rev. ed., 1994). **Chester Pach, Jr. and Elmo Richardson**, *The Presidency of Dwight D. Eisenhower* (1991) presents a useful, brief history. On JFK, see Robert Dallek, *An Unfinished Life: John F. Kennedy, 1917–1963* (2003); Richard Reeves, *President Kennedy: Profile of Power* (1994); and **Seymour Hersh**, *The Dark Side of Camelot* (1997).

There are many studies of Eisenhower's foreign policy, but a good sense of the issues and scholarly debates can be gleaned from **Robert R. Bowie and Richard H. Immerman**, *Waging Peace: How Eisenhower Shaped an Enduring Cold War Strategy* (2000). **John Prados**, *Presidents' Secret Wars: CIA and Pentagon Covert Operations from World War II through the Persian Gulf* (1996), and **Zachary Karabell**, *Architects of Intervention: The United States, the Third World, and the Cold War, 1946–1962* (1999) put an important aspect of policy in a broad perspective. **Walter L. Hixson**, *Parting the Curtain: Propaganda, Culture, and the Cold War, 1945–1961* (1997) and **Kenneth Osgood**, *Total Cold War: Eisenhower's Secret Propaganda Battle at Home and Abroad* (2006) argue that cultural initiatives provided powerful weapons in the Cold War. **Lawrence Freedman**, *Kennedy's Wars: Berlin, Cuba, Laos, and Vietnam* (2000) illuminates the major international crises of the Kennedy years.

For events on the home front, **James B. Gilbert**, *A Cycle of Outrage: America's Reaction to the Juvenile Delinquent in the 1950s* (1986) discusses cultural fears; **Karal Ann Marling**, *As Seen on TV: The Visual Culture of Everyday Life in the 1950s* (1994) and **Thomas Doherty**, *Cold War, Cool Medium* (2003) stress the importance of visual imagery; and **James B. Gilbert**, *Redeeming Culture: American Religion in an Age of Science* (1997) examines another aspect of America's changing culture. **W. T. Lhamon, Jr.**, *Deliberate Speed: The Origins of a Cultural Style in the American 1950s* (1990) advances a provocative interpretation. *Sweet Land of Liberty: The Forgotten Struggle for Civil Rights in the North* (2008), by **Thomas J. Sugrue** refocuses the story of civil rights. The highly readable examination of the struggle by **Taylor Branch**, *Parting the Waters: America in the King Years, 1954–1963* (1988) may be augmented by **James Patterson**, *Brown v. Board of Education: A Civil Rights Milestone and Its Troubled Legacy* (2001); Robert O. Self, *American Babylon: Race and the Struggle for Postwar Oakland* (2003); John D'Emilio, *Lost Prophet: The Life and Times of Bayard Rustin* (2003); and **David L. Chappell**, *A Stone of Hope: Prophetic Religion and the Death of Jim Crow* (2004).

On women and families during the 1950s, **Elaine Tyler May**, *Homeward Bound: American Families in the Cold War Era* (rev. ed., 1999) stresses the new emphasis on domestic life and the family wage. Consult also the relevant pages of Ruth Rosen, *The World Split Open: How the Modern Women's Movement Changed America* (2000). **Leila J. Rupp**, *Survival in the Doldrums: The American Women's Rights Movement, 1945 to the 1960s* (1987); **Joanne Meyerowitz, ed.**, *Not June Cleaver: Women and Gender in Postwar America, 1945–1960* (1994); **Stephanie Coontz**, *The Way We Never Were: American Families and the Nostalgia Trip* (1992); and **Martin Meeker**, *Contacts Desired: Gay and Lesbian Communications and Community, 1940s to 1970s* (2006) work against that grain.

CHAPTER 29

On Lyndon Johnson, see **Robert J. Dallek**, *Flawed Giant: Lyndon Johnson and His Times, 1961–1973* (1998), and **Randall Woods**, *LBJ: Architect of American Ambition* (2006).

The many outstanding overviews of U.S. involvement in Vietnam include **George Herring**, *America's Longest War: The United States and Vietnam, 1950–1975* (rev. ed., 2001); **Robert D. Schulzinger**, *A Time for War: The United States and Vietnam, 1941–1975* (1997); **David Kaiser**, *American Tragedy: Kennedy, Johnson, and the Origins of the Vietnam War* (2000); **Fredrik Logevall**, *The Origins of the Vietnam War* (2001); **James Mann**, *A Grand Delusion: America's Descent into Vietnam* (2001); and **James H. Willbanks**, *Abandoning Vietnam: How America Left and South Vietnam Lost Its War* (2004). *Working-Class War: American Combat Soldiers and Vietnam* (1993) and *Patriots: The Vietnam War Remembered from All Sides* (2003), both by **Christian Appy**, provide a wide range of perspectives. See also **Odd Arne Wested**, *The Global Cold War* (2005), and **Jussi Hanhimaki**, *The Flawed Architect: Henry Kissinger and American Foreign Policy* (2004). **Jeffrey Kimball**, *The Vietnam War Files: Uncovering the Secret History of Nixon-Era Strategy* (2004), collects and skillfully organizes a revealing set of documents. Finally, **David Maraniss**, *They Marched into Sunlight: War and Peace: Vietnam and America October 1967* (2003), moves back and forth, between Vietnam and the home front, during a single, crucial month.

The "movement of movements" during the 1960s can be surveyed, from diverse vantage points, in **David W. Levy**, *The Debate over Vietnam* (rev. ed., 1994); **Lynn Spigel and Michael Curtain**, *The Revolution Wasn't Televised: Sixties Television and Social Conflict* (1997); **Maurice Isserman and Michael Kazin**, *America Divided: The Civil War of the 1960s* (1999); and **Edward K. Spann and David L. Anderson, eds.**, *Democracy's Children: The Young Rebels of the 1960s and the Power of Ideals* (2003). On the civil rights movement and its larger context, begin with **Thomas J. Sugrue**, *Sweet Land of Liberty: The Forgotten Struggle for Civil Rights in the North* (2008). **Taylor Branch** concludes his multivolume history with *Pillar of Fire: America in the King Years, 1963–1965* (1998), and *At Canaan's Edge: America in the King Years, 1965–68* (2006). **William L. Van Deburg**, *New Day in Babylon: The Black Power Movement and American Culture, 1965–1975* (1992), along with **Kathleen Cleaver and George Katsiaficas, eds.**, *Liberation, Imagination, and the Black Panther Party: A New Look at the Panthers and their Legacy* (2001), offer useful overviews, while **Robert Self**, *American Babylon: Race and the Struggle for Postwar Oakland* (2003), provides a superb local study, as does **Gerald Horne**, *Fire This Time: The Watts Uprising and the 1960s* (1995). See also **Robin D.G. Kelley**, *Freedom Dreams: The Black Radical Tradition* (2002).

On the late 1960s and early 1970s, begin with the opening portions of **Bruce J. Shuman**, *The Seventies: The Great Shift in American Culture, Society, and Politics* (2001), and of **Andreas Hillen**, *1973 Nervous Breakdown: Watergate, Warhol, and the Birth of Post-Sixties America* (2006). The year of 1968 is the subject of numerous volumes, including **Carole**

Fink, Philipp Gassert, and Detlef Junker, eds., *1968: The World Transformed* (1998); **Tariq Ali and Susan Watkins, *1968: Marching in the Streets*** (1998); and **Mark Kurlansky, *1968: The Year that Rocked the World*** (2003). On the riddle that was Richard Nixon, see **Richard Reeves, *President Nixon: Alone in the White House*** (2001); **David Greenberg, *Nixon's Shadow: The History of an Image*** (2003); and **Mark Feeney, *Nixon at the Movies*** (2004). **Stanley I. Kutler, ed., *Abuse of Power: The New Nixon Tapes*** (1997), provides evidence of Nixon's approach to politics and constitutional limits, in his own words, along with commentary that updates Kutler's own *The Wars of Watergate*. **John D. Skrentny, *The Minority Revolution*** (2002), details the bureaucratic activism that expanded rights during the Nixon years, while interpretations of activism on the Supreme Court can be found in **Morton J. Horwitz, *The Warren Court and the Pursuit of Justice*** (1999), and in **Lucas A. Powe, Jr., *The Warren Court and American Politics*** (2000).

CHAPTER 30

For differing views of the political trends that came together during the 1980s, see **Garry Wills, *Reagan's America: Innocents at Home*** (rev. ed., 2000); **Burton J. Kaufman, *The Presidency of James Earl Carter*** (1993); **Douglas Brinkley, *The Unfinished Presidency: Jimmy Carter's Journey to the Nobel Peace Prize*** (1998); **John W. Sloan, *The Reagan Effect: Economics and Presidential Leadership*** (1999); **Frances Fitzgerald, *Way Out There in the Blue: Reagan and Star Wars and the End of the Cold War*** (2000); **Lisa McGirr, *Suburban Warriors: The Origins of the New American Right*** (2001); **John Schoenwald, *A Time for Choosing: The Rise of Modern American Conservatism*** (2001); **W. Carl Biven, *Jimmy Carter's Economy: Policy in an Age of Limits*** (2002); **W. Elliott Brownlee and Hugh Davis Graham, eds., *The Reagan Presidency: Pragmatic Conservatism and Its Legacies*** (2003); **Gil Troy, *Morning in America: How Ronald Reagan Invented the 1980s*** (2005); **John Ehrman, *The Eighties: America in the Age of Reagan*** (2005); **Richard Reeves, *President Reagan: The Triumph of Imagination*** (2005); **Mark Bowden, *Guests of the Ayatollah: The First Battle in America's War with Militant Islam*** (2006). See also **Bruce J. Schulman, *The Seventies: The Great Shift in American Culture, Society, and Politics*** (2001); **James T. Patterson, *Restless Giant: The United States from Watergate to Bush vs. Gore*** (2005); and **Sean Wilentz, *The Age of Reagan: A History*** (200&).

Suggestive studies relevant to themes of social and cultural activism include **Juan P. Garcia, ed., *Mexican Americans in the 1990s*** (1997); **John D'Emilio, William B. Turner, and Urvashi Vaid, eds., *Creating Change: Sexuality, Public Policy, and Civil Rights*** (2000); **Ellen Messer-Davidow, *Disciplining Feminism: From Social Action to Academic Discourse*** (2002); **Frank Wu, *Yellow: Race in America Beyond Black and White*** (2002); **Larry Nesper, *The Walleye War: The Struggle for Ojibwe Spearfishing and Treaty Rights*** (2002); **Sara Evans, *Tidal Wave: How Women Changed America at Century's End*** (2003); **Van Gosse and Richard Moser, eds., *The World the 60s Made: Politics and Culture in Recent America*** (2003); **David Carter, *Stonewall: The Riots That Sparked the Gay Revolution*** (2004); **Laura Pulido, *Black, Brown, Yellow & Left: Radical Activism in Los Angeles*** (2006); **Andreas Hillen,**

1973 Nervous Breakdown: Watergate, Warhol, and the Birth of Post-Sixties America (2006); and **Kim Phillips-Fein, *Invisible Hands: The Making of the Conservative Movement from the New Deal to Reagan*** (2009).

CHAPTER 31

The economic ferment of the late 20th and early 21st centuries may be surveyed, from differing perspectives, in **Daniel Yergin, *The Commanding Heights: The Battle between Government and the Marketplace That Is Remaking the Modern World*** (1998); **Randall E. Stross, *Eboys: The First Inside Account of Venture Capitalists at Work*** (2001); **Kevin Phillips, *Wealth and Democracy: A Political History of the American Rich*** (2003); **Joseph Stiglitz, *The Roaring Nineties: A New History of the World's Most Prosperous Decade*** (2003); and **Paul Krugman, *The Great Unraveling: Losing Our Way in the New Century*** (rev. ed., 2004).

An overview of major demographic and social issues can be gleaned, from very different viewpoints, in studies such as **David Hollinger, *Post-Ethnic America: Beyond Multiculturalism*** (1995); **David M. Reimers, *Unwelcome Strangers: American Identity and the Turn against Immigration*** (1998); **Debra L. DeLaet, *U.S. Immigration Policy in an Age of Rights*** (2000); **Joseph Nevins, *Operation Gate-Keeper: The Rise of the "Illegal Alien" and the Remaking of the U.S.-Mexico Boundary*** (2001); **Alice O'Connor, *Poverty Knowledge: Social Science, Social Policy, and the Poor in Twentieth-Century U.S. History*** (2001); and **Hugh Davis Graham, *Collision Course: The Strange Convergence of Affirmative Action and Immigration Policy in America*** (2002).

The much-contested cultural scene comes into view in **Lawrence Grossberg, *We Gotta Get Out of This Place: Popular Conservatism and Postmodern Culture*** (1992); **Fred Goodman, *Mansion on the Hill: Dylan, Young, Geffen, Springsteen, and the Head-On Collision of Rock and Commerce*** (1997); **Robert Kolker, *Cinema of Loneliness: Penn, Kubrick, Scorsese, Spielberg, Altman*** (rev. ed., 2000); **Diana L. Eck, *A New Religious America*** (2003); **Patrick Allitt, *Religion in America since 1945: A History*** (2003); **Virginia Postel, *The Substance of Style: How the Rise of Aesthetic Value Is Remaking Commerce, Culture, and Consciousness*** (2003); **Sam Roberts, *Who We Are Now: The Changing Face of America in the Twenty-First Century*** (2004); **Reynold Farley and John Haaga, eds., *The American People: Census 2000*** (2005); **Jon C. Teaford, *The Metropolitan Revolution: The Rise of Post-Urban America*** (2006); and **Steve Knopper, *Appetite for Self-Destruction: The Spectacular Crash of the Record Industry in the Digital Age*** (2009).

CHAPTER 32

Very different perspectives on the Clinton years appear in **Bob Woodward, *The Agenda: Inside the Clinton White House*** (1994) and *The Choice* (1996); **Theodore Lowi and Benjamin Ginsburg, *Embattled Democracy: Politics and Policy in the Clinton Era*** (1995); **Kenneth Baer, *Reinventing Democrats: The Politics of Liberalism from Reagan to Clinton*** (2000); **Haynes Johnson, *The Best of Times: America in the Clinton Years*** (2001); **David Halberstam, *War in a Time of Peace*** (2001); **Sidney Blumenthal, *The Clinton Wars*** (2003); **Joseph**

E. Stiglitz, *The Roaring Nineties* (2003); **John F. Harris**, *The Survivor: Bill Clinton in the White House* (2005).

The electoral contest that elevated George W. Bush to the presidency is analyzed in **Jack M. Rakove, ed**, *The Unfinished Election of 2000* (2002) and **Jeffrey Toobin**, *Too Close to Call* (2001). For preliminary assessments of how Bush remained in the White House, see **William J. Crotty, ed.**, *A Defining Moment: The Presidential Election of 2004* (2005).

The controversy surrounding George W. Bush's presidency, and especially its relationship to the attacks of September 11, is reflected in titles such as **Bob Woodward**, *Bush at War* (2002); **Craig Calhoun, Paul Price, and Ashley Timmer, eds.**, *Understanding September 11* (2002); **Stephen Hess and Marvin Kalb, eds.**, *The Media and the War on Terrorism* (2003); **Gerald Posner**, *Why America Slept: The Failure to Prevent 9/11* (2003); **Joanne Meyerowitz, ed.**, *History and September 11th* (2003); **Chalmers Johnson**, *The Sorrows of Empire: Militarism, Secrecy, and the End of the Republic* (2004); **Michael R. Gordon and General Bernard E. Trainor**, *Cobra II: The Inside Story of the Invasion and Occupation of Iraq* (2006); **Thomas E. Ricks**, *Fiasco: The American Military Adventure in Iraq* (2006); **Ron Suskind**, *The One Percent Doctrine* (2006); and **Vali Nasr**, *The Shia Revival: How Conflicts within Islam Will Shape the Future* (2006).

For critical, first drafts of very recent history, see **Jacob Weisberg**, *The Bush Tragedy* (2008); **Charlie Savage**, *Takeover: The Return of the Imperial Presidency and the Subversion of American Democracy* (2008); **Phillip Bobbit**, *Terror and Consent: The Wars for the 21st Century* (2008); **Joseph Stiglitz and Linda Bilmes**, *The Three Trillion Dollar War: The True Cost of the Iraq Conflict* (2008); **Jane Mayer**, *The Dark Side: The Inside Story of How the War on Terror Turned Into a War on American Ideals* (2009); **Fareed Zakaria**, *The Post-American World* (2009); **Thomas Ricks**, *The Gamble: General David Petraeus and the American Military Adventure in Iraq, 2006–2008* (2009); **Robert Kagan**, *The End of History and the Return of Dreams* (2009); **William D. Cohan**, *House of Cards: A Tale of Hubris and Wretched Excess on Wall Street* (2009); **Kevin Phillips**, *Bad Money: Reckless Finance, Failed Politics, and the Global Crisis of American Capitalism* (rev. ed., 2009) and **David Sanger**, *The Inheritance: The World Obama Confronts and the Challenges to American Power* (2009).